S0-ADS-611

LAWRENCE
OF ARABIA

The Authorized Biography
of T. E. Lawrence

Jeremy Wilson

Abridged by the Author

COLLIER BOOKS

MACMILLAN PUBLISHING COMPANY
NEW YORK

MAXWELL MACMILLAN INTERNATIONAL
NEW YORK   OXFORD   SINGAPORE   SYDNEY

Copyright © 1989, 1992 by N. Helari

All rights reserved. No part of this book may be reproduced or
transmitted in any form or by any means, electronic or
mechanical, including photocopying, recording, or by any
information storage and retrieval system, without permission in
writing from the Publisher.

Collier Books
Macmillan Publishing Company
866 Third Avenue
New York, NY 10022

Macmillan Publishing Company is part
of the Maxwell Communication Group of Companies.

Library of Congress Cataloging-in-Publication Data
Wilson, Jeremy.
Lawrence of Arabia : the authorized biography of T. E. Lawrence /
by Jeremy Wilson : abridged by the author.—1st Collier Books ed.
p. cm.
Includes bibliographical references and index.
ISBN 0-02-082662-1
1. Lawrence, T. E. (Thomas Edward), 1888–1935. 2. Soldiers—Great
Britain—Biography. 3. Great Britain. Army—Biography. 4. World
War, 1914–1918—Campaigns—Middle East. 5. Middle East—
History—20th century. I. Title.
D568.4.L45W55 1991
940.4'15'092—dc20
[B]   91-35831   CIP

Macmillan books are available at special discounts for bulk purchases
for sales promotions, premiums, fund-raising, or
educational use. For details, contact:

Special Sales Director
Macmillan Publishing Company
866 Third Avenue
New York, NY 10022

First Collier Books Edition 1992

10 9 8 7 6 5 4 3 2 1

Printed in the United States of America

To my wife Nicole
and our children
Peter, Emily, and Edward

Contents

List of Maps

Note

Those who like to keep an appropriate map open while reading will find that most of the places referred to in the war chapters appear on the maps printed in editions of Seven Pillars of Wisdom.

Note to the Abridged Edition

When I began work on this biography, I intended to write a book of about five hundred pages—the length of this abridged edition. I then found that there was no established history of British and French policy towards the Middle East between 1914 and 1921, and that accounts in works by Arab and Zionist historians were often wildly contradictory. It was therefore necessary not only to tell the story of Lawrence's military and diplomatic career, but to set out the historical events in considerable detail. As a result, the text and notes relating to 1914–21 grew to nearly 650 pages and, in some senses, this section of the book became a study of Middle Eastern history rather than a biography. To maintain some kind of balance, appropriate space had then to be given to Lawrence's pre-war and post-war life, and when *Lawrence of Arabia* was completed it was 1,200 pages long.

Now that this full version is available, readers needing details of the military and diplomatic background to Lawrence's career can refer to it. They will find, for example, long accounts of the McMahon-Hussein and Sykes-Picot negotiations, and a complex sub-plot of Anglo-French rivalry in the Middle East. In this concise edition, I have felt free to return to my original intention. The result is a study of Lawrence's life which focuses much more sharply on his personality, values, ambitions and self-judgments, and which many readers may find more immediate and rewarding as biography.

Jeremy Wilson, July 1991

Note on the Transcription
of Quoted Material

Letters, reports, memoranda and printed material.

The wording of quoted text has been transcribed exactly as in the original except that the following conventions have been silently applied, in order to make quoted passages more readable.

In general, the original spelling and punctuation have been reproduced, but obvious errors such as unclosed parentheses have been corrected. In a few cases passages have been lightly re-punctuated in order to make their meaning clear at first reading.

Contractions which might be unfamiliar to general readers have usually been written out in full.

Ampersands have generally been transcribed as 'and'.

The use of capital letters has been brought into line with modern practice (e.g. 'north' rather than 'North'). This kind of capitalisation was often inconsistent, even within a single document, and it would have been a needless source of distraction to some readers.

The fully capitalised form used in military documents for place-names (e.g. DAMASCUS) has not been reproduced.

Numbers lower than 100 have been written as words except where numerals were required by the context. The same rule has been applied to most round numbers over 100.

The use of italics and quotation marks has been standardised throughout the text. For example, book titles which were originally underlined or placed in quotation marks have been printed in italics.

Lawrence frequently wrote rows of dots (typically between five and thirteen) as punctuation. He did this both in the middle of sentences and at the ends. The number of dots has been standardised: three are used . . . in the middle of sentences, and four at the end. . . .

Telegrams.

Cipher telegrams were used by the army and diplomatic service as a day-to-day method of communication. To reduce the time taken encoding, transmitting and decoding these messages, words which could be left out without ambiguity (typically 'the') were frequently omitted. Anyone reading a large number of these telegrams becomes completely unaware of such omissions, since the missing words are unconsciously supplied. However, in a book addressed to general readers it seemed best to reinstate the missing words in the text. My object in doing so has been to prevent readers from being distracted by an irrelevant telgraphic practice, and this purpose would have been defeated by printing the inserted words within square brackets. These insertions are not, therefore, indicated. The references state clearly which documents are telegrams, and in every case give a source for the text as transmitted.

Arabic words and names.

During Lawrence's lifetime it was usual to render Arabic words into English by approximate phonetic spellings. As a result there were widely varying forms. Lawrence deliberately reproduced this inconsistency in *Seven Pillars,* where he wrote: 'Arabic names are spelt anyhow, to prevent my appearing an adherent of one of the existing "systems of transliteration".'

Even today there is no universally accepted method of transliteration from Arabic to Roman script, and it would be difficult to justify altered spellings when quoting from *Seven Pillars* and contemporary documents. I have therefore left Arabic words and place-names as they stand.

I felt that to introduce modern academic spellings such as 'Hijaz' and 'Sharif' into my own text would only add further variants. Instead, I opted in each case for one of the versions used in the documents. In the same way, I have given personal names in one of the forms commonly used by British officials at the time, rather than the fuller form which would be technically correct.

Omissions and insertions.

Omissions have been shown thus . . .

Words inserted in quoted text (other than those inferred in telegrams, see above) are printed within square brackets.

Sense and Nonsense in the Biography of T. E. Lawrence

ROMANCE and enigma seem to have become an inseparable part of T. E. Lawrence's reputation. When I began research specifically for this book, in the mid–1970s, I was often told that my task was hopeless. At this distance in time no one could solve the biographical riddles. This had indeed been the case as long as the official archives relating to Lawrence's military and political career remained under embargo, and biographers were denied access to essential material for the period between 1914 and 1922. While this was so, no final judgment of his role during the Arab Revolt was possible, and very little information at all was available concerning either his work in Cairo during 1915–16 or his involvement in British diplomacy after the war.

In 1968, however, the great majority of these Government papers suddenly became available. At any time thereafter, an authoritative re-assessment of this much-debated figure should have been possible—but for various reasons none was forthcoming. Biographers dipped into the official archives in search of previously unpublished material, but none of them attempted a systematic investigation. One scholar did carry out a serious study of Lawrence's part in the Arab Revolt, but his book was published only in German, and has been ignored by British biographers. Twenty years later, at the centenary of Lawrence's birth, his reputation in the English-speaking world seemed little affected by the release of the archives. This was regrettable, since a proper assessment of his career was long overdue.

In the mind of the general public, both in Britain and abroad, he remains one of the most famous Englishmen of his generation. Yet ever since the 1950s, doubts have been expressed about his real achievement, and some writers have challenged the whole basis of his reputation. In 1962 the popular image of Lawrence was radically changed by David Lean's film *Lawrence of Arabia*, and the process has since been continued by a number of sensational biographies. Many of these have been highly speculative, yet subsequent writers have treated unproven suggestion as historical fact, and added further speculation of their own. In this way layer upon layer of invention has accumulated, leaving a grotesque impression of Lawrence's career. Its outline (with variants) runs something like this:

Illegitimate son of a religious maniac mother who dominates her children by flogging them—is taken up in early childhood by an unscrupulous 'mentor', D. G. Hogarth, and indoctrinated with imperialist views—is sent to Carchemish for training as a spy while pretending to be an archaeologist—goes to Cairo at the outbreak of war as a spy-master—gets involved in the Arab Revolt—is motivated by virulent imperialist (or perhaps pro-Arab, or pro-Zionist) feelings—is sodomised at Deraa (or invents the whole story)—is carried away by blood-lust at Tafas—is involved in treacherous diplomacy at the Peace Conference and under Churchill at the Colonial Office, during which he deceives everyone (or perhaps is manipulated by everyone)—enlists to get away from it all—indulges in masochistic floggings—has debatable sexual inclinations—seeks a substitute mother in Mrs Bernard Shaw—and is finally murdered by the secret service for reasons that can only be hinted at.

The errors of fact and interpretation in these accounts ought to have been plain to anyone familiar with the published sources; but apart from a handful of protests by specialist reviewers, the sensational fictions have rarely been challenged. It seems that ordinary human scepticism has been numbed by the sheer quantity of bizarre claims. The public no longer knows what should be believed and what should be denied and, as a result, many serious-minded people have come to regard the subject of T. E. Lawrence with caution, if not distaste.

Such a state of affairs might be tolerable if Lawrence had accomplished nothing and if his career had lacked any lasting historical significance. But despite his detractors' claims, this is not the case: even at their irreducible minimum, Lawrence's achievements cannot lightly be dismissed. His most severe critics have to admit that he played a role of some importance while serving as a British liaison officer during the Arab Revolt. After the war, fellow-officers who had seen his work at first-hand said that his contribution had been outstanding. Although some of these witnesses may have exaggerated, others were men of high integrity. Their testimony cannot be entirely groundless. He was also involved in diplomatic negotiations which reshaped the Middle East, first during the war itself, then at the Paris Peace Conference, and finally while working in the Colonial Office. There is ample evidence that he played an influential role, particularly in the Cairo Conference settlement of March 1921.

Next, his literary achievement: Lawrence had hoped since childhood to become a writer, and according to his own statements this remained his strongest ambition. Three of his works have been very successful. *Seven Pillars of Wisdom* has sold well over a million copies and has been widely translated. The continuing popularity of this long and relatively expensive book about a First World War campaign is surely remarkable. Barrack-room life in the RAF, the subject matter of his second book, *The Mint*, might seem to have still less appeal. Yet this work too has been translated into several languages, and since 1978 it has been reprinted regularly in *Penguin Modern Classics*. Lawrence's translation of the *Odyssey* has also earned a place in English literature, as one of the most successful renderings addressed to the general public. It has run through many editions, and is still available in bookshops after more than fifty years. Finally, Lawrence was a prolific letter-writer, and editions of his correspondence have been widely read.

Even on this minimal reckoning, Lawrence's military, diplomatic and literary achievements merit biographical investigation. But his life is interesting for another reason as well. He knew and corresponded with many of the leading figures of his time. These included archaeologists such as D. G. Hogarth and Leonard Woolley; military leaders such as Allenby, Trenchard and Wavell; diplomats and politicians such as Nancy Astor, Gertrude Bell, Churchill, Curzon, and Lloyd George; and writers such as Buchan, Conrad, Doughty, Flecker, Forster, Graves, Hardy, Sassoon, and Shaw, to name only a selection. There were also friends in the world of art: Eric Kennington, Augustus John, Paul Nash, William Roberts, and William Rothenstein; the architect Sir Herbert Baker, and H. S. Ede of the Tate Gallery. As long as historians are interested in figures such as these, they will also seek information about Lawrence.

One reason for this curiosity will be that Lawrence's personality and career provoked extreme reactions among his contemporaries, often of passionate loyalty, occasionally of bitter antagonism. Few were able to write about him without revealing something of their own values and prejudices. Yet it is impossible to make sense of these attitudes while the truth about Lawrence is obscured by sensational claim and counter-claim.

In the future, the 'Lawrence of Arabia' legend will itself interest social historians. Public enthusiasm for media idols is usually short-lived, but in Lawrence's case it has endured for more than sixty-five years. Instead of fading, the legend has evolved, keeping pace with changing popular interests. In 1919, Lowell Thomas gave Britain a romantic military hero unsullied by the horrors of the Western Front. Afterwards, when Lawrence wrote *Seven Pillars*, he was thought to exemplify the 'intellectual man of action'. During the Second World War his reputation as a leader again came to the fore, and *Seven Pillars* was included in the standard library issued to British fighting units. By the 1950s, the intense patriotism of the war period was fading, and attacks on conventional values became commonplace (Lord Altrincham, for example, made social history by daring to criticise the Queen's speeches). Predictably, the accumulated Lawrence legend came under attack. Then, in the early 1960s, Lawrence became fair game for amateur psychologists, and when the 'permissive society' focused public attention on private lives there was a glut of salacious allegations. During the 1970s and 1980s the vogue has been for espionage, and it has been claimed that Lawrence became a clandestine 'intelligence operative' before the first World War.

The development of this Lawrence legend shows how a popular topic can take on a life of its own as a result of continuing exposure. Successive accounts alter, as writers vie with one another to say something new. In this process, however, stories are not necessarily improved. It is not just the truth which suffers: often the ingredients which originally made an event worth reporting are sacrificed as well. The improbable figure presented in some recent biographies lacks almost all the qualities that made Lawrence fascinating to his contemporaries.

In reality, his biography has no need of such embellishments. His experiences in the Arab Revolt contained an extraordinary degree of drama: as he said himself, the story he had to tell in *Seven Pillars* was 'one of the most splendid ever given a man for writing.' The renunciations of his later career are hardly less intriguing. In Churchill's words: 'The world looks with some awe upon a man who appears unconcernedly indifferent to home, money, comfort, rank, or even power and fame. The world feels not without a certain apprehension, that here is some one outside its jurisdiction; some one before whom its allurements may be spread in vain; some one strangely enfranchised, untamed, untrammelled by convention, moving independently of the ordinary currents of human action'.

The sensational treatment of Lawrence's life, however entertaining, has helped to conceal his true development and motivation. For example, writers seeking an excuse to dwell on his maltreatment by the Turks at Deraa in November 1917 have suggested that this experience was responsible for the profound depression he felt during the later stages of the war.

It would have been more rewarding to admit that this depression was evident several months *before* the Deraa incident. By placing such emphasis on the events at Deraa, even at the expense of chronology, these writers have been led to discount early evidence of the central dilemma in his wartime career.

Likewise, the claim that Lawrence began working for British Intelligence at Carchemish before the First World War provided biographers with a dramatic new angle on the early years of his adult life. It also supplied an explanation, *deus ex machina*, for his elevation by October 1916 to an influential position in the Cairo Intelligence Department. The result, however, is that attention has been distracted both from his achievements as an archaeologist at Carchemish and from the merit of two years' hard work in Cairo Intelligence during 1915 and 1916. Thus a single biographical fiction makes a nonsense of Lawrence's development during six important years.

As Lawrence once warned Robert Graves, 'I'm rather a complicated person, and that's bad for a simple biography.' Obvious among these complications is the sheer diversity of his career. Normally a figure of such stature would be subject to exhaustive study in university departments, but Lawrence's life was too varied to fit in neatly with modern academic demarcations. As a result, no faculty is really interested in more than a small fraction of his life. Holders of university posts are obliged to work mainly in their own fields, and are naturally unwilling to trespass widely into other academic provinces. Thus while individual scholars may be expert in one aspect of Lawrence's career, they are likely to know little about large parts of his life. A specialist in medieval military architecture would not normally want to pass judgment on twentieth-century diplomatic history. Likewise, there are few archaeologists with knowledge of the Hittite period who could write with any proficiency about the development of high-speed motorboats. How many guerilla leaders have successfully translated the *Odyssey*, or set up a private printing press? The diversity of Lawrence's activities and interests has prevented anything but piecemeal academic research.

While this problem has discouraged academic attention, it cannot, on its own, account for the wary attitude towards Lawrence found in British universities. The situation abroad is different: major historical theses have been published in France and Germany, and there have been several American studies of Lawrence's writing. Caution about him in Britain seems to stem from two causes. First, all scholars prefer to deal with evidence and reasoning, while the Lawrence literature in this country has been saturated with myth and enigma. Secondly, attacks on his integrity have raised far stronger passions in Britain than abroad. British scholars, bombarded by allegations that he was a dishonest eccentric, cannot be blamed for choosing some other subject for research.

Much of this hostility towards Lawrence is rooted in aspects of British culture and history. At different times, his reputation has been savagely attacked by well-defined interest groups in Britain. The first of these to speak out was one associated with the Anglo-Indian administration in Mesopotamia. In 1921, Churchill adopted Lawrence's policy for this region and swept away years of painstaking effort by ambitious imperialists. Lawrence's responsibility for this public humiliation was never forgiven. As a result, thousands of Englishmen regarded him with a deep antagonism (passed down, in some families, to the present generation).

Lawrence also offended a second group. At a time when society was far more rigid than it is today, he rejected his 'proper' place in the social order and chose to enlist. Military rank was then a potent sign of social status, and after the First World War a great many ex-officers continued to use their military titles in civilian life. They were bitterly angry when it was revealed that the famous Colonel Lawrence had joined the ranks of the RAF as A/c Ross. His action seemed to undermine the respect which they considered due to the officer class. The depth of feeling on this issue is difficult to understand today, and has surprised me more than once when talking about Lawrence to people of that generation. Naturally, those who felt threatened by his unconventional attitude took action to defend themselves: in no time, uncomplimentary gossip began to circulate about his social eccentricity. The stories usually included some incident in which, while attempting to be 'clever,' he had behaved with appalling rudeness. I have never been able to substantiate one of these tales: no one seems actually to have witnessed an incident of this kind. Yet the gossip is often repeated, sometimes by biographers who do not realise that its original purpose was derogatory.

More recently, there has been vociferous criticism of Lawrence from British pressure groups associated with the Middle East. Although his true role has been little understood, he clearly occupied a position of some influence in Britain's policy towards the Arabs between 1914 and 1922. This episode in British diplomacy has proved to be extremely contentious, and Lawrence's reputation has been attacked virulently by some pro-Arab and some pro-Zionist writers. In many cases, polemicists have used his name simply to attract attention to their views about much wider issues. As the debate is directly related to the modern conflict over Palestine, there has been far too little disinterested scholarship. Historical interpretations are sharply divided, and Lawrence's biographers have been faced with opposing and incompatible statements by writers whose expertise in these questions is widely acknowledged. In order to resolve this problem I was obliged to go back to the contemporary documents. In the process a fresh view emerged, not only of Lawrence, but of the events themselves.

Much of the controversy about Lawrence in Britain can be traced to these differing viewpoints, and it is essential to be aware of them. In almost every case the hostility stems from an emotional allegiance rather than research and analysis. As a result the criticism has often taken the form of abuse or innuendo instead of reasoned argument.

It has also been claimed that veterans of the Western Front felt slighted by the blaze of publicity given to Lawrence (and to Allenby's Palestine campaigns). Individuals may have had such feelings, but the records suggest no general resentment: the fault clearly lay with the publicists and not with those who had fought in the Middle East. A grudge of this kind may nevertheless have prompted Richard Aldington's vehement attack on the popular Lawrence legend. Aldington was a passionately embittered writer who had suffered deeply as a result of war service on the Western Front. By the 1950s he was living abroad, in self-imposed exile, and he had come to see Lawrence as the hero of a decadent society which he detested. He seems to have believed that if he could destroy Lawrence's reputation, this would in some way deeply wound the British establishment.

In his researches, Aldington compared statements made by Lawrence at different times and to different people with those made by three contemporary biographers. He found many discrepancies between these sources, and presented the variants as evidence that Lawrence had told vainglorious lies. The obvious flaw in this argument was the assumption that Lawrence, rather than his three biographers, was responsible for the anomalies. This was extremely naïve. The earliest biographer, Lowell Thomas, was a popular journalist whose work brimmed over with romantic exaggerations. Lawrence was able to influence the text very little, but thought he could safely assume that intelligent readers would recognise it for what it was; his policy was therefore to refrain from comment. The second biographer, Robert Graves, was a poet and novelist whose book was written very hurriedly under pressure from his publishers. Although Lawrence saw the draft, he warned Graves that he had not had the time to correct all the mistakes. Only the third biographer, Liddell Hart, made any attempt at a scholarly treatment, and it was his project which received the greatest help from Lawrence. Given the differing qualities and aims of these authors, it would be amazing if their accounts agreed in every detail.

Conflicting evidence, as Aldington must have known, is a common problem for historians. Even after a short time-span, remembered versions of an incident hardly ever correspond exactly. Moreover, retrospective accounts are often coloured by self-justification and by wisdom after the event. Material gathered from autobiographies or interviews rarely turns out to be wholly consistent with contemporary sources.

In Lawrence's case, special factors have helped to generate conflicting evidence. First, those who knew him were inevitably exposed to the popular legend; many found it impossible to distinguish this from their own recollections. Interviews and published reminiscences often contain inaccuracies which are difficult to explain in any other way.

Secondly, Lawrence's career brought him into contact with people from all ranks of society. To the public at large, the only remarkable thing about some of his acquaintances was the fact that they had known him. Most of his close friends, particularly those in the RAF and Tank Corps, refused to capitalise on this public interest; but there were a few who traded on it and fabricated incidents and anecdotes to bolster their apparent importance in his life.

Thirdly, even greater distortions occur when people are encouraged to recall something 'new' about Lawrence. No interviewee likes to be found wanting, and wholesale fiction is amazingly common. Sometimes, the details have been very ingeniously worked out to tie in with known events. Fortunately, however, these yarn-spinners have rarely had access to Lawrence's vast unpublished correspondence. While their statements may tally with readily available sources, lesser-known material will usually expose enough invention to cast doubt on everything they have said.

It is curious that while such people will take immense care over a central fiction, they often give themselves away in minor details. This is the case with the much-publicised reminiscences of John Bruce. In pursuit of cash rewards for his story, Bruce embroidered it considerably. Thus in 1938 he sold an article to the *Scottish Field* in which he claimed to have been in India on spying expeditions with Lawrence, who dressed like a native and spoke the local language. The story was a complete falsehood, but Bruce thought it safe because ten years earlier there had been press reports that Lawrence was spying in India. As Bruce had not actually been in India with Lawrence, he had no idea that the press rumours were untrue. He said many other things about his relationship with Lawrence, and could have been an important biographical witness. As it is, however, his testimony can be faulted on so many points that every uncorroborated statement must be regarded with extreme caution.

Bruce's Indian spy 'revelations' also demonstrate how a popular myth can inspire what appears to be substantiating evidence. If there were no reliable contemporary documents to show that the 1928 press stories were false, Bruce's account might be accepted as proof that they were true.

Lastly, accounts of Lawrence's life have often been distorted in order to fit a preconceived theory (for instance that he exemplified some archetype such as the romantic 'hero who rejected worldly rewards'). These oversimplified interpretations rarely stand up to close examination, and usually obscure more than they illuminate.

I have tried very hard to avoid such pitfalls. The surest way to do so was to base my account of Lawrence's career on contemporary documents, using later statements only when they were consistent with these sources. Fortunately, an enormous amount of contemporary evidence has survived, relating to every stage in his life. The documents now available in public and private archives fully justify the claim made some years ago by Paul Adam, one of several French intellectuals who have written on Lawrence: 'By a paradox which is not without logic, the very mystery of Lawrence's case has provoked both research and testimony. As a result we know far more about him than we do about people who were never thought to be mysterious.'

The first object of my research was to collect as much of this contemporary information as possible. I soon found that it was better to copy entire documents than to work from notes. Very often a statement which seemed insignificant on its own turned out to be important when set alongside other material from the same period. Relevant documents are scattered throughout the world, and unless transcripts are brought together in one place, all but the most obvious interrelated statements will be overlooked.

The task of gathering photocopies and transcripts of contemporary documents continued during ten years. At the core of the chronological archive thus formed was Lawrence's own correspondence. He once wrote: 'of course somebody will want to write a life of me some day, and his only source will be such letters as chance has preserved. Had they been all kept, there would be a pretty complete history of events since

1910: volumes of stuff enough to discourage any historian: but chance
will winnow his pile down.' Lawrence was wrong in thinking that his
letters would be discarded. At that time many people retained correspondence as a matter of course, and in his case the letters had a financial
value. Comparing his address book with groups of surviving letters, it
seems unlikely that much has been lost. More than four thousand letters,
telegrams, official memoranda, and minutes written by Lawrence, and
about twelve hundred letters and telegrams addressed to him, are now
preserved in libraries or private collections. I was able to copy the vast
majority of these documents, thanks to their owners and to a request for
such co-operation made on my behalf by Lawrence's youngest brother
and literary executor, A. W. Lawrence.

Copies of many other relevant documents have been added to the
archive, especially for the war and diplomatic periods. This material
was essential if Lawrence's contribution was to be seen in its proper
context. I particularly wanted to discover contemporary opinions about
him exchanged between third parties who were in a position to judge
his work.

By the time the biography had been completed, the archive formed a
sequence of day-to-day records running to about four million words.
Some of the material it contains had not been available to other biographers; a great deal more, though available, seems not to have been consulted. While many of the documents were individually informative, the
most valuable conclusions often came through juxtaposition. Even the
most familiar letters have taken on a new significance when put alongside
other material from the same period.

The archive records in minute detail Lawrence's military activities,
diplomatic negotiations, service work, and writing. This incontestable
primary evidence made it possible to write the biography with little re-
course to later reminiscences. One important result is that the account of
his role in the Arab Revolt no longer relies on *Seven Pillars*. I have
quoted contemporary documents in preference to Lawrence's book, even
though that has proved to be remarkably accurate on questions of fact.

Although I know that many people would have preferred my biography
of Lawrence to be an 'interpretation' of his life, there was an overwhelming case for a carefully researched historical study, and that is the approach I decided to take. As a general principle, I have restricted critical
judgments to straightforward issues where the comment is unquestionably
valid. For example, in April 1929, Lawrence made a great fuss about
newspaper revelations that he was anonymously translating the *Odyssey*.

His astonished indignation was clearly absurd, since for several months previously he himself had been telling friends and acquaintances about his work on this project. There were also several instances, such as the question of Lawrence's sexuality, in which I thought it necessary to state my personal conclusions even though the issues were complex.

A biography such as this must not merely be accurate; it must be seen to be accurate. At the end of my research I could have written a narrative of Lawrence's life in which my conclusions were expressed entirely in my own words. This, however, would have required the reader to place total trust in my reliability, and it would have been only too easy for future writers to challenge my account in order to suggest alternatives. I have therefore adopted the principles set out in Winston Churchill's biography of his father. In the introduction he wrote: 'The style and ideas of the writer must throughout be subordinated to the necessity of embracing in the text those documentary proofs upon which the story depends. Letters, memoranda, and extracts from speeches, which inevitably and rightly interrupt the sequence of his narrative, must be pieced together upon some consistent and harmonious plan. It is not by the soft touches of a picture, but in hard mosaic or tessellated pavement, that a man's life and fortunes must be presented in all their reality and romance.'

I too have used extensive quotation, and the essential points can be seen to rest everywhere on contemporary evidence rather than on some theory of my own. Individual extracts were chosen for a number of different reasons. The first was to give authority to the factual record; the second, to illustrate Lawrence's values, aims, motivation and critical judgment, and to show how he was assessed by his contemporaries. Lastly, there can be more subtle benefits in the use of quotation. Those who have never carried out research in historical archives can have little idea of the human interest to be found in letters, telegrams, and notes written down while the events were still unfolding. There is often a fascinating interplay of personalities, and the documents can be alive with ambition and jealousy, generosity and humour. It is virtually impossible to retain these qualities in paraphrase: however brilliant the historian, accounts which summarise the documents almost invariably make duller reading than the documents themselves. In many cases, therefore, I have used quotation simply to preserve the drama that was so vividly present in the source materials; and also on occasion to illustrate attitudes which are very distant from those held today.

Most of the passages quoted contain a narrative element, but they have not been selected for that reason. I have in no sense attempted to 'tell Lawrence's story in his own words.'

Finally, I would like to say something about the status of an 'official biographer'. The expression is commonly used in publishing circles, but to me it has the aura of an 'official version', inspired and possibly censored by the subject's loving relatives. I greatly prefer the term 'authorised biography', which, for me at least, lacks this unfortunate connotation.

I would not have accepted the role of Lawrence's official biographer if there had been any hint of future censorship, and A. W. Lawrence, as literary executor, insisted from the outset that I should publish whatever conclusions I reached. We agreed that it would be best if my work was totally independent, and I avoided troubling him with questions about his brother's life except as a last resort when the information seemed unavailable elsewhere. When the book was in draft I sent parts of it for comment to several well-qualified critics. I was glad when he agreed to read the chapters describing Lawrence's childhood and work as an archaeologist, and I was grateful for the notes that he and other readers sent me. But the responsibility for the content of this biography is mine and mine alone.

Part I

Archaeology and Travel

1888–1914

*Thomas Edward Lawrence, known to his family as
'Ned', was born in the early hours of 16 August
1888 at a house rented by his parents on the outskirts of Tremadoc in Caernarvonshire. He would
remember nothing of this Welsh birthplace since
the family moved north to Kirkcudbright in Scotland when he was only thirteen months old. A
brother, Montagu Robert ('Bob'), was three years
older than Ned. Another boy, William George,
was born soon after the family had settled in Scotland.*

*Before Ned was three years old the house in
Kirkcudbright was put up for sale by its owners
and the Lawrences had to move again. After a
brief stay in the Isle of Man they travelled to Jersey and set about finding a new home on the
nearby coast of Brittany. In December 1891 they
rented a secluded house called the Chalet du Vallon in Dinard. It was here that T. E. Lawrence
first began to explore the world outside his home.*

CHAPTER 1

Childhood

December 1888–October 1907

DURING the closing decades of the nineteenth century Dinard grew from a small fishing village to a substantial town. The 1894 *Baedeker* described it as 'a modern village, picturesquely situated on a rocky promontory on the left bank of the estuary of the Rance, opposite St. Malo and St. Servan. It has two beaches, with sea-baths, the chief of which, with the Casino, is on the small bay nearest the sea . . . The neighbouring heights, sprinkled with villas, command a pleasing view of the bay of St. Malo, with its islets and reefs.'

At that time many English people found the cost of living in France very low, and settled in Brittany where they could live comfortably on a modest income. By the 1890s there were several large British communities near St Malo, for example at Dinan ten miles up the Rance and at St Servan. The school in Dinan had accepted English pupils since 1820 and published an English-language prospectus.

Dinard, however, had grown primarily as a fashionable resort, popular with wealthy visitors who spent the summer in its villas and first-class hotels. Only a few British families lived there all the year round, but those who did had no need to learn French, since English was generally understood by the local tradespeople.

The Chalet du Vallon was a comfortable house built in 1885. Although near to the town centre, it stood in a secluded garden approached by a long walled path. There were few immediate neighbours, but a school, the École Sainte-Marie, was conveniently close. The Lawrence family seemed to prefer this seclusion to the social life of Dinard. Although the mother, Sarah Lawrence, rarely left the house, neighbours found her a pleasant acquaintance. The father, Thomas Lawrence, was more often to be seen. He was a quiet, reserved man who enjoyed walking and cycling, and probably sailing too, since Lawrence later recalled that 'my father had yachts and used to take me with him from my fourth year'. Children of English and French families in Dinard mixed freely together and were welcomed in each others' homes. The daughter of a neighbouring English family, the Herberts, often played with the Lawrence brothers. The

3

Lawrences met one French family, their landlords the Chaignons, very frequently. Here a lasting friendship gradually developed, which would later prove useful to the English boys.

Ned and Bob Lawrence had an English governess who gave them elementary schooling, which was taken very seriously in the household. These lessons were supplemented when Lawrence was five by an hour's schooling each morning at the École Sainte-Marie. Physical education was also considered important, and Lawrence with three other English boys took the steam ferry twice a week across the Rance to St Malo where they attended a private gymnastics class.

At the end of the nineteenth century St Malo was still an ancient fortified town (much of it had to be rebuilt after the Second World War). Lawrence can scarcely have forgotten the view from Dinard of its imposing ramparts—defences which had successfully resisted an assault by Marlborough's army. Its narrow streets and ancient buildings had changed little since the time when it had been a flourishing port, the home of Jacques Cartier and of the famous *corsaire* Surcouf. Memories of this fairy-tale stronghold may well have kindled his later interest in history and military architecture.

When Mrs Lawrence was expecting a fourth child, in 1893, the family travelled to Jersey for the birth. There was concern that a son born in Dinard might eventually be called up for French military service. The child was a boy and was christened Frank Helier, the second name marking his birthplace.

The following spring, when Bob was eight and Ned nearly six, the family moved to England. Their new home, Langley Lodge, was set in a private estate near the edge of the New Forest, just over a mile south-east of the main road between Totton and Lyndhurst. The surroundings were no less beautiful than at Dinard, and the house was even more isolated. To the north and west lay forest, Southampton Water was a short distance away to the east, and to the south there was sparsely populated countryside as far as the Solent shore nine miles away. The Lawrences were very remote from the mainstream of English life. Southampton, the closest large town, was more than an hour's journey distant.

While the children were now to grow up in English surroundings, Lawrence's years in France would have a great influence upon his attitude towards foreign travel. It was in France that he had begun to form ideas about the world beyond his family. His experience had not been that of a tourist, screened from the French in English-speaking hotels; nor had he been like the children of diplomats and colonial administrators, generally proud of their isolation in a British compound. He had lived in France on equal terms with a foreign people; he had spoken their language and had sensed no barrier. Before he was old enough to become mistrustful, he knew that he was welcomed by both French and English families. As a result he never felt the apprehension about living in foreign countries that was so common among the British. In the late Victorian era the English overseas were generally insular, class-conscious and nationalist. Lawrence himself would later write that they reinforced their national character 'by memories of the life they have left. In reaction against their foreign surroundings they take refuge in the England that was theirs. They assert their aloofness, their immunity, the more vividly for their loneliness and weakness.'

Integration while overseas was rare, and those who sought the company of foreigners rather than their British peers risked denunciation for 'going native'. Lawrence was to become one of those Englishmen who, in his own words, 'feel deeply the influence of the native people, and try to adjust themselves to its atmosphere and spirit . . . They imitate the native as far as possible, and so avoid friction in their daily life . . . They are like the people but not of the people'.

It was in this latter spirit that Lawrence would return during his student years to visit French families, and would tour on his bicycle in France as confidently as in England. The series of journeys which thus began would eventually take him to Palestine and Syria; yet the style of his travelling would remain the same. Before going to the Middle East he would learn Arabic, and he would accept enthusiastically the village hospitality offered to Arab travellers. As a result, he was to gain a better knowledge of Arab ways than most British visitors. This in turn would help him to share the life of the bedouin tribesmen while working as a British liaison officer with the Arab forces during the First World War. The move from Dinard to the New Forest was a happy one for the Lawrence children. Encouraged by their father, they spent three summers in open-air pursuits. From the shore of Southampton Water they could look across at the commercial shipping in Southampton and the many passenger liners which linked this great port to every part of the globe. Sometimes the boys were taken to Lepe where they could see the yachts racing off Cowes. As in France, they made friends with local children, notably the Lauries, whose father was agent of a neighbouring estate.

A governess was again employed to give lessons to the boys, but by 1896, when Bob was nearly eleven, there was a need for more conventional schooling. The family could not afford boarding-school fees for four sons, and there were no good schools within easy reach, so that summer the Lawrences moved to Oxford where the boys could receive an excellent education at little cost.

Ned Lawrence was just eight when he left the New Forest. By then he had developed a liking for the countryside and outdoor activities. As an adult he would often say that his favourite place was London, yet many years later when he bought a house of his own it was to be almost as isolated as Langley Lodge.

The Lawrences' new home in Oxford, 2 Polstead Road, was a large semi-detached red-brick house built about six years previously. Unlike Langley Lodge it was surrounded by streets of suburban houses, all dating from the great expansion of north Oxford during the last years of the nineteenth century. In the autumn of 1896 Bob and Ned Lawrence were enrolled at the City of Oxford High School for Boys, where the great majority of the 150 pupils were fee-paying and came from middle-class families. The headmaster, A. W. Cave, had built up a considerable academic reputation for the school, and of the fourteen boys in Lawrence's year, seven would go on to Oxford University.

Recollections of Lawrence during this period must be treated with caution. All were written at least thirty years later when he had become famous. One impression, however, by the teacher who had been his form master in 1901, reads so like a school report that it may even have been based on contemporary notes:

'I found him quiet, very able at Form work, but lacking the enthusiasm which one generally associates with clever boys. The ordinary Form work was no trouble to him. The work of the Form in my day was mapped out for the special behoof of the under-dog. Lawrence did not come into this category and escaped any special direction or correction that might have been required.

'His mind was not always on Form work, although he gave no trouble. He was evidently forming resolutions as to the conduct of life, for he had already begun to criticise his elders, an awkward and hindering habit in any youth . . . He detested "side" and was severe in his looks on any boy who gave way to "swank".

'He had a strong sense of humour, which must have saved him many times in troublesome boyish days. He knew no fear and we all wondered why he did not play games . . . When the free-wheel bicycle came into use, he was the first boy in the School to have one and to have the first three-speed gear . . .

'He was an enthusiast on physical excellence in human beings, although his own build was not as handsome as that of his brother Will, or as upright, tall and straight as that of his elder brother M.R.

'He was unlike the boys of his age and time, for even in his schooldays he had a strong leaning towards the Stoics, an apparent indifference towards pleasure or pain.'

Lawrence disliked organised games. He later wrote: 'You know, I've never, since I was able to think, played any game through to the end. At school they used to stick me into football or cricket teams, and always I would trickle away from the field before the match ended.' Many years afterwards, when Robert Graves wrote in the draft of his biography of Lawrence that organised games were 'too tame for him', Lawrence emended the passage to read: 'He took no interest in organised games because they were organised, because they had rules, because they had results. He will never compete—in anything.' It is clear that the objection was to competition rather than to physical exertion; Lawrence was good at gymnastics and an accomplished cyclist. His fitness showed when he was made to take part in school athletics. In 1904 he was third (of fifteen) in the two-mile cycle race.

Evidently he was well-liked, and despite his eccentric attitude to games no one could regard him as a weakling. A classmate later wrote: 'How often a group of us, absorbed in some discussion of cricket or football, would gradually become conscious of a silent addition to our number, contemplating us with that provocative smile of his, till one of us would seize him and close in friendly wrestling, to feel even then the strength of those iron wrists.'

In addition to their academic education, the Lawrence boys received a strongly religious upbringing. Both parents were convinced Christians, though their faith had a different emphasis. Lawrence's youngest brother (Arnold Walter, a fifth son who was born in 1900) has written: 'My mother . . . held religious convictions profoundly. She totally accepted the tenets of her brand of Christianity and had no doubt they constituted a complete code of binding rules for conduct; but she could only in small part share in my father's emotional, almost mystical, religious feeling'. She was 'religious by upbringing (a fundamentalist) not by temperament. She went to church only at 11 A.M. on Sundays, with the rest of the family, after "morning prayers" by my father, who was more religious-minded.'

Since moving to Oxford the family had worshipped at St Aldate's, opposite Christ Church, even though several other churches were closer to their home in Polstead Road. The rector of St Aldate's, Canon A. M. W. Christopher, was a prominent evangelical.

Most children received a religious upbringing at that time, but Law-rence was an unusually receptive pupil. Religious instruction gave him ethical values and a thorough knowledge of the Scriptures. He also began during childhood to study the geography and history of the Bible lands.

In the summer of 1904, at the end of his sixteenth year, he sat the Junior Oxford Local Examinations. The mark-sheets survive, providing an interesting record of his ability (the first of the two marks given below shows his performance; the second is the mark awarded to the top candidate in that subject). He gained a distinction in Religious Knowledge (162:188), and passed in Arithmetic (77:100), History (112: 156), English language and literature (210:269), Geography (93:140), Latin (204:341), Greek (186:353), French (205:293), and Mathematics, i.e. algebra and geometry, (122:321). His overall total was excellent, and he was placed in the First Class. Of the 6,720 candidates that year, only seventy-nine obtained a higher total.

Despite this achievement, his contemporaries did not see him as a committed intellectual. According to 'Scroggs' Beeson, his closest schoolfriend, Lawrence 'left no impression of unusual erudition. A happy faculty of perceiving and ingenuously acclaiming new features in the already familiar made him appear rather as novice than mentor.'

It was probably in the autumn of 1904 that Lawrence hurt his leg in a playground scuffle. At first he did not think the injury serious and continued the day's lessons despite considerable pain. His brothers wheeled him home on a bicycle and, when the doctor was called, the leg was found to be broken just above the ankle. It took a long time to mend and as a result he missed the rest of term.

During his convalescence he amused himself by extensive reading, and also by copying medieval designs in poker work (then a popular technique: patterns were burned on wood using specially shaped 'points' heated by a 'poker machine'). The works he read were probably on history and archaeology. According to his mother he had bought two second-hand books on Layard's excavations at Nineveh, and came to know them almost by heart. It may have been these which first attracted him to archaeology, although he had begun to collect rubbings from medieval church brasses a year or two earlier. By the age of fifteen he was well known, at school, 'for his archaeological rummagings in and about

Oxford.' C. F. C. Beeson records that their friendship centred on a shared interest in archaeological research, 'undertaken by Lawrence with a passionate absorption beside which my urge was more akin to the curiosity of a magpie in a Baghdad bazaar.' During their later years at school the two friends cycled over a wide area in search of brass rubbings.

This interest in medieval artefacts took them to Oxford's Ashmolean Museum, where they met the Assistant Keeper, C. F. Bell. He saw them as an inseparable pair, devoting themselves to the kind of antiquarian pursuits recorded in the Annual Report of the Museum for 1906: 'During the past year the considerable disturbance of the ground for the foundations of new buildings in the city, at Hertford College, Jesus College, St. John's College, in High Street and in the Cornmarket on the sites of the Civet Cat and Leopold Arms, has produced many remains of pottery and glass of the 16th and 17th centuries. Owing to the generosity of Mr. E. Lawrence and also C. F. C. Beeson, who have by incessant watchfulness secured everything of antiquarian value which has been found, the most interesting finds have been added to the local antiquities in the Museum.'

It is not unusual for teenagers to take up archaeology with a passionate interest; many people who later become professional archaeologists are first drawn to the subject when fifteen or sixteen. Mindful of this, museum staff welcome young enthusiasts, who are often willing to approach the dullest task with dedication. Given sympathetic guidance, their contributions to museum work can be extremely helpful. This was certainly true in Lawrence's case.

During his later years at school other factors began to shape his personality. The first was physical: unlike his four brothers he stopped growing when he reached 5ft 5ins. This shortness in stature was probably inherited from his mother, although she liked to claim that it had been caused in some way when he broke his leg. Short stature can have an influence on personality, and Lawrence was apt to behave in an unconventional fashion, perhaps in order to be noticed. This characteristic would persist in one form or another throughout his life. He also developed an almost obsessive will-power, and while still at school began to experiment with self-imposed tests of physical endurance, going for long walks and cycle rides, and spending periods without food and sleep. These activities set him apart from other boys.

There was another factor which now led him to distance himself from his contemporaries. During early childhood he had become aware that there was something irregular about the circumstances of his birth. It has been suggested that his suspicions were first roused when he overheard part of a conversation between his father and a solicitor. He probably added gradually to this knowledge over several years, and by his own account he had concluded, before he was ten, that he must be illegitimate. At that age, however, he could not possibly have understood the full implications.

Lawrence was the only one of the brothers who discovered this secret, and as he passed through adolescence he must have become increasingly aware of the social rejection that would follow if the truth were revealed. He was surrounded by the high-minded morality of Victorian Oxford, where bastardy would have been an unthinkable disgrace. His knowledge made him a party to his parents' deception, yet he said nothing to them or to his brothers about what he suspected.

Lawrence's written statements about his illegitimacy were made many years later, after he had heard his mother's version of the facts. There is therefore nothing to justify the common assumption that since childhood he had known the full story. On the contrary, such evidence as there is suggests that he did not. Notes written by C. F. Bell indicate that while Lawrence knew before the First World War that he was illegitimate, he had completely misconstrued his parents' situation.

Bell's notes are in general accurate apart from some trivial errors in dates, yet they contain an account of Lawrence's family background, apparently derived from Lawrence himself, that is wholly incorrect. Bell wrote: 'the details . . . amounted to this: that the "father", Mr. Lawrence, who was known in Oxford, was *not* the boys' father at all, but that Mrs. Lawrence, whom we all knew . . . *was* their mother . . . Mrs. Lawrence had been governess in the house of a man of some position who was the father of the boys—or at least of the elder ones. Mr. Lawrence married her later and adopted the children.'

Since Lawrence's parents had told him nothing directly, and behaved as a normal married couple, this might have seemed the most obvious explanation of the scattered allusions he had heard. Indeed the true facts, which his mother told him in 1919, would have seemed far less probable given the *mores* of the time.

Whatever the extent of his knowledge, it is clear that during adolescence he knew that he was illegitimate. This deprived him of the sense of status and security which most children of his social class would have drawn from their family background and ancestry. As a result he would have to build up his own identity and self-esteem through personal achievement and moral integrity. When considering other ways in which knowledge of his illegitimacy may have influenced his development, it is important to bear in mind that he may not have believed, before 1919, that Mr Lawrence was actually his father. This could help to explain why Lawrence's remarks about his parents suggest that he had felt much stronger emotional ties with his mother than with his father.

The detachment shown in references to his father is all the more surprising since Mr Lawrence lived on private means and was therefore usually at home. While the boys' mother was busy running a large household, their father spent a good deal of time with them and was responsible for many of the interests they developed. In Arnold Lawrence's words: 'his influence can scarcely be overestimated. He was a skilled photographer—his camera is in the Oxford Museum of the History of Science; a handyman—and taught his children carpentry; he regularly bought the best bicycle of next year's model and liked riding 100 miles a day. He knew French grammatically, and in old age quoted Horace to express his own sentiments, and a line of Homer for its metrical felicity. He was interested in current affairs and church architecture; his best friend, H. T. Inman, was author of *Near Oxford*—an excellent guidebook to churches'. From his father Lawrence gained skills and enthusiasms which were later to be very important in his life.

This parental influence extended much further. During his childhood Lawrence acquired certain attitudes towards life which belied the family's income of £300–£400 a year (then equivalent to a middle-rank professional salary). Mr Lawrence himself had been brought up in a wealthy landowning family where he had acquired an aristocratic disdain towards money and the necessity of working for a living. By practising a good deal of financial restraint, he was able to retain these attitudes in later life, and he passed them on, perhaps unconsciously, to his sons. Lawrence wrote home in 1911: 'I fear Father is right about us and our careers: but this idealist disregard for the good things of the world has its bright side. And to say that he had five sons, none making money, would be a glorious boast—from my point of view at least.'

In the tradition of the leisured classes, Mr Lawrence had learned to fill his days with absorbing pastimes. This attitude affected his sons, and Lawrence would always retain an aristocratic habit of seeking fulfilment chiefly in his own pursuits. The lives of all five brothers show an indifference towards the kind of career ambition that would normally motivate men of their social and financial position. Although Lawrence said little about his father, the values he inherited from this tall, gentle, unobtrusive figure were to influence him greatly.

*   *   *

The contrast between Lawrence's father and mother was considerable. Mrs Lawrence's sons knew little about her background, but Lawrence himself later found out that she too had been an illegitimate child. She had been brought up in Perthshire and on the Isle of Skye by her uncle, a minister of the Episcopal Church of Scotland. Able and intelligent, she had been taught to value education highly. Despite her origins she acquired sufficient qualifications to seek work as a governess. This profession offered many openings to girls from Scotland, since the renowned qualities of the Scottish nanny were much appreciated by aristocratic families both in Britain and abroad. It was doubtless her constant encouragement which spurred her five sons to seek academic success.

She worked long hours to maintain the standards she felt proper for their household and, in his letters, Lawrence often showed concern for her, urging her to take more rest. The sacrifice she made for the needs of her family reflected an indomitable willpower, which she applied no less to herself than to those around her. This dominant personality brought her directly into conflict with Lawrence as he grew towards adulthood. He resented increasingly her intrusions into his private affairs and, as he himself had a strong character, their relationship worsened. In 1927, when he had lived apart from her for many years, he wrote a letter which shows how deeply he was scarred by this adolescent conflict: 'Mother is rather wonderful: but very exciting. She is so set, so assured in mind. I think she "set" many years ago: perhaps before I was born. I have a terror of her knowing anything about my feelings, or convictions, or way of life. If she knew they would be damaged: violated: no longer mine. You see, she would not hesitate to understand them: and I do not understand them, and do not want to. Nor has she ever seen any of us growing: because I think she has not grown since we began . . . She has given me a terror of families and inquisitions. And yet you'll understand she is my mother, and an extraordinary person. Knowledge of her will prevent my ever making any woman a mother, and the cause of children . . . the inner conflict, which makes me a standing civil war, is the inevitable issue of the discordant natures of herself and my father, and the inflammation of strength and weakness which followed the uprooting of their lives and principles. They should not have borne children.' The bitterness expressed in this letter can only reflect the feelings of his youth, since afterwards he had lived away from home.

At one point, probably in the autumn of 1905, tension reached such a pitch that Lawrence ran away. On at least two occasions he stated that this was 'because of trouble at home'. The incident undoubtedly marked the end of his childhood dependence on his mother. Once, writing to a friend, he remarked that seventeen was 'the age at which I suddenly found myself. You may have begun a little earlier, since the being torn out of home is an education in itself.'

When he ran away there were no relatives to stay with and enlistment was one of the few courses open to him. A local recruiting office placed him in the Royal Garrison Artillery (part of the Royal Artillery) as a boy soldier and he was posted to the Falmouth Garrison. He served for a time in the small sub-section which manned the fort situated on the opposite side of the River Fal between St Just-in-Roseland and St Mawes. At that date boy soldiers between fourteen and eighteen were recruited by the Royal Artillery to serve as trumpeters. They were taught both trumpet and bugle and, when proficient, blew the various bugle calls that regulated military life.

Lawrence was shocked by the brutality of the men in the RGA: 'every incident ended in dispute and every dispute either in the ordeal of fists (a forgotten art, today) or in a barrack-court-martial whose sentences were too often mass-bullying of anyone unlike the mass . . . I cannot remember a parade . . . without a discoloured eye. Usually five or six men bore fighting damages.'

This experience must have seemed considerably worse than the problems he had run away from: 'the other fellows fought all Friday and Saturday nights and frightened me with their roughness.' It seems that he appealed to his father for help and as a result was bought out.

Many children rebel against their parents and run away from home in their teens; but the incident is testimony to Lawrence's self-confidence, and to the conflict of strong personalities which blocked an easier solution to this adolescent tension between mother and son. Knowledge of his illegitimacy may also have played a part in the decision. He later wrote: 'My mind was not so peaceful then, for I had not tried everything, and made a final choice of the least ill.'

After he had become famous, his mother liked to stress the harmony of their family life during his childhood. She and her eldest son therefore denied that Lawrence had ever run away from home. Lawrence himself evidently knew that it had hurt her, for he regretted mentioning it to one of his biographers, to whom he wrote: 'This is hush-hush. I should not have told you . . . I'd rather keep this out of print, please: the whole episode.'

*   *   *

It was at about this time that the emphasis of Lawrence's schooling changed. In the Junior Locals two years before, he had gained barely a third of the marks of the top candidate in mathematics. As the marks were not disclosed, his school did not know this and had decided to put him up for a mathematics scholarship at Oxford University. However, when he was nearly eighteen he abruptly switched from mathematics to history. Later references in his letters show that this change was his own decision, and the matter may have been contentious. His comments about mathematics suggest that he had no liking for the subject: 'the average intelligence in a month could learn all the arithmetic that he or she will ever need thereafter, till dying day. About one person in a thousand wants to know more. I should isolate these repulsive cases and protect all other children from their contact . . . for me addition, subtraction, and division, with multiplication are enough. Since I dropped maths I've never needed a log. or done an equation, or used a trig. formula'. This dislike of mathematics may have been partly due to missing a school term when his leg was broken. The gap in his knowledge caused by such a long absence would have been a continuing handicap, since the study of maths is cumulative. But the change also reflected something in Lawrence's intellectual make-up. He would never be attracted to pure theory, whether in mathematics, philosophy, economics, or politics. In the same way, though he would learn to read and speak a foreign language, he felt no need to acquire a deep knowledge of its grammar.

Another motive for the change in subject must have been the interest in medieval history which had developed through his enthusiasm for brass-rubbing and archaeology. During his last year at school he read history books borrowed for him by his father from the library of the Oxford Union, and took private coaching from L. C. Jane, a historian whose slightly unconventional approach suited Lawrence well.

In the summer of 1906 he sat the Senior Oxford Local Examinations, a necessary step towards university entrance. While waiting for the results he set out on a bicycle tour of Brittany to visit castles and historic churches. This was the first time he had left England on his own, but he had few anxieties since his base would be the Chaignons' house in Dinard. His elder brother Bob had visited them as a paying guest two summers previously, and Lawrence was to stay with them on the same basis. He intended to spend two weeks travelling with his schoolfriend Beeson, returning to England in mid-August. In the event, however, his visit was to be extended, and he stayed on for nearly a fortnight after Beeson left.

During this holiday he wrote to his family at regular intervals, and the dozen letters which survive total more than twenty thousand words. These contemporary documents provide a much more reliable picture of Lawrence at the close of his eighteenth year than the later reminiscences of family and friends. There are remarks which bear on his relationship with members of his family; there are comments which illustrate different facets of his developing personality; and there is a good deal of material that displays his various abilities, interests and opinions.

At first sight, the letters seem curiously impersonal, and this itself must be a reflection of Lawrence's relationship with his family. He told his mother: 'you want more details of myself; I really have none to give', and again, 'there will be no private or family messages in [this letter], although there have not been anything of the sort in any letters of mine up to the present.' When addressing a letter to his father he wrote: 'it does not make the least difference in style, since all my letters are equally bare of personal information. The buildings I try to describe will last longer than we will, so it is only fitting that they should have the greater space.'

Despite this reserve he shows a good deal of filial affection and much concern for his mother's health. There are also messages for his parents from people they had known when they lived in Dinard twelve years before. Other passages in the letters reflect Lawrence's upbringing. His parents were staunchly Protestant so not surprisingly he found the Bretons 'ignorant and priest-ridden'. His mother's influence is clear in other ways. The family was teetotal, and Lawrence therefore disapproved of alcohol, remarking, for instance, on the drunkenness in Dinard: 'Everyone mixes raw brandy with their cider, and they get fearfully mad with drink.' His expenditure is frequently and carefully accounted for: 'I fear I will be sixpence short in England; I had forgotten the sum charged for bringing the luggage to the Docks Station, when I kept some English money unchanged . . . I am one half-penny short deducting bicycle fare. I shall have to change that sovereign for the half-penny, unless I carry my own luggage to the station, which might perhaps be the easier course.'

Lawrence's father had encouraged his sons to take an interest in current affairs, and several comments reveal the family's Tory opinions, for example: 'The Whites were interested in the Unemployed so I gave them a history of the movement, for it is undoubtedly engineered. Mr. White has no sympathy with them.' References to his elder brother in the letters are less than respectful: 'The people here say that I am much thinner than Bob, but stronger, and have a better accent. Still Bob's fatness is much better than my muscle in their eyes'. Bob had embraced his mother's form of religion and hoped to become a medical missionary. He was at that time an undergraduate at St John's College, Oxford, struggling through the pre-clinical syllabus for a medical degree. He was probably the least academic of the brothers: 'he's queer company', Lawrence later wrote, 'you will not persuade him of anything . . . He is illuminated from inside, not from out. His face, very often, shines like a lamp.' Bob was therefore an easy target. When visiting a castle which had well-preserved latrines, Lawrence teased: 'By the way, did not Bob . . . go and see this castle? What could he have been thinking about not to mention these most attractive domestic conveniences?'

The third brother, Will, was only sixteen months younger than Lawrence and the two were very close. While on holiday that summer, Will came across a mound which appeared to be a barrow, and wrote to Lawrence asking how to excavate it. The reply was helpful though filled with bantering admonitions. It ended encouragingly: 'Let me know how the matter progresses . . . keep an accurate account . . . and mark on a plan where each important article is found. You have my best wishes for success . . . Don't give up at once, if you do not find anything. Digging is an excellent exercise.' Frank, the fourth brother, was now thirteen, and the five-year age gap seems to have prevented the development of a close relationship. Arnold, however, was still a small child, and Lawrence's almost fatherly affection towards him is often reflected in these letters.

Lawrence clearly also revelled in gossip, some of which seems to have been reported home for his mother's benefit: 'The servant question is very acute over here: they take percentages of everything bought and this raises the prices. Mrs. Purvis says that if she buys a franc's worth of vegetables from a woman at the door, on going she will slip a *sou* into the hand of the cook. If she orders anything in the shops the servant goes on her next opportunity and demands her commission which is always given.' This willingness to listen to local chatter seems to have been a feature of Lawrence's personality. It would continue throughout his life and was to help him in a curious way when he began to travel further afield. Any outsider who wants to be accepted in a foreign community must enter into the spirit of its gossip. A few years later, while overseeing Arab workmen, his knowledge of their family scandals would help to make him popular, and during the First World War he would advise British officers serving with the Arab armies to learn 'all you can . . . Get to know their families, clans, and tribes, friends and enemies, wells, hills, and roads. Do all this by listening and by indirect enquiry. Do not ask questions.'

The 1906 letters also show that he already enjoyed making provocative remarks about people. This would be another lifelong trait. He liked resounding statements and he also liked to shock (when he meant to be malicious the tone was much quieter). His letters contain some biting personal assessments: 'I forgot to mention that, owing to paralysis of his eye, [Toby Purvis] squints terribly. He is certainly very clever at making himself pleasant, and has good manners, joined to good powers of observation; but much of his pleasantness lies, I expect, on the surface, and is only shown to strangers. He will be entertaining enough for one drive I hope.' The style of these judgments in letters home displays a degree of youthful arrogance and may also reflect his upbringing. Yet Lawrence's ability to assess character quickly and accurately would later be crucial to his role in the Arab Revolt.

Though constantly aware of his short stature, he took pride in his strength and was pleased when this was admired: 'when he heard of my Fougères ride [Mr Lewis] declared I was very strong and that I had inherited Father's talent . . . I am beginning to be proud of myself.' Mme Chaignon 'got a shock when she saw my "biceps" while bathing. She thinks I'm Hercules'. Again: 'My leg muscles are like steel now. I expect I'll delight Mother when I return. I'm as brown as a berry.'

He was beginning to find vegetarianism attractive. This was not, however, encouraged by his hosts: 'The Chaignons declare I will kill myself if I don't eat more meat; they say all vegetarians fill an early grave, although I'm not a veg. out here, no Frenchman has any opportunity to be.' During the next three years he would adopt vegetarianism seriously; it formed one aspect of the idealism which began to mark much of his thinking.

His letters occasionally reveal a strongly romantic side to his nature. One of the set texts in the English Literature paper for the Senior Locals had been Tennyson's poetry. On August 26 he sent home a string of descriptive passages, mainly from Tennyson and Shelley, to illustrate the evening seascape at Dinard. The letter continued: 'You really must excuse this battery of quotations, but I have got into the habit of quoting any appropriate lines to myself, and this time I thought I would put them on record . . . The sea was of the wondrous blue met with sometimes here, and all was perfect; *there was no-one else there.* This last makes such an addition to one's enjoyment of nature and her prodigal loveliness; all this scene was reserved for me alone: it is a wonderful surpassing thought on which to reflect, I can only wish my mind was more receptive and my emotions more deeply affected. Nature contains that spirit and power

which we can witness but not weigh, inwardly conceive but not compre-
hend, love but not limit, imagine, but neither define nor describe. Nature
is incomprehensible, fleeting, and yet immortal, and a love for it and its
impressions are both ineradicable.' Such passages seem very strange
when set alongside the arid descriptions of castles and churches which
make up the bulk of these letters. At this time, however, Lawrence was
reading Ruskin's *Stones of Venice*, and the content of his letters may be
an unconscious imitation of the book, in which eloquence alternates with
technical accounts of Venetian architecture.

Lawrence's enthusiasm for history was now leading him in new directions. His starting-point had been the intriguing medieval figures to be
found on monumental brasses. From these he had passed quite naturally
to details of costume, heraldry and armour, and to three-dimensional
effigies on tombs. By 1906, however, he was interested in every trace of
the medieval world. Through extensive reading he learned the relationships between churches, ceramic fragments, costume, and military architecture. As Beeson noted: 'Brasses and the bypaths they opened into
mediæval history confirmed the gradual concentration of Lawrence's interest in the development of Gothic architecture and the design of military
buildings in particular.' His main preoccupation was now with 'the minds
of the designers of these defensive works and the extent to which history
had tested their intentions.' This was no casual interest. The 1906 letters
frequently display the discipline of his detailed observation and the knowledge that lay behind it.

Though Lawrence was now a competent photographer he had not taken
a camera on this tour, thinking that it would be difficult to make room for
one on his bicycle with all his other baggage. As it turned out, he realised
that other things were more dispensable and regretted that he had to rely
on commercial picture postcards.

That summer he rode considerable distances on his own machine and
felt fit enough to cycle a hundred miles each day (on one outing, from
Dinard to Fougères and back, he covered 114 miles). But cycling was a
means to an end, and he remarked that: 'A motor bicycle would be very
useful for getting away to the antiquities round about.'

He received his Senior Locals results while still at Dinard. The published
lists showed that he had been placed in the First Class, as in the Junior
Locals two years before. The marks gained show that of 4,645 candidates, only twelve had achieved a higher total. In several subjects he had
done well compared with the candidates who took first place (whose

marks are also given here). In English Language and Literature he shared first place (439 marks) and he had also gained a distinction with equal third place in Religious Knowledge (183:216). Other good results were Arithmetic (84:100), History (193:262), and French (214:278). In Political Economy (171:194) he was in fact second, but all the candidates did badly and no distinctions were awarded. His results in Latin (191:459) and Greek (193:430) probably reflect his attitude towards grammar. His total in mathematics (algebra and geometry) was very poor: (79:239).

When Lawrence learned of his passes and distinctions he wrote home: 'The result is on the whole not as good as I had hoped, although I am quite satisfied with the English. I wonder whether there is any profession in which a knowledge of one's tongue is of the slightest use . . . In the Divinity I had hoped for more. Polit. Econ. is not surprising . . . in the English my essay on Physical Culture in 2000 A.D. evidently went down'.

That autumn was taken up mainly with work for Oxford entrance, although he won a school essay prize on the subject of 'Our Colonies'. He tried for a scholarship at St John's College, but learned early in December that he had not been successful. In January 1907 he sat the examination for Jesus College where, by virtue of his birth at Tremadoc, he would be eligible for a Welsh award. Lawrence was a strong candidate and showed in the interviews that he could speak with authority about medieval pottery and brass rubbings. He won a Meyricke Exhibition, worth £50 a year, in Modern History.

During the Easter holidays, perhaps mindful that he was going to a college with a large Welsh membership, he went on a cycling tour of the Welsh castles, visiting Dinas Bran (Crow Castle), Caernarvon, Harlech, Chepstow, Caerphilly, Tintern Abbey and Raglan. He wrote of the Welsh: 'After ten days in Wales I ought to be able to sum up all the character, habits, peculiarities, virtues, vices, and other points of the Welsh people. I am sorry I cannot do this yet. They seem to me to be rather inquisitive, more dirty, and exceedingly ugly. I am at last discovering where I got my large mouth from, it's a national peculiarity. At the same time they appear honest; I have had no extortionate bills'.

Lawrence left the Oxford High School at the end of July 1907. He was nearly nineteen. Many years later he remarked that he had been educated there 'very little, very reluctantly, very badly', and he told his biographer Liddell Hart that he had found school 'an irrelevant and time-wasting nuisance, which I hated and contemned.' There seems to be a contradiction between these statements and his achievements, explained perhaps by another retrospective comment: 'They drag those "boy" years out too much. In my case they were miserable sweated years of unwilling work: and when after them I suddenly went to Oxford, the new freedom felt like Heaven. I don't think men ever work as hard as boys are made to work (unless they are working for themselves, when it isn't work at all) nor do I think the miseries of grown-up feelings are as bad as those of boys.'

CHAPTER 2

Oxford University
October 1907–December 1910

LAWRENCE entered Oxford University on 12 October 1907 as an exhibitioner at Jesus College. Since he had lived in the city for eleven years it may have been a less momentous step for him than for most of his fellow students. His elder brother Bob was already at St John's College, and Will would go up, also to St John's, in 1909.

The expense of maintaining and educating three fully grown children (with two younger boys following on) placed an increasing strain on the family budget. As Lawrence's Exhibition would not cover the full cost of residence in college he continued to live at home. In one way this decision would greatly diminish the effect of being at university. Normally students learn about living with their peers by being thrown together in an enclosed college environment, but Lawrence was never to participate fully in this life. Moreover, during his three undergraduate years he would take no part in sport or other college activities.

Like many of the most talented undergraduates, he concentrated on his studies. He belonged to the intellectual élite of scholars and exhibitioners which, in 1907, had less in common with the mass of students than would be the case today. Many of his contemporaries from wealthy families did not see academic achievement as the main purpose of attending university.

From the start, Lawrence's main academic contacts were outside the college. His principal tutor, Reginald Lane Poole, was a Fellow of St John's. Lawrence also continued to see a good deal of L. C. Jane, although he did not resume regular coaching with him until shortly before finals. Through his archaeological activities he already had friends at the Ashmolean, notably C. F. Bell and, from March 1908 onwards, E. T. Leeds, a new assistant keeper. Several schoolfriends, such as Beeson, were also up at Oxford, though only E. F. Hall was at Jesus.

For all these reasons it is unlikely that Lawrence spent much time in college during his first two terms, particularly as he was busy with university examinations. Yet it was probably quite difficult to concentrate on

21

academic work at home, as the house was also occupied by three younger brothers. In the summer term of 1908, therefore, he moved into rooms at Jesus. It was only then that he made friends among his fellow undergraduates.

Student behaviour is traditionally unconventional and, taking this into consideration, not many of the exploits credited to Lawrence deserve special mention. During the summer that he spent in college his most notable prank was canoeing along the Trill Mill Stream, which runs under the streets of Oxford. Like many undergraduates before and since, Lawrence posed deliberately as an eccentric. One remarkable scholar, A. T. P. Williams, who was later to beome Bishop of Winchester, recalled meeting Lawrence 'almost always late at night, walking in the quadrangle at Jesus. I do not know when he went to bed; some nights, I am pretty sure, not at all, certainly seldom till well on in the small hours.' Another contemporary, A. G. Prys-Jones, wrote that Lawrence 'sat cross-legged on the floor quietly explaining that he never sat on chairs if he could help it, that he never indulged in the meals known as breakfast, lunch, tea and dinner, nor smoked nor took drinks; in fact he did nothing which qualified him to be an ordinary member of society. But he added, drolly, that he had no objection whatsoever to my doing any of these things'.

One aspect of university life has changed beyond recognition since Lawrence's day: the nature of relationships permitted between the sexes. Although there was a small number of women's colleges at both Oxford and Cambridge, the two sexes had few opportunities to mix freely, and emotional friendships during the undergraduate years were strongly discouraged. These constraints formed part of a wider attitude towards relationships between men and women which was generally accepted, and which could easily be justified as a rational response to progress in medicine. Infant mortality had fallen greatly, notably in the middle and upper classes; yet there was still no sure method of contraception except sexual abstinence. As a result, the emphasis in marital life was on the virtues of companionship rather than on sex. Young men were taught that women were a fit subject for romantic admiration, but that a desire for sexual gratification was sinful. Lawrence would recall how, 'at Oxford the select preacher, one evening service, speaking of venery, said, "And let me implore you, my young friends, not to imperil your immortal souls upon a pleasure which, *so I am credibly informed*, lasts less than one and three-quarter minutes." ' Lawrence was echoing views held sincerely by many Englishmen of his generation when he later wrote scathingly of those 'who regarded our comic reproductive processes not as an unhygienic pleasure, but as a main business of life.'

Young men of the ruling classes were taught that abstinence in general would prepare them for their duties; moral leadership would fall to those who could resist the temptations to which others succumbed. The basis for this view came directly from the Protestant Christianity which Lawrence so wholeheartedly accepted. Before going to university he had taught at St Aldate's Sunday school and served as an officer in the Church Lads' Brigade. Canon Christopher had retired from St Aldate's in 1905, but the Lawrence brothers continued to attend weekly Bible classes at his home.

During Lawrence's three years as an undergraduate he increasingly practised self-denial, exploring and stretching the limits of his physical capability. He tried staying awake for long periods and experimented with fasting. While he took no part in formal sport, he built up his strength and stamina by arduous cycling over long distances. He made no secret of his desire to subjugate his body to his will. E. F. Hall, whose rooms at Jesus Lawrence often used, recalled that: 'He came one evening into my rooms . . . and began to fire a revolver, blank cartridge fortunately, out of the windows . . . one glance at his eyes left no doubt at all that he told the truth when he said that he had been working for forty-five hours at a stretch without food, to test his powers of endurance.'

By June 1908, the end of his first year at Oxford, Lawrence's tutors had formed a good idea of his academic potential. For his final history examinations he would have to sit various set papers, and also to select one of ten alternative special subjects. This choice would not have to be made until mid-November 1909, but Lawrence began to explore the topics long before then. It seems likely that he was at first attracted by the paper on Military History and Strategy. This would have been a natural extension of his enthusiasm for military architecture; he later told Liddell Hart that he had become interested in the subject while still at school. At Oxford he 'read some French study of Napoleon's Italian campaign, and then browsed in his despatches, a series of about twenty-five vols. These interested me in his text-books, and so they got me to Bourcet (?), Guibert, and Saxe, in that order . . . But my interests were mainly mediaeval, and in pursuit of them I . . . went elaborately into siege-manoeuvres'.

When a subject attracted him he would study it with immense energy; but otherwise his work was sound rather than exceptional. L. C. Jane, who probably knew Lawrence's academic abilities as well as any of his university tutors, later wrote: 'I found out in the first week or two that the thing was to suggest rather out-of-the-way books—he could be relied on to get more out of a suggestive sentence in a book than an ordinary man would get from a volume . . . He had the most diverse interests historically, though mainly mediæval . . . Lawrence was not a bookworm, though he read very fast and a great deal: I should not call him a scholar by temperament and the main characteristic of his work was always that it was unusual without the effort to be unusual.'

In 1908 the examiners in Modern History introduced a new option allowing candidates to present a thesis 'on some question within any special subject offered by them in the Examination.' If Lawrence chose 'Military History and Strategy' as his special subject, he would be able to display his knowledge of medieval military architecture in depth, both in a thesis and in the ensuing viva.

Accordingly, in the summer of 1908 he went on the longest of his French cycling tours, to examine medieval castles and fortifications. Bicycles (which could be taken to a distant starting-point by train) had revolutionised European tourism, and Lawrence's 2,400–mile journey was not exceptional. He crossed to Le Havre in mid-July, having worked out a route which would take him to see the most important castles he had not already visited.

Letters home show that he found the journey very enjoyable, despite the fact that he was cycling long distances every day in the summer heat: 'I'm riding very strongly, and feel very fit, on my diet of bread, milk and fruit . . . I begin on two pints of milk and bread, and supplement with fruit to taste till evening, when more solid stuff is consumed: one eats a lot when riding for a week on end at any pace. My day begins early ('tis fearfully hot at mid-day), there is usually a château to work at from 12–2, and then hotel at seven or eight. I have no time for sight-seeing: indeed sometimes I wonder if my thesis is to be written this November or next, I find myself composing pages and phrases as I ride.'

After a fortnight's travelling, he reached the Mediterranean coast at Aigues-Mortes, and wrote home: 'I bathed today in the sea, the great sea, the greatest in the world . . . I felt that at last I had reached the way to the South, and all the glorious East; Greece, Carthage, Egypt, Tyre, Syria, Italy, Spain, Sicily, Crete . . . they were all there, and all within reach . . . of me. I fancy I know now better than Keats what Cortes felt like, silent upon a peak in Darien. Oh I must get down here—farther out—again! Really this getting to the sea has almost overturned my mental balance: I would accept a passage for Greece tomorrow'.

Instead, however, he turned westwards to continue his tour. The walled city of Carcassonne exceeded all his expectations, although he did not at first realise how greatly it had been restored: 'It is of all dates: much Roman work: much Visigothic, a splendid Saracenic tower, some Carlovingian work, and mediæval of all sorts to the end of the fourteenth century . . . This makes it the most interesting and most valuable object-lesson in military architecture (for at all periods it was a first-class fortress) and it happens also to be wonderfully picturesque . . . Also I have a superb plan, showing the different periods of the buildings . . . there is much of the twelfth [century] for me; so much that I cannot satisfy myself upon it: in fact could only do so by carting it back to Oxford and fixing it on Brill hill.'

A few days later he was at Cordes, and sent his family a letter which shows that he already possessed the powers of observation and description that would be so evident in his later writing: 'the streets (two streets paved) are so steep that one can only maintain one's balance with great difficulty, and a strange horse cannot mount. Join these streets by narrow alleys of flights of broken, irregular stairs alternating with tiny squares of gravel about one house (say twenty feet long) each way. In places throw archways over the streets, or make them run under tunnels for fifty yards. Put in eight or ten fortified gates of the fifteenth and sixteenth centuries and fairly complete town walls, built over and round with a tangled ramshackle mass of hovels and ruined cottages. Let every other house be of stone, and of the fourteenth century, with charming flamboyant windows of two lights, divided by exquisitely carved pillars and shapely capitals of a bunch of vine leaves or other naturalistic foliage. Half these windows are blocked up with a mass of broken tiles and mortar; over the others are worm-eaten shutters with splendid iron-work, and hinges of the Renaissance time. Between the windows are string courses, often carved with grotesques, of animals with human heads, hunting scenes etc. The roofs project a couple of feet, with gargoyles grinning down into the middle of the tiny streets, only a matter of two yards wide. These houses are usually of three storeys, and are mixed up with modern houses (modern for Cordes that is), perhaps of the sixteenth century with transomed and mullioned windows, and square-headed or ogee doorways . . . Some of the houses are in ruins, others tottering. There are only three straight ones in the town (these are now the *Mairie*), all the rest lean backwards and forwards, or are shored up by a stable, or a buttress thrown across the streets to a similarly affected house: and so two sick men support each other. Some are of brick, plastered, or have been plastered, for it has usually fallen away, revealing blocked doors and windows, niches, and sculptured blocks built into the later work. All the wood-work is old and weather-warped, much of it quaintly carved, with all sorts of dilapidations.'

On August 28 Lawrence reached Chartres, expecting it to be 'like most French cathedrals spoilt by restoration, so I slipped out before breakfast to "do" it.' A letter written to his parents that evening is one of the most interesting to have survived from this period. Its uninhibited expression of religious feeling contrasts sharply with the reserved tone of other letters to his mother.

'What I found I cannot describe—it is absolutely untouched and unspoilt, in superb preservation, and the noblest building (for Beauvais is only half a one) that I have ever seen, or expect to see. If only you could get an idea of its beauty, of its perfection, without going to look at it! Its date is late twelfth and early thirteenth century. It is not enormous; but the carvings on its three portals are as fine as the best of all Greek work. Till yesterday I would put no sculptors near the Greeks of the fifth century. Today the French of the early middle ages *may* be inferior, but I do not think so: nothing in imagination could be grander than that arrangement of three huge cavernous portals, (thirty-odd feet deep), of gigantic height, with statues everywhere for pillars, bas-reliefs for plain surfaces, statuettes and canopies for mouldings. The whole west wall of the cathedral is chased and wrought like a florentine plaque, and by master hands! You may think the individual figures stiff—the details coarse—everything is hard and narrow I admit, but when you see the whole—when you can conceive at once the frame *and* the picture, then you must admit that nothing could be greater, except it were the Parthenon as it left the hands of Pheidias: it must be one of the noblest works of man, as it is the finest of the middle ages. One cannot describe it in anything but superlatives, and these seem so wretchedly formal that I am half tempted to scratch out everything that I have written: Chartres is Chartres:—that is, a gallery built by the sculptors to enclose a finer collection than the Elgin Marbles. I went in, as I said, before breakfast, and I left when dark:—all the day I was running from one door to another, finding in each something I thought finer than the one I had just left, and then returning to find that the finest was that in front of me—for it is a place absolutely impossible to imagine, or to recollect, at any rate for me: it is overwhelming, and when night came I was absolutely exhausted, drenched to the skin (it had poured all day) and yet with a feeling I had never had before in the same degree—as though I had found a path (a hard one) as far as the gates of

Heaven, and had caught a glimpse of the inside, the gate being ajar. You will understand how I felt though I cannot express myself. Certainly Chartres is the sight of a lifetime, a place truly in which to worship God.'

Lawrence returned to England on September 8, bringing back a large number of picture postcards, photographs, notes, sketches and plans for his thesis.

That autumn the Oxford University Officers' Training Corps was formed. Lawrence was among the first to volunteer. His decision came as a complete surprise to many of his friends, though possibly not to those who knew that he had already been an officer in the St Aldate's Church Lads' Brigade. Like most other young men of his social background, he felt deeply patriotic.

Although he joined this military scheme, there are few signs elsewhere that he took any greater part in undergraduate life during his second year at Oxford. He did not take rooms in Jesus College when he came back from France. His parents had decided to create the quiet surroundings he needed for his studies by building a two-room bungalow at the bottom of the garden. When this was completed it had a grate, electricity, water, and a telephone to the house. He slept and worked there for the next two years, gaining not only a degree of independence, but also the habit of isolation. He read voraciously, and his choice of books went well beyond the scholarly works required for the history course. He studied medieval writings such as the *chansons de geste*, and also enjoyed historical romances about the Middle Ages, reading Maurice Hewlett's *Richard Yea and Nay* over and over again.

That autumn he discussed his survey of French castles with C. F. Bell at the Ashmolean. Bell later wrote: 'We were talking one day about what his next step should be and I said "Why don't you go to the Holy Land and try to settle once and for all the long contested question as to whether the pointed arch and vault were copied or developed from Eastern sources by the Crusaders, or whether it was they who taught their use to the Arabs?" . . . The suggestion was the origin of Lawrence's first visit to the Levant.'

The idea of travelling to the Holy Land appealed greatly to him. In writing a thesis along the lines Bell had suggested he could incorporate all the research he had already done in France. Moreover, he could change his chosen special paper from 'Military History and Strategy' (which, in 1910, was to include a paper he found of little interest, about the Waterloo Campaign) to 'The First Three Crusades, 1095–1193', a medieval subject already close to his heart.

Before the end of the year he had made up his mind to go to the East if possible. By good fortune, an archaeologist and traveller with personal knowledge of the areas he would need to visit had just been appointed Keeper of the Ashmolean. This was D. G. Hogarth, to whom Lawrence was introduced at the beginning of January 1909. Hogarth suggested writing to C. M. Doughty, one of the most experienced Arabian travellers then living, for advice about the practicality of the journey. Doughty's reply was hardly encouraging: 'In July and August the heat is very severe by day and night, even at the altitude of Damascus, (over 2,000 ft). It is a land of squalor, where a European can find little refreshment. Long daily marches on foot a prudent man who knows the country would I think consider out of the question. The populations only know their own wretched life, and look upon any European wandering in their country with at best a veiled ill-will.

'The distances to be traversed are very great. You would have nothing to draw upon but the slight margin of strength which you bring with you from Europe. Insufficient food, rest and sleep would soon begin to tell . . .

'I should dissuade a friend from such a voyage, which is too likely to be most wearisome, hazardous to health and even disappointing.'

Lawrence, however, was determined to go, and made preparations for the journey. Since he would need some spoken Arabic he began to take lessons. He also took lessons in drawing, because he had found that it was often difficult to photograph the features of castles he wished to use as illustrations. His teacher, E. H. New, was excellent company. New had recently illustrated a major biography of William Morris and was working on a series of bird's-eye views of Oxford colleges. It was said that no one knew better than he did where to find good vantage points for such work, and it was probably with his encouragement that Lawrence took to climbing Oxford buildings: 'I used to go up all the towers and roofs, to get new angles of photography for architectural reasons.'

It may also have been through New's influence that Lawrence began to take an enthusiastic interest in the work of William Morris. His letters show that he read works by Morris extensively during the next four years and was strongly attracted by the ideals of neo-medievalism and crafts-manship they advocated, though he seems to have been less affected by their utopian socialism, which was quite alien to his own upbringing.

The notion of running a printing press after Morris's example appealed to Lawrence's romantic nature. Commercial printing had long since abandoned the standards of the early craftsmen who had tried to make their printed books as beautiful as medieval manuscripts. Morris had revived hand-printing and had aimed to 'produce books which would be a pleasure to look upon as pieces of printing and arrangement of type.' Lawrence had no experience of printing, but discussed the idea of setting up a press with several friends, one of whom was Leonard Green: 'We decided that we would buy a windmill on a headland that was washed by sea. We would set up a printing press in the lowest storey and live over our shop. We would print only rather "precious" books . . . they would not be bound except to suit the temperament of the possible purchaser, and then only in vellum stained with Tyrian dye'.

As the date of Lawrence's departure for Syria approached, Hogarth provided an introduction to H. Pirie-Gordon, who had toured part of the region the previous year on horseback; Pirie-Gordon lent Lawrence an annotated map. In the meantime Sir John Rhys, Principal of Jesus College, had asked Lord Curzon, Chancellor of the University, to arrange with the Turkish authorities for *irades*, or letters of safe conduct, to facilitate the journey.

Lawrence left England on 18 June 1909 on board the SS *Mongolia*. He spent the voyage working at his Arabic and, after a delay changing ships at Port Said, finally reached Beirut on July 7. There he made contact with tutors at the American University who assured him that they had been 'taking walking tours in their summer holidays for years, exactly as I proposed to do . . . everybody, from the Consul downwards, tells me that travelling is as ordinary as in Europe.'

He set out on July 8, walking thirty miles down the coast road to Sidon on the first day. His itinerary then took him to Nabatiyeh, where he hired a guide to reach the fortress of Beaufort and thence Banias. After this he went on to Hunin, Tibnin and then Safed, which stands on a hill 2,700 feet high: 'In the day's march I went up and down the height of Mt. Blanc—and Palestine is all like that: a collection of small, irritating, hills crushed together pell-mell, and the roads either go up and down all the time, or wind in and about the rocks of the valleys, and never reach anywhere at all.' From Safed he went eastward to Chastellet, and then down the Jordan valley to the Sea of Galilee. Continuing southward he visited Belvoir, then walked via Endor to Nazareth and eventually Athlit before returning up the coast road to Haifa, Acre, Tyre, Sidon, and Beirut. He completed this section of his tour in three weeks.

In one way he found his journey through the Bible lands disappointing, since the arid landscape bore so little resemblance to the scenery he had somehow expected: 'it is such a comfort to *know* that the country was not a bit like this in the time of Our Lord. The Renaissance painters were right, who drew him and his disciples feasting in a pillared hall, or sunning themselves on marble staircases: everywhere one finds remains of splendid Roman roads and houses and public buildings . . . Also the country was well-peopled, and well watered artificially: there were not twenty miles of thistles behind Capernaum! . . . Palestine was a decent country then, and could so easily be made so again. The sooner the Jews farm it all the better: their colonies are bright spots in a desert.'

He returned to Beirut on August 2 and wrote a 5,000–word letter to his family, to give them 'an idea of Northern Palestine in summer.' They must have been delighted to receive it, not least because of its many Biblical allusions.

The account of his contacts with the local people shows his willingness to adapt to the ways of the country: 'When I go into a native house the owner salutes me, and I return it and then he says something to one of his women, and they bring out a thick quilt, which, doubled, is laid on the rush mat over the floor as a chair: on that I squat down, and then the host asks me four or five times how my health is; and each time I tell him it is good. Then comes sometimes coffee, and after that a variety of questions, as to whether my tripod is a revolver, and what I am, and where I come from, and where I'm going, and why I'm on foot, and am I alone, and every other thing conceivable: and when I set up my tripod (sometimes, as a great treat) there are cries of astonishment and "*Mashallah*"'s, "by the life of the Prophet", "Heavens", "Give God the glory" etc. etc. Such a curiosity has never been seen and all the village is summoned to look at it. Then I am asked about my wife and children, how many I have etc. I really feel a little ashamed of my youth out here. The Syrian of sixteen is full grown, with moustache and beard, married, with children, and has perhaps spent two or three years in New York, getting together enough capital to start him in business at home. They mostly put my age as fifteen, and are amazed at my travelling on foot and alone. Riding is the only honourable way of going, and everyone is dreadfully afraid of thieves: they travel very little.'

Lawrence had averaged twenty-two miles a day, and on one occasion walked thirty-six. He left Beirut for the next stage of his journey on August 6 and reached Tripoli a week later, having spent three or four days at the American Mission School in Jebail where he was welcomed by the principal, Miss Holmes, and her staff: Lawrence's opinion of the American Mission's activities in Syria was to change over the coming years, but in 1909 it was favourable: 'it is doing much the most wonderful work of all in Palestine. It is Presbyterian, and has most brilliant men at the head of it. They recognised that at present conversion of Muslim in Syria was impossible . . . they have opened schools for both parties all over the country. In these the instruction is given in English, and includes many very important matters . . . Thus English is a common language in Syria, and in ten years no other will be needed . . . They have colleges all over Syria, and Asia Minor, and in Constantinople (mostly self-supporting) and in all of them the religious side is emphasised: also every school is a mission station'.

On his way north to Tripoli he had visited castles at Batrun, Mseilha, Enfeh and Tripoli. Then he set off into the interior. On August 16, his twenty-first birthday, he reached the magnificent Crac des Chevaliers, 'which is I think the finest castle in the world: certainly the most picturesque I have seen—quite marvellous: I stayed three days there'. Thence on to Safita and beyond: 'I will have such difficulty in becoming English again, here I am Arab in habits and slip in talking from English to French and Arabic unnoticing'.

On one occasion he was shot at, from about two hundred yards, by 'an ass with an old gun,' but managed to scare off his attacker by firing back (at extreme range) with his pistol: 'I'm rather glad that my perseverance in carrying the Mauser has been rewarded . . . the man simply wanted to frighten me into money-payment'. At the end of the month, when he had reached Latakia, he wrote home reassuringly: 'you may be happy now all my rough work is finished successfully: and my Thesis is I *think assured.*' But from Latakia he struck inland once again to Sahyun, where he stayed two days before going to Aleppo 'by forced marches, 120 miles in five days, which no doubt Bob or Will will laugh at, but not if they had to do it stumbling and staggering over these ghastly roads: it took me thirteen hours of marching per day, and I had an escort with me (mounted) so I lost no time. By the way it is rather amusing to contemplate a pedestrian guarded carefully by a troop of light horse: of course everybody thinks I am mad to walk, and the escort offered me a mount on the average once a half-hour: they couldn't understand my prejudice against everything with four legs.' The escort was a precaution taken after the shooting incident.

Lawrence reached Aleppo, but he was running short of time, and decided to hire a carriage there with two men and two horses to take him inland to Urfa and back. This final stretch of the journey, which lasted only ten days, took him through an area rich in Hittite remains. D. G. Hogarth, who had visited this region the previous spring, was one of the pioneer authorities on Hittite seal stones, and he had asked Lawrence to look out for seals. All kinds of ancient objects could be bought quite readily from villagers, who augmented their meagre incomes by robbing graves and selling their finds to itinerant *antika* dealers based in Aleppo.

On the way back from Urfa, at Seruj, Lawrence's camera was stolen from the carriage while the coachman he had left on watch slept. This was a serious loss, since no picture postcards of these Crusader castles were available and photographs were essential for his thesis. Worse was to come: a few days later while touring villages near the Euphrates in search of Hittite seals he was attacked. 'A beggar followed me from Meyra and bagged all my money and valuables (not content with pounding me behind the ear with a stone and biting open the back of my hand). I recovered most; but with such work that I was too sick of the district, and had (after due baksheeshing) too little cash to spare to search further.'

He was back in Aleppo by September 19, making strenuous efforts through the local authorities to recover his lost camera, but with no success. Three days later he decided to abandon his remaining plans and return to England. In a letter to Sir John Rhys at Jesus College, excusing himself for arriving in Oxford late for the beginning of term, he wrote: 'I have had a most delightful tour . . . on foot and alone all the time, so that I have perhaps, living as an Arab with the Arabs, got a better insight into the daily life of the people than those who travel with caravan and drag-omen. Some thirty-seven out of the fifty-odd castles were on my proposed route and I have seen all but one of them: many are quite unpublished, so of course I have had to make many plans, drawings and photographs'.

He travelled the whole way to England by sea, rather than taking the quicker route across France from Marseilles by train. This gave him the chance to recover his strength before reaching Oxford in mid-October. During the voyage home he drew up a detailed statement of his expenses on the tour, which amounted to £71 8s. 6d.

When the ship called in at Naples, Lawrence visited a foundry which produced bronze copies of classical sculptures. There, he bought 'a Hyp-nos head, very good work, but a bad cast, modern naturally. I asked the price and tumbled down with it to eight francs, little more than the value of the metal.' He brought the Hypnos back to Oxford and found a place for it on a seat in the bay window of his study in the garden bungalow, where it became his most cherished ornament. It was a free-hand copy of the well-known Hypnos in the British Museum bronze room (itself a Roman copy of a Greek work dating from the fourth century B.C.).

Lawrence's letters show that his interest in medieval sculpture had led him to study the Greek masters. Now that he had learned to draw, he began to try three-dimensional work, and this became an occasional hobby. Much later he wrote that he had 'modelled and carved with some hope and vigour . . . and did slowly gain the power to express something of my meaning in clay or stone. And I did thereby come to understand a little the limitations and triumphs of a sculptor's aim.' When his youngest brother Arnold was sixteen, Lawrence would advise him to 'keep up an interest in sculpture. It is finer far than flat work, much more difficult to do and to appreciate, and gives one complete satisfaction where it is well done. I would rather possess a fine piece of sculpture than anything in the world.'

The bungalow gave Lawrence the liberty to work or read late into the night without disturbing his family. 'You know, I think, the joy of getting into a strange country in a book: at home when I have shut my door and the town is in bed—and I know that nothing, not even the dawn—can disturb me in my curtains: only the slow crumbling of the coals in the fire: they get so red, and throw such splendid glimmerings on the Hypnos and the brass-work. And it is lovely too, after you have been wandering for hours in the forest with Percivale or Sagramors le desirous, to open the door, and from over the Cherwell to look at the sun glowering through the valley-mists. Why does one not like things if there are other people about? Why cannot one make one's books live except in the night, after hours of straining? . . . if you can get the right book at the right time you taste joys—not only bodily, physical, but spiritual also, which pass one out above and beyond one's miserable self, as it were through a huge air, following the light of another man's thought. And you can never be quite the old self again. You have forgotten a little bit: or rather pushed it out with a little of the inspiration of what is immortal in someone who has gone before you.'

During the winter of 1909–10 Lawrence completed his thesis, calling it *The Influence of the Crusades on European Military Architecture—to the End of the XIIth Century*. The maximum length allowed was 12,000 words, and the thesis had to be submitted before the Easter vacation began. He had the final draft typed, although this was not a requirement, and illustrated it with numerous plans, sketches, photographs, and picture postcards.

He hoped that his result in finals would be good enough for him to pursue an academic career; the next step would be to prepare a B.Litt. thesis. He had spent a good deal of time during his undergraduate years working on various archaeological projects at the Ashmolean. That spring, for example, he had helped rearrange the Medieval Room. If he chose a research topic that combined his academic knowledge of the Middle Ages with this private interest in medieval pottery, the way might be open to a career in archaeology. Like other undergraduates, however, he felt unwilling to commit himself; indeed he took a certain pride in neglecting plans for a career. He later wrote: 'I fought very hard, at Oxford and after going down, to avoid being labelled'.

His scheme for setting up a private press was also taking shape. He had passed on his enthusiasm for fine printing to Vyvyan Richards and the two were thinking of forming a partnership. The project owed more to the ideals preached by William Morris than to any first-hand knowledge of the tasks involved. A letter written by Lawrence to his father some months later describes the basis for their plans: 'If we are to preserve the utmost elasticity in our relations, we cannot be bound by a written agreement. We must (if such agreement exists) inevitably go outside and beyond it whenever we feel inclined: so that there will always be a contradiction between our theory and our practice . . . There cannot be any fixed hours of work. We both feel (at present) that printing is the best thing we can do, if we do it the best we can. That means, though, (as it is an art), that it will be done only when we feel inclined. Very likely sometimes for long periods I will not touch a press at all. Richards, whose other interests are less militant, will probably do the bulk of the work. The losses (if any) will be borne by us both, according as we are in funds (we will approximate to a common purse): the profits will be seized upon as a glorious opportunity to reduce prices.

'You will see, I think, that printing is not a business but a craft. We cannot sit down to it for so many hours a day, any more than one could paint a picture on that system.'

Lawrence's parents did not approve. Richards was two years older than their son, and they could see no natural basis for this friendship. 'It would be hard to imagine two more diverse minds than his and mine', Richards later wrote. 'I had spent all my boyhood since the age of ten getting classics, with scholarships and distaste, in the orthodox public school way. My father was an inventor and a man absorbed altogether in business; my mother, an American . . . Archaeology, architecture, art—all such matters I scorned. I was one of the leaders in the college games with a proper sense of their importance.'

Towards the end of his life Richards confessed the true basis for his friendship with Lawrence: 'Quite frankly for me it was love at first sight.

He had neither flesh nor carnality of any kind; he just did not understand. He received my affection, my sacrifice, in fact, eventually my total subservience, as though it was his due. He never gave the slightest sign that he understood my motives or fathomed my desires.'

Though Lawrence hid the fact from Richards, he can hardly have been unaware of this difficulty in their relationship. He chose to be tolerant; moreover he had a gift for persuading people to do what he wanted, and skilfully diverted Richards' infatuation into enthusiasm for printing. Although Richards had previously known nothing whatsoever about this craft he had become the instrument of Lawrence's ambition to set up a private press.

The difference in their attitudes towards one another is clear from their own statements. Richards wrote: 'The rest of my life at Oxford was spent in almost daily companionship with my new exciting friend.' Lawrence, on the other hand, while prepared to defend what he saw as Richards' good points, also had many reservations. In a letter to his brother Will, he said: 'Your character of him seems to me very apt and fairly complete: though I must say I think some of the "snobbery" which gives such an unpleasant conceit to his judgments comes rather from lack of understanding, than intentionally. Richards is exceedingly narrow in his outlook and interests, and is too apt to condemn generally where he does not find the particular colour and cast of thought that appeals to him. He is not at all intellectual, but an artist to the finger-tips . . . As soon as you get him on what he thinks really good he loses entirely his critical sense, and becomes a most fiery prophet. He has said things to me of an intimacy and directness which are beyond anyone else I have met. Altogether though he is a most complex and difficult personality, and I do not think he will get any better on acquaintance. He is quite in earnest about the printing: just as I am. I fancy we each of us trust the other entirely in that, without any great love, personally. But he will do his best for the press, and I also, so that only a little *savoir vivre* is necessary to make a very satisfactory partnership. I am most fortunate to have found a man of tremendous gifts, to whom craftsmanship is at once a dream and an inspiration . . . I think even Mr. Jane would be satisfied if our association produced the best book of modern times . . . To do the best of anything (or to try to do it) is not waste of opportunity:—and to be keeper of a museum would not be my best, any more than to teach history: I want something in which I can use all these things instead of being used by one of them.'

Richards' homosexual feelings had no place in Lawrence's emotional life; while still an undergraduate he had fallen in love with a girl he had known since childhood. His affection for her was noted by close friends such as E. F. Hall, who often saw them together.

Lawrence and Janet Laurie had played together at Langley Lodge when he was six or seven. The two families had become close friends and after 1899, when Janet went to boarding school in Oxford, she had been a regular visitor to the house in Polstead Road. In 1901 her father had died, and she had been obliged to return home, but she was always welcomed by the Lawrences in Oxford and continued to see the boys quite often.

These visits were encouraged; Janet was much the same age as Bob, and Mrs Lawrence hoped that they would marry. Janet liked all the boys but had no strong feelings for Bob, who was 'so terribly good'. However, her company had always been enjoyable and she laughed readily; now she had grown into a good-looking if slightly tomboyish young lady. Both Lawrence and his brother Will found her very attractive. She visited Lawrence at Jesus College, and he often saw her at his home.

According to her own account, one evening after dinner when the two had remained behind at table, he bolted the dining room door and asked her quite unexpectedly if she would marry him. Like many of his contemporaries he was deeply secretive about his personal feelings and had an extremely inhibited attitude towards courtship. The depth of his affection now came as a complete surprise to her; she had never thought of him as a husband, and moreover was attracted to his tall and handsome brother Will. She realised that Lawrence was perfectly serious, but in her embarrassment laughed off the proposal. Although he often saw her afterwards he never mentioned the incident again. Some years later however he would prove the strength of his loyalty to her by an act of extraordinary generosity.

On 28 July 1910 the results of the Honour School of Modern History were published in Oxford. Lawrence and nine other candidates had been awarded First Class Honours. As his tutors had hoped, the thesis had been a remarkable success. The research in Syria had made an original contribution to knowledge. He later wrote to his brother Will that, in future, 'I fully expect Theses will be frowned upon: partly my fault, in straining the statute far beyond what ever was intended. Simple pieces of secondary work were supposed.'

L. C. Jane later told Robert Graves that Lawrence 'took a most brilliant First Class, so much so that Mr R. L. Poole (his tutor at Jesus) gave a dinner to the examiners to celebrate it.' C. T. Atkinson, one of the examiners, was probably more objective than Jane: 'The thesis was an excellent piece of work and just "made" what was otherwise a not very exciting First: "safe but rather slight".' Another of the examiners, W. H. Hutton, later wrote: 'I have just looked up his marks. There were ten papers, and a translation paper, and a thesis. His thesis was marked "most excellent", but it was not that which won him his first class, but the other papers which were all good and some very good.' Ernest Barker, a Fellow of St John's who had given Lawrence tutorials on the Crusades, concluded: 'I should doubt if Lawrence ever was, or ever wished to be, an "historical scholar" in the ordinary sense of the word. He was not interested in historic fact just for its own sake. He took the Oxford History School because it came in his way, and because it was a hurdle to be jumped . . . he made it interesting to himself by doing something of his own free choice, and by doing it on the spot: but when the History School was past—well, it was past, and history had served its turn.'

The result was very satisfactory, especially since the thesis had shown that Lawrence had an aptitude for research. Before he could begin post-graduate work, however, he needed finance. This problem would have to be resolved before the next academic year began in October, but first he took a well-earned holiday, cycling for a month in France, accompanied for part of the time by his younger brother Frank.

When they returned, he found that Jesus College was willing to give him money for postgraduate work. The subject of his B.Litt. research was to be 'Mediaeval Lead-Glazed Pottery from the 11th to the 16th Centuries.' The project was formally accepted by the University on November 1. Lawrence travelled that night to Rouen and from there wrote to Leeds: 'I hope . . . that you are aware of your new dignities. You are appointed (with the Regius Professor of Modern History, who was once Mr Oman) to supervise my researches into the origin and intentions of Mediæval Pottery . . . (especially grotesque): and if you get back to Oxford by when I return, I must call on you in cap and gown and receive instruction . . . The greatest and purest joy will be if you are set up at a huge table to *viva* me solemnly on what we have discussed and discovered together.

'It should create a good impression on your mind to know that I am in Rouen looking at medieval pots: Mr Bell got me letters from Mr Salomon Reinach [Keeper of National Museums in France] that make me out to be a sort of god: and they all rush about the museum here offering me keys and cupboards and cups of coffee: the last rather a bore.'

This letter from Rouen contains the earliest known reference to a

dramatic change in Lawrence's plans (though the news will have come as
no surprise to Leeds): 'Mr Hogarth is going digging', Lawrence wrote,
'and I am going out to Syria in a fortnight to make plain the valleys and
level the mountains for his feet:— also to learn Arabic. The two occupations fit into one another splendidly.'

The sudden decision to join Hogarth's excavations at Carchemish in
Syria was a turning-point in Lawrence's life. On October 23 Hogarth had
returned to Oxford from Turkey, where he had finalised official arrangements for the new dig. It is unlikely that Lawrence had known much
about Carchemish before this, although he had passed close to it during
his 1909 walking tour. He would now have learned that the significance
of the site had long been recognised by archaeologists. As the excavations
were to be an important stage in his career, something must be said about
the background to this expedition.

English scholars had known of an ancient site at Jerablus on the Euphrates since the early eighteenth century. By 1872 the ruins had been
identified as Carchemish, capital city of the Syrian Hittites. Four years
later a British Museum Assyriologist visited the site, and made detailed
notes and sketches. In December 1878, the British Consul at Aleppo
began the first investigation of Carchemish on the British Museum's
behalf. However, the work was not properly supervised, and the excavations were carried out unscientifically without adequate records. The
arrangement proved so unsatisfactory that in 1881 the work was abandoned.

Twenty-six years elapsed before the Museum found itself in a position
to undertake proper excavations at Carchemish; but it did not lose interest
in the site, part of which it had purchased. In the autumn of 1907 Sir
Edward Maunde Thompson, then Director and Principal Librarian of the
British Museum, invited Dr E. Wallis Budge, Keeper of the Department
of Babylonian and Assyrian Antiquities, to put forward proposals for
some Hittite excavations. It was felt that the Museum should 'contribute
to the solution of the Hittite problem, which had recently been illuminated by Dr Hugo Winckler's discoveries at Boghaz Keui.'

D. G. Hogarth was asked to visit northern Syria in 1908 and inspect
alternative sites. Even before he left, Budge thought that Carchemish
would be the best choice. Hogarth concluded that, despite the earlier
excavations and some damage done at various times to its visible monuments, Carchemish still probably 'contained more than the other sites
and represented a more important Hittite centre.' One of the chief in-
ducements to dig there was the hope of finding a bilingual text, equivalent

to the Rosetta Stone, which would enable scholars to decipher Hittite script and understand the Hittite language. The Euphrates at Carchemish had been the boundary between the Hittite and Assyrian empires, and therefore between the unknown Hittite language and Assyrian (written in cuneiform) which archaeologists could understand. 'Where more likely', Hogarth asked, 'to find monuments set up in two systems of writing for the edification of two neighbouring races?'

Following Hogarth's report, the Museum had decided to begin work at Carchemish in January or February 1911, but there was no commitment at this stage to long-term excavation. The scheme was for a single trial season, which would establish whether the site was worthy of more extensive works. In March 1910, therefore, Frederic Kenyon, who had taken over as the Museum's Director and Principal Librarian, had applied to the Turkish authorities for a permit. They had agreed, and permission for a two-year excavation was given to Hogarth, who had been nominated by the Museum to direct the work. As usual, there were conditions. All antiquities discovered were to be the property of the Imperial Ottoman Museum (although these objects could be photographed and casts taken). All objects found had to be deposited in a store controlled by the Turkish authorities, and the expedition had to pay the salary of a Turkish Commissaire who would oversee the dig on behalf of the Imperial Ottoman Museum. The administrative clauses stated that the permit was valid for two years, that it was not transferable, and that it would be void unless excavations began within three months of the date of issue.

Since Hogarth was not planning to begin work until February 1911 he could not comply with the last of these requirements. To avoid difficulties, therefore, he had gone to Constantinople in October 1910 and arranged for the starting date to be deferred until February.

Lawrence seems to have heard about the purpose of this visit to Constantinople while Hogarth was still away. Seeing an enviable opportunity to return to Syria, he went to see E. T. Leeds at the Ashmolean, who later recalled that Lawrence had unexpectedly asked him whether there were any digs in prospect 'in the Near East or elsewhere' which he might join. Leeds knew a good deal about Hogarth's Carchemish plans and had replied, 'Why on earth didn't you speak sooner?' He thought the arrangements were probably too far advanced, as R. Campbell Thompson had already been nominated as Hogarth's assistant. It also seemed unlikely that the British Museum would pay the cost of sending an inexperienced archaeologist to the site. When Hogarth returned to England, however, he was asked whether Lawrence could join the dig. Hogarth did not know

Lawrence well at this time, but he had been impressed a year earlier by the Syrian walking tour. Bell and Leeds were confident that Lawrence would make a good archaeologist, and his personality must have seemed to Hogarth well fitted for this career. 'Your true antiquary', Hogarth had written not long before, 'is born, not made. Sometimes an infirmity or awkwardness of body, which has disposed a boy to shun the pursuits of his fellows, may help to detach the man for the study of forgotten far off things; but it is essential that there be inborn in him the type of mind which is more curious of the past than the present, loves detail for its own sake, and cares less for ends than means.'

Hogarth agreed to take Lawrence, but the British Museum could hardly be asked to finance this addition to the party, and absence abroad on work which had nothing to do with the proposed B.Litt. would disqualify Lawrence from the Jesus College scholarship. So Lawrence was now awarded, 'entirely through Hogarth's initiative and wholehearted advocacy,' a Senior Demyship at Magdalen College, Oxford. The award, in effect a junior research fellowship, could run until the summer of 1914 and was worth £100 a year. This meant that if Lawrence went to Carchemish the Museum would not need to pay more than his on-site living expenses.

The dig, however, might not last more than four months, while the award was for four years. To qualify for it Lawrence gave as a research subject 'Norman Castles in the Levant'; additional fieldwork in Syria and Palestine would enable him to expand his undergraduate thesis into a book. Most of his time would nevertheless be spent in Oxford, and the project could run in parallel with his B.Litt. research on medieval pottery.

Lawrence now had two reasons for returning to Syria and for both of them he would need to improve his Arabic. He therefore arranged to spend the first two months of 1911 at the American Mission School in Jebail which he had visited during his 1909 walking tour. He also began to study Assyrian grammar and cuneiform, which would prove useful if Assyrian inscriptions were found at Carchemish.

He had more distant projects as well. One was for an academic book (or possibly two) which he sometimes referred to as 'my monumental work on the Crusades', and elsewhere as *Richard*. There are also references (in letters written many years later) to his having considered writing an account of the background of Christ: 'Galilee and Syria, social, intellectual and artistic, of 40 B.C. It would make an interesting book.' As a diversion from these serious plans he thought of writing a travel book which would recount 'adventures in seven type-cities of the East (Cairo,

Jerusalem, Baghdad, Damascus etc.)' and arrange 'their characters into a descending cadence: a moral symphony.' He had already decided on a title, derived from *Proverbs* (ix.1): 'Wisdom hath builded a house: she hath hewn out her seven pillars'. But 'Seven Pillars of Wisdom' was also a deliberate echo of Ruskin's *Seven Lamps of Architecture,* and there was a clear analogy between the structure of Ruskin's book and the idea behind Lawrence's project. This analogy was of course lost when he later used the title for his war memoirs.

The money from Magdalen would allow Lawrence to advance another of his plans. Before leaving England he talked to Vyvyan Richards, who had now taken a teaching post at Chingford on the border of Epping Forest. They agreed to form a loose business partnership and began to make plans for setting up the press. Before anything could be printed, Richards was to design a new typeface based on the rounded script of the *Book of Kells*, and also to build a neo-medieval hall to house the press machinery. This hall would incorporate roof-beams from an old building in Oxford to be demolished by Jesus College. Lawrence's contribution would be to finance the scheme, but he had no means to do this without help. He hoped that his father would buy a site for the press and lease it to Richards, and would also provide a loan to pay for the building. In the early stages at least, both the partners would earn their livings in other ways: 'Richards and I decided . . . that he would continue teaching for the present . . . we thought it would be wiser, since my power of earning the demyship depends on my health, and my ability to spend it on the press depends on my getting a salary, digging, next year and the year after . . . It is a great battle of the wits, creative, on his side, for he is doing the work, and utilitarian on mine, for I am to provide the materials beyond his keep. It will be a comfort when we get through into smoother water with the whole thing.'

Lawrence left for Syria expecting his father to settle the financial arrangements with Richards, who could then put the building work in hand. He seems not to have foreseen his father's lack of enthusiasm for helping Vyvyan Richards, especially in a scheme which owed so much to romantic idealism and so little to commercial sense.

CHAPTER 3

Beginnings at Carchemish
December 1910–June 1912

ON 10 December 1910 Lawrence sailed for Beirut on board the Messageries Maritimes steamship *Saghalien* which was scheduled to call at Naples, Athens, Smyrna and Constantinople. On the way, the ship developed engine trouble and as a result he had much more time ashore at these ports than he had expected. He seized the chance to visit Athens and explored the Acropolis with the enthusiasm born of a classical education: 'There were no porters, no guides, no visitors. And so I walked through the doorway of the Parthenon, and on into the inner part of it, without really remembering where or who I was. A heaviness in the air made my eyes swim, and wrapped up my senses: I only knew that I, a stranger, was walking on the floor of the place I had most desired to see, the greatest temple of Athene, the palace of art, and that I was counting her columns and finding there only what I already knew. The building was familiar, not cold as in the drawings, but complex, irregular, alive with curve and subtlety, and perfectly preserved. Every line of the mouldings, every minutest refinement in the sculptures were evident in that light, and inevitable in their place . . . and so only this about Athens, that there is an intoxication, a power of possession in its ruins, and the memories that inhabit them, which entirely prevents anyone attempting to describe or to estimate them'.

At Constantinople the *Saghalien* was delayed for several days, and Lawrence used the time to see the city and its museums. He did not reach Beirut until December 21 and arrived at Jebail, his final destination, on Christmas Eve.

At the end of the month Frederic Kenyon, Director of the British Museum, agreed formally to employ Lawrence at Carchemish, and he then wrote to the Treasury seeking approval for the additional cost: 'an offer has been received from Mr. T. E. Lawrence (an Arabic scholar, acquainted with the country, and an expert in the subject of pottery) to join the expedition at Jerablus and to take part in the excavations. Mr. Lawrence is willing to give his services (which will be of very material value) without salary, but I would ask your Lordships to sanction the payment of his actual living expenses while engaged on the excavations, and of his travelling expenses from Beyrout to Jerablus and back'.

Lawrence's knowledge of Arabic was somewhat generously described in this letter, but he was now at Jebail working hard on the north Syrian dialect. During this stay at the American Mission School he made friends with two of the teachers: Miss Fareedeh el Akle, who taught him Arabic, and Mrs Rieder, who encouraged him to improve his French.

Hogarth left England at the beginning of February, travelling out via Turkey. At Beirut he was met by an experienced archaeological overseer who had worked with him on several previous excavations. This was Gregorios Antoniou (generally known as Gregori), a Cypriot from Larnaca. When Lawrence had joined them, they made their way to Aleppo. The train journey gave Lawrence his first close acquaintance with Hogarth, whom he had previously seen as an eminent and distant figure: 'He has been very interesting indeed so far, especially on Arabian geography . . . Mr. Hogarth of course knew all the country by repute, and by books, and we identified all the mountain peaks and wadies and main roads . . . at Dera'at all was sunny, and we had a French *déjeuner* in the Buffet, where Mr Hogarth spoke Turkish & Greek, & French, & German, & Italian & English all about the same, so far as I could judge: it was a most weird feeling to be actually so far out of Europe'. They were delayed by the appalling weather, but at last reached Jerablus on March 11.

The ruins of Carchemish covered ten acres and had lain untouched for thirty years. Lawrence must have been excited by the prospect of finding out what lay beneath the surface. Hogarth later wrote this description of the city as they found it: 'The site . . . is a large oval surrounded by high embankments except on the north-east where the Euphrates flows past it. These embankments, in places as much as twenty-five feet high, conceal city fortifications of crude brick, and are pierced with two gates, one on the south and one on the west. On the north-east by the river but within the enceinte, rises a much higher and more important mound. Its summit is about 130ft above the mean level of the river, and it has evidently served as an acropolis. It is about 320 metres long from NW-SE and falls with a very steep slope to the river and a gentler one towards the town. The top is flattened and shows signs of having carried important Romano-Syrian structures, huge fragments of which have fallen down, and lie on the landward slope.'

Hogarth's object was to find out enough about the site to judge whether the Hittite remains were worth more thorough excavation. He could not attempt any systematic digging in a single season and had not brought the equipment that would be necessary for such work. He knew that Hittite remains had been found at the foot of the mound, including part of a large staircase. The position of this earlier digging was clear from the spoil heaps left behind and from a large stone relief still partly visible above ground. He decided to begin work in the same place, since it seemed likely that there would have been buildings in the vicinity of a stairway. Excavation began on March 13 and soon more than a hundred men were employed. The expedition took over a stone-built house in Jerablus belonging to the local liquorice company. This provided little shelter from the cold weather.

In 1908, when the excavations had first been planned, the Museum had expected Hogarth to run them himself. Now that he was Keeper of the Ashmolean, long absences abroad were no longer possible. He would soon have to return to Oxford, and he could spend only five weeks on the site. It had been arranged that Campbell Thompson, the second-in-command, would take over when Hogarth left. Thompson, however, was a cuneiformist with little experience relevant to these excavations, and Hogarth had some doubts about his capability. After watching him at work for a few days, Hogarth wrote to Kenyon: 'Thompson ought really to have a second helper besides Lawrence. The latter will second him admirably in observing and recording—in fact he is a far better *archaeologist* properly speaking than Thompson—but not in driving'.

Another preoccupation was the Berlin–Baghdad Railway, which was being built by German construction companies. The route had not been fixed when the British Museum applied to excavate at Jerablus in 1908. Now, however, the railway had become a threat. It was to cross the Euphrates at Jerablus, and the workings might endanger part of the site. The bridge would take several years to build, and there was already a construction camp with a team of German engineers. Since the railway company also employed local labour, there was competition between the German and English expeditions.

Lawrence's first duties at Carchemish were a natural continuation of his work on medieval pottery in Oxford: 'It seems likely that I will take particular charge of the pottery found: that would be a business very much to my taste.' Very little pottery came to light during the first few weeks, but he was kept busy and his Arabic was constantly in demand on the site. After a few days he wrote about the dig to his parents: 'Work begins at sunrise (6.0 a.m.), we breakfast first and walk down a little later. Thompson is surveying the site, and will be to the end of the week. Mr. Hogarth does the writing up of the results: I do the squeezing [taking paper impressions] and drawing the inscriptions and sculptures, and (with the great Gregori . . .) direct the men. Work goes on (with an hour for lunch) till sunset. Then home: write up journals: and catalogues: feed, and go to bed. This week has been extra busy putting up shelves, and fitting doors, windows etc. This I have done mostly, being handiest . . . many of the slabs found have been too defaced for photography. These I have been trying to draw on a large scale for reproduction: this has been a big business. One lion's head is very fine work, artistically: also a god or king . . . The district is exceedingly pretty, from the model-village with its spring to the Euphrates, and the plain of Tell Ahmar, and the Taurus, snow-covered, to the north. The whole affair till now has been ideal, or would be if one had time to think about it.'

The digs were yielding many fragments of stone bearing Hittite inscriptions, and Carchemish soon proved extremely rich in these texts. Many years later the distinguished Assyriologist R. D. Barnett would write: 'The collection of inscriptions from Carchemish has proved of the greatest importance in the study and decipherment of this script. Whatever the reasons may be, the Carchemish texts equal or exceed both in number and importance those from all other sites. It certainly seems that at least in the first millennium BC the metropolis of the hieroglyphs was Carchemish.'

The discovery of these indecipherable texts was a continuing source of frustration, especially to Thompson. Despite their hopes of a bilingual inscription, none was found and the site yielded almost nothing in cuneiform. Lawrence, however, was enjoying himself greatly and his letters to England were filled with accounts of entertaining incidents. He was more used to rough living than his companions and watched their discomfort with amusement. On March 27, for instance, he wrote to Leeds about their living accommodation: 'the house . . . is of stone, with mud floors and roof, and from the roof little bits drop all day and all night: and it is full of birds that baptize the bald-heads at their leisure . . . Then there are the cats: Father (who is only suffered, not encouraged) . . . comes in at the holes in the roof and walls by night, and offends lewdly in our beds. Then D.G.H[ogarth] throws a boot towards it and hits Thompson, and plants it in the bath, or knocks the light down: and when he has got out and repaired damages he finds the cat in his bed when he lies down again. So much for Father. Mother is plaintive, and rather a bore: she wails aloud for food, usually about 2 a.m . . . of late she receives sympathy, in spite of one very irregular night, when she woke me up with her claws over the face, and [roused] the rest of the expedition (who sleep together, with piled revolvers) by trying to escape my yells by jumping off the jam-tins through the window . . . Of late Mother has been in the family way, with Thompson a very gallant midwife. Her four kittens . . . make a ghastly noise in the Expeditionary bedroom half the night: I am a tolerable sleeper, but the others get up two or three times each, and draw beads on each other with revolvers.'

The lack of a light railway or lifting tackle imposed great restrictions on the digging. Some parts of the site were totally inaccessible beneath Roman cement foundations. Elsewhere, the Hittite remains lay under tons of shattered Roman masonry: 'Whenever we break fresh ground dozens of these huge blocks have to be moved. Some of them weigh tons, and we have no blasting powder or stone-hammers with us. As a result they have to be hauled, prehistoric fashion, by brute force of men on ropes, helped to a small extent by crowbars. At this moment something over sixty men are tugging away above, each man yelling *Yallah* as he pulls: the row is tremendous'. One of the three Englishmen had to be on the site whenever work was going on, and Lawrence spent most of his time there. This gave him the opportunity to learn more about the local people.

By the end of March, Hogarth had cleared as much of the stairway as he could. The upper part seemed to have been destroyed; in any case it gave out beneath huge stones and earlier spoil heaps that could not be moved. Lower down it was well preserved and he decided to dig at its foot, hoping to find buildings. He cut a trench leading out from the staircase and roughly equal to it in width. This eventually revealed a low wall which continued the line of the stair. Beside the wall were carved slabs, some very broken, which had evidently stood on top of it. In front was a paved surface; it seemed that the wall had formed one side of a roadway approaching the staircase. This part of the site was later christened 'the Lower Palace'.

The reliefs formed a narrative series and showed Hittite warriors in full panoply; these were of great interest since no such pictures had previously been discovered. Among them was a great slab, almost complete, which carried the longest Hittite hieroglyphic text ever found. It seemed, however, that the Hittite city had been very thoroughly ransacked and destroyed, and Hogarth feared that this did not augur well for the excavations.

He began trial diggings on the mound itself in an attempt to find out what lay within it. Pits were dug in the top and headings driven into the sides, but again the diggers faced daunting obstacles. Hogarth could not hope to do more than find out whether there were any remains of early buildings on the mound.

After only two and a half weeks' work he wrote to Kenyon: 'It is too early, of course, to prophesy: but I begin to foresee or suspect two things: (1) that there is no important *primitive* stratum here, except, perhaps, inside the big mound (2) that the earliest and most important building is in the Acropolis mound under at least 20ft. of debris and silt, and probably under much more. To get down to this, or to get into it from the sides of the mound, will be a very heavy task owing to the size and weight of the fallen blocks.' He already had doubts about recommending future seasons: 'I should not advise you to go on here in order to get only Hittite inscriptions of a comparatively late period and Hittite-Assyrian reliefs. You want cuneiform records, and early and fairly well-preserved buildings with their decoration and furniture. These we have not yet got.'

By now Hogarth was more confident about Thompson's ability to take over the dig. Furthermore, 'in certain archaeological points on which he is weak, Lawrence is strong . . . I have found Lawrence an admirable adjutant, and you will be wise to make all the use of him you can. He gets on excellently with Thompson.'

Hogarth was now considering the alternative sites he had visited in 1908, notably Tell Ahmar, which he thought might repay two seasons' work in 1913–14 if Carchemish came to nothing. Lawrence was enthusiastic about this prospect, especially since Hogarth would not be free to work there, 'and the place would be left to Thompson and myself. Thompson is not a digger, so the direction of that part would be my share . . . Mr. Hogarth suggested that a season or half a season with Petrie in Egypt might be valuable experience: and of course it would be. Digging in any case would be always a thing I would try to do, and the more I know of it the better.'

While Lawrence worked at Carchemish, his father was still trying to reach some kind of arrangement with Vyvyan Richards about financing the printing venture. Neither of Lawrence's parents liked Richards, and they would have been happy to see the scheme abandoned. Lawrence, however, stuck to it tenaciously, urging his father on: 'Richards has been a little remiss in the business line I expect: of course he has no time to spare for it . . . I fear very much he will never get it done: in which case I fear my opportunities of doing something good that will count will be very small: at least I am not going to put all my energies into rubbish like

writing history, or becoming an archaeologist. I would much rather write
a novel even, or become a newspaper correspondent:—however there is
still hope that Richards may pull the thing through'.

Despite this outburst, Lawrence was progressing steadily towards an
archaeological career. In due course Hogarth wrote to Flinders Petrie,
head of the British School of Archaeology in Egypt: 'Can you make room
on your excavations next winter for a young Oxford graduate, T. Lawrence, who has been with me at Carchemish? He is a very unusual type,
and a man whom I feel quite sure you would approve of and like. He has
very wide and exact archaeological knowledge, though not of Egyptian
things, and, in view of his being employed in the future by the British
Museum or others, I should very much like him to get some experience
of your School, particularly in tomb digging. I think if you put him to
help, for example, on a prehistoric tomb site you would not repent it. If
he goes to you he would probably come on foot from north Syria. I may
add that he is extremely indifferent to what he eats or how he lives. He
knows a good deal of Arabic, though it is of the northern Syrian variety.
I hope very much that you will be able to make room for him, for about
a month at least, for I can assure you that he is really worth while.'

Lawrence's other plans for the future were gradually changing. When
he came to Carchemish he had had three firm projects. The first was to
prepare an Oxford B.Litt. on medieval pottery; the second, to set up a
printing press with Vyvyan Richards; and the third to develop his thesis
on Crusader castles into a book.

Now, however, he was strongly attracted by the life he was leading at
Carchemish. Outdoor work on the dig was balanced by intellectual luxuries in the evenings, such as talking to Hogarth and Thompson or reading. The idea of combining field archaeology with travel and writing, as
Hogarth had done, appealed to him greatly. He was thinking increasingly
of Doughty's example and began to find himself more interested in the
people of Syria than in its ancient buildings. Before leaving England he
had thought of travelling among the itinerant Soleyb, a people in whose
company he might pass unobtrusively among the Arabs. In May, as the
prospects for a second season at Carchemish faded, he wrote earnestly
about the idea to his parents: 'The Soleyb . . . are not gypsies . . . and
deny all connection with them. They are pagan, and by common consent
the original, pre-Arab, inhabitants of Arabia. They go on foot, often, by
preference, since some have wealth and baggage-camels: are great hunt-
ers of gazelles, hospitable simple folk, in no way fanatical. They are
much despised by the Arabs, who as you will see in Doughty are feather-

brained and rampol-witted. He always has a good word for the Soleyb, but told me he thought their mode of life would be very primitive . . . I am not trying to rival Doughty. You remember that passage that he who has once seen palm-trees and the goat-hair tents is never the same as he had been: that I feel very strongly, and I feel also that Doughty's two year wandering in untainted places made him the man he is, more than all his careful preparation before and since. My books would be the better, if I had been for a time in open country: and the Arab life is the only one that still holds the early poetry which is the easiest to read . . . A spring and summer with [the Soleyb] . . . would be a fresh experience: but I have no intention of making a book of it. I would not even go down in Arabia proper . . . I do not like the modern habit of wrenching all legends into the purpose of anthropology.' Lawrence discussed the idea with Hogarth, who reminded him that the Soleyb were reputed to eat the gazelle they hunted raw. Hogarth later recalled that this 'seemed to give him pause!'

Hogarth and Gregori left Carchemish on April 20, leaving Thompson and Lawrence with a reduced workforce to carry on the dig. On his return to England, Hogarth drafted a long report, setting out the conclusions he had been able to reach. He ended: 'I venture to recommend that the work be allowed to continue under Mr. Campbell Thompson's direction . . . throughout the coming summer, so long as he is able to keep it going economically, or until he has proved that neither the Acropolis nor the ground near its landward foot and on the West of the site is likely to yield adequate return to your expenditure . . . If in the course of May and June, he hits on a favourable spot or on spots where the Hittite stratum can be explored, without too great expenditure, he might well be allowed to continue as long as funds are available . . . A site, so extensive and so notorious as Jerablus, demands, I think, a very full trial, which can hardly last for less than a full season.'

Hogarth must already have realised that a satisfactory exploration was impossible, given the scale of the site, the small workforce that remained, and the obstacles presented by post-Hittite debris. In these circumstances a first season could show that further digs were warranted, but could not definitely prove the contrary. Thompson was now to test a large area by digging pits at intervals in the hope of chancing on something that would justify more thorough excavation, although as Hogarth said, 'pitting over a site, which carried no superficial indication of what its lower stratum contains, is haphazard work at best'.

In mid-May Gertrude Bell visited Carchemish. She was already a traveller and archaeologist of some distinction, and Hogarth's two young assistants did their utmost to conceal their inexperience and the season's disappointing results. Lawrence wrote home: 'she told Thompson his ideas of digging were prehistoric: and so we had to squash her with a display of erudition. She was taken (in five minutes) over Byzantine, Crusader, Roman, Hittite, and French architecture (my part) and over Greek folk-lore, Assyrian architecture, and Mesopotamian ethnology (by Thompson); prehistoric pottery and telephoto lenses, Bronze Age metal technique, Meredith, Anatole France and the Octobrists (by me): the Young Turk movement, the construct state in Arabic, the price of riding camels, Assyrian burial-customs, and German methods of excavation with the Baghdad railway (by Thompson). This was a kind of hors d'oeuvre: and when it was over (she was getting more respectful) we settled down each to seven or eight subjects and questioned her upon them. She was quite glad to have tea after an hour and a half, and on going told Thompson that he had done wonders in his digging in the time, and that she thought *we* had got everything out of the place that could possibly have been got: she particularly admired the completeness of our note-books.

'So we did for her . . . It would have been most annoying if she had denounced our methods in print. I don't think she will.'

Gertrude too wrote home about the meeting, but if their efforts had impressed her, she made no comment: 'I . . . found Mr. Thompson and a young man called Lawrence (he is going to make a traveller) who had for some time been expecting that I would appear. They showed me their diggings and their finds and I spent a pleasant day with them.'

Thompson was planning to finish work at the end of June; without cuneiform inscriptions the dig held little interest for him and he was to get married as soon as the season was over. Towards the end of that month, however, their luck began to turn, and they made a series of interesting finds.

Lawrence's delight over these was shortlived. On June 24 they received a cable from Kenyon halting the dig, and Lawrence wrote to his family dejectedly: 'Have had orders to clear out as soon as possible: so in a fortnight we will shut down the digs. By the terms of the telegram from the British Museum they are so disappointed at our results that there will be no second season. It is a great pity for we had, on the strength of our former orders, just begun important clearances. We will leave the site like a warren, all disfigured with rubbish heaps and with all the work only half done: altogether about the most unsatisfactory job that one can imagine.'

On July 8 Thompson and Lawrence left Jerablus to spend a few days, on Hogarth's suggestion, examining remains at Tell Ahmar, a few hours' journey from Carchemish. They parted company four days later, and Lawrence set off on his own to look at Crusader castles. During the next fortnight he visited the fortifications at Urfa, Harran, Biridjik, and Rum Kalaat, making technical notes on their architecture.

In late July he returned to Jerablus, meaning to finish off one or two small jobs on the site. Once there, he became very ill with dysentery and noted in his diary: 'Cannot possibly continue tramp in this condition.' He was unable to look after himself and was taken in by Sheikh Hamoudi, who had worked as a foreman on the site. Weakened by the privations of his walking tour, Lawrence remained in a serious condition for several days. He cannot have been comforted to know that Hamoudi was advised not to help such a sick man, for fear of blame if things turned out for the worst. Lawrence had to give Hamoudi a note absolving him from any responsibility.

Lawrence continued his diary throughout this illness, noting, for instance, on July 31: 'The Hoja [Hamoudi] awfully good all these days, with me making quite unprecedented demands on his time and patience. But poor man, a most dreadful bore as well, does his best by five or six repeats to get every idea of his into my thick head, which usually understands before he speaks. In the evening tried a little *burghul* well-boiled in milk. Dahoum came to see me'.

Dahoum had worked during the digging season as one of the expedition's donkey boys. He carried water and ran general errands for Thompson and Lawrence. In late June, Lawrence had described him in a letter home as 'an interesting character: he can read a few words . . . of Arabic, and altogether has more intelligence than the rank and file. He talks of going into Aleppo to school with the money he has made out of us. I will try and keep an eye on him, to see what happens. He would be better in the country, only for the hideous grind of the continual forced labour, and the low level of the village minds.

'Fortunately there is no foreign influence as yet in the district: if only you had seen the ruination caused by the French influence, and to a lesser degree by the American, you would never wish it extended. The perfectly hopeless vulgarity of the half-Europeanised Arab is appalling. Better a thousand times the Arab untouched. The foreigners come out here always to teach, whereas they had much better learn, for in everything but wits and knowledge the Arab is generally the better man of the two.'

As this letter shows, Lawrence's views were changing radically. Two years earlier he had sung the praises of the work being done by the American Mission Schools. It seems that Dahoum, a young Arab of fourteen or fifteen, personified all that Lawrence now admired in the native population. The romanticism in his outlook was common enough among Englishmen of that generation. Critics of Victorian achievement pointed out that the Industrial Revolution had been accompanied by a decline in social morality. It is clear from Lawrence's letters that he shared this view; for example he found Blackwood's *Centaur* 'very good, though not "all the way" enough for me: but at the same time more reasoned and definite as an attack on the modern world than anything I've read—bar Morris.' Such attitudes had breathed new life into the philosophical concept of the 'noble savage', and it is clear that Lawrence thought the simple agricultural peasantry in Syria in some way untainted by the vices that had debased the poor in Britain.

He nonetheless encouraged Dahoum's efforts to educate himself, and wrote to the American Mission School at Jebail for help: 'He is beginning to use his reason as well as his instinct. He taught himself to read a little, so I had very exceptional material to work on but I made him read and write more than he ever did before. You know you cannot do much with a piece of stick and a scrap of dusty ground as materials. I am going to ask Miss Fareedeh for a few simple books, amusing, for him to begin on. Remember he is to be left a Moslem.' A month later he amplified this request: 'What I wanted for the donkey boy was a history book or a geography which should be readable and yet Arab . . . nothing with a taste of "Frangi" shall enter Jerablus by my means. I have no wish to do more for the boy than give him a chance to help himself: "education" I have had so much of, and it is such rot: saving your presence! The only stuff worth having is what you work out yourself.' While helping Dahoum, Lawrence was able to improve his own knowledge of Arabic, and he was now planning to return to Jerablus in the winter, with the idea that while travelling 'the strongly-dialectical Arabic of the villages would be good as a disguise'.

It is most unlikely that Dahoum shared Lawrence's romanticism. He saw education as a means to escape from the miserable poverty of the village peasantry, and Lawrence's interest in him must have seemed a miraculous opportunity. He would not have understood his benefactor's strange Victorian ideals. During the days Lawrence spent at Hamoudi's house, when it was feared that he would die, Dahoum came to see him every evening. The care Lawrence received from these two villagers probably saved his life and he did not forget it. Two years later he would take them both to England as a reward and, from this time on, the references to Dahoum in Lawrence's letters show an almost fatherly concern.

On August 3, still very weak, he abandoned any plans for further tramping that summer and decided to return to England. He had found at Jerablus a letter from Hogarth sent on by Thompson which raised strong hopes of a second season. On the way home, therefore, he was already planning his return.

When he reached Beirut, he was delighted to find that the poet James Elroy Flecker had been appointed to the British consulate. Flecker and his wife Hellé had just arrived, and on August 8 Lawrence wrote: 'I have been doing little but talk to them. I had to wait an extra day here because of things for me in the P.O. which was shut when I got there.' After a brief visit to Damascus, Lawrence sailed from Beirut on August 12, travelling by sea to Marseilles and thence overland to England.

He spent the summer recuperating; it was to be several months before his strength fully returned. However, he had plenty to do. One project was *Crusader Castles*, the book he planned to make from an enlarged revision of the successful thesis. He now worked critically through its text, but he failed to find a publisher because the work contained so many plans and photographs.

Since the finds during the final month at Carchemish had been so encouraging, Hogarth wanted to resume the work for a short season. In terms of scholarship the excavations were clearly incomplete, and a third of the £2,000 allocated remained unspent. The most compelling argument, however, was that Turkish law would allow the British Museum to excavate only one site at a time. The Imperial Ottoman Museum wrote to Kenyon expressing its hope that there would be a second season. Clearly Hogarth would not be given permission to work at Tell Ahmar or anywhere else in the Turkish Empire without a more satisfactory ending at Carchemish. It was therefore decided to reopen the excavations for two months in the spring of 1912.

At this stage the British Museum's plans suffered a setback. Campbell Thompson, now married, did not wish to return to Carchemish unless he could be accompanied by his wife, and Kenyon refused to allow this. Hogarth offered the post to Leonard Woolley, then aged thirty-one, who had worked as an Assistant Keeper at the Ashmolean. Woolley would be free to go to Carchemish at the end of February 1912. Hogarth had not been very impressed with Thompson and felt that the change was no loss: 'we have Lawrence, who knows place and people as well as Thompson.'

In the meantime Petrie had agreed to take Lawrence at one of his Egyptian sites during January.

In the autumn of 1911, though he was still unfit, Lawrence decided that he should return to Jerablus and work on his Arabic. Also, Hogarth had recommended building a house for the archaeologists near the site and Lawrence was to supervise its construction before Woolley arrived.

He left England at the end of November and, after a brief visit to Jerablus, took a steamer to Egypt where he joined Petrie at Kafr Ammar some fifty miles up the Nile from Cairo. The site was a graveyard and Lawrence found the work repulsive: 'It is a strange sight to see the men forcing open a square wooden coffin, and taking out the painted anthropoid envelope within, and splitting this up also to drag out a mummy, not glorious in bright wrappings, but dark brown, fibrous, visibly rotting— and then the thing begins to come to pieces, and the men tear off its head, and bare the skull, and the vertebrae drop out, and the ribs, and legs, and perhaps only one poor amulet is the result: the smell and sights are horrible. Digging here is very unlike our Carchemish work—and very much easier. They have nothing of our complications of depth, or of levels, and fragmentary rests of cities or civilisations. I shall be glad to be back in Syria . . . Mr Hogarth was quite right in arranging for no longer: I'm no body snatcher, and we have a pile of skulls that would do credit to a follower of Jenghis Khan. These men are less squeamish than our fellows.'

After a week Lawrence had taken a dislike to both Egypt and the Egyptians, although happily the dig moved to earlier graves in which the bodies had not been mummified. He was nevertheless glad to work under Petrie: 'I like him exceedingly, but rather as one thinks of a cathedral or something immovable but by earthquake. He is a quite inspired archaeologist—and I am picking up hints of sorts all day long.' Petrie was sufficiently impressed by Lawrence to offer him £700 towards the cost of two seasons' excavation in Bahrain and Lawrence later consulted Hogarth about this proposal: 'Prof. Petrie spoke to me two or three times in Egypt about the Persian gulf and south Arabia . . . he declared that he believed the early dynasties came round by sea from Elam or thereabout to Egypt: and that Bahrein was a stage of their going. Finally in my last week with him he suggested my going down there to dig, say next year, as a preliminary season, to be followed by a second on a larger scale, if it seemed promising. He said he could provide the funds.

'I told him I'd ask you about it: and that I'd rather you got what profits were going: he didn't seem to think the ideas were incompatible . . . Of course it could only be if Hittite were not going . . . At the same time I would like to dig in the Persian gulf, and as Bahrein is nominally British, I suppose we might carry off the stuff.'

Lawrence left Kafr Ammar on January 30 and shortly afterwards sent home a diatribe comparing the Egyptians very unfavourably with the men of Jerablus: 'The Egyptian people are horribly ugly, very dirty, dull, low-spirited, without any of the vigour or the self-confident independence of our men. Besides, the fanaticism of the country is deplorable, and the treatment of the women most un-European: most of the Petrie workmen have several wives, and have had many more, and one could not stand or work close to them for a few minutes without catching fleas or lice. Nor could one talk to them with the delicious free intimacy of the men of Carchemish. They either got surly, or took liberties. They were frenetic, and querulous, foul-mouthed, and fawning.'

Unknown to Lawrence, events were taking place in England which would greatly prolong the excavations at Carchemish. After giving a lecture about the site, Hogarth had quite unexpectedly received a cheque for £5,000 towards the cost of continuing work there. This had been sent by Walter Morrison, a wealthy businessman who practised philanthropy on a remarkable scale (for example, he made one of the largest single gifts ever received by the Bodleian Library). Morrison was deeply interested in archaeology; he had been a founder and the chief benefactor of the Palestine Exploration Fund. He met Hogarth regularly since they both served on the PEF committee. The extent of Morrison's generosity never became public in his lifetime because most of his gifts were made under strict conditions of anonymity. With funding assured, work would continue at Jerablus for several seasons, during which the British Museum would contribute a further £2,000, making £7,000 available in all.

When Lawrence reached Jerablus on February 24 he found that the Kaimmakam (Governor) of Biridjik would not give permission for their house to be built. Lawrence could do nothing except wait until the Turks received instructions from Constantinople. In the meantime, he made friends with the German railway engineers and agreed to let them clear away the heaps of stone spoil left on the site after the 1911 season. Since the Germans needed stone for buildings and embankments, and the spoil-heaps hampered the excavations, this arrangement suited both parties.

Woolley arrived on March 13. Lawrence already knew him slightly, as they had met at the Ashmolean some years before. The circumstances of this new contact gave scope for tension. Woolley, eight years older than Lawrence, was coming to take charge, and had greater experience of archaeological field-work. Lawrence, on the other hand, was already familiar with Carchemish and its workforce, and at that point knew much more about Hittite archaeology than Woolley.

To their dismay, the Turkish guards on the site refused to let Woolley begin work. He sent an urgent message to the Kaimmakam asking for permission to proceed, but this met with a curt refusal. It turned out that the Kaimmakam wanted a bribe, thinly disguised as salary for an unofficial Commissaire. To Lawrence's delight, Woolley took the law into his own hands and told the Kaimmakam that he intended to begin work: anyone who obstructed him would, if necessary, be shot. The Kaimmakam gave in, but other difficulties were quickly raised and Lawrence found himself being prosecuted for trespass by one of the people who claimed to own part of the site. The case went before a local Islamic court (which had in fact no jurisdiction over foreigners) and the digging permit was impounded. Woolley's high-handed methods secured its return, and earned Lawrence's admiration.

Lawrence recorded these incidents in letters to England, and they lost nothing in the telling. Woolley had become 'a most excellent person' in his eyes. The Kaimmakam received an official rebuke from Constantinople and there were no further bureaucratic problems.

By the end of April the expedition house was finished and provided not merely accommodation but a photographic darkroom and archaeological store as well. The living quarters were soon decorated lavishly with objects from the site and with a Roman mosaic floor rescued from a nearby field. Lawrence would now be able to live at Jerablus between digging seasons. However, lacking a publisher for his book, he seems to have lost interest in visiting castles in the area and instead planned to return with Woolley to England in mid-June.

At the beginning of May, Hogarth spent nine days at the dig. He wrote back to Kenyon that: 'Lawrence is even more useful this year than last, as he has now quite mastered the local Arabic and through his residence here after the dig last year has come to know all the villagers intimately.'

He commended Woolley and Lawrence for their work, and told Kenyon that Lawrence, 'who now knows the local people and their speech very well, and having had a longer training in Hittite things than Woolley, is an invaluable adjutant to the latter. Both ought, I think, to be secured for the remainder of the excavation.' He recommended that Woolley should be offered thirty shillings a day, and that Lawrence, having 'done an immense amount of work for you in these two seasons, ought also to begin to receive a salary.' He had evidently discussed this with Lawrence and suggested the rate of fifteen shillings a day, which was paid in subsequent seasons.

Lawrence's knowledge of Arabic was increasingly important. There was ample funding for the dig and, if they were to continue on a larger scale, it would be necessary to supervise more men. His responsibility in this area was increasing, and he needed to speak the local dialect fluently with a wide vocabulary. Hogarth asked him to work at it. Lawrence wrote to his friends at Jebail: 'Mr. Hogarth is very anxious to make me learn Arabic; and so I am going to stay here July and August alone.' He planned nevertheless to go home at Christmas 'and to carry Miss Fareedah [el Akle, who had taught him Arabic at the Mission School] away with me for six weeks in England. There will be more digs in February but all through January Miss Holmes [Principal of the School] will be bereft (*inshallah!*).'

Since Lawrence was staying on, Woolley asked him to spend some time working over the season's results and sorting pottery. More than a thousand fragments of carved and incised basalt had been recovered from the area at the foot of the stairway, and the task of fitting them together was very time-consuming. Lawrence was also to visit several villages where Hittite remains had been reported. By this time he was responsible for the expedition's photography. 'We have decided that we cannot do it all ourselves next year, and so I have the training of a boy—Dahoum of course—as well to see to. You have no idea how hard it is to instil elementary optics into his head in imperfect Arabic. He will put plates the wrong side out. However all these are little worries, which are working towards my improvement in Arabic: I hope to be fluent—though still incorrect—by Xmas.'

Woolley closed down the dig early in June. When the men had been paid off, he spent a few days with Lawrence excavating a Hittite cemetery five miles away. Later, having worked for another week clearing up loose ends at Jerablus, the two went to Alexandretta to arrange shipment of their various purchases. Woolley sailed for England on June 20, confident after this first season together that he and Lawrence had formed a successful partnership.

CHAPTER 4

Achievement at Carchemish

June 1912–August 1914

WITH a sense of relief, Lawrence set off back to Carchemish, stopping at Aleppo on the way: 'There is a sort of feeling of blessed peace in the air at the ending of my immediate digging work. Woolley is off and I am my own master again, which is a position that speaks for itself and its goodness . . . I seem to have been months away from Jerablus, and am longing for its peace. You know there one says "I don't want to talk" and there is silence till you break it, or "I want to be alone" and twenty men post themselves around you out of sight that not even a hoopoe or an ant may cry out and break your rest . . . Really this country, for the foreigner, is too glorious for words: one is the baron of the feudal system.'

Lawrence planned to travel during the summer, taking Dahoum as a servant and companion, and by the middle of July he was ready to visit Seruj and Urfa where there were reports of inscribed stones. But then he and several others fell ill with various complaints, and the journey had to be postponed. When they had recovered, he went across to Biridjik, but there he felt feverish again. On his return to Jerablus he had a third attack of fever and 'judged it prudent, in view of the excavations to follow so close, if I rested a bit in the cool'. At the beginning of August, therefore, he abandoned his plans to go on a trek and instead left with Dahoum for Beirut and Jebail, where he stayed at the American Mission School working on his Arabic. Both he and Dahoum were making some progress with writing the language.

While staying in the Lebanon, Lawrence occasionally visited the Fleckers at their summer home in Areya. Hellé Flecker later recalled: 'my husband bore the heat very well, what he again missed was . . . intelligent society . . . [He] was delighted to be able to talk literature and Oxford again'.

As always, Lawrence's letters referred to the books he was reading. Apart from the works he had brought from England, he had access to the Mission School library at Jebail, and well-read friends such as Flecker and R. A. Fontana, the British Consul at Aleppo, helped to broaden his

literary taste. That summer he read Spenser, Catullus, Marot, the *Koran*,
Simonides and Meleager, and a Hewlett novel.

He decided to return to Carchemish at the end of August, when Woolley was expected to arrive. Dahoum, who had now mastered simple
photographic work, would henceforward rank with the expedition's Arab
headmen. As a field archaeologist, Lawrence would need a reliable assistant like Hogarth's Gregori. Dahoum was growing into this role, as
was Hamoudi, who now worked increasingly with Woolley (he continued
to do so for many years afterwards). Although Lawrence took a fatherly
interest in Dahoum, the relationship was that between teacher and pupil,
or master and trusted assistant. The notions which made Lawrence respect the young Arab's simplicity would also mean that he could never
treat Dahoum as an equal.

Reading between the lines of his letters home, it is clear that
Lawrence's parents would have liked him to return to work in Oxford.
When they forwarded details of a vacant academic post, his reply was
revealing: 'I am afraid no "open fellowship" for me: I don't think anyone
who had tasted the East as I have would give it up half-way, for a seat at
high table and a chair in the Bodleian. At any rate I won't'. The previous
day he had written to his brother Bob: 'you know after all, I feel very little
lack of English scenery: we have too much greenery there, and one never
feels the joy of a fertile place, as one does here when one finds a thorn-
bush and green thistle. Here one learns an economy of beauty which is
wonderful. England is fat—obese.'

Woolley was now on his way back from England. Before he arrived,
Lawrence amused himself at Carchemish decorating the lintel of the main
doorway into the house: 'I have carved a great sun disk, with crescent
moon, and wings, on our stone door-lintel—the dining room door that is.
As I had no chisels I carved with a screw-driver and a knife. It is a Hittite
design and use, and looks very fitting.' His delight with this joke would
be renewed each time a visitor to the excavations paused to admire the
forged Hittite relic.

At about this time he wrote, for the new *Jesus College Magazine*, an
article describing his visit with Dahoum that summer to the ruined palace
of Ibn Wardani. They had been shown the building by an old guide and
his son, who had told them of the different scents in each room. The truth
was probably more prosaic, for Lawrence told his parents that 'the palace
of Ibn Wardani has many strange scents about it, as I wrote: it is famous
all over north Syria, and my description is more like the rumour than the
reality'.

Towards the end of the essay Lawrence wrote with evident approval about Arab asceticism, describing for the first time an outlook which he would later refer to as 'the gospel of bareness in materials'. This barren creed appealed to some fundamental element in his nature, and it often recurs in his later writings: 'At last we came into a great hall, whose walls, pierced with many narrow windows, still stood to more than half their height. "This," said he, "is the *liwan of silence*: it has no taste," and by some crowning art it was as he had said. The mingled scents of all the palace here combined to slay each other, and all that one felt was the desert sharpness of the air as it swept off the huge uncontaminated plains. "Among us," said Dahoum, "we call this room the sweetest of them all," therein half-consciously sounding the ideal of the Arab creed, for generations stripping itself of all furniture in the working out of a gospel of simplicity.'

The season's excavations were overshadowed by other worries. Chief among these was fear of local unrest. The Milli-Kurds, a nomadic people who roamed a large tract of land on the far side of the Euphrates (i.e. in Mesopotamia), had a long-standing feud with the Turkish Government. The distraction of the Balkan War seemed to offer them the chance to strike at their overlords, and Lawrence heard that they intended to sack Aleppo. As Woolley wrote later: 'The plan affected me closely, for the line of march proposed by the Kurds was through Jerablus, and as they had promised openly to cut the throats of all the Germans on the Baghdad line between Aleppo and the river, I felt that my own position might be none too secure.' The two archaeologists did their best to make friends with local Kurdish leaders, which was not difficult because many Kurds were working on the dig.

The dig closed down at the Islamic festival of Bairam, and Woolley and Lawrence went to visit Busrawi Agha, an influential Kurdish chief, to plead for protection of their belongings if there was a revolt while they were away. The expedition house was to be kept under guard and, as an additional precaution, all the monuments that could not be removed from the site had been reburied. They left together at the end of November. Lawrence had hoped to bring Fareedeh el Akle home that Christmas, but now had too little money to do so: 'it is no use to take her unless one can show her about.'

On their way home, Woolley and Lawrence had called as usual on F. Willoughby Smith, the American Vice-Consul at Beirut. Lawrence had come to know him through the American Mission School at Jebail and thought that he was very ill-informed about the local situation; he and Woolley now told him of their fears about the Kurds.

Willoughby Smith wrote up their news in a long report which his superior eventually transmitted to Washington. It gives a very detailed account of the history of Kurdish unrest and the nature of the threat to Aleppo, showing that Lawrence and Woolley, concerned primarily for their own safety, had learned a good deal about the Kurdish and Arab independence movements in the Turkish Empire. Within two years this knowledge would become a valuable asset to Lawrence and would influence his thinking during the early stages of the war. The report bears out Lawrence's later claim that: 'The Armenian revolutionaries had come to [me] for help and advice, and [I] had dipped far into their councils. The opposition party of the Kurdish reactionaries against the Young Turks had encouraged [me] to ride in their ranks and seek opportunity in the Balkan crisis.' But his motive for these contacts was self-preservation and not, as some biographers have claimed, work for British Intelligence.

The British Museum was unwilling to let the digs resume unless the situation became more stable. Much thought was given to this before Lawrence was allowed to return to Syria in January 1913. On arrival, he sounded out opinion in Jerablus and Aleppo, but remained very apprehensive about the situation. He had found Aleppo 'quiet politically, but as pessimistic as it can be: what a fortune one would make with a cargo of cheap rifles now! Armenians are arming frantically'.

He wrote to Hogarth: 'I rather hope you will decide to postpone digging till the Autumn.' In England, however, Woolley was very keen to resume the digs. Eventually, Kenyon agreed to let work begin. Lawrence had returned to Carchemish, where he passed the time in various ways. Apart from working on his Arabic, he had made some repairs to the house. A Canadian canoe he had ordered from an Oxford boatyard arrived in February. It had a small motor and henceforward provided much amusement.

The risk of a Kurdish rebellion gave Lawrence good reason to improve his skill with a rifle during these weeks. On February 22 he wrote: 'this afternoon I put four shots out of five with a Mannlicher-Schönauer carbine into a six-gallon petrol tin at 400 yards . . . very good that.' He had probably been given this rifle by R. A. Fontana, the British Consul at Aleppo, as thanks for helping the Royal Navy to smuggle firearms to the consulate.

Shortly before Woolley arrived, Lawrence heard that natives had discovered an ancient cemetery at Deve Huyuk, a village on the railway between Aleppo and Jerablus. He first sent Dahoum across to find out what was happening, and then went himself: 'the people were only plundering, with no idea of what to keep or look for. So that my work there was educational for the more part.' After his visit he wrote excitedly to Hogarth: 'The Hittite graves were full of great bronze spears and axes and swords, that the wretches have broken up and thrown away, because Madame Koch [an Aleppo dealer] . . . didn't buy such things. I got some good fibulae . . . much better than the British Museum ones, some bracelets and ear-rings of bronze, a curious pot or two . . . and as a sideline, some Roman glazed bottles, with associated Greek pottery, and a pleasant little lot of miscellanea . . . tomorrow I return there to gather up, I hope, Hittite bronze weapons in sheaves:— unless the police get there first. It is exciting digging:—a plunge down a shaft at night, the smashing of a stone door, and the hasty shovelling of all objects into a bag by lamp-light. One has to pay tolerably highly for glazed pottery, so I will probably buy no more . . . glass is found, but very dear . . . bronze is thought nothing of'. It turned out later that the weapons discarded by the villagers were made of iron not bronze.

When Woolley reached Aleppo on March 27, Lawrence showed him samples of the finds. Woolley was impressed, and sent Hamoudi, the Carchemish foreman, to supervise the work. Phoenician materials such as those found at Deve Huyuk are relatively rare, so Lawrence and Woolley were delighted.

The fourth Carchemish season began on March 21. Light railways to carry spoil away from the diggings had at last arrived, but Gregori was inexplicably absent (it turned out that the letter telling him of the new season had gone astray). Without him, Woolley and Lawrence were kept extremely busy. Since the Baghdad Railway was now running a three-and-a-half-hour passenger service to Jerablus, they were constantly distracted. Lawrence wrote home: 'we dig furiously, and are inundated by visitors: it makes our day very difficult: we start in the morning early as usual, when it is too cold to do any writing of notes or planning or photography: and then about 10am. comes one batch of visitors, and about 3pm. a second. They are usually foreigners or distinguished people, or people with introductions:—and we have to show them all over: such a dull set!'

The political situation became calmer, almost to Lawrence's regret, and the digs began to yield many important finds. They used dynamite to break up massive Roman concrete foundations. By the time he was twenty-five, Lawrence had learned a good deal about ways to demolish masonry with explosives. On April 26 he wrote home that fifteen new carved reliefs had been found during the month: 'Not bad that, especially as they seem to be working up to a great gate, and that the inner part of the palace is well preserved. Our digs are the richest British Museum dig since Layard's now. . . .'

He had an excellent visual memory. Woolley later recalled: 'He would look at a small fragment of a Hittite inscription which had just come to light and remark that it fitted on to an equally small piece found twelve months before, and although there were many hundreds of such in our store-room he was always right'. In this way he had now succeeded in building up the longest linear inscription yet discovered. A piece of this had been found during March: 'Mr. Lawrence, who was copying this large fragment, was able to join it up with another large (but worn) fragment recovered by Mr. Thompson from a flourmill outside the *Kalaat*, and with smaller fragments found scattered over a wide area in 1911, in the spring and in the autumn seasons of 1912 and during the present season.'

When the harvest began in early May, many of the men left to work in their fields. Woolley gave up major excavations on the site and instead turned his attention to an area just north of Carchemish near the village of Yunus, which had been the ancient city's main graveyard. By excavating this cemetery he hoped to find Hittite and other artefacts in a historical sequence which would make it easier to date the various monuments at Carchemish.

That spring Lawrence was having remarkable success outside the dig. Quite apart from the important Deve Huyuk finds, he had bought a good collection of seals and other Hittite objects for the Ashmolean. Indeed, he had been so successful that he had outstripped Hogarth's purchasing grant, even though he often sold *antikas* to the Ashmolean for less than they had cost. His dedication to Hogarth's collection was not shared by Woolley, and they disagreed over the disposal of seals found in a second cemetery at Deve Huyuk. Lawrence wrote to Leeds: 'the only possible place for decent seals is in the Ashmolean. Therefore I have told Woolley, that I have given the seals to you, and have no intention of asking them back. He talked of writing to Hogarth on the matter, suggesting that the seals be kept neutral for the moment, and of course if Hogarth agreed to that I couldn't very well present them to you by force. Only I should be rather annoyed, because I want the Ashmolean to be the best collection of that sort in the running . . . I'll be glad if you will lump them into the register at once as purchased.'

The number of Hittite seals at Oxford was substantially increased by Lawrence's contributions. Ashmolean records show that between a third and a half of the remarkable collection assembled under Hogarth's direction before the First World War was purchased in the field by Lawrence. He also bought other kinds of *antikas* for the museum, often refusing payment.

He was planning only a short stay in England during the summer. When the graveyard digs were finished he would be busy for a while cataloguing and photographing the many objects found, and there were also the ancient sites at Abu Galgal and elsewhere that he had not been able to visit the previous year. His workload of pottery fragments was enormously increased during the last week of the digs when Woolley and Gregori 'wandered . . . almost to Yunus village, looking for something new, when all of a sudden we found that the surface pottery took a new aspect: we put twelve men on and have had two days' work as yet . . . we have got a pottery factory, with furnaces and wasters, of the latest neolithic period'. Lawrence reported that: 'There are about 11,000 fragments, and there must be about twenty complete pots amongst that lot: we collected together three or four such ourselves. It has, as you may imagine, kept us busy.'

Woolley set out for England in mid-June, very happy with his season's work. Hogarth, who had seen photographs, had written that they were the best things found archaeologically for many years: 'Kenyon is lyrical'. Lawrence stayed on at Carchemish for a while; he had thought of travelling in Asia Minor, but there was now too little time if he was to get back to England. As it was, he had cut his planned visit home to about ten days, having spent less than three weeks there during the previous eighteen months. His parents must have feared that such a long period in Syria was beginning to affect his values. For example, in the first season he had told them that the men had chosen Sunday for their day of rest, 'though they are nominal Mahommedans'. In March 1913, however, he had begun a letter home with the casual remark: 'Today is Friday, which is our Sunday'. This comment (which reached his parents in Oxford a few days after Canon Christopher's death) drew a protest. Lawrence replied: 'You complain of our keeping Friday—but would it be quite considerate to make two hundred workmen miss their day for the sake of the two of us?'

It seems probable that he was already beginning to lose the evangelical fervour that he had learned at St Aldate's. Under the influence of the bedouin culture, his Christianity would be replaced during the next few years by something approaching agnosticism. By 1913 he had already adopted some bedouin attitudes. For example on June 15 he wrote home: 'As for a poor appetite, which in Arnie Father deplores, it is a thing to be above all thankful for. If it were himself who felt no desire to eat, would he not rejoice aloud. To escape the humiliation of loading in food, would bring one very near the angels. Why not let him copy that very sensible Arab habit, of putting off the chewing of bread till the moment that instinct makes it desirable. If we had no fixed meal-hours, and unprepared food, we would not fall into middle-age.'

When he set out for England at the end of June, he took with him Hamoudi and Dahoum, the villagers who had looked after him during his illness two years before. They lived in his garden bungalow at Polstead Road and created a good deal of amusement by cycling round Oxford in their Arab clothes. Hamoudi spent part of the time with Woolley, and Dahoum made himself useful unpacking materials at the Ashmolean. Bell arranged for Dahoum to be sketched by Francis Dodd, and Lawrence was present at the sitting. This was probably the first time Lawrence had seen anyone sit to a professional artist, and it left him with a lifelong fascination for portraiture.

By August 25 he was back in Aleppo. At Jerablus he was joined for several days by his brother Will, who was on the way to a teaching post in India. Will much enjoyed the visit, referring to Lawrence as his 'Bedawi brother', and 'a great lord in this place.' After leaving he wrote reassuringly to his parents: 'You must not think of Ned as leading an uncivilised existence. When I saw him last as the train left the station he was wearing white flannels, socks and red slippers, with a white Magdalen blazer, and was talking to the Governor of Biredjik in a lordly fashion.'

There were other visitors at this time, including Hubert Young, a lieutenant in the Indian Army who stayed on a few days after Will had left. Since the dig was still closed, Lawrence had to devise ways of passing the time. Young recalled going out on the Euphrates in the canoe, competing with Lawrence at target shooting, and carving gargoyles. Lawrence wrote to a friend: 'In the East one has quite a lot of work to keep them fed and amused . . . I couldn't burke the feeding, but I gave each a lump of soft limestone and set them in competition to carve gargoyles for the roof . . . it really is a tip worth trying, since it kept them hard at work for three days.' The carvings were also referred to in a letter from Lawrence to Will: 'I persuaded Young . . . to spend his spare time carving gargoyles for the better adornment of the house. He managed in limestone an ideal head of a woman; I did a squatting demon of the Notre-Dame style, also in limestone, and we have now built them into the walls and roof, and the house is become remarkable in north Syria. The local people come up in crowds to look at them.'

The model for Lawrence's carving had been Dahoum, and when Woolley arrived a few days later he found it shocking. He seems to have jumped to the conclusion that Lawrence had carved the figure while living alone with Dahoum. Many years later, when writing an essay for *T. E. Lawrence by his Friends*, Woolley gave an account of the carvings which is incorrect, and salacious in its insinuation: 'Dahoum . . . was then a boy of about fifteen, not particularly intelligent (though Lawrence taught him to take photographs quite well) but beautifully built and remarkably handsome. Lawrence was devoted to him. The Arabs were tolerantly scandalised by the friendship, especially when in 1913 Lawrence, stopping in the house after the dig was over, had Dahoum to live with him and got him to pose as model for a queer crouching figure which he carved in the soft local limestone and set up on the edge of the house roof; to make an image was bad enough in its way, but to portray a naked figure was proof to them of evil of another sort. The scandal about Lawrence was widely spread and firmly believed.'

This account is factually misleading: it is clear from contemporary letters that Lawrence spent almost no time on his own at the Carchemish house, either in June or September 1913, since there was a stream of visitors. Even without visitors, he would not have been alone there since the expedition cook and his family were permanent residents. The figure was carved when Young and other visitors were present in September, not in June as Woolley states. Finally, the 'queer crouching figure' was intended to look like a gargoyle, not an accurate portrayal of a human form. Taking this into account, and given the fact that other people were present, it seems most unlikely that Dahoum posed in the nude, although this is what Woolley implies.

This passage in Woolley's essay is followed, somewhat incongruously, by a statement that in his opinion Lawrence was not homosexual: 'The charge was quite unfounded. Lawrence had in his make-up a very strong vein of sentiment, but he was in no sense a pervert; in fact, he had a remarkably clean mind. He was tolerant, thanks to his classical reading, and Greek homosexuality interested him, but in a detached way, and the interest was not morbid but perfectly serious; I never heard him make a smutty remark and am sure that he would have objected to one if it had been made for his benefit; but he would describe Arab abnormalities baldly and with a certain sardonic humour. He knew quite well what the Arabs said about himself and Dahoum, and so far from resenting it was amused, and I think that he courted misunderstanding rather than tried to avoid it; it appealed to his sense of humour, which was broad and school-boyish. He liked to shock.'

Lawrence's letters from this period bear out this opinion entirely, and it is legitimate to ask why Woolley should have included the allegations in his essay. Gossip of that kind is common enough but would not normally appear in a serious memoir, especially when it was known to be unjustified. Woolley must have realised that this disingenuous combination of allegation and 'loyal disclaimer' would cause many readers to believe the worst.

The confident manner in which Woolley published his libellously inaccurate account of the carving episode must also raise doubts about his other testimony regarding Lawrence. This is a matter of some importance since Woolley is the only qualified person to have written about Lawrence's work as an archaeologist at Carchemish on the basis of personal knowledge. Woolley's essay in *Friends*, though interesting, has a slightly hostile ring throughout; it gives the strong impression that Lawrence was dilettante in his attitude towards archaeology.

A great many documents concerning the Carchemish excavations have survived and from these it is possible to form an independent view of Lawrence's contribution to the dig. When Woolley's essay in *Friends* is compared with these contemporary sources it becomes clear that he was biased. For whatever reason, the essay deliberately slights Lawrence: it passes lightly over the very large amount of work he did at Carchemish, where he shared the daily tasks almost equally with Woolley; it states that Woolley rather than Lawrence took field notes, without mentioning that it was Lawrence who maintained the detailed catalogues of pottery and sculpture finds; it gives no credit to Lawrence for his extensive buying of *antikas* on behalf of the Ashmolean and the British Museums, though this was an important activity in which, according to the records, Lawrence was much more able than Woolley. While Lawrence is credited with an ability to recognise different fragments of a sculpture or inscription, the essay does not indicate the special value of this ability at Carchemish, where very many of the monuments and inscriptions had been smashed and dispersed when the city was destroyed.

Distorted testimony is a problem faced by all historians, and it is particularly common in statements about Lawrence. When a witness is found to display bias one does not usually have to look very far to find a motive. Woolley may have been influenced by several factors, and he was in any case an inveterate raconteur who thought nothing of improving his yarns. In Lawrence's words, he was 'a curious person . . . he tells the wildest stories as a habit'. A memoir by E. T. Leeds points to other difficulties: 'We all knew our Woolley. Kindly, earnest, extremely hard-working, but one of the ablest drawers of the long bow it has ever been my fortune to meet. Imbued with a passionate belief in his own connoisseurship, resulting in more than one disastrous break in his purchases, he could with difficulty see that tactful disagreement with his diagnoses and downright condemnation were synonymous among friends. If Woolley had only avoided encroachment into the deeper recesses of historical and archaeological research, his fame in the future would be greater even than that he has deservedly won as the best of contemporary excavators abroad. A desire to transform geese into swans has always been his serious failing.' Woolley's monthly reports from Carchemish were studded with superlatives: finds were often described as 'the most important', 'the finest', 'the largest'. It is clear from Kenyon's Carchemish papers that these judgments were not always shared by Hogarth, and that Hogarth discussed the finds independently with Lawrence. Woolley read through these files in the 1920s when he was writing the second volume of the published Carchemish report. He must have discovered and bitterly resented the implicit criticisms.

There was also some coolness, after the war, on Lawrence's side. In 1920 Woolley published an entertaining account of events at Carchemish in his book *Dead Towns and Living Men*. Lawrence made no secret of his dislike of the book, saying it was 'very untruthful, which is not a deadly sin: but a very vulgar book too.' Woolley almost certainly heard about Lawrence's reaction and cannot have been pleased to have his work condemned by a colleague who had since become so famous.

The tone of Lawrence's post-war remarks and of Woolley's essay in *Friends* has led many people to conclude that they had never got on together; but contemporary records show that they worked alongside one another very happily at Carchemish, and that Lawrence enjoyed Woolley's company. There is no note of personal hostility in the surviving pre-war documents, and the occasional disagreements caused by Lawrence's excessive loyalty to the Ashmolean were successfully smoothed over by Hogarth.

*   *   *

The brief digging season of autumn 1913 was extraordinarily fruitful; there were important finds even before the work began. Lawrence wrote: 'We . . . had to cut away a little earth to bank up our railway line, and found out a new line of sculptures in basalt, running in two directions . . . It will make our season a burning success if we find nothing else'.

By now Woolley was convinced that there was much more to be discovered. Hogarth wrote in October urging him to excavate some complete buildings so that plans could be published. This was especially important because there would only be money for one further season. Woolley replied pointing out that it would be impossible to complete the excavations so soon. He wrote to Kenyon in the same vein: 'Things have gone very well indeed, and I think that the promise for the future is excellent . . . It would be heartbreaking to chuck up this work at the present stage. We need at least as much money again before we can begin to think that we have made an impression on the site . . . Moreover I am now convinced that the whole *Kala'at* [mound] is not the whole of Carchemish, but the royal city, outside which lay the bulk of the town; for the greater part of our *Kala'at* must have been given over to great public or royal buildings and as such would repay excavation. Of course one must go at it by degrees; but there is an awful lot to be done, and we can't stop short at this initial stage.' In the hope of attracting further funds, it was decided that Woolley should put a report about the site in *The Times*, while Hogarth would write an article for the *Illustrated London News*.

Work stopped for the winter on December 4. Lawrence and Woolley had suggested to the Museum that they should not go back to England for the three winter months, since the cost of the return voyage was far higher than that of keeping them at Jerablus on half pay. Moreover, there was a great deal of work for them to do at Jerablus. Kenyon accepted the idea, agreeing to full pay for a month followed by half pay during two months' holiday. They decided to spend December at Jerablus and then to travel in January and February. Lawrence planned to go down towards Antioch, looking for *antikas*, while Woolley intended to visit Egypt.

A few days later Lawrence wrote to Vyvyan Richards, confessing at last that he could not join in the printing scheme: 'The fault was in ever coming out to this place, I think, because really ever since knowing it I have felt that (at least for the near future) to talk of settling down to live in a small way anywhere else was beating the air: and so gradually I slipped down, until a few months ago when I found myself an ordinary archaeologist. I fought very hard, at Oxford and after going down, to avoid being labelled: but the insurance people have nailed me down, now.

'All this preface is leading up to the main issue—that I cannot print with you when you want me. I have felt it coming for a long time, and have funked it . . . I have got to like this place very much: and the people here—five or six of them—and the whole manner of living pleases me. We have 200 men to play with, anyhow we like so long as the excavations go on, and they are splendid fellows many of them . . . and it is great fun with them. Then there are the digs, with dozens of wonderful things to find—it is like a great sport with tangible results at the end of things—Do you know I am keen now on an inscription or a new type of pottery? and hosts of beautiful things in the villages and towns to fill one's house with. Not to mention seal-hunting in the country round about, and the Euphrates to rest in when one is over-hot. It is a place where one eats *lotos* nearly every day, and you know that feeling is bad for one's desires to do something worth looking at, oneself.

'Which is the end, I think, of the apologia . . . do write and tell me if there is any hope of your pulling it off on your own? Carchemish will not be finished for another four or five years: and I'm afraid that after that I'll probably go after another and another nice thing: it is rather a miserable come down'.

Although Lawrence abandoned the printing scheme, he seems to have worked on one of his other projects during 1913. This was the proposed travel book about seven cities of the East (the original 'Seven Pillars of Wisdom'). He later wrote that it was 'a queer book, upon whose difficulties I look back with a not ungrateful wryness'. It was probably never completed, though he had now visited all of the seven cities it was to describe (he once listed these as Constantinople, Cairo, Smyrna, Aleppo, Jerusalem, Urfa and Damascus: on other occasions, however, he included Baghdad, which in 1913 he had yet to visit).

On about December 10 a letter arrived from Kenyon which changed Lawrence's and Woolley's winter travel plans. Kenyon asked them whether they would be prepared to accompany a Palestine Exploration Fund survey party making maps in the Sinai Desert south of Beersheba. Woolley replied by cable: 'Both ready survey work January 1st' and sent a letter of confirmation on the same day. 'We should both greatly like to do the work, but I have some misgivings about this place: really we ought to be working on into January'.

They were looking forward to the journey south: 'It will be warm down there, and sunny: which will be pleasant after our snow and frost up

Sarah Lawrence with her four eldest sons at Langley Lodge, *c.* 1894
(l–r Ned, Will, Sarah Lawrence holding Frank, Bob)

The five Lawrence boys in the garden at Polstead Road, 1902
(l–r Frank, Will, Ned holding Arnold, Bob)

left: Portrait of C.M. Doughty by Eric
Kennington, commissioned by Lawrence in
1921 and later presented to the National
Portrait Gallery

above: Crac des Chevaliers, the west face of the
inner ward sketched by Lawrence in August
1909. He called it 'the finest castle in the world'
and spent three days examining it, one of which
was his twenty-first birthday

Oxford University Officers Training Corps, signals section, *c.* 1910.
Lawrence is seated front row left. The semaphore signal in the back row reads
'O[xford] U[niversity] A[rmy] V[olunteers]'

above: Hypnos, the Greek god of sleep. Lawrence bought a cast of this head from a foundry in Naples in 1909, writing later: 'I would rather possess a fine piece of sculpture than anything in the world'
above right: Janet Laurie, a friend since Lawrence's childhood. She claimed that he had proposed to her in 1910
below: The last known photograph of all five Lawrence brothers, 1910 (l–r Ned, Frank, Arnold, Bob, Will)
below right: D.G. Hogarth by Augustus John, a portrait commissioned by Lawrence for *Seven Pillars of Wisdom* and later presented to the Ashmolean Museum

above: Dahoum, Lawrence's future assistant at Carchemish, photographed by Lawrence during the first season in 1911. *above right*: Sheikh Hamoudi, who became Leonard Woolley's assistant at Carchemish and Ur, photographed by Lawrence, 1911

below: Gregori, D.G. Hogarth's assistant in several previous excavations, photographed at Carchemish by Lawrence. *below right*: Two sketches drawn by Lawrence to illustrate the fortnightly report from Carchemish to the British Museum, 12 May 1911

Lawrence and Woolley photographed at Carchemish
by a visitor, Dr Heinrich Franke, in 1913

The Lower Palace wall at Carchemish
reconstructed while waiting for a new digging permit, 1914

above: Doorway to the expedition house, showing the lintel carved by Lawrence in 1912. To his amusement visitors often admired it as a genuine Hittite carving *above right*: Pick men and basket men digging a trench on the summit of the Carchemish mound, 1911. Photograph by Lawrence

below: Lawrence in Arab clothes, including some of Dahoum's, photographed by Dahoum *c.* 1912.
below right: Dahoum photographed by Lawrence on the same occasion

Exterior of the expedition house at Carchemish, *c.* 1913

Living room of the expedition house, 1913–14,
furnished by Lawrence and Woolley with Eastern antiquities

Dahoum sketched by Francis Dodd at the Ashmolean Museum,
July 1913, while he and Sheikh Hamoudi
were on a brief visit to England as Lawrence's guests

here.' But they had little idea what was required of them. Lawrence wrote home: 'we got a wire from the British Museum [a confirmation that they were to go to Sinai] asking us to do the archaeological part of a survey of Arabia Petraea (Gaza-Petra) undertaken by the Palestine Exploration Fund. So we go off in two days . . . not knowing in any respect more than I have told you . . . we are taking down the necessaries and Dahoum with us to make arrangements locally.'

Before leaving they spent a solitary Christmas together at the expedition house: 'Woolley went out into the outer quad (outer at my request) and sang two short carols, and "Auld Lang Syne". The effect was really beautiful, from a little distance'. There would not be another peacetime Christmas for five years.

Acompanied by Dahoum, they set off to join the Sinai expedition on 29 December 1913. At Aleppo, Woolley received a letter from the Palestine Exploration Fund, giving them detailed instructions: 'You are no doubt acquainted with the Survey of Western Palestine on the scale of one inch to the mile, which was carried out by the Society in 1872–77 . . . The southern limit of that survey was a line running approximately from west to east, through Gaza and Beersheba, to Masada on the western shore of the Dead Sea.

'The country, of which the survey is now to be taken in hand, is that south of the previous survey, up to the line of the Egyptian frontier, which extends from Rafah, on the Mediterranean coast about 20 miles south west of Gaza, in a S.S.E. direction, to the head of the Gulf of Akabah. The eastern limit of the new survey will be a line running north through the [Wadi] Arabah, from the Gulf of Akabah to the southern end of the Dead Sea.

'This country, notwithstanding its proximity to Palestine and Egypt, is but little known, and, though it has been crossed by travellers in certain parts, is to a great extent unexplored. A favourable opportunity has now presented itself, and Captain Newcombe R.E., with a party of the Royal Engineers, has obtained permission to make a survey of the district. The topographical work will be carried out by Captain Newcombe, but it is of great importance that an examination of the country should be made from the archaeological point of view, as there are many remains of great interest to the Bible student, and it is for this part of the work that the Committee are desirous of enlisting the services of yourself and Mr. Lawrence . . .

'Speaking generally, the objects of the expedition are as follows:—

1. To produce an accurate map of the country on the scale of half an inch to the mile.
2. To make special plans of important localities, ruins, and other archaeological remains.
3. To take photographs of buildings and other points of interest.
4. To take squeezes and photographs of any inscriptions that may be found.
5. To collect geological specimens, and ancient stone and flint implements.
6. To record carefully all names now in use . . .

'On the conclusion of your work a complete report should be furnished, giving all the information that has been obtained, and including lists in Arabic of all places.'

The archaeologists joined Captain Newcombe on January 10. He later recalled: 'I rode northwards to Beersheba from my Survey camp, to meet the two eminent scientists, who had left their studies of Hittite remains at Carchemish. I . . . expected to meet two somewhat elderly people; I found C. L. Woolley and T. E. Lawrence, who looked about twenty-four years of age and eighteen respectively . . . My letters to them arranging for their reception had clearly been too polite. Undue deference ceased forthwith.'

From Newcombe they learned a good deal more about the military purpose of the survey project, which would cover unmapped territory along the frontier between Egyptian Sinai and Turkish Palestine. They had already guessed (as Lawrence remarked in a letter to his parents) that: 'We are obviously only meant as red herrings, to give an archaeological colour to a political job.'

To Woolley's dismay, no equipment or stores had been provided, so they had to buy what they could for the journey. Fortunately Lawrence had brought his own camera and some squeeze paper from Carchemish. They went first to map the town of Sabaita, and from there worked slowly southwards. Lawrence did not find the journey comfortable: 'over the consequences of much riding of camels I draw thick veils: but take it as a summing up that we are very unhappy: Woolley is the more uncomfortable, since he is a flesh-potter: I can travel on a thistle, and sleep in a cloak on the ground. Woolley can't, or at least, is only learning to, quite slowly.'

Early in February the survey party was to split. Newcombe would cover the southernmost section accompanied by Lawrence and Dahoum.

They would work down to Akaba and then return via the Wadi Araba. Woolley, with another party, would go north-east.

The two archaeologists were able to find almost nothing that related to the Biblical period in which the PEF was interested. The Jews may have spent forty years in this wilderness during the Exodus, but their passage had left no recognisable signs. Lawrence, however, learned a great deal from this six-week journey with Newcombe's survey parties. 'Living with him we got a clear insight into his methods . . . Off by dawn with guides and instruments, he would return to camp at dark, and work perhaps till midnight, arranging and calculating and recording for the benefit of the other parties. He was the prime begetter of the Survey'. Through observing and occasionally helping in this work, Lawrence acquired a grasp of surveying techniques which he would later put to good use.

The map-makers also taught him a great deal about the geology of different landscapes, and he used this knowledge to enrich his writing. Passages in the report of his journey down to Akaba foreshadow the magnificent landscape descriptions of *Seven Pillars*. For example: 'The way down is very splendid. In the hill-sides all sorts of rocks are mingled in confusion; grey-green limestone cliffs run down sheer for hundreds of feet, in tremendous ravines whose faces are a medley of colours wherever crags of black porphyry and diorite jut out, or where soft sandstone, washed down, has left long pink and red smudges on the lighter colours. The confusion of materials makes the road-laying curiously uneven. The surface is in very few cases made up; wherever possible the road was cut to rock, with little labour, since the stone is always brittle and in thin, flat layers. So the masons had at once ready to their hand masses of squared blocks for parapets or retaining walls. Yet this same facility of the stone has been disastrous to the abandoned road, since the rains of a few seasons chisel the softer parts into an irregular giant staircase; while in the limestone the torrent has taken the road-cutting as a convenient course, and left it deep buried under a sliding mass of water-worn pebbles.'

When Newcombe and Lawrence reached Akaba, the Kaimmakam forbade them to work in his area, and though this did not hinder Newcombe a great deal (maps of the locality already existed), it provided Lawrence with a number of adventures. In particular, he wanted to examine the ruined fortifications on Geziret Faraun, a small island known to the Crusaders as Graye, about four hundred yards offshore near Akaba. The

Turkish police prevented him taking a boat but he managed to reach the island on a makeshift raft.

After this episode, to his disgust, he and Dahoum were escorted on the return journey northwards by a lieutenant and a squad of soldiers. He regarded this as a challenge and shook the soldiers off by making forced marches over appalling terrain. There was some point to this expedition, however, as they found what Newcombe was looking for: 'the two great cross-roads through the hills of the Arabah that serve modern raiding parties entering Sinai, and which served the Israelites a bit earlier. Nobody would show them us, of the Arabs, which accounts for our rather insane wanderings without a guide . . .' The journey also gave Lawrence his first chance to visit Petra. It was the place, rather than the monuments, which impressed him, but he wrote little about it, saying: 'you will never know what Petra is like, unless you come out here . . . Only be assured that till you have seen it you have not had the glimmering of an idea how beautiful a place can be.'

From Petra he travelled eastwards to Maan, where, after another minor conflict with the Turkish authorities, he took the railway northwards to Damascus, some 230 miles distant. He would revisit this railway in very different circumstances three years later.

While Woolley and Lawrence were in Sinai, the British Museum had been fortunate in its quest for funds. Without waiting to be prompted by the articles which appeared simultaneously in the *Illustrated London News* and *The Times* on January 24, Walter Morrison offered a further £10,000 for the work, and the full excavation of Carchemish seemed assured. Hogarth intended to visit Jerablus and agree on a plan of campaign to last for several years ahead. He also wanted to talk seriously to Lawrence: 'His Magdalen Senior Demyship is running out. Is he to go on at Jerablus? If so, he will need a higher salary after this year. But does he want to go on with what leads nowhere in particular, and is it right that he should? This must be discussed with him. If he does not wish to go on, *someone else must be found this summer.*' Hogarth was doubtless questioning whether Lawrence should continue in a subordinate position at Carchemish, where most of the credit for successful results would go to Woolley. Lawrence, now twenty-five, might better advance his career by conducting a dig of his own, as Petrie had suggested, or by returning to Oxford and completing his B.Litt. on medieval pottery.

Woolley and Lawrence were back in Jerablus at the beginning of March, but the season's excavation was interrupted almost immediately by a fracas between the German railway engineers and their men. At considerable personal risk, the two archaeologists had succeeded in calming the enraged workmen. They were publicly thanked by the Turkish authorities, but lost a good deal of time making statements to the officials who came to investigate the affair.

The site had now become famous, and eminent visitors arrived by the trainload. By way of recompense, the German railway engineers, who had continued to remove spoil from the digs during the winter, now lent some extra wagons for the light railway, which enabled clearing work to proceed more quickly. In the evenings Woolley and Lawrence worked at their report on Sinai, which was to be published as a monograph. Lawrence planned to spend about six weeks completing it during the summer in England, where he could consult historical source materials. He had decided to stay on at Carchemish and was even planning to learn Kurdish, writing home: 'I don't think that I will ever travel in the West again: one cannot tell, of course, but this part out here is worth a million of the rest. The Arabs are so different from ourselves.'

The flow of visitors continued throughout the season. Guests were received in the expedition house, which through successive enlargements had become a sizeable building. Since there were to be more Europeans in future seasons, a second sitting room was built, as well as a new *antika* store, stable, charcoal store and wash house.

With all this going on, Lawrence's occupations were varied, especially on Fridays when the digs were shut down: 'in the morning we slept later than usual, and then I riveted up a set of points on our light railway till midday. In the afternoon read a little, measured up a building, worked at the plastering of a broken relief, bathed, and shot a little at 200 yds. Now I ought to be reading, but am not.'

In mid-May the site was visited by Stewart Newcombe and his assistant Lieutenant Greig, the two RE officers who had been in charge of the Sinai Survey. Woolley and Lawrence had done their best to interest the surveyors in archaeology and had invited them to see Carchemish on their way back to England. To provide Newcombe with an excuse for this detour Woolley had suggested that the region might yield information of military interest (for example about the engineering of the Baghdad Railway). After a brief visit to Carchemish, the two officers travelled 150 miles westward to the Taurus mountains, hoping to find out about the exact route and construction of the railway through this most difficult terrain.

Lawrence was planning to leave Jerablus on about June 10. 'Both of us', Woolley told Kenyon, 'are glad to have reached the end of the season, being pretty tired and considerably slack in consequence. I want a summer in England to buck me up again'.

Shortly before their departure, a letter arrived from Newcombe, who had reached Constantinople. He had found the railway construction road through the Taurus mountains and had been able to travel along it. But it had proved difficult to obtain much information about the railway itself. He therefore asked Woolley and Lawrence to try and take the same route on their way home.

Early in June, therefore, they took leave of the men at Jerablus and set out via the Taurus mountains for their summer holiday in England. Lawrence was planning to return before the end of August, and the new season would begin in September. Woolley later wrote: 'in June 1914 the catalogue had been brought up to date and of inscribed stone fragments alone more than two thousand had been recorded, and complete type-lists of all Early Bronze Age pottery had been drawn up'. Lawrence left these precious notes behind, but took his camera for the Taurus journey.

By a mixture of bluff and good luck, he and Woolley got on to the railway construction road, where they chanced on a senior Italian engineer who had just been sacked by the Germans. Woolley loved Italy and spoke the language fluently. He made friends with the disgruntled engineer who gave him all the information Newcombe wanted. Woolley later wrote: 'It is the only piece of spying that I ever did before the War.'

Woolley and Lawrence had to spend the next two months in England working on their archaeological report for the PEF. About half the text had been written during the last season at Carchemish, but there was still much to do, especially on the plans and illustrations.

At 11 p.m. on 4 August 1914, twelve days before Lawrence's twenty-sixth birthday, Britain entered the Great War. He would never see Carchemish again. Later, he wrote with nostalgia of his early adult life: 'The first time I left England [in 1906] was a dream of delight . . . I began my own, independent, voluntary travels. France, mainly: then further afield, by slow degrees, until the War cut short that development of me into a sort of Hogarth: a travelled, archaeological sort of man, with geography and a pen as his two standbys.' Yet Lawrence's very words point to the underlying continuity between his pre-war and wartime careers. Geography and writing were to be his principal activities for the next two years, and throughout the war he would draw on his earlier knowledge and experience. There would also be continuity in Lawrence's development as a person. While some people respond to the challenge of war with hitherto unsuspected ability, this was not so in his case. By August 1914 the personal qualities which would bring him fame were already evident.

Part II

The Years of Conflict

1914–1922

Do make clear . . . that my objects were to save
England, and France too, from the follies of the
imperialists, who would have us, in 1920, repeat the
exploits of Clive or Rhodes. The world has passed by
that point. I think, though, there's a great future for
the British Empire as a voluntary association.

T. E. Lawrence to D. G. Pearman
16 February 1928. Pearman was preparing
lectures on the Arab Revolt.

Part I

The Years of Conflict
1914–1922

CHAPTER 5

London and Cairo

August 1914–August 1915

WHEN war broke out in August 1914 most young men of Lawrence's background immediately volunteered for service. His brothers were all affected in one way or another, except for the youngest, who was still at school. Bob had chosen a career in medicine; as soon as he completed his training, he would go to the front. Will, then teaching in India, felt it his duty to return to England as soon as he could and join up. Frank, though still an Oxford undergraduate, had planned a career in the army; he was given a commission straight away. Lawrence also intended to volunteer. First, however, he had to finish work on the Sinai archaeological report.

That summer Turkey held back from the conflict, and some members of the Cabinet hoped that the Sultan might be dissuaded from taking sides with Germany. Lord Kitchener, now Secretary of State for War, asked that the PEF Sinai Survey report should be published as rapidly as possible. It might help to persuade the Turks that the survey had been purely archaeological. Lawrence therefore spent the summer in Oxford. Woolley, as the principal author, was also prevented from enlisting, and the chapters went back and forth between them.

During these weeks Lawrence had second thoughts about his 'youthful indiscretion-book' on seven eastern cities, much of which was now in draft. He decided that it was immature and burned it.

He planned to enlist in September when the Sinai text was complete. By that time, however, the glut of volunteers had become so great that men under six feet tall were being refused. He and Woolley wrote to Newcombe asking whether they might be able to get work in Military Intelligence. They were told to wait, since their specialist knowledge of the Middle East would become useful if Turkey entered the war.

By the third week in October Lawrence had found a war job in London. He began work, as a civilian, in the Geographical Section of the General Staff (GSGS). Hogarth knew the head of the department, Colonel Hedley, and was probably responsible for finding Lawrence this post.

Experienced map officers were in great demand at the front, and ten days after Lawrence joined the Geographical Section only he and Hedley remained there. He found himself working from nine in the morning until late at night. Although the GSGS was busy with maps of France, some of his work was concerned with Newcombe's Sinai Survey. He was well qualified for this, having a knowledge of the area and an ability to work with Arabic place-names. In due course he was commissioned, as a Temporary 2nd Lieutenant-Interpreter.

Turkey finally entered the war at the end of October, and map-making of enemy-held territory in Sinai, Syria and western Arabia was then transferred to Egypt. Lawrence expected to leave for Cairo almost at once.

He had not lost touch with his archaeological work during this period at the War Office; he was concerned about the fate of the Carchemish site and the Arabs who had worked there. When Fontana suggested that the British Museum continue employing the headmen as site guards, Lawrence agreed, telling Kenyon: 'I expect that the issue of the fight with Turkey will transfer all the antiquities at Carchemish to your account . . . that would be only a little item in the peace-bargain . . . and on this presumption it would be worth your while to continue paying the guards'. The Museum made arrangements through a third party to retain Hamoudi, Haj Wahid, Dahoum and others.

In mid-November Lawrence's departure for Cairo was postponed when he was given an urgent job to do: 'I was to have gone to Egypt on Sat last: only the G.O.C. there wired to the W.O. and asked for a road-report on Sinai that they were supposed to have.

'Well, of course they hadn't got it—not a bit of it. So they came to me, and said "write it."

'I thought to kill two or three birds with my stone, so I offered 'em *The Wilderness of Zin* . . . they took it and asked for more.' The report was to cover the whole of northern Sinai, as far west as the Suez Canal. Lawrence had only visited a small part of this area during his work with the Sinai Survey: 'So I'm writing a report from the military point of view of a country I don't know, and haven't visited yet. One of the minor terrors is, that later on I'm to get my own book, and guide myself over the country with it. It will be a lesson in humility, I hope.'

The work was 'an awful sweat, for it has to be done against time, and the maps are not yet drawn. So I have to oversee them also, and try and correlate the two.' It took Lawrence nearly a month to compile the *Military Report on the Sinai Peninsula*. The information it contained was all to be found in the Department's files, but the task of collating and editing it into a 190–page book often meant working far into the night. He finally left for Egypt on 9 December 1914, travelling with Newcombe.

The British authorities in Cairo had made discreet preparations during the months of uncertainty about Turkish intentions. Although Egypt was nominally under Turkish suzerainty, the country was already in effect controlled by Britain, and its security would be of vital interest because of the Suez Canal. On November 2 the British Cabinet had formally abandoned the pre-war policy of maintaining the Turkish Empire in its existing form and, on December 17, Egypt was declared a British protectorate. Sir Henry McMahon, whose previous posts had included that of Foreign Secretary to the Government of India, was nominated High Commissioner.

The main objective of British policy in Egypt was to defend the Suez Canal, but there were two schools of thought as to how this might best be done. One believed that every means should be used to defeat Turkey, and that some kind of pre-emptive attack would be the most effective way to defend British interests. Its leading advocate was Lord Kitchener, who had served as British Agent in Egypt until August 1914 and was now one of the most influential members of the Cabinet. The other school argued for a passive garrison strategy, whereby the British presence in Egypt would be used only to restrain local pro-Turkish movements and to fend off any attack on the Canal. This strategy was supported by three powerful interest groups. First, there were many who believed that Britain's effort should be concentrated on the Western Front, and that 'sideshows' should be avoided. Secondly, there were the French, whose policy towards the Middle East was influenced by fears that Britain would use the war as an excuse to annex regions where France had colonial ambitions (the French were also convinced 'Westerners', because the European war was being fought on their territory). Finally, there was the British imperial administration in India, which had long regarded the Middle East as its own sphere of interest and resented the prospect of initiatives from Cairo in the region.

It is significant that none of those arguing for a passive garrison on the Canal had any direct responsibility for defending Egypt. The authorities on the spot, however, knew that if the Turks mounted a serious offensive, it would be necessary to hold a very long front in a desert region which lacked natural defensive positions. A successful Turkish thrust at any point might easily interrupt traffic through the Canal.

If passive defence was undesirable, there remained the question of

The Turkish Empire in January 1915

deciding how best to disable the Turks. This would not necessarily involve an advance across Sinai; a more damaging and economical attack
might be made elsewhere. The Turkish front in Sinai was supplied by a
very long line of communication. This stretched northwards through the
Palestine railway system, then inland to Damascus, and finally north-
westwards through the Taurus and Amanus mountains before reaching
Constantinople. It was clear from the outset that the best plan might be to
land a British force and attack one of the vulnerable sections of this line.

Another factor was the possibility that Arabs in enemy territory might
be induced to rebel. The Turkish line of communication to Sinai ran for
nearly a thousand miles through Arab provinces. At the outbreak of war

these areas were not strongly held by Turkish troops, and in the more remote parts of the Empire local leaders often exercised a good deal of political power.

Revolutionary Arab nationalist movements had existed for some time before the war, and their aspirations were widely known. A number of schemes for winning independence had been envisaged, but none had been practicable. Such an attempt could only be sustained if there were an external source of arms and ammunition. The most promising course would be a mutiny of Arab troops supported by the general populace; an Arab nationalist rising on these lines would mimic the successful Young Turk revolution of 1908. Such plans seemed feasible because the Turkish army was made up of conscript units, and the Arab provinces were therefore largely garrisoned with local troops.

As long as British policy had been to maintain the Turkish Empire in its pre-war form, no encouragement had been offered to Arab nationalists. When Turkey took sides with Germany, however, the official British attitude changed. It seemed likely that the Turkish Empire would be dismantled if the Allies won the war, and the Cabinet had therefore to consider what kind of future for the region would be most beneficial to British imperial interests. Until the war, Turkey had presented no threat to British maritime traffic through the Suez Canal. A new settlement would have to prevent any potentially unfriendly power from gaining a dominant position in the eastern Mediterranean. One solution would have been for Britain to annex a major portion of the Ottoman Empire, but influential members of the Cabinet argued that there was nothing to gain by taking on the cost of further responsibilities in this region.

During 1914, as it became clear that there was a possibility of war between Britain and Turkey, tentative contacts began between Arab nationalists and British officials in Cairo.

Most significant among these was the correspondence that began with Sherif Hussein, the Emir of Mecca. As guardian of the Holy Places, Hussein was a religious leader revered not only in the Hejaz but throughout the Moslem world. He held a degree of temporal power in and around Mecca, and he had succeeded in whittling away the influence of the Turkish provincial governor. He had been secretly involved in schemes for Arab independence since the early years of the century, and was seen as a potential figurehead by many Arab nationalists. The Turks were aware of these sympathies, but their attempts to neutralise his influence had been unsuccessful.

Early in 1914 one of his sons, the Emir Abdullah, had visited Cairo. In private meetings with Lord Kitchener and Ronald Storrs, Kitchener's Oriental Secretary, Abdullah had asked what the British attitude would be if the Turks attempted to depose his father. At the time, he had been offered no British support, but these discussions paved the way for more fruitful contacts after the outbreak of war.

In September, Storrs had suggested opening a correspondence with Abdullah. This was authorised by London, and Kitchener sent a message for transmission to Abdullah, which asked whether, in the event of war with Turkey, 'he and his father and the Arabs of the Hedjaz would be with us or against us.' The reply from Mecca, while non-committal, was encouraging.

The delicacy of the Sherif's position was well understood in Cairo. The Hejaz had never been self-sufficient economically, and it depended on outside sources for food supplies. For centuries it had relied on support from Egypt and, before the war, its food had come mainly from Egypt and India. Much of the pilgrim traffic had now been interrupted. This had been an important source of income, and Hussein was therefore in considerable financial difficulties. For the present he depended very heavily on Turkey.

The staff in Cairo saw that even if there were no final break between Sherif Hussein and Constantinople, his attitude towards Britain would be extremely important. The reason was that an Islamic jihad against the Allies had been proclaimed on November 14 by the Sultan of Turkey in his role as Caliph. The Turks believed that a Holy War would create a conflict of loyalties among the millions of Islamic subjects in Russia and in French and British colonies. Moslem troops in the Allied armies might refuse to fight against fellow-Moslems on the Turkish side.

The authorities in Constantinople had confidently expected that their call for a jihad would be echoed by the Sherif, whose endorsement, as guardian of the Holy Places, was essential. During the weeks that followed, however, Hussein managed to avoid lending his support, offering a succession of adroit excuses. Britain was very grateful for the Sherif's inaction. Although the full effect of a jihad could not be estimated, the potential danger seemed considerable, especially in Egypt, where pro-Turkish loyalties were widespread and the Canal installations offered a vulnerable target.

By December 15, when Lawrence reached Cairo, co-operation with the Arabs seemed to offer one of the most promising openings for British policy in the Middle East, and the Sherif's friendship was already yielding valuable results. The efforts of British officials in Cairo to foster Arab nationalism had been not merely sanctioned but encouraged by Kitchener and Sir Edward Grey, the Foreign Secretary, in London.

Lawrence and Newcombe were joined in Cairo after a few days by Leonard Woolley, and also by two young Members of Parliament, George Lloyd and Aubrey Herbert. These last were both very knowledgeable about the Turkish Empire; each had served for a time as an honorary attaché at the British Embassy in Constantinople. Lawrence wrote cheerfully to Hogarth: 'There wasn't an Intelligence department it seemed, and they thought all was well without it:—till it dawned on them that nobody in Egypt knew about Syria. This was the day we got there, so they changed their minds about sending us flying as a good riddance—and set us to collect intelligence instead.' This frivolity should not be taken literally; a note in the Cairo GHQ War Diary for December 22 reads: 'Organisation [of] Military Intelligence Department proceeding under Captain Newcombe R.E. with five other officers sent from home. Badly needed.'

Lawrence was pleased with both the posting and his colleagues. It was a youthful team: Newcombe, the senior in rank, was only thirty-four. Lloyd was a year younger, while Herbert and Woolley were thirty-two. The Department was soon extremely busy. Lawrence wrote that he was in the office from morning till night, interpreting information and writing 'little geographical essays. It doesn't sound exciting, but it has been far and away the best job going in Egypt these few weeks.' Since he had worked on maps for two months at the War Office he was given the task of liaising between Military Intelligence and the Survey of Egypt, a civilian department of the Egyptian Government which was responsible for producing maps. Much of the information needed for revisions had to be collected from Intelligence sources, and these liaison duties soon became important.

The work of the Intelligence Department was not restricted to gathering information. From the outset it examined broader questions of strategy. Within days of their arrival, a friend of George Lloyd's visiting Cairo set down opinions which can only have been gleaned from Lloyd himself: 'The Intelligence Department . . . have done invaluable work already collecting and tabulating information and initiating ideas which never could have dawned in the heads of the General or his surroundings . . . A well-run Intelligence Department will really run him as regards policy'.

Although it was new, the Department had replaced an earlier Intelligence office, which had long been advising the British authorities in

Cairo. The continuity with previous work was provided by Gilbert Clayton, Newcombe's chief, who had worked in Cairo Intelligence before the war and had now been promoted Lieutenant-Colonel.

Clayton also controlled a separate Egyptian civil Intelligence service. Through his military and civil responsibilities he was in close contact with both Major-General Maxwell (the GOC) and the High Commissioner. In addition to these duties, Clayton was the Cairo representative of Sir Reginald Wingate, Governor-General of the Sudan (generally referred to by his Egyptian Army rank of 'Sirdar', i.e. C-in-C). Thus Clayton was personally responsible to the three most senior British officials in the Middle East. This multiple role demanded unusual ability and a good deal of tact in dealing with superiors and staff. Lawrence would later write: 'Clayton made the perfect leader for such a band of wild men as we were. He was calm, detached, clear-sighted, of unconscious courage in assuming responsibility. He gave an open run to his subordinates . . . and he worked by influence rather than by loud direction. It was not easy to descry his influence. He was like water, or permeating oil, creeping silently and insistently through everything. It was not possible to say where Clayton was and was not, and how much really belonged to him. He never visibly led; but his ideas were abreast of those who did'. Through Clayton, the enthusiastic specialists recruited to the new Intelligence Department soon found themselves involved in the largest questions of future policy, both military and political.

Lawrence shared fully in this political work. As Newcombe later wrote: 'We worked in the same room together. Lawrence, Woolley and I had breakfast, lunch, and dinner together daily at the Continental Hotel for nine months. So Lawrence knew all that any other of us did and of course read all reports which we all discussed together . . . ''maps'' was only a nominal part of his job: and he was in fact as much in the picture as any of us'.

One of the Department's first tasks was to study schemes for a British landing somewhere on the Syrian coast. The most vulnerable point in Turkish communications with Sinai (and also with Mesopotamia) was clearly Alexandretta. On December 4, before Lawrence and Newcombe arrived, Maxwell had written to Kitchener: 'If any diversion is contemplated, I think the easiest, safest, and most fruitful in results would be one at Alexandretta. There . . . we strike a vital blow at the railways and also hit German interests very hard . . . Alexandretta would not want a very large force. All other places—Rafah, Jaffa, Acre, Beirut—are too far from the Turkish lines of communications.'

The capture of Alexandretta was envisaged purely as a British operation, but it seemed possible that the effect of a landing there might be greatly increased by Arab nationalist action. Information reaching Cairo suggested that if Turkish military communications were cut by British intervention, the Syrian Arabs would seize the opportunity to declare a general revolt.

There was, however, a difficulty in giving direct encouragement to Syrian nationalists. Just as India saw Mesopotamia as a potential colony, France had long-standing imperial ambitions in Syria. The French regarded themselves as protectors of the Maronite Christian community in the Lebanon, where there were substantial French commercial interests, and vociferous French pressure groups were making no secret of their hope to colonise a much wider area.

Politicians in London tended to accept that much of northern Syria would become a French colony after the war, but in Cairo it was apparent that such a policy would lead to difficulties between Britain and the Arab nationalists. At the very least, it was necessary to clarify the British position. Maxwell therefore asked Kitchener 'what the ultimate policy of England regarding Palestine and Syria in connection with the Arab movement will be? . . . I do not want anything said or done which may afterwards prove to have been a breach of faith.' Kitchener replied that no policy had yet been defined, 'but if our troops arrive in Syria we hope they would be well received by the population.' Both Kitchener and Maxwell knew that a British landing might encourage Syrian nationalists to revolt, and that the result could be a new Arab government utterly opposed to French colonisation. If the military arguments for such a landing prevailed, France might have to scale down her ambitions.

Syria was the Arab province Lawrence himself found most interesting, and he became deeply absorbed in the debate about its future. Before the war he had seen for himself how ruthlessly the native villagers were exploited by corrupt Turkish officials, and he had learned a certain amount about nationalist aspirations. His commitment to the ideal of Arab self-rule had already made him an opponent of French ambition. He knew that French colonial administration, unlike British, would tend to destroy Arab culture, language and social structure. Others in the Intelligence Department shared this opposition to France, though possibly not for the same reasons. Aubrey Herbert, for example, wrote: 'This is a war for liberty and small peoples, not for French financiers.'

From the outset, therefore, Lawrence was one of the most enthusiastic advocates of Arab self-government in Clayton's Intelligence Department. When he saw that the Alexandretta scheme might lead to an Arab revolt in Syria, he enthusiastically provided information and arguments that might persuade his seniors to act.

During January the scheme met with general approval. It was discussed in Cabinet on the 13th, and planning went ahead on the basis that the action would be carried out in parallel with naval bombardment of the Dardanelles.

Wartime censorship prevented Lawrence from giving details of these military questions in private letters to England, but he wrote triumphantly to Hogarth: 'Our particular job goes well. We all pulled together hard for a month to twist "them" from what we thought was a wrong line they were taking—and we seem to have succeeded completely: so that we today have got all we want for the moment, and therefore feel absolutely bored.'

The atmosphere in the Intelligence office was in some ways more reminiscent of a university department than a military unit, and professional soldiers often felt uneasy with members of this very intellectual group. This feeling was exacerbated by Lawrence, who abhorred pomposity and inefficiency, and found plenty of both in the military bureaucracy. He was working under considerable pressure and had no time for lengthy regulation procedures. Worse still, regular officers would sometimes find themselves a target for his mischievous humour. At Oxford he had often drawn attention to himself by unconventional behaviour. This quirk had become habitual, and could offend. In his own words: 'When in fresh company, I would embark on little wanton problems of conduct, observing the impact of this or that approach on my hearers, treating fellow-men as so many targets for intellectual ingenuity: until I could hardly tell my own self where the leg-pulling began or ended. This pettiness helped to make me uncomfortable with other men, lest my whim drive me suddenly to collect them as trophies of marksmanship'. Aubrey Herbert's first impression (which probably had a social bias) was of 'an odd gnome, half cad—with a touch of genius'.

Those who worked alongside Lawrence learned to tolerate his eccentricities; most of them knew him well enough to like the personality beneath, and they had a healthy regard for the ability and dedication he brought to his work. Others, outside his immediate circle, were often resentful. Ernest Dowson, who as Director of the Survey of Egypt was in almost daily contact with Lawrence at this period, later wrote: 'for truthful balance it has of course to be recognized . . . that it was not only the pompous, the inefficient and the pretentious whose co-operation Lawrence's ways tended to alienate. Many men of sense and ability were repelled by the impudence, freakishness and frivolity he trailed so provocatively.' These difficulties were aggravated still further by his appearance. He seemed an 'extremely youthful and, to our unseeing eyes, insignificant figure with well-ruffled light hair, solitary pip on sleeve, minus belt and with peaked cap askew'. Such indifference to dress was general in the Intelligence office during 1915. Herbert was described as 'being, after Lawrence, the untidiest officer in Egypt', and Newcombe said that he himself, though a Regular with sixteen years' service 'also wore slacks without a belt (and I believe General Maxwell, G.O.C. did the same).'

As anticipated, early in February the Turks mounted an attack on the Canal. It was beaten off with surprising ease, and the enemy force retired so unexpectedly that the British failed to mount a crushing counter-attack. It was later realised that the Turkish commander had expected that the Canal defences would be crippled by a general Moslem rising in Egypt as soon as his force approached. Since no such rebellion took place he had no alternative but to retire. Afterwards the Turks put out face-saving statements that the attack had merely been a 'reconnaissance'.

During the first weeks of 1915, the future of the Arabian provinces, and of Syria in particular, was widely debated in Cairo. There were vociferous political factions in the city representing pro-French Maronites and various types of Arab nationalist. To British irritation, the pro-French lobby in Cairo was being actively encouraged by French diplomats.

The publicity given to French aims was causing deepening anxiety in the minds of most Syrian nationalists. Early in February Clayton drew up a briefing document on the future of Syria, attaching a statement of non-Maronite Syrian Christian views on the one hand, and the opinion of a well-known Pan-Arab spokesman, Rashid Rida, on the other. The non-Maronite Christian argument was for a British protectorate on the Egyptian model, which would unite Egypt and Syria (including Palestine and Sinai) under one titular Sultan. By contrast, Rashid Rida sought British support for independence in all the Arab provinces of the Turkish Empire, without any form of protectorate. Both, however, were totally opposed to any form of French colonisation; it was suggested that France should be bought off by compensation elsewhere. In the light of these views, Clayton urged that a decision on future policy should be taken as soon as possible, since otherwise Britain might find that commitments had been given which would later prove embarrassing.

However, while British officials in Cairo dealt with day-to-day diplomacy, wider policy was settled by the Foreign Office in London, and ultimately by the Cabinet. During the spring of 1915 the Government began taking steps to formulate a general policy towards the Middle East, but no definite conclusions were reached and after a few weeks the process ground to a halt while wider consultations took place.

While such issues could conveniently be shelved in London, it was impossible to set them aside in Cairo, where the future of Turkey's Arab provinces was a burning question. Lawrence was one of those who hoped to find some way of triggering a nationalist revolt in Syria. Towards the end of March he had an opportunity to send two uncensored letters to Hogarth who, though still a civilian in Oxford, had influential friends in Whitehall. The content of these letters is unusually interesting, since Lawrence was able to discuss freely the topics which are so noticeably absent from his correspondence with family and friends in England.

In the first he urged Hogarth to help revive the Alexandretta scheme, arguing (as did many others) that Alexandretta itself lay outside the area France could legitimately claim. He wrote: 'The French insist upon Syria—which we are conceding to them: there remains Alexandretta, which is the key of the whole place as you know. It's going to be the head of the Baghdad line, and therefore the natural outlet for north Syria and north Mesopotamia: it's the only easy road from Cilicia and Asia Minor into Asia etc. etc. Also it's a wonderful harbour, and thanks to Ras Khanyir on the south can be made impregnable. It is cut off from Syria, and is neither Syria nor Asia Minor. In the hands of France it will provide a sure base for naval attacks on Egypt—and remember with her in Syria, and compulsory service there, she will be able any time to fling 100,000 men against the canal in twelve days from declaration of war . . . The only place from which a fleet can operate against Egypt is Alexandretta, because there is no English port from which one can blockade it. Smyrna and Constantinople are shut in by islands: whereas Alexandretta has only Cyprus in front of it, and the water round that is too deep for a large naval harbour to be built.

'If Russia has Alexandretta it's all up with us in the Near East. And in any case in the next war the French will probably be under Russia's finger in Syria. Therefore I think it absolutely necessary that we hold Alexan-

dretta . . . and thanks to the Amanus [mountains] we needn't hold anything else, either in Syria or in Asia Minor. The High Commissioner is
strongly of the same opinion, and General Maxwell also, when he is
awake and sober. Kitchener has pressed it on us: Winston seems uncertain, and someone . . . in the F.O. is blocking it entirely. I think that
perhaps you can get a move on'. Lawrence suggested tempting Churchill,
then First Lord of the Admiralty, with the prospect of mineral wealth in
the Alexandretta region: 'If Winston settles on a thing he gets it, I fancy:
especially with K's help.'

Lawrence's apparent acceptance of a French Syria was purely tactical,
since he fully expected a large-scale nationalist revolt in the region if
British forces occupied Alexandretta. This is hinted at earlier in his letter,
where he noted that Turkey had 'only 50,000 disaffected troops in Syria
. . . and the whole country is mad against them'. Indeed there were
several other places where the conditions for an Arab uprising seemed to
be ripening. He wrote: 'Idrisi is at open war with the Turks in Asir: Sherif
[Hussein] has almost declared himself, and the Vali and staff of Hedjaz
have taken refuge in Damascus'. This last remark suggests that Cairo
Intelligence had picked up some news of the latest dispute between Hussein and the Vali, which had flared during February when a secret Turkish
plot to depose (and possibly assassinate) the Sherif had come to light.

Lawrence's second letter, on March 22, was more explicit about his
ideas for a widespread Arab movement. His hopes were now pinned on
the Idrisi, who was fighting a neighbouring Turkish-controlled chieftain,
the Imam of the Yemen. Lawrence saw this as a starting-point for wider
action. However, Clayton could not intervene directly, because it had
been agreed that British relations with Arab chieftains on the Red Sea
littoral south of Kunfida would be handled by the Government of India
through its representative in Aden. Kunfida, a port on the Red Sea, was
the most northerly town controlled by the Idrisi, and Cairo was not
therefore empowered to negotiate with him.

Lawrence told Hogarth: 'You know India used to be in control of
Arabia—and used to do it pretty badly, for they hadn't a man who knew
Syria or Turkey, and they used to consider only the Gulf, and the preservation of peace in the Aden Hinterland . . . Egypt (which is one Clayton, a very good man) got hold of the Idrisi family . . . and for some
years we had a little agreement together. Then this war started, and India
went on the old game of balancing the little powers there. I want to pull
them all together, and to roll up Syria by way of the Hedjaz in the name
of the Sherif. You know how big his repute is in Syria. This could be

done by Idrisi only, so we drew out a beautiful alliance, giving him all he
wanted: and India refused to sign. So we cursed them, and I think that
Newcombe and myself are going down to Kunfida as his advisors. If
Idrisi is anything like as good as we hope we can rush right up to
Damascus, and biff the French out of all hope of Syria. It's a big game,
and at last one worth playing. Of course India has no idea what we are
playing at: if we can only get to Assyr we can do the rest—or have a try
at it . . . If only India will let us go. Won't the French be mad if we win
through?'

Others were cautious about the proposal. The Sherif of Mecca was in
dispute with the Idrisi about possession of Kunfida, and this difficulty
stood in the way of the common action Lawrence had envisaged. Through
support for the Idrisi Britain might well alienate Hussein. Eventually, to
Lawrence's disappointment, the plan to send him to Kunfida was abandoned.

At about this time Lawrence wrote a long analysis of the internal factors
which would have to be taken into account when the future of Syria was
decided. He gave a great deal of thought to this paper; its conclusions
were based on his own knowledge of the country and on a vast amount of
diverse information which had accumulated in Intelligence Department
files. He was Clayton's specialist on Syria, and the views he now expressed were destined to have far-reaching influence.

His account began with a long description which emphasised the geographical, cultural, racial, linguistic and religious diversity of Syria. After this he turned his attention to the six major cities. He argued that two
of these, Jerusalem and Beirut, should be set apart because they were too
cosmopolitan to be considered essentially Arab. The people of Jerusalem,
he wrote, 'with the rarest exceptions, are characterless as hotel servants,
living on the crowd of visitors passing through. Questions of Arabs and
their nationality are as far from them as bimetallism from the life of
Texas'. Beirut, on the other hand, 'would be all bastard French in feeling,
as in language, but for its Greek harbour and its American College.
Public opinion in it is that of the Christian merchants, all fat men . . .
Beyrout is the door of Syria, with a Levantine screen through which
shop-soiled foreign influences flow into Syria. It is as representative of
Syria as Soho of the Home Counties'.

There remained: 'Damascus, Homs, Hamah, and Aleppo . . . the four
ancient cities in which Syria takes pride. They are stretched like a chain
along the fertile valleys of the interior, between the desert and the hills;

because of their setting they turn their backs upon the sea and look eastward. They are Arab and know themselves such.

'Damascus is the old inevitable head of Syria. It is the seat of lay government and the religious centre, three days only from the Holy City by its railway. Its sheikhs are leaders of opinion, and more "Meccan" than others elsewhere. Its people are fresh and turbulent, always willing to strike, as extreme in their words and acts as in their pleasures. Damascus will move before any part of Syria. The Turks made it their military centre, just as naturally as the Arab Opposition . . . Damascus is a lode star to which Arabs are naturally drawn, and a city which will not easily be convinced that it is subject to any alien race.

'Hamah and Homs are towns which dislike one another. Everyone in them manufactures things . . . Their industries were prosperous and increasing; their merchants were quick to take advantage of new outlets, or to meet new tastes . . . They demonstrated the productive ability of Syria, unguided by foreigners . . . Yet, while the prosperity of Beyrout has made it Levantine, the prosperity of Homs and Hamah has reinforced their localism, made them more entirely native, and more jealously native than any other Syrian towns . . .

'Aleppo is the largest city in Syria, but not of it, nor of Turkey, nor of Mesopotamia. Rather it is a point where all the races, creeds and tongues of the Ottoman Empire meet and know one another in a spirit of compromise . . . Aleppo would stand aside from political action altogether but for the influence of the great unmixed Arab quarters which lie on its outskirts like overgrown, half-nomad villages. These are, after the *Maidan* of Damascus, the most national of any parts of towns, and the intensity of their Arab feeling tinges the rest of the citizens with a colour of nationalism, which is by so much less vivid than the unanimous opinion of Damascus.'

Lawrence next turned his attention to Syrian politicians, but found little to admire: 'All of them want something new, for with their superficiality and their lawlessness is combined a passion for politics, the science of which it is fatally easy for the Syrian to gain a smattering, and too difficult to gain a mastery. They are all discontented with the government they have, but few of them honestly combine their ideas of what they want. Some (mostly Mohammedans) cry for an Arab kingdom, some (mostly Christians) for a foreign protection of an altruistic thelemic order, conferring privileges without obligation. Others cry for autonomy for Syria.' He saw 'no national feeling' in Syria: 'Between town and town, village and village, family and family, creed and creed, exist intimate jealousies, sedulously fostered by the Turks to render a spontaneous union impossible. The largest indigenous political entity in settled Syria is only the village under its sheikh, and in patriarchal Syria the tribe under its chief . . . All the constitution above them is the artificial bureaucracy of the Turk . . . By accident and time the Arabic language has gradually permeated the country, until it is now almost the only one in use; but this does not mean that Syria—any more than Egypt—is an Arabian country. On the sea coast there is little, if any, Arabic feeling or tradition: on the desert edge there is much. Indeed, racially, there is perhaps something to be said for the suggestion—thrown in the teeth of geography and economics—of putting the littoral under one government, and the interior under another.'

Looking ahead, Lawrence argued that 'an Arab Government in Syria, today or tomorrow, would be an imposed one, as the former Arab Governments were.' However, there were two factors which might help to provide a basis for political cohesion. First, a kind of patriotism based on common language rather than racial or territorial boundaries: 'The heritage of the Koran and the classical poets holds the Arabic-speaking peoples together.' Secondly, there was the Arab consciousness of a shared history, 'the dim distortion of the old glories and conquests of the Arabian Khalifate, which has persisted in the popular memory through centuries of Turkish misgovernment.' Lawrence concluded that these factors would be insufficient in themselves, and sketched out the kind of additional bond he thought necessary: 'only by the intrusion of a new factor, founded on some outward power or non-Syrian basis, can the dissident tendencies of the sects and peoples of Syria be reined in sufficiently to prevent destructive anarchy. The more loose, informal, inchoate this new government, the less will be the inevitable disillusionment following on its institution; for the true ideal of Syria, apart from the minute but vociferous Christian element, is not an efficient administration, but the minimum of central power to ensure peace, and permit the unchecked development of customary law.'

Lawrence's proposed solution does not appear until the final sentence of his paper: 'the only imposed government that will find, in Moslem Syria, any really prepared groundwork or large body of adherents is a Sunni one, speaking Arabic, and pretending to revive the Abbassides or Ayubides.' Lawrence's analysis could lead to only one conclusion: that the Arab Caliphate advocated by Kitchener should include inland Syria and its four principal cities, Damascus, Homs, Hama and Aleppo. He had also suggested that the Arab peoples of the interior need not come under

the same government as the cosmopolitan regions on the coast. Seven
months later these two principles were to be adopted as key elements in
British policy towards the future of the region.

During April Lawrence's job became more demanding when the Department started issuing daily Intelligence Bulletins. The task of putting
these together was to be one of his principal activities. Issues varied in
length between one and eleven pages, and totalled about 150 pages a
month. They carried miscellaneous information of military or political
interest relating to every part of the Turkish Empire. There was a very
wide variety of sources: material was obtained from agents, neutral travellers, air reconnaissance, prisoners, captured documents, and Intelligence reports from other commands.

Another project which interested him at this time was pioneering work
on the use of aerial photography for making maps. If the technical problems could be solved, this would be extremely valuable for mapping areas
behind enemy lines. Experiments were carried out during the spring of
1915 under the supervision of the Survey of Egypt, and the principles
learned were put to the test during the operations in Gallipoli. Newcombe
and Lawrence supported the trials with enthusiasm. Both were well qualified for the work, Newcombe as a survey officer, and Lawrence through
his map liaison duties and personal knowledge of photography. The experiments were successful, and as a result aerial surveying was used
extensively in the Middle East during the First World War.

On May 9 Lawrence's brother Frank was killed in action on the Western
Front. Lawrence wrote to his father: 'to die for one's country is a sort of
privilege: Mother and you will find it more painful and harder to live for
it, than he did to die: but I think that at this time it is one's duty to show
no signs that would distress others: and to appear bereaved is surely under
this condemnation.' Frank had been his mother's favourite, and she was
deeply distressed. Lawrence was evidently hurt by a letter she wrote to
him, to which he replied:

Poor dear Mother
   I got your letter this morning, and it has grieved me very much.
You *will* never never understand any of us after we are grown up a
little. *Don't* you ever feel that we love you without our telling you
so?—I feel such a contemptible worm for having to write this way
about things. If you only knew that if one thinks deeply about
anything one would rather die than say anything about it. You know

men do nearly all die laughing, because they know death is very
terrible, and a thing to be forgotten till after it has come.

There, put that aside, and bear a brave face to the world about
Frank. In a time of such fearful stress in our country it is one's duty
to watch very carefully lest one of the weaker ones be offended: and
you know we were always the stronger, and if they see you broken
down they will all grow fearful about their ones in the front . . .

I didn't go to say good-bye to Frank because he would rather I
didn't, and I knew there was little chance of my seeing him again;
in which case we were better without a parting.

He rarely expressed such personal feelings in his letters home, especially
as he knew that the mail to England was read for censorship by a fellow-
officer. In the same way, he was unable to tell his parents about the more
interesting aspects of his secret political and military work in Cairo. They
had, at best, a partial view of his activities and can have had little idea of
the value and importance of his role. This, for example, was the general
account of his office duties he sent home on June 23: 'I got a letter
yesterday asking for more details of what I am doing. Well, drawing, and
overseeing the drawing of maps: overseeing printing and packing of
same: sitting in an office coding and decoding telegrams, interviewing
prisoners, writing reports, and giving information from 9 a.m. till 7 p.m.
After that feed and read, and then go to bed. I'm sick of pens, ink and
paper: and have no wish ever to send off another telegram. We do daily
wires to Athens, Gallipoli, and Petrograd: and receive five times what we
send, all in cypher, which is slow work, though we have a good staff
dealing with them . . . We have only war work:—European Turkey, Asia
Minor, Syria, Mesopotamia, Arabia, Sinai, and Tripoli:—we all dabble
in them all. One learns a lot of geography, some people's names, and
little else.'

In July, D. G. Hogarth arrived from London. Hogarth, then in his early
fifties, was an acknowledged authority on the geography and history of
the Middle East, but he had been unable to find a useful war job. He had
come to Cairo hoping to be given an Intelligence post with the Gallipoli
expedition. No request came; instead he stayed in Egypt for several
weeks working on a project for Clayton.

While he was there, Lawrence was sent on a brief visit to Athens to
improve liaison with the Levant branch of British Intelligence. He spent
about a week in Greece, leaving again on August 14. Afterwards he wrote
home: 'Athens was very hot, and glare of sun very bad. Otherwise not

dull. I was in office there from 9 a.m. (when shops opened) till 7 p.m. (when shops shut): so I bought nothing, and saw nothing:—except the Acropolis from the window.' For some time after this, 'till the work grew important', he was responsible for liaison with the Levant branch. The journey to Athens was his only break from office work during 1915, except for a brief visit to the Western Desert, where the Senussi, still loyal to Turkey, was a constant problem.

CHAPTER 6

The Arabs Revolt
September 1915–October 1916

AT the beginning of September Newcombe was posted to the Dardanelles. His place at the Intelligence Department was taken for some weeks by Colonel A. C. Parker, a nephew of Lord Kitchener's who had been Governor of Sinai before the war. Lawrence was probably repeating the general opinion when he wrote to his parents that Parker was 'an authority on Sinai and not much else'.

Newcombe's departure meant that Lawrence was now one of the most experienced and knowledgeable officers remaining in Cairo Intelligence. He had been there longer than anyone except Clayton. Lloyd and Herbert had moved to posts elsewhere, and Leonard Woolley, although still in Egypt, had been detailed to handle liaison with the French Navy and rarely visited Cairo. Lawrence's work on the Intelligence Bulletin had given him an encyclopaedic knowledge of the Ottoman Empire, and also of the Turkish Army and its dispositions. Each day an immense amount of military and political information passed through his hands.

Although few people yet spoke of it openly, by the beginning of October the future of the Gallipoli enterprise was being questioned. If the Allies had to withdraw, a large Turkish army would be released for action elsewhere, and those responsible for defending Egypt were very concerned about this possibility. For some months the Cairo Intelligence Department had been monitoring improvements to the Turkish railways in Syria and Palestine. By the end of September an extension to the Palestine railway system was complete almost as far as Beersheba, and from there a metalled road had been constructed as far as the pre-war Egyptian frontier. A new attack on Egypt seemed imminent, and Turkey might soon be in a position to mount and sustain a major offensive against the Canal.

In this threatening situation the attitude of Arab nationalists towards Britain suddenly became very important. Hussein's pro-British stance had already done much to neutralise the Turkish call for a jihad, and a rebellion in any part of the Ottoman Empire would have tremendous

100

propaganda value for the Allies. Even a small amount of unrest in Syria and Palestine would force the Turks to police thousands of square miles of territory and take costly precautions to protect the railway and other installations against sabotage. A more serious revolt would divert enemy forces on a large scale, and considerably reduce the threat to Egypt.

What would happen if the Arabs decided that there were few advantages to be gained from alliance with Britain? A truly neutral attitude was improbable. The Turks were prepared to pay a high price for co-operation in the war effort, and some Arab leaders had already accepted their offers. A more general switch in Arab loyalties would relieve the Turks of many problems and greatly increase the danger to Egypt. It might also lead to an effective jihad.

It seemed to the Cairo staff that the risk of such a change in Arab attitudes was growing. Despite early confidence, the war was not going well for Britain, and the Arabs could be forgiven for thinking it wiser to side with Turkey. Any admission of military failure at Gallipoli would deal a severe blow to British prestige, and this would be exploited ruthlessly by enemy propaganda. The Arabs could have little doubt that if Britain were finally to lose the war, Turkish reprisals in rebel areas would be terrible.

Intelligence seemed to confirm that the Arabs were wavering, and this influenced the stance taken by Cairo officials in the continuing exchange of letters with Sherif Hussein.

Contemporary evidence lends substance to a statement by Hogarth, who had firsthand knowledge of Clayton's staff at this period. He later wrote: 'T. E. Lawrence, whose power of initiative, reasoned audacity, compelling personality, and singular persuasiveness I had often had reason to confess in past years, was still a second lieutenant in the Cairo military intelligence, but with a purpose more clearly foreseen than perhaps that of anyone else, he was already pulling the wires.' Hogarth listed Lawrence alongside McMahon, Clayton, Storrs and Wingate when discussing the key figures in British dealings with Hussein. Elsewhere, he wrote that Lawrence had been 'a moving spirit in the negotiations leading to an Arab Revolt.'

Although the correspondence between the British staff in Cairo was signed by Sir Henry McMahon, each letter and reply was discussed by Clayton, Storrs, Lawrence, and others. Copies were also transmitted to London for consideration by the Foreign Office. In essence, the correspondence was a bargaining process in which Hussein, on behalf of the Arab nationalist movement, tried to extract the best possible undertakings

in exchange for Arab military action against the Turks. Eventually, in
October 1915, the British agreed to support Arab independence in a very
large area which included the Hejaz, most of Syria and most of Mesopotamia. However, this promise was hedged by various reservations.
Notable among these was a clause intended to exclude Lebanon and (by
implication) Palestine, and a statement that Britain could only give assurances in regard to those territories 'in which she can act without
detriment to the interests of her ally France'.

In November, Lawrence received news that his brother Will had been
reported missing. Will, who had returned from India that spring in order
to join up, had been serving in France as a Royal Flying Corps observer
for less than a week. It was to be some time before his death was
confirmed, but there could be little hope that he was alive. The loss
affected Lawrence deeply; the two brothers had been very close.

Before going on active service Will had asked Lawrence to be his
executor, a request which would have had little significance, except that
an uncle had died early in May leaving their father £25,000 (at that date
a very large sum indeed). Mr Lawrence had decided to divide £15,000 of
this between his sons. Although Will had spent the two preceding years
in India, he had been deeply in love with Janet Laurie, the girl for whom
Lawrence also had shown a strong affection in 1910. When Will wrote
that he wished to bequeath his money to her, if he died, Lawrence had
replied: 'I . . . was going to agree, for such a time as Janet remained
unmarried. Today I hear from Father that it's likely to remain so only a
very short time, so that my trust would automatically expire. I don't know
what your feelings in this matter will be: you will however understand
that you cannot well leave anything in such a manner to another man's
wife.' In the event, Will had died before the inheritance was distributed,
and his estate was negligible. Lawrence wrote sadly to Leeds: 'first one
and now another of my brothers has been killed. Of course, I've been
away a lot from them, and so it doesn't come on one like a shock at all
. . . but I rather dread Oxford and what it may be like if one comes back.
Also they were both younger than I am, and it doesn't seem right, somehow, that I should go on living peacefully in Cairo.'

The following spring, the Cairo Intelligence Department found itself with
new preoccupations. The Mediterranean Expeditionary Force had finally
been evacuated from Gallipoli, and as a result there were two separate
armies with their staffs in Egypt. Their combined strength, some 275,000

men, formed the largest Allied army outside France at any time during the war. Medforce was now commanded by Lieut.-General Sir Archibald Murray, while the Force in Egypt remained for the present under Sir John Maxwell. Lawrence commented wryly: 'One could hardly move about for generals! We had 108'. Cairo Intelligence, which had hitherto carried out some tasks for both forces, was likely to face drastic reorganisation. It had been transferred from the Cairo War Office to GHQ at the Savoy. For the time being, however, its structure remained intact, and the threat seemed to diminish in late January when Medforce headquarters were moved away to Ismailia.

Few working papers from the department are now available, but the daily Intelligence Bulletins survive. They show that from the autumn of 1915 onwards Lawrence was handling a growing amount of information about defences on the north-eastern frontier of Turkey (referred to as the Caucasus Front). The Grand Duke Nicholas had taken over command of the Russian forces there in September 1915. On being told of Allied plans to withdraw from the Dardanelles he had decided to launch a big offensive before the Turkish forces opposing him were reinforced by troops released from Gallipoli.

The Russian advance began early in January 1916, and was extremely welcome to British commanders in Egypt. They saw that it might have the effect of stalling Turkish preparations for a large-scale attack on the Canal. This was the background to one of the more obscure incidents in Lawrence's Intelligence career.

Arab troops from Syria and Mesopotamia had been posted by the Turks to the Caucasus Front, and among them were units and commanders known by Cairo Intelligence to be secret enemies of the Ottoman Government. One of Lawrence's tasks was to follow the movements of every Turkish unit, which he did by collating information gathered by Intelligence from prisoners captured on the various fronts. As the Russian plans took shape, he evidently realised that some practical benefit might be gained from the information he possessed. In his own words: 'I . . . put the Grand Duke Nicholas in touch with certain disaffected Arab officers in Erzeroum. Did it through the War Office and our military attaché in Russia.' Erzurum, the principal fortress town of eastern Turkey, was not originally among the Russian objectives. Despite its immensely strong fortifications, it was to be captured by the Grand Duke in mid-February.

Lawrence referred to this incident on several occasions after the war, and it is alluded to in *Seven Pillars*. Fuller details may one day be disclosed if the relevant secret service papers are released. However, the documents already available leave no doubt that he was in a position to provide the Russians with valuable information. Many years later Liddell Hart noted after a talk with Lawrence in which Erzurum was mentioned: 'He put Russian General in touch with Arab on staff.' Lawrence asked Liddell Hart not to publish a full account of the incident as this might endanger relatives of the Arab concerned who were still living in Turkey. (It is for such reasons that secret service papers, when they survive at all, are embargoed for a hundred years.)

By this time it had been decided that there should be a new organisation in Cairo responsible for Arab affairs. This was to be called the Arab Bureau, and headed by Clayton. Even before its structure had been settled, Clayton began to choose a team of specialists, and it was inevitable that Lawrence would be among them. Ever since coming to Cairo he had been actively involved in Arab questions. Clayton, Maxwell and Mc-Mahon all had great confidence in his reports.

An example of Lawrence's work for Clayton at this time was a long unsigned memorandum called 'The Politics of Mecca', sent to McMahon on February 1 for transmission to the Foreign Office. The paper was clearly written to reassure those people in London who feared that the outcome of Sherif Hussein's nationalist ambition might be a formidable Arab empire that would threaten Britain's communications with India. Lawrence wrote that Hussein's activity 'seems beneficial to us, because it marches with our immediate aims, the break up of the Islamic "block" and the defeat and disruption of the Ottoman Empire, and because the states he would set up to succeed the Turks would be as harmless to ourselves as Turkey was before she became a tool in German hands. The Arabs are even less stable than the Turks. If properly handled they would remain in a state of political mosaic, a tissue of small jealous principalities, incapable of cohesion, and yet always ready to combine against an outside force.'

In mid-March 1916 the Mediterranean Expeditionary Force was at last amalgamated with the Force in Egypt. Sir Archibald Murray took command and Maxwell returned home. Both Lawrence and Woolley were mentioned in his valedictory dispatch of March 16. Lawrence's name was also included in a list for the distribution of Allied honours, and he was awarded the French Légion d'Honneur in a citation dated March 18.

The majority of Intelligence work was henceforth to be concentrated at Murray's Ismailia headquarters. Lawrence was one of only seven to remain under Clayton's direct supervision at the Savoy Hotel office in Cairo; he would divide his time between Arab affairs and maps.

Not long after reaching Egypt, Murray had decided to advance across northern Sinai, recognising that fewer troops would be required to hold a line at El Arish than to garrison the whole Canal. Preparations were soon in hand, and morale began to improve.

During the first fifteen months of the war against Turkey, the campaign in Mesopotamia had been conducted quite separately from Britain's military operations in Europe and the Mediterranean. The landing by the IEF 'Force D', in November 1914 had been undertaken by the Government of India. The initial objective had been to secure the British oil installations at the head of the Persian Gulf which were vital to the Royal Navy. Within three weeks of the first landing the lower reaches of the Shatt al Arab (the river formed by the confluence of the Tigris and Euphrates) were under Indian Army control as far north as Basra.

Britain's political objectives in Mesopotamia were theoretically controlled from London by the India Office, while Indian Army headquarters in Simla were responsible for military command and logistical support. In reality, however, policy in Mesopotamia was strongly influenced by Anglo-Indian views.

Imperial rule was the very *raison d'être* of the Anglo-Indian community, and the Government of India was intensely hostile to native independence movements. The Arab secret societies had counterparts in India, where nationalist fervour had led to a spate of 'anarchical crimes' between 1907 and 1909. Strong measures had been taken: seditious meetings, publications and associations were banned, and special tribunals had been set up to deal with native unrest. Trouble had broken out again, however, at the end of 1912. During an official procession a bomb had been thrown at the elephant bearing the Viceroy, Lord Hardinge. He had been seriously injured and only narrowly escaped with his life. During 1914 native revolutionary activities in India had once again increased.

The attitude of the Government of India towards schemes for Arab independence was wholly coloured by these domestic problems. It was impossible for colonial administrators to support nationalists in the Turkish Empire while suppressing identical movements elsewhere. If Arab nationalism were successful, the example would have an incalculable effect on native attitudes in India.

In any case, the Indian administration had imperial ambitions of its own in Mesopotamia. The fertile plains between the Tigris and Euphrates only needed efficient irrigation to yield an immense surplus of grain which might greatly relieve the dangers of famine in India. In sending Sir Percy Cox as Chief Political Officer to Basra, Lord Hardinge had envisaged nothing other than an Indian imperial administration.

Mesopotamia (now known as Iraq, although historically this name applied only to lower Mesopotamia) formed the north-eastern corner of Turkey's Arab empire. It was bordered to the east by Persia, and to the south by the Arabian Gulf; westwards the frontier was defined approximately by the River Euphrates. Between Baghdad and the Syrian city of Damascus, 450 miles to the west, lay desert. The IEF therefore saw little relationship between its activities in Mesopotamia and Arab aspirations in Syria. However, nomadic tribes and trading caravans travelled freely across the central region, and the attitudes of their principal chiefs were affected both by the Arab nationalist movement in the west and by the conduct of the Anglo-Indian invaders in the east.

During 1915 the IEF had been enlarged, and had occupied most of the southern part of the country. It had then been decided that a division commanded by General Townshend should advance up the Tigris to the strategically important town of Kut al Amara, deep inside Turkish-held territory. The advance had seemed feasible because the River Tigris would serve as a line of communication. This objective was ambitious in itself, but it had then been superseded by a still more daring plan, to advance further upstream and take Baghdad.

At first Townshend's move had been remarkably successful. Kut had been occupied in September 1915, and he had then continued northwards, fighting a major action at Ctesiphon, some twenty miles short of Baghdad, on November 22. After this, however, the forces opposing him had been heavily reinforced. Well-trained Turkish troops replaced the half-hearted Arabs he had previously encountered. Townshend had been obliged to retreat to Kut where his force of 17,000 men was quickly surrounded. During the months that followed, the rest of the Anglo-Indian Army, still nearly 200 miles further south, had been unable to relieve him.

In March 1916, the War Office was still confident that the situation could be saved. Kitchener thought it would be useful if disruption were created behind Turkish lines, and accordingly he decided to implement a plan whose very nature demanded the greatest secrecy. He knew that the Turkish élite was not united behind the war effort and, having spent many years in the East, he also knew that corruption was endemic in the

Turkish Empire. It therefore seemed possible that a large well-placed bribe might in some way relax the Turkish Army's grip on Kut.

There were few Englishmen qualified to carry out such a delicate mission. Kitchener settled on Wyndham Deedes, who had worked for three years with the Turkish Gendarmerie in North Africa and had also spent several months in Constantinople attached to the Turkish Ministry of the Interior.

An alternative scheme was suggested by Cairo: steps should be taken to bring about an Arab insurrection in Mesopotamia. There was thought to be considerable nationalist feeling there, and this move would be a natural extension of British policy towards Hussein.

Kitchener decided to follow up both ideas and Deedes, who had been most unwilling to take part in the bribery scheme, must have been considerably relieved. Although he was well qualified to deal with Turks, others were much better informed about the Arab question. Clayton suggested that George Lloyd might be sent, but Kitchener rejected the idea, feeling perhaps that a serving Member of Parliament ought not to be mixed up in such a dubious affair. Instead the choice fell on Lawrence (who later said that he had been chosen because the War Office hoped that Arab co-operation could help at Kut as it had at Erzurum).

There were, moreover, other reasons why it was convenient to send Lawrence to Mesopotamia. A few weeks previously Gertrude Bell had visited India. The Viceroy had suggested that she should go to Basra, where her specialist knowledge of the Arabs might be of help to the IEF Intelligence Department. Such a visit might also help to establish co-operation in Intelligence work between Mesopotamia and Egypt, under the aegis of the new Arab Bureau. She had therefore arrived in Basra on March 3, and had decided that it would be useful to stay on for a while.

While in Cairo during the autumn of 1915 she had observed how the Intelligence Department was using aerial photographs as a basis for maps. She must have mentioned this to the Intelligence staff in Mesopotamia, since the authorities in Basra now asked Cairo to send an officer who could give instruction in the new technique. Lawrence, who had been providing liaison between Royal Flying Corps photographers and the Survey of Egypt, was without doubt the best qualified person. At the same time he was given a brief by Clayton to discuss the Arab Bureau and future Intelligence co-operation. He left Egypt on March 22. Sir Henry McMahon wrote to Sir Percy Cox, the Chief Political Officer in Mesopotamia: 'He is one of the best of our very able intelligence staff here and has a thorough knowledge of the Arab question in all its bearings.'

Before he reached Mesopotamia, the most promising part of his mission had been abandoned, because the Anglo-Indian authorities there refused to countenance any encouragement of Arab nationalist activity. Lawrence remarked obliquely in *Seven Pillars* that co-operation with the Arabs 'was not the way of the directing parties . . . and till the end of the war the British in Mesopotamia remained substantially an alien force invading enemy territory, with the local people passively neutral or sullenly against them.' Kitchener's bribery scheme had no chance of success, and though Lawrence spent six weeks in Mesopotamia, he was unable to help ease General Townshend's predicament at Kut. During the final negotiations before Townshend's surrender he was at the advance British headquarters, and he crossed the lines with two other British officers to negotiate release for Townshend's wounded men. His role in these conversations, however, was unimportant.

He left Basra on May 11, having had fruitful contacts with the Intelligence and map-making departments. During the voyage back to Egypt he wrote a long report about the situation in Mesopotamia. By chance General Webb Gillman, who had been sent out by the War Office to investigate the IEF difficulties, was travelling home on the same ship. During the two weeks they spent together Gillman discussed 'every page' of Lawrence's report while drafting his own submission to the War Office.

At the tragedy of Kut, Lawrence had been a helpless spectator, sharing in the despondency at British headquarters as Townshend's messages charted each step towards the inevitable surrender. He was shocked by the attitude of Indian Army officers towards their native Indian troops and the indigenous Arabs of Iraq, and the visit to Mesopotamia left him with a strong distaste for the Anglo-Indian style of administration. This spectacle of European imperialism at work strengthened his conviction that the Arabs should be given self-determination. He would later oppose sending European troops to the Hejaz, and would do his utmost to keep British officers with strongly imperialist views away from the Arab Revolt.

He rejected not merely the philosophy of imperialism, but also its cost. After the war, looking back on his experiences in Mesopotamia, he was to write: 'We pay for these things too much in honour and in innocent lives. I went up the Tigris with one hundred Devon Territorials, young, clean, delightful fellows, full of the power of happiness and of making women and children glad. By them one saw vividly how great it was to be their kin, and English. And we were casting them by thousands into the fire to the worst of deaths, not to win the war but that the corn and rice and oil of Mesopotamia might be ours. The only need was to defeat our enemies (Turkey among them) . . . All our subject provinces to me were not worth one dead Englishman.'

Lawrence reached Cairo on May 26 and and found that a great deal had taken place during his ten-week absence. For one thing, there had been a major change in organisation. On March 21 it had been agreed that the small branch of Military Intelligence remaining under Clayton's supervision would specialise in political work relating to the Near East. Four days later Hogarth had returned to Egypt, temporarily seconded to Clayton's staff to help set up the new Arab Bureau. For this purpose he took three rooms in the Savoy Hotel no longer required by Military Intelligence.

The Bureau was not yet properly funded and there was no money to pay for the staff it needed. Fortunately much of its work was indistinguishable from that carried out by the specialist Intelligence officers remaining with Clayton, and the Bureau began to function with their help. While the arrangement was satisfactory at this early stage, there was scope for contention as the Arab Bureau workload increased. Although Clayton was in charge of both the Bureau and Cairo Military Intelligence, the former was controlled by the Foreign Office and answerable to McMahon, while the latter was part of the Egyptian Expeditionary Force headquarters staff. In due course GHQ would realise that Intelligence officers were spending a large part of their time working for the High Commission. For the present, however, Lawrence was delighted with a situation which allowed him to give much of his time to Arab affairs.

Hogarth had also brought disquieting news. Unlike anyone in Egypt, he had seen some of the documents connected with negotiations between Britain and France about the future of the Middle East. At the beginning of January 1916 Sir Mark Sykes, an MP interested in the Middle East, and his French counterpart François Georges-Picot had hammered out a draft memorandum as the basis for an Anglo-French understanding on the future partition of the Turkish Empire. This understanding was to become known as the Sykes-Picot Agreement.

While the Hejaz was to be independent, the agreement specified areas of direct French administration on the north Syrian littoral (the 'blue' area) and direct British administration in the regions of Basra and Baghdad (the 'red' area). The interior of Syria and northern Mesopotamia was

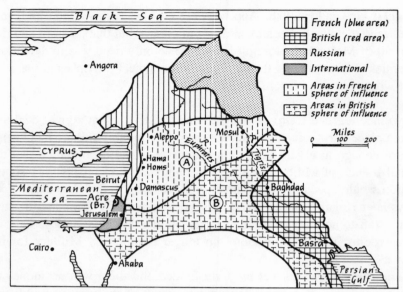

The Sykes-Picot Agreement

divided up into zones of French influence ('Area A') and British influence ('Area B'). Jerusalem and the Holy Places were to be governed under an international administration. The arrangement was less generous to the Arabs than anything hitherto envisaged in Cairo, and could not possibly have been accepted by Hussein. It gave France a vast area of influence in Syria and northern Mesopotamia, and allowed for substantial Anglo-Indian colonisation in Iraq.

The Sykes-Picot draft was widely circulated in Whitehall, but someone in a position of authority decided not to consult McMahon. In this way the Sykes-Picot proposals were shielded from rejection by Hussein or by representative Arab opinion in Cairo.

The overriding need, as the Foreign Office saw it, was to reach an accommodation with France that would reduce Anglo-French tension and remove the grounds for any future French suspicion of British intentions in the Middle East. This last consideration might soon become important. A limited advance across Sinai to positions which would assure a more economical defence of Egypt was already under discussion, and the ultimate defeat of Turkey might well involve a major British thrust into Palestine and Syria.

If the Foreign Office had seen the Syrian Arabs as committed allies in the war against Turkey their interests might well have been respected. The reality was different: Syrian representatives had done nothing except

make noisy political and military demands. Their position was not comparable to Hussein's: he had already helped Britain by refusing to endorse
the jihad, and it was now unlikely that he could recover his position with
the Turks. He would have his Arabian kingdom as a reward. The Syrians,
on the other hand, could offer no practical help to the Allies.

Doubts about any future Arab action were reflected in an important
qualification: 'If the Arab scheme fails the whole scheme will also fail
and the French and British Governments would then be free to make any
new claims.' A clause to this effect was incorporated in a preamble to the
draft text which read: 'It is understood that the putting into effect of these
proposals is contingent on the successful assistance of the Arabs and their
leaders in the establishment of an Arab State or Confederation of Arab
States under the protection of France and Great Britain; and on their
active co-operation with the Allies'.

This clause contradicted the essence of McMahon's pledge to Hussein
three months before. Without decisive action on their part, the Syrian and
Mesopotamian Arabs would not have any claim to self-determination.
However, the new formula had considerable attractions in British eyes.
For the duration of the war the Sykes-Picot Agreement would eliminate
Anglo-French tension over Syria; but afterwards, if the Arabs had taken
no substantial military action, it would be void. The Ottoman Empire
could then be divided up between the Allies on whatever lines seemed
appropriate.

Further protests or demands from Hussein would only interfere with
such a felicitous arrangement. This was doubtless a further reason for
saying nothing to Cairo. From now on McMahon's role should be to
placate the Arabs without making embarrassing concessions. McMahon
would be able to do this more gracefully while he remained unaware of
the Sykes-Picot terms. It would therefore be advantageous to delay telling
him for as long as possible.

The Sykes-Picot text had received British approval on February 4. The
only change was that the draft preamble was scrapped. However, the
condition requiring Arab action was retained in another form, in which it
was even more precise and stringent. Georges-Picot was authorised to
'inform his Government that . . . provided that the co-operation of the
Arabs is secured, and that the Arabs fulfil the conditions and obtain the
towns of Homs, Hama, Damascus and Aleppo, the British Government
would not object to the arrangement.' Knowledge of this proviso was to
have a great influence over Lawrence's actions during the Arab Revolt.

Quite apart from the possible effect on Britain's relationship with the

Arabs, the failure to consult McMahon during the Anglo-French negotiations was to cause deep resentment among British officials in Egypt. The
proposals differed substantially from anything previously agreed between
them and the Foreign Office. All that the Cairo staff could do now was to
plead that the Sykes-Picot terms should remain secret. On May 3 Clayton
telegraphed to the Director of Military Intelligence at the War Office that
'divulgence of the agreement at the present time might be detrimental to
our good relations with all parties and possibly create a change of attitude
in some of them which would be undesirable just at present and would
certainly handicap our Intelligence work. It might also prejudice the
hoped-for action of the Sherif who views French penetration with suspicion . . . it is difficult to foresee the interpretation he might place on the
two spheres of influence.

'Lapse of time, accompanied by favourable change in the situation,
will probably render acceptable in the future what is unpalatable today.'

The British and French Governments had other compelling reasons for
keeping the Sykes-Picot terms secret. The Agreement would have been
interpreted by Ottoman propagandists as evidence of Christian ambitions,
and would have inflamed opinion against the Allies throughout the Islamic world.

On May 24 news came that Hussein's revolt was soon to begin. This was
welcomed in Cairo, where it had been feared that the surrender at Kut
might have persuaded Hussein to postpone action. In reality, the Sherif's
hand had been forced by Turkish moves. He had learned in April that a
force of 3,500 Turkish soldiers would shortly pass through the Hejaz on
their way to the Yemen and he naturally suspected that this expedition
was being sent to nip his revolt in the bud. In early May, while Feisal was
in Damascus, the Turks had without warning executed twenty-one leading Syrian nationalists there.

This was the position when Lawrence returned to Cairo from Mesopotamia. He at once took up his previous work on the daily Military
Intelligence Bulletins and suggested that a supplementary 'Arab Bureau
Summary' could be produced from time to time, covering the areas now
dealt with by the Bureau. The first of these supplements was issued on
June 6, a week after his return. Not long afterwards the new periodical
was given its own name, the *Arab Bulletin*. Hogarth, as acting head of the
Bureau, was to take overall responsibility for the journal; but he was
away when the first issue was assembled. It was signed by Lawrence,
who remained closely involved with the *Bulletin* for the next five months.

He soon felt 'written out, for now I have two newspapers (both secret!) to edit, for the information of Governors and Governments, and besides heaps of writing to do:— and it is enough.'

Sherif Hussein's revolt against the Turks began on June 5. His sons Feisal and Ali attacked Medina and the railway to its north; Hussein took charge in Mecca, while Abdullah moved on Taif. Another force advanced on the Red Sea port of Jidda.

Even at this stage it was clear that the Sherif knew little about military practicalities. A British observer reported that the Revolt was 'about to be undertaken upon inadequate preparation, in ignorance of modern warfare, and with little idea of the obligations which its success would impose on the Sherifial family. In both the organisation of the tribal forces and the provision of armament far too much has been left to the last moment and to luck. If the Arabs succeed, it will be by their overwhelming numbers and by the isolation of the Turkish garrisons'.

Nevertheless, during the first weeks the Arabs were fairly successful. Mecca was cleared of Turks within a few days, although the outlying barracks held out until July 4. Jidda was attacked on June 9, with help from the British Navy, and fell a week later. Abdullah's force quickly captured Taif but the Turkish fort there was strongly held, and showed no willingness to surrender. The only large setback was at Medina, where Feisal's tribesmen found themselves outnumbered and outclassed. The Turkish garrison had now been reinforced, and was under the command of Fakhri en din Pasha, an officer noted for his ruthlessness. It emerged during the attack that Arab tribesmen were terrified of artillery, which they had never experienced before, and the attempt to take Medina failed. An effort to blockade the town was equally unsuccessful. Although Ali's force had torn up long stretches of the Hejaz Railway to the north, the Turks were soon able to repair it.

The 'Arab Bureau Summary' for June 23 recognised that there would probably be a long siege at Medina, although little reliable news had reached Cairo about events there. That day McMahon sent a message to Hussein, congratulating him on 'the strategy and the bravery by which your Highness and the noble Arab nation have been able to achieve the first decisive victory whose results, diligently pursued, should deliver you from the oppression under which you have so long suffered, and restore to you the land which was your birthright since the beginning'.

*   *   *

The start of Arab operations quickly led to tensions between the various British authorities involved in support and liaison work. On June 15 General Murray cabled the War Office to raise the question of control: 'The time now seems to have arrived when operations should come under military supervision. I am supplying, as you know, all possible assistance in supplies and munitions, but I am aware that military assistance cannot be given beyond this. I am prepared, if you wish, to assume such military supervision as it is possible to exercise from here'. The reply from the CIGS, Sir William Robertson, was firmly negative: 'There are many interests involved in the Arab Movement. The Foreign Office, India Office, and the French and Russian Governments are all interested and there are many ramifications of the question.'

This decision had unfortunate consequences. As Lawrence later wrote: 'Sir Archibald Murray . . . wanted, naturally enough, no competitor and competing campaigns in his area. He disliked the civil power [in Egypt] . . . which might yet be a sprag on his rolling wheel. He could not be entrusted with the Arabian affair, for neither he nor his Staff had the necessary competence to deal with so curious a problem. On the other hand, he could make the spectacle of the High Commission running a private war sufficiently ridiculous. His was a very nervous mind, fanciful and even ungenerous. When he found the opportunity he bent his considerable powers to crab what he called the rival show.'

Murray's staff followed this lead, 'and so the unfortunate McMahon found himself . . . reduced to waging his war in Arabia with the assistance of his Foreign Office attachés.'

When Murray discovered the extent to which his Intelligence Staff in Cairo was involved with the administration of supplies to the Revolt, he wrote to McMahon: 'I do not know who is supervising this campaign of the Sherif's against the Turks. It is evident I can do nothing except to give such assistance in material as I am asked for. It is also quite obvious that the branch of my Intelligence Department at Cairo can only be used for purposes of Intelligence, not operations . . . I should be very glad if you will send me a line to tell me who is supervising, or controlling, the action of the Sherif, if anyone.'

There was no accident about the moment Murray chose to make an issue of the role played by Cairo Intelligence. On the morning of June 20, the day McMahon received this letter, Clayton had left Egypt for a month, on a working visit to England. He would discuss the present state of Arab affairs with the War Committee and take part in detailed exchanges of information at the Foreign Office.

Murray was now determined to have a clear demarcation between his own operations and those of the Sherif, and Clayton's ambiguous position could no longer be tolerated. A note in the Ismailia Intelligence Diary for June 24 sets out the General Staff complaint: 'Great confusion arises over the Sherif of Mecca's rebellion. It is in no way under Egyptforce. Yet demands for material are made on us by the High Commissioner and Sirdar independently.

'It is complicated by the fact that the Arab Bureau is under the High Commissioner: and that Clayton is the Sudan Agent of the Sirdar and is, further, liaison between Egyptforce and the Government of Egypt and therefore under us. The Arab Bureau works in the same office as Clayton in his dual regime at Cairo and it is difficult therefore for Egyptforce to know where it stands.'

As one of the Intelligence officers most prominently involved in work on Arab affairs, Lawrence found himself caught up in this power game. The Arab Bureau report for May and June 1916 noted: 'The return of Captain T. E. Lawrence from Mesopotamia late in May greatly strengthened us since, though not definitely attached to the Bureau, he works continually in co-operation with it.' His relations with Ismailia Headquarters became strained, and he began to fear that he would shortly have to choose between the Arab Bureau and Intelligence. On July 1 he wrote home: 'The Reuter telegram on the revolt of the Sherif of Mecca I hope interested you. It has taken a year and a half to do, but now is going very well. It is so good to have helped a bit in making a new nation—and I hate the Turks so much that to see their own people turning on them is very grateful. I hope the movement increases, as it promises to do . . . the army here are very savage at being left out of the Arabia business, and I may have to cut adrift of them, which would reduce my pay a good deal . . . It is curious though how the jealousies and interferences of people on your own side give you far more work and anxiety than the enemy do.'

To make matters even worse, another rivalry was growing between McMahon in Cairo and Wingate in the Sudan, whose staff was involved in shipping supplies to Hussein. All these tensions continued throughout the summer and early autumn of 1916 and were well known to members of the Cairo Intelligence Department. Despite a veil of formal courtesy, the animosity between Murray, McMahon and Wingate was blatantly obvious in the communications which passed between them. These difficulties hampered the efficiency of British material support for the Revolt, which failed to keep up with Hussein's urgent requests.

In late July, following the initial Arab success around Mecca, the Red

Sea ports of Rabegh and Yenbo were taken (in the latter case through action by the Royal Navy). Around Medina, however, the Revolt had settled down to a precarious stalemate. The British were landing supplies at Rabegh and hoping that all was well; but news from the interior was vague and often conflicting, as successive issues of the *Arab Bulletin* show.

In reality, though Cairo did not know it yet, the arms, ammunition, and other supplies landed at Rabegh were not being transported inland. Feisal and Ali therefore soon found themselves in a difficult position, unable to fight effectively or even to feed and pay their forces. As rumours of these problems reached Cairo there seemed an increasing danger of a strong counter-attack by the Turkish Army in Medina, which had now been substantially reinforced from the north.

Although Murray was not responsible for directing Hussein's military actions, the EEF stood to benefit from a successful revolt in the Hejaz, which would reduce the Turkish forces available for defending Sinai. At the beginning of July, Robertson asked the War Committee to consider whether Murray might not undertake operations across Sinai to Akaba on the Red Sea and El Arish in the north. Murray found Akaba of considerable interest, since Turkish units based there would present a serious threat to the right flank of any British force advancing across northern Sinai. Akaba was only seventy miles from the Hejaz Railway, and a British force there might also be of some value to the Sherif. A War Office memorandum of July 1 concluded that British forces established at El Arish and Akaba 'would directly threaten the Turkish communication between Syria and the Hejaz, and would encourage the Syrian Arabs, while at the same time effectively defending the eastern frontier of Egypt.' However, it was thought that for climatic reasons these operations could not be undertaken before October.

On July 6 the War Committee approved the Akaba and El Arish schemes in principle, and instructions were issued to Murray and the naval authorities to concert their plans for the occupation of Akaba. A week later Murray wrote to Robertson: 'I am making a study of the Akaba problem and am in touch with the Navy on the subject. I am surprisingly short of topographical information and have telegraphed to the War Office to send what the Intelligence there has, and I am arranging for Naval reconnaissance'.

In Egypt, Murray's request for information was passed to the Cairo Intelligence branch, where it was dealt with by Lawrence. As fresh information came in, notably as a result of an aerial survey, he realised that the scheme was impossible. He later summarised his conclusions as follows: 'To take Akaba meant a naval expedition and a landing. The landing would not be difficult, but afterwards there was no logical objective. There was no covering position to the beach, which could be shelled always from the hills. The enemy garrison was posted in these hills, in elaborate prepared positions, constructed one behind the other in a series, as far as the mouth of Wadi Itm. If the British advanced to this point they would have effected nothing material, and would be exposed to continual flank attack from the hills. The Turks would be quite secure, for their line of communications with their railway base, seventy miles away, was up this very Wadi Itm, and so they would be able to increase their defending force or to change its disposition at their will.

'The British would be able to deliver themselves from these attacks only by forcing the twenty-five miles of the gorge in the teeth of the enemy, to deny them access to the coastal range. Now the Wadi Itm was from 2,000 to 5,000 feet in depth, and often less than 100 yards in width, and ran between fretted hills of granite and diorite whose sides were precipices hundreds of feet in height. The hundred-yard width of the bed was so encumbered by rocks that in places camels could pass only two abreast. It was winding and blind, afforded innumerable natural positions for defence, and hiding places not merely in the cliffs, but in the boulder-masses on the floor. The many side-ravines allowed easy retirement to forces knowing the country. There was water in these side-ravines, but none in the main valley; another advantage to the defence.

'The Turks had organised the valley in position after position, prepared to cover every foot of these twenty-five magnificently defensible miles . . . The approach Akaba-Maan thus formed a natural defensive position of almost unequalled strength, and the Staff in Egypt estimated that to carry it against a weak enemy might take three Divisions, almost the complete strength of Sir Archibald Murray's army: but success would depend on the speed of the operation, and the Turks might be able to reinforce by rail and route march faster than we could disembark, for the Akaba water-supply was inconvenient, and to land so great an expedition in a harbourless Gulf would not be easy. In fact a British landing there was out of the question'. Naturally, when he realised how large a force would be required, Murray's interest in the scheme evaporated.

Throughout the summer Lawrence collected news about the Revolt, writing brief reports for the *Arab Bulletin*. He also helped to arrange the shipment of British supplies. One of his more entertaining projects was to create a set of Hejaz postage stamps which would proclaim Hussein's independence throughout the world. Lawrence proposed this scheme in mid-July, and not long afterwards had told his family about it: 'It's rather amusing, because one has long had ideas as to what a stamp should look like, and now one can put them roughly into practice. The worst is they can only be little designs, not engraved, so that the finer detail is not possible.' At first he had hoped to use flavoured gum on the stamps 'so that one may lick without unpleasantness', but in the end the only suitable paper available in Egypt was a pre-gummed stock used for the labels that re-sealed censored correspondence. Lawrence and Ronald Storrs enjoyed themselves thinking of suitable illustrations for the stamps. The first stamps were produced during September 1916 and were put into use by Hussein during October.

If the Turks were to crush the Arab Revolt, they would have to advance along the Sultani Road to Rabegh, and then move southwards down the coast. The alternative routes from Medina to Mecca, though shorter, were too mountainous for a substantial force. Their only obstacle on the Sultani Road was an ill-equipped and demoralised Arab force commanded by the Emir Feisal. It seemed no great obstacle to the coming Turkish thrust.

As Feisal had anticipated, the Turks sent out a strong expedition in an attempt to force the Sultani Road. Their progress, however, was hampered both by Feisal's tribesmen and by difficulties in the mountainous section of the route. Arab morale rose, and was further boosted when the fort at Taif surrendered to Abdullah's army on September 22. At much the same time Ali arrived at Rabegh with a thousand men. It was decided that he should remain there and build a defensive position.

At the end of the month the General Staff took decisive action to prevent Cairo Intelligence working on McMahon's projects. Clayton was stripped of his Military Intelligence duties, and left only with the Arab Bureau, which would henceforth be an entirely separate organisation.

Lawrence was keen to remain with Clayton, and was alarmed to learn that Murray's Intelligence chief would not allow him to transfer to the Arab Bureau. This meant that he would in future be completely cut off from Arab affairs. His disappointment was not merely personal: he knew that Hussein's rising was fragile and feared that if deprived of effective staff support in Cairo it might eventually collapse. As he later wrote: 'I was confident in the final success of the Arab Revolt if it was properly advised. I had been a mover in its beginning, and my hopes lay in it, and

I was not strong enough to watch it being wrecked by the jealousies of little-spirited intriguers in Egypt, for their own satisfaction.'

In an attempt to make GHQ change its mind, Lawrence began to behave intolerably towards Ismailia Intelligence: 'I took every opportunity to rub into them their comparative ignorance and inefficiency (not difficult) and irritated them yet further by literary airs, correcting split infinitives and tautologies in their reports.' Clayton had meanwhile put in a request for Lawrence's transfer to his new department, routing it through official channels in London in order to circumvent Murray's staff. He badly needed Lawrence for the Bureau.

While this move was still being arranged, Clayton determined to make use of Lawrence on Arab work. On October 9 he wrote to Wingate that Storrs was about to visit the Hejaz, hoping to see Abdullah and possibly Hussein: 'I propose to send Lawrence with him, if G.H.Q. will let him go. They ought to be of use and, between them, to bring back a good appreciation of the situation'. Storrs was a civil servant with no training in the kind of specialised observation that Clayton needed. The quality of Lawrence's report from Mesopotamia suggested that he would be an excellent person to send.

To avoid difficulties with GHQ, Lawrence applied for leave (this seems to have been the first he had taken since arriving in Egypt nineteen months previously). 'I took this strategic moment to ask for ten days' leave, saying that Storrs was going down to Jidda on business . . . and that I would like a holiday and joy-ride in the Red Sea with him. They hated Storrs, and were glad to get rid of me for the moment. So they agreed at once, and began to prepare against my return some rare place to which I could be banished to rust out in idleness hereafter. Needless to say, I had no intention of giving them such a chance'. By the time Lawrence returned, his transfer to the Arab Bureau would have come through. Meanwhile, GHQ had no idea that he was about to go on an Intelligence mission to the Hejaz.

Storrs and Lawrence left Cairo on October 12, travelling to Suez by train. There they boarded the *Lama* for the three-day voyage down the Red Sea to Jidda and the pitiless heat of Arabia.

Sinai

Gulf of Akaba

Akaba
Khadra
W. Itm
Rumm
km
545 Tell Shahm
572 Mudawara
Dhat el Haj
692 Tebuk

W. Sirhan
Biseita
Jauf
Kaseim
W. Fejr

El Houl

N e f u d

Muweilah
Dhaba
Diraa

Hail

955 Medain Saleh
980 El Ula
W. Hamd'h
Jeida
Fagair
1133 Hedia
Kheibar
Abu el Naam
1173 Istabl Antar
1189
Bowat
1248 1268
Hafira
Owais
Kheif Hussein
1302 Medina
Nakhl Mubarak Bir Abbas
Yenbo
Hamra
Bir Said
W. Bir Ibn Hassani
Jafra

Wejh
W. Kitan
Um Lejj
W. Ais

R E D

S E A

Rabegh

Khalis

Jidda
Mecca
Taif

Miles
0   50   100

The Red Sea Campaign

CHAPTER 7

Intelligence Mission to the Hejaz
October–November 1916

DURING the early autumn of 1916 messages from the Hejaz had alternated between exultation and despondency, and it had gradually become clear that Hussein himself did not know the true state of affairs. The British Representative in Jidda, Colonel C. E. Wilson, had reported that the Arab armies under Ali, Abdullah and Feisal were operating more or less independently of one another. He had found, moreover, that there was a considerable divergence between Hussein's ideas and those held by each of his sons. Clayton hoped that Lawrence, with his fluent Arabic and sympathy for the Arab cause, would bring back a useful assessment of the position.

As it happened, the Sherifian military position had unexpectedly improved at the beginning of October. When the Turks advanced along the Sultani Road farther into the hills, their supply caravans had been attacked by raiding parties from the hostile tribes on either side. This helped Feisal's army to gain the upper hand in a series of engagements which began on October 6 around Bir Abbas, some thirty miles southwest of Medina. Despite the threat of a new advance, the annual pilgrimage to Mecca had taken place without interference.

Although the future of the Revolt seemed uncertain, the Arab Bureau was delighted with the achievement thus far. There could be no doubt that the rebellion in the Hejaz had materially weakened the potential strength of the enemy facing Murray's army in Sinai. A summary pointed out that: 'The equivalent of a Turkish division has been eliminated, all its effectives having been either killed or captured. Turkish rule and control has been replaced in the greater part of the Hedjaz by free Arab rule under the chief of the Descendants of the Prophet. The pilgrim roads from Jeddah, central and southern Arabia have been reopened and for the first time for many years satisfactory and more enlightened government established in the country.

'The Arabs, without the assistance of any non-Arab troops, have secured their independence in the part of Arabia where lies the very heart and centre of their national and religious sentiment'.

Feisal's success at Bir Abbas suggested that it might not be necessary to send European troops to hold the Sultani Road at Rabegh—a project which had been under consideration for some time. Hussein, however, was urging that a brigade should be held in readiness, and that any available Muslim troops should be sent to garrison Rabegh at once so that his Arab units could be used for an assault on Medina.

Lawrence arrived in Jidda on October 16 for the meetings with Sherif Abdullah. The principal British representatives were Storrs and Colonel Wilson. Lawrence took only a minor part in the discussions, but he observed the participants closely. He drafted 'personality' notes for the Arab Bureau, reporting that Abdullah was: 'Aged thirty-five, but looks younger. Short and thick-built, apparently as strong as a horse, with merry dark brown eyes, a round smooth face, full but short lips, straight nose, brown beard. In manner affectedly open and very charming, not standing at all on ceremony, but jesting with the tribesmen like one of their own sheikhs. On serious occasions he judges his words carefully, and shows himself a keen dialectician. Is probably not so much the brains as the spur of his father: he is obviously working to establish the greatness of the family, and has large ideas, which no doubt include his own particular advancement . . . The Arabs consider him a most astute politician, and a far-seeing statesman: but he has possibly more of the former than of the latter in his composition.'

Lawrence was determined, if possible, to see all of Hussein's sons. After this meeting in Jidda, he would go north up the coast and see Ali at Rabegh. It would be difficult, however, to visit Feisal, whose forces were operating inland. Until now, the few British officers who had visited the Hejaz had not been allowed to leave the Red Sea ports. However, with help from Storrs he managed to obtain authorisation to travel inland.

While in Jidda, Storrs and Lawrence dined with Colonel Brémond, head of a French military mission which had arrived there at the end of September. Lawrence did not care for Brémond's attitude to the Revolt. Shortly afterwards he wrote: 'The French military mission . . . say "Above all things the Arabs must not take Medina. This can be assured if an Allied force lands at Rabegh. The tribal contingents will go home, and we will be the sole bulwark of the Sherif in Mecca. At the end of the war we give him Medina as his reward"'.

'This is of course a definite policy, agreeable to their larger schemes. It breaks down, I think, in the assumption that an Allied force at Rabegh would defend Mecca for good and all. Once the Turks are able to dispense with the tribal resistance, they will be able to advance along any of the central or eastern roads to Mecca, leaving the Franco-British force a disconsolate monument on the dusty beach at Rabegh.'

This summary of Brémond's policy was perfectly correct. On the very day he met Lawrence, he cabled to Paris: 'If the Arabs took Medina they would immediately try to go into Syria. It is therefore in our interests that Medina does not fall into the hands of the Sherif of Mecca before the end of the war.' Lawrence knew how much the Arabs stood to lose if their rebellion never reached Damascus, and he was determined that Brémond's policies should not succeed. To this end he urged repeatedly that the French military mission should be withdrawn from Jidda.

Storrs and Lawrence travelled by sea to Rabegh on October 19; there they met Sherif Ali and Colonel Parker. Lawrence was not impressed by Sherif Ali's qualities as a war leader. He described him as: 'Short and slim, looking a little old already, though only thirty-seven. Slightly bent. Skin rather sallow, large deep brown eyes, nose thin and a little hooked, face somewhat worn and full of lines and hollows, mouth drooping. Beard spare and black. Has very delicate hands. His manners are perfectly simple, and he is obviously a very conscientious, careful, pleasant, gentleman, without force of character, nervous and rather tired. His physical weakness makes him subject to quick fits of shaking passion with more frequent moods of infirm obstinacy. Apparently not ambitious for himself, but is swayed somewhat too easily by the wishes of others. Bookish, and learned in law and religion. Shows his Arab blood more than his brothers.'

Lawrence spent only three days in Rabegh before setting out on the hundred-mile journey inland to meet Feisal. Ali had deep misgivings about this expedition and would have refused to let Lawrence go but for the written request Abdullah had sent in Hussein's name.

During the first day's journey, Lawrence with his Arab guides rode from 3 a.m. until midnight, with two three-hour breaks at midday and in the early evening. He was extremely tired by the time he reached Feisal's camp in the mid-afternoon of October 23.

He found the Arab leader in a despondent mood. The Turks had recovered from their defeat at Bir Abbas, and had already succeeded in driving the Arab army back about thirty miles to Hamra. The principal difficulty was still a lack of supplies. Hussein, who had no knowledge of military affairs, had not thought it necessary to make proper arrangements for logistical support before the Revolt began and, as a result, the distribution of British arms and ammunition was extremely haphazard. Feisal found himself once again without the materials he needed to resist a Turkish attack; he felt bitterly let down. Lawrence reported that he had met Feisal 'in a little mud house built on a twenty foot knoll of earth, busied with many visitors. Had a short and rather lively talk, and then excused myself'. Before going to bed he had a second long discussion with Feisal, who was 'most unreasonable'.

Feisal made a strong impression on Lawrence, as he had earlier done on Wilson. After these first meetings Lawrence described him as: 'tall, graceful, vigorous, almost regal in appearance. Aged thirty-one. Very quick and restless in movement. Far more imposing personally than any of his brothers, knows it and trades on it. Is as clear skinned as a pure Circassian, with dark hair, vivid black eyes set a little sloping in his face, strong nose, short chin. Looks like a European, and very like the monument of Richard I at Fontevrault. He is hot tempered, proud and impatient, sometimes unreasonable and runs off easily at tangents. Possesses far more personal magnetism and life than his brothers, but less prudence. Obviously very clever, perhaps not over scrupulous. Rather narrowminded, and rash when he acts on impulse, but usually with enough strength to reflect, and then exact in judgement. Had he been brought up the wrong way might have become a barrack-yard officer. A popular idol, and ambitious; full of dreams, and the capacity to realise them, with keen personal insight, and very efficient.'

It was evident that of all Hussein's sons, only Feisal had the extraordinary mixture of qualities needed to lead the Arab Revolt. Hussein, Ali and Abdullah would be little match for Brémond's skilful manipulation. Feisal, however, was altogether more formidable, and Lawrence did not hesitate to stress the importance of Syria.

This aspect of the conversation is not mentioned in Lawrence's reports to Cairo: in the wake of the Sykes-Picot Agreement the question of Arab action in Syria had become extremely sensitive. There can be little doubt, however, that he was anxious to dispel any feeling of complacency among the Arabs about their limited achievements in the Hejaz. Unlike Feisal, he knew that the Arabs needed to take Damascus, Homs, Hama and Aleppo.

At 6.30 a.m. the following day, Lawrence saw Feisal again, 'and we had another hot discussion, which ended amicably.' Afterwards he wrote to Parker: 'Feisal is a very impatient general, who is very intelligent, and understands things well. Only I'm afraid that some day he will get wild, and spoil the whole show, by trying to go too fast. It's a pity as he is a very nice fellow'.

Lawrence had walked round the Arab camp talking to Feisal's men. His reports gave a vivid picture of the difference between Hussein's rising and a European campaign: 'The forces actually mobilised are continually shifting. A family will have a gun, and its sons will serve in turn, perhaps week by week, and go home for a change as often as replaced. Married men drop off occasionally to see their wives, or a whole clan gets tired, and takes a rest. For these reasons the paid forces are more than those serving, and this is necessary, since by tribal habit wars are always very brief, and the retention in the field of such numbers as the Sherif has actually kept together is unprecedented. Policy further often involves the payment to sheikhs of the wages of their contingent, and many such payments are little more than disguised bribes to important individuals.'

'With the exception of the Bishawi retainers, and the "soldiers" at Rabegh, these forces are entirely tribal. About 10% are camel-corps, and the rest infantry, some of whom are desert tribes, and some hill tribes. I did not see much (or think much) of the desert tribes, but the hill men struck me as good material for guerilla warfare. They are hard and fit, very active; independent, cheerful snipers. They will serve only under their tribal sheikhs, and only in their home district or near it. They have suspended their blood feuds for the period of the war, and will fight side by side with their old blood enemies, if they have a Sherif in supreme command . . .

'The tribal armies are aggregations of snipers only. Before this war they had slow old muskets, and they have not yet appreciated fully the uses of a magazine rifle. They would not use bayonets, but enjoy cutting with swords. No man quite trusts his neighbour, though each is usually quite wholehearted in his opposition to the Turks. This would not prevent him working off a family grudge by letting down his private enemy. In consequence they are not to be relied on for attack in mass. . . . They shoot well at short ranges, and do not expend much ammunition when in contact with the enemy, though there is any amount of joy-firing at home. . . .

'The Arabs have a living terror of the unknown. This includes at present aeroplanes and artillery. The sound of the discharge of a cannon sends every man within earshot to cover. They are not afraid of bullets, or of being killed: it is just the manner of death by artillery that they cannot stand. They think guns much more destructive than they really are, but their confidence is as easily restored, morally, as it is easily shaken. A few guns—useful or useless—on their side would encourage them to endure the Turkish artillery, and once they get to know it, most of their terror will pass. At present they fight only at night, so that the Turkish guns shall be blind . . .

'I think one company of Turks, properly entrenched in open country, would defeat the Sherif's armies. The value of the tribes is defensive only, and their real sphere is guerilla warfare. They are intelligent, and very cheerful, almost reckless, but too individualistic to endure commands; or fight in line, or help each other. It would, I think, be impossible to make an organised force out of them. Their initiative, great knowledge of the country, and mobility, make them formidable in the hills, and their penchant is all for taking booty. They would dynamite a railway, plunder a caravan, steal camels, better than anyone, while fed and paid by an Arabic authority. It is customary to sneer at their love of pay: but it is noteworthy that in spite of bribes the Hejaz tribes are not helping the Turks, and that the Sherif's supply columns are everywhere going without escort in perfect safety.'

Lawrence spent twenty-four hours at Hamra discussing the military situation and future strategy. Afterwards he returned directly to Yenbo, arriving on the morning of October 26. HMS *Lama* did not appear on October 29 as expected, and Lawrence spent five days waiting, using the time to write a series of detailed reports which totalled about seventeen thousand words.

No other reports from British officers in the Hejaz compare with Lawrence's, either for detailed observation or quality of writing. His talent for description had been refined by the discipline of making notes about architecture and archaeological finds, and he now had a remarkable ability to portray what he saw. Work on maps had taught him to record the shape of the landscape through which he travelled, and he kept a detailed log of travelling times and compass bearings throughout his journeys. Later these were used, together with his sketches of hill contours, as a basis for map revisions in Cairo. The route reports included valuable military information such as the location of wells and the suitability of terrain for wheeled vehicles. Although it was normal practice to write notes on 'personalities', his comments were particularly impressive, both for their physical descriptions and their shrewd evaluation of character.

On October 31 HMS *Suva* put in to Yenbo. Colonel Parker, knowing Lawrence's intended route, had come up with her to learn about conditions inland. Afterwards he noted in his diary: 'It appears most important that His Excellency the Sirdar should have first hand information of the nature of the country and the situation and I have therefore advised Lawrence if he can spare the time to proceed to Jiddah and endeavour to obtain a passage, possibly in the [Admiral] C.-in-C.'s ship . . . to Port Sudan, proceeding thence to His Excellency. This he is doing.'

Lawrence left Jidda on board HMS *Euryalus*, the flagship of Admiral Wemyss, who had since June been one of the mainstays and best-informed observers of the Revolt. Having crossed the Red Sea they arrived in Port Sudan on November 5. Here they encountered two other British officers, Major Joyce and Captain Davenport, who were bound for Rabegh with two companies of Egyptian Moslem troops. From Port Sudan Lawrence travelled inland with Wemyss to see Wingate at Khartoum.

By chance, their arrival coincided with the announcement that Wingate was to replace McMahon as British High Commissioner in Cairo in December. McMahon had been identified with the pro-Arab policy conducted from Cairo during the preceding months, and to Lawrence his unexplained removal seemed a victory for French and Anglo-Indian interests in London. He felt uneasy about the future of Britain's promises to Hussein, and later wrote: 'The dismissal of Sir Henry McMahon confirmed my belief in our essential insincerity'.

Nevertheless, McMahon's departure would end the absurd division of military and political responsibility for dealings with the Revolt. From Khartoum, Wingate had been unable to stay in close contact with the latest thinking in Cairo. As a result of these changes, Wingate and Wemyss were to be the two most senior British officers directly involved with the Arab campaign, while Lawrence had just returned from the most extensive Intelligence-gathering mission yet undertaken in the Hejaz. Their meeting was an occasion for far-reaching discussions about the present difficulties and future potential of the Sherifian forces.

By this time Lawrence had strong opinions on these subjects. In particular he argued that the hill passes between Medina and Rabegh gave Feisal's Arab tribesmen a great natural advantage, enabling them to block a much larger conventional force. If properly equipped and advised, the local tribes could make these hills into an impregnable shield and the question of defending Rabegh itself would never arise. He had arrived at Khartoum in an optimistic frame of mind.

Assuming that Rabegh was safe, there remained the long-term question of an Arab offensive. The principal objective would be to capture Medina, the last Turkish stronghold in the Hejaz. This, however, would be a major operation, and every British officer visiting the Hejaz had con-

cluded that it should not be attempted until the Sherifian forces had resolved their problems of communication, organisation and fighting
strength. Lawrence agreed with this view. As things stood, the only hope
was to cut the Hejaz line permanently, leaving the Turks in Medina
without supplies. If this could be achieved, the garrison would eventually
have to surrender.

There seemed to be two areas in which British help to the Arabs could
be made more effective. First, there was an urgent need for military
training and technical advice. Wingate had already decided to increase
the number of Arabic-speaking British officers in the Hejaz. Apart from
Joyce and Davenport, whom Lawrence had already met, there was Major
Garland, an engineer officer from Egypt who was training the Arabs to
use explosives. A still larger staff of advisers seemed to be needed, and
Wingate told the War Office: 'The necessity for the presence at Rabegh
of a small expert military staff to superintend the organisation of Arab
trained bands and to advise on and appreciate the military situation is very
urgent. Colonel Newcombe, an artillery officer and an engineer officer
should be sent as soon as possible . . . If possible Colonel Newcombe's
assistants should have previous experience of Arabs.' The group, under
Newcombe's command, would be known as the British Military Mission.

The other area for improvement was liaison and Intelligence. Britain
would not be able to give the Arabs effective support unless Wingate was
much better informed about the military situation and the true capability
of Hussein's forces. He needed frequent and accurate reports on all aspects of the campaign.

This question was not resolved at the Khartoum meeting, but on November 11, just after Lawrence had left for Cairo, Wingate received a
cable from Robertson at the War Office: 'In view of the importance of
establishing at Rabegh a Military Intelligence system it is suggested that
an officer should be specially detailed to undertake as soon as possible the
work of organising such a system on the spot. Bray [an Indian Army
officer who had recently returned to London after visiting the Hejaz]
thinks that Feisal would welcome the proposal, if judiciously approached,
and it is possible that an organisation of this description might lead to our
obtaining valuable military information about Turks generally. Bray will
probably be sent out to you shortly, but as you may need him to train
Arab bands, it is suggested that unless you have someone available in
Sudan you could obtain an officer from G.O.C. Egypt. The names Lawrence or George Lloyd occur to me as suitable.'

There were, however, other plans for Lawrence's future when he got back to Cairo. Clayton had gone to some trouble to secure his services, and the Arab Bureau report of October 31 had noted that: '2/Lieut. Lawrence, who has since the inception of the Bureau given much unofficial assistance, has been on a mission to the Hejaz . . . On his return he will become a regular member of the staff with propaganda as his special domain. This important subject, which was one of the original objects for which the Bureau was formed, has hitherto been dealt with by Capt. P. Graves of the Military Intelligence, in addition to his ordinary duties. By transferring it to the Bureau and putting it in the hands of an officer who will devote all his time to it, it is hoped that the scope may be considerably enlarged.'

On receiving Robertson's cable about Hejaz Intelligence, Wingate immediately dispatched a copy to Clayton, adding: 'I propose sending Newcombe to Yenbo but in view of the possible delay of his arrival I think Lawrence would do this work excellently as a temporary arrangement. George Lloyd might do well for Rabegh.' Wingate suspected that Clayton would oppose this plan, as is clear from a message he sent to Wilson on the same day: 'I telegraphed to you to ask who you would like to send [to Yenbo]—my own idea is that pending Newcombe's arrival (and he is undoubtedly just the man for that place) Lawrence, who knows Feisal well, would be most suitable, but I can imagine Clayton crying out against it, as I am afraid the Arab Bureau is rather hard put to it.' He was right about Clayton's reaction, and shortly afterwards he received a strong protest: 'The importance of an Intelligence system as suggested is obvious and the establishment of such a system was one of the subjects of Parker's mission. Lawrence was sent there with much the same object. The difficulties at present are apparently the impossibility of getting British officers into the interior and the inaccuracy and unreliability of Arab agents . . . G.H.Q. are prepared to hand Lawrence over to the Arab Bureau and I think his great knowledge and experience of far greater value at headquarters where he will be almost indispensable. The same applies to Lloyd, whose strong points are politics, economics and commerce, and who in addition does not I believe know Arabic.

'I strongly deprecate therefore sending either of these two officers, especially Lawrence.'

There was also opposition to the proposal from Wilson, to whom Lawrence would report if he returned to the Hejaz. Wilson's relationship with Lawrence had got off to a bad start when they had met in Cairo some weeks before. Lawrence had disagreed with Wilson's view that it was undignified for Europeans to wear Arab clothes. There had also been some coolness between them during Lawrence's visit to Jidda. Wilson now argued that if Lawrence returned to the Hejaz it should be to Rabegh rather than Yenbo. Doubtless he preferred to keep this untried newcomer under the scrutiny of a senior officer such as Parker. Wingate, however, insisted that Lawrence should go to Yenbo in order to report on the situation and to arrange supplies. He used the same argument to persuade Clayton: 'It is vitally important to have an officer of his exceptional knowledge of Arabs in close touch with Feisal at this critical juncture; but, as soon as Newcombe arrives, Lawrence will return to the Arab Bureau where I consider his services would be most valuable. G. Lloyd will . . . make a tour to Jidda and Rabegh. With Parker, Joyce and others at Rabegh it is quite possible his services will not be required there permanently'.

Thus when Lawrence reached Cairo in mid-November, his future was uncertain. A few days passed before he was told about the plan to send him to Yenbo; in the meantime he was thoroughly preoccupied with other matters. In the face of a new crisis, the scheme to send European troops to halt a Turkish advance at Rabegh, much favoured by Wingate and Wilson, had once again come to the fore.

None of the authorities in Egypt wanted to send British troops. Clayton was therefore pleased to find that Lawrence had returned from the Hejaz strongly opposed to the scheme. He asked Lawrence to write a memorandum on the subject, and the result was 'a short and very pungent note', part of which read: 'All the forces fighting for the Sherif are made up of tribesmen, and it is the tribal army 3,000 to 4,000 strong under Sidi Feisal . . . that has held up the advance on Mecca or Rabegh of Fakhri Pasha's army for five months. Rabegh is not, and never has been, defensible with Arab forces, and the Turks have not got there because these hill tribes under Feisal bar their way. If the hill tribes yield the Turks need not look to any further opposition to their advance until near Mecca itself. This situation affects our consideration of the scheme to land an Allied force at Rabegh; so long as the tribes hold out such a force is not necessary. If the tribes give way the Turks will reach Rabegh in about four days. This does not give time for the collection, embarcation, transport, disembarcation, and preparation of a position for a British force to hold the front of 6,000 yards of the palm grove at Rabegh. The British force therefore must arrive at Rabegh while the tribes are still resisting the Turks if it is to get there in time. At present the tribes' opinion is chauvinistic. They are our very good friends while we respect their independence. They are deeply grateful for the help we have given them, but they fear lest we may make it a claim upon them afterwards. We have appropriated too many Moslem countries for them to have any real trust in our disinterestedness, and they are terribly afraid of an English occupation of Hejaz. If the British with or without the Sherif's approval landed at Rabegh an armed force strong enough to take possession of the groves and organise a position there, they would, I am convinced, say "We are betrayed", and scatter to their tents.'

Murray was delighted by Lawrence's forthright condemnation of the Rabegh scheme, and without reference to Wingate cabled the entire document to London, sending a parallel wire to Robertson suggesting that he read it. As a result, Lawrence's arguments were before the Cabinet within days. While Lawrence had hoped that his memorandum would undermine support for the Rabegh scheme, he cannot have imagined that it would receive such attention.

On November 19 Lawrence was told of the decision to send him back to Yenbo on a temporary liaison posting. The idea of returning did not appeal to him. In *Seven Pillars* he wrote: 'I urged my complete unfitness for the job.' Meanwhile, Wingate had been angered by news that Lawrence's memorandum about sending troops to Rabegh had been sent to London. He wrote: 'The whole point of this little "storm in a teacup" was evidently an attempt [by Murray] to get out of any responsibility for sending troops to the Hedjaz . . . basing it on Lawrence's views that the landing of Christian troops in any numbers at Rabegh would at once cause Feisal's Arabs to throw in their hands and return to their homes.

'There may be something in what Lawrence says, but he appears to me to have omitted the one and important essential, and that is that the Arabs have no more desire to come under the heel of the Turks again than has the Sherif himself, and when it comes to a matter of almost certain defeat, the Arabs will, in my opinion, welcome any steps taken to save them . . .

'I have no doubt that Lawrence has done all this in perfectly good faith, but he appears to me to be a visionary and his amateur soldiering has evidently given him an exaggerated idea of the soundness of his views on purely military matters.'

Clayton wrote to Wingate in conciliatory terms, placing the entire blame for the memorandum affair on Murray. He even went so far as to claim that Murray had asked Lawrence to write it! No doubt he felt that this diplomatic lie would be helpful, both to himself and Lawrence, since Wingate was about to take over as their superior in Cairo.

News of Lawrence's memorandum had been particularly unwelcome to Colonel Wilson at Jidda, who was not pleased to have his judgment about the need for European troops at Rabegh challenged by a junior from Cairo. His critical attitude owed much to Lawrence's demeanour, which fell so far short of accepted military standards. As Dowson had already noted, Lawrence often antagonised very able regular officers, and Wilson was a case in point. Lawrence's conduct in the Hejaz can be judged by the later comments of Captain Boyle, whose ship had collected him from Yenbo some weeks previously. Boyle wrote of Lawrence's 'off-hand and somewhat rude manner', saying that he had been 'a little astonished when a small, untidily dressed and most unmilitary figure strolled up to me on board the ship I was temporarily commanding and said, hands in pockets and so without a salute: "I am going over to Port Sudan . . . "'

'Looking at him I saw three stars on one shoulder strap, the other was blank, so I pointed out the first lieutenant . . . and told Lawrence to report himself to that officer, which he did. The first lieutenant, who had witnessed this meeting, subsequently speaking of it, said he had "properly told off Captain Lawrence" for his lack of manners.'

On closer acquaintance Wilson would see Lawrence in a different light, but for the present he was furious. He wrote to Clayton: 'Lawrence wants kicking and kicking *hard* at that, then he would improve. At present I look upon him as a bumptious young ass who spoils his undoubted knowledge of Syrian Arabs etc. by making himself out to be the only authority on war, engineering, running H.M.'s ships and everything else. He put every single person's back up I've met, from the Admiral down to the most junior fellow on the Red Sea.'

Such was the atmosphere when Lawrence set out on his second mission to the Hejaz, this time as Wilson's subordinate.

CHAPTER 8

Temporary Posting with Feisal
December 1916–January 1917

BY the beginning of December, Lawrence was in Yenbo. From the outset his role was uncertain, as Wilson had already sent a senior officer, Major Garland, to advise and help train the Arabs based in Yenbo itself. Lawrence decided to join Feisal inland as soon as possible.

The military position had changed since his first visit to the Hejaz. By November Feisal had concluded that his tribesmen would block any Turkish advance through the hills south-west of Medina. The Sherifian leaders had therefore begun to think of an extension northwards to Wejh, a small Turkish-held port two hundred miles up the coast from Yenbo. Possession of this northern base would allow them to attack the Hejaz Railway around El Ula, so far north of Medina that the line could not be protected by Fakhri Pasha's garrison. At the very least this thrust would extend the front and reduce the number of Turkish troops available for action against Rabegh. Feisal hoped, however, to keep the line cut permanently, thereby forcing the Medina garrison to surrender.

Details of this plan had been worked out at a meeting between Feisal, Ali and others at Rabegh. The first stage was to consolidate the Arab front in the hills west of Medina, and various steps had been decided upon to this end. This would prevent any Turkish advance from Medina towards Yenbo, Wejh or Rabegh. Meanwhile Abdullah, with a large force, had set off from Mecca to the region east of Medina. His role would be to attack the railway and to prevent supply caravans sent by pro-Turkish tribes farther east from reaching the town. The Arabs hoped that these measures would contain the Turks in Medina while Sherif Nasir moved on Wejh with a two-thousand-strong force which he had already raised in the area north of Yenbo. Nasir, who came from one of the most influential families in the Hejaz, had already proved himself an extremely capable leader.

Feisal, who was to be based at Kheif Hussein in Wadi Yenbo, would build up his army by new recruitment. If Nasir's force proved insufficient to capture Wejh, Feisal would then be in a position to send reinforcements. Later, when the Arab position south-west of Medina had been secured, Feisal would move his operational base from Yenbo to Wejh.

At the end of November Feisal began to carry out his part of the scheme, moving north into Wadi Yenbo. He believed that the natural strength of his younger brother Zeid's position at Bir Said would allow the force remaining there to keep the Turks in check. Lawrence, who had been told of these plans, rode inland on December 2 expecting to meet Feisal's army at Kheif Hussein. He was astonished, therefore, to find the Arab force much closer to Yenbo at Nakhl Mubarak, one of the date plantations of Yenbo al Nakhl. It was apparent that something had gone badly wrong.

Lawrence explained the débâcle in a report to the Arab Bureau: 'While [Feisal] was in Wadi Yambo in early December the unexpected happened. The Arabs under Sidi Zeid became slack and left a by-road near Khalis unguarded. A Turkish mounted infantry patrol pushed up along it into Wadi Safra . . . The front line of Arabs, hearing news of this enemy six miles in their rear, broke with a rush to rescue their families and property in the threatened villages. Zeid's main body followed suit. Zeid himself fled at top pace to Yambo; and the astonished Turks occupied Hamra and Bir Said unopposed.' As a result of this collapse there was no obstacle to a direct Turkish advance from Wadi Safra to Yenbo, and Feisal had no option but to withdraw almost to the coast.

He must have been pleased, at this difficult moment, to be joined by a liaison officer bringing the promise of more effective British support. Lawrence would be the first British officer to spend time with a Sherifian army inland, and Feisal asked him to wear Arab dress. This was, Lawrence wrote in *Seven Pillars*, so that 'the tribesmen would . . . understand how to take me. The only wearers of khaki in their experience had been Turkish officers, before whom they took up an instinctive defence. If I wore Meccan clothes, they would behave to me as though I were really one of the leaders; and I might slip in and out of Feisal's tent without making a sensation which he had to explain away each time to strangers.' Lawrence, who was already accustomed to wearing Arab clothes, agreed readily and was kitted out with fine white robes indicative of high rank.

He soon realised that there was little hope that Feisal's Arabs would hold the position at Nakhl Mubarak; their morale was gone, and a retreat to the coast seemed inevitable. Moreover, it seemed unlikely that Yenbo itself could be held by Feisal's defeated army, and Lawrence therefore arranged for an urgent message to be sent out to HMS *Suva*, which by good fortune had arrived a few days earlier with stores. Within a short time, five ships had assembled at Yenbo, including the monitor *M.31,* a vessel specially designed for coastal bombardment. Lawrence also requested an air reconnaissance of the area round Wadi Safra and Bir Said.

His earlier optimism about the role of Feisal's army had evaporated. As he feared, the Turks soon attacked the position at Nakhl Mubarak, and by the morning of December 9 the relics of Feisal's army, some fifteen hundred men, had arrived in Yenbo; the rest of the Arab forces had melted away to their villages. With Zeid's men this gave a total of around two thousand to defend the town. While Garland organised some rudimentary defences Lawrence arranged liaison with Boyle's warships.

It seemed that Yenbo would be secure as long as the warships were there, since the Turks would have to cross several miles of flat open sand, some of it soft, before reaching the town. While doing so they would be exposed to ships' guns firing at close range.

For the moment, Feisal and Zeid were trapped in Yenbo, and Abdullah's army east of Medina was too far away to help if the Turks decided to advance. On its own, Ali's force at Rabegh could present little opposition. The crisis was so grave that on December 9 the War Office instructed Murray to hold a brigade in readiness, in case the Government should now decide in favour of a landing at Rabegh.

In the event, the naval presence at Yenbo was sufficient, and the Turks did not follow up their success. The closest they came to a decisive action was on the night of December 11, when they seemed poised to attack. Lawrence wrote in *Seven Pillars*: 'Afterwards, old Dakhil Allah told me that he had guided the Turks down to rush Yenbo in the dark that they might stamp out Feisal's army once for all; but their hearts had failed them at the silence and the blaze of lighted ships from end to end of the harbour, with the eerie beams of the searchlights revealing the bleakness of the glacis they would have to cross. So they turned back: and that night, I believe, the Turks lost their war.'

A week later, aerial reconnaissance observed what seemed to be a Turkish withdrawal from the approaches to Yenbo, and this was soon confirmed by the news that Nakhl Mubarak had been evacuated. At first it seemed that this might be a local measure to avoid further bombing raids from HMS *Raven*'s two seaplanes. However, the withdrawal proved to be more general. It seemed that the Turks might be concentrating their resources against Ali's makeshift force advancing from Rabegh, which had met little opposition thus far. Feisal reoccupied Nakhl Mubarak and almost immediately began a further advance inland, even though his forces were ill-prepared. His hope was to trap the Turkish Army in the hills, between his own force and Ali's.

During these last weeks at Yenbo Lawrence had learnt a good deal from watching Garland teach the Arabs how to use explosives. He wrote in *Seven Pillars* that Garland 'had his own devices for mining trains and felling telegraphs and cutting metals; and his knowledge of Arabic and freedom from the theories of the ordinary sapper-school enabled him to teach the art of demolition to unlettered Beduin in a quick and ready way . . . Incidentally he taught me to be familiar with high explosive. Sappers handled it like a sacrament, but Garland would shovel a handful of detonators into his pocket, with a string of primers, fuse, and fusees, and jump gaily on his camel for a week's ride.'

Garland's health was poor, and in mid-December he went to Cairo on leave. He could ill be spared: ignorance of explosives had proved a great handicap to the Revolt. The Arabs had torn up great stretches of line by hand, but this left the rails undamaged and repairs were easy. Great damage might be done if Garland could go inland himself and decide where to lay the dynamite charges. He was designing special mines with automatic trigger mechanisms, which could be used to blow up trains; but trials were required to perfect them and they needed expert handling. Lawrence hoped that Feisal would eventually see the force of these arguments. It seemed unlikely, however, that the Arabs would allow a Christian officer to take part in attacks on the railway close to the holy city of Medina.

As Feisal began to push forward towards Wadi Safra in the hope of trapping the Turks, news came that Ali's force had taken fright on the strength of a false rumour and had retreated headlong to Rabegh. By December 22, therefore, Feisal was back in Nakhl Mubarak, very angry that the opportunity to catch the Turks had been missed. Fakhri's army seemed to be regrouping for some purpose, and if he decided to advance on Rabegh now, there was little to stop him. Rumours and counter-rumours came in from the hill tribesmen, and in Rabegh emergency plans were drawn up for an evacuation.

During the last days of 1916 it became imperative for the Arabs to take some kind of aggressive action. Since there was no hope of defeating the Turks around Medina, the only feasible course was to attack their lines of communication. The best scheme seemed to be for Feisal to advance on Wejh as quickly as possible with most of his army, and from there to mount a large-scale offensive against the railway. This would surely divert Turkish attention from Rabegh.

The scheme was quite unlike the plans for Wejh that had been discussed in mid-November. Feisal had never envisaged taking his main force to Wejh until strong defensive positions had been created in the hills south-west of Medina. As it was, the armies commanded by Ali and Zeid had proved completely ineffective. The risk of moving now seemed very great. Lawrence later wrote: 'Our fear was not of what lay before us, but of what lay behind. We were proposing the evacuation of Wadi Yenbo, our only defensive line against the Turkish division in Wadi Safra, only fifteen miles away. We were going to strip the Juheina country of its fighting men, and to leave Yenbo, till then our indispensable base, and the second sea-port of the Hejaz, in charge of the few men unfit for the march north, and therefore unfit for anything at all dangerous. We were going to march nearly two hundred miles up the coast, with no base behind and only hostile territory in front . . . If the Turks cut in behind us we would be neatly in the void.' However, a move to Wejh 'now appeared not merely the convincing means of securing a siege of Medina, but an urgent necessity if a Turkish advance on Mecca was to be prevented.'

While Lawrence was discussing the Wejh scheme with Feisal, he thought of another way to menace the Hejaz line. Abdullah's army, far inland, was supposed to be interrupting traffic but was not doing so. In *Seven Pillars* Lawrence wrote: 'If only Abdulla had been threatening Medina properly at this time, the Turkish expedition against Rabegh would have been prevented, but his men had run short of water and food in their attempted blockade of the town on the east, and he had recalled the bulk of them to his own distant base of Henakiyeh.' Lawrence therefore suggested to Feisal that Abdullah should move west to Khaibar, no closer to Medina but much better placed for operations against the line. Then, however, Lawrence had second thoughts, and said that Abdullah might not be able to maintain himself at Khaibar. Feisal, who seems not to have understood him, interjected: 'You mean Wadi Ais . . .'

This was not the first time Wadi Ais had been mentioned: it ran slightly north-of-east from the coast near Yenbo towards the Hejaz Railway, and three weeks previously there had been some talk of sending Nuri as-Said there. No one had thought of it, however, as a base for Abdullah's force; yet the valley was well-watered and accessible from the coast, and it would be easy to keep a large army there supplied with food and arms.

Lawrence urged Feisal to send a message asking Abdullah to go there, since the move would have great strategic advantages. As he wrote in the *Arab Bulletin*, Wadi Ais was 'a natural fortress about 100 kilometres above Medina on the railway line. [Abdullah] would there be astride the Medina lines of communication, and no Turkish advance towards Mecca, Yambo, or even Rabugh would be possible till he had been dislodged'. If at the same time Feisal moved to Wejh, the two Arab armies would dominate a two-hundred-mile stretch of the railway and the Medina garrison would be at their mercy. Feisal was convinced by these arguments, and a messenger was dispatched to Abdullah.

With Abdullah in this new position, the risk of leaving Yenbo so lightly defended would be much smaller, but Feisal was still uneasy. On December 27 Wilson arrived to urge him on, assuring him that the Rabegh garrison, supported by the Royal Navy, would be able to resist any Turkish attack until Feisal had occupied Wejh. The assurance had doubtful weight, but it was sufficient to persuade Feisal.

On the same day, Lawrence wrote to the Arab Bureau enquiring about the British military mission; he knew that Newcombe's arrival in the Hejaz would bring his liaison posting with Feisal to an end. However, it would be useful for Intelligence reasons if he visited the little-known Wadi Ais, and he hoped that this would prolong his stay. He asked: 'Have you any news of Newcombe? The situation is so interesting that I think I will fail to come back. I want to rub off my British habits and go off with Feisul for a bit. Amusing job, and all new country. When I have someone to take over here from me I'll go off'. Newcombe, however, was not yet ready to leave Cairo.

The military mission was to be composed of four officers: Newcombe, an Engineer; two artillery officers, Majors Vickery and Cox; and a medical officer, Major Marshall. Newcombe was to go to Yenbo while the others would be stationed at Rabegh; they would all report to Wilson. In addition, Captain Bray had recently been sent back to the Hejaz.

In Yenbo the Turkish threat seemed to be receding all the time and on 2 January 1917 Lawrence reported: 'The Turks were getting rather nervous in Wadi Safra, I think, as their main force seems to have moved towards Ghayir or Gaha. So we pushed out a strong reconnaissance at midnight towards Wadi Safra. We will hear tonight of the evacuation of the Wadi by the Turks, I expect, and that means the end of the threat on Rabegh probably . . . The Wejh scheme is going strong . . . If Hamra is re-taken and Feisal moves northward, the trick is played!' On the night of

January 3 Lawrence went out with a small raiding party to attack a Turkish post in the hills. There was no engagement at close quarters, but this marked his first personal involvement in the fighting.

Feisal's army finally left Nakhl Mubarak the following day and moved a short distance to Owais. Lawrence returned from his night raid just as it was leaving and he accompanied it for part of the way. Afterwards he wrote: 'The order of march was rather splendid and barbaric. Feisal in front in white. Sharaf on his right, in red headcloth and henna-dyed tunic and cloak, myself on his left in white and red. Behind us three banners of purple silk, with gold spikes, behind them three drummers playing a march, and behind them a wild bouncing mass of 1,200 camels of the bodyguard, all packed as closely as they could move, the men in every variety of coloured clothes, and the camels nearly as brilliant in their trappings—and the whole crowd singing at the tops of their voices a war song in honour of Feisal and his family! It looked like a river of camels, for we filled up the Wadi to the tops of its banks, and poured along in a quarter-of-a-mile-long stream.'

Naval support would be crucial during Feisal's northward advance along the level strip of land beside the Red Sea. There was a shortage of transport camels and the Arab army could not carry the provisions it would need. Feisal waited at Owais while Lawrence arranged with Boyle for the necessary supplies to be put ashore. By January 9 all was ready, and on the same day a message came from Abdullah that he was moving to Wadi Ais.

Lawrence also heard that he was definitely to be relieved. Three days earlier Wilson had cabled to the Arab Bureau: 'I consider the Wejh operations offer a good opportunity to Newcombe and the other two to know Feisal and the various sheikhs . . . I wish him to proceed to Yenbo where Lawrence, who has received instructions from me to hand over to him, will meet him.' Lawrence therefore stayed behind in Yenbo to wait for Newcombe while Feisal marched north.

During the first stages of its march, Feisal's army passed through friendly country. Um Lejj, the half-way point, had already been taken, and he set up camp some miles inland where there was adequate water. Meanwhile Lawrence heard that Newcombe would go straight to Um Lejj rather than to Yenbo, and went there himself on board HMS *Suva*. He wrote home with obvious regret that his liaison job with Feisal was about to end: 'My Arabic is getting quite fluent again! I nearly forgot it in Egypt, where I never spoke for fear of picking up the awful Egyptian accent and vocabulary. A few months more of this, and I'll be a qualified Arabian. I wish I had not to go back to Egypt. Anyway I have had a change.'

Plans were made for a joint attack on Wejh. Five hundred and fifty Arabs judged to be of indifferent fighting quality were to be put on board HMS *Hardinge* and landed on the far side of the town. Their role would be to prevent the Turks escaping northwards while Feisal's main army, now strengthened by men from Sherif Nasir's force, attacked from the south. Arrangements were made for a final rendezvous between the Navy and Feisal's army shortly before the attack.

Although Newcombe was expected at Um Lejj, he had not arrived by the evening of January 17, and the Arab army was due to set out on the following day. Lawrence felt that his duty was to remain ashore with Feisal. He left behind a cheerful letter for Newcombe: 'So I miss you by a day! I'm very sick, but it was either that or miss Wadi Hamdh [which Feisal's army would cross on its way north], with the foreknowledge that I may never see Wadi Hamdh again, and that I will certainly see you at Wejh.

'I prepared Feisul (who is an absolute ripper) carefully for you . . . This show is splendid: you cannot imagine greater fun for us, greater vexation and fury for the Turks. We win hands down if we keep the Arabs simple . . . to add to them heavy luxuries will only wreck their show, and guerilla does it. It's a sort of *guerre de course*, with the courses all reversed. But the life and fun and movement of it are extreme . . . may I suggest that by effacing yourself for the first part, and making friends with the head men before you start pulling them about, you will find your way much easier? . . . After all, it's an Arab war, and we are only contributing materials—and the Arabs have the right to go their own way and run things as they please. We are only guests.'

Newcombe reached Um Lejj during the morning of January 18. When he heard that the Arab army was striking camp a few miles inland he immediately commandeered a horse and set off to join it. Lawrence's diary records that 'Newcombe turned up 1.15.' Thus his temporary duties with Feisal ended earlier than he had hoped. Newcombe, who enjoyed Lawrence's company, asked him to stay on as far as Wejh; the week-long march would provide a useful handing-over period.

Feisal's army of ten thousand Arabs, half of them mounted on camels, formed a magnificent spectacle. The mood of exultation increased when a messenger brought news that Abdullah's force, while moving to Wadi

Ais, had surprised and captured an important member of the Turkish élite together with a valuable baggage caravan. This good fortune called for celebration and for a time Feisal's progress northwards halted.

This unplanned delay must have given Newcombe an early insight into the peculiar nature of Arab operations. As a result, Feisal missed the rendezvous before Wejh previously agreed with Boyle, leaving Admiral Wemyss in an unexpected quandary: 'The non-appearance of Faisal made it incumbent on me to decide whether I should attack without him or await his arrival. I finally decided on the former step, the principal argument in favour of this being the presence of the five hundred Arabs on board the *Hardinge*. It would have been impossible to keep these men any longer on board, owing to the difficulties of feeding them, and also for sanitary reasons.' On January 23, therefore, the Arab landing party, accompanied by Vickery and Bray, was put ashore north of Wejh. These were not Feisal's best troops, but they were able to advance on the town under cover of the ships' gunfire. Although the attack was undisciplined by European standards, the Turkish garrison was eventually defeated. The victory was consolidated by a naval landing party and Wejh was in Allied hands by the time Feisal's main army arrived.

Despite the success, both Vickery and Bray were deeply shocked by the style of Arab warfare they had witnessed. Both were to write bitterly of the lack of discipline and planning. For example, Vickery noted that although Feisal's army 'only embarked on a four days' march, due north, parallel to the coast line, and within twenty miles of it, a great part . . . lost its way and arrived at the rendezvous two days late.'

In the new circumstances, the British military mission lacked a clear role. Its original purpose had been to help train Arab regulars in Rabegh; but that scheme had come to nothing, and after the capture of Wejh the greatest need for military expertise was farther north. In the short term the most useful thing it could do would be to help with attacks on the railway. Feisal had intended to move against the line as soon as possible after reaching Wejh. When he arrived there, however, it was clear that Abdullah's presence in Wadi Ais had reduced the need for immediate large-scale action. Feisal therefore planned a series of smaller raids, while taking steps to consolidate his new position and recruit men from the local tribes. Since the raids from Wejh would reach the line a long way north of Medina, there was increasing pressure on Feisal to allow Newcombe and Garland, the two British officers expert in demolition, to go inland.

*   *   *

It was soon to become evident that the campaign in the Hejaz had been won before the military mission arrived. Following weeks of crisis during which it had seemed that the Turks might march to victory at any time, the repositioning of Abdullah's and Feisal's armies in January had shifted the military balance in favour of the Arabs. The Turks would now be obliged to place troops along hundreds of miles of railway, their only line of communication to Medina. This would leave Fakhri with too few men to conduct an offensive. They were also experiencing difficulties maintaining their advanced positions in the hills south-west of Medina. Sporadic raiding by the hill tribes on Turkish supply columns during January demonstrated that the whole area was hostile, and that a much larger Turkish force would be required if such an extended front was to be secure. An Intelligence summary in the *Arab Bulletin* of January 29 noted that there had now been 'a very considerable measure of [Turkish] withdrawal on all the Rabugh roads, as well as from the Yambo direction . . . We have learned in various ways that much material of all kinds has been or is about to be retired to Medina, and there remains little doubt that Turkish offensive movements towards Yambo and Rabugh are abandoned for the present.

'If this is so, Sidi Abdullah's stroke, which preceded by two or three days our first inkling of Turkish withdrawal in the south-west, probably had something to do with it. Added to uneasiness about communications and shortage of supplies, there is also probably serious sickness in Medina.' From now on the presence of Arab armies at Wejh and Wadi Ais would preclude any further Turkish offensive in the Hejaz. This position could only be reversed by massive reinforcements to the Medina garrison, which Turkey could ill afford.

The British authorities were greatly encouraged. Wingate wrote to Robertson: 'The Arab leaders have always beautiful plans and describe them most plausibly, but—and this is a new and encouraging feature— some of them of late have actually matured.' He felt that the time was ripe to attempt co-ordinated action by all the Sherifian forces against Medina, and Newcombe's staff began to make detailed plans.

Other observers were not quite so optimistic, for while the Turkish position in the Hejaz had deteriorated, this had not been due to any improvement in Arab fighting capability. The projected operation would involve not merely Feisal's army, but the forces commanded by Ali, Abdullah, and Zeid. Vickery wrote: 'The value of the Sheref's Armies as a military force is nil if they are exploited on wrong principles and if they are asked to undertake tasks which would tax trained troops'.

With hindsight, such criticisms seem to throw considerable doubt on the wisdom of attempting operations against Medina *en masse*, yet this remained the official scheme. Despite his own observations, Vickery maintained that: 'The maximum amount of success can only be obtained when all armies work on some concerted plan, controlled and advised from some central channel. Spasmodic operations undertaken by one army not in conjunction with the others cannot give the best results.' It would be some time before the British military hierarchy accepted that Hussein's armies were incapable of such concerted action.

Lawrence could not feel deeply involved in the immediate military activities being planned at Wejh, since he was now preparing to return to Cairo. Feisal, however, was unwilling to see him go. Lawrence had shown a remarkable grasp of the political and military situation; but for him, Abdullah would not have moved to Wadi Ais and the future of the Revolt would still have been precarious. No other British adviser in the Hejaz had the encyclopaedic knowledge Lawrence had gained during two years in the Cairo Intelligence Department. Storrs's autobiography recounts how, during their visit to the Hejaz three months previously, Lawrence had displayed this knowledge to great effect: 'As Syrian, Circassian, Anatolian, Mesopotamian names came up, Lawrence at once stated exactly which [Turkish] unit was in which position, until Abdallah turned to me in amazement: "Is this man God, to know everything?" '

Feisal must also have sensed that Lawrence's commitment to the Arab cause was quite unlike the attitude of other British officers in the Hejaz. The lack of sympathy with the Revolt so often evident in their reports must have been reflected in their behaviour.

Lawrence's reports drew attention to successful aspects of Feisal's campaign. He did not seek to deny Arab shortcomings, but he tried to analyse their causes, and constantly looked for ways to develop the military potential which he sensed was there. This was deliberate: if the only reports reaching London were hostile, lasting damage would be done to Hussein's cause. French and Anglo-Indian interests would cite these criticisms as proof that the Arab Revolt did not deserve support. Lawrence tried in some measure to redress the balance.

Lawrence realised that much of the irritation was caused by cultural differences, such as the Arab indifference towards formal discipline and British Army procedures. Regular army training was not the best preparation for working with bedouin tribesmen. Moreover, the Arabic-speaking British officers sent to the Hejaz had all spent their earlier careers in colonial service, mainly in India, Egypt, or the Sudan. The attitude towards natives prevalent in these places was inappropriate for work in Arabia, where the British were acting as advisers, not masters. Lawrence saw this clearly. He himself, by contrast, had spent his pre-war years as a civilian employer at Carchemish. Although he had not treated the villagers there as equals, neither had he hidden behind his privileged status as an Englishman. He had mixed freely and had sought to build up a relationship of mutual respect. In Carchemish, as in the Hejaz, there was no tradition of discipline in the European sense, and the tribesmen would ignore direct orders. Nevertheless, as Lawrence had discovered, an Arab labour gang could achieve remarkable results if given the right kind of encouragement. This was the lesson he was to apply during the Revolt.

When he had been told to return to the Hejaz two months earlier, he had protested that there was more useful work for him in Cairo. Now, however, he had seen how much depended on the attitude of British liaison officers in the field. There were many things he could do to advance the Arab cause if he remained in the Hejaz, and it was clear that this would be worthwhile, since the Revolt was taking pressure off the EEF. In addition, he had discovered a personal affinity with Feisal, even in matters such as their sense of humour. In background and ability they were very different, yet they complemented one another in many ways. Lawrence's knowledge of the workings in Cairo and ability to get things done there were matched by Feisal's rank and persuasive power among the Arabs. They each had a romantic vision of the Arab national movement, strong enough to transcend everyday setbacks, and they both knew that they were helping to shape momentous historical events. If the Revolt succeeded it would be the most important event in Arab history since the Crusades. Feisal had been born into this role, and alone among his brothers had the qualities needed to perform it. Lawrence was a fascinated outsider who had steeped himself in Middle Eastern history since childhood. In the epilogue of *Seven Pillars* he was to rank historical ambition among his principal motives during the Revolt: 'I had dreamed, at the City School in Oxford, of hustling into form, while I lived, the new Asia which time was inexorably bringing upon us.'

Both Feisal and Lawrence wanted their partnership to continue. On January 25 a cable from Jidda informed the Arab Bureau that: 'Feisal writes to the Sherif asking him to wire you that he is most anxious that

Lawrence should not return to Cairo as he has given such very great assistance.' Since this request came from Feisal himself, Clayton had little choice but to accede. Lawrence left for Egypt on January 27, but he was to return to the Hejaz almost immediately on an indefinite liaison posting.

CHAPTER 9

Looking Northwards
January–April 1917

LAWRENCE was delighted to learn that he would be rejoining Feisal. He wrote home: 'Things in Arabia are very pleasant, though the job I have is rather a responsible one, and sometimes it is a little heavy to see which way one ought to act. I am getting rather old with it all, I think! However it is very nice to be out of the office, with some field work in hand, and the position I have is such a queer one—I do not suppose that any Englishman before ever had such a place.'

His new role would require, among other things, great sensitivity in political questions. Arab aspirations and Anglo-French policy were as far apart as ever, and this chasm might become increasingly obvious as the Revolt moved northwards. Whatever the difficulties, Lawrence's superiors would expect him to keep Feisal enthusiastically on Britain's side.

Lawrence knew far too much of the real situation to underestimate the dangers. To succeed, he must turn his friendship with Feisal into a relationship of deep and unshakeable trust. Until now, his principal task had been to provide effective communication with Cairo; in the future, he would need to do much more.

By chance, a French initiative now gave Lawrence the opportunity to strengthen his influence over Feisal. Earlier that month it had been suggested in Paris that a European expeditionary force might be sent to Akaba. This would advance against the Hejaz Railway, cut off supplies to Medina, and thereby eliminate the Turkish threat to Mecca. To make the proposal more attractive, Paris offered to contribute two Senegalese battalions from Djibouti, as well as Brémond's units camped at Suez.

Both the War Office in London and Murray in Cairo rejected the proposal, and Brémond was informed of this on January 24. He was not, however, convinced: for military and political reasons he favoured a landing at Akaba, and for personal reasons he was keen to find a useful role for his Suez contingent. Unless he did so, the French War Office might soon redeploy it elsewhere, and he would be left with neither a force to command nor any means to exert real influence in the Hejaz.

At the end of January, therefore, Brémond left Jidda for Egypt, determined to get the French plan accepted. In his view, if men could have been spared from the EEF for Rabegh, they could be spared for Akaba. He knew that Wingate saw this as the best point from which to attack the Turkish supply line to Medina. Murray would surely give way if France offered substantial help.

On the way north, Brémond's ship called briefly at Wejh, where he put the scheme to Feisal and Newcombe. Feisal said that, according to the latest Arab intelligence, there were only 150 gendarmes at Akaba, and that he himself intended to capture the town. Newcombe, who had visited Akaba during the Sinai Survey, agreed wholeheartedly that it would be a good location for a new base.

Brémond travelled to Cairo, and on February 3 he found time to call on Lawrence, who was hardly surprised at the Frenchman's persistence. One of Brémond's principal aims was to prevent an Arab nationalist rebellion spreading into Syria. He was therefore deeply anxious about Feisal's move northwards to Wejh. An Anglo-French force advancing inland from Akaba would soon convince local tribes that Hussein's European allies were bent on imperial conquest. French propaganda would reinforce this view, and the Revolt would gain no adherents in the critical region between the Hejaz and Syria. In effect, an Allied landing at Akaba would contain the Arab rebellion inside the Hejaz.

Lawrence saw little likelihood that Murray would drop his resistance to the scheme, as GHQ knew that the terrain between Akaba and the railway seventy miles inland was extremely difficult. However, Lawrence was alarmed to learn that Brémond intended to revisit Wejh and press the plan on Feisal and Newcombe (it is most unlikely that Brémond had told Lawrence of Feisal's unpromising reaction three days earlier). He therefore decided to return to the Hejaz at once. In *Seven Pillars* he wrote: 'I had not warned Feisal that Brémond was a politician [in an earlier draft he wrote 'a crook']. Newcombe was in Wejh, with his friendly desire to get moves on. We had not talked over the problem of Akaba. Feisal knew neither its terrain nor its tribes. Keenness and ignorance would lend an ear favourable to the proposal. It seemed best for me to hurry down there and put my side on its guard.'

Lawrence reached Wejh on February 6 and in discussions with Feisal dealt with the French question once and for all. It might conceivably have been possible to warn Feisal about Brémond's true intentions without disclosing the truth about the Sykes-Picot Agreement, but it would have been very difficult. Lawrence decided to take Feisal into his confidence. He was to be attached to Feisal's staff for the foreseeable future, and it would be better to establish mutual trust at the outset. Sooner or later the truth would emerge, and if he lied now, his relationship with Feisal would be constantly at risk. Moreover, it would be particularly difficult to deceive a man such as Feisal. As Lawrence later wrote: 'lying . . . was the worst gambit against players whose whole life had passed in a mist of deceits, and whose perceptions were of the finest.'

Contemporary evidence, and Lawrence's own later statements, reveal that he must have told Feisal plainly that the McMahon-Hussein correspondence offered no certainty of Arab independence in Syria. France was certain to gain Lebanon, and would rule the interior of Syria as well unless the Arabs captured Damascus, Homs, Hama and Aleppo, the four cities named in the Sykes-Picot proviso. The decision to disclose this secret information to Feisal cannot have been easy, as the consequences might have been very serious indeed. Lawrence was no doubt influenced by his conviction that Feisal would become the Arab leader most closely involved with Syria. Lawrence sensed instinctively that his trust would not be betrayed. The nature of his work during the Arab Revolt demanded many such judgments of character, and from the success he achieved it is clear that he was rarely wrong.

Knowledge of the Sykes-Picot proviso brought about a fundamental change in Feisal's plans. From now on, he knew that it was vital for the Arabs to take Damascus and the other inland cities before the war ended. When the northern campaign began, his forces must give priority to regions east of the Jordan designated by Britain and France as a potential area of Arab self-government. An attempt to seize areas such as the Lebanon might only serve to undermine Allied sympathy for other Arab claims. That would be undesirable, since the Arabs would need Britain's support in order to hold French ambitions in check. Lawrence argued that Feisal would, in any case, be best advised to leave the Mediterranean littoral to the EEF. The coastal regions would be inaccessible to bedouin raiding parties, which could not operate very far from the inland desert. It would be extremely difficult for Arab irregulars to work in harmony with a European army, and the most useful thing Feisal could do would be to secure the right flank of the British advance. This would ensure continuing supplies of money and *matériel* during the campaign, as well as political support after the war. France could make no valid protest as long as the Arab campaign was seen to focus on objectives defined in the McMahon-Hussein correspondence and the Sykes-Picot proviso.

If the Arabs succeeded they would secure the territory allocated to them under the Sykes-Picot Agreement, and would be strongly placed to challenge its least acceptable provisions. At best, there was a real chance that Britain would help the Arabs create a viable and truly independent state in Syria. Lawrence later wrote: 'I had early divulged the existence of this thing [Sykes-Picot] to Feisal, and had convinced him that it was only to be set aside if the Arabs redoubled their efforts against the Turks . . . His only escape was to do so much to help the British that after peace they would not be able for very shame, to shoot such allies down in fulfilment of a secret treaty.

'Then, at least, there would be a modification, in which he would secure something . . . I begged him not, like his father, to trust our promises—though one could not know if Hussein trusted us out of stupidity or craft—but to trust in his own performance and strength . . . Feisal, a reasonable and clear-eyed statesman, accepted my point of view as the normal between nations, and his conviction of the hollowness of promises and gratitude did not sap his energy. Yet I did not dare to take so frankly into confidence the other men in our movement'.

It was against this background that Lawrence tackled the more immediate question of Akaba. He was relieved to hear that Feisal had offered no encouragement to Brémond, but he now learned with some concern that the Arabs had made plans of their own for capturing the town. The Arab leadership had envisaged an operation very similar to the one that had succeeded at Wejh. Lawrence knew, however, that this scheme was open to the same military objections as the one that had been proposed by Brémond. He argued against it, pointing out that the crucial objective was not Akaba itself, but the track leading eastwards through Wadi Itm and up onto the Maan plateau. If, as Feisal hoped, the Arabs were soon to operate in the northern deserts, they would need this line of communication. It would be the only practical route for sending British arms, ammunition, and other supplies inland. Lawrence argued that no action should be undertaken at Akaba unless it was certain to give Feisal possession of Wadi Itm as well.

Lawrence (unlike Feisal, Newcombe, or indeed Brémond) had seen the 1916 air reconnaissance reports on this mountainous track. He explained that the natural strength of Turkish positions in Wadi Itm was so great that a force trying to advance from the coast would face almost insuperable difficulties. There was no need for the Turks to keep these defences manned or to maintain a large garrison at Akaba (the village itself was in any case undefendable). There would be ample warning of any enemy approaching from the west, and this would leave more than enough time to send a defending force from Maan. The landing Feisal proposed at

Akaba would not merely fail to take Wadi Itm; it would bring the whole Turkish scheme of defence into operation. As a result, the inland route so essential to future Arab campaigns would be irretrievably lost.

Lawrence's rejection of the Arab scheme would have carried little weight if he had been unable to propose anything better. However, he was ready with a tentative suggestion which held out a much better promise of success. He had studied military strategy sufficiently to look at such problems from more than one angle, and he saw that in the case of the Wadi Itm there was indeed an alternative option. Assault on the Turkish defences by a force landed at Akaba would be futile, but the Wadi Itm track might well be captured through a surprise attack at the *inland* end. Given a sufficient force of local tribesmen, the Akaba road could be seized near Maan itself. This would prevent Turkish troops going out to man the Wadi Itm defences. If a blocking action could be maintained, even for a relatively short time, it would be a small matter to pick off the few permanent Turkish posts along the road down to Akaba. Thus the prepared defences in Wadi Itm would fall into Arab hands without a fight. No European invader could carry out such a coup; but in the extraordinary circumstances of the Arab Revolt, the scheme might well be possible. The area around Maan was so thinly populated that a mounted Arab force could reach its objective without detection, striking quickly and with devastating effect.

Two things, however, would be necessary. First, before the attack, utmost secrecy, since if rumours reached the Turks, they would immediately garrison the Wadi Itm. Secondly, after the wadi had been taken, a large Arab force would have to be brought to Akaba as soon as possible. This would be needed to hold the Maan road against the inevitable Turkish counter-offensive. The only way to get such a force to Akaba in time would be by sea.

At this stage neither Lawrence nor Feisal could be certain that the scheme was really feasible. The idea was simple, but its implementation would call for local knowledge and co-operation. Fortunately, they would soon have direct contacts with tribal leaders from these areas, and such questions could then be answered. In the meantime, the project must remain secret. Such secrecy was not easy to achieve in the Arab army. The nomadic tribesmen moved freely between areas controlled by Feisal and those controlled by the Turks. Both Feisal and Lawrence knew of this, and from time to time they profited from it in order to send the Turks misleading information. However, it often meant concealing their real intentions from Feisal's entourage until disclosure was absolutely necessary. Lawrence was equally cautious about reporting these Akaba plans to

Cairo. Akaba was strategically a key point, and he knew that the prospect of Arab control there would be opposed in some quarters. During the months ahead there were to be several occasions when the subject of Akaba had every reason to appear in Lawrence's reports, but he would find it politic to remain silent.

At this stage, he thought that the capture of Akaba should be part of a much larger general movement northwards which could not yet begin. First, the Arabs must carry out the concerted operation against Medina that had been planned for so long. Feisal's role in this would be to cut the Hejaz line permanently at El Ula, 100 miles east of Wejh. The armies of Ali and Abdullah would then close in on Medina and isolate the city. Once Fakhri Pasha was cut off from all hope of rescue, he would surely surrender. Only after the fall of Medina should the Revolt move northwards, driving the Turks back up the railway, first to Maan, and later to Damascus and Aleppo. It was at this later stage that a supply base at Akaba would become necessary. Feisal seemed to accept the change of plan.

Despite an initial hesitancy, tribal leaders from a wide area were soon declaring for Feisal, and by mid-February he was effectively in control of all the land between Wejh and the railway. He was also, with encouragement from Lawrence, seeking support farther north in the regions towards Maan. As a result, a continuous stream of visitors arrived. Lawrence wrote that on February 17: 'There came in to Feisul . . . five chief men of the Sherarat [a tribe from the area north-east of Tebuk], with a present of ostrich eggs; the nephew of Ibn Jazi [chief of the central Howeitat living around Maan] with his felicitations on the capture of Wejh; a cousin of Nawaf's [the son of Nuri Shalaan, chief of the Rualla] with a horse as a gift from him to Feisul; Ahmed abu Tageiga with the respectful homage of the Western Howeitat [from the Red Sea coast below Akaba]; the cousin and ten principal sub-chiefs of Auda abu Tayi [chief of the eastern Howeitat, based around Maan], to present his compliments to Feisul, and consult with him what they could best do to further his plans . . . and some more men of the Billi and Wuld Ali. The whole country is full of envoys and volunteers, and great sheikhs coming in to swear allegiance, and the contagion of their example is chasing away the last hesitations of the Billi . . .

'Feisul swore the Abu Tayi sheikhs on the Koran to wait while he waited, march when he marched, to show mercy to no Turk, but to everyone who spoke Arabic, whether Baghdadi or Aleppine, or Syrian, and to put the needs of Arab Independence above their lives, their goods,

θ 153 →

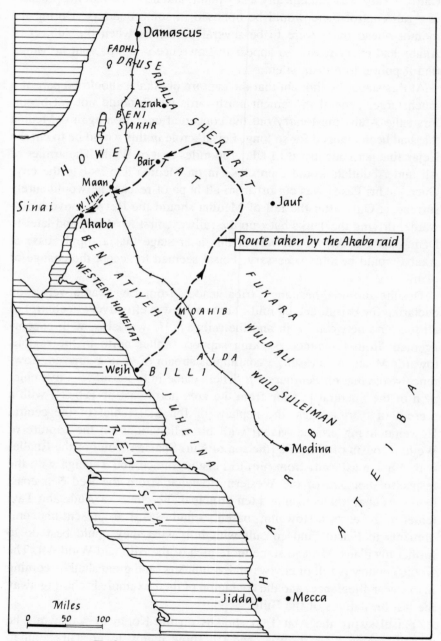

Damascus

FADHL

O DRUSE

RUALLA

Azrak

BENI
SAKHR

SHERARAT

HOWE Bair

Maan

W. Itm

Sinai

Akaba

Jauf

Route taken by the Akaba raid

BENI ATIYEH

WESTERN HOWEITAT

MOAHIB

FUKARA

WULD ALI

AIDA

Wejh

BILLI

WULD SULEIMAN

JUHEINA

RED SEA

Medina

HARB

ATEIBA

Miles

0   50   100

Jidda

Mecca

Tribes of the Hejaz and southern Syria

or their families. He also began to confront them with their tribal enemies, and force them to swear internal peace for the duration of the war.'

The support of these northern and eastern tribes was extremely important. In the short term, it would broaden the impact of the forthcoming
railway offensive and help to prevent the Turks from mounting a crushing
counter-attack at any one point. In the long term, it would be essential for
the campaign northwards. Lawrence later wrote: 'If we wanted to get
beyond Tebuk towards Maan or Akaba (and we did badly), it was clear
that we must find a way round by the east, and for this we should require
the favour of the nomads there. Our route would run first through the Billi
and Moahib country so far as the railway, and would then cross part of the
district of the Fejr. We had the Fejr. Beyond them lay the various tribes
owning obedience to Nuri Shalaan, the great Emir of the Ruwalla, who,
after the Sherif and ibn Saud and ibn Rashid was the fourth figure in the
desert . . . His favour would open to us Wadi Sirhan, the famous roadway, camping ground, and chain of water holes, which in a series of
linked depressions extended from Jauf, Nuri's capital, in the south-east,
northwards to Azrak . . . near Jebel Druse, in Syria. It was the freedom
of this Wadi Sirhan we needed, to get from our Fejr friends to the tents
of the Eastern Howeitat, the famous abu Tayi, of whom Auda, the greatest fighting man in all Arabia, was chief. Only by means of Auda abu
Tayi could we swing the tribes from Maan to Akaba so violently in our
favour that they would help us take Akaba and its hills from their Turkish
garrisons; only with his active support could we come from Wejh to
Maan. Since our Yenbo days we had been longing for him and trying to
win him . . . Auda was an immense chivalrous name, but an unknown
quantity to us, and in so vital a matter . . . we could not afford a mistake.
He must come down and see us, so that we might weigh him and frame
our future plans actually in his presence.' The scheme to take Wadi Itm
from the east was too secret to be entrusted to messengers, and Auda was
therefore sent an invitation to come to Wejh.

Although no major operation against the line had yet begun, preparations were in hand for several small expeditions. Feisal had given permission for Garland and Newcombe to accompany raiding parties.
Through their expert knowledge of explosives, they would greatly increase the damage done to the railway and to rolling-stock. This was the
first time the Arabs had allowed any British officer other than Lawrence
to go inland.

It was not until February 18 that Brémond arrived. He had had little
success promoting his Akaba landing scheme in Cairo, and the main

purpose of this new visit to Wejh was to improve his position with Feisal. He was very anxious to find a way of influencing Arab planning, and at the very least he wanted full reports on the activities of this northern Arab army. After some discussion, Feisal agreed to accept three machine-gun instructors. When Brémond's visit was over, Lawrence returned briefly to Cairo: he needed wireless equipment and other materials at Wejh, and also wanted to finish clearing up his affairs in the Arab Bureau.

He arrived in Egypt to find that the General Staff had just reached an agreement with Wingate that would greatly affect the future of the Arab Revolt. The background to this decision was Murray's advance across northern Sinai during December 1916. The EEF was now preparing for a major offensive against the Gaza-Beersheba line. If this succeeded, the road would be open for a British advance into Palestine in the autumn and Murray's forces would soon be in direct contact with the Arabs of Palestine and Syria. For this reason it was agreed on February 21, the day before Lawrence reached Cairo, that any action by the Arabs in areas to the north would be controlled by Murray. Wingate would be responsible only for Sherifian operations in the Hejaz, to the south of the Akaba-Maan line.

From Lawrence's point of view this change was extremely important. Feisal would not be able to carry out a campaign in Syria without British money and supplies, yet when the Arab campaign reached Akaba it would suddenly lose the benefit of Wingate's wholehearted enthusiasm. Murray's attitude was less certain: the Revolt had never been very popular at EEF headquarters, and if Feisal were to gain the support he needed, the Arabs would have to prove that they could make a worthwhile contribution to Murray's success.

Before Lawrence left Cairo, news came that Garland, with a party of Arabs, had succeeded in derailing a train during a night raid on the Hejaz line. Although in the darkness Garland had been unable to assess the damage, the engine had overturned and fallen down a small embankment. The value of this operation was readily understood in the Arab Bureau. A few months earlier it had been estimated that there were only about 40 locomotives, 700 box wagons and 600 trucks on the entire thousand-mile narrow-gauge railway system south of Damascus. This rolling stock was used to supply not merely the force in Medina, but the Turkish Army in Palestine and Sinai. According to Arab Bureau calculations, 'about ten locomotives will be engaged in the Damascus-Beyrout sector. The remaining thirty will have to work [from Damascus] to Beersheba and Medina. To run one train a day to each place would take about twenty engines (running time to Beersheba about forty hours, and to Medina about 100 hours). In addition a certain number of engines will be under repair, and engaged in local construction, breakdown, or armoured-train work.' Turkish locomotives were therefore important targets: each engine put out of action would significantly reduce the enemy's ability to move men and supplies.

Garland's report once again drew attention to the difficulties experienced by British regular officers when working with bedouin tribesmen. He criticised the state of the camels, the slow progress, and the tribesmen themselves: 'It is of course obvious to anyone knowing Arabs at all, that military work of any kind is difficult with the best of them. The majority of them show no respect, tending rather to insolence, and, I suppose from their traditional weakness for looting, seem to regard the stranger as legitimate plunder. In military operations they continually incur unnecessary risks by their stupid conduct, such as singing and shouting within hearing of the enemy, approaching enemy positions (as we did the railway line) up the middle of broad wadis that could be seen for miles by any outpost on the top of any of the small *jebels* [hills] adjoining the line . . . And of course it is quite useless for the Britisher to endeavour to introduce military ideas, or in any way to command; he can only make tactful suggestions, and hope by example to get them to do as he wants. It requires much patience and perseverance, and a lot of fraternization, for they strongly resent the application of the term ''soldier'' to themselves.' Despite his value as an explosives expert, Garland's difficulty in coming to terms with Arab ways was to prove a continuing handicap, and he was later withdrawn from guerilla operations in the Hejaz. Lawrence once remarked that he was 'a sick man, an ex-Sergeant, not very good, apt to stand on his dignity at the wrong moment. Not the type for the job.'

As Lawrence travelled back to Wejh, at the end of February, he was unaware of the new problem that awaited him. It seems that Feisal had been perturbed by knowledge of the Sykes-Picot proviso, and had become anxious to move as soon as possible against Damascus, Homs, Hama and Aleppo. He was also under pressure from Syrians on his staff who wanted to spread the campaign northwards. As a result, the question of Syria now occupied his entire attention, and he had begun to abandon the cautious step-by-step policy Lawrence had advocated. Reports confirmed that the Akaba region was almost free from Turkish troops, and this seemed to present a golden opportunity.

Within a few days of Lawrence's departure, Feisal had set aside warnings about the Wadi Itm defences, and had raised the subject of Akaba with Vickery, then the only British officer remaining at Wejh. Vickery, like Newcombe, felt that action at Akaba would help the Arabs to tackle the railway. He wrote to Clayton: 'I should be very glad of instructions on the question of taking Akaba with troops from Sherif Feisal's army.

'Sherif Feisal is very anxious to occupy the town as he thinks—with some reason too—that its capture and occupation by him would have an excellent political effect on the Syrians. He has also been asked to take the town by the Howeitat.

'He further considers, and I agree with him, that the farther north he proceeds, the farther north on their line of communication must the Turks go. [If] Sherif Feisal threatens [the Hejaz Railway] from Wejh, Dhabba and (when taken) Akaba . . . the Turks must defend their line, and without reinforcements they can only do this by withdrawing from their posts south of Medina, and by weakening their garrison at Medina. The longer the line which they have to guard against raids, the more scattered will be their troops, and they will be weak everywhere and strong nowhere . . .

'I told the Sherif that I could give no promise or undertaking for any assistance . . . without referring the matter to you. I told him this as I understand there are some difficulties in the question of an attack or occupation of Akaba.'

Although Feisal had stated that there was no urgency, this report shows that he did not think it necessary to wait for the fall of Medina before going north. In talking to Vickery, he had presented the taking of Akaba as a helpful step in the campaign against Medina, even though it was in reality a move in the opposite direction. This impatience exactly reflected the mood of Syrians in his entourage such as Nesib el Bekri, a Damascus landowner who had been deeply involved in secret Arab independence movements before the war. For Nesib, the revolt in the Hejaz was almost irrelevant, and its outcome was in any case now assured. The real prize would be Syria, his own country. He saw that a northern rebellion at that moment would catch the Turks unprepared, but he knew too little about military affairs to realise how quickly a revolt would die unless it could be supplied with money, arms, ammunition, and other necessities.

Since the outset, inattention to such matters by the Arab political leadership had crippled operations in the field. Feisal himself had little grounding in military strategy, and in reply to Nesib he could only cite the opinions of European advisers such as Lawrence, which were inevitably regarded as suspect.

When Lawrence reached Wejh on March 3, he must have realised how greatly Feisal had been swayed. The situation was easily rectified, but the incident served as a warning for the future. Many years later he remarked that Feisal 'always listened to his momentary adviser, despite his own better judgment.' Lawrence's reports contain no allusion to this wavering over Akaba, or anything further about Feisal's northern plans. In view of the reports by Vickery, Newcombe, and others during the same period, this silence can only have been a deliberate policy. He must nevertheless have been very anxious to know how Cairo would respond to Vickery's request for guidance.

Operations against the railway were now gathering pace. In early March it was learned that demolition parties from Abdullah's force in Wadi Ais had destroyed a bridge and several sections of line north of Medina. A few days later Lawrence heard that Newcombe had destroyed 2,500 metres of line. The Arab Bulletin of March 12 noted that there had been at least seven recent attacks at widely spaced points along the railway.

In the morning of March 8, while he was busy with administrative arrangements at Wejh, an urgent message arrived from Cairo. British Intelligence had learned that orders had been issued for the evacuation of Medina. The Turks had realised that it would be impractical to defend the whole length of the railway, now that it was threatened by Arab armies from both Wejh and Wadi Ais. Instead, they were planning a staged withdrawal five hundred miles northwards to a new defensive position south of Maan.

This should have been excellent news: when the Turks left, Hussein's armies would have achieved every objective they had been fighting for in the Hejaz. However, the proposed withdrawal was extremely unwelcome to Murray, who was on the point of launching his attack on Gaza. Although his army was superior to the Turkish force on the Gaza-Beersheba line, this advantage might easily be lost. He had little reserve strength because many of his troops had been transferred to the Western Front during the preceding months. If the Turks now gave up Medina and the southern half of the Hejaz Railway, they would be able to transfer a large number of experienced and well-armed men to the Sinai front. This would radically change the balance of forces there.

Clayton had therefore sent orders to Wejh that every effort must be made to prevent the Medina garrison from going north. If the city could not be captured, the Turkish force must be kept where it was or destroyed as it attempted to withdraw.

When the message arrived, Lawrence was the senior British officer present in Wejh. Newcombe and Garland had not yet returned from their raids on the railway, and Vickery had left for service in Europe. The task of persuading Feisal to take urgent action was made more difficult because Clayton did not wish the Arabs to be informed of the intended Turkish withdrawal. They had been hoping that Medina would be abandoned, and Clayton must have feared that if the news leaked out nothing would be done to stop Fakhri leaving. Compliance with the request from Cairo would prolong the status quo in the Hejaz, perhaps for a considerable time, and this would be a great sacrifice for the Arab leadership. Continued Turkish occupation of Medina, the second most holy city of Islam, had become a symbol of Arab weakness. Moreover, if existing plans were followed, a delay in ending the Hejaz campaign would put off the moment when Feisal could advance into Syria.

The instructions placed Lawrence in an awkward predicament, since all Feisal's thoughts were now directed towards the north. He realised that it would be impossible to persuade Feisal to take effective action against the line unless the true situation was explained. It seemed safe to do so because there had now been a great increase in trust between them. According to *Seven Pillars*, Lawrence appealed to Feisal's sense of honour, arguing that while Britain had done many things to assist the Arab Revolt, it was now Murray's turn to ask for assistance. While Lawrence may well have pitched his request in these terms, he doubtless dropped hints of another, much stronger, argument. He now knew that the whole future of the Arab campaign in Syria would depend on Murray's goodwill. If Feisal could hold the Medina garrison, Murray would be under a deep obligation.

Feisal agreed to do everything possible. Detailed plans were hurriedly drawn up, and messages sent out to Sherifs Ali and Abdullah, as well as to tribal leaders, asking them to attack the railway above Medina and to destroy any Turkish force that left the town. If the line could be kept out of action, it would be almost impossible for the Turks to move. There was no British liaison officer with Abdullah, whose military performance during the past few weeks had been very disappointing. Lawrence therefore decided to go up to Wadi Ais himself.

He wrote to Colonel Wilson explaining that the urgency of the order had left little time to make all the necessary arrangements: 'I hoped to get it up to Newcombe, but cannot, as he is coming in, without saying by what road . . . In the circumstances . . . I got Feisul to take action. In spite of General Clayton's orders I told him something of the situation. It would have been impossible for me to have done anything myself on the necessary scale. One must inform one's G.O.C.!'

After giving details of the action to be taken, Lawrence concluded: 'The plan (spur of the moment, I wish one had had more notice) is to get something going at once against the [Turkish] water arrangements, to give time for concentration. For this purpose these light advance parties are going up, to risk anything to gain time. Then when the camels [requested for the El Ula operation] come, and Ali has moved, the main forces of the three brothers will be from Medina to El Ula along the line, and the Turks will find movement most difficult . . . I'm afraid it will be touch and go. I am taking some Garland mines with me, if I can find instantaneous fuse, and if there is time, I will set them, as near Medina as possible: it is partly for this reason that I am going up myself, and partly with a view to smashing Hedia [the only station with a water supply for two hundred kilometres south of El Ula], if it can anyhow be done. Feisul will do anything he can. Only it's fearfully short notice.'

Although he had no experience as an officer in the field, he was now preparing to take an active part in operations. The mines Garland had invented for blowing up trains were still at an experimental stage, and no Arab had been trained to use them. In this unforeseen emergency, it might even become necessary for him to assume command of an Arab force, and he wrote in his notebook: 'Feisul has authorised me to bring down the Fagair troops to Abdulla, use them myself, or send them north as I think best.'

On March 10 Lawrence with a small escort set out for Wadi Ais. The long ride inland to Abdullah's camp was particularly unwelcome, as he had a severe outbreak of boils on his back, the result of unfamiliar diet and spartan living conditions. Not long after setting out he went down with dysentery and began to suffer bouts of high fever. Some of the notes he made on this journey are barely legible.

On the second evening, while camped in the Wadi Kitan, he found himself in one of the most unpleasant predicaments that he would face during the whole war. The small party which accompanied him had been assembled in haste, and it contained a motley selection of Arabs from different regions. Tensions between them were inevitable and, following a quarrel, one of the Ageyl was murdered by a Moroccan. Lawrence realised that justice would have to be done quickly before the other men took matters into their own hands. He described his feelings in *Seven Pillars*: 'Then rose up the horror which would make civilized man shun justice like a plague if he had not the needy to serve him as hangmen for wages. There were other Moroccans in our army; and to let the Ageyl kill one in feud meant reprisals by which our unity would have been endangered. It must be a formal execution, and at last, desperately, I told Hamed that he must die for punishment, and laid the burden of his killing on myself. Perhaps they would count me not qualified for feud. At least no revenge could lie against my followers; for I was a stranger and kinless.' Lawrence was appalled by the gruesome task, but there was no alternative. He was now very feverish, and his hand was so unsteady that it took three shots to carry out the execution. The memory of it would remain with him for the rest of his life. Had the incident occurred later in the campaign, when he had been hardened by the experience of fighting, it might have been easier; but this was the first man he had killed in the Arab cause.

He reached Abdullah's camp four days later and handed over letters from Feisal. After explaining the plans for urgent action against the railway, his strength gave out completely. Dysentery was followed by a heavy bout of malaria, and it would be a few days before he recovered sufficiently to do anything further. During this period of enforced idleness his mind distanced itself from day-to-day preoccupations, and he began to see the Arab Revolt in a broader perspective.

There had been a fundamental change since he had last thought deeply about Arab strategy in the Hejaz. Until now, every long-term plan had centred on the need to drive the Turks from Medina. Yet just when this objective was within reach, Murray had ruled against it. The new aim was to keep as many Turks as possible away from the Palestine front. As Lawrence pondered this, he began to see wider implications. Why should the Arabs take Medina at all? The Turkish garrison no longer presented any threat to the rest of the Hejaz, and as long as it remained where it was, it could not be used against the British in Sinai. The Turks had also to hold the Hejaz Railway, and this would mean constant patrolling against Arab attacks. The five-hundred-mile track south of Maan ran through desert where bedouin raiding parties could come and go as they pleased. As raids increased in frequency, thousands more Turkish soldiers would be needed to defend the line. The immobilisation of so many men and weapons would be a positive handicap to the Turks. It would therefore be in Britain's interests to keep Fakhri Pasha's garrison in Medina: not only at this time, but as long as the war continued.

Lawrence summarised this conclusion in *Seven Pillars*: 'We must not take Medina. The Turk was harmless there. In prison in Egypt he would cost us food and guards. We wanted him to stay at Medina, and every other distant place, in the largest numbers. Our ideal was to keep his railway just working but only just . . . The factor of food would confine him to the railways, but he was welcome to the Hejaz Railway, and the Trans-Jordan railway, and the Palestine and Syrian railways for the duration of the war, so long as he gave us the other nine hundred and ninety-nine thousandths of the Arab world.'

Such tactics would also help to minimise Arab losses; British advisers in the Hejaz had noted how badly Arab morale suffered when casualties were heavy, and had argued in favour of guerilla action rather than conventional engagements. Lawrence now believed that, given time, Arab guerilla raids could actually win the war: 'The death of a Turkish bridge or rail, machine or gun or charge of high explosive, was more profitable to us than the death of a Turk . . . Most wars were wars of contact, both forces striving into touch to avoid tactical surprise. Ours should be a war of detachment. We were to contain the enemy by the silent threat of a vast unknown desert, not disclosing ourselves till we attacked. The attack might be nominal, directed not against him, but against his stuff; so it would not seek either his strength or his weakness, but his most accessible material.'

According to this strategy, the Revolt should be extended as widely as possible: there was no longer any virtue in postponing a campaign in Syria until Medina fell. Indeed, if the Hejaz campaign were to be prolonged indefinitely, simultaneous action in the north would be essential. Otherwise, the Arabs might not have a chance to occupy Damascus before the end of the war. A change in British policy along these lines would accommodate Feisal's growing impatience to take action in the north. Nevertheless, the rebellion in Syria must be properly planned.

Lawrence would be unable to begin work on this new strategy until he got back to the coast. For the moment, his priority was to see that sufficient action was taken to prevent the Turks leaving Medina. On March 22 he was well enough to write to Wejh: as illness had prevented him from attacking the line, it was all the more important that some kind of action was being taken at El Ula. Without continuous prompting, Feisal might well lose interest in the railway. Indeed, the Arab leader could be forgiven for hoping privately that the Turks would manage to leave Medina. Lawrence therefore addressed an urgent letter to whichever British officer was now with Feisal: 'Please beg him not to remain in Wejh unless it is absolutely necessary. The effect both on Arabs and Turks of knowing him to be near the line would be very great: and if he left his heavy baggage in Wejh he could fall back on it in case of need, quickly. He has aeroplanes now, and Wejh is very easy to defend. Also if the Turks pushed west from El Ula I would get Sidi Abdullah to march up the line towards El Ula—which would have the effect of bringing the Turks back. In fact I hope most strongly to find him at [Wadi] Jayadah or Ainsheifa [on the western approach to the railway] soon.'

The tone of these remarks seems to hint at another aspect of Feisal's character. Years afterwards Lawrence admitted that 'Feisal was a timid man who hated running into danger, yet would do anything for Arab freedom—his one passion, purely unselfish . . . it made him face things and risks he hated. At the original attack on Medina he had nerved himself to put on a bold front, and the effort had shaken him so that he never courted danger in battle again.' In his wartime reports Lawrence did his best to conceal this timidity, knowing that the British military establishment would despise a leader with any taint of cowardice. But others had already noted the weakness. For example, before the move to Wejh an RFC officer had written: 'Sherif Feisal has greater breadth of character [than Ali] and no more strength. He is easily frightened and lives in constant dread of a Turkish advance though he seems to conceal that fear from his army.'

As regards his own plans, Lawrence wrote in a second note on March 22: 'I hope to go down to the railway tomorrow for a preliminary reconnaissance, and after that will be able to say what can be done: but in any case I will stay here a bit, as it is most important that the Turks should not be able to concentrate much of their Medina force at El Ula against [Feisal], and I am afraid if I do not stay here not much will be done.'

This visit to Wadi Ais had confirmed Lawrence in his earlier impression that Abdullah would be more useful to the Arab cause as a politician and diplomat than as a military leader. Later, in a detailed report to Colonel Wilson, he wrote: 'The conditions in his camp were, I thought, unsatisfactory. He had a force of about 3,000 men, mostly Ateiba. They seem to me very inferior as fighting men, to the Harb and Juheina . . .

'Sidi Abdulla himself gave me rather the same impression . . . [he] spends his time in reading the Arabic newspapers, in eating, and sleeping, and especially in jesting with one Mohamed Hassan, an old Yemeni from Taif . . .

'He takes great interest in the war in Europe, and follows the operations on the Somme, and the general course of European politics most closely . . . He takes little interest in the war in the Hedjaz. He considers the Arab position as assured, with Syria and Iraq irrevocably pledged to the Arabs by Great Britain's signed agreements'. Lawrence thought Abdullah unwise to put so much faith in the vague McMahon-Hussein commitments over Syria and Iraq, but refrained from telling him so.

As regards operations against the railway, Abdullah's attitude was 'hardly favourable. His Ateiba knew nothing of the country in which they were, and their Sheikhs are nonentities . . . Of his five machine guns only two were effective for lack of armourers or spares . . . His regular troops (seventy Syrian deserters, the gunners, and machine-gunners) lack nearly all equipment, and he had taken no steps to help them. His Ateiba were two months in arrears of pay, simply through *laissez faire*, for the gold was present in the camp to pay them up in full. He understands very little about military operations . . . Since his arrival in Wadi Ais, Sidi Abdulla had not ordered any attack on the railway. The destruction of the bridge over Wadi Hamdh near Abu el Naam was the work of Dakhilallah el Gadir, permitted certainly by Abdulla but not suggested or encouraged in any way by him.' Fortunately, Lawrence had been able to work up some enthusiasm among Abdullah's retainers, notably Dakhilallah el Gadir and Sherif Shakir. He described these two as the 'outstanding personalities of Abdulla's camp . . . thanks to their help I was able to influence him to take rather more interest, and feel rather more responsible in Hedjaz affairs than formerly.'

From what he had seen at Wadi Ais, Lawrence must have felt that no operation against Medina could succeed if it depended on large-scale action by Abdullah. This conclusion only served to strengthen the case for his new strategy of leaving the Turks in Medina indefinitely.

However, while his report contained severe military criticisms, Lawrence also stressed his regard for Abdullah's talent in other fields: 'I hope that in making . . . strictures on Sidi Abdulla's behaviour, I have not given the impression that there is anything between us, he treated me like a prince . . . I had come straight from Feisal's headquarters where one lives in a continual atmosphere of effort and high thinking towards the better conduct of the war—and the contrast with this of Abdulla's pleasure-loving laughing entourage was too great to be pleasant. One must remember however, that Abdulla is the head and cause of the Hedjaz revolt and neither his sincerity nor his earnestness can be called in question.'

Towards the end of March, Lawrence was fit enough to set out on the first of two expeditions against the railway. Hedia and its water supply were too strongly held to attack with the resources Abdullah offered, and it was decided instead to raid the station at Abu el Naam. After observing the Turkish garrison there for a day and a half, Lawrence realised that even here the Arab force led by Sherif Shakir was insufficient to attempt capture, so a different plan was adopted. Under cover of darkness, Lawrence laid one of the Garland mines and cut the telegraph wires. Early the following morning, while a train was in the station, the Arabs attacked with a mountain gun and a howitzer. Some damage was done, and when part of the station surrendered, the Arabs were able to take twenty-four prisoners. Lawrence reported: 'I think that the attack—as an experiment—justified itself. It had the effect in the next three days, of persuading the Turks to evacuate every out-post and blockhouse on the line, and concentrate the garrison in the various railway stations, which facilitated the work of the dynamite parties.'

On the second raid the Arab party was led by Dakhilallah el Gadir. The line was again blown up at several points, and Lawrence laid his second Garland mine. By mistake he buried the trigger mechanism a fraction of an inch too deeply, and a train passed without setting it off. After dark he dug it up: 'a most unpleasant proceeding: laying a Garland mine is shaky work, but scrabbling along a line for 100 yards in the ballast looking for a trigger that is connected with two powerful charges must be a quite uninsurable occupation.' He relaid the mine, and its charges later isolated a Turkish repair train.

Although he had failed to destroy a locomotive, his two expeditions did a good deal of damage, and he had been able to show the Arabs the type of operation that would cause most disruption. He arranged with Shakir and Dakhilallah that the line would be raided frequently, causing the maximum dislocation to the Turks: 'Dynamiters have been ordered to blow up not more than five rails per night, and so something every night . . . I think a constant series of petty destructions of rails is the most efficient means of keeping the line out of order. Large demolitions are no more difficult to repair and the blowing up of culverts is a waste of time and explosives.'

When Lawrence returned to Wadi Ais from his second expedition, he found an urgent handwritten message from Feisal. He decided to go back to the coast as quickly as possible.

Feisal had good reason to wish that Lawrence was in Wejh. During the preceding three weeks he had faced mounting difficulties in several areas. As Lawrence had feared, his attention had again swung towards the north, and he had shown little interest in operations on the railway. This had soon brought him into conflict with a new British arrival, Major Joyce.

Joyce had reached Wejh on March 17. He was to act as Senior British Officer, responsible for the armoured cars and the RFC flight that would shortly move up from Rabegh, where he had been based during the previous four months.

Joyce was annoyed to discover how much time Feisal was giving to delegations from tribes far outside the present theatre of operations, and despite Joyce's efforts to focus attention on El Ula, it was the end of March before Feisal's army moved inland. As for Feisal himself, Joyce reported that he 'insists that his presence in Wedj is absolutely essential at present, meeting the deputations from northern and eastern tribes which arrive nearly every day, and he considers it most important that he should be here to receive them'. Joyce evidently hoped to curb these activities, because he continued: 'The whole of Sherif Faisal's endeavours, with the exception of the actual occupying of a portion of the line, are now concentrated on the north with the idea of getting the tribes in this region to co-operate and make a general attack on the line between Derra and Tabuk. His ambitions probably go even further and aim at getting the whole line south of Damascus.

'I feel sure it would be advantageous if the limits of the Hedjaz operations could be defined as soon as possible. The further north they extend entails more money and more rifles . . . in order to save disappointment and possible friction later, I feel certain that something definite should be laid down.

'I have endeavoured to confine Faisal to local ambitions and military operations, but from somewhere he has developed very wide ideas and I would like to feel certain they are in accordance with the general plan.'

One of the reasons for Feisal's concern about the north was growing alarm over French activities. Syrians in Feisal's entourage were increasingly worried by rumours that France intended to invade Syria and take control there (such thoughts had doubtless occurred to Feisal when Brémond offered to send French colonial troops to Akaba). There now seemed to be evidence of definite preparations, and in reality the authorities in Paris were seriously considering such a project. A French officer, charged with preparing a feasibility study for landings on the Syrian coast, had recently been interviewing Arab representatives in Alexandria, Cairo and Port Said. He had wished to assess potential Arab reaction, and the motive for his questions must have been obvious. Moreover, there were firm plans to send a contingent of French support troops to join the

EEF. Its role would be to ensure that the tricolour was present during any advance through Palestine, and the first units were about to arrive in Egypt. Feisal had undoubtedly heard something of these new initiatives, possibly from Arab contacts in Egypt, but more probably from the French machine-gun instructors at Wejh.

Arab anxiety increased when Brémond appeared briefly at Wejh on April 1. The effect of this visit can be judged by a report from Wejh written a few days later. It said that Feisal had 'expressed considerable alarm at a rumour which had reached him to the effect that the French were about to land sixty thousand men in Syria. He feared that if this were true England would cease to supply him with arms and munitions, and that the French would take Syria without the assistance of the Arabs.

'He expressed the utmost apprehension of such a contingency and went so far as to say that, if it should come to pass, he would first fight the Turks, and then the French.'

Feisal must have feared that the Arabs would lose Syria altogether unless they acted quickly to secure the northern cities. According to this report, he had now 'told the . . . Sheiks of the northern tribes that he hopes to move north in about two months' time and that they must all be ready to rise against the Turks, each in his pre-arranged place, on a date to be decided upon later. All they need do at present is to get their people ready and wait. Meanwhile, he would have the necessary arms ready and would arrange with the Druses and also with the Arabs north near Aleppo, Hama, and Homs.'

There was still another factor which caused Feisal to recall Lawrence. By March 23 he knew that Auda abu Tayi would shortly arrive in Wejh. Auda was the Howeitat chief who would say whether or not Lawrence's scheme for taking Akaba was feasible, and whose co-operation would be essential if the plan were to be put into action.

When Lawrence reached Wejh, he would also find a reply from Clayton to the message about Feisal's Akaba ambitions, sent by Vickery five weeks previously. The note, addressed to Lawrence, read: 'With reference to the attached letter from Major Vickery, the situation has changed somewhat since it was written and the move to Akaba on the part of Feisal is not at present desirable.

'It is essential that he should concentrate his energies on immediate operations against the Railway, and a move on Akaba as is proposed, might distract him from this objective . . . the sea-planes and ships for transport which are asked for are not available, so that in any case, the operation cannot be carried out at present.

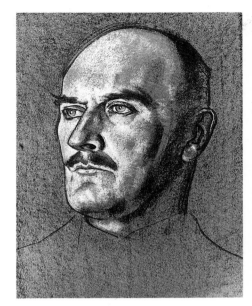

above: Tragic end to an impossible mission: the last radio messages from Kut, 29th April 1915
above right: Allenby by Eric Kennington, a portrait commissioned by Lawrence for *Seven Pillars of Wisdom* and later hung on the staircase at Clouds Hill
below: Gilbert Clayton, head of Cairo Intelligence during 1915 and 1916. One of the most important figures in Lawrence's career
right: S.F. Newcombe in the Hejaz as leader of the British Military Mission, 1917

The Hejaz railway ran through desert for hundreds of miles. Arab attacks forced the Turks to deploy thousands of troops to patrol it

Feisal's camp at dawn, photographed by Lawrence in January 1917. He wrote: 'Most sunrise pictures are taken at sunset, but this one is really a success'

above: Auda aby Tayi, the famous Howeitat chief with whom Lawrence developed the successful plan to attack Akaba

right: Emir Feisal, Hussein's third son. Lawrence wrote: 'I felt at first glance that this was the man I had come to Arabia to seek'

below: Hussein, Sherif and Amir of Mecca. Very few photographs survive of this key figure in the history of the Arab movement

The Arab force on its way to triumph at Akaba, 1917, one of the most important events of the Revolt

Lawrence with his Arab bodyguard, 1918. This personal bodyguard was recruited after Lawrence's capture at Deraa and subsequent escape

Lawrence at Damascus, October 1918: 'Our war was ended'. He left Damascus in the same Rolls-Royce tender after only four days

below left: Lawrence, D.G. Hogarth and Alan Dawnay in Cairo, 1918. Hogarth was then running a branch of the Arab Bureau in Palestine, and Dawnay was responsible to Allenby for liaison with the Arab forces. *below right*: T. E. Lawrence sketched by Augustus John during the Peace Conference in Paris. This drawing epitomised the popular image of 'Lawrence of Arabia'

Churchill, Gertrude Bell and Lawrence, from a larger group photograph taken during
an excursion on camel-back to the Pyramids, 20 March 1921

The Cairo Conference, March 1921. Front row centre, l–r: Sir Herbert Samuel, Winston Churchill, Sir
Percy Cox. Second row left: Sir Arnold Wilson, Gertrude Bell; centre: Jaafar Pasha, Lawrence

Feisal with his delegation and advisers at
the Peace Conference. Second row l–r:
Rustum Haidar (Feisal's secretary), Nuri
Said, Capitaine Pisani (France), Lawrence,
and Captain Hassan Kadri

Sherif Feisal by Augustus John, painted
during the Peace Conference at Paris, 1919,
and subsequently used by Lawrence as
frontispiece to the subscribers' *Seven Pillars*

l–r: T.E. Lawrence, Sir Herbert Samuel and the Emir Abdullah in Transjordan after the Cairo Conference, 1921

'I appreciate Major Vickery's arguments in favour of the occupation of Akaba, but, on the other hand, his arguments to Feisal, as to the difficulty of retaining Akaba against hostile attack are equally convincing.

'It is questionable whether, in the present circumstances, the presence of an Arab force at Akaba would be desirable, as it would unsettle tribes which are better left quiet until the time is more ripe.'

At the very least, it would have been unwise to encourage Feisal to think of taking Akaba without new instructions from Cairo. Newcombe, who had known Clayton for several years, could probably guess at the unspoken objection behind this message. The truth was that Clayton, like many others concerned about the future defence of Egypt, wanted to see Akaba in British, not Arab, hands.

CHAPTER 10

'A Useful Diversion'

April–July 1917

FEISAL must have been pleased by Lawrence's sudden enthusiasm for action in Syria, which corresponded exactly with his own feelings. Lawrence no longer insisted on carrying out the El Ula scheme: he saw no need to capture Medina or even to block the railway before extending the Revolt.

The other British officers at Wejh were much less receptive to these new ideas. As Newcombe was away, Lawrence had to put his case to Joyce and Bray. Both men were certain that if the Arabs occupied El Ula and Medain Saleh, Medina would fall. From the standpoint of European military thinking, the Arab position seemed so strong that the surrender of Fakhri's garrison was a foregone conclusion. All that remained was to work out the final details for co-operation between the various Arab forces.

In this atmosphere of high expectation, Lawrence's new ideas were dismissed. The El Ula attack was scheduled for mid-May, and neither Joyce nor Bray had time to think deeply about the possible benefits of his strategy. In any case, British policy on such issues was determined in Cairo, and there could be no radical change of course without approval from Clayton and Wingate, four hundred miles away.

There was, however, limited agreement when he suggested that someone might be sent north to raise a tribal force and attack the railway near Maan. Such raiding, if successful, would hamper any movement of Turkish reinforcements down from Maan to El Ula. As Lawrence wrote in *Seven Pillars*: 'Neither my general reasoning . . . nor my particular objections had much weight . . . All I gained was a hearing, and a qualified admission that my . . . offensive might be a useful diversion.'

Privately, Lawrence was now convinced that Feisal's immediate objective should be the Akaba-Maan supply route which would open the door to operations further north. As the Howeitat leader Auda abu Tayi was now at Wejh, it was at last possible to assess the scheme for approaching Akaba from inland.

Lawrence quickly saw that Auda was as remarkable as his reputation, and that he had the personality, tribal strength, and local knowledge needed to carry out the Akaba scheme. The vivid description of him in *Seven Pillars* is closely based on Lawrence's contemporary reports: 'He must be nearly fifty now (he admits forty) and his black beard is tinged with white, but he is still tall and straight, loosely built, spare and powerful, and as active as a much younger man. His lined and haggard face is pure bedouin: broad low forehead, high sharp hooked nose, brown-green eyes, slanting outward, large mouth . . . pointed beard and moustache, with the lower jaw shaven clean in the Howeitat style. The Howeitat pride themselves on being altogether bedu, and Auda is the essence of the Abu Tayi [tribe]. His hospitality is sweeping . . . his generosity has reduced him to poverty, and devoured the profits of a hundred successful raids. He has married twenty-eight times, has been wounded thirteen times, and in his battles has seen all his tribesmen hurt, and most of his relations killed. He has only reported his "kill" since 1900, and they now stand at seventy-five Arabs; Turks are not counted by Auda when they are dead. Under his handling the Toweihah [tribesmen] have become the finest fighting force in western Arabia . . .

'In his way, Auda is as hard-headed as he is hot-headed. His patience is extreme, and he receives (and ignores) advice, criticism, or abuse with a smile as constant as it is very charming. Nothing on earth would make him change his mind or obey an order or follow a course he disapproved'. When the Akaba scheme was explained to him, Auda pronounced that it was feasible, and in discussions during the third week in April he and Lawrence began to work out detailed plans.

Lawrence only hinted about the nature of this project to his British colleagues, and maintained a complete silence about the proposed operation in his reports to Cairo. His reason for doing so can only have been Clayton's letter about Akaba, which he had now seen for the first time; he was well qualified to read between the lines of this forthright opposition to an Arab attack on the town. During the preceding months the two of them must have discussed Akaba on many occasions, and he surely knew about the strategic considerations on which Clayton's attitude was based. They were spelled out in an internal memorandum written by Clayton at about this time: 'the occupation of Akaba by Arab troops might well result in the Arabs claiming that place hereafter, and it is by no means improbable that after the war Akaba may be of considerable importance to the future defence scheme of Egypt. It is thus essential that Akaba should remain in British hands after the war.'

Lawrence must have suspected that if he told Cairo of his plan, he would receive an unequivocal order to abandon it. Failing that, there would be a lengthy debate, and the French might be consulted. He can have had no illusions about their reaction: if Brémond got wind of an Arab move on Akaba, he would urge the French Government to use every possible channel of influence to block it. In this process the scheme would inevitably be publicised and, once the Turks had been forewarned, the inland approach to Akaba would become impossible, now or in the future.

Lawrence had now reached a point of no return. In *Seven Pillars* he wrote: 'I decided to go my own way, with or without orders.' Having seen Clayton's letter, he could not encourage Feisal to take Akaba without acting against a direct command from a superior officer. Yet he was sure that the capture of Akaba was in the best interests of both the Arabs and the British. Everything in Syria would be lost to the Arabs unless Feisal managed to carry the campaign northwards out of the Hejaz. Likewise, if the Arab Revolt never spread to Syria, the EEF would have to fight its way northwards without the benefit of Arab assistance. His decision had not been taken lightly. He had given much thought to the scope for future co-operation between Murray and Feisal. If the Arabs succeeded in as big a venture as Akaba, Murray would realise how valuable they could be.

In summary, Lawrence felt that he could see the justification of his proposed action better than those in Cairo. Clayton's letter about Akaba was five weeks old, and it could be argued that the objections actually stated there did not apply to the inland scheme. Once Feisal had taken Akaba, the immediate military benefits would outweigh considerations about the future defence of Egypt. Above all, Akaba would be vital to the progress of Feisal's campaign: without it, the Arab Revolt might be confined to the Hejaz for the duration of the war. Lawrence concluded that it must be taken as soon as possible, without warning, and without British help.

He had originally imagined that the attack on Akaba would follow a general Arab advance up the railway towards Maan. Now, it would have to be captured in a separate operation, long before Feisal's main force moved northward. The venture would therefore be more difficult and more risky. He and Auda worked out a scheme to travel north-east with a small party, joining the Howeitat in their spring pastures near Maan. A fresh tribal force would be raised there, which would first create a noisy diversion around Maan itself, and then take control of the route down to Akaba. In *Seven Pillars* Lawrence described this trek as 'an extreme example of a turning movement, since it involved a desert journey of six hundred miles to capture a trench within gunfire of our ships: but there was no practicable alternative . . . Auda thought all things possible with dynamite and money, and that the smaller clans about Akaba would join us. Feisal, who was already in touch with them, also believed that they would help if we won a preliminary success up by Maan and then moved in force against the port.'

By chance, while these deliberations were taking place, Lawrence obtained valuable Intelligence about the state of the Wadi Itm defences. On April 20 the Royal Navy had put a landing party ashore at Akaba, in order to investigate rumours that a German officer had arrived and was engaged in laying a minefield offshore. The naval party overpowered the local defences and took eleven prisoners.

Captain Boyle brought the prisoners to Wejh, and Lawrence was able to interrogate them. They gave exact information about the disposition and strength of Turkish forces in the area. It transpired that the permanent garrison based in Akaba totalled only 330 men from the Turkish Gendarmerie, and that the great majority of these were Arabs. Better still, the posts along the track to Maan were very lightly held. This news confirmed Lawrence's hopes: as long as the Turks could be prevented from sending in reinforcements, the defences of Akaba and Wadi Itm against an attack from inland were negligible.

This was excellent news, and Lawrence felt that the expedition should set out as soon as possible. He had already concluded that his own presence would be indispensable, as this was the surest way to see that the party held to its objective. The bedouin were notoriously rapacious, and neither Akaba itself nor the barren track that led there offered much prospect of loot. Around Maan, however, there were richer targets, and the tribesmen might well be tempted by them.

On his own, Lawrence could not guarantee that the expedition would stay on course. He could not reveal to the Howeitat the full reasoning behind the Akaba plan, and Auda might choose to ignore him. This problem was diminished, however, when Feisal appointed Sherif Nasir as overall leader of the expedition. Nasir was widely respected, and had earned his place as one of the most trusted leaders in the Arab army. He was well aware of Lawrence's special status with Feisal, and he knew how greatly the Revolt depended on British help. It was most unlikely that he would ignore Lawrence's advice.

There was another very important reason for Lawrence to accompany the expedition. If Akaba were captured, supplies and reinforcements would be needed urgently, and these could only be brought in by British ships. Somehow, news of the successful coup would have to be taken to Egypt. If one of Boyle's patrol vessels passed Akaba at the right moment, something might be done to attract its attention. However, alternatives had to be considered. Akaba was several days' journey from Wejh, even by the shortest route, and it seems likely that Lawrence realised at the outset how much quicker it would be to ride directly across Sinai to Suez. If he went himself, he would be able to state exactly what was needed, and use his influence to see that it was sent quickly.

Only Feisal and a handful of the Arab leaders knew what was being planned. As far as the British were concerned, Lawrence's northern expedition was a purely Arab affair, directed primarily against Maan. It was tolerated because few men would be withdrawn from Joyce's railway enterprise. Lawrence later wrote: 'the venture was a private one. I had no orders to do it, and took nothing British with me. Feisal provided money, camels, stores, and explosives.'

Such was the lack of interest in Lawrence's activities that his British colleagues failed to grasp the implications of the plan, even when they learned its essential details. In late April, C. E. Wilson accompanied Feisal to a meeting with Abdullah at Fagair. Lawrence, who would not be involved in the railway operations, remained behind, but Auda went, probably to speak on behalf of the northern tribes in any wider discussions. During the journey to Fagair, Wilson travelled in the same armoured car as Auda, who told him a certain amount about the northern scheme. Wilson's subsequent report, which was mainly about the forthcoming railway operations, contained almost casual statements about the expedition: Auda was to travel north, 'probably' accompanied by Lawrence; the first aim would be to disrupt the railway around Maan, which would then be captured; if this succeeded, the force could clear out the Turkish posts down to Akaba. Neither Wilson, nor Clayton when he read the report, seems to have realised what the true objective was, although all the elements of the Akaba plan were there. Doubtless they assumed that, like many other ambitious Arab schemes, it would come to nothing.

While Feisal and Auda were away, Lawrence took an armoured car and spent several days locating the wreck of an RFC plane that had crash-landed in Wadi Hamdh. He did not get back to Wejh until May 3, by which time the Fagair party had also returned.

To his complete surprise, he learned that Sir Mark Sykes, co-author of the Sykes-Picot Agreement, had spent a few hours there on the previous day, and had talked at length with Feisal. During these conversations,

Sykes had tried to obtain Feisal's consent to various propositions related, as Feisal must instantly have recognised, to the secret Anglo-French agreement over Syria. Afterwards, Sykes had left for Jidda, where he was to meet Sherif Hussein.

Lawrence probably knew something of the background to this visit. Five months earlier, in late December 1916, Britain and France had agreed that when the EEF advanced into Palestine, a French political officer would be appointed to Murray's staff. More recently, when the French Government had learned of the planned assault on Gaza, they had nominated François Georges-Picot to this post.

The prospect of having to deal with Georges-Picot was most unwelcome to Murray's staff, and it had been decided that a British political officer should be appointed as well. He would be Georges-Picot's only channel of communication with GHQ. In the first instance Sykes had been nominated for this delicate liaison job, although it was hoped that a replacement could be found.

Ironically, when Sykes and Georges-Picot arrived in Egypt on April 22, the EEF was still blocked outside Gaza, with no immediate prospect of advancing into Palestine. However, before setting out from England, Sykes had made arrangements to meet a small number of (carefully selected) Syrian Arabs. In Cairo, he and Georges-Picot began a series of talks with these representatives. Their aim was to bring the Arabs to a point at which the content of the Anglo-French agreement would seem acceptable.

At these meetings, the Arabs were presented with the idea that, after the war, Britain and France would help them to create an independent inland state or confederation. This would depend on its two European allies for protection, and would give in return financial and other concessions—in practice, those embodied in the Sykes-Picot Agreement. However, Sykes and Georges-Picot took care not to reveal that Britain and France had already divided the proposed autonomous area into two spheres of influence. As Sykes put it, the task was 'to manoeuvre the delegates, without showing them a map or letting them know that there was an actual geographical or detailed agreement, into asking for what we are ready to give them.'

Sherif Hussein, who had earlier been informed that a French political officer would join Murray's army, had found out that discussions were to take place in Egypt. He was alarmed, and asked for explanations. Accordingly, after hurried consultations with the Foreign Office, it had been agreed that Sykes should go down to Jidda for talks. He would reveal certain aspects of Anglo-French policy, in much the same way as he had done in Cairo. He would also, if possible, secure the Sherif's agreement to a further meeting, at which Georges-Picot would be present. Sykes had therefore left Egypt on April 30, and had called at Wejh to see Feisal on the way south.

As previously agreed with Georges-Picot, Sykes had explained the position to Feisal in very general terms, stressing that the Arabs would 'have to deal with an indivisible Entente; that, under whatever overlord, an enlightened progressive régime must be established in Syria; and that certain districts of the latter, which present peculiar difficulties, must remain under special tutelage in any event.'

Sykes probably found these discussions quite uncomfortable: Feisal, an acute politician, already knew more about the Anglo-French agreement than Sykes meant to divulge, and his questions were doubtless very penetrating. Sykes, who invariably reported such meetings in the best possible light, wrote afterwards that he had 'explained to [Feisal] the principle of the Anglo-French Agreement in regard to Arab Confederation. After much argument, he accepted the principle and seemed satisfied'. Following his subsequent meeting with Hussein, Sykes cabled Picot: 'I am satisfied with my interviews with Sherif Feisul and the King of the Hejaz, as they both now stand at the same point as was reached at our last joint meeting with the three Syrian delegates in Cairo.'

Lawrence left no record of the conversation he had with Feisal on his return to Wejh. Nor is there any account in his notebooks of the discussions which took place on the morning of May 7, when Sykes made a second brief visit on his way back from the meeting with Hussein in Jidda. Lawrence's pocket diary merely notes that he saw Sykes and Wilson that day. Despite this silence (which is maintained in *Seven Pillars*), there is contemporary evidence that he was extremely alarmed by the way Sykes was handling the discussions with the Arab leaders, and later comments by Sykes suggest that, during this meeting at Wejh, Lawrence disagreed with him openly.

By this time several other British officials in the Hejaz either knew or suspected that some kind of Anglo-French agreement had been reached. Those who were dealing directly with the Arabs had been expressing their concern about the situation for some months. Now that the Arabs were taking serious steps towards a campaign in Syria, the need to settle the question of future French involvement was becoming increasingly urgent. Lawrence had solved his own dilemma by telling Feisal the essentials of the Sykes-Picot Agreement. In March, Wilson had urged that the position should be made as clear as possible to the Sherif, writing: 'I feel very strongly that the settlement of Syria etc., should not be arranged behind his back, so to speak: he is, in my opinion, well deserving of the trust of the British Government and I feel sure we will greatly regret it in the future if we are not quite open and frank with him now over the whole matter.' Like Lawrence, Wilson believed that a policy of deception was morally indefensible and that it would almost certainly be counter-productive.

Despite these warnings, Sykes had not come to the Hejaz with any intention of clearing up Arab misunderstandings. He remained sublimely confident that a policy of vagueness and deceit could be continued. In his reports and in conversation with British and French officers, he made no attempt to disguise his cynicism about Allied commitments to the Arabs. Thus Brémond heard from Lieutenant Millet, an English-speaking officer of the French military mission at Jidda, that Sykes had 'received him in a most friendly manner, giving an impromptu briefing. Sir Mark . . . claimed that all the tribes in the Damascus-Aleppo-Baghdad triangle would prove very good in combat, and were merely waiting for weapons to attack the Turks; naturally, one would allow them to continue in the belief that they were fighting for their independence.' To Millet's objection that this would raise difficulties in the future, Sykes had replied: 'I am not looking so far ahead; to do a good job, one must seek the immediate benefit . . . For the moment, our task is to beat the Germans wherever we can. As for dividing territories, we will always be able to make arrangements when the war is over.' Millet noted that Sykes seemed to regard as unimportant any concessions made at this moment to the Sherif and the Arabs in general. His conclusions about Sykes were damning: 'no subtlety, crude common sense, simplistic politics, scant knowledge of the people and places involved, great self-satisfaction.'

Within a month of this visit to the Hejaz (and after further experience of Sykes's opportunist diplomacy), both Wilson and Newcombe were to protest in very strong terms. Newcombe would write that Sykes's policy 'entails throwing great responsibility on our government to see the . . . Arab cause through to the end: otherwise we are hoodwinking the Sherif and his people and playing a very false game in which officers attached to the Sherif's army are inevitably committed and which I know causes anxiety in several officers' minds: in case we let them down.'

The disingenuous attitude displayed by Sykes made these British officers deeply aware of their own moral responsibility. They would be

expected to give whatever assurances were needed to keep the Arabs
fighting on Britain's side; but while doing so they would know that their
Government did not intend to keep its promises. Lawrence was more
deeply troubled than his colleagues, as he was about to set out on an
expedition that he himself had advocated, whose sole aim was to take the
Revolt out of the Hejaz and into Syria. As a result, Arab tribesmen would
soon begin to sacrifice their lives for territory over which France was to
lay claim.

He had little time to think over this problem while the Akaba expedition was making its final preparations. On May 9, two days after meeting
Sykes, he set off north-east with Sherif Nasir, Auda abu Tayi, and a party
of about forty-five Arabs. They took 20,000 sovereigns with them to
finance recruiting, and a large quantity of explosive.

It was only when the long camel ride began that Lawrence had the
opportunity to reflect, and he was soon tormented by doubts. These were
aggravated by the cheerful presence of Nesib el Bekri, a passionate be-
liever in Syrian independence, who was to accompany the expedition on
its first stage. He was travelling north to carry out a mission of his own,
aiming to strengthen support for Feisal among the leaders there.

Four days into the journey, Lawrence suffered an outbreak of boils and
high fever, similar to the one he had experienced two months earlier
during the ride to Wadi Ais. The illness did nothing to improve his
troubled state of mind. On May 13 he noted cryptically in his diary: 'The
weight is bearing me down now . . . pain and agony today'. In this
mood, the trust and comradeship of his companions became a burden
rather than a solace, and he felt increasingly isolated. His sense of guilt
and depression seems to have been accentuated by illness and by the
desolate landscapes through which the expedition was passing.

After riding for ten days, they reached the Hejaz Railway near Diraa,
and blew up a section of the line before passing on into the desert beyond.
On May 20 they began to cross a barren plain known as El Houl. Lawrence wrote in *Seven Pillars*: 'We, ourselves, felt tiny in it, and our
urgent progress across its immensity was a stillness or immobility of
futile effort. The only sounds were the hollow echoes, like the shutting
down of pavements over vaulted places, of rotten stone slab on stone slab
when they tilted under our camels' feet, and the low but piercing rustle of
the sand, as it crept slowly westward before the hot wind along the worn
sandstone, under the harder overhanging caps which gave each reef its
eroded, rind-like shape.

'It was a breathless wind, with the furnace taste sometimes known in

Egypt when a khamsin came; and, as the day went on and the sun rose in the sky it grew stronger, more filled with the dust of the Nefudh, the great sand desert of Northern Arabia, close by us over there, but invisible through the haze. By noon it blew a half-gale, so dry that our shrivelled lips cracked open, and the skin of our faces chapped; while our eyelids, gone granular, seemed to creep back and bare our shrinking eyes. The Arabs drew their head-cloths tightly across their noses, and pulled the brow-folds forward like vizors with only a narrow, loose-flapping slit of vision.

'At this stifling price they kept their flesh unbroken, for they feared the sand particles which would wear open the chaps into a painful wound: but, for my own part, I always rather liked a khamsin, since its torment seemed to fight against mankind with ordered conscious malevolence, and it was pleasant to outface it so directly, challenging its strength, and conquering its extremity. There was pleasure also in the salt sweat-drops which ran singly down the long hair over my forehead, and dripped like ice-water on my cheek. At first, I played at catching them in my mouth; but, as we rode further into the desert and the hours passed, the wind became stronger, thicker in dust, more terrible in heat. All semblance of friendly contest passed. My camel's pace became sufficient increase to the irritation of the choking waves, whose dryness broke my skin and made my throat so painful that for three days afterwards I could eat little of our stodgy bread. When evening at last came to us I was content that my burned face still felt the other and milder air of darkness.'

In the late morning of May 24, while crossing a desert of dried mud flats called the Biseita, they realised that one of the party had gone missing. His loaded camel was still following on, but the saddle was empty, and no one had seen him dismount. It seemed that the man, whose name was Gasim, must have dozed off and fallen to the ground. He would be unable to rejoin the caravan because it left no trace on the hard ground, and mirages made it impossible to see very far in the desert. Unless someone went back to look for him, he would certainly die. Lawrence felt he had to take upon himself the responsibility of finding Gasim, who was one of his own men. He decided to turn back, telling no one and hoping that an exact compass course would bring him to the expedition at its next camp. In *Seven Pillars* he wrote: 'I looked weakly at my trudging men, and wondered for a moment if I could change with one, sending him back on my camel to the rescue. My shirking the duty would be understood, because I was a foreigner: but that was precisely the plea I did not dare set up, while I yet presumed to help these Arabs in their own revolt. It was hard, anyway, for a stranger to influence another people's national movement, and doubly hard for a Christian and a sedentary person to sway Moslem nomads. I should make it impossible for myself if I claimed, simultaneously, the privileges of both societies . . . My temper was very unheroic, for I was furious with my other servants, with my own play acting as a Beduin, and most of all with Gasim'. After riding for a time Lawrence found Gasim, half-maddened by the desert sun. They regained the expedition safely.

The most difficult part of the journey was over when they reached the Wadi Sirhan, a long series of depressions with occasional wells and vegetation. Auda knew that they would find the Howeitat there, and three days later they reached the first encampment. Here Auda left them for a few days, while he went to explain their purpose to Nuri Shalaan, paramount chief of the region. During Auda's absence, Nasir and the remainder of the party moved northwards from camp to camp, recruiting men for the operations at Maan and Akaba. At each place there were tribal feasts, which Lawrence described in his notebook with increasing revulsion.

It was not just the feasting that Lawrence resented. The work of recruiting involved constant affirmation that the Arabs were fighting for their independence. As British liaison officer with Feisal, he was asked again and again to give assurances on this point. On June 2 he noted: 'All day deputations, fusillades [of welcome], coffee, ostrich eggs. Dined with Auda. Lies.' He found his position impossibly difficult, not least because he feared the outcome of the forthcoming meeting between Sykes, Picot and Hussein. He could not be sure what would happen, but there seemed little likelihood that Sykes would put Britain's relationship with Hussein on a more straightforward footing. Lawrence's clearest statement of the dilemma is in *Seven Pillars*, where he wrote: 'Arabs believe in persons, not in institutions. They saw in me a free agent of the British Government, and demanded from me an endorsement of its written promises. So I had to join the conspiracy, and, for what my word was worth, assured the men of their reward . . . In this hope they performed some fine things, but, of course, instead of being proud of what we did together, I was continually and bitterly ashamed.

'It was evident from the beginning that if we won the war these promises would be dead paper, and had I been an honest adviser of the Arabs I would have advised them to go home and not risk their lives fighting for such stuff'.

Lawrence's contemporary notes show that he soon found his role in the recruiting process intolerable. On June 5, he wrote: 'Can't stand another day here. Will ride north and chuck it.' The significance of this entry is clarified by a message scribbled in the notebook he was to leave behind: 'Clayton. I've decided to go off alone to Damascus, hoping to get killed on the way: for all sakes try and clear this show up before it goes further. We are calling them to fight for us on a lie, and I can't stand it.'

In full knowledge of the risks involved, he planned to make a secret journey northward, still deeper into enemy territory. He would travel among tribesmen whose loyalty to the Sherif was questionable, and who knew that the Turks had put a price on his head. If he failed to return, the notebook containing his message to Clayton would probably find its way back to Cairo.

Unlike Newcombe and Wilson, he was not a professional soldier. He had no habit of unquestioning obedience to help him cope with his predicament. Instead, he had been brought up to believe in uncompromising standards of personal conduct, and these now conflicted with a patriotism he felt no less deeply. The manner in which Britain was prepared to treat the Arabs bore no relation to the chivalrous kind of warfare Lawrence had imagined and admired during his childhood. He was being forced to play a role that undermined the whole basis of his self-esteem. As an illegitimate child, he had inherited no sense of security or social position from his family. His future public status, no less than his self-respect, would depend on what he made of himself. Although he despised conventional careers, he had hoped for honourable distinction, and the war had seemed to offer such an opportunity. He later wrote that in August 1914 he 'had meant to be a general and knighted, when thirty'. Now, however, it was unthinkable that he should accept honours earned in such a manner.

In the published text of *Seven Pillars* this acute personal crisis is given little prominence. The Akaba campaign is described in a succession of triumphal chapters so enriched by lavish descriptions of the desert landscape that the journey takes on an epic quality. After writing the book, Lawrence explained to a friend that he had felt it 'a fault in scale to represent the Arab Revolt mainly as a personal tragedy to me.' An early draft, however, deals much more openly than the final text with the reasons for his northern journey: 'I wanted an excuse to get away from the long guiding of people's minds and convictions which had been my part since Yenbo six months before. It should have been happiness, this lying out, free as air, with life about me striving its uttermost whither my own spirit led: but its unconscious serving of my purpose poisoned everything for me. A man might clearly destroy himself: but it was repugnant that the innocence and the ideals of the Arabs should enlist in my sordid service for me to destroy. We needed to win the war, and their inspiration had proved the best tool out here. The effort should have been its own reward:—might yet be, for the deceived—but we the masters had promised them results in our false contract, and that was bargaining with life, a bluff in which we had nothing wherewith to meet our stake. Inevitably we would reap bitterness, a sorry fruit of heroic endeavour.

'My ride was long and dangerous, no part of the machinery of the revolt, as barren of consequence as it was unworthy of motive . . . At the time I was in reckless mood, not caring very much what I did, for in the journey up from Wejh I had convinced myself that I was the only person engaged in the field of the Arab adventure who could dispose it to be at once a handmaid to the British army of Egypt, and also at the same time the author of its own success . . . I knew that when we had taken Akaba I would have to lead the movement, either directly or indirectly . . . Accordingly on this march I took risks with the set hope of proving myself unworthy to be the Arab assurance of final victory. A bodily wound would have been a grateful vent for my internal perplexities, a mouth through which my troubles might have found relief.'

Despite these confused and self-destructive motives, he knew that his journey might serve a useful purpose. He wanted to assess for himself the spirit and resources of the leaders who had sent messages of support to Feisal. He later wrote: 'while I still saw the liberation of Syria happening in steps, of which Akaba was the indispensable first, I now saw the steps coming very close together, and . . . planned to go off myself . . . on a long tour of the north country to sound its opinion and learn enough to lay definite plans. My general knowledge of Syria was fairly good, and some parts I knew exactly: but I felt that one more sight of it would put straight the ideas of strategic geography given me by the Crusades and the first Arab conquest, and enable me to adjust them to the two new factors in my problem, the railways in Syria, and the allied army of Murray in Sinai.'

Lawrence also intended to recommend a policy of restraint to the northern leaders. In the Hejaz, the Revolt had begun without adequate preparation, and Hussein had only been saved by the Royal Navy. In Syria, no such help would be at hand. If the northern tribes rebelled too soon they would be defeated, and there would be terrible reprisals. Lawrence knew that Nesib el Bekri would go north to these same leaders, telling them how successful Feisal had been and holding out the promise of a rapid victory. During an argument with Lawrence on June 3, Nesib had turned against the Akaba plan, proposing instead to raise a rebellion around Damascus. Nesib lacked funds and arms, but anti-Turkish feeling in Syria was very strong, and Lawrence feared what might happen.

The military aspects of Lawrence's extraordinary journey were later summarised in a report to Clayton. From this source, as well as his pocket diary and later statements, it appears that his total itinerary was rather more than three hundred miles. Starting from Nebk, he rode north via Burga (east of Jebel Druse) and reached Ain El Barida near Tadmor about June 9. There he enrolled a small group of Arabs under Sheikh Dhami of the Kawakiba Aneza, and rode with them to Ras Baalbek, fifty miles north of Damascus, arriving on June 11. They damaged a small plate-girder bridge there near the station, using about 4lb of explosive: 'The effect on the traffic was of course very slight, but the Metowila of Baalbek were most excited, and it was to arouse them that I did it. The noise of dynamite explosions we find everywhere the most effective propagandist measure possible.' A month later British Intelligence in Switzerland obtained information about these events from a Turkish officer who had left Damascus on June 19 and passed through Constantinople ten days later. According to his account, which was clearly exaggerated: 'The whole province of Baalbek is in a state of revolt and Baalbek itself has been occupied by the Turkish troops from Gaza. Six battalions of the third division have been withdrawn from that front for the purpose of quelling the insurrection in this province. The station at Ras Baalbek has been burned. The Vali of Damascus has been sent to enquire into the trouble there. Nedjib Bey, son of Mahommet Said, chief of the Metuali tribe at Hermel, was responsible for the revolt and attack on Baalbek.'

Turning southwards, Lawrence travelled to the outskirts of Damascus. There, on about June 13, he met Ali Riza Pasha Rikabi, a high official in the city who was also a secret Arab nationalist, and warned him against the kind of premature rising that Nesib el Bekri might advocate. After this, he continued south, visiting Druse leaders. As he passed through each tribal territory, he was provided with a new escort.

His final call was at Azrak, a desert oasis about fifty miles east of Amman, where he saw Nuri Shalaan. Nuri's influence was so great that his co-operation, whether open or covert, would be essential to Feisal's northern campaigns. Although he was sympathetic to the Arab cause, the economic welfare of his tribes depended on Turkish goodwill, and at this

stage he could not have openly declared for Feisal even if he had wanted
to. Moreover, like many Arab nationalists in the north, he was deeply
mistrustful of British and French intentions. These doubts were continually fuelled by Turkish propaganda.

Nuri was, by any standards, a grim figure. Lawrence wrote in *Seven
Pillars*: 'he was very old; livid, and worn, with a grey sorrow and remorse upon him and a bitter smile the only mobility of his face. Upon his
coarse eyelashes the eyelids sagged down in tired folds, through which,
from the overhead sun, a red light glittered into his eye sockets and made
them look like fiery pits in which the man was slowly burning. Only the
dead black of his dyed hair, only the dead skin of the face, with its net of
lines, betrayed his seventy years.' Nuri's rule was absolute, and he had
killed two of his brothers in his rise to power: 'he had none of the
wheedling diplomacy of the ordinary sheikh; a word, and there was an
end of opposition, or of his opponent.'

Lawrence found this visit to Azrak very distressing. He later wrote:
'The abyss opened before me suddenly . . . when in his tent old Nuri
Shaalan bringing out his documents asked me bluntly which of the British
promises were to be believed. I saw that with my answer I would gain or
lose him: and in him the fortune of the Arab movement: and by my
advice, that he should trust the latest in date of contradictory pledges, I
passed definitely into the class of principal. In the Hedjaz the Sherifs were
everything, and ourselves accessory: but in this distant north the repute of
Mecca was low, and that of England very great. Our importance grew:
our words were more weighty: indeed a year later I was almost the chief
crook of our gang.'

It seems that Nuri extracted some kind of personal pledge from Lawrence: if Britain failed the Arabs, Lawrence would submit himself to
dreadful retribution, perhaps even death. When asked, years later, what
the pledge had been, he replied: 'Prefer not to reveal'. Whatever it was,
the bargain was to cause him a great deal of anguish later in the war. At
the time, however, it may have seemed a way out of the moral dilemma
that had spurred him to make this northern journey.

Lawrence returned safely to Nebk on June 18, and took up the responsibilities he had been unable to evade. From now on, he would do everything in his power to see that Britain honoured her commitments: 'I
salved myself with the hope that, by leading these Arabs madly in the
final victory I would establish them, with arms in their hands, in a
position so assured (if not dominant) that expediency would counsel to

the Great Powers a fair settlement of their claims. In other words, I presumed (seeing no other leader with the will and power) that I would survive the campaigns, and be able to defeat not merely the Turks on the battlefield, but my own country and its allies in the council-chamber. It was an immodest presumption . . . it is clear that I had no shadow of leave to engage the Arabs, unknowing, in such hazard. I risked the fraud, on my conviction that Arab help was necessary to our cheap and speedy victory in the East, and that better we win and break our word than lose.'

By the time he reached Nebk, the recruitment had been completed. The expedition, now a substantial force, moved to Bair. From there, Nasir began to make contact with tribesmen to the west of Maan. Their help would be needed in the operation to take control of the road towards Akaba. While this was going on, Lawrence took a small raiding party to blow up the railway much farther north. His aim was to give the impression that Nasir's force, whose presence near Maan had been reported to the Turks, would shortly move up into the Hauran. He set out from Bair on June 20.

After three days he left the main group, making a detour which was scarcely less hazardous than his earlier journey. Taking only one or two companions, he visited the Yarmuk valley, in the hope of damaging an important bridge carrying the railway which branched west from Deraa into Palestine. He had no success, but the reconnaissance was useful.

He returned to Bair on June 28, to find that Nasir was ready to carry out the first stage of the Akaba plan. The main force moved to Jefer, some thirty miles east of Maan, where it was to wait in readiness. Meanwhile, the tribesmen Nasir had previously contacted to the west attacked and captured Fuweila, a Turkish post which covered the head of the pass between Maan and the descent towards Akaba. This was where the track leading down towards Wadi Itm was to be blocked.

As soon as news came that this had been done, other parties began raiding north of Maan and attacking the railway to the south. It was hoped that these operations would distract Turkish attention from the Akaba road, but they failed to do so. The Turks in Maan learned very quickly about the trouble at Fuweila and, by coincidence, were in a position to do something about it. They had just been reinforced by a fresh battalion, and this was immediately sent out. It drove the tribesmen out of Fuweila and occupied the important springs at Aba el Lissan nearby.

When Nasir, Auda, and Lawrence heard the news, they realised that they must defeat or at least contain this unwelcome force. As long as it was free to move, the Akaba plan would be hopeless. By dawn on July 2, their forces had surrounded the Turkish battalion at Aba el Lissan, and all day long Arab snipers harassed it from hiding places on higher ground. Finally, at dusk, the position was charged, and the terrified defenders scattered. Three hundred Turks were killed and 160 taken prisoner, while the Arabs lost only two men. Lawrence himself took part in this last stage of the battle, but during the charge he accidentally shot his camel in the head and was thrown to the ground.

When he interrogated some of the prisoners he learned that Maan itself was very lightly defended. It seemed that the Arabs might easily capture the town, and some of their leaders were keen to try, as they had little food and Maan offered rich prospects of loot. Lawrence, however, re-sisted the temptation. Once taken, Maan would be impossible to hold. He wrote in *Seven Pillars*: 'We had no support, no regulars, no guns, no base nearer than Wejh, no communications, no money even, for our gold was exhausted, and we were issuing our own notes, promises to pay ''when Akaba is taken'', for daily expenses. Besides, one did not change a strategic scheme to follow up a tactical success. We must push to the coast, and reopen sea-contact with Suez.'

The decision to leave Maan alone marked, in effect, the end of the adventure, since the fall of Akaba was now a foregone conclusion. Hav-ing set up a garrison at Aba el Lissan, the victorious Arab force made its way downwards, across the Guweira plain and into the Wadi Itm, where many of the Turkish posts proved to be empty. The only real opposition was at Khadra, the main fortified position at the mouth of the wadi. However, the defences there had been designed to resist an attack from the sea, not from inland, and the outnumbered Turks found themselves in a hopeless situation. After some negotiation they surrendered, and on July 6, eight weeks after leaving Wejh, the Arabs entered Akaba.

They found little food in the town for their own needs, let alone those of their 650 Turkish prisoners. Apart from the ruins of a sixteenth-century stone fort, the place was merely a village of mud and rubble houses. Supplies were required very urgently, and as soon as the necessary de-fensive posts had been established, Lawrence set out with a small party along the old pilgrimage road across Sinai to Suez. They completed the 160-mile journey from Akaba almost without stopping, in forty-nine hours.

He was not expected. Only four days earlier, Clayton had written: 'It is not known what are the present whereabouts of Captain Lawrence, who left for the Maan area or Jebel Druse area some time ago'.

Lawrence travelled up from Suez to Cairo by rail. At Ismailia station, where he had to change trains, he noticed a party of high-ranking officers, one of whom was Admiral Wemyss. Although Lawrence was haggard and virtually unrecognisable in Arab dress, he managed to catch the eye of Wemyss's Flag Captain, Burmester. Within hours a storeship was on its way to Akaba.

CHAPTER 11

The Consequences of Akaba

July–August 1917

BY July 9, when Lawrence reached Suez, he had been out of touch with events in Egypt and the Hejaz for two months. During this period, the earlier hopes of military success on both these fronts had been dashed.

In Sinai, Murray's army had been rebuffed a second time at Gaza, with heavy losses. When the scale of the defeat became known in London, Murray had been recalled, and on June 28 General Sir Edmund Allenby arrived in Cairo to take his place.

In the Hejaz, the promised operations against Medina had failed to materialise. During the spring and summer of 1917 a succession of bitterly pessimistic assessments had come in from Newcombe, Garland, Hornby, and other British officers in the field. As early as May, Newcombe had concluded that, of the forces at his disposal, only seven people (including himself) were actually doing any harm to the Turk, 'and our feeble efforts only annoy him slightly. Meanwhile I am asked to be patient with the bedouin, and not to punish or be severe . . . It is obvious from this and former reports, that either all of us are wasting our time here, instead of getting on with the war, or an entirely new line must be taken.' He had demanded that a particular Arab should be disciplined, failing which he had asked that he himself should be posted away from the Hejaz.

The general despondency among British officers in the Hejaz must have led the Cairo staff to doubt that Hussein's armies were capable of achieving very much more. Nonetheless, it had now been agreed in principle that Feisal should be allowed to raid the northern railways if he could find a way of doing so. These were the main Turkish lines of communication to Palestine and the Hejaz, and Arab action against them would be useful to the British army blocked outside Gaza.

Lawrence reached Cairo at midday on July 10 and immediately called on Clayton, who was astonished to see him. Their first discussion was taken up with the question of sending supplies and money to Nasir, and other steps necessary to consolidate the Arab position at Akaba. Lawrence spent little time explaining how the town had been captured. Instead, he handed Clayton a brief report on the expedition and his secret journeys farther north.

Within hours, the Arab victory was the talk of GHQ. Such news was especially welcome after the failure at Gaza. When his success was set alongside the dismal results from the Hejaz, it was obvious that Lawrence had a special talent for leading the bedouin. Recognition of this fact gave new authority to his ideas about future action, and he set out a scheme of operations which the Arabs of Syria might be able to undertake in conjunction with an advance by the British Army in Palestine.

Clayton was naturally impressed that a force of tribesmen had been able to take Akaba without British foreknowledge or support. He therefore considered these proposals very carefully. In due course General Allenby sent for Lawrence, partly to congratulate him on the Akaba victory, and partly to question him about these new and interesting projects.

Despite his recent achievements, Lawrence must have been extremely anxious about the meeting, since the future of Feisal's northern campaign was in the hands of the EEF. If Allenby were unsympathetic, the Revolt might yet be confined to the Hejaz. Lawrence therefore sketched the future military value of Arab co-operation in generous terms. There were rumours that the Cabinet wanted Jerusalem captured by Christmas, and he stressed the contribution that the Arabs could make to such a victory by cutting Turkish lines of communication at Deraa.

The meeting undoubtedly had its comic side. Allenby, a cavalry general fresh from the Western Front, was then fifty-six. He was a large man, every inch a commander, whose ferocity when angered was legendary. He must have been surprised when Lawrence arrived dressed in white silk Arab skirts and head-cloth, resplendent with gold-bound headrope and dagger. However, this unconventional garb had not been a matter of choice: Lawrence's army uniform had been ravaged by moth while stored in Cairo, and he had not yet been able to replace it.

Following these discussions, detailed proposals were drawn up at the Arab Bureau. Clayton then drafted a memorandum on the subject for Allenby. Having noted Lawrence's view that a revolt in Syria was not dependent on further military achievement in the Hejaz, he listed the objectives that might be achieved by Arab guerillas working far behind Turkish lines in Syria, notably the destruction of railway bridges and other damage to Turkish lines of communication. In addition, Lawrence thought that if one of the larger Yarmuk bridges could be demolished, it would be possible to launch 'a general attack on Deraa and the three railways running north, south, and west from it, from the Gebel Hauran, by a force of probably 8,000 Arabs and Druses. These, while not "storm-troops," are respectable fighting men, and should be able to occupy most of the area and the approaches to it. Their success would lead to risings of a local character in the hills between the Jordan and the Hejaz Railway, from Deraa to opposite Jericho, and to similar risings in the hills along the Nazareth–Damascus roads.'

There were, however, two very important conditions which would have to be met if these plans were to be implemented. First, Allenby must provide the necessary material and financial support. Second: 'The above operations are entirely contingent on a decision to undertake major operations in Palestine with which the movement of the Arabs must synchronise. If minor operations only are intended in Palestine, the Arab operations as suggested above would probably lead to the destruction of many of the Arab elements, and most certainly to that of the Druses, were they to take action. Unless operations of such magnitude as to occupy the whole of the Turkish Army in Palestine were undertaken, the proposed Arab operations must be abandoned.' In other words, the British must not trigger an Arab revolt in Syria and then allow it to fail.

Neither Clayton nor Allenby believed that all the actions Lawrence proposed would take place, but even a few of them would be useful. Allenby telegraphed details to the War Office, noting: 'Captain Lawrence . . . is quite confident that provided the necessary measure of material assistance is afforded by us, this could be successfully carried out.' The possible benefits to British efforts in Sinai and Palestine were obvious, and here Allenby repeated Clayton's memorandum almost word for word: 'There is no doubt that Turkish railway communications south of Aleppo would be seriously disorganised even by the partial success of Lawrence's scheme, whilst its complete success would effectively destroy [the Turks'] only main artery of communication between the north Syria and Palestine and Hedjaz fronts, and possibly extensive local risings throughout the Jordan Valley might be produced.'

The capture of Akaba brought Lawrence high commendations, not least from officers who had personal experience of working with the Arabs. C. E. Wilson, who only seven months earlier had described him as a 'bumptious young ass,' now cabled to Wingate: 'I recommend strongly that Lawrence be granted a DSO immediately for his recent work . . . I am confident that the . . . successes gained against trained troops, which should have excellent results on general operations, are due to his personality, gallantry, and grit.'

The achievement that most impressed the staff in Cairo, however, was his journey into Syria. When Wingate cabled news of the fall of Akaba to the War Office he described this secret reconnaissance as 'little short of marvellous.' Lawrence's feats were admired in London, and three days later Wingate informed him that, 'The Chief of the Imperial General Staff has requested me to convey his congratulations on your recent exploit and I do so with the liveliest satisfaction. It was a very gallant and successful adventure which it has been my pleasant duty to bring to the notice of the higher authority for special recognition, and I sincerely trust this latter will not be long delayed. I hope you are taking a rest and making up some of the arrears of sleep which you must be badly in need of.'

The 'special recognition' Wingate had recommended was a Victoria Cross. In a telegram to the War Office he pointed out that the Turks had put a £5,000 reward on Lawrence's head. Knowledge of this had 'considerably enhanced the gallantry of his exploit. He was moving among a highly venal population, of whom some at least were definitely hostile. In spite of this, he seized every opportunity of damaging the railway, interviewing tribesmen and obtaining information regarding the country and its inhabitants, and finally successfully directed the operation in the Maan region, the result of which was that 700 Turks were destroyed and 500 captured.

'I strongly recommend him for an immediate award of the Victoria Cross, and submit that this recommendation is amply justified by his skill, pluck and endurance.'

The irony of this praise was completely lost on Lawrence's superiors. They would have been shocked to know that he had made the northern journey hoping that it would end his involvement in the Arab war. He was relieved, therefore, when a technicality prevented the award of a VC (the journey had not been witnessed by another British officer). Instead, he was shortly afterwards appointed a Companion of the Order of the Bath and promoted to the rank of major. Although the medal was primarily intended for the northern ride, this could not be publicised. Significantly, however, the CB was backdated to the day in early June when he had set out on the northern journey. His letters home show total rejection of this decoration, which he refused to acknowledge.

The essential next steps in Lawrence's scheme were to move Feisal's headquarters up to Akaba and make sufficient defensive arrangements to hold the track through Wadi Itm against recapture. This would provide access to the Syrian interior, enabling raiding parties to harass the Turkish lines of communication. In the longer term, the settled peoples south of Damascus could be prepared for the Revolt. Lawrence later wrote: 'When the Hauran joined us our campaign would be well ended.

'The process should be to set up another ladder of tribes, comparable to that by which we had climbed from Wejh to Akaba: only this time our ladder would be made of steps of Howeitat, Beni Sakhr, Sherarat, Rualla, and Serahin, to raise us to Azrak, the desert oasis nearest Hauran or Jebel Druse. We needed to reach more than three hundred miles—a long stride without railways or roads, but one which would be made safe and comfortable for us by an assiduous cultivation of desert power, the control by camel-parties of the desolate and unmapped wilderness of mid-Arabia from Mecca to Aleppo and Bagdad.

'In character our operations . . . should be like naval war, in their mobility, their ubiquity, their independence of bases and lack of communications . . . Camel raiding-parties, self-contained like ships, might cruise without danger along the enemy's cultivation frontier, and tap or raid into his lines where it seemed easiest or fittest or most profitable, with always a sure retreat behind them into the desert-element which the Turks could not explore . . . Our fighting tactics should be always tip and run: not pushes, but strokes. We should never try to maintain or improve an advantage, but should move off to strike again somewhere else. We should use the smallest force in the quickest time at the farthest place . . .

'The necessary speed and range at which to strike, if we were to make war in this distant fashion, would be attained through the extreme frugality of the desert men, and their high efficiency when mounted on their female riding camels . . . Our six weeks' food would give us capacity for a thousand miles out and home.'

The transfer of Feisal's base from Wejh to Akaba would mean the end of the El Ula scheme. After some debate, however, Lawrence gained his point. Doubtless the advantages to Allenby of a northern campaign outweighed the irritation of a continuing stalemate in the Hejaz. It was therefore agreed that Wejh would be closed down, and that Joyce should move up to Akaba as senior British officer.

Another major change proposed by Lawrence was that in future Feisal and his army should be placed directly under Allenby's command. In the north, Feisal would have to co-operate with the EEF rather than the forces of Ali or Abdullah. Moreover, Akaba was seven hundred miles from Mecca, but only one hundred miles from Allenby's advance headquarters. It was logical to place the Arab northern army under Allenby's overall command, if Hussein would accept this arrangement. Lawrence therefore set off for Jidda on July 17, to seek Hussein's agreement and to talk with Wilson about plans for the move to Akaba.

On the following day, a cable was received in Cairo from the War Office approving Lawrence's northern proposals. Allenby's reply, on July 19, shows that Arab action now played a significant part in his plans for a September offensive: 'The advantages offered by Arab co-operation on the lines proposed by Captain Lawrence are, in my opinion, of such importance that no effort should be spared to reap full benefit therefrom.'

Lawrence called in at Wejh on his way south to Jidda, hoping to see Feisal. He was taken by air to the inland headquarters set up by New-combe and Joyce near the railway. Feisal was delighted to learn that there was now approval for large-scale northern operations, and at Lawrence's request wrote letters to Hussein urging the transfer of his army to Allen-by's command. He also took steps to send Arab reinforcements to Akaba straight away.

On July 22 Lawrence reached Jidda where he discussed with Wilson personnel and other requirements for the new base at Akaba. Wilson readily agreed to this move, having always favoured the idea of a Syrian campaign. He knew that action against the railway in the north would directly affect Turkish supplies to Medina, and for the present he was thoroughly disillusioned about the chances of further success in the Hejaz. He offered to transfer five of his most experienced British liaison officers to Feisal's army in Syria.

He had originally intended to send Newcombe to Akaba as well, but after discussing the matter with Lawrence he wrote: 'I understand that his services will not be required for the Emir Feisal's operations'. New-combe's recent reports, seen by Lawrence in Cairo, suggested that his period of usefulness with the Arabs was at an end. Not long after this he left the Hejaz for service with the EEF.

The duties of the officers transferred to Akaba were set out by Clayton as follows: 'Captain Lawrence—to serve with Beduin troops and to advise and, as far as possible, direct their operations.

'Lieut. Col. Joyce—to advise and control the trained Arab troops under Jaafar Pasha. These troops will be concentrated at Akaba and will form the garrison of that place. Should future developments require it they will be available for service in the Hauran as support to the Druses.

'Capt. Goslett, A.S.C.—to be supply officer at Akaba and in charge of all consignments sent from Egypt or the Hejaz.' Captain W. E. Marshall, chief medical officer in the Hejaz, and H. S. Hornby, an engineer experienced in railway demolition, were also to accompany the northern army.

Arrangements had already been made to transport part of Feisal's regular army to Akaba. The remainder, under Jaafar Pasha, would be taken there in late August with Feisal himself.

A few days earlier, Wilson had written to Hussein, asking for a meeting: 'Captain Lawrence, of whom your Highness has heard, has arrived here today; he was with Sherif Nasir, and has himself been north of Damascus and seen various Sheikhs. He saw Emir Faisal at Wedj and has seen His Excellency the High Commissioner and His Excellency the General Officer Commanding in Chief in Egypt . . . Captain Lawrence and I go to Cairo in four days' time and I would much like to have the honour of meeting your Highness with Captain Lawrence before we go, as there are matters for which your Highness's approval is necessary.' Thus it came about that on July 28 Lawrence met the Sherif of Mecca for the first time.

Both Lawrence and Wilson had expected Hussein to make difficulties over the transfer of Feisal's army to Allenby's command. In the event, however, Hussein did not oppose the idea, and signed a letter confirming Feisal's appointment as Supreme Commander of all Arab forces operating northwards from Akaba: 'The Emir Faisal will have a free hand to deal direct with the British General Commander-in-Chief in all military matters, which will facilitate the co-operation between my army and that of Great Britain.' This diplomatic formula maintained the fiction that the Arab forces were operating as an independent command, while ensuring that in future the British would be able to direct Feisal's operations without needing to secure Hussein's approval.

Characteristically, Hussein took up the rest of this meeting with a lengthy and none-too-lucid exposition of his religious views. Although he claimed to have renounced any ambition for the Caliphate, it was clear that he was still hoping for some position of greater spiritual authority in the Arab world. Lawrence found this unexpected topic of considerable interest, and wrote a detailed account of the conversation.

On the following day Hussein asked to see Lawrence again, and used the meeting to give his version of the discussions with Sykes and Georges-Picot in May. Lawrence had doubtless heard from Wilson and others that the talks had been singularly unsatisfactory. Far from setting out the true political situation in clear, unambiguous terms, Sykes and Georges-Picot had left the matter more confused than ever. The only agreement to emerge had been a vague understanding that France would act in Syria on the same basis as Britain in Baghdad. Both Georges-Picot and Hussein had been delighted with this formula, but only because each put a completely different construction upon it. Georges-Picot, familiar with the Sykes-Picot terms, thought that Britain intended to impose direct rule in Baghdad: he could therefore claim that Hussein had agreed to direct French rule throughout Syria. Hussein, on the other hand, was working on the basis of his correspondence with McMahon. He believed that permanent British rule of Baghdad was not intended, and that by this new understanding France had relinquished her claims in both Syria and Lebanon. This deceitful formula had been suggested by Sykes, who doubtless regarded the 'agreement' as a personal triumph. When Wilson discovered the role that Sykes had played, he was disgusted.

While Lawrence was at Jidda, an alarming message was received from Egypt. In Clayton's words: 'It was reported by Agent "Y" during the week, that Auda Abu Tayi (who was Captain Lawrence's right-hand man during the recent operations in the Maan-Akaba area) had written to the Turks giving as his reason for rebelling, that presents had been given [by the Turks] to Nuri Shalaan and not to him, but that he was now willing to come in under certain conditions, and had written twice to the G.O.C. 8th Army Corps [in Maan] asking for a present.'

This news was most disturbing. Auda had been entrusted with the defence of Guweira, an important post on the route from Akaba to Maan. The Turks had already recaptured Aba el Lissan, and were bombing the Arab forces closer to Akaba. If the Howeitat abandoned their positions before Feisal's regulars arrived, there would be little to prevent the Turks retaking the Wadi Itm. Such an outcome would be fatal to the whole northern campaign. Lawrence travelled up to Akaba as quickly as possible and went inland to confront Auda with knowledge of this treachery. There were embarrassed explanations from both Auda and Mohammed el Dheilan, another Howeitat leader. Lawrence seems not to have been convinced of their innocence, but he laid stress on the bounty that Feisal would shortly distribute, and hoped that the shock of such rapid discovery would discourage them from further wavering.

After this hurried visit to Akaba, Lawrence spent a week in Egypt, where he and Wilson took part in further detailed discussions at the Arab Bureau. He had by this time decided that his experiences during the Revolt would make a magnificent subject for a book. The idea had been forming in his mind for some while, and ever since his permanent posting to Feisal in February, he had made descriptive jottings. He mentioned the project to Wilson and others during their talks in Cairo.

There was also a more immediate writing project: in an attempt to pass on the secrets of his success in dealing with the Arabs, Lawrence drew up a set of guidelines called 'Twenty-seven Articles'. These were published in the *Arab Bulletin* later that month. It is clear from these 'articles' that Lawrence had now assumed a role of covert leadership: 'Your ideal position is when you are present and not noticed. Do not be too intimate, too prominent, or too earnest. Avoid being identified too long or too often with any tribal sheikh, even if C.O. of the expedition. To do your work you must be above jealousies, and you lose prestige if you are associated with a tribe or clan, and its inevitable feuds. Sherifs are above all blood-feuds and local rivalries, and form the only principle of unity among the Arabs. Let your name therefore be coupled always with a Sherif's, and share his attitude towards the tribes. When the moment comes for action put yourself publicly under his orders. The Bedu will then follow suit . . . The foreigner and Christian is not a popular person in Arabia. However friendly and informal the treatment of yourself may be, remember always that your foundations are very sandy ones. Wave a Sherif in front of you like a banner, and hide your own mind and person. If you succeed you will have hundreds of miles of country and thousands of men under your orders, and for this it is worth bartering the outward show . . .

'While very difficult to drive, the Bedu are easy to lead, if you have the patience to bear with them. The less apparent your interferences the more your influence. They are willing to follow your advice and do what you wish, but they do not mean you or anyone else to be aware of that. It is only after the end of all annoyances that you find at bottom their real fund of good will.'

Lawrence returned to Akaba on August 17, just after his twenty-ninth birthday. Three days later Doynel de Saint-Quentin, of the French military liaison staff in Egypt, drew up a confidential summary of his career and achievements for the War Office in Paris. He wrote: 'This officer, whose name has often appeared in correspondence from Cairo, is probably the most outstanding figure of the British army or administration in the east.'

CHAPTER 12

The First Syrian Campaign
August–December 1917

BY mid-August the transformation of Akaba into a military base was well under way. The Navy had stationed HMS *Humber* there as guardship and headquarters, and the presence of a British warship did much to bolster Arab morale. Meanwhile, other vessels of the Red Sea Patrol ferried men, animals and stores up from Wejh.

Nasir had been steadily recruiting, and when he was joined by Feisal hundreds of new volunteers came in every day. Lawrence wrote: 'The slide of Arabs towards the Sherif . . . has become immense, almost impossible, since Feisul arrived. He is unable even to see all the head sheikhs of the newcomers.' One result of the increasing numbers at Akaba was that supply problems became acute.

Although the Turks had kept up some pressure against Arab outposts, there had not yet been any major offensive. It was known, however, that they were preparing for action, and in the meantime aircraft flying from Maan were doing a great deal of damage to Arab morale. On August 28 and 29, however, four RFC aircraft raided Maan, Fuweila and Aba el Lissan. This unexpected attack again checked the Turks.

The Arab military situation was nonetheless worrying. Although Akaba itself could be protected, the important defensive line was far inland. The future of the Syrian campaign depended on local bedouin who would fare badly if the Turkish forces at Maan launched a full-scale attack.

Lawrence was confident that the Turks at Maan would not risk a full-scale attack until they had been substantially reinforced, and he saw that offence might be the best form of protecting Akaba from attack. He therefore proposed a raid on the Railway between Maan and Mudowwara, 113km farther south, writing: 'There are seven waterless stations here, and I have hope that with the Stokes and Lewis guns we may be able to do something fairly serious to the line. If we can make a big break I will do my best to maintain it . . . As soon as the Railway attack is begun a force of "regulars" will enter the Shobek–Kerak hills [north-west of Maan] and try to occupy them.

'If these operations are part-successful, the Turkish force at Fuweileh

195

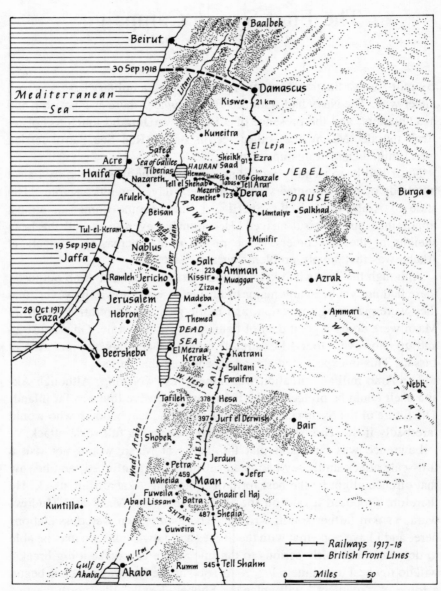

Baalbek

Beirut

Mediterranean Sea

30 Sep 1918

Litani

Damascus

Kiswe • 21 km

• Kuneitra

El Leja

Safed
Acre
Sea of Galilee
Haifa
Tiberias
Nazareth
HAURAN
Sheikh • Saad
91 • Ezra
Hemme • umkeis
Tabas • *JEBEL*
Tell el Shehab • 106 • Ghazale
Tell Arar
Mezerib
Remthe • 123 • **Deraa**
DRUSE
Burga •

Afuleh •

Beisan •

• Umtaiye • Salkhad

Tul-el-Keram

Wadi Fara

ADWAN

• Minifir

19 Sep 1918

Nablus •

River Jordan

Jaffa

Salt •
223
Kissir •
Ziza •
Amman
• Muaggar

• Azrak

Ramleh • Jericho

Jerusalem
Hebron •

Madeba •

Themed •

• Ammari

28 Oct 1917
Gaza

DEAD SEA

El Mezraa •
Kerak •

Katrani

Sultani •

• Faraifra

W. Hesa

RAILWAY

Beersheba •

Tafileh • 378 • Hesa

Wadi Araba

397 • Jurf el Derwish

• Bair

• Nebk

WADI SIRHAN

Shobek •

HEJAZ

• Jerdun

• Petra
459
Waheida •
Fuweila •
Maan
• Jefer

Kuntilla •

Abael Lissan • Batra •
• Ghadir el Haj

SHTAR

487 • Shedia

• Guweira

| Railways 1917-18
|---|
| British Front Lines |

W. Itm

Gulf of Akaba
Akaba

• Rumm 545 • Tell Shahm

0　　Miles　　50

The Syrian Campaigns

will probably be withdrawn, or reduced, and our position at Akaba then becomes safe.'

On September 1, Clayton came down to Akaba and held lengthy discussions with Lawrence and Feisal about the strategic situation. While there, he produced a dramatic letter from Sykes, which raised all kinds of issues in Lawrence's mind. Sykes had been greatly upset by events which had taken place in London during his absence in the Middle East. He wrote: 'I found that the Foreign Office had been carefully destroying everything I had done in the past two years. Stimulating anti-*Entente* feeling, and pushing separate negotiations-with-Turkey ideas. Indeed I just arrived in the nick of time.'

If Lawrence had not already heard rumours of the secret moves to make peace with Turkey, this letter provided sufficient warning. Even while Sykes had been writing, Aubrey Herbert had been holding discussions with a Turkish representative in Geneva. In the event, nothing ever came of these talks, but contacts between Britain and Turkey were to continue throughout the remainder of the war, and at times it seemed that a peace treaty was within reach.

Lawrence realised that the fate of the Arabs might be greatly influenced by such negotiations. He later wrote: 'I had always the lurking fear that Great Britain might . . . conclude its own separate peace . . . with the Conservative Turks. The British Government had gone very far in this direction, without informing her smallest ally. Our information of the precise steps, and of the proposals (which would have been fatal to so many of the Arabs in arms on our side), came, not officially, to me, but privately. It was only one of the twenty times in which friends helped me more than did our Government'.

Sykes's letter to Clayton continued with an exhortation to uphold the Anglo-French alliance: 'there is only one possible policy, the *Entente* first and last, and the Arab nation the child of the *Entente*. Get your Englishmen to stand up to the Arabs on this . . . Colonialism is madness and I believe Picot and I can prove it to them. Lawrence's move [i.e. the capture of Akaba] is splendid and I want him knighted. Tell him now that he is a great man he must behave as such and be broad in his views. Ten years' tutelage under the *Entente* and the Arabs will be a nation. Complete independence means Persia, poverty and chaos. Let him consider this, as he hopes for the people he is fighting for.'

The anti-imperialist note in this letter was a new element in Sykes's rhetoric, and it has to be seen in the context of events elsewhere in the world. On April 1 the United States had entered the war, infuriated by German attacks on merchant shipping. However, President Wilson had stated unequivocally that America would not tolerate a scramble for new colonies in the wake of victory. In a speech to the American Senate, he had warned: 'No peace can last, or ought to last, which does not recognize and accept the principle that governments derive all their just powers from the consent of the governed, and that no right anywhere exists to hand peoples about from sovereignty to sovereignty as if they were property.'

A similar policy had been adopted by Russia, now under Kerensky's provisional government after the fall of the Tsarist regime in March. Kerensky demanded an assurance that Britain agreed with the policy of self-determination laid down in Wilson's speech. The British Government complied, fearing that Russia would be prompted to stop fighting; it also expressed its willingness 'to examine and, if need be, to revise' any existing agreements that were found to contravene Wilson's principles.

Liberal-minded Englishmen readily accepted that if the Central Powers were defeated, the future of their colonies should be resolved according to the principle of self-determination. This new form of idealism had quickly entered the political debate about Britain's proper war aims, and Sykes was very sensitive about it. His secret agreement with Georges-Picot was a flagrant contradiction of Wilson's policy, and association with such an imperialist measure could pose a threat to his own political career. A few days before writing to Clayton, he had drawn up a memorandum demanding that in future the agreement should be called the Anglo-French-Arab Agreement, not the Sykes-Picot Agreement.

Sykes's letter to Clayton also contained a passing reference to the Zionist question. It was well known that he was interested in this subject, and the British staff in Egypt also knew that some kind of discussions on the matter were taking place in London. Jewish ambitions in Palestine were common knowledge in Cairo, where Aaron Aaronson, a prominent figure in the movement, was hoping to set up a Zionist office. Lawrence had good reason to be interested in a question that so obviously affected the aspirations of the Palestinian Arabs.

On September 7, he wrote to Sykes at length, asking both about Zionist aims and about the future of the Sykes-Picot Agreement. He sent this letter to Clayton, with the comment: 'Some of it is really thirst for information, and other is only a wish to stick pins into him . . . One must have the Jewish section cleared up: and I fancy we may (if we win) clear up the French section ourselves.'

Lawrence wrote to Sykes: 'General Clayton showed me a letter from you which contained a message to myself—and this has prompted me to ask you a few queries about Near East affairs. I hope you will be able to give me an idea of how matters stand in reference to them, since part of the responsibility of action is inevitably thrown on to me, and unless I know more or less what is wanted there might be trouble.

'About the Jews in Palestine, Feisal has agreed not to operate or agitate west of the [Wadi] Araba–Dead Sea–Jordan line, or south of the Haifa–Beisan line . . .

'You know of course the root differences between the Palestine Jew and the colonist Jew: to Feisal the important point is that the former speak Arabic, and the latter German Yiddish. He is in touch with the Arab Jews (their H.Q. at Safed and Tiberias is in his sphere) and they are ready to help him, on conditions. They show a strong antipathy to the colonist Jews, and have even suggested repressive measures against them. Feisal has ignored this point hitherto, and will continue to do so. His attempts to get into touch with the colonial Jews have not been very fortunate. They say they have made their arrangements with the Great Powers, and wish no contact with the Arab Party. They will not help the Turks or the Arabs.

'Now Feisal wants to know (information had better come to me for him since I usually like to make up my mind before he does) what is the arrangement standing between the colonist Jews (called Zionists sometimes) and the Allies . . . What have you promised the Zionists, and what is their programme?

'I saw Aaronson in Cairo, and he said at once the Jews intended to acquire the land-rights of all Palestine from Gaza to Haifa, and have practical autonomy therein. Is this acquisition to be by fair purchase or by forced sale and expropriation? The present half-crop peasantry were the old freeholders and under Moslem landlords may be ground down but have fixity of tenure. Arabs are usually not employed by Jewish colonies. Do the Jews propose the complete expulsion of the Arab peasantry, or their reduction to a day-labourer class?

'You know how the Arabs cling even to bad land and will realise that while Arab feelings didn't matter under Turkish rule . . . the condition will be vastly different if there is a new, independent, and rather cock-a-hoop Arab state north and east and south of the Jewish state. I can see a situation arising in which the Jewish influence in European finance might not be sufficient to deter the Arab peasants from refusing to quit—or worse!'

As regards the French, he wrote: 'The Arabs can put their revolt through without French help, and therefore are disinclined to pay a price only to be made known to them in the future. You say they will need French help afterwards in the development of Syria—but do you really imagine anyone in Syria (bar Christians) wants to develop Syria? Why this craze for change? A slow progress, utilising only the surplus resources of Syria itself, seems to me more desirable than foreign borrowing, and a forcing-bed of public enterprises; and I think this point of view will be uppermost in the minds of the Damascus Government . . .

'I don't think the Sykes-Picot [Agreement] can stand as things are. The Sherif will succeed, given time and a continuance of our help: he will take by his own efforts (don't assume virtue for the mules and cartridges we supply him: the hands and heads are his) the sphere we allotted to our foreign-advised "independent Syria", and will expect to keep it without imposed foreign advisers. As he takes this sphere of his, he will also take parts of the other spheres not properly allotted to an Arab state. His title to them will be a fairly strong one—that of conquest by the means of the local inhabitants—and what are the two Powers going to do about it?'

Clayton decided not to send this letter on to Sykes. Instead, he wrote back to Lawrence: 'Mark has, as far as I can gather from Hogarth, rather dropped the Near East just now and the whole question is, for the moment, somewhat derelict. All the better, and I am somewhat apprehensive lest your letter to Mark may raise him to activity. From all I can hear the Sykes-Picot agreement is in considerable disfavour in most quarters . . . I am inclined . . . to think that it is moribund. At the same time we are pledged in honour to France not to give it the *coup de grâce* and must for the present act loyally up to it, in so far as we can. In brief, I think we can at present leave it alone as far as possible with a very fair chance of its dying of inanition. As you know, I have been of this opinion from the beginning . . . The Sykes-Picot agreement was made nearly two years ago. The world has moved at so vastly increased a pace since then that it is now as old and out of date as the Battle of Waterloo or the death of Queen Anne. It is in fact dead and, if we wait quietly, this fact will soon be realized: it was never a very workable instrument and it is now almost a lifeless monument. At the same time we cannot expect the French to see this yet, and we must therefore play up to it as loyally as possible until force of circumstances brings it home to them.'

On September 7 Lawrence set out from Akaba intending to raid the railway south of Maan. By far the most important target was Mudawara station, where there was the only significant water supply in 150km of the line between Maan and Dhat el Haj (itself 84km north of Tebuk). If the water installations at Mudawara could be destroyed, it would become extremely difficult for the Turks to work traffic over this section. To cross it, trains would have to carry so much water that they would be able to transport little else. In Lawrence's eyes, an attack on Mudawara had several merits. First, it would divert Turkish resources that might otherwise be used in attempts to retake Akaba. Secondly, it would be a severe blow against the Turkish line of communication to Medina. Thirdly, a really successful raid would do much to re-establish Arab morale.

As so often in these bedouin operations, he found that his original plan could not be carried out. He had hoped to raise a force of three hundred Howeitat at Guweira, sufficient to capture the station at Mudawara. However, the scheme was frustrated by tribal friction, lack of commitment to Feisal, and the fact that some of the men he had hoped to recruit had not yet been paid by Auda for earlier services. Eventually, Lawrence was obliged to return to Akaba. After some negotiations, he managed to raise a smaller force, but when he reached Mudawara on September 17 he quickly realised that he would be unable to take it. Instead, he moved to another point on the railway and the following day successfully mined a train, using for the first time an electric exploder rather than an automatic detonator. Two English machine-gun instructors working at Akaba had accompanied the expedition, and their accurate fire contributed greatly to the success of the operation.

Lawrence returned to Akaba on September 22. A few days later he wrote to his Oxford friend E. T. Leeds: 'I hope when the nightmare ends that I will wake up and become alive again. This killing and killing of Turks is horrible . . . you charge in at the finish and find them all over the place in bits, and still alive many of them, and know that you have done hundreds in the same way before and must do hundreds more if you can.'

On September 27 he set off for another raid. In addition to Arab tribesmen, he took Captain Pisani, the French gunner who had come to Akaba, and three educated Syrians who were to be taught to use explosives. He hoped that by training them he would free himself from the need to take part in attacks on the line, as he would be more usefully employed carrying out liaison duties at Feisal's headquarters. Again, there was severe damage to an engine, which Lawrence judged to be beyond repair.

*   *   *

When he returned to Akaba, on October 8, he found a telegram requesting him to go to EEF headquarters in Sinai. An aeroplane was sent from
Suez to collect him, and on October 12 he reached GHQ, at that time to
the north of El Arish. There he found Clayton and Hogarth, and was
briefed on plans for a major autumn offensive. As expected, orders had
come from London for the capture of Jaffa and Jerusalem, in the hope that
this would induce Turkey to withdraw from the war.

The decision to advance left Lawrence in a depressing quandary. In
July, when he had sketched out his ideas for Arab action, he had expected
Feisal to establish himself at Akaba without difficulty. In the event,
however, there had been severe problems over supply and sickness, and
Arab morale was very low. So long as the Wadi Itm route was insecure,
it would be impossible for the Arabs to embark on large-scale action
elsewhere in Syria. After these discussions, Hogarth wrote: 'Feisal does
not get any bigger—even T.E.L. admits that . . . [Lawrence] is not well
and talks rather hopelessly about the Arab future he once believed in.'

Another difficulty was that no one could tell whether or not the EEF
would advance very far. If it did not, an Arab revolt in Syria would be
fatally isolated. On the other hand, if Allenby proved to be successful, it
was important that the Arabs should be ready, on their side, to exploit any
Turkish retreat that followed. By determined action in the north, they
would be able to turn defeat into chaos. Lawrence later wrote: 'Such
would be our moment, and we needed to be ready for it in the spot where
our weight and tactics would be least expected and most damaging. For
my eyes, the centre of attraction was Deraa, the junction of the Jerusalem–
Haifa–Damascus–Medina railways, the navel of the Turkish Armies in
Syria, the common point of all their fronts; and, by chance, an area in
which lay great untouched reserves of Arab fighting men, educated and
armed by Feisal from Akaba . . . We were certain, with any management, of twelve thousand men, enough to rush Deraa, to smash all the
railway lines, even to take Damascus by surprise.'

A decisive action against the railway junction at Deraa would help
Allenby greatly and, as Lawrence knew, the tribes were only too willing
to rise. On the other hand, if the EEF failed, the consequences would be
terrible. Lawrence was therefore faced with a dilemma which Clayton
and Hogarth could well understand. In *Seven Pillars* he wrote: 'Not for
the first time or last time service to two masters irked me. I was one of
Allenby's officers, and in his confidence: in return, he expected me to do
the best I could for him. I was Feisal's adviser, and Feisal relied upon the

honesty and competence of my advice so far as often to take it without argument. Yet I could not explain to Allenby the whole Arab situation, nor disclose the full British plan to Feisal.' In an early draft of this passage Lawrence continued: 'Of course, we were fighting for an allied victory, and if in the end the sake of the English—the leading partner— was to be forwarded only by sacrificing the Arabs on the field of battle, then it would have to be done unhesitatingly; but it was hard to know just when it was the end, and necessary; and, in this case, to cast the die and lose meant to have ruined Feisal's cause.' If the Arabs took Deraa, and later had to give it up, there would be 'horrible massacres of all the splendid peasantry of the district. They would have formed the bulk of our forces in the operation and were not beduin, able to fall back into the desert when the raid ended or miscarried. They were prosperous towns-folk and villagers, who lay open, themselves, their families and their property, to the revenge of a peculiarly barbarous enemy. Accordingly they could only rise once, and their effort on that occasion must be decisive. To call them out now was to risk the best asset Feisal held for eventual success, on the speculation that Allenby's first attack would sweep the enemy before it'.

Before leaving GHQ Lawrence decided, with Clayton's support, that such a rising could not at present be justified. Instead, he proposed to go himself with a bedouin raiding party and try to destroy one of the larger railway bridges in the Yarmuk gorge. If this could be carried out at the moment of Allenby's attack, the Turkish army in Palestine would be deprived of its line of communication and retreat towards Damascus at a most critical moment. Should the EEF then succeed, a more favourable moment might arise for calling a general revolt. This scheme was put to Allenby, who approved it, and asked that the bridge should be blown up on November 5 or one of the following three days. Lawrence therefore flew back to Akaba on October 15 to make his preparations.

Neither Hogarth nor Clayton was very sanguine about his chances of destroying the bridge. Hogarth wrote shortly afterwards: 'I doubt if he will manage to get north again. Recent successes have drawn rather too many troops down onto the Maan section of the railway.' For Clayton, one of the greatest worries was Lawrence's personal safety. Raids on the desert railway involved little physical risk, except at the moment of action. What was now proposed, however, was a journey through an area of settled villages deep inside enemy territory. George Lloyd, who had gone to Akaba to see if he could be of any assistance, wrote to Clayton on October 20: 'Lawrence is quite fit but much oppressed by the risk and the magnitude of the job before him. He opened his heart to me last night and told me that he felt there was so much for him still to do in the world . . . that it seemed horrible to have it all cut off, as he feels it will be—for he feels that while he may do the job he sees little or no chance of getting away himself—I tried to cheer him up, but of course it is true . . . He is really a very remarkable fellow—not the least fearless like some who do brave things, but, as he told me last night, each time he starts out on these stunts he simply hates it for two or three days before, until movement, action and the glory of scenery and nature catch hold of him and make him well again.' Clayton wrote back: 'I am very anxious about Lawrence. He has taken on a really colossal job and I can see that it is well-nigh weighing him down. He has a lion's heart, but even so the strain must be very great. Well, he is doing a great work and as soon as may be we must pull him out and not risk him further, but the time is not yet, as he is wanted just now. The first real issue in this theatre of the war is at hand and much will depend on the doings of the next month.'

Lawrence spent ten days in Akaba before setting out on the Yarmuk expedition. Shortly before he was due to leave, the plans were radically changed when the Emir Abd el Kader arrived in Akaba offering the support of his followers. Abd el Kader was an Algerian who controlled a number of villages on the north side of the Yarmuk valley, peopled by Algerian exiles. With their support, a small raiding party could in effect command the central section of the Yarmuk line. The opportunity seemed too good to miss, and it was decided that Abd el Kader would join the expedition, despite his reputation as a Muslim fanatic. Afterwards, a warning came from Brémond that he was in the pay of the Turks. This added to Lawrence's anxiety, but there was nothing to substantiate the charge and in the end it was ignored: Brémond's feelings towards a declared enemy of France were naturally suspect.

The expedition left Akaba on October 24 with an experienced raider, Sherif Ali ibn el Hussein of the Harith tribe, as its Arab leader. Much of the force was to be recruited farther north, but Lawrence also took a party of Indian machine-gunners who had been serving for several months in the Hejaz. When the Yarmuk bridge was attacked, their steady fire could be used to hold back any Turkish reinforcements while the bedouin over-powered the guards. He also thought it wise to take an explosives specialist who would know how best to destroy the steel girder bridge, and he chose Lieutenant Wood, a sapper officer who worked as base engineer at Akaba. In this way, the operation would still have a good chance of success even if Lawrence were killed or wounded.

When they reached Jefer, Lawrence found to his annoyance that it was impossible to raise an escort of tribesmen. In *Seven Pillars* he spoke in vague terms of Howeitat dissatisfaction. A contemporary report, however, shows that he was unable to persuade them to join the Yarmuk raid because there was no prospect of loot. The party moved on to Bair, where they were able to recruit some Beni Sakhr before travelling towards Azrak, the desert oasis from which the raiding party would set out.

The expedition encountered some Serahin tribesmen who directed them to their encampment near Azrak. These tribesmen were willing to join Feisal, but were very unenthusiastic about the proposed expedition. Moreover, their news about the local situation in the Yarmuk valley was disquieting. Lawrence's original objective had been the most westerly bridge, at Hemme, which he had reconnoitred in June. It transpired that this would now be impossible, as the surrounding district was filled with Turkish wood-cutters collecting fuel. Under the current plan, one of the central bridges was to be attacked using Abd el Kader's villagers; but the Serahin were doubtful of this scheme and extremely mistrustful of Abd el Kader. There remained a third possibilty: an attempt on the nearest bridge, at Tell el Shehab. This would be much more dangerous than Abd el Kader's scheme, because the approach would have to be made through settled country. If there were rain, it would be difficult to escape across the muddy terrain. In addition, there was a feud between the Serahin and local villagers.

With deepening reservations, Lawrence decided to keep to the existing plan, but it was then noticed that Abd el Kader had disappeared. Lawrence feared, correctly as it turned out, that he had gone over to the Turks. This put the whole expedition in jeopardy, since he knew all their plans. It would now be folly to approach the Algerian villages and, with acute misgivings, it was agreed that the bridge at Tell el Shehab was the only remaining option.

The British staff at Akaba and in Cairo knew nothing of these developments, but they were nevertheless extremely apprehensive. On November 4 (the day that Abd el Kader disappeared) Joyce wrote to Clayton: 'Lawrence by now must be very near his objective. I hope he is lucky. Fortunately he has got brains as well as dash and the two I trust will pull him through, but one cannot help feeling anxious.' Hogarth too was worried: 'I only hope and trust TEL will get back safe. He is out and up against it at this moment. If he comes through it is a V.C.—if not—well, I don't care to think about it!'

The distance from Azrak to Tell el Shehab was about eighty miles, of which the last section would be the most dangerous. This could not be attempted before dusk, leaving little time to carry out the attack and escape before dawn. Nevertheless, the expedition reached its objective safely on the night of November 7, and the early stages of the operation went according to plan. Then, as the demolition party crept towards the bridge in the darkness, someone dropped a rifle. The noise alerted the Turkish guards, and in the firing that followed the Serahin tribesmen panicked. Fearing that the explosive would blow up if hit with a bullet, they threw it into the ravine. Without any means to destroy the bridge, there was no point in continuing the engagement, and Lawrence gave orders for everyone to leave as quickly as possible. He was bitterly disappointed, but grateful when the raiding party escaped without loss.

Lawrence was determined to find some way of compensating for this failure. He had little explosive, and his range of action was restricted because the expedition was running short of food. The best he could do was to blow up a train near Minifir on the line between Deraa and Amman. This would not affect traffic to Palestine, but it would be good for Arab morale.

The circumstances for the attack were not ideal: in order to save food he had been obliged to send the Indian machine-gunners back to Azrak, and this meant that the raiding party had no machine-gun cover. There were further problems when they reached the railway, and two trains went by unscathed before Lawrence managed to trigger the mine. The account in *Seven Pillars* shows how little glamour there really was in these raids: 'Round the bend, whistling its loudest, came the train, a splendid two-engined thing of twelve passenger coaches, travelling at top speed on the favouring grade. I touched off under the first driving wheel of the first locomotive, and the explosion was terrific. The ground spouted blackly into my face, and I was sent spinning, to sit up with the shirt torn to my shoulder and the blood dripping from long ragged scratches on my left arm. Between my knees lay the exploder, crushed under a twisted sheet of sooty iron. In front of me was the scalded and smoking upper half of a man. When I peered through the dust and steam of the explosion the whole boiler of the first engine seemed to be missing.

'I dully felt that it was time to get away . . . but when I moved, I learnt that there was a great pain in my right foot, because of which I could only limp along, with my head swinging from the shock. Movement began to clear away this confusion, as I hobbled towards the upper valley, whence the Arabs were now shooting fast into the crowded coaches. Dizzily I cheered myself by repeating aloud in English "Oh, I wish this hadn't happened".

'When the enemy began to return our fire, I found myself much between the two. Ali saw me fall, and thinking that I was hard hit, ran out, with Turki and about twenty men of his servants and the Beni Sakhr, to help me. The Turks found their range and got seven of them in a few seconds . . . We scrambled back into cover together, and there, secretly, I felt myself over, to find I had not once been really hurt; though besides the bruises and cuts of the boiler-plate and a broken toe, I had five different bullet-grazes on me (some of them uncomfortably deep) and my clothes ripped to pieces.

'From the watercourse we could look about. The explosion had destroyed the arched head of the culvert, and the frame of the first engine was lying beyond it, at the near foot of the embankment down which it had rolled. The second locomotive had toppled into the gap, and was lying across the ruined tender of the first. Its bed was twisted. I judged them both beyond repair. The second tender had disappeared over the further side; and the first three waggons had telescoped and were smashed in pieces.

'The rest of the train was badly derailed, with the listing coaches butted end to end at all angles, zigzagged along the track. One of them was a saloon, decorated with flags . . . The Turks, seeing us so quiet, began to advance up the slope. We let them come half-way, and then poured in volleys which killed some twenty and drove the others back. The ground about the train was strewn with dead, and the broken coaches had been crowded: but they were fighting under the eye of their Corps Commander, and undaunted began to work round the spurs to outflank us.

'We were now only about forty left, and obviously could do no good against them. So we ran in batches up the little stream-bed, turning at each sheltered angle to delay them by pot-shots . . . Ali was angry with me for retiring slowly. In reality my raw hurts crippled me, but to hide from him this real reason I pretended to be easy, interested in and studying the Turks . . .

'At last we reached the hill-top. Each man there jumped on the nearest camel, and made away at full speed eastward into the desert, for an hour.'

Lawrence was fortunate to have escaped with his life. Afterwards, the party made its way back to Azrak, arriving there on November 12. Rather than return to Akaba, he decided to stay in the north until the moment was right for another raid, and also in case some further action might be appropriate, should the Turks collapse under Allenby's attack. During November, however, the winter rains set in, and he was able to guess that Allenby's advance had been halted by the bad weather.

For Lawrence, the Yarmuk failure was a bitter disappointment. In July, he had offered Allenby a general rising to help the EEF advance. Then, fearful that the British would fail, he had decided to hold back, substituting the more limited bridge-blowing operation. In the end, he had been able to achieve almost nothing. The Turkish line of communication between Damascus and Palestine remained intact.

It was some time before messengers from Akaba brought news to Azrak of Allenby's offensive. The EEF had been victorious on the Gaza–Beersheba line but, as many had feared, their advance had soon run into difficulties. Despite severe casualties and losses of *matériel*, the Turks had retreated in reasonable order and were soon fighting a strong rearguard action. Allenby had not been halted definitively, but a further advance would be a slow and more costly affair. In late November, a two-week pause was necessary while reserves were brought up to the front; both sides were preparing to fight for Jerusalem.

Now that Feisal's army had reached Azrak, Lawrence was determined that the place should remain in their hands. In *Seven Pillars* he wrote: 'Partly it would be a preaching base, from which to spread our movement in the north: partly it would be a centre of intelligence: partly it would cut off Nuri Shalaan from the Turks . . . Azrak lay favourably for us, and the old fort would be a convenient headquarters if we made it habitable, no matter how severe the winter.'

Much time was taken up in entertaining visitors and encouraging them to take part in the Revolt. Ali ibn el Hussein was far more suited to this than Lawrence, who decided to leave again after only two days. He was accompanied by Sheikh Tallal, from the village of Tafas south of Damascus. With Tallal as guide, Lawrence set out on a brief tour of the Hauran country, so that he could see the lie of the land for himself. After circling Deraa he decided to look at the defences and installations inside the town. On November 20, therefore, he parted company with Tallal and took two villagers as companions. There seemed no great danger in wandering through the busy town dressed inconspicuously as a local

Arab, and Lawrence was by this time well used to travelling among the peasantry behind Turkish lines.

His earliest account of what then happened is given in a letter to a fellow officer, written eighteen months later. It begins: 'I went into Deraa in disguise to spy out the defences, was caught, and identified by Hajim Bey, the governor, by virtue of Abd el Kadir's description of me. (I learned all about his treachery from Hajim's conversation, and from my guards.) Hajim was an ardent paederast and took a fancy to me. So he kept me under guard till night, and then tried to have me.'

This is at variance with the later *Seven Pillars* version in one important respect: it states plainly that he was recognised, as indeed he must have been. Arab clothes were good enough as a disguise at a distance, but neither Lawrence himself nor any of his fellow-officers in the Revolt ever claimed that he could pass close scrutiny as an Arab.

Moreover, his identity was by this time well known to the Turks, who had long offered a reward for his capture. The hunt for him had recently been stepped up, and the price on his head increased to £20,000.

It seems that Lawrence was first arrested in Deraa purely on suspicion of being a deserter from the Turkish Army. He countered by claiming to be a Circassian, exempt from military service, but this excuse was not accepted, and he was held in a guardroom. In the evening, when he was taken to the Bey, he found out that he was expected to submit to homo-sexual advances. He later wrote: 'Incidents like these made the thought of military service in the Turkish army a living death for wholesome Arab peasants, and the consequences pursued the miserable victims all their after-life, in revolting forms of sexual disease.' He resisted the Bey's attentions, and eventually the soldiers were ordered to take him away 'and teach him everything'.

He was severely beaten and, when he could resist no longer, he was sexually abused. The whole ordeal may not have lasted very long—an early draft of *Seven Pillars* suggests that the beating took no more than ten minutes—but it affected him very deeply. It stopped when Hajim Bey called, and the soldiers 'splashed water in my face, lifted me to my feet, and bore me, retching and sobbing for mercy, between them, to his bedside: but he now threw me off fastidiously, cursing them for their stupidity in thinking he needed a bedfellow streaming with blood and water, striped and fouled from face to heel . . . So the crestfallen cor-poral, as the youngest and best-looking of the guard, had to stay behind, while the others carried me down the narrow stairs and out into the street

. . . They took me over an open space, deserted and dark, and behind the Government house to an empty lean-to mud and wooden room, in which were many dusty quilts. They put me down on these, and brought an Armenian dresser, who washed and bandaged me in sleepy haste. Then they all went away, the last of the soldiers whispering to me in a Druse accent that the door into the next room was not locked.'

Despite the injuries he had received, the instinct of self-preservation drove him to explore this second room, which turned out to be a dispensary. A window on the far side offered a way out. His earliest account of the incident ended: 'I escaped before dawn, being not as hurt as [Hajim] thought. He was so ashamed of the muddle he had made that he hushed the whole thing up, and never reported my capture and escape. I got back to Azrak very annoyed with Abd el Kadir'.

At the time, his strongest emotion must have been an overwhelming sense of relief that he had managed to get away. In the future, however, other aspects of the experience would cast a deepening shadow, and later events would show that this brutal homosexual rape had inflicted terrible psychological damage. Lawrence had been sexually inexperienced (in 1917 this was the norm among young men from the middle classes, not the exception). What had taken place left him with profound feelings of guilt and shame. He would later write: 'in Deraa that night the citadel of my integrity had been irrevocably lost.'

Immediately afterwards, there were few outward signs of this psychological injury: some of the consequences would take years to manifest themselves. As long as the Arab campaign lasted, his attention was focused almost entirely on his responsibilities, and he had little opportunity for introspection. It was only later, when the war was over, that the events at Deraa would come to dominate his most intimate thoughts.

As for his physical injuries, their after-effects were no worse than other hardships of the campaign, and in a few days he had recovered. During the previous twelve months he had endured repeated illness and had been wounded several times, but he had made it his practice to carry on as best he could.

He did not stay long at Azrak. A few days after sending a report on the northern operations down to Akaba with Lieutenant Wood, he decided to go there himself, and he reached the camp at midnight on November 26. Finding that Joyce was on the point of leaving for a reconnaissance inland, he joined the expedition and spent a few days 'motoring, prospecting the hills and valleys for a way Eastwards for our [armoured] cars'. They returned to Akaba on December 3 and from there Lawrence was flown to the British advance GHQ, fully expecting to be criticised for the Yarmuk failure.

In reality, Clayton was much less disappointed than Lawrence about the Yarmuk expedition. He took a wider view of the developing situation, and seems to have felt that Lawrence's personal safety was almost as important to the British as the fate of the Yarmuk bridges. Although Feisal had made no specific contribution to Allenby's attack, there was no doubting the general value of Arab operations, both now and for the future. The Sherifian forces were engaging troops that the Turks desperately needed to defend Jerusalem. British Intelligence received frequent reports about Turkish dispositions, and these showed the large numbers of troops that were being held down by the Arabs. Clayton wrote: 'the enemy forces operating at Medina and on the railway line of communications . . . or the greater part of them, would have been available to reinforce the enemy's Palestine armies, if it were not for the Arab Revolt.

'The [Turkish] Hejaz Expeditionary Force and the two Composite Forces with Headquarters at Tebuk and Maan have a ration strength of over twenty-three thousand. They are made up in the main of regiments containing, until lately, over 90% of Turks, and even now, rarely under 80%, and include the picked force of three thousand Anatolian troops sent down originally in spring 1916 . . . Although the Arabs have not yet succeeded in overcoming the resistance of Medina and the line of communication, the continuance of their Revolt has cost the enemy, through deaths, wounds, sickness and captures, quite a full Division, and at the present moment his strength is barely sufficient to hold on to what, for politico-religious reasons, he will not resign except in the last extremity . . . At the same time the maintenance of these forces and of supplies to them makes a heavy call on railway plant and rolling stock and on the reserves of food and stores at Damascus, a great proportion of which would otherwise be available for the Palestine front.

'This being so, the [Arab] operations by which these enemy forces are being held in place . . . are of direct assistance to the Palestine campaign.'

The EEF was now within sight of Jerusalem and, as Lawrence later wrote, Allenby 'was so full of victories that my short statement that I had failed to carry a Yarmuk bridge was accepted as sufficient, and the rest of my failure could remain concealed.'

While Lawrence was with Allenby, extraordinary news came in: the Turks had quite unexpectedly pulled out of Jerusalem during the night, and civilian officials had come to the British lines in search of someone who would accept their surrender.

Lawrence was still at headquarters on December 11, when the ceremonial British entry took place. In a draft of *Seven Pillars* he wrote that Allenby 'was good enough, although I had done nothing to forward his success, to allow Clayton to take me with him as his Staff Officer for the day. The personal Staff tricked me out in their spare clothes till I looked like an ordinary major in the British Army, and Dalmeny lent me red tabs, and Evans gave me a brass hat, so that for once I had the gauds of my appointment; and then I shared in what for me was the most memorable event of the war, the one which, for historical reasons, made a greater appeal than anything on earth.

'It was strange to stand before the tower with the Chief, listening to his proclamation, and to think how a few days ago I had stood before Hajim, listening to his words. Seldom did we pay so sharply and so soon for our fears. We would have been by now, not in Jerusalem, but in Haifa, or Damascus, or Aleppo, had I not shrunk in October from the danger of a general rising against the Turks. By my failure I had fettered the unknowing English, and dishonoured the unknowing Arabs in a way only to be repaired by our triumphal entry into a liberated Damascus. The ceremony of the Jaffa Gate gave me a new determination.'

CHAPTER 13

The Dead Sea Campaign
December 1917–February 1918

THIS dramatic climax to the EEF advance into Palestine made the prospects for total victory in the East seem much more real. Writing to an Oxford friend, Lawrence began to speculate about his career after the war: 'one is getting terribly bound up in Eastern politics, and must keep free. I've never been labelled yet, and yet I fear that they are going to call me an Arabian now. As soon as the war ends I'm going to build a railway in South America, or dig up a South African goldfield, to emancipate myself. Carchemish will either be hostile (Turks will never let me in again) or friendly (Arab), and after being a sort of king-maker one will not be allowed to go digging quietly again. Nuisance. However the war isn't over yet, and perhaps one needn't worry one's head too soon about it.'

Before leaving GHQ, Lawrence discussed the strategic situation with Allenby. He was told that a further British advance would be impossible before mid-February 1918, because new supplies were needed, and casualties had to be made good. After that, the EEF would consolidate its position by moving against Jericho, so that its inland flank reached the northern end of the Dead Sea. No large-scale offensive would take place until later in the year.

In the meantime, however, the Arab forces could be usefully employed. The first objective Allenby laid down was to occupy the region at the southern end of the Dead Sea, closing that route to a possible Turkish attack on his army from the rear. This scheme had been mooted for some time and, as it happened, Lawrence had just heard from Joyce that operations had begun. The idea of moving into this region appealed strongly to Feisal, who wished to establish support for the Revolt among the settled villages. The area would be valuable to the Arabs because it produced grain, and its loss would be a serious blow to the Turks, who depended on it for the timber used as fuel on the Hejaz Railway south of Maan. Lawrence explained that Arab forces were moving out of Akaba already, with the aim of taking first Shobek and then Tafileh, a village close to the southern end of the Dead Sea. An elaborate three-pronged operation for this purpose had been worked out by Joyce and Feisal some weeks previously.

Allenby's second request was that by the middle of February the Arabs should put a stop to Turkish lighter-traffic on the Dead Sea. This was being used to carry food from the Kerak region to Jericho.

Lawrence himself suggested a third objective: if possible, the Arabs would take control during March of the whole region between the Dead Sea and the railway. The EEF could then supply the Revolt directly from Palestine and, in preparation for the final offensive, Feisal's main force could be moved from Akaba to the northern end of the Dead Sea.

This visit to Cairo also enabled Lawrence to catch up on Intelligence about recent political developments. Among the most serious questions to be faced were those that had been raised by the Bolshevik Revolution of early November. The new Russian regime was vehemently opposed to the war and had taken immediate steps to reach an armistice with the Central Powers. This meant that Turkey would soon be able to transfer troops from the Caucasus Front to Palestine and Mesopotamia.

The Revolution had another disconcerting consequence. Within days of seizing control, the Bolsheviks had published secret Allied treaties including the Sykes-Picot Agreement. During the following weeks, these texts had appeared in newspapers throughout the world. The Sykes-Picot terms were a gift to Turkish propaganda, and British officials had waited anxiously for Arab reaction.

It was feared that Arab support might disappear completely unless the Allies took some step to counteract the damage done by the Sykes-Picot revelation. The situation was made still more fraught by the publication, at much the same time, of the Balfour Declaration, which provided for a Jewish 'national home' in Palestine.

While Lawrence was in Cairo, news arrived which confirmed that the Turks were trying to use Sykes-Picot as a means of detaching the Arabs from the Allied side. Hussein passed on to Wingate the text of a letter which Jemal Pasha had recently sent to Feisal, alluding to the Sykes-Picot terms and offering talks.

No reply had been sent but, by passing the letter on to Cairo, Hussein was clearly warning the British that he now had the option of making peace with Turkey. Wingate decided that Lawrence should return to Akaba and discuss the matter with Feisal, in case 'any further confirmation of the new Turkish policy could be obtained by interchange of verbal messages between [Feisal] and Jemal.' Lawrence himself may well have made this suggestion.

He reached Akaba on Christmas Day, and encouraged Feisal to send Jemal a reply. In his view, the correspondence would provide an insurance, in case Britain's secret negotiations with Turkish conservatives bore fruit. In the draft *Seven Pillars* he wrote: 'Feisal, with my full assistance, sent back tendentious answers to Jemal, argumentative enough to cause to continue the exchange: and it continued brilliantly.' In due course, Turkish nationalist officers began writing separately to Feisal, and Jemal was forced to concede more and more of the Arab demands. Very little about these 'long complicated negotiations' was disclosed either to Cairo or to Hussein. Lawrence wrote: 'We feared that the British might be shaken at Feisal's apparent mistrust of them in entertaining separate negotiations, after their own model. Yet, in fairness to the fighting Arabs, we could not close all avenues of accommodation with Turkey.'

Lawrence's account of this correspondence does not mention one important aspect of the situation. For a time, the Sykes-Picot revelations were very damaging indeed to Britain's relationship with the Arabs. It was inevitable that Arab leaders, threatened with European domination after the war, would open contacts with Muslim Turkey. If Lawrence had opposed such moves, he would not have prevented them, and the issue might have destroyed the trust between himself and Feisal. It must have seemed better that any exchanges took place with his full knowledge, and if possible under his influence.

Lawrence had returned to Akaba during a lull in Arab operations. Expeditions towards Shobek were on their way, but had not yet launched their attacks. Meanwhile another force was beginning to push forward against the Turks at Aba el Lissan.

During the preceding months, the Akaba base had been greatly developed. The armoured cars, no longer needed at Wejh, had been transferred there, and a motor-track had been constructed from Akaba through Wadi Itm up onto the Guweira plain. A permanent advance headquarters had been established there for Feisal's army.

At the end of December, Joyce decided to attempt an experimental raid on the railway with the cars. If they could cross the terrain between Guweira and Mudawara, a long stretch of the line would be at their mercy. A secondary objective was to divert Turkish attention from the operations at Aba el Lissan.

The experiment of getting to the line succeeded and, from this time on, the cars could dominate the line to Medina. For the moment, however, Lawrence was happy to leave the line working intermittently. The attack on Aba el Lissan was successful too, and by January 6 the pass was once again in Arab hands, and the Turks were soon forced back to within three miles of Maan itself.

On his return to Akaba, Lawrence began to form a personal bodyguard. The price on his head was steadily rising, and this greatly increased the risk to his safety when moving through areas where local allegiance was doubtful. Sooner or later someone would be tempted by the reward, and after the experience at Deraa he was determined never again to fall into Turkish hands alive.

Accompanied by this new bodyguard, on January 10 Lawrence set out for Aba el Lissan, where he waited for news of the Shobek and Tafileh operations. When he heard that Nasir had successfully cut the line, he rode north to join the Arab forces. By the time he reached Tafileh the village had been in Arab hands for five days: the first objective of the Dead Sea campaign had been achieved. Sherif Zeid had now arrived to represent Feisal, bringing orders that the expedition should push on as soon as possible towards Kerak, about thirty miles farther north.

Lawrence soon realised that this might be difficult, as the local situation was far from satisfactory. Among the bedouin, tribal loyalty was everything, and the men could usually be relied upon to follow their chiefs. In settled villages like Tafileh, things were very different. Political loyalties were complex, and winning the populace over to Feisal's cause would be a long and delicate process. He reported to Clayton: 'The local people are divided into two very bitterly opposed factions, and are therefore terrified of each other and of us. There is shooting up and down the streets every night, and general tension . . . We have about five hundred men in the place, and are quite secure, of course. Flour and barley are, however, dear . . . and very difficult to find . . . There is a great lack of local transport . . . Zeid is rather distressed by the packet of troubles we are come in for . . . and is pulled here and there by all sorts of eager newcomers all intriguing against one another like cats.'

Lawrence still hoped that Kerak and Madeba could be under Sherifian control by January 26. However, this would depend on the attitude of local leaders farther north. If it were necessary to take the villages by force, more funds would be needed to raise a sufficient body of men, and this would involve further delay.

On January 23 the Turks quite unexpectedly sent out a large expedition to recapture Tafileh. The first contacts with Arab outposts took place during the following afternoon, and by nightfall the attackers were threatening the village itself. Next morning, the Arabs began a counter-attack which steadily grew in vigour. After a day of hard fighting, the Turks were driven back into Wadi Hesa, a precipitous ravine lying to the north of Tafileh. During the night the survivors of the attacking force were harried mercilessly by local Arabs, and many others died of wounds or exposure. Lawrence later estimated that up to a thousand Turks may have perished; some two hundred were captured, along with valuable field artillery. Arab losses were about twenty-five killed and forty wounded.

This was the first time that an Arab force to which Lawrence was acting as adviser had fought a battle on conventional lines. He had taken a key role in the day's events, overturning Jaafar Pasha's original idea of moving from the village to a defensive position farther south. After some indecision, Zeid had put his weight behind Lawrence's plan.

Although the outcome had been a crushing defeat for the Turks, Lawrence wrote in *Seven Pillars* of his bitter regrets about the decision to fight an orthodox battle, when he could probably have avoided an engagement altogether. His chosen tactics had been 'villainous, for with arithmetic and geography for allies we might have spared the suffering factor of humanity . . . We could have won by refusing battle, foxed them by manoeuvring our centre as on twenty such occasions before and since . . . By my decision to fight, I had killed twenty or thirty of our six hundred men, and the wounded would be perhaps three times as many. It was one-sixth of our force gone on a verbal triumph, for the destruction of this thousand poor Turks would not affect the issue of the war . . . This evening there was no glory left, but the terror of the broken flesh, which had been our own men, carried past us to their homes.'

Lawrence also saw that the battle would delay the northward advance, and the inevitable pause for recuperation would use up the limited funds available. There had been a miscalculation at the outset about the money required, and both he and Zeid now urgently appealed for more.

A few days earlier a small force under Abdullah el Fair had been instructed to destroy the Turkish lighters used to carry produce up the Dead Sea from Kerak to Jericho. Since then there had been no news, and as there was no immediate prospect of an advance, Lawrence decided to go himself and see what was happening. As a result of his prodding, the operation got under way. On January 28, the second of Allenby's requirements was met, two weeks ahead of time, with no Arab casualties.

Lawrence had calculated that some £30,000 would be necessary if the advance were to continue. When the winter weather turned to snow, making immediate action even less likely, he decided to return to Guweira and collect the money himself.

His arrival, on February 5, coincided with a visit by Lieutenant-Colonel Alan Dawnay, who had recently been given responsibility for liaison between the EEF and the Revolt. The increasing scale and complexity of the campaign in Syria called for expert staff work, and Dawnay's role would be to direct a small 'Arab Operations' team in Cairo. He would work closely with the Arab Bureau, which continued to handle Intelligence.

This appointment brought a strength to the Revolt which it had hitherto lacked. There would now be a relatively senior officer in Cairo working exclusively on the Arab campaign. Dawnay was able to translate the suggestions put forward by Lawrence and others into formal plans which could be acted upon swiftly at headquarters. In addition, he had the standing to see that requests for supplies, air reconnaissance, bombing raids, etc. were given prompt consideration. Lawrence later wrote: 'Dawnay was Allenby's greatest gift to us . . . He was a professional soldier and so had the class-touch to get the best out of the proper staff at G.H.Q. . . . He married war and rebellion in himself: in the way that . . . it had been my dream every regular officer would do it. Yet in three years' practice only Dawnay succeeded, and he on his first visit . . . He spent twenty days in Akaba and Guweira, and went back with despatches to Allenby, showing all our needs (far more and other than we thought) in stores and funds and arms, and personnel and direction . . .

'Indeed, his taking charge of us was a revolution in our history. Hitherto the Arab movement had lived as a one-wild-man show . . . Henceforward Allenby counted it as . . . part of his tactical scheme'. Dawnay now concluded that there was scope for two quite different types of Arab operation. The first was loosely organised guerilla action, carried out mostly by local men. The Revolt had hitherto consisted almost entirely of such operations, and, in the near future, they would be used to complete the Dead Sea campaign. Secondly, there was scope for more conventional action, to be carried out by Jaafar Pasha's Arab regulars. By the end of January the regular force at Akaba totalled more than three thousand men. It was equipped with artillery and machine guns, and could also call on the French artillery detachment, British armoured cars, and two British-crewed 10-pounder guns mounted on Talbot lorries. In addition, the RFC flight of six aircraft at Akaba was by this time carrying out reconnaissance and bombing missions with great effect.

Hitherto, the regulars had served mainly to secure Feisal's base against attack from Maan. This danger had now passed, and Jaafar, Nuri, and other senior officers believed that the time had come to embark on more ambitious operations. Consequently, it was agreed that preparations should be made for an offensive against the Turkish forces centred on Maan. The objectives would be: 'The destruction of the enemy's 1st Composite Force and the capture of Maan, with a view to the permanent isolation of all Turkish forces south of the latter, the ultimate capitulation of whom should, in these circumstances, become merely a question of time.'

The British officers had argued that a frontal attack on the Maan defences should be avoided. Instead, the Arab regulars should try to cut the railway north of Maan compelling the Turks to leave their prepared defences in order to restore supplies. Fighting would then take place on ground more favourable to the Arabs. If, at the same time, the British armoured cars attacked the line south of Maan, the chances of reducing the garrison to surrender seemed excellent.

Another aspect of the Syrian operations which Dawnay sought to clarify was the structure of command among the various British officers involved. In a separate report, he noted that the existing arrangements had grown up piecemeal to meet immediate needs. As a result, some officers were carrying out duties which bore little relation to their original appointments, and there were anomalies in rank.

In particular, the duties of Joyce and Lawrence clearly called for redefinition. During recent months, Lawrence had spent very little time at Feisal's headquarters, and Joyce had taken over much of his original role as military adviser. As Lawrence later wrote: 'It was Joyce who ran the main lines of the Revolt, while I was off on raids, or making plans for advances. I acted as his main source of Intelligence.'

Similarly, when Joyce came to Akaba, his main duty had been to work as Base Commandant, responsible for supporting Feisal's army. He was also there to advise and control the Arab regulars training under Jaafar Pasha. Now that Feisal's headquarters had been moved inland to Guweira, and the regulars were about to undertake offensive operations, the actual work of Base Commandant at Akaba was being carried out by a subordinate, Major Scott.

Dawnay recommended that Joyce, who was in command of 'all British troops in the area, also *de facto* director of Arab operations in the field,' should be reclassified as a Special Service officer, grade one, while Lawrence should be classified as a Special Service officer, second grade.

*   *   *

After the discussions with Dawnay, Lawrence returned to Tafileh with a small party of Arabs, each of whom carried two thousand of the thirty thousand sovereigns allocated to the Dead Sea operations. Rain and blinding snow turned the three-day journey northwards over muddy tracks into a test of endurance, and several of the camel-men dropped out. Some were delayed for several days.

By the time Lawrence reached Tafileh on February 11, he was exhausted. To his disappointment, he found that no preparations had been made for an advance. It seemed that the tactical advantage of the Tafileh victory had been entirely wasted.

After discussing the situation, Lawrence concluded that Zeid's force no longer had the capacity or the will to take the northern villages on their own. The Turks would first have to be weakened by bedouin attacks from east of the railway, which Lawrence decided to organise.

He thought that the money he had brought up from Guweira would be sufficient to finance his own plan and also to meet Zeid's legitimate needs: 'This £30,000 will last the northern tribes this month, and have enough over to carry us into the middle of March.'

Two days later the weather improved, and he set off on a reconnaissance of the south-eastern shore of the Dead Sea, to look at possible approaches to Kerak from this side.

After this, he decided to examine the lie of the land between Tafileh and the northern end of the Dead Sea. He took a sheikh from Kerak as his guide, and in two days they travelled to the edge of the Jordan valley and back. The results were entirely satisfactory.

He rode back to Tafileh on February 18, but when he explained the favourable situation to Zeid, the latter was unimpressed. It soon transpired that during Lawrence's absence all the money he had brought had been allocated by Zeid and his advisers to local sheiks who, in Lawrence's opinion, had little claim to it. He demanded that the money be returned, but Zeid refused. This open rejection of Lawrence's authority left him with no alternative but to leave.

For the second time, he would be unable to fulfil a promise he had volunteered to Allenby. The loss of such a huge sum meant that there was no longer any hope of taking the northern villages. Worse still, without a further advance, most of the territory already taken would soon be recaptured by the Turks.

He had always feared that the moment would come when one of the principal Arab leaders ignored his advice. This one act might destroy his authority completely. Only a week before, he had warned of the danger in a letter to Clayton. Now, he felt that his only course was to quit the Arab operations. Perhaps he would take the home leave he had already been promised, and return later to Intelligence duties at GHQ.

As he was preparing to set off, Joyce arrived unexpectedly with Marshall, the British doctor from Akaba. Joyce tried to persuade Zeid to release the money, but had no success. He therefore agreed to close down Lawrence's affairs and disperse the bodyguard. On February 19, Lawrence left for the British lines at Beersheba, accompanied by an escort of only four men.

When he reached Allenby's headquarters, he found Hogarth waiting for him. 'To him I said that I had made a mess of things: for me the play was over, and I had come to beg Allenby to find me some smaller part elsewhere . . . The fault lay in my sick judgment, bitterest because the occasion was Zeid, own brother to Feisal and a little man I really liked. I now had left no tricks worth a meal in the Arab market-place, and wanted . . . to pillow myself on duty and obedience, irresponsibly.

'Since landing in Arabia I had had options and requests, never an order: and I was surfeited, tired to death of free-will . . . For a year and a half I had been in motion, riding a thousand miles each month upon camels, with added nervous hours in crazy aeroplanes, or rushing across country in powerful cars. In my last five actions I had been hit, and my body so dreaded further pain that now I had to force myself under fire. Generally I had been hungry: and lately always cold: and that and the dirt had poisoned my hurts into a festering mass of sores.

'However, these worries would have taken their due petty place had it not been for the rankling fraudulence which had to be my mind's habit: that pretence to lead the national uprising of another race, the daily posturing in alien dress, preaching in alien speech: with behind it a sense that the ''promises'' on which the Arabs worked were worth what their armed strength would be when the moment of fulfilment came. The fraud—if fraud it was—was shared with Feisal in full knowledge: and we had comforted ourselves that perhaps peace would find the Arabs in a winning position (if such poor creatures, unhelped and untaught, could defend themselves with paper tools), and meanwhile we conducted their necessary, honourable war as purely and as cheaply as men could . . . but now by my sin this last gloss had been taken from me in Tafileh. To be charged against my conceit were the causeless and ineffectual deaths of those twenty Arabs and seven hundred Turks in Wadi Hesa. My will had gone, and I feared longer to be alone, lest the winds of circumstance or absolute power or lust blow my empty soul away.'

Years later, Lawrence told Liddell Hart: 'I was a very sick man, again, you know: almost at breaking point.'

CHAPTER 14

A Dangerous Pause

February–June 1918

WHEN Lawrence saw Clayton, he realised at once that he would not be allowed to give up his work with the Arabs. There was no place for defeatism in the mood now prevailing at Allenby's headquarters. The Cabinet had recently decided that victory in this theatre should be given first priority, even if this meant that no offensive could be undertaken on the Western Front. They hoped that a British advance to Damascus and Aleppo would force the Turks to sue for peace, and Allenby had been instructed to resume the offensive as soon as possible. Plans were already in train for an advance to Beirut, Damascus and beyond. Arab co-operation would be essential.

Allenby told Lawrence of his new requirements. As the EEF moved northwards, there would be a lengthening eastern flank needing protection. Feisal's army would not be able to concentrate on this task until it had closed down the present campaign. This meant disposing of the Turkish forces at Maan as rapidly as possible. Once this had been done, the whole of the Hejaz Railway southward to Medina would fall into Arab hands.

To Lawrence's delight, Allenby now agreed to provide seven hundred camels from the Egyptian Camel Transport Company, together with their drivers, equipment and British officers. With this transport, the Arab regulars could operate some eighty miles in advance of their supply base.

The capture of Maan would bring the first phase of Arab operations to an end. The regulars would then be moved to a new base north-east of the Dead Sea, where they could draw supplies from Jericho. If the seven hundred camels lent by Allenby could be retained, this force would be in a position to raid a large section of the railway south of Deraa.

After these discussions, Lawrence travelled to Jerusalem, where he spent two days with Ronald Storrs, now Military Governor of the city. During this visit, he was introduced by Storrs to a young American who was gathering material for a series of illustrated lectures about the war. This was Lowell Thomas, an experienced journalist and skilled public speaker, who had arrived in Palestine a few weeks earlier with his photographer, Harry Chase. Thomas had been thrilled by rumours of the Arab Revolt and was delighted to meet one of its leading personalities.

The Thomas mission was no ordinary exercise in wartime journalism. It had first been planned in the spring of 1917 with the express purpose of increasing popular support for the war effort in America, and it had the backing of influential figures in the US Administration. The authorities in Whitehall were keen to help Thomas, in the hope that his work might promote a better understanding of Britain's part in the struggle. In August 1917, the head of the British Bureau of Information in New York had commended Thomas and Chase to the Department of Information in London: 'the two gentlemen . . . are about to go to Europe for the purpose of getting material for so called "travelogues." These are very popular in this country and consist in a sort of penny reading illustrated with living and moving pictures . . . the Secretary of War [is] very anxious that these gentlemen should meet with success. Accordingly, anything that you could do for them would be well worth doing . . . I do think it is important to put our case through as many channels as possible . . . and as this project has the blessing of the Administration I think it would be wise to give them some really good interviews. Let them go to really interesting places and try to show up in a good light as compared with the French.'

Thomas had first visited the Western Front, but found that the grim realities of trench warfare offered little material to suit his purpose. On December 10, having learned of British successes in Palestine, he had written to John Buchan, then Director of the Department of Information in London: 'I am here in Europe at the head of a mission authorised by the United States Government, to gather data and photographic material for a series of illustrated patriotic lectures to be delivered throughout America to help arouse the country to complete support of the Allies . . . A bulletin received to-day states that your Army has captured Jerusalem. From the standpoint of the material we are gathering this event is of the greatest importance, and if it can be arranged, I want to go there at once, accompanied only by my photographer . . . These lectures are to be delivered by me, hence to make them effective pictures must, at least partially, be of things I see personally and which have not already been used for general publication. I have letters from the Secretaries of War, Navy and State requesting that all possible facilities be given my mission.'

Clearly, Thomas was offering Britain an excellent opportunity to 'show up in a good light'. The Department of Information therefore applied to the EEF and the War Office, and on December 21 Thomas and Chase were given permission to visit Palestine. They sailed from Italy on about January 12.

When Lawrence met Thomas in Jerusalem, the circumstances of the mission were explained to him. Lawrence was enthusiastic about publicity for the Revolt, and understood how important American opinion might be in the ultimate settlement. He talked about the progress of the campaign and the politics of Arab nationalism, and also agreed to pose for Harry Chase on the balcony of the Residency.

Thomas was intrigued by what he had learned and decided to find out more. Soon after Lawrence's departure he persuaded Allenby to authorise a visit to the Arab forces at Akaba. The decision to grant this request was probably influenced by pressure from London for more coverage of the Revolt. On March 2, for example, the Foreign Office had cabled: 'Can you supply as soon as possible a good article on Feisal's operations for world consumption?'

On March 4, Lawrence went briefly to Akaba to see Feisal. He explained the new plans agreed with Allenby and discussed the problems he had experienced with Zeid. When he had left Tafileh a fortnight earlier, he had realised that the Turks would be able to recapture the village without difficulty. The latest news suggested a build-up of enemy strength in the region, but Lawrence no longer cared. His attention was focused on Maan in the south and Amman in the north. If the Turks sent troops to Tafileh, they would weaken their forces at one or the other of these places.

Some time before, it had been decided that an understudy would have to be found for Lawrence. His role with the tribes had become so important that he was unable to take leave, and there was no one who could replace him if he were killed or seriously wounded. He had suggested that Hubert Young might be a good choice. Young, who spoke Arabic fluently, was still serving in Mesopotamia, where the two had last met in April 1916. At that time Young had resented Lawrence's manner and, in particular, his disrespectful attitude towards regular soldiers. However, Lawrence now wrote that Young 'should be the right sort of man: the work is curious, and demands a sort of twisted tact, which many people do not seem to possess. We are very short-handed, and it will make things much easier if he fits in well.'

Young arrived in Cairo early in March, and was surprised at the scale of Arab operations: 'I found that Lawrence was only one of the many

British officers who were helping the Arabs . . . as soon as the Sherifian revolt took definite military shape, a special liaison staff was formed at General Allenby's G.H.Q. to deal with what were known as Hejaz operations . . . Dawnay was officially the chief staff officer, just as Joyce was officially the senior British officer with Feisal's army, but Lawrence really counted more than either of them with Allenby and Feisal, and used to flit backwards and forwards between G.H.Q. and Feisal's headquarters as the spirit moved him.'

It was no doubt in recognition of this extraordinary role that Lawrence was now promoted Lieutenant-Colonel. He also learned that he had been awarded a DSO, for his part in the battle of Siel el Hesa outside Tafileh. On March 15 he returned to Akaba to finalise preparations for the new Arab offensive. It was agreed that the Maan operation should go ahead on the plan drawn up with Dawnay three weeks previously. Jaafar Pasha's Arab regulars were to occupy the railway north of the town, while Joyce, with the British armoured cars, went south to Mudawara. Joyce hoped to do so much damage there that Turkish communications with Medina would be broken permanently. Lawrence, for his part, would be responsible for arranging the tribal follow-up to a thrust by Allenby's forces across the Jordan to Amman.

While waiting for the operations to begin, he travelled up to the Shobek region for a few days to look at the situation. During this tour, unpleasant news came from Ali ibn el Hussein, who had passed the winter at Azrak: two of the men there had died of cold. One was an Indian machine-gunner, the other Lawrence's young servant Ali. It was Ali's friend Othman who brought the news. The two had enrolled themselves in Lawrence's service during the journey to Akaba. In *Seven Pillars* (where they are called Daud and Farraj) Lawrence described their high spirits and incessant practical jokes, which must have appealed to his own sense of mischief. Now, however, Othman had changed: 'These two had been friends from childhood, in eternal gaiety: working together, sleeping together, sharing every scrape and profit with the openness and honesty of perfect love. So I was not astonished to see Farraj look dark and hard of face, leaden-eyed and old, when he came to tell me that his fellow was dead; and from that day till his service ended he made no more laughter for us. He took punctilious care, greater even than before, of my camel, of the coffee, of my clothes and saddles, and fell to praying his three regular prayings every day. The others offered themselves to comfort him, but instead he wandered restlessly, grey and silent, very much alone.'

* * *

Lawrence returned to Akaba on March 21. To his surprise, Lowell Thomas arrived shortly afterwards with Harry Chase, who began taking large numbers of photographs and asked Lawrence to sit for further portraits. Thomas doubtless explained that the impact of an illustrated lecture is greatly increased if the slides change frequently, and that he might therefore need several different photographs of some subjects. Lawrence agreed to the portrait sessions, but he saw to it that Chase also photographed the Arab forces and their leaders.

After the war, Thomas would imply that he and Chase had spent a considerable time with Lawrence, working as correspondents accredited to the Arab campaign. He would even claim to have been present during battles against the Turks. The truth was rather different: he spent less than a fortnight with Feisal's army and saw Lawrence for only a few days. Before Thomas and Chase completed their work in Akaba, Lawrence had travelled inland. He later wrote that Thomas 'saw a scoop in our side-show, and came to Akaba (1918) for ten days. I saw him there, for the second time, but went up country to do some other work. He bored the others, so they packed him off by Ford car to Petra, and thence back to Egypt by sea.'

As it happened, Thomas's visit took place during one of the dullest periods of the entire Revolt. The March War Diary of Hejaz Operations noted: 'Sherif Feisal's army did not succeed in attacking the Turks . . . A very sudden and deep fall of snow about March 24th in this area made further operations impossible . . . The main activity . . . has been in establishing supply dumps at Gueira and Abu Lissal, with a view to extended action against Maan.' Two small expeditions earlier in the month had come to nothing because of snow and rain.

It would be eighteen months before Lawrence discovered the real reason that Thomas and Chase had come to Akaba. Thomas knew, with the instinct of a practised journalist, that there would be little popular interest in Arab military achievements and political claims to Syria. However, these would provide a romantic backdrop for the story that was really forming in his mind: that of a young English archaeologist who had become the 'Uncrowned King of Arabia'. Doubtless he was able, like all skilled journalists, to conceal the true drift of his enquiries by displaying profound interest in everything his interviewees talked about. Yet his real intentions are revealed in the glamorous portrait photographs of Lawrence taken by Chase.

It is doubtful that Thomas managed to get many personal details from

Lawrence himself, but other British officers freely expressed their admiration for him, and unwittingly provided material to fill out this 'human angle'. Thomas later wrote: 'During the time that Mr. Chase and I were in Arabia, I found it impossible to extract much information from Lawrence himself regarding his own achievements. He insisted on giving the entire credit to Emir Feisal and other Arab leaders, and to his fellow adventurers, Colonel Wilson . . . Joyce, Dawnay, Bassett, Vickery, Cornwallis, Hogarth, Stirling, etc., all of whom did magnificent work in Arabia. So to them I went for much of my material, and I am indebted to various members of this group of brilliant men whom General Clayton used in his Near Eastern Secret Corps. Eager to tell me of the achievements of their quiet scholarly companion, they refused to say much about themselves, although their own deeds rivalled those of the heroes of *The Arabian Nights*.' Lawrence commented bitterly: 'His spare credulity they packed with stories about me. He was shown copies of my official reports, and made long extracts or summaries of them. Of course he was never in the Arab firing line, nor did he ever see an operation or ride with me.'

On April 2 Lawrence set out northwards from Aba el Lissan. He was accompanied by his bodyguard, and baggage camels loaded with food and ammunition. The projected EEF raid on Amman was intended to divert attention from the Arab operations further south. As Lawrence did not know exactly when the raid would take place, he planned to stay in the desert east of the line until news reached him.

Although Lawrence did not know it, by the time his expedition set out the EEF raid on Amman had gone badly wrong. Salt had been captured, but bad weather hampered further progress. The Turks recognised the expedition as a threat to the railway, and by the time the attack on Amman took place their positions had been reinforced. Although some damage was done, a strong counter-attack forced the raiding party to a precipitate withdrawal. Even Salt had been abandoned.

When Lawrence learned what had happened, he realised that nothing useful could be done in the north. He therefore returned south with his bodyguard, hoping that they might be able to help with the attack on Maan.

On the way back, his party marched for some distance along the railway. Near Faraifra they came upon a small Turkish patrol and there was a brief skirmish. During this, Othman (Farraj of *Seven Pillars*) whose lifelong friend Ali had died only weeks before, rode forward in advance of the main party. As he neared the Turks, he fell from his camel. In *Seven Pillars*, Lawrence described what followed: 'I was very anxious about Farraj. His camel stood unharmed by the bridge, alone . . . We reached it together, and found there one dead Turk and Farraj terribly wounded through the body, lying by the arch just as he had fallen from his camel. He looked unconscious; but, when we dismounted, greeted us, and then fell silent, sunken in that loneliness which came to hurt men who believed death near. We tore his clothes away and looked uselessly at the wound. The bullet had smashed right through him, and his spine seemed injured. The Arabs said at once that he had only a few hours to live.

'We tried to move him, for he was helpless, though he showed no pain. We tried to stop the wide slow bleeding, which made poppy-splashes in the grass; but it seemed impossible, and after a while he told us to let him alone, as he was dying, and happy to die, since he had no care of life. Indeed, for long he had been so, and men very tired and sorry often fell in love with death . . .

'While we fussed about him Abd el Latif shouted an alarm. He could see about fifty Turks working up the line towards us, and soon after a motor trolley was heard coming from the north. We were only sixteen men, and had an impossible position. I said we must retire at once, carrying Farraj with us. They tried to lift him, first in his cloak, afterwards in a blanket; but consciousness was coming back, and he screamed so pitifully that we had not the heart to hurt him more.

'We could not leave him where he was, to the Turks, because we had seen them burn alive our hapless wounded. For this reason we were all agreed, before action, to finish off one another, if badly hurt: but I had never realized that it might fall to me to kill Farraj.

'I knelt down beside him, holding my pistol near the ground by his head, so that he should not see my purpose; but he must have guessed it, for he opened his eyes and clutched me with his harsh, scaly hand . . . I waited a moment, and he said, "Daud will be angry with you," the old smile coming back so strangely to his grey shrinking face. I replied, "Salute him from me." He returned the formal answer, "God will give you peace," and at last wearily closed his eyes.'

As Lawrence approached Maan, he found that the attack had already begun. Here too, there had been departures from the agreed plan, and the fighting continued indecisively for some days, while the RAF bombed the town and defences. Then, on April 17, Nuri as-Said led a storming party into the main Turkish positions about the station. The defences were formidable, and the Arabs found themselves caught in the fire of well-positioned machine guns behind concrete emplacements. There was insufficient artillery cover from their own side, and they were forced to retreat with heavy losses. Afterwards, the Arabs could only entrench their positions outside the town, and the situation at Maan settled into a stalemate. Despite this unsatisfactory outcome, Lawrence and the other British officers thought that the regulars had put up an impressive fight.

Another element in the plan was an attack by armoured cars on the railway farther south; this operation began on April 18. Joyce was ill, and Dawnay stepped in as commander. The raid involved not only British and tribal forces, but also the newly formed Egyptian Camel Corps under F. G. Peake. Lawrence asked to go too, ostensibly as an interpreter because Dawnay spoke no Arabic. In reality, he was worried that there might be friction between the various racial elements. As he later wrote: 'I knew that one row would spoil the delicate balance of the Arab front: and that rows would come unless ceaseless vigilance were exercised. I was one of the very few people intimate enough with the Arabs to be ceaselessly with them without boring them into sulks. So I tried to godfather every mixed expedition. Dawnay didn't want me hanging about.'

On this occasion his fears proved well founded. After the capture of Tell Shahm station on April 19, the bedouin set about looting, as was their habit. According to Dawnay's report, while this was going on 'a somewhat dangerous situation arose between the Arabs and the Egyptians; serious consequences were, however, averted by skilful handling of the Bedouin by Colonel Lawrence.'

Demolition work on the railway continued for several days, and by April 25 a hundred kilometres of line between Maan and Mudawara had been systematically destroyed. Lawrence had not stayed for this second stage of the operations. When the irregular tribesmen went home, he had seen little risk of further trouble, and on April 22 returned to Aba el Lissan. His concern now was that the Maan operations were vulnerable to counter-attack from the north. The limited damage done by the British at Amman had soon been repaired, and there was little to prevent the Turks bringing strong reinforcements down the line towards Maan, where Feisal's army was already facing superior numbers.

In order to delay such a move, Lawrence proposed that bedouin forces should mount frequent raids on the railway north of Maan. He himself was unable to organise this, as he was about to go to Palestine for meetings at GHQ. Instead, he asked Young to coordinate the various regular and tribal elements in the area. He later wrote: 'I wanted Young to try his prentice hand at it, so gave him the idea and my notions of what to use for the job.'

When Lawrence reached GHQ on May 2, he learned to his astonishment that the EEF had just launched a further attack on Salt. This had been prompted by Beni Sakhr envoys who had come to the EEF offering Arab help on a large scale. The British action had been taken on the spur of the moment, without reference either to Lawrence or to Dawnay's staff in Cairo.

Lawrence was alarmed, because he knew that there was no likelihood of substantial help from the Beni Sakhr. A day later his worst fears were confirmed: the Arabs had done almost nothing. As a result the Turks had been able to seize the roads by which General Chauvel's expedition had advanced; it was lucky to escape with only 1,650 casualties. After this blunder, the General Staff resolved to leave future co-operation with the bedouin to Lawrence.

There was other disquieting news at British headquarters. Some weeks earlier the German Army had launched a major offensive on the Western Front. The War Office had begun to recall men and equipment to Europe and, by March 27, Allenby had been told to fall back for the present on a scheme of active defence. This placed a question mark over the timing of the coming offensive.

Any delay would be unwelcome to Feisal, whose confidence had been badly shaken by the earlier British retreat from Salt. The new fiasco would unsettle him further, and Lawrence decided to fly at once to Akaba and explain how it had happened. He soon learned that his anxieties were justified. Two days earlier the Turks had sent out a messenger with a white flag to the Arab lines in front of Maan. He was carrying a letter to Feisal from Jemal Pasha, written immediately after the new British defeat at Salt. It hinted at concessions to Arab nationalist demands if Feisal would change sides. Lawrence's explanations saved the situation, and he hurried back to GHQ to see what could be done about future plans.

If he was hoping for better news, he was disappointed. A second German offensive had begun in Europe on April 9, and Allenby had now been asked to release another fourteen battalions without waiting for the Indian relief troops. Altogether, sixty thousand officers and men were being withdrawn from the EEF.

Allenby explained that the new Indian units he was expecting were not fully trained, and lacked any previous experience of warfare: 'When these drafts came he would reorganise or rebuild his army on the Indian model, and perhaps, after the summer, might be again in fighting trim; but for the moment this was too far to foresee: we must, like him, just hold on and wait.' For Lawrence, ten weeks' planning lay in ruins: he would have to tell Feisal that the promise of an early victory had been false. The news would be a severe blow. Lawrence had been counting on Allenby's forward movement to resolve the dangerous stalemate at Maan. Now, however, the Turks would be free to concentrate their attention on Jaafar Pasha's army. If they were allowed to move south, the Arabs might soon be driven back off the Maan plateau.

In the longer term, the delay might have a decisive effect on Arab morale and allegiance to the Allied cause. Since the autumn of 1917, the Anglo-Arab alliance had been under great strain. The cause was Arab knowledge of the Sykes-Picot terms and of the Balfour Declaration. These agreements affected Syria, Lebanon, Mesopotamia and Palestine. If they were implemented, only the Arabian Peninsula would be autonomous. In other words, the richest and most fertile of the Arab provinces had been reserved for the Allies, and political independence was to be denied to the overwhelming majority of Turkey's subject peoples. Arab leaders felt cheated of much that they had been fighting for, and bitterly angry that they had not been consulted about these agreements.

Their principal reason for continuing the alliance with Britain was a belief that the Allies would win the war. During the spring of 1918, however, this was open to doubt. The EEF advance to Jerusalem and Jericho had been impressive, but there it had stopped, to be followed only by two disastrous raids across the Jordan. Arab suspicions that the Allies might be weakening had been reinforced by news of the successful German offensive in Europe.

It was inevitable that signs such as these would cause the Arab leaders to reconsider the likely outcome of the war they were fighting.

If Britain were forced to make peace with Turkey from a position of weakness, what would happen to Arab aspirations? Syria and much other Arab territory would end the war in Turkish hands, and the Arabs might be left to strike the best deal they could, having fought the war on the losing side. At present, a change in Arab allegiance would still be valuable to Turkey, and in exchange, Feisal could surely negotiate a more favourable outcome than the Sykes-Picot terms.

Lawrence was acutely aware of this danger and feared that a military standstill would precipitate an Arab *rapprochement* with the Turks. If nothing could be done in Palestine, Feisal must be persuaded to take the initiative himself.

This problem was on his mind when he paid another visit to GHQ on May 15. While discussing the position with Allenby, he learned that an Imperial Camel Corps Brigade whose services he had asked for in February was soon to be reorganised as a conventional cavalry force. As he reflected on this news, he realised that the change would release a large number of riding camels. If these could be given to the Arab regulars, who had proved their worth at Maan, Feisal would be able to strike at objectives much farther afield. Lawrence asked for the camels, saying that they would enable him to 'put a thousand men into Deraa' whenever Allenby pleased.

More important still, such a force would enable the Arabs to mount their own northern offensive, without waiting for Allenby. While they might not be able to hold what they captured, they could cripple Turkish communications and might build up a popular rising whose momentum would drive the Turks back to Damascus and beyond. At that point, Allenby would be strongly tempted to join in, thereby consolidating the Arab position. If he did not, Feisal could still save the situation by making a separate peace with Turkey. Lawrence knew that the Arabs would see this too: a successful raid on Damascus would in no way weaken their position *vis-à-vis* the Turks: on the contrary, Feisal's bargaining power might be greatly improved.

There was, however, a problem which would have to be solved before such a scheme could be put into effect. The men Lawrence had in mind for the ICC camels would have to be drawn from the Arab regulars at present serving outside Maan. But it would be most unwise to weaken Jaafar Pasha's forces there, which were already outnumbered by the Turkish defenders. To get over this difficulty Lawrence proposed to bring up most of the regular Arab units still serving with Ali and Abdullah in the Hejaz.

With these reinforcements, and the extra men now being recruited in Palestine and elsewhere, the number of Arab regulars in the north could be brought up to about ten thousand. This army would then be divided into two, the larger part continuing the siege of Maan while a carefully picked mounted force operated in the Deraa-Damascus sector.

As details of the offensive were worked out at Feisal's headquarters, Lawrence became fairly confident that the initial movement would break the deadlock on the Palestine front. Even a small advance there would place the Turkish forces at Salt in such an exposed position that they would probably have to withdraw. This in turn would give the Arabs control of the hill country east of the Dead Sea, and allow them to link up with the British around Jericho for a final campaign.

Lawrence could only speculate about the outcome of the later stages of his offensive. In *Seven Pillars* he wrote that the ICC camels were 'an immense, a regal gift; the gift of unlimited mobility. The Arabs could now win their war when and how they liked.' Privately, however, he realised that the camel raiders might never reach Damascus. In this case, the gain would be slight and the cost very heavy. As he later wrote: 'Practically, I was proposing that we use up the Hauran Arabs to let us reach Jericho, half-way to our Damascus goal. It was an expensive plan therefore but the alternative was stagnation for English and Arabs in their present line throughout next winter.'

It would be some time before these operations could begin. In the meantime, it was necessary to protect the Arab position outside Maan from a Turkish counter-attack. For the moment, this was being done by repeatedly cutting the railway to the north. Co-ordination of these operations had originally been entrusted to Young, but it had soon become evident that he was unsuited to such a delicate task. As Lawrence had seen in other instances, regular army training was of little help when working with Arab irregulars. In Young's case there was also a problem of temperament. He possessed too little patience to deal successfully with the bedouin: in his eagerness to get things done, he gave strings of exacting orders and expected them to be obeyed. This approach led to constant difficulties, and he had exhausted himself riding backwards and forwards trying to keep different groups working together in the most effective fashion. Eventually, he had fallen ill and was sent back to Egypt. Lawrence left Feisal's headquarters on May 28 to take his place.

By this time he had taken other steps to help safeguard the Arab position on the Maan plateau. During his last visit to GHQ he had asked for frequent bombing raids on Amman and Katrani, and the RAF was responding very generously. In *Seven Pillars* Lawrence wrote: 'Routine attacks upon the Hejaz Railway were arranged, and the Royal Air Force kept at this dull and troublesome business from now till the fall of Turkey. They served a valuable strategic purpose, by causing heavy damage and uncertainty along the line, and so making any large concentration either of men or stores dangerous in the sector north of Maan. Much of the inactivity of the Turks in this our lean season was due to the disorganisation of their railway traffic by air bombing.' Using an advance airfield near Guweira, the RAF flew missions as far north as Jurf, while aircraft from Palestine attacked the line south of Amman. The Air Force also flew very frequent reconnaissance missions which provided exact information about enemy troop movements.

The cumulative effect of these operations on the ground and in the air was everything that Lawrence had hoped. After a short time with the raiding parties north of Maan, he concluded that these would be sufficient to prevent any major Turkish counter-attack for at least two months. There was little he personally could contribute, so he turned his attention to the forthcoming Arab offensive. During the first week of June, he carried out a reconnaissance of the Moab plateau between the Railway and the Dead Sea, returning afterwards to Aba el Lissan.

While he had been away, a further message from Jemal Pasha had reached the Arab headquarters. Without telling Lawrence, Feisal had begun to take these exchanges with the enemy very seriously. Lawrence later wrote: 'Djemal was willing to give independence to Arabia, and auton- omy to Syria, and half the riches of Turkey to Feisal, if the Arab Army would rejoin the Turks against the British'. Years later, Lawrence dis- cussed these secret negotiations with Liddell Hart, who made notes of the conversation. These jottings are confused, probably because Lawrence only gave a condensed summary. In part, however, the notes clearly refer to the situation in June: 'Feisal never told [Lawrence] about his negoti- ations in the summer of 1918—Feisal was definitely "selling us". He thought the British were cracking . . . [Lawrence] heard through agents in camp. [He] stopped it when getting dangerous; pretended to take it as a piece of political tactics . . . Feisal could not carry on when the English knew.'

Another important diplomatic contact had taken place while Lawrence was away. This was a visit to Feisal's camp by Dr Chaim Weizmann, a leading British Zionist. Some weeks earlier, Weizmann had arrived in Palestine at the head of a Zionist Commission authorised by the Eastern Committee of the War Cabinet. Among the Commission's objects was 'the establishment of good relations with the Arabs and other non-Jewish communities in Palestine'.

Clayton, who was now closely involved in the administration of Pal- estine, hoped that the mission would help to reduce hostility between Jews and Arabs. He had written to London on February 4: 'I have urged

Lawrence to impress on Faisal the necessity of an *entente* with the Jews. [Feisal] is inclined the other way, and there are people in Cairo who lose no chance of putting him against them.' Subsequently, Lawrence had told Clayton: '[As] for the Jews, when I see Feisul next I'll talk to him, and the Arab attitude shall be sympathetic, for the duration of the war at least. Only please remember that he is under the old man, and cannot involve the Arab kingdom by himself.' He would advise Feisal to visit Jerusalem when the demands of the campaign permitted, and 'all the Jews there will report him friendly. That will probably do all you need, without public commitment, which is rather beyond my province.'

Lawrence's place at the Feisal-Weizmann meeting had been taken by Joyce. It was only later, during a visit to Allenby's headquarters, that he had an opportunity to meet Weizmann.

After a brief stay in Akaba, Lawrence left for Egypt on June 10. While passing through Cairo, he spoke to Wingate about bringing Arab regulars up from the Hejaz. Afterwards he travelled to GHQ, meaning to discuss final details of the northern offensive.

When he arrived, on June 19, he found that the mood of Allenby's staff had changed completely. A programme of rapid training for the new Indian troops was yielding excellent results, and plans had advanced much farther than had seemed possible a few weeks before. It had just been decided that a new offensive could be launched in September. This meant that Lawrence's Arab initiative, with all its attendant risks, was no longer necessary.

CHAPTER 15

Preparations
June–September 1918

THE decision to launch a major attack in the autumn of 1918 had been taken only four days before Lawrence reached GHQ, and detailed plans had not yet been made. However, Allenby's requirement east of the Jordan had not changed. The main objective of the Arab forces would be the railway junction at Deraa. If this could be isolated, Turkish lines of communication to their Seventh and Eighth Armies in Palestine would be cut.

Lawrence found the Arab Bureau mulling over a new Foreign Office declaration to the Arab nationalists. A few weeks earlier, a memorandum had been received from seven Syrians resident in Cairo. They claimed to represent the secret nationalist committees in Damascus and, hence, 'four-fifths and more of the total inhabitants of Syria'. The seven, who preferred to remain anonymous, protested strongly about the Sykes-Picot division of Arab territory into British and French zones. They had asked for clarification of recent pronouncements in favour of self-determination made in speeches by Lloyd George and President Wilson, and requested assurances that Britain intended to give the Arabs complete independence in Arabia, Syria, and Mesopotamia. Despite professions of loyalty to Hussein, the writers gave clear hints that they would be opposed to Sherifian rule in Syria, and asked whether the future regional governments would be decentralised, on the American model, or whether some leaders were to be given more influence than others.

The response from London had been carefully worded. It began by dividing the Arab areas referred to in the memorandum into four categories. The first two were areas 'which were free and independent before the war', and areas 'emancipated from Turkish control by the action of the Arabs themselves during the present war'. In these cases, the British Government would 'recognise the complete and sovereign independence of the Arabs inhabiting those areas and support them in their struggle for freedom'.

In the third category were areas 'occupied by the Allied forces during the present war.' Here, the undertakings were much more vague: it was

237

Britain's 'wish and desire' that the future government should be based on 'the principle of the consent of the governed'. Finally, there were 'Areas still under Turkish control', where it was also Britain's 'wish and desire' that the Arabs should gain their 'freedom and independence'. At first sight, this document was a flagrant contradiction of the Sykes-Picot Agreement. On closer scrutiny, however, it can be seen to contain a subtle ambiguity.

The crucial issue was whether any further areas of Syria and Lebanon captured by the Arabs before war ended would be regarded as coming into the second category: 'areas emancipated from Turkish control by the action of the Arabs themselves during the present war'. If so, the British were now pledged to recognising 'complete and sovereign independence' in these regions, despite the earlier Sykes-Picot undertakings.

However, Sir Mark Sykes, who had drafted the reply, meant the wording 'during the present war' to allow a second interpretation. While the obvious sense was 'during the whole of the present war', he had carefully phrased the document so that this vital clause could also be understood to mean 'during the present war up until now'. According to this alternative interpretation, Syria was excluded from the area of guaranteed independence. Sykes probably considered this ambiguity pardonable because he had persuaded himself that in the political atmosphere now prevailing, neither Britain nor France would attempt to impose colonial rule in their respective Sykes-Picot areas.

A few days later, Wingate received from Hussein's agent in Cairo an angry enquiry about the present status of the Sykes-Picot Agreement. As the Sherif had already known about the Agreement for some time, Wingate feared that this sudden reaction might be an attempt to pick a quarrel with Britain. He cabled to the Foreign Office saying that he had 'advised the agent to say that the Bolsheviks found . . . a [Russian] Foreign Office record of old conversations and a provisional understanding (not a formal treaty) between Britain, France and Russia early in the war to prevent difficulties between the Powers in prosecuting the war with Turkey. Jemal, either from ignorance or malice has . . . omitted its stipulations regarding the consent of the native populations and the safeguarding of their interests, and has ignored the fact that the subsequent outbreak and success of the Arab Revolt, and the withdrawal of Russia, has for a long time past created a wholly different situation.' He asked: 'Can I add that we regard the Agreement as dead for all practical purposes?' The Foreign Office approved the line Wingate had taken, but had to refuse his final request, pointing out that until or unless the Sykes-Picot Agreement was modified, Britain was bound to uphold its terms.

A meeting with two of the Syrians was arranged for June 25, and Hogarth read them the British Government's declaration as well as the reply Wingate had given to the Sherif's agent. As a result, both statements gained wide circulation. Taken together, their content led many people, including Lawrence, to believe that the declaration should be taken at its face value and that the Sykes-Picot Agreement was a dead letter.

Although the role to be played by Feisal's army under Allenby's new scheme would be less onerous than an independent offensive, Lawrence still thought it would be advisable to obtain additional regulars from the Hejaz. The extra men would help to secure the position at Maan until the autumn, and would enable the Arabs to send a large force northwards when the offensive began. He decided to go ahead with his visit to the Hejaz and put the case to Hussein personally.

By this time, however, he was beginning to realise that it might be extremely difficult to persuade the Sherif to transfer these units. The Hejaz was now embroiled in a dispute with ibn Saud, the Wahhabi leader of the Nejd on Hussein's inland frontier. Like Hussein, ibn Saud had formally broken with the Turks, but this had involved him in little fighting. Turkish strength in Arabia lay along the Hejaz Railway, in Hussein's territory. While the Sherifians had fought a long and hard campaign, ibn Saud had concentrated on increasing his personal influence in the Arabian Peninsula. Although he was nominally on friendly terms with the Sherif, there had been growing tension along their common frontier, and several incidents had taken place.

Hussein had made no secret of his aspirations to some kind of supremacy throughout the Arab world and, in his view, Britain bore a large share of the responsibility for the difficulties he was having with ibn Saud. The latter was receiving liberal support from the Government of India which, in pursuit of its 'divide and rule' policies, was deliberately building up ibn Saud as a counterbalance to Hussein in the Arabian Peninsula.

Lawrence sailed for Jidda on June 21, taking letters to the Sherif from Wingate and Allenby supporting the request to move troops to Syria. However, he soon realised that his mission was hopeless. In addition to Hussein's problems with ibn Saud, his relationship with Feisal had deteriorated sharply in recent months, no doubt because of Feisal's increasing dependence on Syrian and Iraqi officers who were opposed to the Sherif's wider political ambitions. Since early May, he had refused to allow Feisal to visit him, inventing one excuse after another. He now declined to meet Lawrence, on the pretext that it would not be correct to leave Mecca during Ramadan. They spoke by telephone, but Lawrence found that each time he tried to discuss the object of his mission, Hussein pretended that the line was faulty and broke off the conversation. Lawrence decided that it would be useless to pursue the matter. He left Jidda on July 1 and reached Cairo five days later.

From Cairo he went to Palestine, to discuss details of the forthcoming offensive with Allenby and Dawnay. The EEF had by this time a very considerable advantage in strength over the Turks, and Allenby knew it. Nevertheless, surprise would be the key to a cheap and speedy victory. As it happened, the abortive raids on Amman and Salt that spring had persuaded the Turks that the EEF intended to attack in that sector. Allenby, who learned of this Turkish appreciation from Intelligence sources, decided to do everything possible to sustain it. Meanwhile, he would build up his forces secretly along the Mediterranean coast. The real plan was to attack there in overwhelming force on September 19. He expected the Arabs to isolate Deraa three days beforehand. This would further convince the Turks that the weight of his own attack would fall in the east.

Returning to Cairo, Lawrence found time to reply to a letter from Vyvyan Richards, the friend with whom he had once planned to run a private press. Nine months before, in September 1917, he had mentioned to his parents that he might take up the printing scheme again after the war. He had then written: 'I can honestly say that I have never seen anyone doing anything so useful as the man who prints good books.' Now, however, his plans were less certain. He was convinced, as he explained wearily to Richards, that the kind of life he had thought of leading was forever closed to him. This letter is perhaps the earliest surviving document which reflects the mood that later took him into the ranks of the RAF: 'You guessed rightly that the Arab appealed to my imagination. It is the old, old civilisation, which has refined itself clear of household gods, and half the trappings which ours hastens to assume. The gospel of bareness in materials is a good one, and it involves apparently a sort of moral bareness too. They think for the moment, and endeavour to slip through life without turning corners or climbing hills. In part it is a mental and moral fatigue, a race trained out: and to avoid difficulties they have to jettison so much that we think honourable and brave: and yet without in any way sharing their point of view, I think I can understand it enough to look at myself and other foreigners from their direction, and without condemning it. I know I'm a stranger to them, and always will be: but I cannot believe them worse, any more than I could change to their ways . . .

'Anyway these years of detachment have cured me of any desire ever to do anything for myself. When they untie my bonds I will not find in me any spur to action . . .

'A house with no action entailed upon one, quiet, and liberty to think and abstain as one wills—yes, I think abstention, the leaving everything alone and watching the others still going past—is what I would choose today, if they ceased driving one . . .

'Those words—peace, silence, rest and the others—take on a vividness in the midst of noise and worry and weariness like a lighted window in the dark . . . A long quiet like a purge and then a contemplation and decision of future roads, that is what is to look forward to.'

By the beginning of July, the Turks had put an end to the Arab blockade of the railway north of Maan and had begun repairing the line. Both Dawnay and Lawrence knew that it was vital to prevent them from mounting an attack on Jaafar's force around Maan before the autumn offensive began. Otherwise, the whole northern scheme might founder: Feisal could not be expected to move regulars towards Deraa as long as his line of communication from Akaba onto the Maan plateau was under threat. Thinking over this problem, Dawnay suggested to Lawrence that two companies of the Imperial Camel Corps should be used to put on a show of force east of the Jordan.

Lawrence took to the idea immediately, and Dawnay therefore asked for General Staff approval. This was obtained, with the stipulation that the men must, if possible, be returned to Palestine by August 25, so that they would be available for Allenby's autumn offensive. For the same reason, they were not to be employed in any operation that might involve heavy casualties.

Dawnay and Lawrence worked out details of a long raid by the Camel Corps which would do as much as possible to worry the Turks in the short time available. They decided that the first objective should be the water installations at Mudawara station, and the second either a large railway bridge or the tunnel near Amman. Little was known, however, about these northern targets, and if they proved impossible, the Camel Corps would try to do serious damage to the railway farther south.

The real value of the expedition would be psychological. The Turks would probably not realise that these widely separated attacks had been carried out by the same force. As a result, they would be more uncertain than ever of Feisal's true strength. The natural reaction would be extra caution, and this would make them think very hard before launching an offensive southwards towards Maan.

Another matter discussed by Lawrence and Dawnay was the plan to take Deraa. Several factors had changed since Lawrence had first developed his scheme for an attack by camel-mounted Arabs, and he now proposed that only five hundred regulars should be withdrawn from Maan. They would ride north to Azrak in a single journey, taking with them a supply column of fifteen hundred camels, the French artillery, machine guns, two armoured cars and two areoplanes. The force would operate as a self-contained unit, carrying all the supplies it could not obtain locally. It would take a fortnight to reach Deraa, via Azrak, and another week to cut the railways with the help of the Rualla.

Some weeks before this, Dawnay had seen the need for an additional British officer to organise the line of communications inland from Akaba. It was clear that Jaafar Pasha's operations would be greatly assisted if the supply caravans were run more efficiently, and any kind of northern offensive would place still greater strains on transport resources. In early June, therefore, Dawnay had suggested to Joyce that Hubert Young would be suited to this work: 'His clear military mind would be specially well adapted to this class of work: his knowledge of Arabic would not be wasted, as he would be dealing, largely, direct with the Arabs; moreover, his present nominal position as understudy to Lawrence has never up to now really panned out entirely satisfactorily, and I am not sure, taking the personal factor into account, that it is ever likely to; also, and lastly, one doesn't see any apparent alternative'. Another British officer, Major Stirling, was about to join Joyce's staff, and Dawnay proposed the following division of responsibilities:

'*Yourself* [Joyce], directly in charge of the whole show.
'*Lawrence*, running his peculiar brand of Lawrentian stunt, and carrying on as usual.

'*Young*, i/c communications and administrative understudy to yourself.

'*Stirling*, in charge of the travelling circus [British units in the
northern operation], and doing the bulk of the reconnaissance work
and so forth.'

Young had arrived in late June. As before, he proved to be an able but
very demanding chief, who found it frustrating to deal with the
independent-minded Arabs in charge of supply caravans. Joyce was worried by the constant rows, but Dawnay nevertheless urged him to make
the best use of Young's ability.

Joyce had also complained that he was not being sufficiently consulted
about schemes submitted by Lawrence to GHQ, even though he would
have to play a large part in their execution: 'I am quite prepared to accept
any responsibility as regards all British and European personnel . . .
being the senior officer here, that of course is my job. As regards the
whole show, I think Colonel Lawrence must accept a share of the
responsibility—he pipes the tune with GHQ and then disappears and
leaves working out . . . details to other people, and these may or may not
work when put into practice.' Dawnay had replied that he had discussed
the question with General Bartholomew, 'and I think that you may now
feel absolutely assured that in future no scheme or plan will receive
official sanction . . . until examined and recommended by yourself . . .
That is to say, that although "wild cat" schemes may and will be
discussed—academically—their acceptance will in future rest on your
approval after thorough examination by us both.

'Moreover, that, I honestly believe, is what Lawrence himself would
wish—as he is absolutely satisfied in his capacity of the inexhaustible
fountain of ideas, and perfectly content to leave to others the more practical business of irrigating the fields.'

Despite this assurance, Joyce was not consulted about the new plans
for the Deraa operation and the Camel Corps raid until the main outlines
had been finalised and submitted to GHQ. Details were taken to Akaba by
Stirling, who arrived on July 19.

When Joyce received these plans, he telegraphed Cairo asking that no
final decision about the northern operations should be taken until an
alternative, drawn up at Guweira, had also been considered. Thus, when
Lawrence returned to Akaba on July 28 after a seven-week absence, he
was shown an elaborate nine-page scheme, worked out largely by Young.

It contained detailed schedules (down to the last camel-load) for trans-
porting food, ammunition, and forage, which were to be stockpiled in
dumps in advance of the movement of five hundred camel-mounted regulars northward to Azrak. The supply system envisaged was so complex
that the 'flying column' could not even set out until September 29, and
would reach Azrak on October 7 or 8.

Lawrence must have seen at a glance that the scheme was impossibly
complicated. Its precise interdependent timetables would be reduced to
chaos by the dislocation inevitable in Arab operations. He said plainly
that he thought it unworkable. Moreover, even if by some miracle it did
succeed, the regulars would arrive at Deraa three weeks too late to meet
Allenby's requirement. He therefore insisted on the alternative he had
worked out with Dawnay.

Joyce was furious at this new *fait accompli,* and in the discussion that
followed he sided with Young, who had spent many hours calculating the
transport schedules. They argued, with some reason, that inadequate
supply had always been the cardinal weakness of Arab operations. Lawrence refused to give way, and the atmosphere became very tense. There
was also disagreement about the Camel Corps raid. The transport arrangements, as set out by Young, would be stretched to the limit by the
forthcoming offensive, and it was argued that there was no spare capacity
to put in the dumps required by the Camel Corps. Joyce said that the
result would be a further delay to the main autumn campaign.

The argument seems not to have reached any immediate conclusion.
Young later wrote: 'Relations between Lawrence and ourselves became
for the moment a trifle strained, and the sight of the little man reading the
Morte d'Arthur in a corner of the mess-tent with an impish smile on his
face was not consoling.' The documents suggest that it was three days
before Joyce gave in. He cabled Dawnay on August 1: 'It is evident after
discussion with Lawrence, that operations must be accelerated . . . The
scheme as outlined [by us] has as a result to be cancelled and a short raid
with a reduced force substituted . . . Time does not permit of forward
dumps being put in. Our supply [calculations] for personnel and animals
are therefore quite unsound. In the past, unsupported raids . . . have had
a bad effect on the Arab movement . . . Sherif Feisal is prepared to make
the attempt but expects full support should premature action result in
reprisals on the tribes concerned.' He had also accepted the Camel Corps
scheme.

Young resigned himself to doing things Lawrence's way, at any rate in
this instance. He focused his attention on Jaafar Pasha's supply lines, and

earned generous praise in *Seven Pillars*, where Lawrence wrote: 'Using his full power, he grappled with the chaos. He had no stores for his columns, no saddles, no clerks, no veterinaries, no drugs and few drivers, so that to run a harmonious and orderly train was impossible; but Young very nearly did it, in his curious ungrateful way. Thanks to him, the supply problem of the Arab regulars on the plateau was solved.'

The Camel Corps raiding party reached Akaba on July 31. Although Lawrence would not be involved in their attack on Mudawara, he guided them for the first stage of the journey, to Wadi Rumm. During this ride he struck up what was to be a lasting friendship with their commanding officer, Robin Buxton who, like himself, had studied history at Oxford. Buxton gave his first impressions of Lawrence in a letter to England: 'He is only a boy to look at, has a very quiet sedate manner, a fine head but insignificant body. He is known to every Arab in this country for his personal bravery and train wrecking exploits. I don't know whether it is his intrepidity, disinterestedness and mysteriousness which appeals to the Arab most, or his success in finding them rich trains to blow up and loot. After a train success he tells me the army is like Barnum's show and gradually disintegrates. At any rate it is wonderful what he has accomplished with the poor tools at his disposal.

'His influence is astounding not only on the misbeguided native, but also I think on his brother officers and seniors. Out here he lives entirely with the Arab, wears their clothes, eats only their food, and bears all the burdens that the lowliest of them does. He always travels in spotless white, and in fact reminds one of a Prince of Mecca more than anything. He will join us again later I hope as his presence is very stimulating to us all and one has that feeling that things can not go wrong while he is there.'

On Lawrence's side, the thoughts provoked by this ride with the Camel Corps were later recorded in *Seven Pillars*: 'I stayed at Rum with the Camel Corps for the first day, feeling the unreality there of these healthy-looking tommies, like stiff-bodied schoolboys in their shirts and shorts . . . Three years of Egypt and Sinai had burned all the colour out of their faces, to a deep brown—in which their blue eyes flickered weakly like sky-gaps, against the dark possessed gaze of my men. For the rest they were a broad-faced, low-browed people, blunt-featured beside the decadent Arabs, whose fine-curved shapes had been sharpened by generations of breeding to a radiance ages older than these primitive, blotched, honest Englishmen . . .

'Late the next day I left them, and rode for Akaba, passing again through the high-walled Itm, but now alone with my silent, unquestioning fellows, who rode after me like shadows, harmonious and submerged in their natural sand and bush and hill; and a home-sickness came over me, reminding me vividly of my outcast life among these Arabs, exploiting their highest ideals and making their love of freedom one more tool to help us win England the victory over her enemies.

'It was evening, and the low sun was falling on the straight bar of Sinai ahead, its globe extravagantly brilliant in my eyes, because I was dead-tired of life, longing as seldom before for the peaceful moody sky in England. This sunset was fierce, stimulant, barbaric. Its intense glow revived the colours of the desert like a draught—as indeed it did each evening, yet seeming ever a new miracle of strength and heat—while my longings were for weakness and chill, and grey mistiness, that I might not be so crystalline clear, so sure of the wrong which I was doing.

'We English who lived years abroad among strangers . . . idealised our country so highly, that when we returned, sometimes the reality fell too short of our dreams to be tolerable. When away, we were worth more than other men by our conviction that she was greatest, straightest and best of all the countries of the world, and we would die before knowing that a page of her history had been blotted by defeat. Here, in Arabia, in the war's need, I was selling my honesty for her sustenance . . .'

The sense of guilt about his role had never been far from his thoughts, and he could imagine the personal recriminations that would follow if, when the war was ended, the Arabs were denied what he had promised them. These forebodings now came to him very strongly, because he was to see Nuri Shalaan in order to discuss the role to be played by Rualla tribesmen in the attack on Deraa. He could not forget the pledge he had given at their last meeting, a year before. Nuri now knew, because of the Sykes-Picot revelations, that Lawrence had not told the whole truth, and he might demand fulfilment of whatever penalty had been agreed between them. Lawrence later wrote: 'There was a particular and very horrible reason (not published) for my distress at this moment.'

On August 7, he was flown from Guweira to Jefer, where the talks with Nuri were to take place. The anxiety he felt is clear from his description of the flight in *Seven Pillars*: 'The air was thin and bumpy, so that we hardly scraped over the crest of Shtar [the head of the pass near Aba el Lissan]. I sat wondering if we would crash, almost hoping it. I felt sure Nuri was about to claim fulfilment of our dishonourable half-bargain, whose execution seemed more impure than its thought. Death in the air would be a clean escape; yet I scarcely hoped it, not from fear, for I was too tired to be much afraid: nor from scruple, for our lives seemed to me absolutely our own, to keep or give away: but from habit, for lately I had risked myself only when it seemed profitable to our cause.

'I was busy compartmenting-up my own mind, finding instinct and reason as ever at strong war. Instinct said "Die", but reason said that was only to cut the mind's tether, and loose it into freedom: better to seek some mental death, some slow wasting of the brain to sink it below these puzzlements. An accident was meaner than deliberate fault. If I did not hesitate to risk my life, why fuss to dirty it? Yet life and honour seemed in different categories, not able to be sold one for another: and for honour, had I not lost that a year ago when I assured the Arabs that England kept her plighted word?'

To his relief, when they reached Jefer, Nuri greeted him amicably, making 'no mention of my price'. But the Rualla leader had not forgotten their previous discussion, and he brought out copies of the Sykes-Picot Agreement and the declaration to the seven Syrians of Cairo. Lawrence later wrote: 'Old Nuri Shalaan, wrinkling his wise nose, returned to me with his file of documents, asking in puzzlement which of them all he might believe. As before, I glibly repeated "The last in date", and the Emir's sense of the honour of his word made him see the humour. Ever after he did his best for our joint cause, only warning me, when he failed in a promise, that it had been superseded by a later intention!'

Feisal was at this meeting also, and for two hours Lawrence shared with him the task of preaching revolt to the Rualla sheikhs. Afterwards, Lawrence was flown back to Guweira, and by nightfall he had travelled down to Akaba.

News came that Buxton's Camel Corps had succeeded in taking Mudawara, the Turkish post that had survived so many previous expeditions. They had attacked before dawn, and had captured the station with the loss of only seven men killed. By evening, the wells and railway installations had been destroyed.

Afterwards, the British force had set off north-eastwards towards Jefer. Lawrence and Joyce drove out to meet it there on August 11, and a conference was held to decide which of the northern targets to attack. In the end they chose the most difficult: a railway viaduct near Kissir, south of Amman. This meant making another 120-mile journey behind Turkish lines. As the raid would bring British troops into contact with Arab tribesmen, Lawrence was to accompany it.

When the Camel Corps reached Bair on August 15 it was found that the dump of stores placed there in readiness had been looted by bedouin tribesmen. The loss was serious, since it meant that the raiding party would have to be scaled down.

The next day was Lawrence's thirtieth birthday but, according to Buxton's notes, he was ill with a high temperature. He chose to pass most of his time alone, thinking about what he had made of his life. During the preceding months he had become prone to morbid introspection and, in his feverish state, this exercise in self-judgment gave him little satisfaction.

The Camel Corps continued northwards, and on August 20 was within eight miles of Amman. During the final stage of the journey there was an alarm when the column was sighted by two German aircraft: as a result Buxton knew that his attack could no longer take the Turks by surprise. To make matters worse, a bedouin tribe which had yet to declare for the Revolt was camped in the area they would have to cross in order to reach the railway viaduct. Two Arabs, sent forward to find out what the situation was, reported that there were also three strong Turkish patrols in the district.

Taken together, these factors greatly increased the risk of heavy fighting and casualties. Therefore, with much regret, the rest of the operation was abandoned. Although the target itself had not been touched, the raiding party had already served its main purpose. The Turks would be alarmed by exaggerated rumours of its strength, and would soon turn their energies to preparing a defence of Amman rather than attacking Jaafar Pasha.

On August 26 Lawrence arrived back in Aba el Lissan, to find that preparations for the Deraa raid had been completed. At this critical juncture, however, Feisal's army was thrown into confusion because of an unexpected intervention by Hussein. The ageing Sherif had published in the *Qibla*, his newspaper at Mecca, a statement to the effect that Jaafar Pasha had never been appointed Commander-in-Chief of the regular Northern Army and held no such position.

The truth was that Jaafar's appointment had been made by Feisal in 1917, but that Hussein had never approved of it. Lawrence saw the intervention as an attempt by Hussein to assert his authority over Feisal. He later wrote: 'This gross insult to all of us had been published by King Hussein . . . out of pique at his son's too-great success, and to spite the northern town Arabs, the Syrian and Mesopotamian officers, whom the

King despised and feared. He knew they were fighting, not to give him dominion, but to set free their own countries to govern themselves'.

As a result of the announcement Jaafar immediately resigned, and so did all his officers. Feisal might have been prepared to ignore the snub, but the Syrians and Iraqis in his army opposed Hussein's political ambitions, and seized the opportunity to humiliate the Sherif by forcing a retraction of the offensive statement. In view of their attitude, Feisal felt that he too must resign, which he did in a telegram to his father of August 29. This development led in turn to problems with the irregular forces, who had previously been unaffected by the squabble.

From the British point of view, the position was extremely worrying. Unless the columns moved off for Azrak without delay, the Deraa raid would not take place on the date Allenby had requested. Everything possible was being done to persuade Hussein to make a conciliatory gesture, but the northern operation could not be held up until he gave in. For the moment, the British officers at Aba el Lissan had assumed direct command. Lawrence cabled to Cairo on August 30: 'According to plan, the convoy and advanced guard of the September scheme are going forward on our orders, without Sherifian approval . . . I think that the situation can be held together another four days. If Feisal can be satisfied by then, operations may continue, if not I will do all possible to withdraw these advanced posts.' In this manner a supply caravan and the first assault column set out, accompanied by Pisani's artillery, on September 3. They were one day late.

In the meantime there was a tedious correspondence with Hussein, who was in no hurry to withdraw his remarks. Lawrence was bitterly angry that so much planning had been put in jeopardy. This was the Arabs' one chance of victory in the north, and they would lose a great deal if they threw it away. He later wrote: 'King Hussein behaved truly to type, protesting fluently, with endless circumlocution . . . It was intolerable to be at the mercy of so crass a person.'

Hussein's cipher messages passed through the hands of British radio operators and were decoded secretly before being passed to the Arab secretariat. Lawrence had been taking advantage of this to re-copy them, corrupting the most offensive passages so that they became unintelligible. Finally, on September 4, he decided that no further delay could be tolerated. In *Seven Pillars* he wrote: 'there came a long message, the first half a lame apology and withdrawal of the mischievous proclamation, the second half a repetition of the offence in a new form. I suppressed the tail, and took the head marked "very urgent" to Feisal's tent'.

This intervention resolved a crisis which no one wanted to see prolonged. A few days later Joyce reported to Cairo: 'Lawrence and Nasir left for the north on September 6th . . . Recent satisfactory telegrams have greatly relieved the situation . . . unless anything unforeseen arises I confidently expect to leave on the 9th with Feisal.'

CHAPTER 16

A Hollow Triumph
September 1918

LAWRENCE and Nasir travelled up to Azrak in an armoured car with Lord
Winterton, a Camel Corps officer who had recently transferred to Arab
operations. Nasir, rather than Feisal, was to take charge of the Arab
irregulars in this final campaign. As Lawrence later wrote: 'In accord
with my year-old principle, Feisal would be kept in the background, in
reserve, to be risked as a last card only if the situation was overtaxing our
strengths, or if we were certainly victors. Until then, to fill his place, we
needed an experienced and popular Sherif in command, since we would
have contingents of Rualla, of Serahin, of Druses, and of Howeitat tribesmen . . . besides masses of peasant horse and foot from the villages of the
Hauran'. During the next few days the Arab striking force assembled at
Azrak in readiness for the assault. There were in all nearly 1,000 men,
including the specialist British, French and Indian units.

Unless there was some wholly unexpected misadventure, the northern
breakthrough Lawrence had worked towards for so long was about to take
place. However, he did not share in the general mood of elation. He had
begun to lose the sense of purpose that had been driving him. In *Seven
Pillars* he wrote: 'Everyone was stout and in health. Except myself. The
crowd had destroyed my pleasure in Azrak, and I went off down the
valley . . . and lay there all day in my old lair among the tamarisk, where
the wind in the dusty green branches played with such sounds as it made
in English trees. It told me I was tired to death of these Arabs; petty
incarnate Semites who attained heights and depths beyond our reach,
though not beyond our sight. They realised our absolute in their unre-
strained capacity for good and evil; and for two years I had profitably
shammed to be their companion!

'To-day it came to me with finality that my patience as regards the false
position I had been led into was finished. A week, two weeks, three, and
I would insist upon relief. My nerve had broken; and I would be lucky if
the ruin of it could be hidden so long.'

The motivation that had sustained him until this final campaign had
been largely personal. Ever since coming to Cairo Intelligence at the end

of 1914 he had dreamed of bringing freedom and dignity to the peasant villagers of Syria, a population which had been exploited for centuries by corrupt Turkish administrators. It seems that in his mind he had distilled this idea into a simple, untarnished image: that of his friend and protégé at Carchemish, Dahoum—the boy who had once helped to save his life. When faced by the difficulties and horrors of the battlefield, most men drew moral strength from some such concept; a symbol of the values and loyalties they were fighting for that could be called to mind in an instant. Many found this image in religious belief or the memory of loved ones at home. But by this time Lawrence had few religious convictions, and he had lived away from England since 1910. His closest personal allegiances were not in Oxford, but in Carchemish, where he had lived so happily before the war.

At the end of *Seven Pillars* he wrote: 'The strongest motive throughout had been a personal one . . . present to me, I think, every hour of these two years.' This private motive also appears in the book's dedication: 'I loved you, so I drew these tides of men into my hands . . . to earn you Freedom'. The meaning of both passages is clarified in a letter written while he was drafting *Seven Pillars*: 'I liked a particular Arab very much, and I thought that freedom for the race would be an acceptable present.'

By the time the final offensive began, Lawrence knew that Dahoum was dead. This is clear from several post-war statements. He said, for example, that the personal motive referred to in the dedication had ceased to exist 'some weeks before' the capture of Damascus. Other remarks suggest that this does not refer to the date of Dahoum's death but to the date he learned of it. He told Liddell Hart: 'The unhappy "event" happened long before we got to Damascus', and two years after the Armistice he wrote: 'Dahoum died some years ago, during the war, of fever'.

In reality, Dahoum may have died a long time before. In 1916 there had been a severe famine in northern Syria followed by a typhus epidemic. Leonard Woolley, who went to the Jerablus region at the end of 1918, found that nearly half of the old Carchemish labour force had perished, and it was reported to him that almost a third of the population had died during 1916.

Dahoum had remained at the site as one of the guards, and salary records for the first two years of the war show that he worked there on and off until October 1916. After this, no records survive; but Woolley's post-war reports state that, apart from Hamoudi, none of the men who had originally been appointed to watch over the site had been there during the later part of the war.

Carchemish is some two hundred miles north of Damascus, and it is most improbable that Lawrence heard the news directly. On the other hand, British Intelligence received a constant flow of local information from Turkish prisoners and deserters. The Arab Intelligence office at Allenby's advance headquarters had been built up by Hogarth, who was interested in any news of Carchemish. If he had learned of Dahoum's death, he would have seen to it that Lawrence was told.

Lawrence knew that the presence of a large force at Azrak could not be kept secret from the Turks. He was confident, however, that they would see it as further proof that the Arabs were about to launch an attack on Amman, which was almost due west of Azrak and much closer than the real target, Deraa. This impression had been carefully fostered, as it would reinforce the Turkish expectation that the EEF was planning a third attack on Salt.

By the time the Arab forces were assembled, it was clear that they would not be able to attack Deraa in the way Lawrence had hoped. His plan had been to take the town by direct assault, under cover of an aerial bombardment; but messages from Palestine now warned that the RAF would be unable to provide very much air support. Moreover, the large force of Rualla irregulars which he had expected had not had time to gather, mainly because of the delays created by the *Qibla* affair. At a conference held on September 11, the original plan was dropped. Instead, the Arabs would 'carry out a flying attack on the northern, western, and southern railways at Deraa, with our regular troops, the Rualla horse . . . and such Hauran peasants as should be brave enough to declare for us.'

The first step would be to make a break in the railway between Amman and Deraa. This would strengthen Turkish fears of a threat to Amman, and prevent the reinforcement of Deraa from the south. A raiding party consisting of Peake's Egyptians and the Gurkha Rifles left Azrak on September 13 to carry this out, assisted by the armoured cars. Although the expedition ran into problems, the line was successfully cut on September 16. Meanwhile, the main column had continued its advance, with the object of breaking the line between Deraa and Damascus. This too was carried out successfully, with only one Arab killed. In *Seven Pillars* Lawrence wrote: 'So . . . ten miles of the Damascus line was freely ours . . . It was the only railway to Palestine and Hejaz and I could hardly believe our fortune; hardly believe that our word to Allenby was fulfilled so simply and so soon.' Demolitions to the line were so extensive that it would remain closed during several vital days.

Once the railway north and south of Deraa had been cut, only the branch line westwards into Palestine remained. Nuri's regulars were sent to attack this, and Lawrence joined them with his bodyguard. The station at Mezerib, west of Deraa, was carried by assault. Lawrence later reported: 'As our only demolition parties were on the Damascus line, still demolishing, we could not do anything very extensive, but cleared the station, burnt a lot of rolling stock and two lorries, broke the points and planted a fair assortment of "tulips" [mines] down the line.' Lawrence and Young also cut the main telegraph lines into Palestine, an essential part of Turkish military communications. The damage would probably not be repaired before Allenby's surprise offensive began.

Later that night, Lawrence took a demolition party a few miles farther west, hoping to blow up the bridge at Tell el Shehab, where he had failed a year previously. They approached under cover of darkness, but found that a trainload of German and Turkish reserves had just arrived from Palestine. For a second time, Lawrence had to leave the bridge intact; but his disappointment was tempered by knowledge that these troops, sent up to reinforce Deraa against Arab raids, would weaken Turkish resistance west of the Jordan.

By the morning of September 19, the expedition was safely back in the Arab camp at Umtaiye in Jebel Druse. That was the day of Allenby's attack.

Although the Arab advance position had seemed well chosen when the plans were made, it was proving to be very vulnerable to Turkish aircraft. The Arabs were defenceless, since both of the British aircraft that had accompanied them had now been grounded (in one case after heroic action against enemy machines). Some remedy was urgently needed.

It had been arranged that an RAF machine would fly from Palestine to Azrak on September 21, to bring news of the EEF advance. Lawrence went down to meet it, hoping to fly across to Allenby's headquarters and arrange for air cover. The aeroplane brought news of a quite extraordinary victory. As planned, the EEF had attacked in overwhelming force in the early hours of September 19, taking the Turks completely by surprise. There had been little organised resistance and, by noon, all semblance of orderly retreat had ended. Allenby's cavalry had then broken through and swept northwards to close off the enemy's main lines of retreat. The only remaining escape route was eastwards across the Jordan, and Allenby hoped that the Arabs would close it.

The aeroplane brought several messages. One, from Allenby to Feisal, read: 'I send your Highness my greetings and my most cordial congratulations upon the great achievement of your gallant troops about Deraa, the effect of which has, by throwing the enemy's communications into confusion, had an important bearing upon the success of my own operations.

'Thanks to our combined efforts, the Turkish Army is defeated and is everywhere in full retreat . . .

'Already the Turkish Army in Syria has suffered a defeat from which it can scarcely recover. It rests upon us now, by the redoubled energy of our attacks, to turn defeat into destruction.'

There was also a letter from Dawnay to Joyce which enclosed Allenby's new instructions for the Arab forces. Dawnay wrote: 'the whole Turkish army is in the net, and every bolt-hole closed except, possibly, that east of the Jordan by way of the Yarmuk valley.

'If the Arabs can close this, too—and close it in time—then, not a man, or gun, or wagon ought to escape—*some* victory!'

He went on to spell out Allenby's requirements: '(1) he wants the railway *south* of Deraa smashed, *as completely as you are able* to smash it, in order to eliminate that flank once and for all; (2) he wants the tribes to close the gap across the Yarmuk valley between Lake Tiberias and Deraa, which may be used by parts of the 8th Army Corps from the Amman area and by remnants of other troops who succeed in making their way across from west of Jordan. (3) Above all he does NOT wish Feisal to dash off, on his own, to Damascus or elsewhere—we shall soon be able to put him there as part of our own operations, and if he darts off prematurely without General Allenby's knowledge and consent, to guarantee his action, there will be the very devil to pay later on, which might upset the whole apple cart. So use all your restraining influence, and get Lawrence to do the same, to prevent Feisal from any act of rashness in the north, which might force our hand and in the wrong direction. The situation is completely in our hands to mould now, so Feisal need have no fear of being carted, provided he will trust us and be patient. Only let him on no account move north without first consulting General Allenby—that would be the fatal error.' The letter ended: 'All good luck to you, Joyce, again my *best* congratulations to you all. Give a good fruity message from me to Feisal, and my love to Lorenzo, and Frank Stirling.'

As Lawrence had hoped, he was able to fly across to EEF headquarters. It was fortunate that he did so, because the military situation was changing from hour to hour and the information received at Azrak was already out of date. During the night of September 20, a large part of the Turkish

7th Army, together with remnants of the 8th, had attempted to escape eastwards. This movement had been detected at dawn on the 21st when British pilots reported a long transport column moving down the Wadi Fara from Nablus towards the Jordan valley. They were attacked from the air with devastating effect, and those men who escaped amounted to little more than an exhausted rabble without transport or supplies; most would be picked off by Arab villagers. One of the main tasks Feisal had been requested to undertake was no longer necessary.

The victory in Palestine was so complete that Allenby decided to push forward immediately, before the Turks had a chance to regroup. His next objectives would be Deraa and Damascus. To defend them, there were at present only the regular Turkish garrisons, plus any remnants that might reach these towns from the defeated armies in Palestine.

To the south, however, was the Turkish 4th army, based east of the Jordan at Maan, Amman and Salt. This had not, so far, been involved in any of the fighting, except some skirmishes with Arab raiding parties around Deraa. As soon as its commanders realised what had happened in Palestine they would guess Allenby's next move and see the danger of being cut off. They would respond by pulling back northwards, hoping to make a stand at Deraa or Damascus. Allenby was keen to forestall such a move, and this was why he had asked Feisal to destroy the railway south of Deraa.

He now told Lawrence that cavalry units of the EEF would shortly drive eastwards across the Jordan. The New Zealanders under Major-General Chaytor would occupy Salt and Amman, hoping to intercept the retreat of the 4th Army. An Indian force, under Major-General Barrow, would move on Deraa, while Australian troops under Lieutenant-General Chauvel would advance on Kuneitra, farther north. When these places had been taken, the forces under Chauvel and Barrow would close on Damascus, while Chaytor continued his holding operation at Amman.

For the present, the Arabs were to co-operate with these movements, and in particular with action against the Turkish 4th Army. Allenby again stressed that there was to be no independent Arab offensive. Lawrence was told firmly not to carry out his 'saucy threat to take Damascus, till we were all together.' He was assured, however, that Feisal would be given the opportunity to set up an Arab government in Damascus.

Before leaving GHQ, he asked for the air cover so badly needed by the Arabs. Two fighting aircraft were sent out to the advance base near Deraa immediately; Lawrence flew back in one of them. In addition, it was arranged that a Handley-Page bomber would fly across bringing petrol and spares.

By this time, the Arab achievement at Deraa had been reported back to London. It was discussed at a meeting of the War Cabinet on September 20. The minutes record that 'The attention of the War Cabinet was again called to the work which Colonel Lawrence was doing with the Arab forces, and General Wilson undertook to make enquiries with regard to suitable recognition being given to Colonel Lawrence for his valuable services.'

While this was by no means the first time that Lawrence had been discussed by the Cabinet, he was still totally unknown to the general public. Four days later, however, his name was published in a French newspaper, the *Echo de Paris*, and its startling claims were immediately picked up by the London press. The *Evening Standard*, among others, translated the French report, heading it 'An historic Lawrence': 'Side by side with General Allenby and the French Colonel de Piépape [commander of the French contingent in Palestine] we must mention Colonel Lawrence as having played a part of the greatest importance in the Palestine victory. The name of Colonel Lawrence, who placed at the disposal of the British leader his experience of the country and his talent for organisation, will become historic in Great Britain.

'At the head of the cavalry force which he had formed with Bedouins and Druses, he cut the railway at Deraa, thus severing the enemy communications between Damascus and Haifa and the eastern side of the Jordan.'

One result of Allenby's unexpected advance was that attention in London and Paris was suddenly focused on the future of Syria. On September 23, the French Ambassador in London called to see A. J. Balfour, the Foreign Secretary. Balfour noted afterwards that Cambon had spoken of 'the situation which seemed likely to be created in the immediate future by General Allenby's success in Palestine. The Turkish Armies in that country had apparently been now destroyed, and there seemed every probability that General Allenby would penetrate into Syria. Syria, as M. Cambon reminded me, was, by the Sykes-Picot Agreement, within the French sphere of influence, and it was extremely important from the French point of view that this fact should not be lost sight of in any arrangements that General Allenby, as Commander-in-Chief, might make for the administration of the country he was presumably about to occupy.'

In response, Balfour had given Cambon a statement setting out the Cabinet's position: 'The British Government adhere to their declared policy with regard to Syria: namely that, if it should fall into the sphere of interest of any European Power, that Power should be France. They also think that this policy should be made perfectly clear both in France and elsewhere.

'The exact course which should be followed by the two Governments in case General Allenby takes his forces into Syria should be immediately discussed in Paris or London. But it is understood that in any event, wherever officers are required to carry out civilian duties, these officers should (unless the French Government express an opinion to the contrary) be French and not English; without prejudice of course to the supreme authority of the Commander-in-Chief while the country is in military occupation.'

This statement was telegraphed to Allenby on September 25, with a reminder of those clauses of the Sykes-Picot Agreement which applied to inland Syria. At the same time, he was sent the text of a Foreign Office message to Paris: 'If General Allenby advances to Damascus, it would be most desirable that in conformity with the Anglo-French Agreement of 1916 he should if possible work through an Arab Administration by means of French Liaison.'

It is clear from the records that these steps were forced on the British Government by French demands that the Sykes-Picot Agreement should be applied at once. They did not reflect any enthusiasm in London for French ambitions, which were now seen to be an acute embarrassment *vis-à-vis* the Arabs.

On September 22 Lawrence returned to Azrak where he met Feisal and explained the need to break the line south of Deraa, in order to hold up any northward movement by the Turkish 4th Army. During the following two days armoured cars, Arab regulars and large forces of tribesmen attacked the railway many times, until it was impossible for trains to travel between Amman and Deraa.

As Allenby had foreseen, the Turks decided to abandon Maan and began to move northwards by train, but before they could reach Amman, it too was evacuated. When the retreating forces arrived at the break in the railway, they had to continue their journey by road. As a result, their movement soon became very slow and disorganised.

Once the line south of Deraa was damaged beyond repair, Lawrence made up his mind to press northwards. If the Arabs took up a position north of Deraa and prevented the railway there coming back into service, that garrison too would find itself in extreme difficulties. It would have to choose between a retreat by road, leaving most of its stores and equipment behind, or making a stand in the town, where it would quickly be surrounded by Barrow's cavalry.

Lawrence planned, after cutting the railway, to move north-west of Deraa to Sheikh Saad, where the Arab force would be able to watch over the Turkish line of retreat. From this vantage point, they could attack any units of the Turkish 4th Army trying to go north, and also remnants of the Palestine Armies still moving up through the Yarmuk valley.

Once this scheme was under way, there would be no purpose in retaining the present base in Jebel Druse; the armoured cars, which could not operate in the Hauran, would be sent back to Azrak. Operations in the north would be carried out by Nuri as-Said's regulars and tribal forces.

On September 25 Lawrence wrote to GHQ: 'The [Turkish] force coming up from Amman is presumably about four thousand strong. Of this we hope to knock out nearly half. I think the others will not stand at Deraa (where they will find about two thousand of the relicts of the Palestine Army) but will go off to Damascus at once. Please tell the C.G.S. that I am acting on this idea and raising the west side of the Hauran . . .

'Will you get news to me as soon as you can of General Allenby's intentions as to following up the Turks? We can do it, and I think should do it to the Nth, but we would be glad to have a small force of British cavalry with us.'

On the same day, Allenby issued new instructions to Feisal. He knew that the Arab forces had fulfilled much of their previous assignment and that Lawrence was moving north. The Foreign Office had now confirmed that there was to be an Arab administration in Damascus, and there no longer seemed any reason to stop Feisal going there. Allenby therefore sent an urgent message: 'There is no objection to Your Highness entering Damascus as soon as you consider that you can do so with safety.

'I am sending troops to Damascus and I hope that they will arrive there in four or five days from today.

'I trust that Your Highness' forces will be able to co-operate, but you should not relax your pressure in the Deraa district, as it is of vital importance to cut off the Turkish forces which are retreating North from Maan, Amman and Es Salt.' This letter was taken to Feisal by air, but Lawrence seems not to have been aware of it for some days.

Allenby's administrative plans for Syria were set out in a résumé cabled to London shortly afterwards: 'As regards the "A" area [reserved for French influence], notably the city of Damascus, I shall recognise the local Arab administration which I expect to find in existence and shall appoint a French liaison officer as required . . .

'I hope by the above procedure to safeguard French and Arab interests while ensuring that supreme control remains in my own hands as C.-in-C.' The way was now open, therefore, for Feisal to set up an Arab government in Damascus. It could assume responsibility for civil administration as soon as the Turks left.

Allenby took other steps to ensure that this was allowed to happen. At his final meeting of corps commanders, on September 26, he made it clear that EEF forces were to stay out of Damascus. The orders given to forces closing in on the city included a specific instruction: 'While operating against the enemy about Damascus care will be taken to avoid entering the town if possible . . . Unless forced to do so for tactical reasons, no troops are to enter Damascus. Brigadiers will arrange a picquet on all roads from their areas in to the town to ensure this order being carried out . . .

'Damascus will be left under the . . . civil administration and no national flags will be flown.'

Soon after the Arab forces reached Sheikh Saad, news came that Deraa was being evacuated by road. A little later a British aeroplane dropped a message that two columns of Turks were approaching. As Lawrence afterwards reported: 'One from Deraa was six thousand strong, and one from Mezerib, two thousand strong. We determined that the second was about our size, and marched the regulars out to meet it just north of Tafas, while sending our Hauran horse out to hang on to the skirts of the large column . . . We were too late (since on the way we had a profitable affair with an infantry battalion) to prevent the Mezerib column getting into Tafas. They strengthened themselves there, and as at Turaa, the last village they had entered, allowed themselves to rape all the women they could catch. We attacked them with all arms as they marched out later, and bent the head of their column back towards Tell Arar. When Sherif Bey, the Turkish Commander of the Lancer rearguard in the village, saw this he ordered that the inhabitants be killed. These included some twenty small children (killed with lances and rifles), and about forty women. I noticed particularly one pregnant woman, who had been forced down on a saw-bayonet. Unfortunately, Talal, the Sheikh of Tafas, who . . . had been a tower of strength to us from the beginning, and who was one of the coolest and boldest horsemen I have ever met, was in front with Auda abu Tayi and myself when we saw these sights. He gave a horrible cry, wrapped his headcloth about his face, put spurs to his horse, and rocking in the saddle, galloped at full speed into the midst of the retiring column, and fell, himself and his mare, riddled with machine-gun bullets, among their lance points.

'With Auda's help we were able to cut the enemy column in three. The third section, with German machine-gunners, resisted magnificently, and got off, not cheaply . . . The second and leading portions after a bitter struggle, we wiped out completely. We ordered ''no prisoners'' and the men obeyed, except that the reserve company took two hundred and fifty men (including many German A.S.C.) alive. Later, however, they found one of our men with a fractured thigh who had been afterwards pinned to the ground by two mortal thrusts with German bayonets. Then we turned our Hotchkiss on the prisoners and made an end of them, they saying nothing. The common delusion that the Turk is a clean and merciful fighter led some of the British troops to criticize Arab methods a little later—but they had not entered Turaa or Tafas, or watched the Turks swing their wounded by the hands and feet into a burning railway truck, as had been the lot of the Arab army at Jerdun. As for the villagers, they and their ancestors had been for five hundred years ground down by the tyranny of these Turks.'

That night, Arab horsemen were sent into Deraa 'with orders to scatter any Turkish formations met with on the road, and to occupy the place.' Lawrence did not follow immediately, because he had to return to Sheikh Saad. Later, he rode down to Deraa, arriving at dawn on September 28. He found the town in a state of chaos, with Arabs looting and killing. Working with Nasir, he began to make the first administrative arrangements, appointing a military governor, forming a police force, and placing guards over the remaining stores.

After this, he went out westwards to make contact with General Barrow's forces, which were advancing on Deraa without knowing that the Turks had left. The task of halting a division engaged in preparations for an attack was not simple. Lawrence later told Liddell Hart: 'This was a difficult situation to carry off. I took one man with me, only . . . and behaved with histrionic nonchalance, being treated first as enemy, then as native, then as spy'. Eventually, however, he found his way to Barrow's staff.

When Barrow went into Deraa there was a disagreement. Lawrence had always hoped to occupy the town before the EEF reached it and to establish an Arab administration there. Barrow, however, knew nothing about Arab politics and thought only in terms of restoring order to the situation. Many of the Arabs now in Deraa had been at Tafas and they were still wreaking vengeance on the Turks. Barrow was horrified to find them looting a hospital train that had been caught there by the cutting of the line. He later wrote: 'In the cab of the engine was the dead driver and a mortally wounded fireman. The Arab soldiers were going through the train, tearing off the clothing of the groaning and stricken Turks, regardless of gaping wounds and broken limbs, and cutting their victims' throats . . . it was a sight that no average civilised human being could bear unmoved.'

Lawrence made it clear that he did not want Barrow to take control of Deraa. He later justified this by stressing the need to let the Arabs establish their own government: 'My head was working full speed in these minutes, since now or never was the moment to put the Arabs in control, to prevent those fatal first steps by which the unimaginative British, with the best will in the world, usually deprived the aquiescent native of responsibility, and created a situation which called for years of agitation and successive Reform Bills and riotings to mend.

'. . . my play was for high stakes, high beyond [Barrow's] sight, and I cared nothing what he thought of me so that I won. By being personally objectionable to the great men I transferred their anger from my cause to my manner, and gained from them all that I wanted, so long as it was not for myself'. Despite Lawrence's protests, however, Barrow ordered his men to restore order at the station.

By this time, Lawrence's behaviour and judgment were almost certainly affected by exhaustion, as he had slept very little during the four preceding nights. He later wrote to Stirling, his companion during the final days of the advance: 'before the end I was very weary, and moved in a haze, hardly knowing what I did. Up to Deraa, perhaps, I fought: after that clearly the crisis was solved in our favour, and the last advance and entry into Damascus were almost formalities . . . things which had to be passed through, but which required no grip or preparation. Didn't you notice that I was three-parts vacant then?'

On September 29, Barrow's cavalry set off on the seventy-mile advance to Damascus. It had been agreed that Nuri's regulars would march up the railway to cover his right flank, while the irregulars continued to harry the Turkish columns attempting to retreat northwards. Lawrence stayed behind to see Feisal, who was due to arrive in Deraa later that day.

Early next morning he set off with Stirling in a Rolls-Royce tender to rejoin the Arab forces. About ten miles south of the city, they caught up with the Arab irregulars, still on the tail of a surviving Turkish column.

'Aircraftman Ross' by William Roberts, autumn 1922. Probably the only portrait of Lawrence during the period at RAF Uxbridge described in *The Mint*

Charlotte Shaw, wife of the playwright, who developed a very deep affection for Lawrence. She sent him countless presents and poured out her soul to him in letters. Every one of his replies is noted in her diaries

T.E. Lawrence by Augustus John, 1923. When Lawrence saw this picture on exhibition in London he said that it made him look like a 'budding sergeant'

Thomas Hardy by Augustus John, painted at Lawrence's suggestion in 1923. Hardy was delighted to learn that the portrait had been given to the Fitzwilliam Museum

Turkish concentration of troops, earmarked for Maan when supply Nasir
conditions would let them move. This supply reserve was being put forward
in by rail from Damascus, as well as the bombing attacks of the
Royal Air Force from Palestine permitted.

To make head against them, Nasir, our best guerilla general, had
been appointed, in advance of Zeid, to do something great against
the railway. He had camped in Wadi Hesa, with Hornby, full of
explosives, and Peake's trained section of Egyptian Army Camel
Corps to help in demolition. Time, till Allenby recovered, was what
we had to fight for, and Nasir would very much help our desire if he
secured us a month's breathing space by playing the intangible ghost
at the Turkish Army. If he failed we must expect the relief of Maan
and an onslaught of the reinvigorated enemy upon Aba el Lissan.

New Chapter

For six weeks we marked time Zaid
& Jaffar, with their regulars, continued
a profitable battering upon the Maan sector
Sherif Nasir, accompanied by Peake & Hornby
moved forty miles northward and occupied
eight miles of railway in one happy thrust.
By intensive demolition the very foundations
of the line thereabout were destroyed and
the Turkish contemplated offensive against
Feisal in Aba-el-Lissan was brought to
nought. Dawnay and myself took advantage
of the lull to go up again to Allenby.

A proof page from the subscribers' *Seven Pillars* marked up by Lawrence for *Revolt in the Desert*. This
is from the original pencil draft, not the fair copy sent to Jonathan Cape

Lord Trenchard, who did his best to help Lawrence serve in the RAF despite opposition from successive Air Ministers

above: Lawrence very rarely signed photographs but two signed prints of this one survive. *above right*: Lawrence at Miranshah in December 1928. He had broken his wrist at Cranwell and wrote on the back of this photograph, 'nursing my right wrist which hurt for so long that nursing it became a habit'

Lawrence at Karachi, reading *Ulysses*. He was pleased to find that his fellow airmen appreciated good books, and lent freely

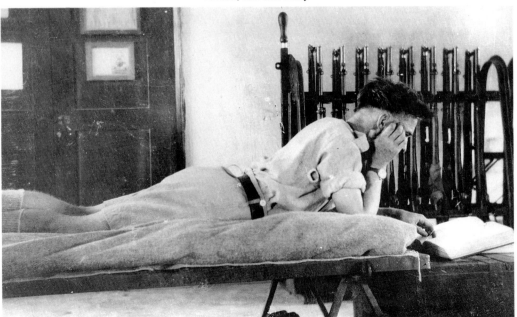

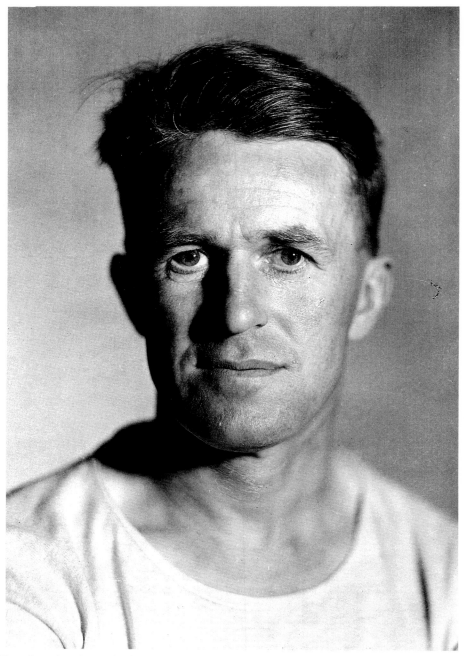

One of a series of portrait photographs by Howard Coster, October 1931. Coster had always wanted to photograph Lawrence, and recognised him one day in London. He chased after Lawrence and persuaded him to sit

In his report on this final advance, Lawrence described the fate the Turkish 4th Army had suffered at the hands of the Arabs: 'In all, we had killed nearly five thousand of them, captured about eight thousand . . . and counted spoils of about one hundred and fifty machine guns and from twenty-five to thirty guns.' One column of about a thousand men had nevertheless succeeded in escaping to the east. It was dealt with a few days later by forces from the EEF.

By the night of September 30, the escape routes from Damascus were virtually closed, with Chauvel's Australians on the north and west, and Barrow to the south-west. The Arabs camped that night at Kiswe, a few miles south of the city. Those Turks inside who had not already fled were trapped.

There seemed no reason for the Arab forces to enter Damascus that night. The roads were dangerous, and the arrival of so many exhausted men would only add to the state of confusion. However, messengers were sent in to make contact with Feisal's secret supporters. Lawrence wished to make sure that a provisional administration was set up, so that the city should be under Arab control before Allenby's representatives went in. It seems also that he feared there might be physical opposition to Christian troops from fanatical elements angered by rumours of the Sykes-Picot terms. He later wrote: 'In their envelopment of Damascus the Australians might be forced, despite orders, to enter the town. If anyone resisted them it would spoil the future. One night was given us to make the Damascenes receive the British Army as their allies.'

In any case, Lawrence knew that Feisal's army would be allowed to occupy the city. Nasir and Nuri Shalaan went in at about 7.30 a.m. on October 1. Lawrence and Stirling had meant to accompany them, but had been detained on the way. As Stirling later recalled: 'We stopped the car by a small stream and got out to wash and shave. No sooner had we completed our ablutions than a patrol of Bengal Lancers appeared round the shoulder of the hill, galloped up, and made us prisoners.

'Lawrence was in full Arab kit. I had on the Arab head-dress . . . and a camel hair *abaya*, or cloak, which concealed the ordinary khaki uniform I was wearing underneath. Unfortunately I could not speak a word of Urdu, but I tried to indicate that I was a British officer by pulling back my cloak and displaying the red gorget patches on my collar. The only effect this had was to provoke a prod in the back with the point of a very sharp lance. We were driven as captives across country until we were lucky enough to meet a British officer of the regiment to whom we explained our identity.'

It was 9 a.m. before Stirling and Lawrence drove into Damascus. Lawrence wrote that they found the streets 'nearly impassable with the crowds, who yelled themselves hoarse, danced, cut themselves with swords and daggers and fired volleys into the air. Nasir, Nuri Shaalan, Auda abu Tayi and myself were cheered by name, covered with flowers, kissed indefinitely and splashed with attar of roses from the house-tops.'

When they reached the Town Hall, they learned that an Arab government had been proclaimed the previous afternoon, even before the last Turkish and German forces had left. Lawrence had expected that the new administration would be formed by Ali Riza Rikabi, whose nationalist sympathies had been so well disguised that he had been a senior official in Damascus under the Turks for most of the war. However, Ali Riza had made his way to Barrow's headquarters on September 29. His place had been taken provisionally by another respected nationalist, Shukri el Ayoubi. The Sherifian flag had been hoisted, and the new administration had declared its allegiance to Hussein, as King of all the Arabs.

Nasir, Nuri, and Shukri were not the only Arab leaders at the Town Hall. There was also a rival group, led by the Algerians, Abd el Kader and his brother Mohammed Said. Lawrence had suffered personally from Abd el Kader's treachery, and he knew that the two Algerians had been working for the Turks right up to the end. Before leaving Damascus, Jemal Pasha had appointed Mohammed Said governor. However, the brothers had thought it politic to change sides, and had put themselves at the head of the Arab administration. On Lawrence's orders, they were removed.

Soon after this, General Chauvel drove into the city, knowing that Lawrence was already there. They met at the Town Hall, and Lawrence introduced Shukri as the military governor, saying that the Arab forces would take responsibility for public order. He encouraged Chauvel to keep his Australian troops outside the town.

Chauvel wrote to GHQ about these arrangements. As he understood them, his orders had been 'to instruct the Wali to carry on the civil administration of the city, providing such military guards and police only as were required for the protection of property'. His report stated: 'On arriving at the Serail at 9.30 a.m. I met Lieut. Col. Lawrence who introduced me to Shukri Pasha, whom he told me was the Military Governor. I understood that this official was the Wali, and I issued him instructions through Lt. Col. Lawrence to carry on the civil administration of the city, and informed him that I would find him any military guards and police that he required.

'Lt. Col. Lawrence offered to assist, to advise me of what guards were required, and to supervise the carrying out of these instructions. I asked Lt. Col. Lawrence to assist in these matters because I had no Political Officer at the moment at my disposal . . .

'Lt. Col. Lawrence returned . . . to my Headquarters about 5 p.m. and informed me that Shukri Pasha was not, as I thought, the original Wali, but had been appointed by him that morning . . . all Turkish officials had fled from Damascus about noon on the 30th. The Arabs of Damascus had declared for the King of the Hedjaz on the evening of the 30th.

'I said I could not recognise the King of the Hedjaz in the matter without further instructions, but I was agreeable to Lt. Col. Lawrence, with the Military Governor, carrying out the civil administration as a temporary measure pending instructions to the contrary being received from General Headquarters.'

Lawrence too reported on the situation: 'Shukri Pasha el Ayoubi was appointed Arab Military Governor, as all former civil employees had left with Jemal Pasha on the previous day. Martial law was proclaimed, police organised, and the town picketed . . . I have no orders as to what political arrangements should be made in Damascus, and will carry on as before till I hear further from you . . . G.O.C. Desert Mounted Corps [Chauvel] has seen above, and agrees with my carrying on with the town administration until further instructions.'

It is clear from the retrospective accounts given by both Chauvel and Lawrence that there was considerable tension between the two men. Chauvel knew no more than Barrow about the political status of the Arabs. He was shocked by the scenes of Arab indiscipline and looting in the city, and angered to find that Lawrence, a relatively junior officer, seemed to have taken control in Feisal's name. His own troops had been engaged in hard fighting during the previous days, and he was determined that they should be honoured as the captors of Damascus. Despite Allenby's orders, some of his units had found an excuse to pass through the outskirts of the city early that morning, and the Australians were loudly proclaiming the glory of having been 'first in'. Chauvel was annoyed when Lawrence pointed out that the Arabs had taken possession of Damascus hours before any EEF troops had entered.

Lawrence had already made up his mind to escape from his role with the Arabs as soon as possible. On the evening of October 1 he wrote a brief report on the events of the past three days. He ended: 'If Arab military assistance is not required in further operations of the Desert Corps, I would like to return to Palestine as I feel that if I remain here longer, it will be very difficult for my successor.'

During the next two days he struggled to ensure that the Arabs achieved some semblance of order. He wrote in *Seven Pillars*: 'Our aim was a façade rather than a fitted building. It was run up so furiously well that when I left Damascus . . . the Syrians had their *de facto* Government'. Above all, he wished to establish the principle that the Arabs should receive technical or other help only when they asked for it, rather than have European control imposed on them. The task was not easy, partly because the Turks had left acute difficulties behind them.

Another problem was public disorder. Much of this was caused by Druse peasantry from outside the city who saw the victory as an occasion for riot and plunder. However, there was also political conflict. On the night of October 1, Abd el Kader and Mohammed Said attempted to raise a rebellion against the Sherifians and their Christian allies. This was put down by the Arab Army during the following morning, and the situation was finally calmed at noon by a march-through of Chauvel's forces, with an Arab contingent at their head.

By this time, Beirut had also been evacuated by the Turks. On September 30, before Lawrence reached Damascus, Mohammed Said had sent a message to nationalists there, urging them to proclaim an Arab government. This move was warmly supported by other Damascene politicians including Ali Riza Rikabi, who had taken over the leadership from Shukri on October 2. Lawrence did not learn of this until the next day, and he regretted it, because he knew it would cause trouble with the French.

When Allenby and members of his staff visited Damascus on October 3, he approved the arrangements Lawrence had set up and confirmed Ali Riza's appointment as governor. By this time he had received detailed instructions from London about the political status of the Arabs and the attitude he should take towards any administration they formed: 'In accordance with the engagements into which His Majesty's Government have entered with the King of Hejaz, and in pursuance of the general policy approved by them, the authority of the friendly and allied Arabs should be formally recognised in any part of the areas "A" and "B" as defined in the Anglo-French Agreement of 1916, where it may be found established, or can be established, as a result of the military operations now in progress.' The 'belligerent status of the Arabs fighting for the liberation of their territories from Turkish rule' should now be recognised. Accordingly, 'in so far as military exigencies permit, the regions so liberated should properly be treated as Allied territory enjoying the status of an independent State (or confederation of States) of friendly Arabs . . . and not as enemy provinces in temporary military occupation . . .

'It would be desirable to mark the recognition and establishment of native Arab rule by some conspicuous or formal act such as the hoisting and saluting of the Arab flag . . .

'Our policy should be to encourage the setting up of either central, local or regional Arab administration, as the case may be, and work, at least ostensibly, through them entirely. For this purpose there need be no hesitation to accept a merely nominal authority when no other can for the moment be established.'

Despite these concessions to the idea of self-determination, the instructions continued: 'if . . . the Arab authorities request the assistance or advice of European functionaries, we are bound under the Anglo-French Agreement to let these be French in Area "A". From this point of view it is important that the military administration should be restricted to such functions as can properly be described as military, so as to give rise to no inconvenient claim to the employment where unnecessary of French civilians. It is equally important to keep our procedure on the same lines in that of Area "B" which lies east of the Dead Sea and of the Jordan Valley depression, so as not to give the French the pretext for any larger demands in Area "A".'

Allenby had come to Damascus to implement these instructions, and it had been arranged that Feisal would arrive in the city on the same day. They met for the first time at the Victoria Hotel. Also present were Chauvel, Nuri as-Said, Nasir, Joyce, Lawrence, Stirling, Young and Cornwallis.

Lawrence wrote little about the meeting in *Seven Pillars*, mentioning only that 'Allenby gave me a telegram from the Foreign Office, recognising to the Arabs the status of belligerents; and told me to translate it to the Emir: but none of us knew what it meant in English, let alone in Arabic: and Feisal, smiling through the tears which the welcome of his people had forced from him, put it aside to thank the Commander-in-Chief for the trust which had made him and his movement. They were a strange contrast: Feisal, large-eyed, colourless and worn, like a fine dagger; Allenby, gigantic and red and merry, fit representative of the Power which had thrown a girdle of humour and strong dealing round the world.'

Fuller notes of the meeting were made by Chauvel. Regrettably, these appear to survive only in a revised form written up some years later. There are discrepancies between this and the contemporary documents, so Chauvel's account cannot be regarded as completely reliable. He wrote: 'Lawrence acted as Interpreter. The Commander-in-Chief explained to Feisal:

'(a) That France was to be the Protecting Power over Syria.

'(b) That he, Feisal, as representing his Father, King Hussein, was to have the Administration of Syria (less Palestine and the Lebanon Province) under French guidance and financial backing.

'(c) That the Arab sphere would include the hinterland of Syria only and that he, Feisal, would not have anything to do with the Lebanon, which would be considered to stretch from the Northern boundary of Palestine (about Tyre) to the head of the Gulf of Alexandretta.

'(d) That he was to have a French Liaison Officer at once, who would work for the present with Lawrence, who would be expected to give him every assistance.

'Feisal objected very strongly. He said that he knew nothing of France in the matter; that he was prepared to have British assistance; that he understood from the Adviser whom Allenby had sent him that the Arabs were to have the whole of Syria including the Lebanon but excluding Palestine; that a country without a port was no good to him; and that he declined to have a French Liaison Officer or to recognise French guidance in any way.

'The Chief turned to Lawrence and said: ''But did you not tell him that the French were to have the Protectorate over Syria?'' Lawrence said: ''No Sir, I know nothing about it.'' The Chief then said: ''But you knew definitely that he, Feisal, was to have nothing to do with the Lebanon?'' Lawrence said: ''No, Sir, I did not.''

'After some further discussion, the Chief told Feisal that he, Sir Edmund Allenby, was Commander-in-Chief and that he, Feisal, was at the moment a Lieut.-General under his Command and that he would have to obey orders . . .

'After Feisal had gone, Lawrence told the Chief that he would not work with a French Liaison Officer and that he was due for leave and thought he had better take it now and go off to England.'

At first sight, the statements about Anglo-French arrangements attributed to Lawrence in this document seem curious. Chauvel implies that, when challenged, both Lawrence and Feisal denied any knowledge of the Sykes-Picot terms. But the Agreement had by this time been public knowledge for nearly a year, and it would have been absurd for either Feisal or Lawrence to pretend not to know about it (although Feisal could maintain that he had never been told officially). It seems likely that

Chauvel misconstrued what he heard, and it has to be borne in mind that at that time he knew almost nothing about the political background to the discussion. The probable explanation of these exchanges is that Lawrence and Feisal now heard for the first time about the interim arrangements for Syria, which the British and French Governments had only recently agreed to. The details Allenby announced must have come as a shock. They seemed to amount to an imposition of the Sykes-Picot terms, despite the fact that Lawrence's superiors had repeatedly told him that the Agreement was as good as dead.

The remark Chauvel attributed to Feisal about the Lebanon must also be considered in its proper context. Feisal would not have been able to admit, particularly in front of other Arab leaders, that he was prepared to recognise any form of French claim to the Lebanon. Such a concession would have led to an immediate breach with his father, and would have alienated Arab nationalists throughout Syria. If, therefore, such a remark was made at this meeting, it must be regarded as evidence of a political stance, rather than a reflection of Feisal's private knowledge or opinion.

CHAPTER 17

The Peace Conference
October 1918–September 1919

As Lawrence drove away from Damascus, he knew that Feisal's position would be extremely difficult. There would be problems both with the French liaison staff and with Syrian politicians who had no wish to see their personal influence diminished by a Sherifian head of state. The latter were now trying as hard as they could to assert their own authority.

Allenby and Clayton inadvertently made the situation worse by trying to prevent Feisal getting involved in local politics. At first, they restricted him to a purely military role, making Ali Riza Pasha governor of all the occupied territories in Sykes-Picot areas A and B. He was to report directly to Allenby. This proved to be a tactical error, as Ali Riza was a Syrian political leader with no reason to feel loyal towards Britain.

Lawrence later wrote: 'Upon the taking of Damascus, Feisal and myself lost control. The Syrians (Ali Riza and the Bekri brothers) took charge, and galloped (metaphorically) straight for the coast. My intention had been to occupy from the gap of Tripoli northward to Alexandretta, and I had told Feisal that in the welter which would follow victory he would stand a very decent chance of getting this area eventually allotted to the Syrian kingdom upon terms. I still think that it was a possibility, and that the precipitate occupation of Beyrout and Lebanon wholly threw away the local people's chances. Shukri was sent to Beyrout by Ali Riza. I was much too engaged in struggling with difficulties of Damascus to attempt to cope with Ali Riza'.

Lawrence reached Cairo on October 8, and a week later left for England. By chance, one of his fellow-passengers during the voyage from Port Said to Taranto was Earl Winterton, who wrote to Lord Robert Cecil, assistant secretary of State for Foreign Affairs, on the second day out: 'Lawrence, as you probably know, has been chief political officer to Feisal and may be described as "the Soul of the Hedjaz" . . . But for him the Arab movement could never have succeeded as it has done.

'He is very anxious to see you and A. J. Balfour [the Foreign Secretary]. May I bring him to the F.O.? Could you let your secretary write to me at the House of Commons when I could see you. Lawrence is *au fait* with the whole Damascus-Beirut-Aleppo position as no-one else is and joins exceptional intellectual brilliance to a unique personal knowledge of the Arabs and Arab movement.'

Lawrence travelled north from Taranto by rail. As the journey by troop train often took ten days, he had arranged before leaving Egypt for promotion to the 'special, temporary and acting' rank of full colonel. This entitled him to take a sleeping berth on an express, which reached Le Havre in only three days.

He arrived in England on about October 24 and went to Oxford to see his family. This was the first time he had been home in nearly four years. On the following Monday he set to work, making use of Winterton's introduction. His object was to see that the Sykes-Picot Agreement was overturned. After meeting him, Cecil wrote: 'Colonel Lawrence . . . impressed upon me that Faisal and the Arabs (to whom he always referred as "we") had taken Beyrout, Latakia, and Antioch without any assistance by means of local risings. He also declared that Damascus had been militarily at the mercy of Faisal ever since November of last year, and that he could have taken it then and made peace with the Turks upon terms which would have been very favourable. He declared that he had seen letters which had passed between Djemal and Faisal, and which made this clear beyond a doubt. He denounced in unmeasured terms the folly (or, as he called it, the levity) of the Sykes-Picot Agreement, the boundaries of which were, he said, entirely absurd and unworkable . . .

'I spoke to him about Mesopotamia, and he urged that it should be put under an Arab Government of as little practical activity as possible. He suggested that one of King Hussein's sons should be Governor. Abdullah would do very well . . .

'He was violently anti-French, and he suggested that, if there were to be fresh conversations, it would be well to have both Arab and Zionist representatives present, as well as Americans and Italians.'

Lawrence made other visits during this first week in England, hoping to win as many friends as possible for the Arab cause. On October 29, he addressed the Eastern Committee of the War Cabinet. To his irritation, Lord Curzon, chairman of the committee, began the proceedings with a eulogy of his achievements in Arabia. Lawrence was in no mood for such praise, and his reply was brusque. The Committee asked him about 'the views that were entertained by the Arab chiefs concerning the settlement of the conquered territories and Franco-Arab relations in particular'. He began his reply by describing Feisal's pro-British stance and successful co-operation with Allenby; in the future, however, the Arab attitude would depend on the extent to which Britain backed up French claims: 'The French representatives had made it perfectly clear to Feisal that they intended to build up a colonial empire in the east . . . Feisal and the Arab leaders relied upon our declaration of [June] 1918 [to the seven Syrians] . . . regarding the disposal of all territory actually captured by Arab arms. In this declaration we had promised unlimited Arab sovereignty for such areas'.

Lawrence went on to make a series of suggestions: Abdullah should be set up as ruler of Baghdad and lower Mesopotamia, with Zeid in a similar position in upper Mesopotamia and Feisal in Syria. The Committee minutes record: 'In regard to Upper Mesopotamia, whence most of the best officers and men in Feisal's [regular] army had been drawn, [Lawrence] was convinced that a separate province or kingdom would have to be established distinct from Lower Mesopotamia and from Syria.' The Arabs, Lawrence said, believed that France was 'getting into Syria under General Allenby's wing, and although he did not like it, Feisal would probably be content to leave Beirut and the Lebanon to French tutelage provided that there was no question of French annexation. Tripoli is the part which the Arabs will make a fight for, as . . . the Tripoli-Homs railway is the only Syrian railway with real commercial possibilities'. As regards French advisers, 'Feisal took the view that he was free to choose whatever advisers he liked. He was anxious to obtain the assistance of British or American Zionist Jews for this purpose. The Zionists would be acceptable to the Arabs on terms.' Following this discussion, Lawrence was asked to write a memorandum setting out his suggestions in more detail.

He must have realised very soon that the Cabinet would find it difficult to give their full support to Feisal. Britain already had an embarrassing list of desiderata to lay before the Peace Conference. Among them were Mosul in northern Mesopotamia (allocated to France under the Sykes-Picot Agreement) and Palestine (placed by Sykes-Picot under an international administration). Both these cases would involve concessions by France, and it would be awkward for Britain to oppose French ambitions in Syria as well. Moreover, while the Foreign Office might well sympathise with Feisal, the India Office would not. The Anglo-Indian lobby still intended to add Mesopotamia to the Empire, and was opposed to Arab nationalist leaders there or anywhere else. Lawrence saw that the best hope for Arab independence lay with the Americans. At the Peace Conference, President Wilson would surely prefer the cause of Arab self-determination to that of European imperialism.

*   *   *

On the day after the Eastern Committee meeting, Lawrence went to Buckingham Palace for an audience with King George V. Allenby had recommended him for a knighthood, but Lawrence had already told the military secretary at the Palace that he would accept no honours. When he arrived, he found to his dismay that the meeting was to be a private investiture. His discussions in Whitehall during the preceding days had done nothing to weaken his objections to taking decorations from the British Government. According to a contemporary note made by the King's private secretary, he told the King 'that he had pledged his word to Feisal, and that now the British Government were about to let down the Arabs over the Sykes-Picot Agreement. He was an Emir among the Arabs and intended to stick to them through thick and thin and, if necessary, fight against the French for the recovery of Syria.

'Colonel Lawrence said that he did not know that he had been gazetted or what the etiquette was in such matters, but he hoped that the King would forgive any want of courtesy on his part in not taking these decorations.' The King seems to have taken no offence, and subsequent letters show that he bore Lawrence no ill-feeling. In later years, according to Lawrence, the incident was to become one of George V's favourite stories, developed into 'an account which tells how each time he pinned one on and turned round for the next, he found the last taken off.' Lawrence admitted, however, that the Queen had been 'very huffy'.

While Lawrence's feelings were sincere, his gesture was ill-considered. It was seized upon by political opponents who spread hostile gossip during the succeeding months, to the effect that he had refused the honours at a public investiture and that the King had been caused acute embarrassment. This rumour did Lawrence much harm, although it drew attention in some quarters to the depth of his feelings about British conduct towards the Arabs.

He spent the following weekend working on his memorandum to the Eastern Committee, a most important opportunity to influence the Cabinet. The document was submitted on November 4. It began with a summary of the historical events (written from memory and not entirely accurate) and presented the Sherifian case in strong terms. Lawrence stressed the risks taken by Hussein in rebelling against the Turks, the sacrifices made by the Arabs during the Revolt, and their contribution to Allenby's victory. His paper then examined the principal regions in which the Arabs aspired to independence, and set out his views on a settlement in detail.

*   *   *

During the first days of November diplomatic events gathered pace, as the Allied governments and interested pressure groups all sought to increase their influence at the coming Peace Conference. There was some prospect of talks about the Syrian question before the Peace Conference opened. On November 8, Lawrence sent an urgent message about this to Hussein: 'I believe there will be conversations in Paris in fifteen days' time between the Allies about the question of the Arabs. General Allenby has telegraphed that you will want to have a representative there. If this is so, I hope you will send Feisal, since his splendid victories have given him a personal reputation in Europe which will make his success easier. If you agree please telegraph him to get ready to leave Syria at once for about one month, and to ask General Allenby for a ship to take him to France. You should meanwhile telegraph to the Governments of Great Britain, France, America and Italy telling them that your son is proceeding at once to Paris as your representative.'

On the following day an Anglo-French Declaration, mooted since August, was at last released. Though this brief statement was couched in legalistic prose, the Foreign Office hoped that it would calm Arab nationalist fears about Allied intentions. In its final form it read: 'The aim which France and Great Britain have in view in prosecuting in the East the war let loose by German ambition is the complete and final liberation of the peoples so long oppressed by the Turks and the establishment of national governments and administrations deriving their authority from the initiative and free choice of the native populations.

'In order to give effect to these intentions, France and Great Britain have agreed to encourage and assist the establishment of native governments and administrations in Syria and Mesopotamia, already liberated by the Allies, and in the territories which they are proceeding to liberate, and they have agreed to recognise such governments as soon as they are effectively established. So far from desiring to impose specific institutions upon the populations of these regions, their sole object is to ensure, by their support and effective assistance, that the governments and administrations adopted by these regions of their own free will shall be exercised in the normal way. The function which the two Allied Governments claim for themselves in the liberated territories is to ensure impartial and equal justice for all; to facilitate the economic development of the country by encouraging local initiative; to promote the diffusion of education; and to put an end to the divisions too long exploited by Turkish policy.' Although, in British eyes, this Declaration would preclude direct imperial rule, the 'functions' claimed by the Allies were so vaguely defined that they could be used to justify almost any form of colonialism.

Behind the scenes, the French Foreign Office, was demanding that the Sykes-Picot terms should be fulfilled to the letter: 'on no point, whether at Damascus, Aleppo, or at Mosul, is [France] prepared to relinquish in any way the rights which she holds through the 1916 Agreement, whatever the provisional administrative arrangements called for by a passing military situation.'

On November 21, Lawrence attended a further meeting of the Eastern Committee. The Peace Conference was imminent, and everyone present understood the need to reach a firm decision about policy without further delay. His chief ambition at this stage was to ensure that Feisal, now on his way to Europe, got a fair hearing in any international debate about the future of the Turkish provinces. America would be in a position to dominate such discussions, and although President Wilson's militant idealism held little attraction for France and Britain, it might prove a lifeline to the Arabs. Lawrence had convinced key members of the Eastern Committee before this meeting that it would be in Britain's best interest for Feisal to attend the Peace Conference. Only Hussein, the argument ran, could reassure President Wilson that the Arabs wanted Britain to assume the stewardship of Mesopotamia and Palestine.

On December 1, the French and Italian prime ministers arrived in London. They were honoured with a military procession which passed through cheering crowds. After arriving at the French Embassy, Lloyd George found himself alone for a time with Clemenceau, the French premier. According to a later note by the Cabinet secretary, Clemenceau had asked what they might talk about, and Lloyd George, seizing the opportunity, had replied: ' "Mesopotamia and Palestine" . . . "Tell me what you want" asked Clemenceau. "I want Mosul" said Lloyd George. "You shall have it" said Clemenceau. "Anything else?" "Yes, I want Jerusalem too" continued Lloyd George. "You shall have it" said Clemenceau "but Pichon will make difficulties about Mosul." '

The episode was typical of Lloyd George, an artful politician who knew what he wanted and seized an opportunity when he saw one. Characteristically, he took this action without any kind of brief from the Foreign Office, and he made no formal report despite the importance of this verbal 'gentleman's agreement'. Worse still, he was vague about the concessions he had made in return. Later, it would transpire that Clemenceau had asked that Britain should not oppose a unified French ad-

ministration in the whole of Syria, including the inland area reserved for
an independent Arab administration. As far as Lloyd George was concerned, no British interests were threatened by this request and he had
readily agreed.

Doubtless he believed that he had secured a valuable bargain, for his
heart had long been set on a British administration in Palestine. In reality,
however, the agreement was worth far more to Clemenceau. France's
greatest fear had been that America would overturn the Sykes-Picot
Agreement. If this happened, and the future of the Middle East were
decided on the principle of self-determination, the French would certainly
lose Syria, and possibly Lebanon as well. Britain, on the other hand, with
support from Hussein, would be very well placed to receive stewardship
of Mosul and Palestine. Now, by handing Mosul and Palestine to Lloyd
George, the French premier had simply given away what he would have
lost anyway. In exchange, he had obtained a commitment which cut the
ground from under the feet of those inside the Foreign Office who wanted
to see the whole Sykes-Picot Agreement scrapped. This was exactly the
kind of bilateral settlement Lawrence had been seeking to avoid. In two
areas, it is true, British territorial desiderata had been met, but this had
only been achieved by sacrificing the hopes of the Arabs.

Three days later, before the French concessions over Mosul and Palestine were known to any but Lloyd George's closest associates, Lawrence attended another meeting of the Eastern Committee. On the agenda
was Britain's future policy with regards to Syria. The minutes show that
most of those present had no idea that the matter had already been decided, over their heads, by Lloyd George.

By the end of the meeting, however, it was clear that the Cabinet was
prepared to offer the Syrian Arabs nothing more than sympathy. On the
other hand, it would be willing to help Feisal obtain a hearing at the Peace
Conference, on the tacit understanding that he would support British
stewardship of Mesopotamia and Palestine. If he used this opportunity to
appeal for American help over Sykes-Picot, that was his affair.

From this point onwards, Feisal was on his own, and his aims during
the Conference were quite independent of those pursued by Britain. The
Foreign Office nevertheless thought it important to attach someone to his
entourage who could persuade him whenever possible to act in Britain's
interests. On December 5 Sir Eyre Crowe, a senior Foreign Office official, minuted: 'I venture to recommend strongly . . . that we ought to
have Colonel Lawrence available at the Peace Conference for purposes of

advice in regard to [the] Arab question of which he knows more than anyone else.

'Colonel Lawrence himself is apparently anxious to be with Feisal, and we have everything to gain from such an arrangement. It is a question whether Col. Lawrence should be in Paris in the capacity of a member of Feisal's staff (he holds an appointment from him to this effect) or as an adviser of the British Delegation. I favour the latter arrangement, but perhaps this need not exclude the former.' Lord Hardinge noted: 'Col. Lawrence should certainly be in Paris and available as adviser. Probably he would be able to give an opinion as to the position in which he could be most useful or whether he could combine both.' Lawrence's name was added to the list of the British Delegation, Political Section, as one of the 'advisers on special subjects'.

While these deliberations had been taking place, Feisal had been on his way to England via France, where his journey had been deliberately held up by a lengthy official tour. On December 7, however, Lawrence travelled to Paris to accompany him to England, and they arrived in London three days later.

Over the next few days, Lawrence accompanied Feisal to an audience with King George V and arranged meetings with influential politicians. Afterwards they went on an official tour to Edinburgh and Glasgow.

By this time, Lawrence had begun to promote Feisal's cause in the British press. On December 15 he sent an article on Arab affairs to *The Times*, and in a covering letter wrote: 'Feisul will probably be in London on Thursday and then I'll try and arrange you something useful.

'The points that strike me are that the Arabs came into the war without making a previous treaty with us, and have consistently refused to listen to the temptations of other powers. They have never had a press agent, or tried to make themselves out a case, but fought as hard as they could (I'll swear to that) and suffered hardships in their three campaigns and losses that would break up seasoned troops. They fought with ropes around their necks (Feisul had £20,000 alive and £10,000 dead on him. I the same: Nasir £10,000 alive, and Ali el Harith £8,000) and did it without, I believe, any other very strong motive than a desire to see the Arabs free. It was rather an ordeal for as very venerable a person as Hussein to rebel, for he was at once most violently abused by the Moslem press in India and Turkey, on religious grounds.'

Despite these efforts, the year 1918 did not end happily for Feisal, who was soon told officially that 'if the French Government insisted on its rights under the [Sykes-Picot] Agreement, Great Britain would not be in a position to refuse.'

Lawrence arrived in Paris for the Peace Conference on about January 9, 1919. He was given rooms in the Hotel Continental, some distance from the Majestic and Astoria which were the main hotels used by the British Delegation. He was to remain in Paris, fighting for the Arab cause, until late May. Long afterwards he would describe these months as 'the worst I have lived through: and they were worse for Feisal. However he learnt the whole art of politics, from them. Perhaps I did, too!'

Since 1915, Lawrence had been living and working among people to whom the future of Syria was a central issue. In Paris, attention was focused on Germany and Austria, and the disposal of the Ottoman Empire was of secondary importance. The fate of Syria seemed peripheral; it rarely featured on the official agendas.

While there was little scope for formal discussion, there were many opportunities to argue Feisal's case for Arab independence in private meetings with statesmen and journalists. Thus most of Lawrence's work took place behind the scenes. At first, there was a flurry of activity, arranging interviews and acting as Feisal's interpreter, but as the weeks went by the pace slowed. Lawrence used his free time to begin the first draft of an account of the Arab Revolt. Between January 10 and mid-May he wrote what are now Books 2–7 and Book 10 of *Seven Pillars of Wisdom*.

While there was little progress towards a resolution of the Syrian question, a number of memoranda were submitted to the Conference by interested parties, and some of these papers were widely circulated and discussed. The attitudes of Britain, France, America and the Arabs can readily be summarised from these documents.

Whatever the private feelings of British Delegates, the Cabinet had decided to remain neutral in the Franco-Arab dispute. It was thought probable that France would gain Lebanon, but if America took a hand and the future of Syria was established on the principle of self-determination, the prospects for France seemed uncertain. Acting as a disinterested observer, Britain refused to take any action in Syria or to sanction any move by France that might prejudge the Peace Conference decision. In practice, this meant that the British Government refused to hand over military control of Syria to France, or even to allow an increase in the number of French troops stationed there. French participation in the administration of Syria was limited to the presence of the advisers appointed under the Anglo-French understanding reached just before the capture of Damascus. However, British taxpayers were bearing the cost of keeping Allenby in Syria, and Lloyd George made it clear early in the Conference that he hoped the future of these regions would be decided as rapidly as possible.

Despite the formal British position, there were widely differing views on the Syrian question within the British Delegation. The majority, concerned mainly with the future of Europe, felt that no vital British interests were at stake in Syria, and that the wrangle was harming Anglo-French relations.

Hardline Anglo-Indian imperialists such as Sir Arthur Hirtzel, an India Office official, wished to turn Mesopotamia into a colony. They hoped that concessions to the principle of self-determination would be nothing more than cosmetic and that the Arabs would be content with the vague assurances contained in the Anglo-French Declaration. France had similar ambitions in Syria and, now that the Mosul question had been resolved, there was little conflict between French and Anglo-Indian views.

At the beginning of the Peace Conference the French position was that there would be no concessions in the Middle East beyond those already made by Clemenceau to Lloyd George. On the contrary, France was keen to gain recognition for the principle Lloyd George had accepted, that her colonial administrators would have a free hand to govern both coastal and inland Syria as one unit. For this reason, there were attractions in exchanging the Sykes-Picot arrangements for a Mandate over the whole of Syria. In this case, it might be possible to eliminate the distinction between the coast and the inland area reserved under Sykes-Picot for an independent Arab administration. The French Foreign Office began to press for this modification.

The intransigence of the French Government over Syria was greatly aggravated by domestic popular feeling. Pressure groups with special interests in the Lebanon launched a well-orchestrated campaign in the French press. As a result there were frequent articles attacking Britain, Feisal, and even Lawrence; the Syrian issue became a *cause célèbre*.

Thus the background to Feisal's efforts at the Peace Conference was one of deepening antagonism between Britain and France. At first, Arab prospects seemed reasonably good: with Lawrence's help, Feisal was able to put his case to leading members of the American Delegation and to the press. It was not difficult for the Americans to feel sympathetic, and

the Arabs, who had made great sacrifices to fight off their Turkish oppressors, were now cast as victims of French imperial greed. Feisal was
almost always accompanied by Lawrence, who prepared the English
drafts of his memoranda, correspondence, and telegrams, and acted as
interpreter in private meetings and in public. To the Americans, Feisal
seemed elegant and gifted, while amazing stories circulated about Lawrence, 'that young successor of Mohammed . . . the twenty-eight year
old conqueror of Damascus, with his boyish face and almost constant
smile—the most winning figure, so everyone says, at the whole Peace
Conference'.

American accounts of Feisal and Lawrence at this time are infused with
romanticism: 'Lawrence . . . has been described as the most interesting
Briton alive, a student of medieval history at Magdalen College, where he
used to sleep by day and work by night and take his recreation in the deer
park at four in the morning—a Shelley-like person, and yet too virile to
be a poet.' His strategy of befriending Americans was so successful that
French observers became deeply concerned, and steps were taken to
present the French view to President Wilson.

Another problem for Feisal was the tactical alliance that Lawrence had
encouraged him to form with the Zionists. Although this had seemed at
first to promise a great deal, it soon became more of a liability than an
asset. The apparent moderation of Chaim Weizmann's views, and the
measured undertakings of the Balfour Declaration, were overshadowed at
the Peace Conference by much more extreme demands. There was, moreover, a flagrant contradiction between the principle of self-determination,
as applied to the existing Arab population of Palestine, and Zionist ambitions. Many Zionists spoke openly of their hopes to take over Palestine
and govern it in the interests of a new Jewish community that had yet to
arrive.

The Zionist lobby was powerful in America as in Britain, and the Great
Powers continued to ignore this conflict of principle, discouraging those
who drew attention to it. Stephen Bonsal, one of the aides in the American Delegation, was embarrassed when Lawrence brought to him a draft
memorandum in which Feisal expressed mounting anxiety on the matter.
In outline, according to Bonsal's memoirs, the memorandum ran: 'If the
views of the radical Zionists, as presented to the [Peace Conference],
should prevail, the result will be a ferment, chronic unrest, and sooner or
later civil war in Palestine. But I hope I will not be misunderstood. I
assert that we Arabs have none of the racial or religious animosity against
the Jews which unfortunately prevail in many other regions of the world.

I assert that with the Jews who have been seated for some generations in Palestine our relations are excellent. But the new arrivals exhibit very different qualities from those "old settlers" as we call them, with whom we have been able to live and even co-operate on friendly terms. For want of a better word I must say that new colonists almost without exception have come in an imperialistic spirit. They say that too long we have been in control of their homeland taken from them by brute force in the dark ages, but that now under the new world order we must clear out; and if we are wise we should do so peaceably without making any resistance to what is the fiat of the civilised world.'

On March 20 the Powers took their first decision of any importance about Feisal's case. President Wilson suggested that an inter-Allied commission should visit Syria in order to establish the wishes of the people. This decision, which the Foreign Office had long been hoping for, promised to absolve the Cabinet from any further embarrassment over the question. Britain would go on maintaining a position of strict neutrality, yet the Commission was certain to find that France was unacceptable to the great majority of Syrians as a Mandatory Power. Feisal's wishes would then be granted.

Needless to say, France used every possible device to block this move. Clemenceau immediately suggested that the Commission should not confine its attention to Syria, but should also visit Mesopotamia and Palestine. When Zionists heard that it was to consult the Palestinian Arabs, they threw all their influence against it. Likewise, the India Office opposed a visit to Mesopotamia. Within days, a considerable body of opinion was mobilised against the Commission scheme.

On April 7, Lawrence's concentration on these matters was distracted when a telegram warned him that his father was seriously ill with pneumonia. He left for Oxford immediately, but arrived to find that his father had died. Shortly afterwards he returned to Paris. A week later he went home again, and it was only then that the Hejaz Delegation learned what had happened. Feisal wrote in his diary: 'The greatest thing I have seen in him, which is worthy of mention as one of his principal characteristics, is his patience, discretion, zeal, and his putting the common good before his own personal interest. When he came to take leave I asked the reason for his departure. He said, "I regret to say that my father has died and I want to go and see my mother." I enquired when his father had died and he said, "A week ago—I received a telegram saying that he was ill, and left straightaway, but when I arrived I found that he had died two hours previously. I did not stay in England until the funeral because I realised that you were here alone and that there is much work to be done. I didn't want to be far from you, in case things happened in my absence. I didn't tell you this at the time in case it upset you, so I tell you now. I shall return on Friday.'' Consider such honesty, such faithfulness, such devotion to duty and such control of one's personal feelings! These are the highest qualities of man, which are found in but few individuals.'

In late April Feisal left for Damascus to prepare for the arrival of the Commission. There was little to distract Lawrence from writing his account of the Revolt. As he worked, he realised that he needed to visit the Arab Bureau in Cairo in order to check his narrative against the messages and notes in its files.

When he learned that the RAF was about to send fifty Handley-Page bombers from France to Egypt, he arranged to travel with them, and in mid-May joined one of the first squadrons to set out. He told colleagues in the British Delegation that he was going to Cairo to get his belongings, 'and was coming back in a week.'

On May 18 the British Embassy at Rome cabled to the Foreign Office: 'Two Handley-Page machines in one of which was Colonel Lawrence arrived last evening at Rome aerodrome after nightfall. [His aircraft] struck a tree and was wrecked. Colonel Lawrence escaped with a broken collar bone. Aviation Officer Prince was killed on the spot. Spratt [the 2nd pilot] died in hospital from skull fractures. Two mechanics escaped with shock. Lawrence will be in hospital for four or five days and remain here till convalescent. The second machine landed safely.'

Lawrence's injuries were remarkably slight. On examination, he proved to have a cracked shoulder blade and some strained muscles. Four days after the accident the British Ambassador in Rome reported: 'He is at present in the military hospital but I hope to move him to the Embassy in a few days. The medical view is that the cure will take about three weeks. He is however anxious to proceed on his mission earlier if possible.'

By May 29, Lawrence was well enough to leave Rome with the next flight of Handley-Page bombers. Although his left arm was in plaster, he was able to write, and he passed his time drafting the introductory chapters of *Seven Pillars*. At Taranto there was a delay while the machines were overhauled. Afterwards, the squadron flew on by easy stages, spending a week in Athens. In early June it reached Crete, where Lawrence decided that he would break his journey to visit the ruins of Knossos, travelling on to Egypt with one of the later squadrons.

In mid-June, the Foreign Office learned that Lawrence was waiting at Suda Bay, in Crete, for a flight which had not yet arrived. While he was still there, another aircraft called, carrying a diplomat from London to Egypt. This turned out to be H. St. J. B. Philby, who was on an urgent mission to mediate in the continuing frontier dispute between King Hussein and ibn Saud. Lawrence joined him for the flight to Cairo.

Hussein's quarrel with ibn Saud had been smouldering for months, with repeated border incursions by one side or the other. In late May, a Sherifian army under Abdullah had been attacked while sleeping in its tents, and was virtually destroyed. The British Government was embarrassed, since Hussein was a key figure in its Middle Eastern policy, while ibn Saud was the protégé of the India Office. It had therefore been decided that the parties should be persuaded to accept arbitration.

Lawrence himself would have become involved in the affair, had anyone been able to contact him earlier. On June 5, the Foreign Secretary had cabled to Allenby (who had now effectively taken over as British High Commissioner in Egypt): 'In view of the paramount importance of checking the Wahabi threat to the Holy Places and the difficulty of providing King Hussein with adequate support, I consider that every effort should be made to assist him to organise his own forces to the best advantage. Colonel Lawrence from his unequalled experience in directing Arab operations would, in my opinion, be invaluable in the Hedjaz and I recommend that he should be [despatched] to Jeddah forthwith to assist in Hussein's operations if this has not already been done.' Allenby had agreed with the suggestion, but was unable to do anything until Lawrence arrived. Later, it had been suggested in London that Lawrence should undertake the role of mediator, but as he had still not reached Cairo, Philby had been sent instead.

By June 28, both Lawrence and Philby were in Cairo, where they stayed at the Residency. As originally planned, Lawrence remained in Egypt for only a few days, most of which he spent searching through the files of the Arab Bureau.

During his absence there were important developments affecting the Syrian question. France refused to participate in the Inter-Allied Commission unless the British forces in Syria were first replaced by French troops. This move placed Lloyd George in an embarrassing position, and he decided that if no French Commissioners went, the British should stay away also. Consequently, the only Allies represented were the Americans, whose Commissioners were Dr H. C. King and C. R. Crane. Accompanied by a small staff, they had spent two weeks in Palestine before arriving in Damascus on June 25 for a visit which lasted ten days.

By then, however, their conclusions were of purely academic interest. As most observers recognised, there was little likelihood that America would accept any of the Middle East Mandates. The Syrians were still clamouring for British stewardship, but Lloyd George was tied by the gentleman's agreement he had made with Clemenceau. He decided to clarify the position by stating that the Cabinet would under no circumstances accept a Mandate for Syria. The only possible outcome, therefore, was that Syria would go to France.

When he returned to Paris, Lawrence found that there was nothing to do there, and he travelled on to Oxford. On June 10 he had been been elected to a Research Fellowship of All Souls College. The conditions had been drawn up by the Warden and D. G. Hogarth in as vague a fashion as possible: during his tenure he was to 'prosecute his researches into the antiquities and ethnology, and the history (ancient and modern) of the Near East'. The Fellowship was worth £200 a year, a comfortable income for a single person. It would run for seven years, and carried the right to rooms in college.

By the beginning of September there was still no prospect of an American decision about accepting Mandates, and President Wilson, now in failing health, was preoccupied by domestic political difficulties. Lloyd George was unwilling to finance Allenby's troops in Syria indefinitely, knowing that the territory would almost certainly go to France. He therefore announced that he would shortly travel to Paris to try and settle the Syrian question. At the suggestion of the British Delegation, Feisal was urgently requested to return to Europe, though he could not possibly arrive in time for the proposed discussions.

Lawrence was not recalled, and when he learned of the forthcoming meeting, he feared that France was at last to get the bilateral agreement with Britain she had been seeking since before the Conference. Under the guise of a Mandate, her imperial rule would be extended to cover the whole of Syria. Whatever the shortcomings of the Sykes-Picot Agreement, it had been better than this. On September 8 he wrote to the editor of *The Times*, arguing that the situation should be resolved through revision of the original Anglo-French Agreement, and that the Arabs themselves should take part in this process. If he was hoping to delay any significant action over Syria until Feisal reached Europe, he failed. On September 13, Lloyd George told Clemenceau that, in the absence of a Peace Conference decision about the Mandates, Britain would shortly have to withdraw her troops from Syria. An *aide-mémoire* on this subject was drawn up on that day. It began: 'Steps will be taken immediately to prepare for the evacuation by the British army of Syria and Cilicia . . . Notice is given, both to the French Government and to the Emir Feisal, of our intentions to commence the evacuation of Syria and Cilicia on the 1st November 1919.

'In deciding to whom to hand over responsibility for garrisoning the various districts in the evacuated area, regard will be had to the engagements and declarations of the British and French Governments, not only as between themselves, but as between them and the Arabs.

'In pursuance of this policy, the garrison in Syria west of the Sykes-Picot line and the Garrisons in Cilicia will be replaced by a French force and the garrisons at Damascus, Homs, Hama, and Aleppo will be replaced by an Arab force.

'After the withdrawal of their forces, neither the British Government nor the British Commander-in-Chief shall have any responsibility within the zones from which the army has retired.'

CHAPTER 18

An Honourable Settlement
September 1919–August 1922

DESPITE Feisal's protests and entreaties, Britain could no longer take responsibility for the affairs of Syria. When he reached London it was explained to him that his only course was to reach the best settlement he could with France. After a month of fruitless negotiations he left for Paris.

Lawrence, who now found himself unable to help the Arabs in any way, was affected deeply by his sudden political isolation. In Paris, observers had been impressed by his personality, intelligence, and energy. By the autumn, however, the strain had taken its toll. He lived at Oxford, dividing his time between All Souls and his home in Polstead Road. His mother later related how he 'would sometimes sit the entire morning between breakfast and lunch in the same position, without moving, and with the same expression on his face.'

His depression must have been aggravated by the knowledge he had recently acquired about his father's true identity. Until his father's death, he had never discussed his illegitimacy with either parent. Now, however, he had heard his mother's version of the family history. It seems probable that since childhood he had doubted whether Mr Lawrence was his natural father. If so, he must have learned with mixed feelings that the man he had known as Mr Lawrence had been Sir Thomas Chapman, rightful heir to large estates in Ireland, and also his true parent. Chapman had abandoned his wife, children, social position, and fortune in order to spend the rest of his life with the woman he loved.

A letter written by Lawrence some years later doubtless reflects the things his mother now told him: 'My father was on the large scale: tolerant, experienced, grand, rash, humoursome, skilled to speak, and naturally lord-like. He had been thirty-five years in the larger life, and a spendthrift, a sportsman, and a hard rider and drinker . . . Father had, to keep with mother, to drop all his old life, and all his friends. She by dint of will raised herself to be his companion: social things meant much to him: but they never went calling, or on visits, together. They thought always that they were living in sin, and that we would some day find it out. Whereas I knew it before I was ten, and they never told me: till after my Father's death something I said showed Mother that I knew'. When the references to his illegitimacy in Lawrence's letters are taken together, they leave no doubt that he was bitterly aware of the social standing that might, in other circumstances, have been his by right.

By a supreme irony, while he was trying to come to terms with the failure in Paris, London audiences were being treated to a romanticised version of his wartime career: 'At this moment,' they were told, 'somewhere in London, hiding from a host of feminine admirers, reporters, book publishers, autograph fiends and every species of hero-worshipper, is a young man whose name will go down in history beside those of Sir Francis Drake, Sir Walter Raleigh, Lord Clive, Charles Gordon, and all the other famous heroes of Great Britain's glorious past. His first line of defence against these would-be visitors is an Amazonian landlady who battles day and night to save her illustrious guest from his admirers . . . The young man is at present flying from one part of London to another, dressed in mufti, with a hat three sizes too large pulled down over his eyes, trying to escape from the fairer sex.

'His name is Thomas E. Lawrence.

'The Germans and Turks were so impressed with Lawrence's achievements in Arabia that they expressed their admiration and appreciation by offering rewards amounting to over one hundred thousand pounds on his head—dead or alive. But the wild sons of Ishmael regarded their quiet, fair-headed leader as a sort of supernatural being who had been sent from heaven to deliver them from their oppressors, and they wouldn't have betrayed him for all the gold in the fabled mines of King Solomon . . .

'From personal observation and from the lips of a group of equally daring and adventurous British officers who were associated with him, I discovered that Lawrence had accomplished more toward unifying the peoples of Arabia than all of the sultans and emirs since the days of the Great Caliphs six hundred years ago.

'His success was largely due to his genius for handling men, and his peculiar training, which made it possible for him to transform himself into an Arab.'

The speaker was Lowell Thomas, the American journalist who had visited Akaba in March 1918 looking for lecture topics that would encourage his countrymen to support the war. His project had never served its original purpose, since he had returned to America long after the Armistice. By then, there was little interest in the European battlefronts.

He had given his illustrated talks in New York, but found that the only ones which were popular were the accounts of Allenby in Palestine and Lawrence in Arabia.

By chance, the lectures had been heard by an astute English impresario, Percy Burton, who realised that there would be a British public for romantic tales of the campaigns in Palestine and Arabia. He had met the stiff terms demanded by Thomas, and the travelogue had opened at the Royal Opera House, Covent Garden, on August 14.

Burton's expectations were rewarded. The *Daily Telegraph* wrote: 'Thomas Lawrence, the archaeologist, who went out to Arabia and, practically unaided, raised for the first time almost since history began a great homogeneous Arab army . . . we should have thought of merely as one of many who did their duty in these five stirring years. Even the fact that the Turks, under the instigation of their Teutonic masters, set a price of £50,000 on the head of this Englishman who was rousing Arabia from her long lethargy, would probably soon have been forgotten. Now, thanks to Mr. Lowell Thomas and his moving pictures, Thomas Lawrence is definitely marked as one of the elect. In the opinion of the young American lecturer, the name of Thomas Lawrence will go down to remotest posterity beside the names of half a dozen men who dominate history.'

Lawrence, who had played no role whatsoever in bringing this publicity to London, was disconcerted. The lectures attracted full houses for month after month, and it would have been inhuman not to have been intrigued. Yet their style was distasteful and much of the content absurd. During his tour of Palestine, Lowell Thomas had been shown copies of the *Arab Bulletin*, and had noted details from some of Lawrence's raiding reports. In a series of articles published that autumn in the American magazine *Asia*, he claimed to have accompanied Lawrence on expeditions against the railway, giving vivid details. Lawrence called this 'red-hot lying', and persuaded Thomas to omit the most outrageous inventions before the articles were published in England. In exchange, he told Thomas a little about his background, including a version of his father's family history that owed something to the truth he had recently discovered. On the strength of this information, Thomas would later claim that Lawrence had helped him with the articles.

As Lawrence's fame grew, even the politicians who had failed him were keen to associate themselves with his legend. Articles by Thomas in the *Strand Magazine* were prefaced by a comment from Lloyd George: 'Everything that Mr. Lowell Thomas says about Colonel Lawrence is true. In my opinion, Colonel Lawrence is one of the most remarkable and romantic figures of modern times.'

Lawrence's true reaction to Thomas can be judged from a contemporary letter: 'I am painfully aware of what Mr. Lowell Thomas is doing. He came out to Egypt on behalf of the American Government, spent a fortnight in Arabia (I saw him twice in that time) and there he seems to have realised my "star" value on the film. Anyway, since, he has been lecturing in America and London, and has written a series of six articles about me, for American and English publications. They are as rank as possible, and are making life very difficult for me, as I have neither the money nor the wish to maintain my constant character as the mountebank he makes me.

'He has a lot of correct information, and fills it out with stories picked up from officers, and by imagination . . . [He] asked me to correct his proofs: but this I decided was impossible, since I could not possibly pass one tenth of it, and he was making his living out of it. He then asked me what view I would take about misstatements, and I said I would confirm or deny nothing in public. The stuff seems to me too obvious journalism to weigh very deep with anyone serious . . . I am sitting still while he calls me an Irishman, and a Prince of Mecca, and other beastlinesses, and it seems hardly possible to begin putting it straight.' However, Lawrence also admitted to a certain influence with Thomas: 'I don't pay him . . . but I could kick his card-house down if I got annoyed, and so he has to be polite. As a matter of fact he is a very decent fellow—but an American journalist, scooping.'

Lawrence's reputation had been so well established in Government circles by the end of the war that he could easily have obtained personal publicity before this, had he wished. However, he had rarely given interviews, except on Arab questions, and had usually chosen to provide material for articles anonymously. A journalist interviewing him in December 1918, shortly after his return to England, had written: 'Colonel Lawrence, like most men who "do things," is a man of the most charming and unassuming manners, and his extreme modesty and dislike of talking about himself make the interviewer's task a somewhat difficult one. His first remarks, in fact, were directed to "throwing down" the stories concerning himself which had appeared in the press, on the ground that he was having too large a share of the limelight cast upon him. "The stories told about me are very often untrue," said the Colonel, "and they are not quite fair, as I was not the senior British officer out there. There were four or five colonels senior to myself, and the fact that they happened to stay out there and I came home has rather spoilt the perspective of my seniors, who have remained in the east.'' ' Paradoxically, a reputation for personal reticence was now fuelling his popularity.

More than a million people, including royalty and leading politicians, went to the Lowell Thomas travelogue in London. To make way for other bookings, it moved from the Royal Opera House to the Albert Hall, then to the Philharmonic Hall, and finally to the Queen's Hall. At first, Thomas had called it 'With Allenby in Palestine, including the Capture of Jerusalem and the Liberation of Holy Arabia'. Then, as the figure of Lawrence caught the popular imagination, the title became 'With Allenby in Palestine and Lawrence in Arabia'. The phenomenal success must be attributed in part to the skill of Thomas's delivery and the excellence of the slides and motion pictures. But there was also a romance about the war in Palestine and Arabia which provided audiences with a welcome relief from the horrors of the Western Front. The Palestine campaigns had been dubbed 'The Last Crusade', and it was in this almost religious context that Lawrence now found himself cast as a national hero. After lecturing in London for more than four months, Thomas went on tour in the provinces and later the British Empire. During the years that followed, more than four million people would hear him deliver his epic account of Lawrence's Arabian adventures.

One consequence of this sudden fame was that Lawrence began to receive large numbers of unsolicited letters. Some were from admirers, some from women who wanted to marry him, some from people who hoped that he would help them to find work, and some from the demented. He was invited by fashionable hostesses to attend their social functions, and by British and overseas universities to give lectures.

Understandably, he wanted none of this, and he replied to few of the letters. Almost every invitation was refused. He would much rather not have had the publicity in the first place, and he now studiously avoided the press. Percy Burton was offered a large sum by Lord Northcliffe if he would secure a personal interview with Lawrence for *The Times*. Lawrence declined, writing: 'I'm afraid I can't do this. I never care what people say of me or about me, but I try not to help them to do it, and I will not do it myself. It is unpleasant to see one's name in print—and, in spite of the very nice way Lowell Thomas does it, I much wish he had left me out of his Palestine show. I'm very sorry for appearing so sluggish.'

The friendships Lawrence sought during this period were in the world of art and letters. Wishing to improve *Seven Pillars*, he was spending much

of his time reading the work of contemporary writers and trying to analyse their technique. After a dinner at All Souls in November he met
Robert Graves, who had become a member of St John's College. He
showed great interest in Graves's poetry, and his comments were evidently of some value. Graves later wrote that he had been 'for years the
only person to whom I could turn for practical criticism of my poems. He
had a keen eye for surface faults, and though I did not always adopt his
amendments, it was rarely that I did not agree that something was wrong
at the point indicated.' Through this friendship Lawrence was soon introduced to Robert Bridges, Edmund Blunden, Robert Nichols, and other
poets. In the same way he sought out prose writers and painters.

Towards the end of the year, the draft of *Seven Pillars* was nearing
completion: only the chapters covering the spring and summer of 1918
remained to be written. He had sent the manuscript piecemeal to Alan
Dawnay, then at Sandhurst, asking for corrections. One day late in November he went down to Camberley to discuss Dawnay's criticisms with
him. Afterwards, he was to take the draft back to Oxford. As he had
nothing to carry it in, Dawnay lent him an official attaché case. At
Reading, Lawrence had to change trains, and while waiting he sat in the
cafeteria. When he went out, to catch the Oxford train, he forgot the
attaché case. On arrival at Oxford he phoned Reading station, but there
was no sign of the missing case or its contents. It had been taken by a thief
and was never recovered.

The loss was serious: the bag contained all but three of the book's
eleven sections as well as photographs, negatives, and wartime notes
relevant to the later chapters. This would have been a terrible blow in any
circumstances, but Lawrence was already depressed. When he phoned
Dawnay that evening he was distraught.

Within days, however, he had been persuaded by Hogarth (one of the
three people who had read the lost text) that *Seven Pillars* must be
rewritten and, on December 2, he began redrafting it from memory. The
work was not done at All Souls, where there were many distractions, but
in a room on the upper floor of 14 Barton Street, Westminster. This
house, in a quiet street close to the Houses of Parliament, was the property of Westminster School, but had been let as offices to Sir Herbert
Baker, one of the leading architects of the day. Baker had met Lawrence
in Oxford and, not needing the top floor of the Barton Street house, he
had offered it to him as a London base.

During the first two months of 1920, Lawrence wrote out a new version
of *Seven Pillars*. He later stated that he had recreated 95 per cent of the

text in only thirty days. A great help in this task was his set of the *Arab Bulletin*, which contained many of his best wartime reports. By incorporating almost everything he had written for the *Bulletin* somewhere in *Seven Pillars*, he was able to write large sections of the text very easily. The reports were detailed, and provided the basis for almost all the descriptions of raids and journeys. He was also able to use the few notes of his own that had survived; some were original, others copied in 1919 from the Arab Bureau files in Cairo. Despite this, the new version of *Seven Pillars* owed much less to contemporary materials than the one that had been lost. To enrich it, he used lavish description: 'the sense of the country and atmosphere and climate and furniture of Arabia hung so tightly about me that I put too much of them into the story, in hopes that they would make it life-like.'

Lawrence's life at Barton Street was deliberately frugal: he believed that his creative power would be intensified by hunger and lack of sleep, and preferred to work at night, wearing a flying suit to keep warm. The attic room contained little furniture and no cooking facilities. He lived off sandwiches bought from refreshment stands in nearby stations, and washed at the local public baths. He later wrote: 'I got into my garret, and . . . excited myself with hunger and cold and sleeplessness more than did de Quincey with his opium.'

During the spring he set about correcting the text, as best he could; here again, the *Bulletin* was invaluable. He tried very hard to be historically accurate, and long afterwards would write: 'All the documents of the Arab Revolt are in the archives of the Foreign Office, and will . . . be available to students, who will be able to cross-check my yarns. I expect them to find small errors, and to agree generally with the main current of my narrative.' Nevertheless, he remained deliberately silent about certain aspects of the story. For example, as Feisal's Arabs might soon be in conflict with French forces in Syria, he carefully refrained from giving specific details of their wartime tactics and equipment.

This was not the only way in which *Seven Pillars* reflected his concern about French colonial ambitions. The book had now assumed a strongly political role: it was to serve as a record of the Arab war effort, justifying Feisal's claims to self-government. Lawrence did not entirely conceal the Arabs' failings during the war, but his treatment was sympathetic, and there was much that he glossed over. The documents show that *Seven Pillars* often tells less than the whole truth, concealing politically damaging matters such as Feisal's weakness of character. Lawrence also played down the enormous contribution made to the Revolt by non-Arab personnel. He did not assess the achievements of the Indian machine-gunners, the armoured cars, the French artillery unit, and above all the RAF, whose bombing and reconnaissance had been a decisive factor during the northern campaign.

This emphasis on the Arab achievement cannot be excused by the claim that Lawrence was writing only about his personal experience of the war. In his liaison role he had been directly and continuously involved with the non-Arab contribution. His decision to present such a one-sided account doubtless reflects the bitterness of his experience at the Peace Conference and his own commitment to the Arab cause. Yet the same political message might have been put across, with less risk of criticism, by stressing that there had been a large degree of inter-dependence. While Feisal's success owed much to British help, the EEF also owed much to Feisal. The needs of the Western Front had starved Allenby of troops, and without the contribution made by Arab forces east of the Jordan his advance through Palestine would have been difficult, if not impossible.

In late April, when Lawrence had roughed out most of the new *Seven Pillars* draft, he returned to Oxford for a month. Before long, he was involved in Middle Eastern politics again.

The Paris Conference had produced no agreement over Mandates, and the matter was being settled at an Allied meeting then taking place in San Remo. As expected, Britain was to get Palestine and Mesopotamia, while France took the whole of Syria. After negotiating some kind of *modus vivendi* with Clemenceau at the end of 1919, Feisal had returned to Damascus in January to find himself attacked by nationalists for selling out to the French. During his long absence in Europe, local support had begun to fade, and the internal situation was rapidly deteriorating.

If the Syrian politicians had been less short-sighted, they would have realised that their only hope of preserving any form of autonomy was to reach an accommodation with France. As it was, however, Feisal gave in to the extremists. After wavering for a few weeks, he disowned the understanding he had reached with Clemenceau, thereby earning lasting mistrust from the French.

On March 8, a 'General Syrian Congress' proclaimed Feisal King of an 'independent and integral Syria', which was supposed to include not only Lebanon, but also northern Mesopotamia and Palestine. The claim to these latter regions caused as much irritation in Britain as it did in France, and was roundly dismissed at San Remo. Both the Foreign Office and the

India Office now viewed Damascus as a hotbed of rabid nationalism which threatened to unsettle the whole region.

Worse still, Feisal's control over inland Syria had weakened. Attacks on French personnel and property occurred with increasing frequency. The French administration made it clear that they would not tolerate such conduct, and the end of Feisal's regime seemed therefore merely a question of time.

As far as France and the Government of India were concerned, the allocation of Mandates at San Remo was simply a sharing-out of imperial gains. This action denied the claims of Arab nationalism and made nonsense of all that had been said in Britain and the United States about self-determination. Lawrence later wrote: 'The Sykes-Picot treaty was the Arab sheet-anchor. The French saw that, and worked frantically for the alternative of the mandate. By a disgraceful bargain the British supported them, to gain Mesopotamia. Under the Sykes-Picot treaty the French only got the coast: and the Arabs (native administration) were to have Aleppo, Hama, Homs, Damascus, and Trans-Jordan. By the mandate swindle England and France got the lot. The Sykes-Picot treaty was absurd, in its boundaries, but it did recognise the claims of Syrians to self-government, and it was ten thousand times better than the eventual settlement.'

To Lawrence, at least, Arab fury about the San Remo Mandates was predictable. He had already warned, seven months previously, of his disquiet about the effect of Anglo-Indian methods in Mesopotamia, writing: 'if we do not mend our ways, [I] will expect revolt there about March next.' Others, too, thought that the Anglo-Indian administration in Mesopotamia should be changed. Among them was Sir Hugh Trenchard, head of the RAF. Air power had proved a successful and relatively cheap method of maintaining order in Somaliland, and Trenchard was keen to extend the operations of his fledgling Service by taking over similar duties in Mesopotamia. On April 21 he discussed his ideas with Lawrence, who afterwards wrote to Lord Winterton (then a Conservative member of the House of Commons): 'I think he is right in all points, and after quite a lot of talk I feel inclined to back his scheme. It means Salmond as High Commissioner in Bagdad (a happy deliverance from the Indian Civil Service tradition) with probably the Colonial Secretary nominally responsible, and with an Arab army under an Arab–British administration to defend the country.

'Trenchard sounded to me clean and honest . . . and means to play fair by the local people. He thinks as little of the worth of bombing as we did!'

A month later Lawrence was one of the most prominent figures among an informal group of politicians and experts who urged Lloyd George to take control of Britain's Middle Eastern interests out of the hands of the Foreign Office and the India Office. He helped to canvass for signatures to this appeal, writing to Philby: 'It happens to be—politically—the right moment for pressure towards a new Middle East Department, since some reshuffling of spheres is certain to happen quite soon: and the enclosed [draft letter to Lloyd George] is a step taken under advice, to add pressure from outside, to what is going on inside. They have asked me to get your name on the list: other "experts" invited are Hogarth, [Lionel] Curtis, [Arnold] Toynbee, and myself. I have no doubt you will agree, so I won't bother to argue. It is a step necessary before a new policy can be put in force, and when we get it through, then we'll have to open up a battery of advice on the new men.'

Now that he wanted to influence the Government, Lawrence suddenly found his popular reputation useful. Newspapers were only too willing to publish anything he wrote about the Middle East. On May 28 he began a press campaign with a piece in the *Daily Express*, which was followed up with articles in the *Sunday Times* and elsewhere.

During the interval between the Peace Conference and this new involvement in Eastern politics, Lawrence had made plans for his own future. In fulfilment of a promise made years before, he had bought the land which his friend Vyvyan Richards was renting at Pole Hill in Essex, on the edge of Epping Forest. It was here that, as young Oxford graduates, the two had planned to set up a private press. With the income from All Souls and the £5,000 given to him by his father in 1916, the dream of printing fine editions seemed at last to be within Lawrence's grasp. His rooms at All Souls were soon furnished with books from the great private presses: a series of Kelmscotts, including the famous Chaucer, a Doves Press Bible, the latest titles from the Ashendene, and works from many other well-known craftsmen. He began to talk of producing an edition of poems by Meleager, translated from the original Syrian.

Richards was still teaching at a school in Chingford, and they were now thinking of putting up a building at Pole Hill to house the press and provide simple living accommodation. They did not expect to begin printing before 1921 at the earliest.

Lawrence offered to raise enough money to finance the building, and his letters show that as early as February 1920 he was intending to do this by publishing a popular abridgement of *Seven Pillars* in the United States.

By the end of June the scheme had taken definite shape, and he offered the book to the American publisher F. N. Doubleday, whom he had met in London shortly after the war.

By midsummer he felt that the redrafted text of *Seven Pillars* had been corrected sufficiently to serve as a basis for the abridgement, and he decided to spend August and September at All Souls, working on the shorter text. He invited Richards to visit him there whenever possible: 'Your critical faculty would be invaluable: because though it's only a cheap book written to buy Pole Hill and build its house, yet it's got to have my name on it—therefore I don't want it to be despicable.'

Lawrence completed several chapters of the abridgement during August. Then, in the first week of September, he abruptly stopped. There is very little evidence relating to this decision, which was nevertheless a turning-point in his career. The most likely explanation is the simplest: his sole purpose was to raise money to finance the press at Pole Hill and if, as seems probable, he began to doubt that the book would earn the sum he needed, he had no reason to go on with it.

Lawrence's financial position at this time was much less secure than most people believed. In principle, his annual revenue amounted to £200 from All Souls and roughly another £150 interest from the £5,000 investments given to him by his father. At that time £350 was a very adequate income for a single person, and as recently as March 20 Lawrence had confidently described himself as 'a person who doesn't care sufficiently about money to try hard to make any. My father was kind to me, and spent none of the capital he received from his father . . . and unless I marry non-self-supporting wives or have children, all will be well with me.'

In addition to these sources of income, he should have had a sizeable capital sum resulting from the accumulation of unspent army pay during the five years between October 1914 and August 1919. This surplus might well have amounted to £2,000 and, if he had invested it, his total income would have been over £400. However, he had not done so. A series of land purchases at Pole Hill had probably cost him more than £2,000 between September 1919 and May 1920. During the same period, he had built up a valuable collection of private press books, worth hundreds of pounds, even at the prices then prevailing. He had also acquired one of Augustus John's two oil portraits of Feisal. What he paid is not recorded (there is even a story that he exchanged the painting for a diamond). At that time, however, the market value of the portrait was about £600.

By the summer of 1920 all Lawrence's savings from his wartime pay must have been spent. This would not have been a very serious matter, but at about this time he also gave away a large part of the capital received from his father.

The gift was in the spirit of a request made by his brother Will who had been killed during the war. In 1915, Will had asked Lawrence to be his executor, saying that he wanted to bequeath all his money to Janet Laurie. This had been a confidential arrangement between the two brothers: there was no mention of Janet in the written will, which named Lawrence as sole beneficiary. After his brother's death, Lawrence had doubtless carried out this private request, but the sum involved was negligible because Will had died shortly before his father had divided £15,000 between the brothers.

During the spring of 1920, Lawrence must have learned that Janet Laurie, now married, was in need of money. It seems that he then gave her the £3,000 that Will had expected to receive from his father. This extraordinary act of generosity must reflect his affection for Will, who had been the closest of his brothers, and also for Janet, perhaps the only girl to whom he had ever felt a deep attachment.

The gift of so much capital reduced Lawrence's income, and there is ample evidence of this sudden poverty in letters written during the summer and autumn of 1920. In his new financial circumstances he would have needed a much larger sum than before if he were to set up a private press at Pole Hill with Richards. He had never expected the press itself to be profitable, and in addition to the capital cost of the building and equipment, he would require a sufficient investment income to cover all his personal expenses. To meet these outgoings he now needed a capital sum of at least £5,000.

A. S. Watt, Lawrence's literary agent, would not have been willing to hazard a guess about likely earnings from the abridgement until he had seen a sample. By the end of August, Lawrence had seven chapters ready, and he must have sent them to Watt for evaluation before meeting Doubleday, who was due to arrive in Britain in the middle of September.

Lawrence wanted to confine publication to America and, because of this, Watt's estimate was almost certainly disheartening. 'Lawrence of Arabia' was famous in Britain, but still relatively unknown in the United States. Yet to earn the money required, the abridgement would have to be a best-seller there. This was something no literary agent would have been prepared to guarantee. Watt must have told Lawrence that the income he was hoping for could only be assured if the book were published in the British market.

Lawrence was totally opposed to this. He had earlier written: 'Unless I am starving (involuntarily) there will be no London publisher. My whole object is to make money in U.S.A. and so avoid the notoriety of being on sale in England.' He saw that there was little point in continuing the abridgement. Moreover, the task he had set himself was proving more difficult than he had expected: after more than a month, barely a quarter of the proposed 150,000-word text had been completed. He abandoned the project and, in its place, began at the beginning of September to write a new polished draft of the complete *Seven Pillars* text.

During the two preceding years he been a regular visitor to London art galleries, and had sat for Augustus John, William Orpen, Derwent Wood, and William Rothenstein. He had thought of using portraits rather than photographs to illustrate the *Seven Pillars* abridgement, and he now hoped to commission portraits for an edition of the complete text.

For this purpose he made contact with Eric Kennington, whose work as an official war artist was highly regarded. He asked whether it might be possible to draw portraits based on photographs of the Arab personalities in *Seven Pillars*. Kennington, whose previous knowledge of Lawrence had been derived from the Lowell Thomas lectures, was fascinated by the project, but he rejected the idea of working from photographs. Instead, he suggested that he should visit the Middle East and draw the Arabs from life. Lawrence explained how much this would cost, but Kennington said that he would shortly have earned enough from other work to pay his own way.

At the beginning of October, Lawrence wrote an introduction to a new edition of Doughty's *Travels in Arabia Deserta*. This marked the successful conclusion of a long campaign to have the book reprinted. During the war, the Arab Bureau had possessed a copy of the original edition. Doughty's account had proved to be an invaluable source of information, and ever since returning to England Lawrence had been urging it on publishers: 'The whole book is a necessity to any student of Arabia, but it is more than that. It's one of the greatest prose works in the English language, and the best travel book in the world. Unfortunately it's solidly written (not dull at all, but in a queer style which demands care at first), and because of its rarity is far too little known . . . It has of course an immense reputation amongst the elect.'

At first he had thought of having a new edition produced by the Government Press in Cairo, but this had proved impossible. However, he had been more fortunate when he approached the Medici Society, which had published a number of fine limited editions. There he had met Jonathan Cape, who was working for the firm but was keen to set up an imprint of his own. It had eventually been agreed that Cape and the Medici Society would co-publish a new edition, provided that Lawrence wrote an introduction. It was to be issued in January 1921 at nine guineas. If the first printing (of only five hundred copies) sold out rapidly, the cost of typesetting would be paid off and further impressions could be issued at a much lower price.

During the summer and autumn of 1920, Lawrence had continued his press campaign against the Middle East settlement, writing in the columns of *The Times* and the *Observer*. The rebellion in Mesopotamia was then at its height, and he pointed out that the oppressive Anglo-Indian administration had done nothing to cultivate Arab sympathy. It had barred educated Arabs from responsible work in the civil service or defence forces, imposing a form of colonial rule that was even less sympathetic to local aspirations than that of pre-war Turkey. He was greatly saddened when the French, no doubt encouraged by this Anglo-Indian example, drove Feisal's Arab administration out of Damascus.

At the end of the year, it was decided that Winston Churchill should be put in charge of the Colonial Office and given responsibility for Mesopotamia, coastal Palestine and the inland region known as Trans-Jordan. On January 8 he invited Lawrence to join him as an adviser on Arab Affairs. Lawrence's initial response was not enthusiastic. After his failure at the Peace Conference he had resolved to seek no further role in Arabian diplomacy or administration, and his present thoughts were mainly of writing and printing. Only a week before, he had written: 'I've long given up politics.' However, he eventually accepted the post, seeing it as an opportunity to salve Britain's reputation in part, at least, of the Arab world. At first he tried to make a condition that Britain's wartime promises to the Arabs would be honoured. The condition was refused, and he later wrote that he had only accepted because 'Winston . . . offered me direct access to himself on every point, and a free hand, subject to his discretion. This was better than any condition, because I wanted the best settlement of the Middle East possible, apart from all the promises and treaties.'

Churchill knew little about the Arab world, yet his greatest need was to reduce the cost of the colonial administration in Mesopotamia. Lawrence had assured him that he could save millions by turning the country into an autonomous Arab kingdom under Feisal and, as the latter was now in London, Churchill asked Lawrence to discuss the scheme with him privately.

One problem was that France was acutely hostile towards the idea of making Feisal ruler in Mesopotamia. Anglo-French tension over the Middle East had been aggravated during the winter by Abdullah. In November 1920 he had moved to Maan, at that time within the boundaries of the Hejaz, with the avowed intention of raising an army to drive the French out of Syria. Alarming rumours about his activities were picked up by both French and British Intelligence. Churchill hoped that Feisal would help by using his influence to calm the situation.

Lawrence began work in the Colonial Office on February 18. That day a seven-point outline agenda was drafted for a Middle East conference to be held in Cairo, and he spent most of the following week adding detail to this framework, working closely with Hubert Young, who shared his office. They saw to it that the agenda was framed in such a way that the conference would arrive at the desired conclusions. Some years afterwards, Lawrence told his biographer Liddell Hart that everything had been staged before the meetings began. He had settled not only the questions to be considered, but the decisions to be reached: 'Talk of leaving things to the man on the spot—we left nothing'.

As long as Churchill continued to back him, Lawrence could not fail. If he had worries on this count, they were groundless. Churchill's performance was everything that he could have hoped for, and item after item on the Cairo Conference agenda was settled by unanimous agreement. Feisal was to be presented to the people of Mesopotamia (now to be called Irak) for election as leader of an Arab administration which, with help from British advisers, would move towards autonomy.

In early March, while the Cairo discussions were in progress, news came that Abdullah had crossed the frontier into Trans-Jordan, and was now in Amman. It was decided that he should be offered some kind of political role as governor there or, if he refused, that an alternative Arab governor should be appointed with his approval.

At Churchill's request, Lawrence travelled from Egypt to Trans-Jordan, where he met Abdullah and explained the main lines of Britain's future policy in the region. Both men then went to Jerusalem, where a series of meetings with Churchill took place. The result was that Abdullah agreed to act as ruler in Trans-Jordan and to do his best to halt all anti-French activity. In exchange for this he would receive British financial and military aid. The arrangement was to run for a period of six months while Feisal sought popular approval in Iraq.

One of the principal decisions of the Cairo Conference had been to adopt Trenchard's scheme of using air power to enforce law and order in Iraq. This overseas role would be very important to the status of the RAF during the coming years, and Trenchard would not forget that Lawrence had been one of his most influential supporters. It was hoped that an equally economical solution could be applied in Trans-Jordan, which had sunk into a state of near-anarchy after the end of Feisal's administration in Damascus. Effective policing would be necessary in order to halt the continuing raids into French Syria, and a local force of Arab regulars was already being trained. Meanwhile Abdullah's authority was to be established with armoured cars and RAF support from Palestine.

By May 11 Lawrence was back in London. Everything he had hoped for when he joined the Colonial Office had been achieved. In Mesopotamia, the administration was taking the steps necessary to ensure that Feisal would be chosen by the people as their ruler, while in Trans-Jordan 'we kept our promises to the Arab Revolt and assisted the home-rulers to form a buffer principality'. The India Office victory of 1919 had been overturned.

He later wrote: 'I take most of the credit of Mr. Churchill's pacification of the Middle East upon myself. I had the knowledge and the plan. He had the imagination and the courage to adopt it and the knowledge of the political procedure to put it into operation'. Lawrence saw the settlement as 'the big achievement of my life: of which the war was a preparation.'

Although he had agreed to remain with Churchill for a year, he had no further personal ambitions regarding the Middle East. Daily routine in Whitehall held no appeal for him either, and he was relieved to learn that he would shortly be sent abroad again, even though the main purpose of his new mission was unattractive. His services were to be lent to the Foreign Office so that he could negotiate a treaty between Britain and Sherif Hussein.

When the Middle East Department was formed, Churchill had hoped that the Hejaz would be included in its responsibilities. However, the Foreign Office had pointed out that this might be taken by some as evidence that Hussein's kingdom was not fully independent. The Colonial Office was nevertheless obliged to take Hussein's attitude into account and to secure, if possible, his agreement to the Cairo Conference settlements in Mesopotamia, Trans-Jordan, and Palestine. A draft treaty covering these points had been drawn up by the Foreign Office. In exchange for Hussein's co-operation, it offered financial subsidies and guarantees against military incursions by ibn Saud.

On July 8, Lawrence set out for Jidda bearing what Curzon described as a 'special full power under the Royal Sign Manual and Signet, authorising and empowering you to negotiate and conclude, with such Minister or Ministers as may be vested with similar power and authority on the part of His Majesty the King of the Hejaz, a treaty between the United Kingdom and the Kingdom of the Hejaz, for the settlement of matters now under discussion between the two countries.' In the event that Hussein found clauses of the draft treaty unacceptable, Lawrence was to refer the matter back to Curzon. In addition, he was to persuade Hussein to sign the Treaty of Versailles and a declaration recognising the French position in Syria. While in the region, he might also be sent to Aden, which had recently become a Colonial Office responsibility, to negotiate a settlement between Britain and the Imam of the Yemen.

The final stage of his mission would be a return to Trans-Jordan. The six-month period during which Abdullah had agreed to act as ruler would end in September, and there was some uncertainty as to what would happen afterwards.

Through no fault of his own, the Hejaz mission proved to be one of the least successful episodes in Lawrence's life. It proved impossible to negotiate with the ageing Hussein, who changed his mind between one meeting and the next, constantly retracting agreements that had already been reached. When the discussions halted for the Muslim Pilgrimage, Lawrence visited Aden, but the situation there was not yet ripe for any diplomatic initiative. He returned to Jidda, where Hussein remained obdurate, despite attempts at reasoned persuasion by Ali and Zeid. As the situation was clearly hopeless, the Foreign Office agreed to let Lawrence move on to Trans-Jordan, leaving Hussein to contemplate what his future might be when British support was withdrawn. Lawrence was profoundly disappointed by the failure, and the bitterness towards Hussein expressed in *Seven Pillars* almost certainly reflects this episode.

He arrived in Jerusalem on October 2 and after ten days went on to Amman, where he found that the situation was better than he had been led to expect. Taxes were being paid, and local policing was satisfactory. Abdullah, who doubtless saw little in prospect elsewhere, was prepared to stay on for some months, and perhaps even longer.

Lawrence took over as British representative in Trans-Jordan, working to consolidate Abdullah's position. He also arranged to take up the Hejaz

Treaty negotiations again, on the basis that Abdullah would represent Hussein. During the last week in November further modifications to the text were agreed, and on the 28th Lawrence cabled Churchill: 'Abdulla being only plenipotentiary, his signature without royal ratification is as valueless as my own. Abdulla accepts the treaty as modified by my telegrams . . . He swears that Hussein will ratify . . . but I . . . have my doubts. It may, however, seem to you worth letting [him] try. If I receive your concurrence . . . we can sign it in the next few days before I start home.' The treaty was signed by Lawrence and Abdullah on December 8. Four days later Lawrence left for Egypt, and by Christmas Eve he was back in London.

By the end of 1921, Feisal was King in Iraq, where he reigned until his death in 1933; Abdullah had been established as ruler in Trans-Jordan, where he too would become a monarch in 1946. Hussein refused to ratify the Anglo-Hashemite Treaty and in 1924, deprived of British support against the growing power of ibn Saud, he was forced to abdicate; he died in exile seven years later. Mecca was taken by ibn Saud's forces in 1924, and the Hejaz was eventually absorbed into the new Kingdom of Saudi Arabia. French rule in Syria encountered increasing difficulties, and one administration after another collapsed in the face of local opposition. In 1936, France set up an Arab administration on the lines that Lawrence and Churchill had initiated in Mesopotamia.

For Lawrence, the Arabian chapter was closed. In the last days of 1921 he returned to the Colonial Office, knowing that the year he had promised Churchill had only two more months to run.

CHAPTER 19

The Decision
January–August 1922

AT the beginning of January 1922, Lawrence wrote to Sir Hugh Trenchard: 'You know I am trying to leave Winston on March the first. Then
I want about two months to myself, and then I'd like to join the R.A.F.—
with the ranks, of course.

'I can't do this without your help. I'm thirty-three and not skilled in the
senses you want. Probably I couldn't pass your medical. It's odd being
too old for the job I want when hitherto I've always been too young for
the job I did. However my health is good: I'm always in physical and
mental training, and I don't personally believe that I'd be below the
average of your recruits in either respect. If you think so that will end it.

'You'll wonder what I'm at. The matter is that since I was sixteen I've
been writing: never satisfying myself technically but steadily getting better. My last book on Arabia is nearly good. I see the sort of subject I need
in the beginning of your Force . . . and the best place to see a thing from
is the ground. It wouldn't "write" from the officer level.

'I haven't told anyone, till I know your opinion: and probably not then,
for the newspapers used to run after me and I like being private. People
wouldn't understand.

'It's an odd request this, hardly proper perhaps, but it may be one of
the exceptions you make sometimes. It is asking you to use your influence
to get me past the Recruiting Officer! Apologies for making it: if you say
no I'll be more amused than hurt.'

Other letters written at about this time show that he was not planning
to remain in the RAF for very long. He intended after an interval to return
to *Seven Pillars* and to his scheme for a private press. Not long after this
approach to Trenchard, he wrote to Eric Kennington: 'The real trouble is
about my book, which is not good: not good enough to come out. It has
grown too long and shapeless, and I haven't the strength to see it all in
one piece, or the energy to tackle it properly. After I've got out of the
Colonial Office and have been fallow for a time my interest in it will
probably come back and then I'll have another go at it'.

*   *   *

The motives that lay behind his decision to enlist were complex. He himself recognised that there was no easy explanation, and wrote some months later to a friend: 'Honestly I couldn't tell you exactly why I joined up: though the night before I did . . . I sat up and wrote out all the reasons I could see or feel in myself for it, but they came to little more than that it was a necessary step, forced on me by an inclination towards ground-level, by a little wish to make myself a little more human . . . by an itch to make myself ordinary in a mob of likes: also, I'm broke, so far as money goes . . . All these are reasons, but unless they are cumulative they are miserably inadequate. I wanted to join up, that's all . . . It's going to be a brain-sleep, and I'll come out of it less odd than I went in'.

As his decision stemmed from both conscious and subconscious motives, there is little to be gained by attempting to set these out in a logical fashion. Nevertheless, it is possible to identify many of the factors which influenced him at this time.

One was his disinclination to follow a conventional career—an attitude he had doubtless inherited from his father. His years in the East had reinforced this outlook, leaving him with a contempt for possessions and wealth: 'The gospel of bareness in materials is a good one', he had written in 1918.

He had no ambition to remain in the Colonial Office: in any case, his mentality was that of a crusading politician rather than a civil servant. Now that the special circumstances of the war had passed, he was free to please himself, and he did not like having to advocate or implement ideas he disagreed with. He later wrote: 'the life of politics wearied me out, by worrying me over-much. I've not got a coarse-fibred enough nature for them: and have too many scruples and an uneasy conscience. It's not good to see two sides of questions, when you have (officially) to follow one.'

Academic life might have seemed a natural alternative, but he had never felt attracted to the idea of a university post, and had rejected this option before the war. He had tried living at All Souls during 1919 and 1920, but felt ill at ease there and had spent most of his time at Barton Street. He now decided to give up his rooms in the college.

As an archaeologist, his enthusiasm had been for field-work rather than academic study. Shortly after the Armistice he had spoken of rejoining Woolley for further excavations at Carchemish. By the end of the Peace Conference, however, France had taken control in Syria, and it was obvious that he would not be allowed to go back.

Finally, it is worth noting that Lawrence sometimes spoke of himself as a person only rarely moved by ambition. Years later, he wrote: 'When I want a thing, I'm prepared to lose everything to get it. Hence I succeed, *when I want to*. But that is, fortunately for my peace and comfort, seldom.'

In 1922 he had only one wish: despite the problems he was facing with *Seven Pillars*, he still hoped to make a reputation for himself as a writer. There was nothing new about this ambition. Ever since leaving Oxford in 1910 he had toyed with literary projects of some kind. His latest scheme, for a book about the RAF, was certainly real; and at that time the idea of writing a study of the Air Force as seen from the ranks was a novel one. While it is unlikely that Lawrence would have enlisted for this reason alone, he undoubtedly took the project very seriously and it seems to have played a significant part in the conscious reasoning behind his decision.

Another motive was probably fear of solitude. He did not have a close relationship with any surviving member of his family, nor did he have dependents of his own or hope of marrying. After the homosexual rape at Deraa in November 1917, the consummation of a marriage would have been utterly abhorrent to him. The incident had left him with an aversion for physical contact, which was noticed by many of his friends. Nevertheless, since the end of the desert campaigns he had often felt intensely lonely. The popular reputation created for him by Lowell Thomas had driven him increasingly into isolation, and he had spent months on his own in Barton Street working on *Seven Pillars*. On other occasions he had been hurt when cold-shouldered by political adversaries. Like many other ex-servicemen, he began to long for the spirit of comradeship that he had known during the war: a spirit that is rarely found in civilian life.

According to Lawrence, the idea of enlisting had first occurred to him when working with British units during the later stages of the desert campaign: 'These friendly outings with the armoured car and Air Force fellows were what persuaded me that my best future, if I survived the war, was to enlist.' He also wrote: 'My ambition to serve in [the Air Force] ranks dates—concretely—from 1919: and nebulously from . . . 1917, before there was an Air Force.' There is some evidence to confirm that enlistment had been in his mind during 1919, but at that time he was still considering other possibilities such as the printing scheme. The final decision to join the RAF seems to date from the beginning of 1922.

As he himself admitted, these rational motives for his enlistment were barely sufficient, and he was undoubtedly influenced by other factors which were to some degree subconscious. Among these were psychological problems that had existed for some time. Although he usually made light of his illegitimacy, he would occasionally speak of it with great bitterness to close friends. Likewise, he was acutely aware of his short stature. In the draft of *Seven Pillars*, he wrote: 'I was . . . ashamed of my awkwardness: and of my physical envelope: and of my solitary unlikeness which made me no friend or companion, but an acquaintance: complete, angular, uncomfortable'. He probably knew that people referred to him slightingly as 'little Lawrence', and he seems to have regarded both his illegitimacy and his short stature as real handicaps which would in some way prevent him from taking a more prominent place among the ruling élite.

His sensitivity over these questions was heightened by the state of depression from which he was suffering when he returned to England in December 1921. For some time he had been in poor health, and this had aggravated his sense of disillusion with Hussein and the other Arab leaders. He had drifted into a negative mood which left him disappointed with the outcome of his diplomatic negotiations and irritated by the shortcomings he now saw in his *Seven Pillars* draft. During his work for Churchill, he had also been draining his energies in a struggle to improve the book. Yet it revived the worst of his wartime experiences, and the stress of recreating them under such unfavourable conditions had disturbed the balance of his mind. Subconscious forces, which he might otherwise have been able to cope with, began to play an increasingly important role in his motivation.

Like many soldiers who have lived through horrific battlefield experiences he was suffering from the after-effects of war, and for several years he had dreadful nightmares. Although relatively common, this malaise was inadequately understood by the medical profession at that time, and went largely untreated. Lawrence recognised it, both in himself and in many of his friends.

In his depressed condition, one incident in particular had come to dominate his thoughts. He had been able to put the Deraa episode out of his mind during much of the Syrian campaign, but since returning to civilian life he had found himself brooding over it. The experience had left him with profound feelings of uncleanliness, confusion and guilt. His account of it was among the first *Seven Pillars* chapters he had drafted, and he later said that he had rewritten the description nine times. In the version he finished in 1922, he wrote that he had been left feeling 'maimed, imperfect, only half myself. It could not have been the defilement, for no one ever held the body in less honour than I did myself. Probably it had been the breaking of the spirit by that frenzied nerve-shattering pain which had degraded me to beast level when it made me grovel to it, and which had journeyed with me since, a fascination and terror and morbid desire, lascivious and vicious, perhaps, but like the striving of a moth towards its flame.' Such thoughts gave rise to a new and very damaging sense of personal worthlessness.

In Lawrence's mind, the destruction of his sense of integrity at this most intimate level seemed to reflect the moral degradation he had accepted during his wartime role with the Arabs. Churchill's settlement could not absolve him from responsibility for the lies he had told, nor from their terrible consequences. He would never be able to forget the sacrifices made by those who had believed in him. His memories of events such as the death of his young servant Othman, so painfully described in *Seven Pillars*, must have been an insistent reminder of what he had done.

It was this tormenting knowledge that made public adulation so intolerable. The association between praise and guilt had been forged at Damascus, where the populace had welcomed him as a liberator, believing that he had helped to bring them lasting freedom. He was now desperate to escape from his public reputation, and believed that he could do so by enlisting under an assumed name.

The idea of anonymity seemed to intrigue him in itself. In *Seven Pillars* he wrote: 'There was a special attraction in a new beginning, an everlasting endeavour to free my personality from its accretions, and to project it unencumbered on a fresh medium . . . The hidden self was reflected clearest in the still water of another man's yet incurious mind. Considered judgments, which had in them of the past and the future, were worthless compared with the first sight, the instinctive opening or closing of a man as he looked at the stranger. Whence came our pleasure in disguise or anonymity'.

The wish to submerge his real identity was one aspect of the 'inclination towards ground-level' and 'itch to make myself ordinary in a mob of likes' he spoke of at the time of his enlistment. This feeling too is discussed in the draft of *Seven Pillars*, where he wrote: 'I liked the things beneath me and took my pleasures, and my adventures, downward. There seemed a level of certainty in degradation, a final safety. Man could rise to any height, but there was an animal point beneath which he could not fall. It was a solid satisfaction on which to rest. The force of things, and an artificial dignity, denied it me more and more, but there endured the after-taste of a real liberty from one youthful submerged fortnight in Port Said, coaling steamers by day with other outcasts of three continents and curling up by night to sleep on the breakwater by [the statue of] de Lesseps, with the sea surging past my head.'

Lawrence chose to spend large parts of his adult life among people who shared none of the advantages of his background. He recognised this fact and sought to understand it; yet his explanations of this 'downward urge' seem inadequate, especially in relation to his enlistment. If he had thought about it deeply, he would surely have realised that his education and experience would always guarantee him a special position among the men in the ranks. In practice, therefore, his 'inclination towards ground level' would take him into situations where his intellectual superiority would be effortless and unrivalled. It is clear from his post-enlistment letters that he made no attempt to evade this special status: on the contrary, he seems to have cultivated it. This pattern of behaviour suggests that Lawrence suffered from a deep sense of insecurity.

In the draft *Seven Pillars* he also described a longing for roles that were truly subservient and self-abasing: 'Always in working I had tried to serve . . . It was part of my failure never to have found a chief to use me. All of them were weak, and through incapacity or fear or liking, allowed me too free a hand. I was always hoping for a master [for] whom I could have fought till I dropped at his feet to worship . . . I used myself as I would have let no man use another: but needed over me one yet harder and more ruthless, who would have worn me to the last fibre of my strength. To him I could have given such service as few masters have had, and I would have given it zealously, for voluntary slavery was a deep pride of a morbid spirit'.

This curious statement seems to invite two quite different comments. first, it is clear from 'Twenty-seven Articles' and other writings that Lawrence had been far from subservient when acting as confidential adviser to influential men. Throughout his military and diplomatic career he had tried to manipulate his superiors in order to attain his personal objectives. With both Feisal and Churchill, he had seen himself as a 'power behind the throne'. Allenby had known nothing of Lawrence's personal motives in the Arab Revolt, yet, through Lawrence, he had helped to advance the cause of Arab freedom. In this respect, therefore, the passage quoted above must be regarded as misleading.

By 1922, however, a confused desire for some form of self-abasement seems to have become a powerful element in Lawrence's emotional condition. In a letter to a friend written shortly after his enlistment, he said: 'partly I came in here to eat dirt, till its taste is normal to me'. There were to be many further references to this motive during the next few years, and these later allusions suggest that it formed part of an essentially masochistic disorder unleashed by his experience at Deraa.

Such was Lawrence's state of mind in January 1922. He appears to have believed that a spell in the ranks would help cure his malaise, and told Robert Graves that enlistment was little different from going into a monastery.

Trenchard replied to his letter about enlistment on January 11: 'With regard to your personal point, I understand it fully, and you too, I think. I am prepared to do all you ask me, if you will tell me for how long you want to join, but I am afraid I could not do it without mentioning it to Winston and my own Secretary of State, and then, whether it could be kept secret I do not know . . . What country do you want to serve in, and how? I would make things as easy as anything.

'Let me know if I may mention this to my two Secretaries of State and come and see me.'

Lawrence did not immediately press the matter: at the time he was still working for the Colonial Office, and before taking any new direction he wished to complete the revision of *Seven Pillars*. Having lost the previous draft, he decided to make copies of the new version. He learned that for little more than the cost of having it typed, the *Oxford Times* printers could typeset the whole text in double-column and run off a small number of copies on a proofing press. He was attracted by this unusual idea, and during the spring of 1921 eight sets of proof pages were printed.

Among the preliminaries to the book was the dedication, which was addressed 'To S.A.' The earliest surviving outline of its content is a note jotted down in 1919: 'A(?) I wrought for him freedom to lighten his sad eyes: but he had died waiting for me. So I threw my gift away and now not anywhere will I find rest and peace.' There can be little doubt that the initial 'A' represented Dahoum, whose real name was Ahmed.

By 1922 Lawrence had given a great deal of thought to this dedication. In conscious imitation of Shakespeare, whose sonnets were dedicated to an unidentified 'Mr. W.H.', he became evasive about the identity of 'S.A.', the dedicatee of *Seven Pillars*. It is difficult to reconcile the various statements he made on the subject, but it seems that 'S.A.' had by this time become a wider concept which embodied both his affection for Dahoum and his feeling for Syria and its peoples.

Churchill finally allowed Lawrence to leave the payroll of the Colonial Office on July 1, while retaining him for a time as an honorary adviser. Afterwards Lawrence wrote: 'I liked Winston so much, and have such respect for him that I was determined to leave only with his good-will:—and he took a long time to persuade!' On July 4 he sent in his formal resignation, to which Churchill replied a few days later. Both letters were published in the *Morning Post*.

As soon as he had secured his independence, Lawrence contacted Trenchard, and by July 21 both Churchill and the Secretary of State for Air had agreed to the enlistment. Three weeks later Lawrence arranged to present himself at the recruiting office on August 22. This date was later put back, at his own request, until the end of the month.

In his last weeks of freedom, Lawrence commissioned further portraits for *Seven Pillars*. The subjects were to be his British colleagues in the Revolt. He told Clayton: 'Kennington went east for me, and did about twenty Arabs: and I want about a dozen Englishmen to balance them.

'English people all look alike, in dress anyway: so to make an extra variety I'm out to have the dozen drawn by different artists. They include Newcombe, Alan Dawnay, Hogarth, Boyle (R.N.) . . . Bartholomew, and that sort of man.' These five sitters were to be portrayed by William Roberts, William Rothenstein, Augustus John, Eric Kennington and Colin Gill. Clayton's portrait was to be by William Nicholson, and Lawrence commissioned others from John Singer Sargent, Henry Lamb, Frank Dobson and Gilbert Spencer.

In the process of gathering illustrations for *Seven Pillars*, Lawrence was gradually becoming one of the most significant private patrons of contemporary artists in Britain. Moreover, this generosity was not exclusively related to his book: he did his best to place their work in national collections. For example, he purchased a bust of Osbert Sitwell by Frank Dobson for the Tate, and presented a portrait of Doughty by Augustus John, which he had himself commissioned, to the National Portrait Gallery.

In late August the binders delivered the first three copies of *Seven Pillars*. Lawrence sent one of them privately to Edward Garnett, a very experienced editor and judge of contemporary writing. Garnett was working as a consultant to Jonathan Cape's new publishing house. When Garnett praised the book, Lawrence replied very frankly about his literary ambitions: 'Confession is in the air. Do you remember my telling you once that I collected a shelf of "titanic" books (those distinguished by greatness of spirit, "sublimity" as Longinus would call it): and that they were *The Karamazovs*, *Zarathustra*, and *Moby Dick*. Well, my ambition was to make an English fourth. You will observe that modesty comes out more in the performance than in the aim! . . . . I had hopes all the while that it was going to be a big thing, and wrote myself nearly blind in the effort. Then it was finished (pro tem) and I sent it to the printer, and when it came back in a fresh shape I saw that it was no good'.

Another critic Lawrence hoped would read *Seven Pillars* was Bernard Shaw, whom he had met by chance earlier that year. When he wrote asking whether he could send it, Shaw agreed, but asked for a delay until September.

The date for Lawrence's enlistment was now approaching, and he received detailed instructions from Air Vice-Marshal Sir Oliver Swann, the RAF officer responsible for personnel. He was to go to the Air Force recruiting office in Covent Garden at about 10.30 a.m. on August 30: 'You will say that you wish to see Mr. Dexter from whom you have had a letter. Flight Lieut. Dexter will interview you and will fill up the necessary forms—you should tell him the particulars we have arranged upon (not the whole truth, nor your real name). He will advise you as to the age to give and what trade to enter in—(Dexter knows you are being specially entered and will help, but does not know all the facts, which do not concern him).

'You will then be medically examined at Henrietta Street. Do not mention any disability. If you are failed, Fl. L. Dexter will arrange matters.

'You will have to produce two references as to character and previous employment during the last two years. They will not be investigated but it is necessary for you to have them in order that someone may not say that your papers are not correct.

'You will be sent to Uxbridge with a draft of recruits. At Uxbridge you will be attested and medically inspected. You will have to declare that what you have stated on the attestation form is correct and you will have to swear allegiance to the Crown. You will have a slight educational exam if you are entering as an aircraft hand.

'I think there will be no difficulty after leaving Henrietta Street. No one will know about you . . . but if any difficulty arises, as a last resort, ask that Mr. Dexter of Recruiting Depot be communicated with by telephone.'

Lawrence's enlisted name was to be Ross, a pseudonym he had used with strangers as early as 1920 in order to escape from the reputation created by Lowell Thomas.

*   *   *

Lawrence had already been in poor health when he approached Trenchard about the enlistment in January. By the end of August, after the further stress of completing *Seven Pillars*, he was not far from a nervous break-down. He later wrote: 'I nearly went off my head in London this spring, heaving at that beastly book of mine.' In this precarious state of mind, he had lived for several months without adequate food or sleep. As a result he was in no condition to pass the RAF medical examination, still less to face the rigours of the recruits' training course.

Part III

Writer and Serviceman

1922–1935

CHAPTER 20

Aircraftman Ross
September 1922–January 1923

ON 4 September 1922 the *Daily Mail* reported that: 'Colonel T. E. Lawrence, the British officer who organised and led an Arabian army against the Turks during the war, has . . . left London for a destination abroad.' In reality, he had presented himself on August 30 at the RAF recruiting office in Henrietta Street, Covent Garden.

He had hoped to pass into the RAF without using the special arrangements that had been set up in advance, but he failed the medical examination. Following Swann's intervention, he was eventually accepted and, as 352087 A/c Ross, was posted to the RAF training depot at Uxbridge for three months' basic training.

He immediately began to make notes for his projected book about the Air Force. The first section was to be a description of the training course, but the experience he recorded during these weeks came as a shock. Uxbridge recruits were subjected to rigorously disciplined physical training and spent much of their time on 'fatigues'. Many of their tasks were distasteful, and some had little point except to keep the men occupied. Whether they were usefully employed or not, their duty was unhesitating and unprotesting obedience.

Both physically and by temperament, Lawrence was unsuited to the Uxbridge regime. Training that was designed to toughen younger and fitter men drove him almost to breaking point, and he often felt the temptation to escape. He had to meet harsh discipline with stronger self-discipline, but he refused to give up: 'My determined endeavour is to scrape through with it, into the well-paid peace of my trade as a photographer to some squadron.'

The distractions of RAF training did not make him forget about *Seven Pillars*, and he waited with excitement as the first group of readers passed judgment on the text. To his surprise, one reaction was a series of comic sketches: 'Kennington was moved to incongruous mirth, reading my book, and a dozen Bateman-quality drawings came of it. To my mind they are as rare, surprising and refreshing as plums in cake . . . and lighten up the whole. It's good that someone is decent enough to find laughter in a stodgy mess of mock-heroic egotism . . . It's Kennington pricking the vast bladder of my conceit.'

Edward Garnett's letters continued to be full of praise. Some years previously he had abridged Doughty's *Travels in Arabia Deserta* to about half its length for a popular edition, and he now offered to shorten *Seven Pillars* in the same way. While Lawrence was still dissatisfied with the book as a whole, a well edited abridgement would provide him with a private income. He cautiously agreed: 'It's very good of you to be willing to try and cut it down. I think that I may have to publish something after all: for I'm getting too old for this life of rough and tumble, and the crudeness of my company worries me a bit. I find myself longing for an empty room, or a solitary bed'. He sent a set of unbound sheets of the 'Oxford' Seven Pillars as a working copy.

The first draft was ready in only five weeks, and Lawrence visited Garnett in London to collect the marked-up sheets. A fortnight later he wrote: 'With all the drawings (over fifty now) I feel less and less inclined to publish the whole work, and almost decided not to publish anything. My mind wobbles between the need for money and the desire to be withdrawn, and it's a pitiable exhibition on my part. I wish the beastly book had never been written.'

After only ten weeks on the recruits' course, Lawrence was posted to the RAF School of Photography at Farnborough. Before leaving Uxbridge he had begun to see the basic training in a new light. It had produced a corporate spirit among the men which he had not anticipated, and by the time he was posted to Farnborough he was 'getting keen on the R.A.F. Was writing freely about Uxbridge when they snatched me away from it.'

He soon realised that the Uxbridge notes would form a harsh opening to his study of the RAF. The book had been one of his main justifications for enlisting, but he now felt uncertain about its future. For the time being he lost interest in it and gave up writing notes. Instead he was becoming reconciled to the idea of publishing the *Seven Pillars* abridgement, 'and I shall very much despise myself if I do. Only to face thirty-five years of poverty hurts even more than to smash my self-respect. Honestly I hate this dirty living: and yet by the decency of the other fellows, the full dirtiness of it has not met me fairly.' The thought of asking to leave injured his pride: 'Isn't it a sign of feebleness in me, to cry out so against barrack-life? It means that I'm afraid (physically afraid) of other men:

their animal spirits seem to me the most terrible companions to haunt a man: and I hate their noise. Noise seems to me horrible. And yet I'm a man, not different from them; certainly not better. What is it that makes me so damnably sensitive and so ready to cry out, and yet so ready to incur more pain?'

The thought of publishing an abridgement of *Seven Pillars* made him increasingly careless of his future in the ranks. In November he wrote with great self-assurance to Swann, complaining about his training. He had arrived at Farnborough one day too late for the beginning of a photography course; instead of allowing him to join it, the Commanding Officer had ordered him to wait until the next course two months later. Lawrence wrote a second letter of protest on November 19, telling Swann plainly that unless he could join the class already in progress he would like to be posted somewhere else. Swann (mindful that Lawrence's presence in the ranks had Trenchard's blessing) dutifully requested the Farnborough CO to see that A/c Ross proceeded at once with photographic training.

This initiative was one of the actions which helped to give away Lawrence's identity. The CO at Farnborough, Wing-Commander W. J. Y. Guilfoyle, was surprised that Swann should be so interested in the affairs of A/c Ross. When he looked at Ross more closely, he thought that he saw an uncanny resemblance to the famous Colonel Lawrence. Not long afterwards this suspicion was confirmed when Ross was identified as Lawrence by a visiting officer who had served in Cairo during the war. Guilfoyle and his adjutant Charles Findlay agreed to keep their discovery to themselves, hoping that Lawrence's course of training at the School of Photography would pass off without incident.

By this time, however, Lawrence seemed to be inviting exposure. He told relative strangers that he was serving in the ranks. Some people, including Edward Garnett, knew his pseudonym and address. Incredibly, he had written a tantalising letter about his secret enlistment to his acquaintance R. D. Blumenfeld, editor of the *Daily Express*: 'This letter has got to be indiscreet—shockingly so . . . please keep it as a personal one, from me to you . . . I found I was quite on the rocks: and so I enlisted, as a quick and easy way of keeping alive . . . Do keep this news to yourself. No one in camp knows who I am, and I don't want them to'. Revelations of this kind made it almost certain that gossip about his enlistment would reach the wrong ears.

In order to be able to visit London from Farnborough, Lawrence had bought a motorcycle and sidecar, 'an old crock of a Triumph'. He would often give other airmen rides into town and back. This mobility was to become increasingly important to him.

A second letter to Blumenfeld, who had offered him some work, was even more indiscreet: 'No, please don't publish my eclipse. It will be common news one day, but the later the better for my peace in the ranks . . . As you say, it reads like cheap melodrama, and my life so far has been that, nearly, since the odd circumstances of my birth. Some day I'll tell you stories about myself—if you will hear them.

'Meanwhile I'm excogitating a new book—in no way personal—on the spirit of the Air Force; a most remarkable body: and am hoping to take advantage of my obscurity to produce an abridgement of my old war-book on Arabia.'

Lawrence's over-confident behaviour in the ranks began to invite a confrontation with the authorities. He thought the calibre of the officers at Farnborough too low for them to have moral authority over the very able men under their command, and did not trouble to conceal his contempt. Findlay recalled an occasion when 'I had to reprimand him for the part he played in a silly and pointless incident. The Orderly Officer, a young lad, was carrying out the usual inspection of dress and arms before mounting the guard, in the course of which he told an airman that he was not satisfied with his turn-out. The airman [it was Lawrence] replied to the officer in a foreign language, which elicited the inevitable titter from the other members of the guard. This was certainly not in keeping with his expressed desire to remain unnoticed.'

Lawrence could risk the consequences of such insolence because he had now decided to publish the *Seven Pillars* abridgement, which was to be called *War in the Desert*. He told Bernard Shaw on November 30 not to trouble himself unduly about reading the complete *Seven Pillars*, and two days later he wrote to Garnett again, about the abridgement: 'Mention the book to Cape, by all means: but tell him that it will be a costly production, and that I am making Curtis Brown my agent in disposing of it. Of course I'd be very glad if he got it: but it seems to me a speculation unjustifiably large for his resources.'

In due course Lawrence heard from Shaw: 'Patience, patience . . . The truth is, I havnt read it yet. I have sampled it . . . My wife seized it first, and ploughed through from alpha to omega. It took months and months and months; but it carried her through. But the time it took warned me that I must dispose of certain other reading jobs, in respect of which I was tied to time, before tackling it . . . However, I know enough about it now to feel rather puzzled as to what is to be done with it . . . Obviously there are things in it that you cannot publish. Yet many of them are things that WONT die . . . One step is clear enough. The Trustees of the British Museum have lots of sealed writings to be opened in a hundred years . . . You say you have four or five copies of your magnissimum opus. At least a couple should be sealed and deposited in Bloomsbury and in New York . . . But an abridgment will have to be made for general circulation. There is a need for the main history of the campaign for working purposes.' This advice must have seemed a valuable endorsement of the Garnett project, and if Lawrence still entertained any doubts, he set them aside. He wrote telling Shaw about the abridgement, and also about his RAF enlistment.

Eventually, Fleet Street papers began to investigate the rumours that Lawrence was serving in the ranks; it did not take them long to trace him to Farnborough. On December 16 Guilfoyle reported to Swann that reporters from the *Daily Mail* and *Daily Express* had visited the camp. It would be a matter of time before the story became front-page news, and Guilfoyle could only wait for the storm to break.

Hearing of the proposed *Seven Pillars* abridgement, Bernard Shaw began to take initiatives of his own. On December 17 he wrote telling Lawrence of approaches he had made to his own publishers, Constable, with a view to interesting them in *Seven Pillars*. The letter did not reach Lawrence until Christmas Day, and his arrangements for publication were meanwhile advancing with Cape. On December 21 Lawrence wrote to Buxton: 'I've decided to sell an abridgement (rather less than one third) of my Arabian narrative, and this will bring in some thousands (perhaps £6,000) next year. After that I'm quite likely to chuck the R.A.F. but meanwhile I hang on to it with no more expenses than artists and a motor-bike'. He was now very sure of himself. On Christmas Day he wrote to Herbert Baker that he was 'at Farnborough, suffering many things just lately, and provoking my persecutors by laughing at them. It isn't quite so provoking as being meek—but I can't do the meek touch.'

Two days later, however, the story of his enlistment finally broke. A front-page headline in Blumenfeld's paper, the *Daily Express,* read ' "UNCROWNED KING" AS PRIVATE SOLDIER: LAWRENCE OF ARABIA: FAMOUS WAR HERO BECOMES A PRIVATE: SEEKING PEACE: OPPORTUNITY TO WRITE A BOOK.' Yet, despite the sensational opening, the article gave no precise information about his whereabouts, stating wrongly that he was serving in the Army.

A follow-up story the next day was far more damaging. It revealed that

Lawrence was serving in the RAF at Farnborough as A/c Ross, and gave colourful details of his life there, based entirely on speculation. It is conceivable that R. D. Blumenfeld provided the tip-off for this exposure. Later, in a rather confused account, he claimed that while he was away 'someone in the office learned the story which could not of course be a secret long'.

On December 27, the day of the first *Daily Express* story, Lawrence replied to Bernard Shaw's letter about *Seven Pillars*, making it clear that Cape was first in the running for the abridgement. Before receiving this letter, Shaw had learned from an article in the *Daily News* that negotiations with Cape for *Seven Pillars* were well advanced. He seems to have been extremely put out that his *démarche* on behalf of Constable had been frustrated. He wrote again to Lawrence, enclosing the article from the *Daily News*: 'The cat being now let out of the bag, presumably by Jonathan Cape with your approval, I cannot wait to finish the book before giving you my opinion and giving it strong. IT MUST BE PUBLISHED IN ITS ENTIRETY UNABRIDGED. Later on an abridgment can be considered . . . But anyhow you must not for a moment entertain the notion of publishing an abridgment first, as no publisher would touch the whole work afterwards; and I repeat THE WHOLE WORK MUST BE PUBLISHED. If Cape is not prepared to undertake that, he is not your man, whatever your engagements to him may be.'

Shaw offered no excuse for this volte-face. Just four weeks earlier he had told Lawrence that an abridgement should be published, with copies of the whole text placed under embargo in selected libraries. Now, his argument was that abridgement would prevent any future publication of the whole text. It is not difficult to discern, behind his repeated criticisms of Cape, a desire to deny them success and to secure *Seven Pillars* for his own publishers.

Whatever Shaw's motivation, the effect on Lawrence of such a harangue must have been devastating. Shaw was one of the most influential literary figures of the age. Garnett, hitherto Lawrence's trusted adviser, earned his living by working for a publisher, whereas Shaw was the outspoken champion of authors' rights. Lawrence had always felt some misgivings about the abridgement. Now, he began to fear that he was being manoeuvred by Cape and Garnett into a commercial trap; worse still, that he had to choose between giving permanence to the abridgement or to the full text of *Seven Pillars*. During the last weekend in the year he discussed the position with his agent, Raymond Savage, and then on January 1 he wrote to Cape withdrawing from the project.

If Lawrence had received Shaw's letter a few days later, the contract for the abridgement would already have been signed. He would then have had the money he needed to leave the Air Force and pursue his other plans. The decision not to publish left him without an income and meant that he would have to remain in the ranks or seek some other kind of paid work. Without realising it, and for motives which were at best trivial, Shaw had checked Lawrence at the very moment of decision. By doing so he changed the course of Lawrence's life.

Shaw, however, had little thought for the harm he might be doing. On December 31 his wife Charlotte had written to Lawrence, for the first time, in what was clearly an attempt to support her husband's point of view: 'How is it *conceivable, imaginable* that a man who could write the *Seven Pillars* can have any doubts about it? If you don't know it is "a great book" what is the use of anyone telling you so . . .

'Your book must be published as a whole. Don't you see that? . . . Publish the book practically as it is, in good print, in a lot of volumes. I am sure Constables will do it for you that way. Both G.B.S. and I have lots of experience about books and we would both *like* to put it at your service.'

Not content to let the matter rest, Shaw wrote again on January 4: 'As to the book, bear two things in mind about me. First, I am an old and hardened professional; and you are still apparently a palpitating amateur in literature, wondering whether your first MS is good enough to be published, and whether you have a style or not. Second, I am entitled to a reasonable construction; and when I say, as I do, that the work must be published unabridged, I do not mean that it shall be published with the passages which would force certain people either to take an action against you or throw up their jobs. The publisher would take jolly good care of that if you were careless about it . . . You must get used to the limelight . . . And the people have their rights too, in this matter. They want you to appear always in glory, crying "This is I, Lawrence, Prince of Mecca!" To live under a cloud is to defame God.

'Moral: do your duty by the book; and arrange for its publication at once. It will not bounce out in five minutes, you know. You have the whole publishing world at your feet, as keen as Constables, who have perhaps more capital than Cape. Subject to that limitation you can choose where you will.'

Cape, unaware of Shaw's activities, protested strongly to Lawrence over the sudden and unexplained cancellation of the abridgement. But by this time Lawrence had other reasons to do nothing. Trenchard visited

Farnborough on January 3 and warned him that his position in the Air Force was becoming untenable. Four days later Lawrence wrote to Cape that he could not publish anything while he remained in the RAF: 'That rules out this year, at any rate.'

His mind was in a state of confusion. He had often said that the purpose of the abridgement was to escape from the Air Force, but now something had changed. For the first time, he had discovered what it was like to be the object of sensational press exposure. Hitherto, journalists had eaten out of his hand, and this had led him to the dangerous illusion that he could influence them as he pleased. None of the publicity he had received after the war had prepared him for the shock of his present situation.

When his identity was revealed the officers felt awkward and embarrassed, but most of the men stood by him and shielded him from the press with friendly solidarity. Lawrence wrote: 'It would be hard to remain inhuman while jostling all days and nights in a crowd of clean and simple men. There is something here which in my life before I'd never met—had hardly dreamed of.' The RAF now suddenly appeared to be a haven, and he clung to it desperately.

Though he did not realise it, some aspects of his position began to resemble the life he had enjoyed so much at Carchemish. Two particular friendships were with A. E. Chambers and R. A. M. Guy. 'Jock' Chambers had an intelligent and enquiring mind which nowadays would have won him a place at university. Lawrence recognised his ability and encouraged him to educate himself through reading. Guy was less intellectual, though he too liked reading. Lawrence enjoyed his company, and once wrote of him: 'the little man embodies the best of the Air Force ranks as I picture them.'

It has been suggested, by writers who have seen only a small part of the surviving correspondence between Lawrence and Guy, that the basis of this friendship was homosexual. This claim raises two issues: first about the nature of Lawrence's relationship with Guy, and secondly the more general question of Lawrence's sexual inclination during these years in the ranks. As regards Guy, the suggestion of homosexual attraction rests on three pieces of 'evidence': Guy's good looks, the nicknames by which Lawrence addressed him, and a passage from one of Lawrence's letters.

The first question, of Guy's appearance, was discussed in the biography by John Mack: *A Prince of Our Disorder*. He quoted Jock Chambers as saying that Guy was 'beautiful, like a Greek God'. A few weeks before Mack's interview, Chambers made a very similar statement to me: that Lawrence had once joked to him of Guy's looks, saying 'they were almost angelic, but the effect was shattered by his vile Birmingham accent'. Taken on its own, this observation is hardly evidence for homosexual passion.

Guy, who was short and fair-haired, was called 'Rabbit' or 'Poppet' in the ranks, where nicknames based on physical appearance are very common. The choice was often cruel: on occasions Lawrence himself had to tolerate being addressed as 'Shortarse'. Several biographers have implied that 'Rabbit' and 'Poppet' were used exclusively by Lawrence, apparently without realising that these were ordinary service nicknames.

The final piece of 'evidence' is a letter to Guy in which, according to one biographer, Lawrence 'wrote ecstatically about their closeness'. It is misleading, however, to cite this letter without explaining the context. The letter was written about a year after Lawrence had left Farnborough. He had met Guy briefly some weeks previously, and in parting must have said something which Guy took to imply that they would not meet again. It is quite possible that this was in fact what Lawrence had meant to say, because his subsequent correspondence with Guy shows that he made little effort to stay in touch.

Guy valued his friendship with such a famous personality, but that was not his sole motive for wishing to remain in contact with Lawrence. In every camp there were servicemen who preyed on Lawrence's generosity, and Guy's appetite for cash is a constant theme in their correspondence. He was planning to marry a girl in Birmingham, and Lawrence had already given a modest sum of money to help the young couple. After Lawrence's rather definite farewell, Guy had evidently written a letter of protest. When Lawrence replied (as it happened this was at Christmas), he clearly meant to reassure Guy while confirming the distance between them. Hence the frequently quoted remark: 'When I said "This is the last" I meant that again for an overwhelming time we were going to be apart. Letters don't work, nor do casual meetings, for the shadow of the near end lies over them, so that the gaiety is forced and the talk foolish. You and me, we're very un-matched, and it took some process as slow and kindly and persistent as the barrack-room communism to weld us comfortably together. People aren't friends till they have said all they can say, and are able to sit together, at work or rest, hour-long without speaking.

'We never got quite to that, but were nearer it daily . . . and since S.A. died I haven't experienced any risk of that happening'. Thus, when taken in context, the meaning of Lawrence's remark is exactly the opposite the interpretation suggested by some biographers.

Thus none of the evidence cited as proof of a homosexual affair between Lawrence and Guy stands up to examination. While Guy seems to have been very ready to ask for money, he was only one of the many people Lawrence helped financially.

There has been a good deal of speculation about the more general question of Lawrence's sexual orientation during these service years. Close friendships between people of the same sex are common in all walks of life and inevitable in all-male communities such as the armed services. It is patently absurd to suggest that all such friendships must be homosexual, yet this is the essence of many allegations about Lawrence. There is a popular belief that the service environment is attractive to homosexuals but, as a matter of fact, the lack of privacy would make it far more difficult to conduct a homosexual affair in the ranks than in civilian life. Lawrence dealt with this misconception in *The Mint*: 'Report accuses us of sodomy, too: and anyone listening in to a hut of airmen would think it a den of infamy. Yet we are too intimate, and too bodily soiled, to attract one another. In camps all things, even if not public, are publicly known: and in the four large camps of my sojourning there have been five fellows actively beastly. Doubtless their natures tempted others: but they fight its expression as the normal airman fights his desire for women, out of care for physical fitness.'

Throughout his life Lawrence was deeply influenced by the ethical standards he had learned in childhood, and he set a great value on integrity in his dealings with other people, especially those who would naturally have looked up to him. He would probably have been shocked and bitterly ashamed if he had suspected that there was any sexual motive behind his friendships in the ranks. In later years, when he came to believe that carnality played an important role in all human motivation, he seems to have avoided close friendships with anyone.

In 1927, Lawrence would describe himself in a letter to a friend as 'really celibate'; he went on to say: 'Celibacy is unnatural, in the real sense, and it overturns a man's balance: for it throws him either on himself (which is unwholesome, like sucking your own tail, in snakes) or on friendship to satisfy the urge of affection within . . . and such friendship may easily turn into sex-perversion. If I have missed all these things, as I hope and you seem to suggest—well then, I'm barrenly lucky. It has not been easy: and it leads, in old age, to misery'.

All the evidence suggests that during these post-war years Lawrence felt a deep revulsion towards the physical aspects of sex; yet despite the strength of this personal view, he refrained from criticising other people's conduct provided that it did not affect himself. Tolerance, however, does not imply personal approval or involvement. On this issue, as on the question of imperialism, Lawrence's attitude was ahead of his time.

During January 1923 the publicity about his presence in the RAF continued. His future in the ranks seemed extremely uncertain and he again toyed with the idea of making money from *Seven Pillars*. Heeding Shaw's advice, he 'began to think of publishing, not an abridgment, but the whole story . . . So I sketched to Cape the possibility of a limited, privately-printed, subscription edition of two thousand copies, illustrated with all the drawings made for me by some twenty of the younger artists.'

Cape responded quickly, sending a new contract to sign; but before Lawrence had done so, the RAF decided that A/c Ross placed junior officers at Farnborough in an impossible situation. Lawrence was sent briefly on leave, and by the end of January he was a civilian once more.

From this time on he would be regarded by the world's press as an enigmatic figure, whose motives and influence were open to endless speculation; but his behaviour does not bear out this claim. Before 1922 he had sought press attention on behalf of the Arab cause, but the campaign had long since served its purpose and the resulting publicity seemed to have died. Following the discovery of his enlistment, however, popular interest refocused inescapably on his own life. He clung to a naïve conviction that the Fleet Street editors he had befriended in the past would help him, and from time to time he would plead with them to be left alone; but the effect was never lasting. The threat of unwelcome publicity soon imposed very real restrictions on his personal freedom, yet his attempts to escape from it almost invariably made matters worse.

CHAPTER 21

Private Shaw, Publisher

January 1923–December 1924

ALTHOUGH Lawrence had half-expected the RAF decision, it still came as a shock. He appealed for reinstatement, first to Trenchard and then to Sir Samuel Hoare, the Secretary of State for Air; but Hoare was adamant, and hoped that Lawrence would find a job more suited to his talents.

Lawrence went into hiding at a small hotel in Frensham, Surrey, and from there sent another appeal to Trenchard: 'I've been looking round, these last few days, and find an odd blank:—there is nothing I can think of, that I want to do, and in consequence, nothing that I will do! And the further I get from the R.A.F. the more I regret its loss.' Trenchard's reply was negative. He had already offered Lawrence a commission in the Air Force, and now he suggested work as an Armoured Car officer. However, Lawrence was determined to return to the ranks.

At about the same time Lawrence wrote telling Garnett that he had abandoned his publishing plans: 'Of course everything in connection with Cape and the *Seven Pillars* is over. I now feel that I was an ass ever to have dreamed of publishing anything.' Yet the book had become his main interest in life and, although he had very little money, he now wrote to several artists and sitters to commission new portraits.

On 17 February 1923 Sir Philip Chetwode wrote from the War Office to say that it would be possible for Lawrence to enlist in the Tank Corps as a private soldier. The Tank Corps did not seem a bad substitute for the RAF. Moreover, Lawrence knew that men had sometimes been allowed to transfer from the Tank Corps to the Air Force. Chetwode wrote that Colonel Sir Hugh Elles, who commanded the Tank Corps Training Centre at Bovington in Dorset, would be in London the following week and had suggested that he and Lawrence should meet. Chetwode concluded: 'If you come to a satisfactory arrangement, would you call here at the War Office to see General Vesey the Director of Organisation, as there are certain matters which he would have to arrange with you before the affair is carried through.'

One of these matters was the question of a new pseudonym. The previous one, John Hume Ross, had been chosen before Lawrence first enlisted, but when he went to make the administrative arrangements for re-enlistment 'the recruiting Staff Officer in the War Office said I must take a fresh name. I said, ''What's yours?'' He said ''No you don't''. So I seized the *Army List*, and snapped it open at the Index, and said ''It'll be the first one-syllabled name in this'' '. He was to become 7875698 Private T. E. Shaw.

Before returning to the ranks, he took the surviving manuscript of *Seven Pillars* to Oxford and presented it to the Bodleian Library. He had known the librarian, Dr Cowley, since before the war. Afterwards he wrote: 'In giving my MS to the Bodleian I acted perhaps unhumorously, taking myself a little too seriously as a classic. Cowley was equal to the occasion, and never smiled at all throughout the transaction. Whether he has a treasure or not the next century can tell.'

On March 12 Lawrence arrived at Bovington Camp, where all Tank Corps recruits had to go through their eighteen weeks' basic training. As an Air Force recruit he had been subjected to a good deal of anti-Army propaganda, so even before he reached Bovington he was expecting to dislike what he found.

After a week he wrote to Lionel Curtis, a friend at All Souls: 'My mind moves me this morning to write you a whole series of letters, to be more splendid than the *Lettres de Mon Moulin* . . . What should the preliminaries be? A telling why I joined? As you know I don't know! Explaining it to Dawnay I said ''Mind-suicide''.'

The letter (which was followed over several months by four others in the same vein) reveals only too clearly Lawrence's state of confusion: 'perhaps there's a solution to be found in multiple personality. It's my reason which condemns the book and the revolt, and the new nationalities: because the only rational conclusion to human argument is pessimism such as Hardy's, a pessimism which is very much like the wintry heath, of bog and withered plants and stripped trees, about us . . . What I would say is that reason proves there is no hope'. He was now re-reading Thomas Hardy's novels, and the mood of this letter probably owed something to their influence. Hardy lived only a few miles from Bovington, and Lawrence was eager to meet him. On March 20 Lawrence wrote asking Robert Graves for an introduction.

A week later, in another letter to Curtis, Lawrence reflected upon the differences he saw between the enlisted men at Bovington and those he had known in the RAF: 'There we were excited about our coming service.

We talked and wondered of the future, almost exclusively . . . The fellows were decent, but so wrought up by hope that they were carried out of themselves . . . There was a sparkle round the squad.

'Here every man has joined because he was down and out: and no one talks of the Army or of promotion, or of trades and accomplishments. We are all here unavoidably, in a last resort . . . and each of us values the rest as cheap as he knows himself to be.'

He went on to sketch out the conclusions he had now drawn about the shallowness of civilisation: 'Can there be profit, or truth, in all these modes and sciences and arts of ours? The leisured world for hundreds, or perhaps thousands of years has been jealously working and recording the advance of each generation for the starting-point of the next—and here these masses are as animal, as carnal as were their ancestors before Plato and Christ and Shelley and Dostoevsky taught and thought. In this crowd it's made startlingly clear how short is the range of knowledge, and what poor conductors of it ordinary humans are.'

Lawrence applied this argument to himself, with profound bitterness, seeing intellectual activity as a deceptive superstructure which served to conceal a 'black core . . . of animality.' He reached a conclusion that had never previously appeared in his writing: 'It isn't the filth of it which hurts me, because you can't call filthy the pursuit of a bitch by a dog, or the mating of birds in springtime . . . but I lie in bed night after night with this cat-calling carnality seething up and down the hut, fed by streams of fresh matter from twenty lecherous mouths . . . and my mind aches with the rawness of it . . . We are all guilty alike, you know. You wouldn't exist, I wouldn't exist, without this carnality. Everything with flesh in its mixture is the achievement of a moment when the lusty thought of Hut 12 has passed to action and conceived . . . A filthy business all of it, and yet Hut 12 shows me the truth behind Freud. Sex is an integer in all of us, and the nearer nature we are, the more constantly, the more completely a product of that integer. These fellows are the reality, and you and I, the selves who used to meet in London and talk of fleshless things, are only the outward wrappings of a core like these fellows.'

The romantic Victorian concepts that he had so willingly adopted in his youth were falling away one by one. His evangelical Christianity had faded before the war; at Uxbridge he had written: 'Hungry time has taken from me year by year more of the Creed's clauses, till now only the first four words remain.' The vision of the 'noble savage', a guiding principle during his Carchemish years, had crumbled during the Arab Revolt: 'I was tired to death of these Arabs; petty incarnate Semites who attained heights and depths beyond our reach, though not beyond our sight'. He had abandoned his belief in the progress of mankind, one of the fundamental tenets of his Victorian upbringing, and now he had concluded that romantic love, a concept he had been brought up to revere, was nothing more than animal lust. Like many others of his generation he had accepted these values uncritically. The disintegration of his beliefs had taken him to the brink of nihilism.

As soon as the new recruits were allowed out of camp, Lawrence brought his motorcycle to Bovington, finding a release from his grim thoughts by riding through the Dorset countryside. Alec Dixon, a corporal at the camp, later wrote: 'One Wednesday afternoon Shaw appeared in the lines with a powerful Brough motor-cycle of the latest design, the cost of which represented, to a private soldier, about two years' pay . . . Now where, the N.C.Os. asked one another, did that bloke Shaw get hold of that bike?

'Three days later the Brough again appeared in the lines, but this time with a side-car, a rakish affair of polished aluminium. The N.C.Os. goggled, and did some more mental arithmetic. The recruits, dazzled and impressed by these toys, were much too excited to count their cost. They stood in an admiring circle round the Brough and watched enviously while its owner wriggled himself into a flying suit of sleek black leather. There was a shy murmuring among the spectators; someone whispered "joyrides". Shaw, now gloved and helmeted, turned to them with a grin. "Joyrides?" he said thoughtfully. "Of course! Who's going to be the first?"

'So, one by one, the recruits were taken out in the sidecar. . . Seventy miles an hour was nothing to Shaw . . . and *couldn't* that little bloke ride a motor-bike! . . . Within a week he was known throughout the camp as "Broughie" Shaw, a nickname that clung to him for the remainder of his stay at Bovington.'

As he could now make visits outside camp, he wrote on Robert Graves's recommendation to Mrs Thomas Hardy, saying: 'It feels rather barefaced, because I haven't any qualifications to justify my seeing Mr. Hardy: only I'd very much like to. *The Dynasts* and the other poems are so wholly good to my taste.

'It adds to my hesitation that I'm a private in the Tank Corps, at Wool, and would have to come across in uniform.' Mrs Hardy replied favourably, and on March 29 Lawrence went to tea at Max Gate. It was the first of many visits.

There were other matters to distract Lawrence from camp life. The five *Oxford Times* copies of *Seven Pillars* were still circulating, and successive readers told him that it was remarkable. Reassured of his skill as a writer, he wrote to Jonathan Cape asking for literary translation work from French into English.

Garnett must have heard of this request, for he tried to bring Lawrence back to *Seven Pillars*. Lawrence replied: 'Revise the book? Do you know, I've now reached the happy point of being really sorry that ever I wrote it! Apologies: I must be exasperating to work with: but what can I do about it? Any idea of working over it again must wait . . . this atmosphere is hostile to everything.'

It was inevitable that Lawrence would be noticed in the camp. Alec Dixon recorded that: 'My idle speculation about Private Shaw quickened to curiosity when I found that he exerted—or appeared to exert—a remarkable influence over his fellow recruits. It was significant that the recruits eschewed swearing and smutty backchat whenever Shaw paid them a visit . . . it was clear to me that his quiet manner and noncommital grin had captured the imagination of the men with whom he lived.' From his experience at Farnborough, Lawrence knew that revelation of his identity would do him no harm in the ranks, and after a few weeks at Bovington he let the secret out.

He found that the Tank Corps left him with a large part of the day to himself. This took him towards a new stance: that service life, while uninteresting, was also undemanding, providing him with food and lodging yet leaving him free to give his mind to other things. On May 12 he spelt out the philosophy which was to sustain him for some years: 'I'm fit, and the sort of job I do doesn't worry me, since the only adventures and interests I have are in my head, and the army leaves you all your thinking-time to yourself . . . I quite agree that you can't get satisfaction for life out of working for a living . . . In my case I try to write, and read half my spare time, and get interest in looking at the others doing things, and wondering why they do them. . . it's what they call the reflective mind . . . I've . . . found that the way out lay in the freedom of my mind. Give the world the use of your body and keep the rest for yourself.'

Despite this intellectual self-justification Lawrence suffered from fits of deep depression. He told Lionel Curtis: 'I consume the day (and myself) brooding, and making phrases and reading and thinking again, galloping mentally down twenty divergent roads at once, as apart and alone as in Barton Street in my attic . . . When my mood gets too hot and I find myself wandering beyond control I pull out my motor-bike and hurl it top-speed through these unfit roads for hour after hour. My nerves are jaded and gone near dead, so that nothing less than hours of voluntary danger will prick them into life: and the "life" they reach then is a melancholy joy at risking something worth exactly 2/9 a day.'

At the end of May, Jonathan Cape took up Lawrence's request for translation work, sending an awesome proposal: an English rendering of J. C. Mardrus's four-thousand-page *Mille et une Nuits* (*The Arabian Nights*). Lawrence, who felt very critical of the existing English translations, was enthusiastic, describing it as 'a great chance'. In the meantime Cape asked him to translate *Le Gigantesque*, a novel by Adrien le Corbeau describing the life cycle of a giant sequoia tree. Lawrence agreed, but once he started work on it, he found that literary translation was more demanding than he had anticipated. After a month he wrote to Cape: 'I started gaily: did about twenty pages into direct swinging English then turned back and read it, and it was horrible. The bones of the poor thing showed through.

'So I cancelled that, and did it again more floridly. The book is written very commonplacely, by a man of good imagination and a bad mind and unobservant. Consequently it's banal in style and ordinary in thought, and very interesting in topic . . . it's infuriating to find second-class metaphysics, and slip-shod writing, on so extraordinarily good a theme. I'd like to wring Le Corbeau's neck.'

He sent Cape the first half of the manuscript on August 11: 'I still feel it very deficient, both as English and as a work of fiction. However I also feel that it's better than the French. If the man had had a grain of humour.' To follow this work, which Lawrence titled *The Forest Giant*, Cape proposed a book called *Sturly*, by Pierre Custot. The *Arabian Nights* project fell through when Cape discovered that a translation had already been made by E. Powys Mathers and was on the point of publication. Lawrence was very disappointed: 'I'm sorry about Mardrus. I'd have done you something very good there.' This was another turning-point, for work on *The Arabian Nights* would have filled his off-duty time for several years, keeping him from the final revision of *Seven Pillars*.

Lawrence was constantly being reminded of his war book, for instance when the Hardys read and praised it. On August 15 he wrote to Mrs Hardy: 'It is meant to be the true history of a political movement whose essence was a fraud—in the sense that its leaders did not believe the arguments with which they moved its rank and file: and also the true history of a campaign, to show how unlovely the back of a commander's mind must be.

'So what you said cuts right across my belief, and has puzzled me. Will you tell me what you would do—publish or leave private—if yourself or Mr. Hardy had written such a book? Apologies for bothering you: but the value of the book would give me an income which would keep me out of the army: and I'm wondering since Sunday whether perhaps I may be able to enjoy it.'

At about this time Gertrude Bell strongly urged Lawrence to issue *Seven Pillars* in some form, and he began to contemplate the project again. Shortly afterwards he wrote to Kennington: 'I've asked some friends to see if there isn't an interested millionaire who would put up £2,000 and let me produce a privately printed edition with all the portraits complete. There is a chance of this in the fairly near future.' D. G. Hogarth, Alan Dawnay, and Lionel Curtis, who all lived in Oxford, discussed the position and decided that the best plan would be a sub-scription edition of three hundred copies priced at ten guineas. Lawrence, however, did not like the idea of raising the cost through subscriptions; he wrote to Gertrude Bell that he was 'turning over in my mind the alternative—to publish Garnett's abridgement . . . and do the subscrip-tion edition with its profits.'

He asked Cape to send him the draft of *War in the Desert*: 'I'd like to read it again and see if I can screw myself up to let it appear.' Then, on August 23, he wrote to Hogarth: 'What am I to do? Publish the Garnett abridgement after all, with such restrictions as seem fit to me, and use its profits to publish a limited illustrated complete edition . . . publish noth-ing . . . or print privately?'

On September 13 Lawrence completed *The Forest Giant* and sent it to Cape, writing: 'At last this foul work: complete.' He had found it almost impossible to concentrate on translation work in the camp, and had shared an attic room rented by Alec Dixon in a private house in Moreton, a few miles away. Dixon was due to be posted away from Bovington, and Lawrence looked for somewhere else to work. He soon heard of a cottage at Clouds Hill, a mile north of Bovington Camp. It belonged to the Moreton estate and had been built in 1808 as a farm labourer's cottage. By this time, it had fallen into a very dilapidated condition, and a Tank Corps sergeant, Arthur Knowles, had leased it with some neighbouring land where he had built a bungalow for his family. A condition of the lease had been that the original cottage should be restored, and work had already begun when Lawrence first heard that the old cottage would become available. During the summer a new agreement was made under which Lawrence rented the cottage for ten shillings a month and paid for the completion of the repairs. It would provide him with 'a warm solitary place to hide in sometimes on winter evenings.'

During the autumn he ran short of money and had to lay up his motorcycle. This kept him from pleasures such as visiting the Hardys, and from the exhilaration of putting the Brough through its paces. Worse still, he was giving much of his spare time to translation, and as a result he had little time for reading, one of the few pleasures which distracted his thoughts. It was also a long time since he had been to a concert or listened to a gramophone record. In a fit of depression he wrote to Lionel Curtis: 'My thoughts are centering more and more upon the peace of death, with longing for it. Is it, do you think, that at last I am getting old? Do old people secretly dwell much upon their inevitable end?'

His one remaining pleasure was writing. He told Garnett of the 'frenzied aching delight in a pattern of words which happen to run true. Do you know that lately I have been finding my deepest satisfaction in the collocation of words so ordinary and plain that they cannot mean anything to a book-jaded mind: and out of some of such I can draw deep stuff. Is it perhaps that certain sequences of vowels and consonants imply more than others: that writing of this sort has music in it? I don't want to affirm it, and yet I would not deny it: for if writing can have sense (and it has: this letter has) and sound why shouldn't it have something of pattern too? My sequences seem to be independent of ear . . . to impose themselves through the eye alone. I achieved a good many of them in *Le Gigantesque*: but fortuitously for the most part.'

At the beginning of October Robin Buxton suggested an alternative scheme for *Seven Pillars*. A hundred and twenty copies might be printed and illustrated with all of Lawrence's pictures, for sale to subscribers for about £25 each. Lawrence asked Lionel Curtis to see Buxton and discuss the idea.

While these plans were being considered, Lawrence would have time to tackle the translation of *Sturly*, a novel about life under the sea. He wrote to Cape accepting the task on October 11, with the warning that 'It will take a while to do well, for the wretched man catalogues innumerable French fishes . . . and my French never extended into scientific ichthyology!'

By the end of October the roof of the cottage at Clouds Hill was completed. The building was extremely simple: the ground floor and first floor were each divided by the central chimney which had a single flight of stairs beside it. At each level there was a large room with a fireplace on one side of the chimney, and a smaller room on the staircase side. To begin with Lawrence used only the upstairs rooms, storing lumber and firewood below. He sold the gold Arabian dagger he had carried during the Revolt to Lionel Curtis and used the money to pay for improvements at Clouds Hill. There were even plans for a bathroom, but this scheme was postponed. A more immediate task was the replacement of rotten floorboards. On November 5 he wrote to Jock Chambers: 'At present one chair and a table there. Am hoping for a book case this week, and a bed next week but cash isn't too plentiful and needs are many.'

By this time Lawrence had more or less accepted the Hogarth-Dawnay-Curtis scheme for a three-hundred-copy edition of *Seven Pillars* priced at ten guineas. The £3,000 subscription money would cover the cost of printing the text and illustrations. Whittingham & Griggs, a specialist printing firm, would need a year to reproduce the pictures by the high-quality colour collotype process, thus giving Lawrence time to revise and shorten the text.

Meanwhile, however, Robin Buxton was still canvassing friends about the possibility of finding one hundred and twenty subscribers at a higher price. Lawrence encouraged him: 'I'd rather the few copies: I had rather one copy at £3,000 than 10 at £300, or 30 at £100 or 300 at £10 . . . it is only what people will subscribe. I hate the whole idea of spreading copies of the beastly book'.

The scheme to publish *Seven Pillars* in an expensive subscription edition had led Lawrence to take a radical decision. He could not stomach the idea that subscribers might think that the high price reflected personal greed on his part. No one must say that he was making money out of his own legend, and he therefore decided not to take a royalty from the book. He presented this extraordinary decision, which had unquestionably been made for reasons of pride, as a matter of principle, and now repeatedly told people that he could not accept money from the book or any other part of his share in the Arabian adventure. Hitherto, *Seven Pillars* had been an investment which he could have turned at any moment into a personal fortune, simply by signing a publication contract. By contrast, the subscription scheme would allow him to print *Seven Pillars* lavishly, but it would also deny him the book's earning-power. In future, if he wished to escape from the ranks, he would have to obtain money some other way.

During November Hogarth, Curtis, and Buxton weighed the chances for their subscription schemes. Towards the end of the month Lawrence heard from Buxton that a hundred thirty-guinea subscribers could certainly be found. However, they could not be asked to pay the whole sum in advance, and Buxton's support would therefore be crucial. Liverpool & Martin's Bank, where he was a branch manager, would help finance the book's production.

Lawrence, Curtis, Hogarth and Dawnay met in Oxford on December 9 and agreed that one hundred copies of *Seven Pillars* should be offered to subscribers at thirty guineas each. Afterwards, Lawrence told Robin Buxton that he himself, 'a man of straw,' was 'to be solely responsible for the printing, production, and distribution of the book. This because it must inevitably be libellous. Civil Libel Actions break down because I have no money: criminal, because prison wouldn't seem to me worse than the Tank Corps . . . I propose, in my letter of conditions to each subscriber, to explain that my proposed edition of 100 copies is based on the estimate of £3,000 for the cost of production, with a 10% margin for eventualities: but that if the book costs less I'll distribute fewer than 100 copies: and if more as many more as are required to meet the bill: the price always remaining thirty guineas, and the total proceeds always equalling the total cost.'

The decision to publish *Seven Pillars* gave Lawrence a substantial project to work on, and placed him in a position of great personal responsibility. At thirty guineas, it would be a very expensive book; the modern equivalent can be estimated by relating the price to the average cost of a novel, then 7/6d. On that basis, the *Seven Pillars* subscription in 1990 would be approximately £650, and the gross projected turnover of the edition equivalent to about £65,000. This was a business venture of some scale for a private soldier, and it would involve a good deal of administrative work in addition to the tasks of revising the text and supervising the book's production.

Hogarth, Curtis and Buxton now set about finding subscribers, demonstrating their confidence that Lawrence would see the project through. If he failed, their only security was the Garnett abridgement, which could be published to meet his financial obligations although it would hardly recompense the disappointed subscribers. For this reason Lawrence had agreed at the Oxford meeting to appoint Hogarth his literary executor.

While friends looked for subscribers, Lawrence put the production work in hand. He arranged with Manning Pike, a printer introduced to him by Kennington, to buy printing machinery and equipment. Once the portrait plates had been printed by Whittingham & Griggs, he planned to sell some of the most valuable originals, notably John's oil of Feisal. Since the pictures were his own property he expected the balance in his personal bank account to be handsomely in credit within a year.

He found these arrangements for producing *Seven Pillars* very satisfactory: 'It will be rather a fine volume, and unless I'm wrong, a celebrated one some day.' Cheered by the prospect, he bought a new Brough Superior, his second. The old one had been borrowed without permission by one of the Bovington soldiers and wrecked: 'I've tried now for a valiant six weeks to do without a motor bike . . . and I find that it was indeed the safety valve I'd thought it.' The new Brough would cost £150, and Lawrence raised part of the cost by selling a copy of the Fourth Folio Shakespeare from his library.

By mid-January, a month after the decision to publish, a dozen subscribers had been accepted. But Lawrence's mood of optimism was soon overshadowed by the grim realities of life in the Tank Corps. He wrote to Hogarth in January: 'The Xmas spectacle of camp took out of me the zest I had won at Oxford', and told Wavell that the festivities had been 'like sleeping—or lying rather—in a public lavatory with choked drain . . . and it was even worse than the usual lavatory . . . for there seemed to be a heavy sea on, and all the *habitués* were in need of stewards with little basins.' Clouds Hill had become an essential haven: 'When things are unspeakable I fly out in the evening and debauch myself with canned music till my mind is sick'.

On January 2, while the Shaws were visiting Bournemouth, they had come across to see Lawrence at the cottage. A few days later he received a parcel of books from Charlotte Shaw, the first of many such gifts. A small library began to accumulate at the cottage, although his valuable private press books remained in storage with Vyvyan Richards at Pole Hill.

Pike would soon need revised text to begin work on *Seven Pillars*, but Lawrence was still busy with other writing. The translation of *Sturly* should have been finished at the end of December 1923, but had been held up while he made arrangements for *Seven Pillars*. In addition he was asked by Edward Garnett to write an introduction to *The Twilight of the Gods*, a collection of short stories by Garnett's father, Richard, now to be issued in a new illustrated edition. By the end of January he had hardly started the *Seven Pillars* revision. Realising that he had over-committed himself, he abruptly dropped the time-consuming translation work, writing to Cape that he had burned the draft rendering of *Sturly*.

When he at last tackled *Seven Pillars* he was shocked by the quality of his own writing, which he now saw from a different standpoint. His views about style had changed radically, and the epic manner he had once striven for seemed overwrought and false. Translation work had taught him to see instantly through literary pretension. Moreover, his mind had become attuned to a far simpler form of English through daily contact with men in the ranks. *Seven Pillars,* he realised, was written in a style very unlike that of the contemporary literature he had come to admire.

He had kept the letters Garnett and others had written to him about the book and, on rereading them, he must have realised that they avoided the question of its style. Their comments had been on generalities, praising such qualities of the book as his observation and self-revelation. Now that he saw the text so differently, he found little to comfort him in such opinions.

In mid-February, however, he received a very different type of letter about *Seven Pillars*. It was sent by E. M. Forster and contained detailed comment. Forster wrote at great length, illustrating his criticisms with passages from the text. One important criticism he offered was that 'your reflective style is not properly under control. Almost at once, when you describe your thoughts, you become obscure, and the slightly strained sense which you then (not habitually) lend words, does not bring your sentence the richness you intended, imparts not colour but gumminess.'

Lawrence had now not only recognised the problem of style, but found someone who could help him. He later said: 'detailed criticism is the only stuff worth having—plain praise being the most useless and boring stuff in the world—but the only people who can give you detailed criticism fit to help you are other craftsmen working themselves upon your job.'

Several of Lawrence's letters written in February and March 1924 refer to an illness which was sufficiently serious to put him on the camp sick list, and from which he did not fully recover for some weeks. At the time he was preoccupied, not merely with *Seven Pillars*, but with an overload of clerical duties in the camp. As often happens, physical illness triggered a psychological depression, and he suffered a deepening malaise from this time on. Despite flashes of good humour directed towards particular correspondents, the overall mood of his letters was to grow blacker and blacker. One factor was despair that he was still attracting attention as 'Lawrence of Arabia'. He had again been discovered by a *Daily Express* reporter, who, on February 27, published details of his life at Bovington.

Another influence on his mood was the constant sense of degradation he felt in the Tank Corps. On March 1, a year after his dismissal from the RAF, he appealed to Trenchard to be allowed back.

His depression was doubtless aggravated by the task of revising *Seven Pillars*, whose subject matter was painful to him, and whose style was such a constant disappointment. Moreover, during the first months of 1924 it seemed as though the plans for a thirty-guinea subscription edition had been over-optimistic. By mid-March, three months after the start of the project, only twenty-six subscribers had been found, while the de-tailed cost-estimates he had now obtained were higher than expected.

As he grappled with these worries, Lawrence's thoughts turned in-wards. On March 26, having recovered from what appeared to be a mixture of malaria and influenza, he sent a letter to Charlotte Shaw which clearly displays his mood. The core of the letter is a passage which shows how profoundly his outlook on life was still influenced by the homosexual rape he had suffered at Deraa six years before. He wrote: 'I'm always afraid of being hurt: and to me, while I live, the force of that night will lie in the agony which broke me, and made me surrender. It's the indi-vidual view. You can't share it.

'About that night. I shouldn't tell you, because decent men don't talk about such things. I wanted to put it plain in the book, and wrestled for days with my self-respect . . . which wouldn't, hasn't, let me. For fear of being hurt, or rather to earn five minutes respite from a pain which drove me mad, I gave away the only possession we are born into the world with—our bodily integrity. It's an unforgiveable matter, an irre-coverable position: and it's that which has made me forswear decent living, and the exercise of my not-contemptible wits and talents.

'You may call this morbid: but think of the offence, and the intensity of my brooding over it for these years. It will hang about me while I live, and afterwards if our personality survives. Consider wandering among the decent ghosts hereafter, crying ''Unclean, Unclean!'' . . . There's not a clean human being into whose shape I would not willingly creep. They may not have been Colonel Lawrence . . . but I know the reverse of that medal, and hate its false face so utterly that I struggle like a trapped rabbit to be it no longer . . . it's my part to shun pleasures . . . through lack of desert. There's expiation to be made'. Such were the thoughts that underlay his everyday state of mind.

In late April Trenchard responded to Lawrence's appeal for readmis-sion into the RAF with an unexpected offer. The Secretary of State for Air, now Lord Thomson, a socialist, was as unwilling as Hoare had been to allow Lawrence to rejoin the Air Force. Instead, at the beginning of May, Trenchard offered Lawrence the job of finishing an official history, *The War in the Air*, whose author had died after completing the first volume. Lawrence declined. He knew that the project was hemmed in by political difficulties, and he had no taste for such a responsibility.

Now that he thought there would be no return to the RAF, he became even more depressed. This mood was aggravated by continuing poor health, and there were further problems with *Seven Pillars*. By the middle of May, five months after the decision to reprint *Seven Pillars*, there were still only thirty-four subscribers, barely a quarter of the number needed. Buxton began to fear that the target would never be reached, and that the project might end in a large financial loss. Moreover, the original scheme to complete the book within about a year was clearly unrealistic.

As Lawrence grew more depressed and introspective, he also began to reflect on his illegitimacy. He wrote to Harley Granville-Barker: 'My genuine, birthday, initials are T.E.C. The C. became L. when I was quite young and as L. I went to Oxford and through the war. After the war it became a legend: and to dodge its load of legendary inaccuracy I changed it to R. In due course R. became too hot to hold. So now I'm Shaw: but to me there seems no virtue in one name more than another. Any one can be used by anyone'. On August 3, writing to Jock Chambers, he signed himself 'T.E.S. (ex J.H.R. ex T.E.L. ex E.C.)'. For some months he had been signing letters simply 'T.E.', and occasionally 'T.E.?' and from now on he told people quite readily that Lawrence had been an assumed name.

On May 18, while recovering from another attack of fever, he summarised his predicament in a letter to Edward Garnett: 'I'm sick just at present—in mind and body—and hate myself and all the circumstances of life. If only there was some way out of the *Verboten* notice-boards which stand in thickets about all my roads.' He was, however, making some headway with the revision of *Seven Pillars*. By the end of June, two of the eleven Books had been passed for typesetting. His enthusiasm for fine printing made him take great care over the appearance of each page and, as a result, the project continued to incur additional costs. More subscribers would be needed to cover the mounting expense, and Lawrence decided to print two hundred copies of the text and plates.

Finally, in late September, the introductory Book of eight chapters was in page proof. Lawrence sent copies out to several people who were qualified to criticise the standard of printing. One of these was Charlotte Shaw, who had offered to help with the proof-reading. To his delight she showed the chapters to her husband, and reported soon afterwards that he had taken to them 'like a duck to water, and is working at them as if they were his own'. It seems likely that this was the first time Shaw had given serious attention to any part of the book. He returned the proof after ten days with a forthright letter, criticising Lawrence's punctuation and, above all, his libels: 'I spent fifteen years of my life writing criticisms of sensitive living people, and thereby acquired a very cultivated sense of what I might say and what I might not say. All criticisms are technically libels; but there is the blow below the belt, the impertinence, the indulgence of dislike, the expression of personal contempt, and of course the imputation of dishonesty or unchastity which are and should not be privileged, as well as the genuine criticism, the amusing goodhumoured banter, and (curiously) the obvious "vulgar abuse" which *are* privileged. I have weeded out your reckless sallies as carefully as I can.'

Shaw also urged that the first chapter should be omitted, a proposal which caused Lawrence some misgivings. The chapter contained an important, if over-modest, statement about his position in Arabia, and paid tribute to the other British officers who had served there. He now wrote to Charlotte: 'I'm sorry to lose the list of names . . . It was my only homage to the fellows who helped the show. Perhaps it can be stuck in somewhere, someday. I began the book with that flat chapter, since those usual trumpet-like sentences are too loud for my manner. I like things which creep in silently.' He was less impressed by Bernard Shaw's punctuation scheme, which he did not adopt.

The page proof had also gone to Robin Buxton, who had shown growing concern about the finances of the project and its very slow progress. In a letter of October 7 Lawrence admitted to Buxton that the revenue from a hundred and ten subscriptions would no longer cover the cost.

To get round this problem, Lawrence offered the land he owned at Chingford to the bank as security. In addition, he once again raised the possibility of issuing an abridgement: 'The idea in my mind was that I could assign to the Bank . . . the right to publish an abridgement . . . and to apply the profits of such transaction to meeting any charges they had against either of my accounts . . . any surplus going, of course, to my brother, who is to inherit my debts and assets, if there are any assets ever.'

These difficulties and the effects of a year's overwork compounded the depressive illness from which Lawrence was suffering. By the end of 1924 his mind was no longer balanced, and the complex forces driving him downwards now led to even more extreme forms of self-degradation.

It was to be many years before this secret penance came to light. In May 1968 John Bruce, who had served with Lawrence in the Tank Corps, approached the *Sunday Times* with sensational testimony. He claimed to have been a key figure in Lawrence's life between 1922 and 1935. After some negotiations the newspaper acquired an eighty-five-page typed account of the alleged events in which Bruce had been involved.

Parts of the document were clearly invention, for instance it was stated that Bruce had accompanied Lawrence on spying expeditions in India disguised in native dress. Other parts, which contained extraordinary claims, could not possibly be verified. To protect itself the *Sunday Times* requested Bruce to make a legal declaration that he was telling the truth. In consequence any attempt to point out the inventions in Bruce's testimony would amount to an accusation of perjury.

Extracts from the Bruce document, omitting obvious errors, were published in the *Sunday Times* on 23 June 1968. It was alleged that Bruce had met Lawrence in 1922, that he had been engaged to act as a kind of bodyguard and that, while serving in the Tank Corps, he had administered the first of a series of beatings.

There is independent evidence that Lawrence did arrange to have himself beaten, on a small number of occasions and over a period of several years (Bruce claimed to have administered nine beatings between 1923 and 1935). This evidence has been discussed by John E. Mack, a professor of psychiatry, in his book *A Prince of Our Disorder*. Put simply, Mack's conclusion was that the beatings were a form of penance through which Lawrence attempted to come to terms with the homosexual rape at Deraa in 1917. Mack does not, however, suggest that this was Lawrence's only motivation, and he points to other psychological factors that may have been involved.

The matter is clearly very complex. Since Lawrence himself left no explanation, and there is no opportunity for detailed psychiatric questioning, speculation as to the causes of this behaviour can lead to no conclusive result. Doctors have told me that someone who goes through a deeply traumatic experience will react in a way which is determined by factors in that person's unique psychological make-up. Such a reaction may involve 'abnormal' private behaviour which appears to verge on insanity. Yet, however strange it may seem to others, this course may be the surest path by which that individual can maintain psychological equilibrium.

There is no case for attempting to speculate in this historical biography about a psychological question already discussed by Mack with much greater professional authority. The argument for not doing so is particularly strong because psychiatrists stress that very private behaviour of this nature is not neccessarily reflected in a person's everyday life. In Lawrence's case, no one knew of it except for a handful of people directly involved, and there appears to be no way in which his submission to these beatings affected his career. It was a symptom rather than a cause of his state of mind. As Mack has written: 'There is a temptation in this age of science and psychology to try to explain everything about human beings, or to show how each of the parts of a person's personality relates to the others. There is a false scientism in this, for we are not integrated in our personalities to nearly the same extent as we are in our bodies. Some qualities in all of us—in Lawrence certainly—must stand by themselves without explanation.'

CHAPTER 22

Ambitions Fulfilled
January 1925–December 1926

LAWRENCE was spending a great deal of time on *Seven Pillars*, but by the beginning of 1925, a year after the project had started, only the first three of the eleven Books were in type, and not a single page had passed its final proof. Nevertheless, he told Charlotte Shaw of his hopes to have the text printed by September and the book distributed soon afterwards. Events were to show that this new estimate was as wildly optimistic as the first.

His mental state was now such that he had begun to think re-entry into the RAF the only future worth living for. On February 6 he wrote to Trenchard at length, asking for a transfer: 'Please don't turn me down just because you did so last year and the year before . . . I don't really believe that you will go on refusing me for ever. People who want a thing as long and as badly as I want the R.A.F. must get it some time. I only fear that my turn won't come till I'm too old to enjoy it. That's why I keep on writing.'

Two weeks later he wrote to Buxton thanking him for his help with the *Seven Pillars* overdraft. But although the bank was prepared to continue the existing level of borrowing, it was opposed to any increase. Lawrence knew that he would have to raise money in some other way since he was powerless to speed up the work of printing, which was being done on a small treadle-operated press. In the belief that the book would be finished by Christmas, he argued that an extra loan of £100 from Buxton, together with £300 he hoped to raise by selling some rare books, would see him through. He wrote: 'I'm prepared for a loss of about a thousand pounds on the edition. This added to the overdraft of £1,300, with interest, will leave me about £2,500 to find in January next . . . I have two irons in the fire for the clearing up. Chingford is up for sale, and might bring the whole figure. If it has not done so by Christmas I'll take the offer of an abridgement of about half *Seven Pillars* to Cape, who was willing to go £7,000 last time, and would probably go £3,000 this time, for a limited agreement, which would suit my scruples better than outright disposal.'

These problems were aggravated by his printer, Manning Pike, who had an unhappy marriage and was given to fits of temperament during which he would do no work at all. Lawrence knew that the only hope of progress was to flatter and encourage him.

In March, he decided to sound out the idea of an abridgement. Despite previous disappointments Cape was interested, and they agreed on a text running to 125,000 words, less than half of *Seven Pillars*, to be published under a different title in spring of 1927. Cape suggested a contract under which he would pay £1,500 on signature and a further £1,500 six months later. Lawrence undertook to complete the abridgement by March 1926, which meant that he would tackle it after work on the subscribers' *Seven Pillars* had been finished. When the abridgement contract was agreed, he cancelled the sale of his private press books: 'I'd rather keep them than anything I've ever had.'

Later that month the appeal to Trenchard seemed to bear fruit. A new Conservative Government had been elected in October 1924, and Samuel Hoare was once again Secretary of State for Air. Trenchard promised to raise the question of a transfer when the new Minister returned to England in May after a lengthy overseas tour.

This news was a great boost to Lawrence's morale. He told Buxton on March 26: 'Brough has brought out a new and most wonderful 'bike, which will do 112 m.p.h. so long as the tyres will stand it. I'm going to blow £200 of Cape's on that.' In the same euphoric mood, he told Charlotte Shaw about the possibility of returning to the Air Force: 'Such a thing would push me up into the seventh level of happiness. May is to be the month of decision. Perhaps a good thing may at last happen!'

Then, on May 16, Lawrence heard that Hoare had again refused to allow him back into the RAF. He was shattered, and wrote to Buxton: 'The R.A.F. has finally made up its mind, that I am not, and will never be, considered fit to serve in it again. This, of course, affects my stay in the army, by removing the motive of it. So I may buy myself out in the autumn, to have full-time for the last three months, to finish the *Seven Pillars* business. After it is over I will be able to square up its account and to pay off any deficit there may be in my private account . . . I'm most grateful to you and your Bank for making this last two years possible: and your reliance on my not pegging out (deliberately that is) without settling all up, shan't be disappointed.'

The RAF rejection dashed the hopes that had been sustaining him during the preceding weeks, and his black depression returned. He was prepared to try any steps that might reverse the decision. Knowing that

John Buchan was friendly with the Prime Minister, he had written to Lionel Curtis a few days earlier: 'John Buchan: do you ever see him? Could I? Without seeming to wish to? Naturally, in other words.' It had been impossible to arrange a meeting before Hoare had made up his mind, but on Sunday May 17, the day after he had learned about the refusal, Lawrence met Buchan in London. He evidently begged for help, and he followed this up two days later with a letter: 'I don't know by what right I made that appeal to you on Sunday. It happened on the spur of the moment. You see, for seven years it's been my ambition to get into the Air Force . . . and I can't get the longing for it out of my mind for an hour. Consequently I talk of it to most of the people I meet.' Buchan wrote to Baldwin but his appeal carried too little weight to change Hoare's mind.

The printing of *Seven Pillars* began to run more smoothly when Pike was joined by an experienced pressman, Herbert Hodgson. Hodgson's first act was to have an electric motor fitted to the press, and he proved to be as good a craftsman with presswork as Pike was with typesetting. As a result the text and delicate line illustrations of *Seven Pillars* were printed with great skill.

Now that there was to be money from the abridgement, Lawrence decided to commission more illustrations. When the typeset text was divided into pages, he could see where there were blank spaces at the ends of chapters. He commissioned tailpiece drawings to fill these spaces from Kennington, Paul Nash and, later, William Roberts.

Although he was still busy working through the 1922 text making revisions for the new typesetting, he now had to correct three or four stages of proof. The work was taking him five hours a day over and above his Tank Corps duties. By mid-June he was little more than half-way through the revision, having just completed the section in which he described the distressing events at Deraa. He wrote to Edward Garnett in a mood of deep depression: 'What muck, irredeemable, irremediable, the whole thing is! How on earth can you have once thought it passable? My gloomy view of it deepens each time I have to wade through it. If you want to see how good situations, good characters, good material can be wickedly bungled, refer to any page, passim. There isn't a scribbler in Fleet Street who wouldn't have got more fire and colour into every paragraph.

'Trenchard withdrew his objection to my rejoining the Air Force. I got seventh-heaven for two weeks: but then Sam Hoare came back from

Mesopotamia and refused to entertain the idea. That, and the closer acquaintance with the *Seven Pillars* (which I now know better than anyone ever will) have together convinced me that I'm no bloody good on earth. So I'm going to quit: but in my usual comic fashion I'm going to finish the reprint and square up with Cape before I hop it! There is nothing like deliberation, order and regularity in these things.

'I shall bequeath you my notes on life in the recruits' camp of the R.A.F. They will disappoint you.'

Lawrence must have written this letter with the intention of making his friends take some action. He knew that a suicide threat would be a potent weapon against Hoare. Garnett was naturally alarmed and immediately wrote to Bernard Shaw appealing for help. Shaw forwarded Garnett's letter to Baldwin, pointing out that if Lawrence carried out his threat there would be an appalling scandal.

As it happened, public interest in Lawrence was running high at that moment. In May, Hutchinson had published a popular biography called *With Lawrence in Arabia* by Lowell Thomas, based on his earlier slide lectures. A great deal of the book, according to Lawrence, was 'either invention or gossip', but it had the effect of rekindling public interest.

Suddenly and unexpectedly, he heard from Buxton that Air Vice-Marshal Sir Geoffrey Salmond (whom Lawrence had known since the war) had intimated that the RAF was reconsidering the question of a transfer. Lawrence wrote to Buxton by return: 'Will you ask him about it? I gathered that I was finally turned down, and have been making all my plans on that basis.' A week later he knew that a transfer was possible, and wrote to Charlotte Shaw: 'I live in suspense. Trenchard, the Air Chief has told me to come and see him on Wednesday, to receive a sugar-plum. I can't think what it is. He knows that I want a bad job from him, not a good one.'

At his meeting in London on July 1 he was told that he could rejoin the RAF. Afterwards he wrote: 'Now I feel inclined to lie down and rest, as if there was never going to be any more voyaging. I suppose it is something like a ship getting into harbour at last. The impulse to get that book finished by Christmas is over. I may be living on for years now, and so why hurry it? Also there isn't any longer any need for the book. I was consciously tidying up loose ends, and rounding the oddments off . . . and now it seems there aren't any loose ends or oddments.

'Don't get worried over this: a few days will see me square again, and I'll realise that it will be as well to finish all the consequences of the Arabian business before pushing off into the R.A.F. You see, if I can clean up the Arab mess, and get it away, behind my mind, then I can be like the other fellows in the crowd. Perhaps my mind can go to sleep: anyway I should be more ordinary than I have been of late. The relief it will be, to have the fretting ended.'

During his last weeks at Bovington he worked hard at revising the remaining text of *Seven Pillars* and correcting the proofs. There would be little time for working on the book if, as he expected, he had to repeat two months' basic training when he rejoined the RAF. By July 27 he had completed the revisions to Book IX, the first fourteen chapters had been printed, and the text up to the end of Book VIII (another eighty-three chapters) was in various stages of proof. Before leaving Bovington he sent the two final Books for typesetting.

He rejoined the Air Force at Uxbridge on August 18, just after his thirty-seventh birthday. Three days later, orders came for his immediate posting to the RAF Cadet College at Cranwell in Lincolnshire. He was delighted, and celebrated by ordering a Brough motorcycle of the latest type. It would be his fourth Brough Superior.

At Cranwell he joined B flight, which consisted of fifteen men, a sergeant, and a corporal. Lawrence was to act as runner and clerk. Now that he was back in the RAF and the subscribers' *Seven Pillars* was nearing completion, he had time to take stock. Although he professed to be happy with the prospect of five more years in the ranks, within weeks he was to send Charlotte Shaw one of his most despairing letters: 'Do you know what it is when you see, suddenly, that your life is all a ruin?' The reason for this sudden change of mood was that he had been to London to meet Feisal, who was visiting England, and they had taken lunch with Lord Winterton. 'Winterton of course had to talk of old times, taking me for a companion of his again, as though we were again advancing on Damascus. And I had to talk back, keeping my end up, as though the R.A.F. clothes were a skin that I could slough off at any while with a laugh.

'But all the while I knew I couldn't. I've changed, and the Lawrence who used to go about and be friendly and familiar with that sort of people is dead. He's worse than dead. He is a stranger I once knew. From henceforward my way will lie with these fellows here, degrading myself (for in their eyes and your eyes and Winterton's eyes I see that it is a degradation) in the hope that some day I will really feel degraded, be degraded, to their level. I long for people to look down upon me and despise me, and I'm too shy to take the filthy steps which would publicly shame me, and put me into their contempt. I want to dirty myself outwardly, so that my person may properly reflect the dirtiness which it conceals . . . and I shrink from dirtying the outside, while I've eaten, avidly eaten, every filthy morsel which chance threw in my way . . . My reason tells me all the while, dins into me day and night, a sense of how I've crashed my life and self and gone hopelessly wrong: and hopelessly it is, for I'm never coming back, and I want to'.

Despite this, Lawrence's letters show that he soon found contentment at Cranwell. He made no secret of his identity, and the men's curiosity quickly wore off. By November 3 he was able to write to Edward Garnett that he felt 'absurdly happy'.

He was now working on the last pages of *Seven Pillars* and, on November 17, wrote to Charlotte Shaw eagerly looking forward to the end of his task: 'Isn't it wonderful? the job is nearly over. Your part finishes with what you have in your hand. Mine is to 1st revise IX (nearly through) and X, and to page-proof VI, VII, VIII, IX and X. After that index and map: and binding: and then peace.'

He spent Christmas alone, as the rest of B flight were on leave, passing his time correcting proofs and reading. By the close of the year it seemed that the new text of *Seven Pillars* would be completed, at long last, within a month, although there was still work to be done on the illustrations.

Lawrence now turned his attention to the Cape abridgement. Under the terms of the contract, he had to deliver the text by the end of March 1926, and he began work on it in January, deleting passages in pencil on a proof of the subscribers' *Seven Pillars*. Fortunately, the task was easy, for he had twice before (in 1920 and with Garnett in 1922) shortened the text in this way.

Despite his later belittling statements about the abridgement, implying that he had given it little thought, his very nature forced him to make as good a job as possible of the new version. This was to be the first significant work published under his name, and he would not have risked hostile reviews by slipshod editing. Indeed, the Cape project was a special challenge. He felt that in *Seven Pillars* he had failed to create a work of the 'titanic' class: his more modest aim in the abridgement was to create an uncomplicated adventure story. He was determined to succeed in this easier genre, not only for his self-esteem, but also because he was relying on the abridgement to clear his debts.

On March 8 he finished correcting the last *Seven Pillars* proofs, but the illustrations were still behind schedule. Whittingham & Griggs told him they could not complete their part of the work before July.

It was as well that he had finished the text corrections, for ten days later he broke his right arm. He was turning the starting-handle of a car when the engine backfired, breaking off the tip of his radius and dislocating his wrist. Fortunately, by this time he had also completed the Cape abridgement as far as the final Book of *Seven Pillars*. He was never to recover full movement of his right hand, and for the next month could only write with difficulty, often asking one of the other aircraftmen to act as secretary.

When he finished making the Cape abridgement in late March he decided to keep the pencil working draft. With help from two friends, another proof of *Seven Pillars* was marked up with all the cuts and linking passages for the abridgement. This operation, which consisted mainly of blacking out the deleted passages with Indian ink, provided the basis for a deliberately misleading statement he later gave to Cape's house journal *Now and Then*: 'The abridgement . . . was made by him in seven hours at Cranwell in Lincolnshire on March 26 and March 27 1926, with the assistance of two airman friends, A/A Knowles and A/c Miller'. When he had first agreed to the Cape abridgement, he had planned that it would appear several months after distribution of the subscribers' *Seven Pillars*; but this now seemed unlikely since work on the illustrations was still causing delay.

In late May he learned that he was to be posted to India that autumn. This seemed to be for the best, because it meant that he would be out of reach of the publicity surrounding Cape's issue of the abridgement. Work on *Seven Pillars* was not going so smoothly. When the General Strike affected power supplies, and Whittingham & Griggs were held up still further, Lawrence resigned himself to the possibility that they might not finish the plates until September.

At the end of August Lawrence thought that copies of *Seven Pillars* would be ready for dispatch to the binders on September 15. However, there were yet further delays and the text was still not ready on September 25 when he learned that he had inadvertently libelled Ronald Storrs. The offending passage had to be rewritten, and four pages had to be reset, proofed and reprinted. To add to his problems, Kennington found fault with some of the plates. As a result, the binding date had to be put off until the end of October. There was good news, however, when Raymond Savage obtained offers worth £2,000 from the *Daily Telegraph* and *Asia Magazine* for serial rights of the Cape abridgement. Savage had also arranged that the American copyright edition of *Seven Pillars* should be set up and printed by George H. Doran, who was publishing the Cape abridgement in New York. The contract was for twenty-two copies, two of which would be needed for copyright deposit. The remainder were to be so expensive that none would sell; in this way *Seven Pillars* would remain in print on Doran's list, and copyright would be secure.

On October 18 Lawrence wrote to Pike: 'Keep at it. We are really last-lapping. Get the Table of Contents done: make a title-page which pleases you, and don't send it me: and then print and print and print.' On November 4 he began the month's leave to which he was entitled before going to India. He had planned a last visit to many friends before this five-year absence overseas. But work on *Seven Pillars* took priority.

A few copies were completed by the binders during November, and Lawrence sent the very first of these to the Royal Library at Windsor, insisting that the advance cheque sent by the Royal Librarian should be returned.

Another free copy, with a special inscription, went to Trenchard, who wrote: 'the part I like almost best is the expression "from a contented admirer and, whenever possible, obedient servant". This is a delightful touch from the most disobedient mortal I have ever met.'

The month's leave passed quickly. Lawrence had to spend most of it helping Pike collate the remaining copies, making up the individual sets of pages and plates. He managed a brief visit to Clouds Hill and spent an hour with Thomas Hardy, the last time they would meet. Kennington had asked him to pose for a bronze portrait bust, and somehow Lawrence made time for five sittings. In London he saw the Shaws and a few other friends. As a leaving present Charlotte gave him a notebook she had filled with philosophical meditations.

He sold his motorcycle, which had been damaged in a skid during this leave. Not long before he had sent a testimonial to George Brough, its manufacturer, writing that he had 'completed 100,000 miles, since 1922, on five successive Brough Superiors, and I'm going abroad very soon, so that I think I must make an end, and thank you for the road-pleasure I have got out of them.'

During his last days in London, Lawrence made over the copyright of the Cape abridgement, to be called *Revolt in the Desert*, to a charitable trust, appointing Robin Buxton, D. G. Hogarth and Edward Eliot (a London solicitor recommended by Buxton) as Trustees. He later told Hogarth that he had 'made the Trust final, to save myself the temptation of reviewing it, if *Revolt* turned out a best seller.'

This renunciation would eventually deprive Lawrence of a considerable fortune, but it was implicit in the decision he had taken in 1923 not to take any personal royalty from the subscribers' edition of *Seven Pillars*. It would be unthinkable to profit from an abridgement which some subscribers feared would devalue their costly investment. He suggested that if publication produced surplus revenue, the major beneficiary should be the RAF Benevolent Fund set up by Trenchard in 1919. In due course the *Revolt* Trustees would establish an Anonymous Education Fund, administered by the RAF Benevolent Fund, 'for the benefit of children of Royal Air Force officers, past and present, preference being given to the children of officers who lost their lives or were invalided as a result of service.'

In another letter to Hogarth, Lawrence set out his ideas for the Trust's management: 'There is no power on earth which can call in question your disposal of the cash: so let's have some fun with it: so far as fun can be had without bothering Eliot, Robin and yourself. Simple fun. Let's hope there will be thousands of pounds. The more, surely, the merrier. Chucking away things is the best of sport. Here in the ranks I see many hard cases, which could be palliated by a cheque: however I promise not to bother you. I rather envy you the job. It will, as you say, go on for years: till I die and the *Seven Pillars* is reprinted'.

On December 1 he wrote to his mother: 'This is my last free night in England, and I'm writing to you, very late, in the top of Barton Street, where Baker has let me stay during this month. It should have been leave, preparatory to going overseas: but for me it has been a very hard month of work on that big book of mine. It is not finished: but every copy is at the binders, so that my share is over. All that remains is to send off the copies, and that my printer, Pike, will do for me . . . Getting it over has been a big relief. I have spent £13,000 on it, altogether, and the responsibility of that has been heavy'.

A week later he sailed for India on board the troopship *Derbyshire*.

CHAPTER 23

Voluntary Exile

January 1927–January 1929

On January 7 he reached his destination, an RAF depot seven miles outside Karachi. The first letters written there show mixed reactions: the accommodation was 'comfortable, almost magnificently-built, and cool . . . It seems a quiet place, though the stone floors and high ceilings are noisy and distant, hospital-like, after the homeliness of Cranwell.' A fortnight later, however, he was finding the depot 'dreary, to a degree, and its background makes me shiver. It is a desert, very like Arabia: and all sorts of haunting likenesses (pack-donkeys, the colour and cut of men's clothes, an oleander bush in flower in the valley, camel-saddles, tamarisk) try to remind me of what I've been for eight years desperately fighting out of my mind. Even I began to doubt if the coming out here was wise. However there wasn't much chance, and it must be made to do. It will do, as a matter of fact, easily.' Lawrence was posted as a clerk to the Engine Repair Section, where all the RAF aircraft engines in India were sent for overhaul.

Indian servants made the men's beds and cleaned their boots and brasses. Lawrence had no taste for this racial servitude and wrote to Fareedeh el Akle, who had taught him Arabic at Jebail before the war: 'This country, India, is not good. Its people seem to feel themselves mean. They walk about in a subdued, repressed way. Also it is squalid, with much of the dirty industrialism of Europe, with all its native things decaying, or being forcibly adjusted to Western conditions. I shall be happy only when they send me home again'. He made up his mind not to leave the camp.

In much the same spirit, he had been trying for some time to persuade his mother and elder brother Bob to give up missionary work in China, to which they had devoted their lives since the early 1920s. His renewed contact with a subject race seems to have added bitterness to his views. He was glad to see the 'anti-foreign' bias of Chinese politics and wrote to his mother: 'Salvation comes from within a nation, and China cannot be on the right road till, like Russia, she closes her eyes and ears to teaching, and follows her own instincts to their logical and absurd limits. So long as she permits outsiders to teach or preach in her boundaries, so surely is she an inferior nation. You must see that. People can take from one another, but cannot give to one another.'

Lawrence needed a pastime to fill the off-duty hours at Karachi and now, having signed away a potential fortune by making over the copyright of *Revolt* to a charitable Trust, he found himself short of cash. The men were kept on low pay until their documents arrived from England, and the cost of postage for his usual correspondence would be a heavy burden. He also wanted to build up a new collection of gramophone records. On February 1 he wrote to Cape asking about translation work.

The first mails to arrive from England brought letters from recipients of *Seven Pillars*. Among them was one from Allenby, who wrote: 'I congratulate you on a great work; fit record of your splendid achievements in the war.' Lawrence was relieved by the letter. He told Charlotte Shaw: 'it has been a fear of mine that his sense of proportion (a very sober and stern quality in him) somehow associated my person with the ridiculous reputation raised about it by the vulgar. You see, my campaign and fighting-efforts were entirely negligible, in his eyes. All he required of us was a turn-over of native opinion from the Turk to the British: and I took advantage of that need of his, to make him the step-father of the Arab national movement—a movement which he did not understand and for whose success his instinct had little sympathy.'

The *Revolt* Trustees had arranged to exhibit the originals of the *Seven Pillars* illustrations at the Leicester Galleries. They hoped that sale of the pictures would raise money to help pay off the overdraft. Without consulting Lawrence, Bernard Shaw had written a preface to the catalogue, and this contained several factual errors, including a statement that the subscribers' *Seven Pillars* was a limited edition of one hundred copies. There were in reality 170 'complete' copies, and Lawrence had given away a further thirty-two 'incomplete' copies, lacking some of the colour plates. Shaw's inaccurate claim helped to boost the value of the subscribers' copies, which climbed within weeks to more than ten times the original price.

Shaw also used the Leicester Galleries preface to repeat his view that the Government should provide Lawrence with an income. Lawrence remonstrated with Charlotte: 'I devoutly hope that G.B.S. does not get his pension scheme through. I manage my own life beautifully, it seems to me . . . As a general rule, you must agree, money matters do not enter hugely into my thinking.'

In another context, however, money matters were very much in his thoughts. Everything he owned was mortgaged to the bank, legally or morally, against the *Seven Pillars* overdraft. His financial position in future years would depend entirely on the success of *Revolt in the Desert* which was to be published in March. If *Revolt* failed, Lawrence would 'be hopelessly in debt, and forced to leave the R.A.F. (which is my condition of contentment) to earn money and become solvent.' Unless he did so, the bank would sell his land at Pole Hill. He could not afford to let that happen, since he hoped that this capital would one day provide a modest income for his retirement.

His friends were concerned about what he would do to occupy himself, now that *Seven Pillars* was finished. Lawrence himself must have been pondering this question and he was at no loss for a reply when Buxton wrote inviting him 'to divulge your feelings about your life': 'Well: I feel that the writing complication is past: and with it the last vestige of responsibility for what I did in Arabia. Under Winston I put in order the actual situation in the Middle East, to my full content. In the *Seven Pillars* I've put on record my "why" and "how". So now that is all over, and I'm again a private person, and an insignificant one . . .

'When my health drives me out of it (or Trenchard drives me out!) I'll try and get some quiet job, near London, which is the place I like. A night-watchman, door-porter, or else something like a chauffeur: though I will soon be too old for anything exposed. Perfection would be to do nothing: to have something like a pound a day from investments, and live on it, as I very well could . . . Desires and ambitions and hopes and envy . . . do you know I haven't any more of those things now in me, for as deep down as I can reach? I am happy when I'm sitting still, in complete emptiness of mind. This may sound to you very selfish . . . but the other fellows find me human, and manage to live with me all right. I like so much the being left alone that I tend to leave other people alone, too.'

Revolt in the Desert was published in England and America in early March. The book was advertised widely, and in America the tone of Doran's publicity owed much to Lowell Thomas. English reviewers heaped praise on it, and advance orders for the Cape edition exhausted three printings. Charlotte Shaw sent Lawrence a selection of press clippings. On April 7 he replied: 'The knock-out of the week was your sheaf of reviews of *Revolt in the Desert* . . . It feels altogether incredible: because I know that I'm not any of the things they call me.' His first reaction was one of self-questioning: 'I think the book reviews . . . have worried me . . . I've only been jarred by the improbabilities they spray out. "Genius" comes once in each, ten times in some. Who are they to judge genius? I haven't the slightest awareness of any in myself. Talent, yes, a diversity of talent: but not the other quality which dispenses with talent, and walks by its own light'. The praise, which was almost universal, strengthened his self-confidence about writing. He became fascinated by the reviews, and commented in great detail on some of the criticisms. Yet he found them unhelpful in the very area which mattered to him most: their assessment of his ability as a writer.

Revolt became a best-seller in both Britain and America. Lawrence had predicted that the combined royalties from Cape and Doran would pay off his debt within two or three years; in the event the overdraft was covered within weeks, and *Revolt* would earn a huge surplus before the end of 1927.

Reactions to *Seven Pillars* were no less pleasing. Churchill wrote in May, comparing it with the third volume of his own war memoirs, *The World Crisis* (which had been published a week before *Revolt* and was another of the season's best-sellers): 'when I put down the *Seven Pillars*, I felt mortified at the contrast between my dictated journalism and your grand and permanent contribution to English literature. I cannot tell you how thrilled I was to read it. Having gone on a three days' visit to Paris, I never left my apartment except for meals, and lay all day and most of the night cuddling your bulky tome. The impression it produced was overpowering . . . No wonder you brood in haughty anti-climax! I think your book will live with *Gulliver's Travels* and *Robinson Crusoe*.'

As Lawrence had foretold, the reviews of *Revolt* brought a new wave of public curiosity about his life, and he began to receive many letters from strangers. He rarely replied; his isolation at Karachi was leading him to write more than ever to his friends. One correspondence in particular found a new basis during the first few months of 1927. For two years he had been exchanging letters regularly with Charlotte Shaw about the proofs of *Seven Pillars*. Now that he was in India, Charlotte sent him parcels of books. Lawrence read and commented on them: 'Such a comfort: one can write about books. That will solve the problem of our continued correspondence: which otherwise would have been difficult'.

The Shaws had no children, and Lawrence was young enough to be Charlotte's son. He liked her and admired G.B.S., and she gradually became one of his most intimate correspondents. It has been suggested that it was Lawrence who took the initiative in this friendship, but the reverse is true. It was of Charlotte's making: she wrote far more frequently than he did, and showered him with gifts of books, gramophone records and food hampers. She attached great importance to their relationship, using symbols in her private diary to note the dates she sent him letters and parcels, and those on which she received his replies.

On his side there was always an element of reserve. For example, he told E. M. Forster: 'Her valuation of my work amazes me: and makes me fear that she hangs it as a cloak about the peg of my personality, and wants to over-estimate the cloak, for the sake of being able to over-like the peg. Woe's me. This peg distrusts all human affection.' He wrote to her regularly, but often had difficulty finding something interesting to say: 'Perhaps if I keep a pencilled sheet handy I may be able to jot down enough in the course of a week, for it to be worth posting you. It isn't right that I should just report a bald existence to you. What's the good of two people communicating, if they haven't anything to say to one another?' Although Charlotte Shaw knew that Lawrence destroyed almost all her letters to him, she carefully preserved his replies.

Lawrence accepted Charlotte Shaw's presents but made sure that he was never in her debt. Over the years he gave her several manuscripts, in addition to a copy of the 'Oxford' *Seven Pillars* which he left with her on indefinite loan. Ultimately, the financial value of these gifts would far exceed the cost of her presents to him. He saw himself as a donor, not a recipient, of charity, and as soon as his financial positon improved, he arranged to give money to Private Palmer, a friend from his time in the Tanks Corps, who hoped to leave the RAF and establish himself in civilian life, and to Manning Pike, whose printing business was on the point of failure.

In April Lawrence wrote to Edward Eliot, the solicitor who had been appointed Trustee of *Revolt in the Desert*, asking about the formalities required to change his surname legally to Shaw. When Eliot replied that the process was simple and could be carried through without publicity, Lawrence decided to go ahead with it. The letter he wrote to Eliot on June 16, in which he described his parents' situation, reveals something about his sense of ancestry: 'I'm in some doubt as to my previous name, for I've never seen my birth certificate . . . My father and mother . . . called themselves Lawrence, at least from 1892 onwards. I do not know whether they did so when I was born or not . . . Of course if Father registered me as Chapman, that will do, and there's no need to have the intermediate stage of Shaw, between Lawrence and it: for eventually, I suppose, Chapman it will have to be. There is a lot of land in that name knocking about: and I don't want to chuck it away, as Walter Raleigh, for whom

T.E. Lawrence on one of his Brough Superior motorcycles, talking to the manufacturer, George Brough, in October 1930

T.E. Lawrence during his last RAF years, at Scott Paine's Yard in Southampton.

An RAF 200 Class seaplane tender. The success of this innovative planing-hull design soon led to the introduction of similar but larger launches. All these high speed RAF boats were used for Air-Sea rescue work during the Second World War.

The RAF 200 Class design modified and armour-plated to serve as a target for bombing practice. When the press publicised Lawrence's association with these boats in October 1932 he was returned to more mundane duties

ground floor plan.

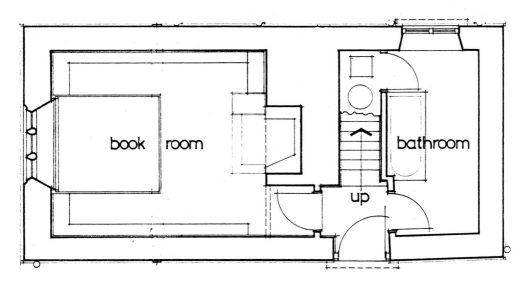

book room

bathroom

up

first floor plan.

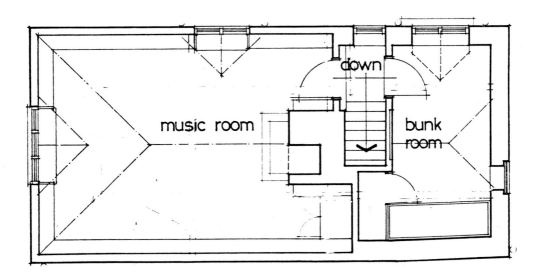

music room

down

bunk room

Clouds Hill: (*top*) ground floor plan; (*below*) first floor plan

Clouds Hill, 1935. Lawrence had written, 'it will be a very habitable and restful place. I am fond of it, and hope to live there after I leave the RAF'

The music room at Clouds Hill, photographed shortly after Lawrence's death. During the preceding years he had modified the cottage to suit his requirements exactly

T.E. Lawrence, photographed by Flight Lieutenant R.G. Sims at Hornsea near Bridlington during the winter of 1934–5. Sims, a keen photographer, took what was to be the last series of portrait photographs

T.E. Lawrence sketched by Augustus John at Friern, near Fordingbridge, in January 1935. Lawrence had 100 collotype plates made from this drawing as the frontispiece for an edition of *The Mint*, but he was destined never to print it.

T.E. Lawrence photographed as he left the RAF at Bridlington in February 1935. When he reached Dorset he found Clouds Hill besieged by the press

I have a certain regard, gave it to my father's first Irish ancestor. I have a feeling that it should be kept in the line.'

Lawrence felt increasingly that the completion of *Seven Pillars* had closed a period in his life. When he realised that his overdraft would be paid off before the end of the year, he persuaded the three Trustees to halt English publication of *Revolt* as soon as possible, hoping that this would quell public interest in him and bring forward the date at which he could return to England.

It was not just in English-speaking countries that *Revolt* sold well. Translations were published in many languages, and during Lawrence's lifetime the abridgement was reprinted several times in French, German and Italian. As early as June 1927 *Revolt* had sold 30,000 copies in England and 120,000 in America. Lawrence must have reflected wryly from time to time that if he had published Garnett's abridgement five years earlier he would now be living in very different circumstances.

Doran and Cape were keen to exploit Lawrence's commercial value, and they decided to commission a popular biography. When Hogarth wrote to Lawrence about this in mid-May, Lawrence was alarmed: 'Dimly behind my mind lay the certainty that some Lytton Strachey of the future would attempt a life of me: but I did not expect more than Lowell Thomas' futile effort in my life-time. And there are so many things in my life that I do not want told.' His thoughts turned to Robert Graves, who was almost always short of money. By chance, the same idea had also occurred to friends in England, and on June 3 Graves sent Lawrence a telegram: 'Cape and Doran want schoolstory of Revolt shall I decently to prevent others no formal imprimatur from you but veto for manuscript Kennington will illustrate'. Lawrence cabled back the one word 'yes', and wrote: 'There may be money in it: which is my reason for wishing you to get it. From all other points of view I'm sorry. Doran should have had more sense . . . I would like to see your text, if time admits, before it goes to press: preferably in typescript. There are certain things which must not be said. Not that I care, but other people have such odd views. And politically about Arabia, there may be a touch or two which I'd suggest your adding. Your book quite likely won't be just a school edition: and if so I may try and persuade you to act as a vehicle in correcting some mistakes the public have made about the direction of my hopes.' One of Lawrence's chief worries about an independent and possibly sensational biographer must have been the question of his family background, since the truth could quite easily have been uncovered.

Graves was not only a friend, but also very substantially in Lawrence's debt. As Graves had been given only a short time to complete the book, Lawrence sent him detailed autobiographical notes. In these he gave the truth about his parentage, adding: 'As widow and mother are both yet alive this story is not for publication. You'll have to dodge the birth somehow.'

These notes were both helpful and almost entirely accurate. Graves cannot have hoped for so much assistance. At this stage Lawrence seems to have believed that he could be relied upon to exercise discretion and good taste: 'He is a decent fellow, does not know too much about me: will think out some psychologically plausible explanation of my spiritual divagations: and will therefore help to lay at rest the uneasy ghost which seems to have stayed in England when I went abroad'. With a little subtle direction, Graves might produce an acceptable, even useful book. As Lawrence wrote candidly in August: 'Graves is smaller than I am, and so will do mainly what I have asked him.'

The project almost immediately became much larger than Graves had expected. Lowell Thomas's publishers announced that a children's version of his book *With Lawrence in Arabia*, to be called *The Boys' Life of Colonel Lawrence*, would be published in September. As there was unlikely to be a market for two children's books on Lawrence that autumn, Cape and Doran agreed that Graves's book should be transformed into a longer popular study. It was hurriedly expanded to three times the length originally proposed; just over three-quarters would be a paraphrase from *Seven Pillars*. In this way, by the time *Revolt* had sold out, Cape would have a profitable substitute; Graves too would benefit from the new scheme.

Reassured by the success of *Revolt*, Lawrence now had other writing projects in mind. He contributed a series of reviews to the *Spectator* and he wrote to F. N. Doubleday asking for translation work: 'I'd like to make pocket money, to supplement my R.A.F. pay of a pound a week, out of writing . . . the trouble is I live so far from London that there's great delay in anything I do. However if Heinemann ever contemplate a leisurely translation of a French book, by an anonymous translator, I'd be grateful for the chance of doing it.'

Before he received Doubleday's reply, however, Lawrence had taken up a literary project of his own. The notes he had made in 1922 on the RAF recruits' training depot at Uxbridge had been untouched for a long time, but soon after arriving in India he had asked a friend to post them out to him. During June and July, while Graves worked on the biography in England, Lawrence began the difficult task of transforming the notes into prose.

He received the first third of Graves's typescript on July 26 and returned it four days later with his comments. He was disappointed by the amount of paraphrase from *Seven Pillars*, and remarked to Graves that he had seen 'a few questions of fact, where Woolley or Lowell Thomas or someone had led you astray. I put a few bright bits in the margin, in case you want to hunt the popular taste . . . I wish you were not hurried. With time you could have written a decent *history* of the Arab Revolt, which would have put my personal contribution in the background.'

Graves had not been able to resist the temptation to include other material from *Seven Pillars* which would be unfamiliar to readers of *Revolt*, and he had borrowed Kennington's longer 'Oxford' text to work from. To Lawrence's dismay, the second batch of typescript contained even more of this unwelcome matter. He wrote to Graves on August 3: 'I . . . will, I fear, have troubled you with my suggestion that you "go easy" on *Seven Pillars* material. But it seems to me only logical . . . [*Revolt*] contained all that I wanted the public to know . . . Regard *Revolt* as your maximum, rather than as something to be supplemented by the *Seven Pillars*. Please don't set the example of nibbling at its copyright!' The following day Lawrence wrote about the typescript to Charlotte Shaw: 'I hate reading it. I correct little, excise little: add less. He avoids G.B.S.' prophecy that he would only be retelling my story in his words, by telling it in my words.'

After he had seen the final batch of typescript Lawrence sent a brief letter to Graves which barely conceals his disappointment with the work: 'Of course you have "done me very well"—but I don't really care a hoot about that. The thing that was really important was for you to do yourself really well, and I don't feel that it's up to the level of your other prose. In the rushed circumstances it could not be: and you will doubtless pull it together in the revise'. A letter to Charlotte Shaw the following day is more frank: 'Every page of R.G.'s own had inaccuracies. I corrected it till I was sick: and let as much more slip. Eighty per cent of the book was what I'd call a bare parody or précis of *Revolt*: I do not think it was quite right to make so free with another's work.'

Despite his reservations, Lawrence's attitude towards the biography was philosophical. It would extend the British publicity he had hoped to quell by withdrawing *Revolt in the Desert*; but some such book was unavoidable, and he could console himself with the thought that it 'might have been done 5,000 times worse by someone merely sensation-hunting'. As it was, even Graves's commercial instincts had proved unexpectedly crude; for example, his first draft had contained a version of the Deraa incident. After this, their relationship never recovered its former intimacy. When *Lawrence and the Arabs* was eventually published, in December 1927, Lawrence told Graves that it was 'the only book about myself in which I will lend help'; but a few years later he would give wholehearted assistance to a more serious study by the military historian Liddell Hart.

Lawrence appears nevertheless to have drawn some benefit from the Graves project. The task of reviewing his life, particularly the Arab period, seems to have helped him come to terms with the moral issues that had troubled him for so long. At no time after this did he express the bitterness and remorse about his wartime role that occurs so frequently in the early post-war letters.

Working in the office of the Engine Repair Section, Lawrence had quickly proved himself 'a little gift from Providence to the paper-laden officer in charge.' The station adjutant noted a distinct literary polish in memoranda coming from the engineering section, and Lawrence was brought in, at first on a part-time basis, to help with paperwork in the Orderly Room.

As he worked through the Uxbridge notes, he came to feel that they could not stand on their own; they painted too bleak a picture of life in the ranks of the RAF. To counter this he now planned a final section describing his experiences as a qualified aircraftman at Cranwell. He had made a few pages of notes while at Cranwell, some of which he had sent to Charlotte Shaw: 'little yellow slips, dealing with colour-hoisting parade, and a guard, and Wing Commander Jago's sermon about Queen Alexandra . . . There are only a few hundred words, in all, I think.' He asked her to copy these for him so that they could be included. Another chapter was to be based on an article he had written at Cranwell about racing an aeroplane on his Brough motorcycle. Months before, he had sent the article, anonymously, to a motorcycling magazine, and to his chagrin it had been rejected.

By this time he had settled down fairly comfortably at Karachi. He found it a 'good place in which to mark time, for the food is good, and there is no attempt to control our deportment in camp . . . I have found a sheltered occupation, which delivers me from working parade, first thing in the morning, and from most of the ceremonials.' He had even improvised a water-heating system using a fifteen-gallon drum and a blow lamp, so that he could take hot baths every day.

Friends were sending books out to India regularly, and Lawrence lent them freely to the other men. That autumn he wrote to Charlotte Shaw: 'Very special things I can keep, under lock and key, in my box. The rank and file have to stand out on a wall-shelf, beyond my bed. We have all things in common, you know, in our life. So it is as if there was an invisible notice on the wall ''Please take one''. All the book-hungry men (hungry for more than the fiction library can give them) slide quietly in and out of my end of the room, borrowing or returning. We are rough, and dirty handed, so that some of the volumes are nearly read to death. You can tell the pet ones, by their shabbiness. I suppose I have had 150 in all, here: of which nearly two-thirds are from you. Of them perhaps fifty are now on loan: I have just counted the survivors—eighty-eight— including many of my pet things. Spenser, and Malory and Morris do not go out much. Though a Glasgow marine-boiler expert, who has read only the *Scientific Engineer* since he came to our room, and scowls drunkenly at the rest of us, took up the *Well at the World's End* once, and read it for nearly six weeks, millimetre by millimetre. It made him beam at me with happiness. Reminded him, he said, of Glasgow. Upon no other reader, probably, has it had that effect.' Lawrence enjoyed recommending books to the airmen: 'They would read, avidly, anything in their reach. Only there are no guides for them, to books: and so many books . . . Everybody reads rubbish when he is tired, and isolated in camp: it would be an insult to give a good book only the dregs of our attention. So magazines and shockers are read: but my little library of queer books is almost as much used as the thousand-volume fiction library which the H.Q. maintains. It's because I tell 'em about books, and make them see them, as they reflect us.'

There were many people who thought Lawrence's talents were wasted in the ranks, especially after the completion of *Seven Pillars* and the success of *Revolt in the Desert*. For the first time since 1923, he was in a position to earn a large amount of money if he chose. During 1927 he received several proposals for well-paid work. In November, for example, he was offered $100,000 for a seven-week lecture tour in the United States, and a month later an American offered him £5,000 (enough capital for him to retire on) for one of the five surviving 'Oxford' copies of *Seven Pillars*. But his only stated ambition, after completing his years in the ranks, was to take a night-watchman's job in London. From time to time he reminded his friends of this: 'Don't forget I rely on someone to recommend me as bachelor-night-caretaker of a block of city offices or buildings in

1935: it is March 1935 which sees my sorrowful departure from the
R.A.F.'

On November 9, he received a telegram from Buxton telling him that
D. G. Hogarth had died. He was deeply saddened by the news: 'the
background of my life before I enlisted has gone. Hogarth sponsored my
first tramps in Syria—then put me on the staff for Carchemish, which
was a golden place—then moved me to Sinai, which led to the War
Office: which sent me to Cairo on the Staff: and there we worked together
on the Arab business, until the War ended: and since then whenever I was
in a dangerous position I used to make up my mind after coming away
from his advice. He was very wise for others, and very understanding,
and comfortable, for he knew all the world's vices and tricks and shifts
and evasions and pretexts, and was kindly towards them all. If I might so
put it, he had no knowledge of evil: because everything to him was fit to
be looked at, or to touch. Yet he had his own position and principles, and
was unmoveable on them. Till I joined up he did everything for me. It
was the first thing I did entirely on my own. So lately I have seen little
of him: but I always felt that if ever I went back to living I'd be able to
link up with him again.'

During November and December, in the aftermath of Hogarth's death,
Lawrence made little progress with the Uxbridge notes. He seems, however, to have decided on a title for them during this period, since they are
referred to as *The Mint* in a letter to Edward Garnett written on November
30. The title was meant to convey the way in which raw recruits were
transformed at Uxbridge into airmen. Lawrence later told Trenchard that
he had called the notes *The Mint,* 'because we were all being stamped
after your image and superscription.'

Unknown to Lawrence, another literary proposal was taking shape. Its
origins lay in the set of *Seven Pillars* proofs which he had sent to Doran
in New York eighteen months previously to serve as a text for typesetting
the US copyright edition. When the American printing had been completed, Doran passed the English proofs to a friend, who in turn gave
them to Bruce Rogers.

Rogers was one of the world's outstanding typographers. He was almost as well known in England as in America, since he had been for a
time printing adviser to the Cambridge University Press. In 1927 he was
working independently, and had been commissioned by Random House
to design and print a fine edition of any important book he chose. After
some thought he had decided on Homer's *Odyssey*.

At first, as he later explained to Lawrence, he had thought of using one of the established translations, then, 'it suddenly came to me that if the swing and go of your English in the *Seven Pillars* which held me to it when I was not specially interested in some of your expeditions, could be applied to the *Odyssey*, we would get a version that would out-distance any existing translations.'

Rogers had never met Lawrence, but approached him through a mutual acquaintance, Ralph Isham. The latter wrote to Lawrence: 'You will be glad to know that it is not your name they want but your translation. They are willing either to give the name you now use, as translator, or to give no name at all, whichever you wish. I do not know how you are at Greek but I thought this scheme might just fit into your present scheme of things and the honorarium of £800 is not to be grown on every tree in India.'

The offer was extremely attractive to Lawrence: he knew the *Odyssey* well, and had the Greek text with him. His work on *The Mint* was nearly complete, and for some time he had been thinking of taking on a new translation project. The *Odyssey* was not just an ephemeral novel like *The Forest Giant* and *Sturly*: it was one of the world's great works of literature, and the task would be worthy of all the effort he could give. He replied to Isham on January 2: 'When your letter came, I took the *Odyssey* down from the shelf, (it goes with me, always, to every camp, for I love it) and tried to see myself translating it, freely, into English. Honestly, it would be most difficult to do. I have the rhythm of the Greek so in my mind, that it would not come readily into straight English. Nor am I a scholar; I read it only for pleasure, and have to keep a dictionary within reach. I thought of the other translators, and agreed that there was not a first-rate one. Butcher and Lang . . . too antique. Samuel Butler . . . too little dignified, tho' better. Morris . . . too literary. That only shows the job it is. Why should my doing be any better than these efforts of the bigger men?'

He was delighted at the chance to work with Bruce Rogers, whose 'dressing of the book will make it glorious, so that even an inferior version would pass muster . . . I have for years admired him from ground level; and have even been able at intervals to buy books of his production'. He concluded: 'let me make stiff terms, in the hope of being refused an honour which I feel too great for me to carry off successfully. I cannot refuse so profitable an offer bluntly.

'1. I should need two years in which to complete the translation, after I began work on it.

'2. I do not feel capable of doing it as well as Homer would have liked; and shall feel unhappy if it turns out botched.

'3. I could not sign it with any one of my hitherto names. It must go out blank, or with a virgin name on it.

'4. I would do the first book, within six months of having concluded the agreement with the publishers; and if they were not satisfied with it, I would agree to let the contract go, upon their paying me the fraction of £800 which the first book bears to the whole . . .

'My strongest advice to you is to get someone better, to do you a more certain performance'.

By the end of January Lawrence was about two-thirds of the way through the *The Mint*. As with *Seven Pillars*, he was now finding it difficult to recapture the spirit of his original draft: 'These are painful chapters. I wonder how I came to write them. They are so much too emotional for my present mind.' A fortnight later the typescript of the middle section had been finished, and the final chapters were taking shape. He aimed to have the book completed by the end of March. His letters show that he was now thinking increasingly of the *Odyssey*. For example, on February 25 he wrote: 'Translating Homer is playing with words, which, as you know, have always fascinated me: playing with them like a child with bricks . . . Meanwhile the old *Mint* staggers on. I think it has a certain historical interest, as the document of a recruit of 1922. The R.A.F. makes documents for every one of its airmen: I have made a document for it: only it might not say thank you! Still, even that's only fair, for we don't thank it for ours: they're mostly records of the poor little faults it calls "crimes". I hope, though, that something of my feeling for the R.A.F. will carry across the mass of contrary examples in which I seem to dissemble my love!'

The notes were completed on the evening of March 14, and he wrote to Charlotte Shaw two days later: 'I have looked back through the book: I sat up very late last night, trying to judge it: and found it good prose. It is monotonous. So is life in the R.A.F. Monotony in life is good: in books apparently bad . . . Anyway I have successfully made this unprintable. The people are all real, though the names are not: or only a few of the names'.

He intended to present the *Mint* manuscript to Edward Garnett, who had encouraged him with the project since its beginning. He now wrote: 'I wonder what Garnett will do with the book. It is an embarrassing gift, surely? When he asked me for it, in 1922, I was nobody: and he didn't think it was as big a thing as this. He will get a shock.'

When *The Mint* reached England, Trenchard had agreed to read it, although he had considerable misgivings about its content: 'I feel rather that what you have probably written is what is quite comprehensible to you and to me as we both understand the position, but it would be seized upon immediately by the Press *if they got hold of it*, and they would say what a hopeless Air Force it was—how badly it was run—what hopeless officers we had, etc., when I know that is not what you mean at all, *though I have not seen what* you have written. I am certain you will believe that this is the sort of thing the Press will do *if what* you have written is ever published.

'And the Air Force is still young. It cannot go on continually being abused by everybody, and I have enough of it as it is regarding accidents and one thing and another.

'I do not feel a bit annoyed with you. I feel I always thought you would do it, though I hoped you would not. Anyhow, I am going to see Garnett when I can, and I hope he will not publish it or let it be published'.

Lawrence instructed Garnett to offer the book to Cape for publication 'without one word excised or moderated. Can you, as his reader, arrange this? I'd rather no one read it but you (and David Garnett . . .): and I want him to refuse it, so as to free me from the clause in his contract of the *Revolt in the Desert*, tying me to offer him another book. I hate being bound by even an imaginary obligation.' To make absolutely sure that Cape would refuse, Lawrence demanded an advance on royalties of one million pounds.

On April 12 Bernard Shaw wrote about *The Mint*, making little attempt to hide his distaste for the book: 'As it cannot be published as a work of literary art (except possibly by Werner Laurie in a three guinea subscription edition as pure bawdry) the only thing to be considered is how and where to place it on record and to secure it from destruction . . . This being done, everything will be done that you could possibly have contemplated when you did the job; and you may dismiss it from your mind and go on to something else . . . Still, though you are wobbling between your conceptions of the thing as a verbatim report for the archives and a work of art, I think you had better discard the latter unless you are prepared to rewrite a good deal of it with humour enough to make it bearable and decency enough to make it presentable'. Shaw suggested various ways of preserving the text for the historical record, but his letter showed clearly that Lawrence's unvarnished description of life in the ranks had run up against a streak of prudishness in his character.

Garnett had no such reservations. When he first read the manuscript he

cabled Lawrence that it was 'a classic'. He followed this with an enthusiastic letter: 'Well, you've gone and done it this time! And knocked all
your feeble pretences of not being a writer, etc. etc. into final smithereens
. . . It is a most *perfect* piece of writing. I call it a *classic*, for there's not
a word too much. It's elastic, sinewy, terse: and spirit and matter are the
inside-out of its technique, perfectly harmonious throughout—
inseparable, as in all first-rate stuff. It's very original in its effect, for
having given us the essential in its living body, it smites one much harder
than if you had made "a book" of it, or told us more . . . the descriptions
of the men . . . are wonderfully drawn, mere thumbnail sketches, with
the lines bitten in with a marked precision. Then, the atmosphere that
grows more hard and bitter and north-easterly as the men get branded, or
"minted" in the struggle. There's nothing like it in the least in English:
there may be in French? . . . The *book has a perfect spiritual balance*.
For a *book* it is. One has no feeling of "notes" at all. The "lubricant"
you have added, does right away with any scrappiness. It all flows, one
out of another perfectly'. Fearful that Trenchard might destroy the *Mint*
manuscript after reading it, Garnett arranged to have typescript copies
made.

On April 19, or shortly before, Lawrence abruptly decided to apply for
transfer to another camp. He wrote to Sir Geoffrey Salmond, the AOC in
India, asking to be sent up-country, perhaps to Peshawar on the North-
West Frontier. A week later he explained the request in a private letter to
Trenchard: 'Nothing has gone wrong yet: but since you are far away, and
not entitled to do anything I'll tell you why. A conversation between an
officer and a civilian in a club after dinner was improperly repeated to me.
The officer has never spoken to me. Our section officers—there have been
six in all in E.R.S. in the sixteen months—have been very decent to me.
I think I deserve it, for I work hard, and intelligently.

'However this one is reported to have sworn he "had me taped" and
was "laying to jump on me" when he got the chance. It was after dinner.
They had all dined. I have no means, or wish, to check the story.

'But I'm pretty tired of fighting, and of risks: and my past makes my
service character brittle. People easily believe ill of a man who has been
an unconventional officer . . . and now prefers not to be an officer. So
I'm going to run away to a squadron. They are small, and officers mix
with airmen, and aren't so likely to misjudge a fellow. I told Salmond I
had private reasons.

'Don't think me a funk. At worst it's only over-caution.'

In reality, Lawrence had good reason to be alarmed by what he had heard, even though he was uncertain whether to take it seriously. The person involved, whose identity he did not reveal either to Salmond or to Trenchard, was apparently the station Commanding Officer.

He was moved from Karachi to Peshawar on May 26. Two days later he was sent to Miranshah, an outpost in Waziristan near the Afghan border, seventy miles to the south-west. The RAF detachment he joined was the smallest in India: 'We are only twenty-six, all told, with five officers, and we sit with seven hundred India Scouts (half-regulars) in a brick and earth fort behind barbed wire complete with searchlights and machine guns. Round us, a few miles off, in a ring are low bare porcelain-coloured hills, with chipped edges and a broken-bottle skyline. Afghanistan is ten miles off. The quietness of the place is uncanny—ominous, I was nearly saying: for the Scouts and ourselves live in different compartments of the fort, and never meet: and so there's no noise of men: and no birds or beasts— except a jackal concert for five minutes about 10 p.m. each night, when the searchlights start. The India sentries flicker the beams across the plain, hoping to make them flash in the animals' eyes. So sometimes we see them.

'We are not allowed beyond the barbed wire, by day, or outside the fort walls, by night. So the only temptations of Miranshah are boredom and idleness. I hope to escape the first, and enjoy the second: for, between ourselves, I did a lot of work at Karachi, and am dead tired.

'Here they employ me mainly in the office. I am the only airman who can work a typewriter, so I do Daily Routine Orders and correspondence: and act postman, and pay clerk, and bottle-washer in ordinary. Normally flights do two months here, and get relieved: but I will try and get left on. It's the station of a dream: as though one had fallen right over the world, and had lost one's memory of its troubles. And the quietness is so intense that I rub my ears, wondering if I am going deaf.'

The reduction in Lawrence's RAF workload was very welcome. When he left Karachi, two men working the standard five and a half hour day were needed to replace him. He was now a proficient typist, and his reputation for handling routine correspondence and administration meant that he was posted to the office as soon as he reached Miranshah.

Lawrence used his extra time to begin working on a specimen section of the *Odyssey* for Bruce Rogers. The sample was to be Book I (there are twenty-four Books in all) which he hoped to finish by the end of July. It would take him five drafts to reach a satisfactory working text, and he planned a final revision when the Book was completed. The calm at

Miranshah was a perfect setting for this kind of work, and Charlotte Shaw helped by sending him a selection of *Odyssey* translations.

Progress with the sample was quicker than he had expected, and he sent the completed Book I off to Ralph Isham on June 30. He assured Isham that he would not be offended if the specimen were rejected, even though it had been hard work: 'Only the unusual size of the translation fee would reconcile me to doing twenty-four Books like this: and I shall, on the whole, be glad if they call it not good enough. Homer is a very great and exacting leader.' The slow postal services between India and the United States meant that it would be at least two months before Lawrence had news of the publishers' decision.

At Miranshah he had found a new contentment, and for the present, no other life seemed as attractive. He decided to extend his stay in the RAF for as long as possible. His seven-year period of enlistment was calculated from the date he had joined the Tank Corps, 12 March 1923, rather than his transfer to the RAF in 1925. He could therefore expect to be discharged on 12 March 1930. It would be possible, however, to extend his service by a further five years, and he decided to do so.

In the first week of September he at last heard about the specimen Book of the *Odyssey*. Isham wrote: 'I am very enthusiastic over your translation as are also the publishers and I am afraid that there is little chance of your getting out of this job of work through any hope that you may have entertained that the answer would be "no".' Although arrangements for publication had yet to be settled, Isham asked Lawrence to go ahead, offering his personal guarantee that the terms of the contract would be satisfactory. The scheme was that Rogers would print a limited de luxe edition, to be followed by general trade publication for which Lawrence would receive additional royalties over and above the initial £800 fee.

Isham enclosed a £35 cheque for the sample, and also an American newspaper article which claimed that Lawrence was engaged in covert diplomacy: 'Disguised in Arab garb, but known to every chieftain in the desert plains and hills between the Suez Canal and the Afghanistan frontier, the former Colonel Lawrence is continuing his peregrinations in the Middle East.' Such reports were common and often originated in the French press, which habitually presented Lawrence as a secret agent working to undermine French imperial ambitions. For example, it had been claimed a few years previously that Lawrence was trouble-making in Morocco during the Riff rebellion there.

In India, the press had already referred to the fact that Lawrence was serving on the North-West Frontier. This presented sensational journalists with a golden opportunity, and on September 26, under a four-decker headline, the London *Evening News* published a fantastic account of his activities:

'LAWRENCE OF ARABIA'S SECRET MISSION.
COUNTERING RED ACTIVITIES IN THE PUNJAB.
POSE AS A SAINT.
WARDING OFF THE EVIL EYE AND CURING ILLNESS.

Evening News Telegram.   BOMBAY, Wednesday

'Lawrence of Arabia—one time of Oxford University, then the "Uncrowned King of the Arabian Desert" and a Colonel in the British Army, next a plain mechanic in the R.A.F., in which he enlisted in 1922 for a term of seven years as Aircraftman Shaw—has undertaken a new job now.

'Like most of the jobs that Lawrence has undertaken in his picturesque life, it is an out-of-the-ordinary one.

'He is, according to messages from Lahore, moving about the Punjab in disguise studying the activities of Bolshevist agents, whose secret headquarters are said to be in Amritsar. It has long been known that the Bolshevists have an eye—a very wide-open eye—on India.

'Lawrence's present home is in a queer house in a remote street in Amritsar. It is luxuriously furnished, and women in quest of wonder-working charms are among his frequent visitors. They bring their babies to him to ward off the Evil Eye; they ask his advice in the curing of illness.

'Lawrence poses as a great Pir (Mohammedan saint or spiritual guide) who has visited many Moslem lands and the tombs of all the great saints. The native gossips say that he is such a religious man that he is always recounting his own deeds.

'It is so unlike Lawrence to "recount his own deeds" that of a certainty he must have some hidden purpose in doing so.'

The article was so patently absurd that it could cause little harm; indeed it provoked letters to newspapers from people knowledgeable about India pointing out that 'spying in Amritsar is valueless. There is nothing to spy on.' Nevertheless, it was repeated in America and elsewhere. Rival popular newspapers were keen to pick up the story, and four days later the fiction was given a new twist by the *Sunday Express* under the headline 'LAWRENCE OF ARABIA'S SECRET AFGHAN MISSION'. It was claimed that: 'The everlasting mystery of the movements of Colonel T. E. Lawrence

. . . was deepened last night by a statement circulating in well-informed quarters in London that he is engaged on a secret mission in Afghanistan attempting to facilitate the negotiation of a treaty between Great Britain and that country.

'Earlier in the week it was reported that Colonel Lawrence was in Amritsar, posing as a Mohammedan saint, and investigating Communist activities in the district . . .

'It is, in fact, confidently asserted that this Colonel Lawrence, the romantic figure who gathered the wandering tribes of the Arabian desert and led them against the Turks, is in Afghanistan studying Afghan life for the British Government . . . Colonel Lawrence, it is explained, is making an intimate study of the views of the hillmen, the merchants, and the peasants. He is living with them, concealed beneath a mocha stain and the turban and robes he knows so well.' The article ran on in the same vein, exploring the possible implications of Lawrence's supposed new role. It too was repeated in American newspapers, but no further evidence was produced, and the story seemed to die.

Since these allegations involved British government policy, they were noted in the India Office, and in the ensuing weeks the *Sunday Express* claims were the subject of a series of exchanges between the India Office, the Foreign Office, and the British Minister in Kabul, Sir Francis Humphrys.

The rumours would not die and the question of Lawrence's activities was even taken up by *Pravda*, which commented: 'The appearance of Colonel Lawrence in any Mussulman country always marks a new British Imperialist intrigue and provocation.' A few days later, an India Office official minuted: 'It would not be a bad thing if this Aircraftman could be found employment in the R.A.F. elsewhere than on the N.W. Frontier.'

By now there was a rebellion in Afghanistan which had become an international news story. It was clear that a firm response would be needed if allegations about Lawrence's involvement in this uprising were not to be a diplomatic embarrassment. A semi-official *démenti* in strong terms was published in India, where all the rumours were originating, and on December 14 Sir Francis Humphrys was authorised to deny categorically that Lawrence had ever been in Afghanistan. By now, however, circulation of the story was beyond control. On December 16, the *Empire News*, a thoroughly sensational newspaper based in Manchester, published the confirmation of Lawrence's presence in Afghanistan which the world's press had been waiting for. It appeared in a long report purportedly based on information provided by Dr Francis Havelock, 'the well-known medical missionary who has just returned from the wild Afghan hills'. The article stated that Havelock had encountered in Afghanistan both Lawrence ('the most mysterious man in the Empire . . . the ultimate pro-Consul of Britain in the East') and Trebitsch Lincoln ('ex-spy, ex-British M.P., ex-forger, the tool of the Soviet Government in China'). The article was wholly fiction, but its substance was repeated on December 27 by a press agency, the Free Press Mail Service, and distributed throughout the world. It was claimed that Lawrence and Lincoln were fighting on opposing sides in Afghanistan: 'The battle is now joined between the Apostle of Hatred and the Apostle of Peace. Lincoln has gold and rifles. Hillmen love both. Lawrence has unknown resources and a silver tongue'.

For a while, Lawrence remained unaware of the growing storm. By late December he had completed Books I–III of the *Odyssey*. After reading them through, on Christmas Day, he wrote to Emery Walker: 'I have spent five hundred hours over these fourteen thousand words, and have reached a sort of finality—arriving at that negation of improvement, when after a cycle of alternatives one returns to the original word.' He started work on Book IV on Boxing Day, hoping to be able to maintain his pace and finish Book VI by the end of March.

However, his tranquil existence at Miranshah now came to an abrupt end. On 3 January 1929, Sir Francis Humphrys cabled to Delhi and London pointing out that the increasing speculation about Lawrence's activities appearing in the Indian press was being repeated in Afghanistan, where suspicions about covert British support for the Shinwari rebellion were 'naturally encouraged by Russian and Turkish Ambassadors and, I am told, even by my French colleague . . . Contradiction of this nonsense will no longer produce the desired effect, and I should be relieved of much embarrassment if Lawrence could be transferred to a place distant from the frontier until the civil war in Afghanistan subsides.'

On January 8, Lawrence was flown from Miranshah to Lahore. His disgust at this latest press fantasy was tempered by pleasure: it had given him the chance to cut short a five-year posting overseas. He was put on board a passenger liner, the SS *Rajputana*, which sailed for England on January 12. By this time allegations and denials of his role in Afghanistan were appearing almost daily in the world's press.

CHAPTER 24

Plymouth
January 1929–February 1931

LAWRENCE spent the voyage home working on the *Odyssey*, and was able to translate three more Books. The Air Ministry, knowing that the press would try to interview him as soon as he reached England, decided to take him off the ship when she put in at Plymouth on February 2, before reaching her final destination at Gravesend.

He was met by Wing Commander Sydney Smith, whom he had first met in very different circumstances during the Cairo Conference of 1921. Smith's attempts to keep Lawrence's whereabouts secret failed at almost every step. As soon as they boarded the London train they were recognised, and by the time it reached Paddington a crowd of journalists was waiting, and there was a farcical chase in taxis, which lasted nearly an hour. Despite this, the journalists were disappointed.

By this time, the confusion about Lawrence's activities had spread to the House of Commons. Ernest Thurtle, Labour MP for Shoreditch, had asked a question about Lawrence's enlistment under a false name. More Parliamentary questions followed, and there seemed little prospect that the issue would die down. Lawrence, who could foresee the likely consequences, decided to tackle Thurtle personally. He therefore visited the House of Commons and explained himself to Thurtle and other Labour MPs.

Lawrence was now told that he would be posted to Sydney Smith's station, RAF Cattewater, at Plymouth. First, however, he was due for a month's leave, which he planned to spend visiting old friends. The problem of transport was resolved when he received a letter informing him that a new Brough SS-100 was waiting for collection, paid for anonymously.

The motorcycle was very welcome as it would enable him to travel, yet he deeply resented the idea of accepting such an expensive present. Although he could easily have earned a substantial income, he had chosen to live in poverty, and a gift of this size seemed to be charity which he had no right to accept. He guessed correctly that Charlotte Shaw was behind the scheme. For more than five years she had been showering him with expensive presents, and he saw that the Brough would put him under a still deeper obligation. He made up his mind to refuse it.

The anonymous donors had named Buxton as their spokesman, and on February 6 Lawrence went to see him. As it happened, there was enough money in Lawrence's bank account to pay for it. However, he was also planning to complete the purchase of Clouds Hill. If he used his reserve for the Brough, he would probably need to borrow money for the cottage. Buxton offered to provide an overdraft for Clouds Hill, and the question of accepting the motorcycle as a gift was dropped.

While in London he made several visits to the Shaws, and met Bruce Rogers for the first time. On his way down to Plymouth he called in to see Clouds Hill again, finding it 'as lovely as ever'. That day, he paid the balance of the purchase price, £350.

RAF Cattewater was to be one of the most enjoyable of Lawrence's postings. The station itself was small and isolated. He wrote to H. S. Ede: 'Cattewater proves to be about 100 airmen, pressed tightly on a rock half-awash in the Sound; a peninsula really, like a fossil lizard swimming from Mount Batten golf-links across the harbour towards Plymouth town. The sea is thirty yards from our hut one way, and seventy yards the other. The Camp officers are peaceful, it seems, and the airmen reasonably happy. That is good hearing for me, as I am to share their good fortune.'

The original military base at Cattewater had been closed down shortly after the Great War, and Sydney Smith had now been sent there to reopen it as a seaplane station. Lawrence was attached to the headquarters section, and during the first weeks his duties were mainly clerical. His experience as clerk to the Engine Repair Section at Karachi proved valuable in setting up the new station workshops. When not in the office, he served as crewman in one of the motorboats used as tenders to ferry personnel round the seaplane anchorage.

There was much less free time at Cattewater than in India. Weekend leave was from 1 p.m. on Saturday until midnight on Sunday. This made it impractical to visit friends in London. One compensation was friendship with his CO. As Sydney Smith already knew and liked Lawrence, he was able, in private, to set aside the formal relationship between a Wing Commander and an A/c 1. Smith's work was very demanding, and he saw in Lawrence a highly capable and trustworthy assistant. He therefore delegated to Lawrence work that was well beyond the level of responsibility normally accorded to an aircraftman. Moreover, Lawrence frequently visited the Smiths' house, and soon became a close family friend.

This unusual state of affairs attracted much less attention in the small headquarters section than it would have done in a squadron, and the friendship made a great deal of difference to Lawrence's life at Cattewater.

Apart from his station duties, Smith had been nominated by the RAF as its representative on the Royal Aero Club committee set up to organise the international Schneider Trophy seaplane race. The competition was scheduled to take place over the Solent early in September. Smith took Lawrence as his personal assistant for this work, and during April both men became engaged in what proved to be a major administrative task. Lawrence attended meetings in London and elsewhere and had to draft countless letters and minutes.

In his role as clerk to the marine and workshop section, he was soon given an attic office of his own. Although there was little free time, he managed to rough out Books VII and VIII of the *Odyssey* during March and April. He planned to get them to Emery Walker by the end of that month.

On April 13, however, his growing contentment was disturbed by a hostile piece in the popular weekly magazine *John Bull*, which alleged that he was 'not much troubled with duties, but divides his time between "special leaves of absence" in London, tinkering with a "super sports" motor-bicycle and literary work. The last takes the form of translating Homer's *Odyssey* into English'. This was the first time that he had been subjected to such belittling treatment at the hands of the British press, and he was hurt by it. After a second article in the same vein he wrote to a service friend: 'as for choking off the Press—he will be my friend for life who finds how to do that. I do nothing—and they talk. I do something—and they talk. Now I am trying to accustom myself to the truth that probably I'll be talked over for the rest of my life: and after my life, too'.

The renewed publicity left him in no mood to apply himself to the *Odyssey*, and on May 1 he wrote about the situation to Bruce Rogers: 'Today I had meant to send you Books VII and VIII: instead of which I must tell you of my worries. It's been published (in *John Bull*, of all the world's press!) that I'm doing an *Odyssey*: and since that day I haven't done a stroke . . . I had not expected this trouble, before publication: *After*, yes: but somehow that didn't matter. You'll realise, I hope, that I can't carry on as it is.

'Will you see Walker and Merton, and present them the difficulties as they stand? I want to be as reasonable and helpful as possible, and only hope that their more sober experiences may find a road out of what seems, to me, rather a deep hole.'

This letter, which contained a broad hint that Lawrence might abandon the translation, was hardly fair. During the preceding months he had described the project openly to friends in the English literary world, many of whom had links with the press. The fact that the author of *Seven Pillars* was now working on the *Odyssey* must by this time have been common literary gossip, and wider publicity was therefore inevitable. Lawrence had been warned by Bruce Rogers at the outset that anonymity could only be preserved if everyone concerned took great care, and he must surely have realised that he himself had probably been responsible for letting the news out. However, by this time other factors were involved in his reaction. One of the most important was the knowledge that further press comment might lead to his dismissal from the RAF.

Bruce Rogers drafted a careful reply, discussing the problems he himself had experienced with the press. He also emphasised that people other than himself were involved in the scheme: 'I have given your letter to Walker and Merton to read and they were both tremendously upset by it.' Substantial sums had already been spent on typesetting and special paper. He concluded: 'I think we shall have to go on, somehow. If you cannot produce any more at present, let it rest for a time. We have already enough copy to go on with for some time, and my own part of the work is far behind its schedule . . . These rumours will not persist . . . and they will be forgotten before the book appears.'

Lawrence's reply suggests that another reason for his attempt to drop the translation may have been his increasing RAF workload. He wrote: 'I understand, and shall complete the translation as well as I can do it, and (if possible) by April next year. Only they put extra jobs on me here, one after the other, and so I have little spare time. I have not done anything since I wrote you that letter trying to get off the job.'

As the Schneider Trophy approached, Lawrence became busier and busier, and in the early summer his letters often spoke of tiredness. At the end of July, he wrote to Bruce Rogers explaining that the *Odyssey* had been held up by preparations for the race, and that his time was wholly committed until mid-September.

The Schneider Trophy was the world's premier air race and received international attention. The speed record had been broken in every preceding Schneider contest.

The rules required a race over at least 150 nautical miles. That year, the competitors took off in succession to fly seven laps round a fifty-kilometre diamond-shaped course in the Solent, starting, and finishing, off Ryde on the Isle of Wight. Although four nations had entered, the French and American teams had been withdrawn, and only Britain and Italy competed. The trophy was won, for the second time in succession, by a British machine.

In the organisation of this famous event, the reputation of the Royal Aero Club was at stake. Smith and Lawrence played a central role during the final preparations at Calshot and on the yacht *Karen* that was used as race headquarters. Lawrence later wrote that 'the actual days and nights at Calshot were unmixed work. I hardly slept, and do not remember eating much'. To everyone's relief, however, the event passed off without a hitch.

The *Karen* had been lent by Major Colin Cooper. One of its tenders, used on ferry duty during the contest, was a Biscayne Baby speedboat built in America by the Purdy Boat Company. This should have been capable of 45 knots, but the 100hp engine needed attention. Lawrence, who had greatly enjoyed driving the boat, offered to give it an overhaul, and was surprised when Major Cooper decided to make a present of it, jointly to Lawrence and Sydney Smith. They renamed it the *Biscuit*.

Lawrence's presence at the contest had involved some risk of publicity, but the accredited press had been told not to photograph him, and neither pictures nor stories were published in British newspapers. Unfortunately, this was not enough to satisfy Lord Thomson. While visiting Calshot he spotted Lawrence acting in a supervisory role and talking to visiting VIPs. Thomson, who had been a high-ranking army officer before and during the war, was vehemently opposed to Lawrence's presence in the ranks. They met briefly during the contest, and the encounter seems to have left Thomson with a strong desire to rid the Air Force of this unconventional serviceman. Lawrence returned to Plymouth with uneasy premonitions, and a week later these were confirmed. Trenchard wrote asking to see him.

As he had feared, he was told that his future in the RAF was again in doubt, and he called on influential friends in London, asking them to take up his case. One of these was Sir Robert Vansittart, now private secretary to the Prime Minister. Vansittart did not like Lawrence very much, but he knew that they were second cousins (on Lawrence's father's side), and he offered to put in a good word. Another acquaintance with useful contacts was Captain B. H. Liddell Hart, the military historian and strategist, whose correspondence with Lawrence had begun in 1927 over a contribution to the *Encyclopaedia Britannica*. As military correspondent of the *Daily Telegraph*, Liddell Hart was well placed to talk discreetly with high-ranking officials in Whitehall.

On September 30, Lawrence was told by Trenchard that he would be reprieved, but there were conditions: in future his employment in the RAF was not to go beyond the duties of an aircraftman; he was not to leave the United Kingdom, and he was not to visit or speak to any of the 'great', notably opposition politicians such as Winston Churchill and Lady Astor. Lawrence was pleased to learn that the ban did not extend to Bernard Shaw; but apparently Shaw, when he heard of this, felt rather slighted. For the second time that year, Lawrence had narrowly avoided dismissal from the ranks. He was entitled to a long leave and he decided to stay in London for nearly seven weeks, working for much of the time in Barton Street on the *Odyssey*.

During a visit to Liddell Hart, he learned that Jonathan Cape had suggested that there was room for another biography about him. Liddell Hart asked Lawrence what his reaction would be, emphasising his own interest in the military history of the Revolt. As Lawrence did not condemn the project outright, Liddell Hart wrote to him the following day asking whether he would be prepared to help with such a biography. This time, Lawrence's reply was unenthusiastic, and in particular he argued that a new book would increase his difficulties with the RAF. He offered nevertheless to point out errors. Liddell Hart must have been discouraged by this response, because he shelved the project for three years.

By this time, Lawrence was beginning to look ahead to 1935, when his term of enlistment would end. He had recently decided to sell his land at Pole Hill, near Chingford, as Vyvyan Richards had moved to a new job in Wales. If the capital which Pole Hill represented was invested, it might produce enough income to live on.

The land would have been worth about £7,000 if sold to a builder, but Lawrence had always hoped that it would one day become part of Epping Forest, which it adjoined. He had offered it to the Forest for the £4,000 he had spent on it, and the purchase had now been agreed in principle.

On the way back to Plymouth at the end of his leave, he called at Clouds Hill. With money in prospect, he had begun to think of improvements to the cottage, and he asked a local firm to draw up plans for a two-room extension: 'A new wing will not harm either the smallness or the quietude of Clouds Hill, or its simplicity.'

That winter he settled down to finish the *Odyssey*. As with *The Forest Giant* six years earlier, he found that the effort to make a good translation gave him unexpected insights into the original text. Satisfaction with his work was therefore tempered by what he felt were shortcomings in the Greek: 'what a set of worms the ancient Greeks paint themselves to be. In my version I underline all strong words, and fade away the weakness, so that my translation will be not so much a copy as an intensification, dramatically. I try to make the poor yarn take up its bric-à-brac and walk . . .

'I have got into a rhythm in the work. The fair copy represents the fourth writing, and is the fourteenth revision; by and large I do five lines an hour, if you take the length of a book, and the total hours I have spent before the fair copy is ended . . . During the last three or four working weeks I have got in forty hours each week on *Odyssey*, and done my forty-eight R.A.F. hours too'.

He was so busy with the translation that he hardly noticed the effect of Lord Thomson's restrictions. In any case, after two years in India he was happy just to be back in England. That spring, he had written: 'There is something about southern England which makes me, in every valley, on every ridge, say "Oh, I want to have a room here, and sit in it looking and looking!" '

During the next few months he continued to give most of his spare time to the *Odyssey*. The project was viewed without enthusiasm by his literary friends, who thought that he should write something new of his own. Embarrassed, he frequently told them that the translation was only a pot-boiler, undertaken to raise cash. Letters to Charlotte Shaw and Bruce Rogers, however, show the immense care he took over it. Many previous translators had tried to capture the spirit of the *Odyssey* in English but, as he worked on through the text, he felt increasingly that they had failed. For the time being his ambition was to create a new and better rendering.

He had found little time for reading during these months, although he usually liked to follow the work of contemporary novelists. At the end of January 1930, however, he had to spend three days on RAF business in London, and while there he bought a copy of *Her Privates We*, a novel about life in the trenches on the Western Front published under the pseudonym 'Private 19022'. He was fascinated by the book: '*Her Privates We* knocked me all of a heap with delight. It's the true and honourable thing, so far as the "other ranks" are concerned. I never thought to see it. That's what my little *Mint* should have been and wasn't.' He thought he recognised the writing style and, aided by a hint from a bookselling friend, guessed that the author was Frederic Manning. This was confirmed in a telephone conversation with Peter Davies, the book's publisher.

Lawrence wrote enthusiastically to Manning, and as a result they became friends. He liked Peter Davies too, and allowed publication of a leaflet quoting his praise of *Her Privates We*; he also lent both of them a typescript of *The Mint*.

One of the reasons Lawrence had chosen life in the ranks was because it offered security, but it could not protect him from financial troubles. Having used up his bank balance, a year earlier, to pay for the Brough motorcycle, he had been obliged to borrow in order to pay for Clouds Hill. He had expected that this expense, together with others that had followed, would be covered by the sale of Pole Hill; but the Epping Forest authorities had postponed the purchase, and although five months had passed, no end to the delay seemed in sight. His overdraft was now £6oo, and increasing steadily through accumulated interest charges. His morale seems to have suffered badly, as it had done in 1925 when he ran into difficulties over the production cost of *Seven Pillars*. The anxiety showed in many ways, but most obviously in a reluctance to leave camp. Whenever he did so, he spent money he now needed to save. Knowledge that he was famous and could easily earn all the money he needed should have been a comfort, but instead it was an irritation. He wrote bitterly to Jonathan Cape: 'Gods, I have written twenty letters this week. At £20 each [their value to collectors at that time], that's £400 I've given away: not to speak of the labour in vain'.

His public reputation remained an embarrassment, as when, for example, he received a letter from the University of St Andrews offering him an honorary doctorate. At first he thought the proposal was a student hoax, and he returned it with a none-too-formal rejection.Then a second letter arrived, this time from J. M. Barrie, Lord Rector of St Andrews. Lawrence realised that his first response had been a gaffe, and made his apologies. However, he had no intention of accepting the degree. Apart from the difficulty of getting leave for the ceremony, there would inevitably be unwelcome publicity.

Despite his troubles with Lord Thomson, Lawrence had remained on friendly terms with Ernest Thurtle. Now that Labour was in power, Thurtle was campaigning against the wartime death penalty for cowardice. Lawrence wholeheartedly supported this cause. Throughout his years in the RAF he had done his best to improve the conditions of service, for example by urging Trenchard to modify the uniform worn by the other ranks. He encouraged Thurtle's present efforts, even sending a statement that could be quoted in Parliament. It read: 'I have run too far and too fast under fire (though never fast enough to suit me at the time) to dare throw a stone at the fearfullest creature. You see, I might hit myself in the eye.' He was delighted when the reform eventually passed into law, and suggested further changes, including the end of compulsory church parade.

By late March, he was once again giving most of his time to RAF duties. During the previous four months the Brough had only clocked up eighty-six miles. He wrote: 'Even Homer has flopped. The Wing Commander has given me more work lately, and the America speed-boat [the *Biscuit*] . . . is now approaching readiness, and the last touches are given to her by my little party as and when we have spare time . . . *Odyssey* is left undone because I do not feel up to doing it, just now'. By the beginning of April, work on the *Biscuit* was completed, and possession of this speedboat gave him a new kind of freedom. He began to spend hours exploring the creeks off Plymouth Sound, sometimes going even farther afield. At Easter he wrote that the *Biscuit* was 'really a sea-car, a two-seater. I get a great deal of new satisfaction out of her.' Often, he went alone, but sometimes he took Mrs Sydney Smith or one of her friends. As with the Brough, he liked occasionally to open out the throttle and experience the thrill of speed, but usually he was content just to know that the power was there.

There was one important respect in which he was now more at ease than in the earlier post-war years. The immorality of his wartime role no longer troubled him deeply. He wrote to Manning: 'We do these things in sheer vapidity of mind, not deliberately, not consciously even. To make out that we were reasoned cool minds, ruling our courses and contemporaries, is a vanity. Things happen, and we do our best to keep in the saddle'.

In early September, the sale of Pole Hill went through. He asked Buxton to clear the overdraft and invest the balance so that it would bring 'about £70 or £80 per annum, perhaps, and grow fatter with the years'.

That autumn, he spent a few days of his leave at Collieston on the Scottish coast. There is evidence that this visit formed part of a self-prescribed therapy for the *malaise* he had been suffering from that year. John Bruce, whom he had paid to administer beatings in the Tank Corps some years before, had been hired to organise a gruelling daily routine of swimming and riding. At the end of the stay, according to Bruce, Lawrence received a severe birching.

This episode seems to have been another manifestation of the abnormal behaviour referred to in Chapter 21. During the coming years, he arranged to have himself instructed in a number of outdoor pursuits under very peculiar conditions. For example, he would write under a false name to a swimming or riding instructor, requesting private lessons for an adult 'nephew', and asking for full reports on the nephew's progress and conduct; the nephew was Lawrence himself. These activities were not physically punitive, but he was always to be observed and reported on. The reports sent back to the fictional uncle were seen only by Lawrence.

These fantasy-world arrangements might suggest that Lawrence was mentally unbalanced, were it not for the undoubted sanity of his everyday life and work. It therefore seems likely that they were subtle forms of the masochistic disorder triggered by the violent homosexual rape he had suffered at Deraa in 1917. They may have been a substitute for birchings, to which he submitted himself very rarely, or perhaps for the rigorous barrack-room discipline which was no longer a dominant feature of his service life.

After a week in Scotland, he spent a few days in London, returning to Mount Batten (the new name for Cattewater) on the evening of October 2. Three days later, rumours began to spread in the camp that the new British R.101 airship had crashed. Many famous passengers had been on board. When the news was confirmed, Lawrence wrote: 'Last night was an awful night. I tried to do *Odyssey*, and then to read: but the wind and the rain (I was duty crew, and so partly responsible for the craft at moorings in the Cattewater) prevented any hope of quietness. We never dreamt the airship would leave. I knew so many people in her. I wonder who are saved.' Among those killed in the disaster was Lord Thomson.

At the beginning of November he suddenly received an urgent appeal from Bruce Rogers about the *Odyssey*; the delays were beginning to cause serious difficulties. He replied that he would try to finish by March, 'subject to the R.A.F. leaving me alone to work all my spare time. It will, of course, be done as well as I can do it.' He now returned to the translation in earnest, working on it about forty-five hours a week.

On February 4, Lawrence happened to be standing on some rocks by the shore at Mount Batten when he saw an RAF Iris III flying boat crash into the sea while coming in to land. He ran to the rescue launch, which was one of the first boats to arrive on the spot. The aircraft had sunk in about twenty-six feet of water. Half the crew managed to escape, but the remainder were trapped inside the hull. The horrified boat crew could only watch, while 'six of us crushed together in the crushed canister of the hull were bubbling out their lives. Great belches of air spewed up now and then, as another compartment of wing or hull gave way.'

The crash caused much bitterness at Mount Batten. The pilot at the time had been a senior officer, Wing Commander Tucker, who was under instruction. He had refused to hand over the controls to his instructor, Flight-Lieutenant Ely, for the landing. Lawrence commented that the crash was 'due to bad piloting, on the part of a man who (as we all knew) should never have flown with passengers. He would not be convinced of that. Fortunately he died with the rest.' It was hoped that by bringing out the truth at the subsequent enquiry, regulations about senior officers under instruction would be changed. Lawrence wrote to a friend: 'I propose to say just what I saw, and what it meant . . . I think such a case had better not happen again, and I have facts enough to prevent it happening again, if I publish them.'

In addition to the Air Ministry Inquiry, there was a public inquest in which Lawrence was called as a witness. Under questioning, several people voiced doubts about Tucker's competence, and the whole matter was reported in the press. When Lawrence was asked whether he, personally, would have objected to flying with Tucker, he replied: ' "Had I been ordered to do so I should have flown with him." '

' "But you would not have flown with him as a matter of choice?" '
' "No Sir, not as a matter of choice." '

The crash and its aftermath had taken still more of Lawrence's time, and on February 25 he wrote to Bruce Rogers: 'The upshot of all this is no more *Odyssey*. I am still working on Book XXI and it will be the end of April before I finish, if all goes well after this ten days'.

CHAPTER 25

Last RAF Duties
February 1931–March 1935

LAWRENCE was sent to test a new fast motorboat designed and built by the British Power Boat Company at its yard in Hythe, on the western shore of Southampton Water. At that time, high-speed boats from this small company led the field in Britain. It had been founded in 1927 by Hubert Scott-Paine, one of the pioneers of the British seaplane industry. He had always been fascinated by the sea, and at Hythe he applied his knowledge of aircraft to hull design and construction, developing successful racing boats such as *Miss Britain III*. His other great strength was salesmanship, and during the winter of 1929–30 he had suggested to the RAF that his firm's new 35ft hard-chine hull design would make an excellent seaplane tender, much faster and cheaper to build than the traditional displacement hull types then in use. After some discussion, the RAF ordered an experimental 37ft 6in boat. At preliminary trials this achieved almost seventeen knots. It had been decided to undertake service trials with a seaplane squadron.

Scott-Paine was anxious to conceal these trials for as long as possible from rival yards in the Solent, and it was therefore agreed that the new boat, known as RAF 200, should be sent for evaluation to Plymouth. This choice was no accident. Ever since Lawrence and Sydney Smith had acquired the *Biscuit*, they had been complaining about the slowness of the boats used for work with seaplanes. The value of faster craft in rescue work had been underlined by the recent Iris flying boat crash. Lawrence had already met Flight-Lieutenant W. E. G. Beauforte-Greenwood, Head of the RAF Marine Equipment Branch.

When putting together a trials crew for the prototype, it was natural for Beauforte-Greenwood to ask for Lawrence, whose experience in high-speed boats was probably unique in the lower ranks of the Air Force. Lawrence's personal enthusiasm for faster RAF craft would be an asset, as would his flair as a mechanic and his ability to write clearly about technical matters.

When the Plymouth trials had been completed, RAF 200 was returned to Hythe so that new and lighter engines could be fitted. Lawrence was sent to the yard with the trials mechanic, Corporal Bradbury, to put these engines through fifty-hour tests.

He had not expected to stay at Hythe very long, but went from one task to another, and it was not until June 6 that RAF 200 was ready for further trials at Mount Batten. By then many improvements had been made and tested. Beauforte-Greenwood wrote to Sydney Smith thanking him for the part Lawrence had played: 'May I express to you my great appreciation for all the assistance you have been good enough to afford my branch by allowing Shaw to run the trials of the new speed-boat for the R.A.F. at Hythe. I can assure you that the help which has been given, together with the reports, have been most useful and resulted in bringing us up to date and at least 4–5 years ahead of the Admiralty. Such an advance would have been impossible without the aid which you have so readily given us, and I thank you very much indeed'.

It is clear from this letter that Lawrence rather than Corporal Bradbury was considered to be responsible for the trials, even though he was merely an aircraftman in rank.

At the end of July, after a further series of trials, he took twenty-eight days' leave. He was determined to complete the *Odyssey* and had arranged to seclude himself once again in Barton Street. By working day and night on the translation, he managed to finish it by August 15.

He had expected to be sent to Hythe when his leave ended, because eight further 200 Class boats had been ordered, but a fire at the British Power Boat Company's works on August Bank Holiday had destroyed all but one of them.

With the pause in boat construction, it seemed as though he might spend several months at Mount Batten, and he wrote: 'I hope to be able to read a lot this winter, and hear some gramophone music, and ride the bike . . . it is rather fine to be owner of all one's 24 hours daily again . . . It is going to be so good, being on my own . . . I hope there will be good books published.' However, a 200 Class boat (No. 201) that had been completed just before the British Power Boat Company fire arrived at Mount Batten for more trials during October.

Soon afterwards, Lawrence became involved in trials with a 16ft fast dinghy and, by November 21, he was back in Hythe. He found the work exhausting, and wrote to Charlotte Shaw: 'We drive all the daylight hours, and by night are dirty, tired, with salt-smarting eyes . . . Testing a marine engine, in a new and open hull, is hard work, and difficult. On a rough day it is utterly comfortless: and what I call comfortless, probably is!' He calculated that in testing these new RAF boats he had travelled the distance to New York and back.

Apart from a short break at Christmas, Lawrence had to remain at Hythe. By the New Year he foresaw that testing of one kind or another would go on until April or May.

Many of the letters he wrote during these months were concerned with technical matters, and it is clear that he was working in a field which gave him great satisfaction. In the past, service life had merely been a refuge: his main interests had been elsewhere, in reading, writing, and a voluminous correspondence. Now, however, he was personally committed to his work, not only because it was worthwhile, but because he enjoyed helping to solve mechanical problems. He soon began work on an instruction book for the 200 Class, a project which kept growing in scale: 'I have tried to meet the needs of boat builders, fitters, electricians and drivers, in all points of repair and maintenance and every half-hour I remember something else!' The notes soon reached about fifteen thousand words.

In early February, George Brough wrote offering a very attractive trade-in price for his present motorcycle in exchange for a new SS-100. He collected the new machine three weeks later, and afterwards wrote gratefully to Brough: 'I think this is going to be a very excellent bike. The crowds that gape at her, just now, will stop looking after she gets dirty: and that may be soon, if only the R.A.F. give me spare time enough to use the poor thing.'

In reality, he was to have very little free time. A succession of boats would be ready for testing during the spring and, later, there were to be two special boats, based on the 200 Class hull but armour-plated for work as practice-bombing targets. He was looking forward to these, as they promised to be 'curious and rather exciting'.

The first target-boat began trials in June. Lawrence found it 'a great success—and it bristles with new ideas. That may keep me longer on boats. Had it failed, or done no more than was asked for, they would have sent me back to Plymouth. But it did 36 m.p.h. and is completely stable.'

During the holiday months in summer the press has often made up for a lack of news by printing exaggerated or far-fetched stories. The summer of 1932 was no exception. In mid-August there were reports that Lawrence had gone to Tibet on a mission. As an India Office official remarked: 'During the last few years his wraith has appeared in Kurdistan, Southern Persia, Afghanistan, and, I think, Soviet Turkistan, and in fact,

almost everywhere where there was trouble which could be attributed to
the Machiavellian designs of the imperialistic British Government. If the
legend has struck deep roots in proportion to the extent of its branches, it
seems likely to enjoy quite a respectable spell of immortality!'

This nonsense was harmless compared with an outburst in the *Sunday
Chronicle*. This paper, which liked to print 'human news-features of a
colourful, picturesque and unusual type about living people' ran a large
headline on August 28 which read:

'COLONEL LAWRENCE: MAN BEHIND BRITAIN'S PLANES, CARS,
AND SPEEDBOATS: HIGH-SPEED PROBLEMS FOR
"AIRCRAFTMAN SHAW".'

Beneath this was an article which could hardly have been better calculated to offend the Air Ministry: 'Colonel Lawrence, once the Uncrowned King of Arabia, is now the uncrowned King of speed . . .
Aircraftman Shaw . . . is living in a little red-brick cottage in the village
of Hythe, near Southampton. The real secret reason why Colonel Lawrence is here is that he is the Government speed expert, the man to whose
steely brain the most abstruse problems of speed, either in the air or on
the water, are referred . . . "Aircraftman Shaw is a great authority on
internal-combustion engines" a noted expert told me to-day. The truth is
that his brain is the ultimate Government testing shop for all problems
affecting high-speed aero and marine engines. It is whispered that more
than half Britain's success in the races for the Schneider trophy was due
to his research work . . . his true identity is unknown even to his landlady
. . . She regards him simply as a somewhat mysterious young man who
suddenly disappears without warning, remains away for months, as suddenly reappears perhaps at midnight . . .

'Sometimes Aircraftman Shaw takes classes of young officers in technical instruction. Their embarrassment is comic. They do not always
know his identity, but they realise that the man of technically far inferior
rank is obviously an authority and clearly a person of great importance.'

As the article was patently invention, the sensible reaction would have
been to ignore it, but some officers thought differently. Protests were
made at the Air Ministry, and eventually it was decided that Lawrence
should be returned to normal duties at Plymouth.

He was not immediately aware of this, because on August 31 he had
left for a few days' holiday. His first stop was the Malvern Festival where
he went to see a new play by Bernard Shaw, *Too True to be Good*. It was

not popular with the critics or the public, but was entertaining to Lawrence because he himself was parodied in the second act as 'Private Meek', a soldier who always knew much more about what was going on than his Commanding Officer. During the preceding months he had read the play in draft, and had amused himself suggesting the kind of things that Meek might have said to his superiors.

It was only when he returned to Hythe that he heard of the change in his RAF fortunes. Despite his irritation, the move seemed at first to have compensations. After working on boats for several months, he was happy with the thought of spending time reading and catching up with his correspondence.

Among the mail he found at Plymouth was an invitation from a new organisation to be called the Irish Academy of Letters. Lawrence's name had been put forward as a possible Associate, and W. B. Yeats had written inviting him to accept. Hitherto, Lawrence had always spoken of England as his home, had taken pains to point out that his father's family had never inter-married with the Irish. In recent years, however, his sense of loyalty to Ireland had grown because Charlotte Shaw had frequently written to him about Irish topics and sent him the work of Irish writers. He now replied to Yeats accepting the nomination: 'I am Irish, and it has been a chance to admit it publicly—but it touches me very deeply that you should think anything I have done or been to justify this honour . . . Thanks again. It's not my fault, wholly, if I am not more Irish: family, political, even money obstacles will hold me in England always. I wish it were not so.'

Public recognition of Lawrence's writing increased at the beginning of November, when the Bruce Rogers *Odyssey* was published. An American trade edition, in which his name was given as translator, was issued by Oxford University Press. It was instantly successful. The Emery Walker limited edition published in England attracted little notice in the press, but it was a magnificent example of book production.

After a while, Lawrence began to regret that he was no longer testing motorboats. Then he caught bad flu which dragged on for several weeks. Sydney Smith had left Mount Batten, and Lawrence had no particular reason to feel at home there. In a disconsolate mood, he began to think of leaving the Air Force. He first hinted at this in a letter written only five weeks after his return to Plymouth: 'My R.A.F. time runs out on March 12 1935: so that is quite a bit yet. I have been not at all well lately and am wondering if I can stick it out.' He began to talk about his plans to retire to Clouds Hill. His mother and elder brother had decided to take up missionary work in China again, so the cottage would soon be unoccupied. During the winter, he instructed builders to repair the roof and damp-proof the walls of the large downstairs room, hitherto used as a kitchen. His plans to add on a room for books had been abandoned because of the recession. Instead, he decided to have shelving installed downstairs.

If he chose to leave the Air Force, he already had a guaranteed income from investments. It would be meagre, but probably sufficient. In addition, there would now be money from the *Odyssey*. He was entitled to a third share of the royalties from the American trade edition. He began to think of bringing a water supply to the cottage and installing a water heater and bath.

While this work was going on, the cottage was uninhabitable, and he would have to remain at Mount Batten. Although he found little interest in his RAF work, Lawrence was not idle. To occupy himself, and earn a little money, he agreed to edit for Cape a book by an unknown author, Ian Tyre, about wartime experiences in Palestine and Syria. Another pastime was correspondence with his friends. During the winter of 1932–3, he exchanged letters with Nancy Astor, Herbert Baker, Maurice Baring, John Brophy, Robin Buxton, Jonathan Cape, F. N. Doubleday, Edward Elgar, Feisal, David and Edward Garnett, Robert Graves, James Hanley and C. J. Greenwood (Hanley's publisher), Mrs Thomas Hardy, Wyndham Lewis, L. B. Namier, Stewart Newcombe, Bruce Rogers, William Rothenstein, Charlotte Shaw, A. P. Wavell, Henry Williamson, and Lord Winterton. Lawrence knew that these friendships, which contributed so much to his contentment, had nothing to do with his life in the RAF: they would continue whether he remained in the Service or not.

Just before Christmas he told Bruce Rogers: 'The large sale for our *Odyssey* will, as you say, mean a big royalty payment next March. I had, in my more hopeful moments, dreamt of its being adopted as a school text-book in the States. Our Oxford Press here makes a better income out of obscure text-books than most publishers do out of novels. They sell and sell for twenty years, making a clear £100 or so a year'.

By mid-February the success of the American *Odyssey* had exceeded his wildest expectations. It had sold eleven thousand copies, and a fifth printing was in the shops. Publishers were urging him to authorise a trade edition in England, but he consistently refused to do so. The money earned in America was more than sufficient for his needs, and even enabled him to find £200 to help a friend who was facing bankruptcy.

He wrote to Buxton on February 16 that he was 'repairing and altering my cottage, against the day of retiring, which may be very soon. This station is not pleasant, now.' Twelve days later, however, he was still thinking he might go to another unit: 'I still wonder about moving, but will not settle that for a month yet, and might retire into civil life instead.'

In the event, he made up his mind only a week later, and on March 6 submitted a formal request for discharge: 'I, No.338171 A/C Shaw, E., respectfully request that I may be granted an interview with the Commanding Officer, to ask him to forward my application to be released from further service in the Royal Air Force as from the sixth of April, 1933.' It was a decision he immediately began to regret. He wrote to Charlotte Shaw: 'This morning I decided I had better end my self-argument, so I have put in a request to be discharged from the R.A.F. . . . and am homesick already, with the change and loneliness to come . . .

'My move will be to Clouds Hill, where I shall try to stay till my heart and head settle down again. I have not been into ways and means, so cannot say how I shall live: but the *Odyssey* has postponed that question till next year.'

The Air Ministry had formally approved his premature discharge but, after various contacts with high-ranking officers, Lawrence was half-expecting the offer of more interesting work. He wrote on April 3: 'Here is Monday come, and my discharge due on Thursday, and not an indication from Air Ministry if I am to or not. Extraordinary people.

'I am carrying on as if to go, and have got rid of all my kit, except what I stand in. This last Saturday I ran a car-load of books, records, clothes and tools to my cottage, which is still in the throes of the builders, but looking peaceful despite it. I think it will do, as a harbour.'

On April 15 the *Daily Mail* reported that he had left the RAF. Four days later, however, he was called to the Air Ministry and offered a posting to the RAF Marine Aircraft Experimental Establishment, at Felixstowe, where he would continue to work on the boat-building programme under Beauforte-Greenwood. This he accepted, and the necessary orders were issued two days later. To reduce the risk of publicity, it was decided that in future he would wear plain clothes whenever he was working away from an RAF station.

He arrived at Felixstowe on April 28. His new duties were: 'generally to watch the Air Ministry's interests at contractors' yards during the construction of marine craft, various types of bombing target, moorings, engines, and equipment'; to 'assist in preparation of trial reports and notes on running and maintenance of various types of craft', and to 'assist in production of craft and equipment generally and in particular the high speed vessel for crashwork, life saving and also salvage of boat planes.'

At the outset, he hoped that the job would prove less gruelling than his previous spell in boats. Soon, however, he was giving many more hours to the job than duty required. Some months later, when the RAF began to consider his ultimate replacement, it was thought that two men would be needed to carry on with his work.

During his last two years in the RAF he travelled frequently, visiting different boatyards, engine builders and other suppliers. There were also frequent meetings at the Air Ministry in London. He had so little free time that his letters became short and obviously hurried; for the first time since 1919, he gave up any thought of literary work. He had finished editing Ian Tyre's book in March, and refused to start anything else, saying repeatedly that all such projects would have to wait until after he had left the Air Force.

He took very few days off, but if he was within reach of Dorset he would visit Clouds Hill at the weekend: 'And there I potter about, like any other retired Colonel, doing little jobs about the place. It is not quite equal to my past reputation, but fits well enough with my present.'

He was now arranging for a water supply to the cottage. The only source within reach was a stream on the far side of the road, about a hundred feet away. To bring this supply uphill without power (there was no electricity at Clouds Hill) he bought a small water-ram which would be driven by the stream itself.

Unfortunately, as the work progressed, the dollar exchange-rate fell, and so the sterling value of his *Odyssey* receipts was much less than he had expected. By the autumn he was obliged to borrow in order to finance the improvements to Clouds Hill, and towards the end of the year he decided to stop using a building firm, although there was more he wanted to do. Pat Knowles, the eldest of Mrs Knowles's sons, was now living with her and had offered to do jobs much more cheaply.

In April 1933 Liddell Hart at last began writing the military biography of Lawrence that Cape had proposed three years earlier. During the spring and summer he asked Lawrence to answer detailed questionnaires, sometimes in writing, sometimes orally, and afterwards he sent sections of the book in typescript for comments and corrections. Liddell Hart was much more thorough and discerning than Graves had been, and he was not under the same pressure over deadlines. He was able to consult British officers who had served in the Middle East during the war and he obtained access to some of the military documents. Lawrence quickly realised that this was to be a serious work of history and gave Liddell Hart all the help he could.

All went well with the project until August, when Cape, having read the draft, asked 'for less military consideration and more life'. Lawrence protested, both to Liddell Hart and to Cape, but to little avail.

There were few other distractions from RAF work in 1933, but his itinerant work gave him opportunities to see some of his friends and, conversely, an excuse to avoid many of the people who wanted to meet him. When Feisal visited London in June, Lawrence and Newcombe met him for lunch. Admiral Snagge, who had served in the Red Sea Patrol, was also there.

Feisal was only fifty, but he suffered from heart disease. He went to Switzerland for medical treatment, and died there on September 11. Not long afterwards Lawrence wrote: 'I think of his death almost with relief—as one would see enter the harbour a good-looking but not sea-worthy ship, with the barometer falling. He is out of it, intact'.

Lawrence had no immediate plans for literary projects, but in early December, he wrote to Charlotte Shaw: 'something happened to me last night, when I lay awake till five. You know I have been moody or broody for years, wondering what I was at in the R.A.F., but unable to let go—well, last night I suddenly understood that it was to write a book called "Confession of Faith" . . . embodying *The Mint* and much that has happened to me before and since as regards the air . . . It would include a word on Miranshah and Karachi, and the meaning of speed, on land and water and air. I see the plan of it. It will take long to do. Clouds Hill, I think. In this next and last R.A.F. year I can collect feelings for it. The thread of the book will only come because it spins through my head: there cannot be any objective continuity—but I think I can make it whole enough to do. *The Mint*, you know, was meant as notes for something (smaller) of the sort. I wonder if it will come off. The purpose of my generation, that's really it. Anyway I shall tell no one else . . . Three years hence we'll know.' He had recently written to another friend: 'When I have left the R.A.F. and entered upon the emptiness of my cottage, desperation may well make me write something, and seek an anonymous printing of it.'

He spent Christmas week of 1933 at Clouds Hill, which was warmed by its two log fires. Much of his time was passed upstairs, reading, writing letters, and listening to the gramophone. Pat Knowles and another local friend would occasionally join him. On December 23 Jock Chambers, whom Lawrence had met at Farnborough in 1922, arrived unexpectedly. They spent the holiday clearing up after the builders, taking long walks, chopping wood for the fire. On the evening of Christmas Day they shared a tinned chicken with Pat Knowles.

During 1934 Lawrence was to have little energy to spare for anything except his RAF duties. He wrote: 'These boats occupy too much of my time. Yet I feel, as I do them, that they will be the last tangible things I do.' Meanwhile, despite mounting expense, work continued at Clouds Hill. A water reservoir, built as a fire precaution, was completed in February, and Pat Knowles began building a glass roof over it. Lawrence decided to extend this at one end to provide a kind of conservatory where he could work.

Press interest had been reawakened by the appearance of Liddell Hart's biography in early March, and he was alarmed when a *Daily Express* journalist began to pry into his ancestry, pointing out how evasive biographers had been on this point. He realised that the scattered statements already in print gave such useful leads that an astute researcher might easily discover his relationship to the Chapman family. The probing and exposure that might result would be quite intolerable. Although weeks passed without a follow-up, he knew that the cutting would be on the files of every major newspaper, and that the quest for his true identity might be taken up again at any time. As a result, he grew more fearful than ever of publicity and was perturbed to hear in late April from one of the trustees of *Revolt in the Desert* that another scheme was afoot to film the book.

By the mid-thirties extreme right-wing politics were gathering strength all over Europe. In England, there was Oswald Mosley's British Union of Fascists. As with all such movements, some adherents spent their time trying to attract famous people who might be persuaded to endorse the political programme. In May, Lawrence refused an invitation to a Fascist dinner, commenting frivolously: 'I want your movement to hurry up, and put an end to the license of the daily Press. It will be glorious to dance on the combined cess-pit that holds the dead *Daily Express*, *Daily Chronicle* and *Daily Herald*.'

As his reply had not seemed totally negative, the Fascists tried again. This time he wrote more firmly: 'Politics in England mean either violent change (I care not enough for anything to lead me into that) or wasting twenty years of one's time and all one's strength on parading to the House of Commons. The meanest Government servant has more power than any unofficial M.P. [i.e. a Member of Parliament not holding Ministerial office]. So I can't afford politics, either.

'I'm sorry you think the youth now growing up lacking in character and guts. I have now served for twelve and a half years in the R.A.F. and nearly lost what withered heart I possess, (at forty-five), to my fellows, here. They are so definite and happy, I think. They seem to get much more out of life than my contemporaries did, twenty-five years ago. I should have called them a cleaner and better generation. I don't see how anybody in daily touch with working fellows could have dismal thoughts of England . . .

'No, please don't make me any part of your Club. I'm prepared only to serve . . . and I'm very tired: even of serving.'

None of the Fascist approaches to Lawrence bore fruit, and Mosley himself would later write: '. . . Neither did I meet nor have any communication with T. E. Lawrence, despite many later rumours to the contrary . . . I knew nothing of him apart from reading the *Seven Pillars of Wisdom*'.

In November Lawrence received another proposal for his future. It too was wholly inappropriate to his talents and ambitions. Montagu Norman, Governor of the Bank of England, had conceived the idea that he would make an excellent Secretary for the Bank. Norman had never met Lawrence, but asked a mutual acquaintance, Francis Rodd, to act as intermediary. Lawrence refused the offer graciously but firmly. That month he had moved to Bridlington for what was to be his last RAF work, supervising the winter overhaul of ten fast launches. There was a great deal to be done and barely enough time to do it.

As the end of his Air Force service drew near, he quite frequently referred in letters to his uncertainty and anxiety about the future. He did not write obsessively about it, but repeated similar thoughts to many different correspondents. From these remarks it is possible to discern the main lines of his thinking about the years ahead.

His final two years' work on boats had been extremely tiring: fatigue is a constant refrain in his letters during 1934. He therefore knew that, above all, he needed a rest. He also believed that it would be foolish to take any major decision before he needed to: 'I have determined to keep my mind wholly blank about futures, till the time comes.' Friends were

showering him with suggestions of literary work, Government appointments, and so on, but he refused to make any commitment. If he waited
long enough, someone was certain to make a proposal that appealed to
him. For the present, that had not happened. At the end of the year he
wrote: 'here I am still strong and trenchant-minded, but with nothing in
my hand.'

Until he knew what he wanted to do, he would live at Clouds Hill. He
believed that the 'last thing desirable is activity for the sake of activity.
I hope I have enough mind for it to be quietly happy by itself. So I shall
not do anything until it becomes necessary'.

This first stage of his retirement was to be a deliberate experiment. He
wrote to Cape: 'I am promising myself a huge rest and sample-time, to
see if (a) I am happy doing nothing, and (b) if I have money enough for
it. Granted (a) and (b) you'll hear no more of me. My heart tells me that
I am finished.' Yet he had also written: 'The finding myself outside what
has been my frame and support for thirteen years will be a test of my
stability: and we shall see what happens. I am very much afraid for
myself, and rather miserable.'

The reason for this fear is apparent from other letters: despite his
elaborate preparations at Clouds Hill, he was not sure whether he would
be able to bear living alone. The risk, as he told Charlotte Shaw, was that
he would 'go back to the self of 1920 and 1921, a crazy pelican feeding
not its young but its spirit-creations upon its bodily strength. I had hoped,
all these years, that I was not going to be alone again.'

Another problem would be lack of money. He had hoped that by 1935
his accumulated capital would produce an income of £3 a week. However, he had spent lavishly on Clouds Hill and in helping needy friends.
The interest rate had now fallen and, as a result, he would have to live on
only twenty-five shillings a week, just over a third of what he had planned.
This would be a very real handicap. He wrote to Frederic Manning:
'Candidly, the prospect of unalloyed leisure terrifies me, for I shall not
have enough money to kill time with travel and motor cars and calls and
meals.' As he would be unable to afford much use of his Brough, he
bought a pedal cycle.

Meanwhile several projects hovered at the back of his mind: he could
write a major work about the RAF, or try a biography of Roger Case-
ment, the Irish patriot hanged as a traitor by the British in 1916. He had
mentioned this last several times to Charlotte Shaw during recent years.
One thing that was certain was that he would miss the Air Force, which

had provided him with a home and companionship and interesting work for twelve years.

During the weeks he spent in Bridlington, he lived at a small hotel that was let to the Air Force for billets during the winter months. He became friends with Flight-Lieutenant Sims, a retired officer working as Adjutant at the RAF training station of which Bridlington was an outpost. They had in common an interest in photography and a love of classical music, and Lawrence was soon spending most of his weekends with the Sims family at their cottage in the village of Hornsea.

On December 21 he had to go to London for a meeting at the Air Ministry, and afterwards he went briefly to Clouds Hill. Jock Chambers was expected, but because of bad weather did not come. Lawrence shared his Christmas chicken with Pat Knowles and they talked over his plans for the cottage and for installing a small printing press, which was to be in operation by the beginning of 1936. It was to be housed in a first-floor building constructed over the water tank, and the first book printed would be a private edition of *The Mint*.

By the end of the year he was back in Bridlington, but in late January he went south again to see Alexander Korda, who was responsible for the new plan to film *Revolt in the Desert*. Lawrence was determined to stop its production, if at all possible, and found to his delight that Korda made no difficulty: 'He was quite unexpectedly sensitive . . . seemed to understand at once when I put to him the inconveniences . . . and ended the discussion by agreeing that it should not be attempted without my consent . . . You can imagine how this gladdens me.'

Afterwards he went to Fordingbridge, where he sat for Augustus John in RAF uniform. John painted a small portrait in oils and drew a three-quarter length charcoal sketch. Lawrence liked the sketch greatly, and arranged to have a hundred copies printed as frontispiece to his projected edition of *The Mint*.

In late January, he received a letter from Robert Graves, who had been asked by *The Times* to draft a two-thousand-word obituary of Lawrence which would be held on their files in case of need. Graves suggested that Lawrence might like to write it himself, promising that no one would know. During these last weeks Lawrence had been thinking deeply about his life, and he now wrote: 'don't give too much importance to what I did in Arabia during the war. I feel that the Middle Eastern settlement put through by Winston Churchill and Young and me in 1921 . . . should weigh more than fighting. And I feel too that this settlement should weigh less than my life since 1922, for the conquest of the last element, the air, seems to me the only major task of our generation; and I have convinced myself that progress to-day is made not by the single genius, but by the common effort. To me it is the multitude of rough transport drivers filling all the roads of England every night, who make this the mechanical age. And it is the airmen, the mechanics, who are overcoming the air, not the Mollisons and Orlebars [two renowned pilots]. The genius raids, but the common people occupy and possess. Wherefore I stayed in the ranks and served to the best of my ability, much influencing my fellow airmen towards a pride in themselves and their inarticulate duty.

'That for eight years, and now for the last four I have been so curiously fortunate as to share in a little revolution we have made in boat design . . . When I went into R.A.F. boats in 1929, every type was an Admiralty design . . . Now (1935) not one type of R.A.F. boat in production is naval. . . We have found, chosen, selected or derived our own sorts: they have (power for power) three times the speed of their predecessors, less weight, less cost, more room, more safety, more seaworthiness . . .

'Now I do not claim to have made these boats. They have grown out of the joint experience, skill and imaginations of many men. But I can (secretly) feel that they owe to me their opportunity and their acceptance. . . . In inventing them we have had to make new engines, new auxiliaries, use new timbers, new metals, new materials. It has been five years of intense and co-ordinated progress.'

He said nothing in this letter about his literary achievements or ambitions, believing perhaps that this was an area in which Graves would reach his own judgments. His true feelings may be gathered from a statement made to Edward Garnett some years previously: 'And in the distant future, if the distant future deigns to consider my insignificance, I shall be appraised rather as a man of letters than as a man of action.'

A few of the Englishmen who had taken part in the Arab Revolt liked to keep in contact with Lawrence, and when they wrote to him he generally made a point of replying. One of these was T. W. Beaumont, who had served as a gunner in the Hejaz Armoured Car Company.

It seems that Beaumont wrote to Lawrence for the first time in 1931, as Lawrence's reply to this letter indicates that there had been no contact between them since the war. Beaumont wrote again, and Lawrence sent him three further replies, of which the most recent was dated 31 January

1935. None of these letters was of any great consequence but, in the last, Lawrence mentioned his impending retirement.

A few days after sending it, he was warned by the Air Ministry that someone from the press had been making enquiries about his movements. Then, on February 17, the *Sunday Express* published an article which quoted extensively from the letter to Beaumont, giving the date that Lawrence would leave the RAF, and news of his plans to retire to Clouds Hill.

The article alerted every newspaper to Lawrence's imminent retirement, with consequences that Lawrence cannot have begun to imagine as he worked out his last days at Bridlington.

CHAPTER 26

Clouds Hill
April–May 1935

LAWRENCE cycled away from Bridlington on 25 February 1935, five days earlier than the date announced by the *Sunday Express*. He was able to go early because he had not made use of his full annual entitlement to leave. The night before he left, he had written a mild rebuke to Beaumont, whose lack of discretion had so unfortunately stirred up newspaper interest in his activities: 'Your contribution sent the pressmen scurrying about Bridlington, I believe: but vainly. They are proper tripe hounds, keep clear of them, for your own sake.'

Had Lawrence's departure been unnoticed for a few weeks, it would have been stale news, hardly worth reporting. As it was, the advance warning turned his retirement into a media event. Journalists from every popular paper were on his track, determined to secure at least as much coverage as their rivals.

As he cycled southwards, Lawrence had little idea of the reception that was in store for him when he reached Clouds Hill. But for the moment, because of his early start, the press was unable to locate him. He meant to visit Frederic Manning in Lincolnshire and then go on to Cambridge and London. On February 28, however, he learned that Manning had died. The news seemed to bear in some peculiar way on his own predicament.

When he reached Clouds Hill he found, to his horror, that journalists and photographers were waiting for him. He left again immediately, and cycled to London, where he rented a room as 'Mr. T. E. Smith'. Then, in the belief that the journalists would eventually grow tired of watching Clouds Hill, he decided to spend a few days touring southern England on his bicycle.

The unexpected press attention was an additional strain at a moment which he would in any case have found very difficult. His dislike of publicity had grown steadily since 1922, when it had cost him his place in the RAF. Unscrupulous journalists had caused him great difficulties in 1929 and again in 1933. Now, they had shattered the privacy of his only home.

400

His fragile mental equilibrium had been dealt a heavy blow, and his fear of the press became almost irrational. The sense of being hunted added to his unhappiness about leaving the Air Force. He was afflicted with a growing sense of hopelessness, and during the next few weeks his letters became increasingly miserable. Nevertheless, he was still able to see his predicament from a rational viewpoint. Thus he wrote to T. B. Marson on March 6: 'At the moment I'm hiding in London, with pressmen besieging my cottage in Dorset . . . and I feel lost and aimless and *cold* somehow. Ah well, that will pass.'

On March 14 he paid five shillings for a year's membership of the Youth Hostels Association, and set off for Dorset to explore the situation at Clouds Hill. When he arrived the following day he found no pressmen, and sent a telegram to Ralph Isham, then visiting England, inviting him to come down. On March 17, however, a Sunday, the journalists and photographers appeared again. They shouted at him to come out and speak to them, banging incessantly on the door. Eventually, in a state of utter rage, he made his escape through the rear of the garden after hitting one of his persecutors in the eye. He cycled as far as Romsey that night and on the next day reached London.

It seemed that whenever he returned to Clouds Hill the press would follow him. The only solution would be to use what was left of his influence, and appeal directly to those who were really responsible for this nuisance. He therefore went to see the Press Association and the London photographic agencies, begging them to call off their men.

By the beginning of April he was back at Clouds Hill. There was no sign of the press and he began trying to settle down. He told a friend that he was 'hoping to stay here quite a while, finishing off my cottage after my own liking. There is pleasure (and engrossment) in arranging and fixing one's surroundings. I find I spend nearly the whole day, beginning job after job and laying them aside, part-done. The sense of infinite time, all my own, is so new.'

After a few days he began to settle into a régime, and he started inviting friends, telling them: 'I think I am going to be happy and comfortable here'. Jock Chambers promised to stay for a fortnight, arriving in late April; in May his place would be taken by E. M. Forster, and after that Lawrence was expecting a friend from Cranwell.

By April 20, after three weeks without interference from the press, Lawrence was beginning to recover his balance. Letters continued to arrive from literary friends, all of whom were willing to suggest interesting projects. For the time being, however, the only thing Lawrence felt

certain about was that he wanted to remain at Clouds Hill. He wrote to
Bruce Rogers on May 6 that he was sitting in his cottage 'rather puzzled
to find out what has happened to me, is happening and will happen. At
present the feeling is mere bewilderment. I imagine leaves must feel like
this after they have fallen from their tree and until they die. Let's hope
that will not be my continuing state.

'Money is very short, and this is the only spot, apparently, where I can
afford to live: but it is too soon to judge of that. In a few months' time
I will know for sure if my savings are enough, or not. Meanwhile I am
practising a not un-amusing penury—or parsimony, rather. Also I work
enough at wood cutting and gathering, pipe-laying and building, to tire
me out thoroughly by each early afternoon . . . and then follows a heav-
enly laze, in the sun, if available, or by my fires if not.'

Two days later he learned there were real prospects of further work for
the Government. Ramsay MacDonald was shortly to retire as head of the
National Government, and Stanley Baldwin would take over. Lawrence
received a letter from Nancy Astor, who wrote: 'I believe when the
Government re-organizes you will be asked to help re-organize the Defence forces. I will tell you what I have done already about it.

'If you will come to Cliveden Saturday, the last Saturday in May
[actually June 1], you will never regret it. Please, please come. Lionel
[Curtis], Pat [Mrs. Curtis], Philip [Lord Lothian], and, for the most
important, Stanley Baldwin. Please think about this.' He replied by return: 'No: wild mares would not at present take me away from Clouds
Hill. It is an earthly paradise and I am staying here till I feel qualified for
it. Also there is something broken in the works, as I told you: my will,
I think. In this mood I would not take on any job at all. So do not commit
yourself to advocating me, lest I prove a non-starter.'

On May 11, a Saturday, Lawrence received a letter from Henry
Williamson, announcing that he would be driving from Devon to London
in three days' time, and proposing to call at Clouds Hill unless the
weather was wet. Williamson wrote that he wanted to leave the typescript
of an unpublished work by the late V. M. Yeates, whose *Winged Victory*,
a book about air fighting in the war, had been greatly admired by Lawrence.

The only way Lawrence could be sure of getting a reply to Devon
before Williamson set out was to send a telegram. In mid-morning of
Monday May 13 he rode his Brough to the post office at Bovington Camp
and sent a wire which read simply: 'Lunch Tuesday wet fine cottage one

mile north Bovington Camp'. At the same time he sent off a parcel of books to Jock Chambers, who had returned to London.

On the way back to the cottage, while riding at about 40 m.p.h., he suddenly came upon two boy cyclists in a dip in the road. He swerved to avoid them, but one was knocked down and fell without serious injury. Lawrence himself was thrown from his machine. When help arrived, he was taken unconscious to the camp hospital at Bovington.

Lawrence had suffered very severe brain damage in the accident. He remained in a coma for six days while his strength gradually failed and finally, on 19 May 1935, he died. Had he lived, he would have been almost completely paralysed, and would have known nothing whatsoever of his past.

His funeral took place at St Nicholas' Church in Moreton, on May 21. Six friends from different periods of his life acted as pall bearers. They were Ronald Storrs, Eric Kennington, Corporal Bradbury, Private Russell, Pat Knowles, and Stewart Newcombe. Among those present were Winston Churchill, Nancy Astor, Alan Dawnay, Lord Lloyd, Lord Winterton, Sir John Salmond, Philip Graves, Lionel Curtis, Mrs Thomas Hardy, A. P. Wavell, Jonathan Cape, Bruce Rogers, B. H. Liddell Hart, Augustus John, and Siegfried Sassoon.

That day a message from George V to A. W. Lawrence was published in The Times. *It read: 'The King has heard with sincere regret of the death of your brother, and deeply sympathizes with you and your family in this sad loss.*

'Your brother's name will live in history, and the King gratefully recognises his distinguished services to his country and feels that it is tragic that the end should have come in this manner to a life still so full of promise.'

Envoi

His best epitaph is perhaps from Pliny's letter to Tacitus (xvi. 6):
*Equidem beatos puto quibus deorum munere datum est aut facere
scribenda aut scribere legenda; beatissimos vero quibus utrumque.*
Happy are those who can do things worth recording, or write
things worth reading: most happy those to whom it is given
to do both.

Sir Arnold Wilson

I am not a very tractable person or much of a hero-worshipper, but
I would have followed Lawrence over the edge of the world. I loved
him for himself, and also because there seemed to be reborn in him all
the lost friends of my youth. If genius be, in Emerson's phrase, a
'stellar and undiminishable something', whose origin is a mystery and
whose essence cannot be defined, then he was the only man of genius
I have ever known.

John Buchan

I think he would always have grinned at the idea of anyone
'mothering' him. But, in the end, he was very dreadfully lonely. The
strangest contact of my life.

Charlotte Shaw

405

Note on T. E. Lawrence's Ancestry

Lawrence's Father

Thomas Robert Tighe Chapman, Lawrence's father, was born on 6 November 1846. He was the second son of William Chapman (1811–89) and Martha Louisa Vansittart.

Lawrence's early knowledge of the Chapman family history seems to have been derived from *Debrett*. According to the 1918 edition: 'This family was originally settled at Hinckley, in Leicestershire; but John Chapman, and his brother William, through the influence of Sir Walter Raleigh, their cousin-german, received large grants of land in Ireland, and settled in that country. Benjamin, the son of William Chapman, was an officer of cavalry in Cromwell's army, and for his services received the castle and estates of Killua, sometime the seat of the family. The 3rd baronet sat as M.P. for Westmeath . . . 1830–41. Sir Benjamin James, 4th baronet, sat as M.P. for Westmeath . . . 1841–7 and was Lord-Lieutenant of that county. The 5th baronet, Sir Montagu Richard, was High Sheriff of County Westmeath.' (*Debrett's Illustrated Baronetage*, London, 1918, p. 135). The Chapman family motto is curious, both in itself and as a comment on Lawrence's life after the First World War. Translated from the Latin, it reads: 'Virtue thrives under oppression'.

Lawrence's father was brought up to the life of a gentleman landowner, at a large manor house called South Hill, near the village of Delvin, County Westmeath. The family also maintained a town house in Dublin. The size of the Chapman fortune should not be judged by the relatively modest South Hill estate (173 acres). When the family land was sold in 1949 it totalled over 1,230 acres, in nine different locations. A better indication of the family's wealth is given by the valuation at probate of the estate of Francis Robert Chapman, Lawrence's uncle, who died in 1915. This amounted to £120,296, equivalent in 1990 to a sum of at least £3 million. All sources show that the Chapman family belonged to the upper tier of the Anglo-Irish landowning class. Through successive generations it had intermarried with families of comparable stature in England and Ireland. Thus Lawrence was a blood relative, on his father's side, of many Englishmen from distinguished backgrounds. For example Robert Vansittart, later Baron Vansittart, was his second cousin.

Thomas Chapman was educated at Eton (as were his two brothers). It was expected that he would run the family estates and from 1866–8 he studied at the Royal Agricultural College at Cirencester. His elder brother, William, joined the army and served in the 15th Hussars, but in May 1870 he died. Thomas then assumed the position of eldest son, and his younger brother Francis was trained to run the estates. In 1873 Thomas married Edith Sarah Hamilton, from another landowning family in County Westmeath. There were four daughters: Eva Jane Louisa (b. 1874); Rose Isabel (b. 1878); Florence Lina (b.1880) and Mabel Cecele (b. 1881).

Lawrence's Mother

At some time in the late 1870s, a young Scotswoman known as Sarah Lawrence entered the Chapman household, having been engaged to work as governess to the daughters. Her industry, capability and cheerfulness were much appreciated.

This was by stark contrast to the conduct of Chapman's wife, who developed an increasingly militant obsession with religion which made life extremely difficult for those closest to her. Most accounts agree that by the mid-1880s Edith Chapman had become a bitter and vindictive woman who subjected her family and servants to very frequent prayer meetings and disapproved of all but the most genteel pleasures. Thomas Chapman, for his part, had by that time become a heavy drinker. In due course he fell in love with Sarah Lawrence, who was fifteen years his junior.

While the history of the Chapman family is well documented, much less is known about Sarah Lawrence. She was herself illegitimate, born on 31 August 1861 in Sunderland, County Durham and registered at birth as Sarah Junner. Her mother's name was Elizabeth, and census records for Sunderland made in April of that year, show that Elizabeth Junner was at that time working as a servant in the household of one Thomas Lawrence, who was by profession a Lloyd's surveyor.

There can be little doubt that Sarah Junner was the child of Thomas Lawrence's eldest son, John. Her birth certificate gives the name Junner both as the maiden name of the mother and as the surname of the father. As the name is unusual, this in itself is curious. However, Elizabeth Junner had been listed in the census only four months before the birth as an unmarried servant living in the Lawrence household. The profession of the child's father is given on the birth certificate as shipwright journeyman, and this corresponds to the profession given in the census for John Lawrence: that of ship's carpenter. The girl was given the name Sarah, which was the name of John Lawrence's mother (and also of one of his sisters). It must also be significant that when Sarah Junner grew older, she used the name Lawrence rather than the name Junner. It may be that the Lawrence family concerned itself with her education after her mother, who became an alcoholic, had died.

The 1861 census reveals a little more about Sarah Lawrence's parents. John Lawrence was born at Chepstow in 1843; his father Thomas at Swansea in 1808; his mother Sarah at Chepstow in 1811. Sarah appears, therefore, to have been half-Welsh. Elizabeth Junner, Sarah's mother, was born in Scotland in 1833. A family called Junner is mentioned in the 1861 census, living in Sunderland at 14 Hamilton Street. As the name is so uncommon it seems possible that these were her parents. If so, her father was John Junner, a retired master mariner born at Franfield, Sussex, in about 1807, and her mother Jane Junner, born at Monkwearmouth in about 1813.

The break-up of the Chapman household

In 1885 Sarah Lawrence became pregnant. She therefore left the Chapman household to live in rooms Thomas Chapman rented for her in Dublin. In December that year a son was born. He was christened Montagu Robert; both names are found in the Chapman pedigree.

For a time, Thomas Chapman continued to live at home while also seeing Sarah and his child. Eventually, however, Mrs Chapman discovered what had taken place. When faced with the choice of leaving his wife and daughters or giving up Sarah and his son, Thomas decided to go with Sarah. Soon afterwards he took her to live in Tremadoc in Wales, where their second son, christened Thomas Edward, was born in August 1888.

Thomas Chapman's subsequent financial position

On March 30 of that year, Chapman had signed an Indenture under the terms of which he assigned his life interest in the family estates to his younger brother Francis (their father, William Chapman, did not die until 1889). In exchange, Thomas Chapman was to receive an annuity of £200 for the rest of his life. It seems that he also possessed or afterwards inherited other capital. According to his own statement, this amounted by the beginning of 1916 to rather more than £20,000. It would have produced, at prevailing interest rates, an income of about £1,000 per annum. This substantial figure contradicts Lawrence's later claim that his parents lived in straitened circumstances: it seems that Mr Lawrence's revenues during the boys' childhood amounted in reality to much more than the £400 per annum that Lawrence spoke of to his biographer Liddell Hart.

In 1914 Mr Lawrence became the seventh and last Chapman baronet. When he had separated from his wife, twenty years previously, it would have been difficult to foresee that the title might pass to him. At that time it was held by an uncle, Benjamin Chapman, who had two sons. They were each in turn to inherit it (becoming respectively 5th and 6th baronets) but neither had children.

Lawrence's father probably expected that the five sons Sarah bore him would eventually inherit a reasonable share of the Chapman fortune. He must therefore have been disappointed when his younger brother Francis, who died in 1915 without having married, bequeathed to him only £25,000 of the £120,296 Chapman estate. (Other specific bequests under the will included £10,000 to the Adelaide Hospital in Dublin, and £25,000 divided between the four Chapman daughters, Lawrence's half-sisters, who were also the residuary legatees.) When Mr Lawrence received this £25,000 inheritance, he shared part of it among his sons. In a draft of the letter he sent to Lawrence he wrote: 'I am glad to say that circumstances allow me to hand over to Bob, you and Arnie exact equal portion of the same Securities as described on another page . . . I should mention that my capital will be increased by less than a third, so that I can never make any of you wealthy but I am very thankful I can do what I am doing and by your having this money now it enables you when this war is over to decide more freely on your future proceedings.' Mr Lawrence stated that the securities given to each of his sons would provide them with incomes of about £270 per annum.

Caroline Margaret Chapman

The last part of this history concerns Mr Lawrence's younger sister, Caroline Margaret Chapman (Lawrence's aunt). She had married her cousin, Montagu Chapman, who became 5th Chapman baronet. He died in 1907 without children, and four years later she drew up a will setting out the terms under which the Killua estate was to be broken up. In this will she arranged to bequeath £20,000 to her brother Thomas (Lawrence's father), making further generous legacies to his daughters in Ireland.

This separate provision for the Chapman girls leaves little doubt that she intended Mr Lawrence's £20,000 to pass, ultimately, to his sons. It is not unreasonable to suppose that he knew of these legacies and that he would have discussed them with Sarah Lawrence. If this is the case, it might account for some otherwise unexplained remarks in Lawrence's letters (see below).

Caroline Margaret Chapman was seriously ill for several years: a codicil to her will dated June 1916 was signed with a cross and witnessed by two nurses. She died in 1920, some months after the death of Lawrence's father. As he had predeceased her, the £20,000 bequest was passed, not to his sons, but to the residuary legatees under her will: his four Chapman daughters.

It seems possible that, following his father's death, Lawrence had learned from his mother of this bequest, and that this explains his remark in a letter to Eric Kennington of 1.10.1921: 'A lump of money I was expecting has not (probably will not) come.' The loss of the bequest may also explain the bitterness of the allusion to the Chapmans inserted by Lawrence in Liddell Hart's biography: 'The father's family seemed unconscious of his sons, even when after his death recognition of their achievement might have done honour to the name.'

If Lawrence did know of his aunt's bequest to his father (and I can discover no other 'lump of money' that he could have been expecting at that time) then it is less surprising that he should previously have given £3,000 of his earlier inheritance to Janet Hallsmith (née Laurie).

Alleged 'New Evidence' Relating to the Deraa Incident

Some months after the first edition of this book was published, a new 'contro-versial' biography of Lawrence appeared: *The Golden Warrior*, by Lawrence James (Weidenfeld & Nicolson, 1990). An advance press release informed reviewers that James 'provides documentary evidence that Lawrence concocted the story of his homosexual rape and torture at Deraa'. If true, this discovery would have great importance, bearing out the accusations of dishonesty made by a succession of Lawrence's detractors since the mid-1950s.

On page 214 of *The Golden Warrior*, James writes: 'It seems absolutely certain that Lawrence fabricated the incident at Dera'. It turns out, however, that this assertion rests on a single piece of documentary evidence: the service diary of the 10th Motor Section of the Royal Field Artillery, a British unit at Akaba. According to James, the diary records that on 21 November 1917 (the *Seven Pillars* date for the Deraa incident) Lawrence and Colonel Joyce were taking part in an armoured car reconnaissance up Wadi Itm, many miles from Deraa.

War diaries should be written up while the events are taking place, but this RFA diary was put together after an interval of six months, on 1 May 1918. The first page gives a description of the formation of the unit and its departure from Suez on board the SS *Ozarda* which arrived at Akaba, according to the diary, on 21 November. That date is demonstrably wrong. The log of the Akaba guardship HMS *Humber*—an impeccable source—shows that the SS *Ozarda* reached Ak-aba at 7.25 a.m. on 20 November, and began unloading at once. As this is one day earlier than the date given by Lt. Brodie in the RFA diary, it gives the lie to James's argument (page 386) that 'the dates of embarcation and disembarcation are most unlikely to have been forgotten'. Such an error, written after six months, must also cast doubt on the accuracy of Brodie's recollections written twenty years later still, for *T. E. Lawrence by his Friends* (Cape, 1937). There, Brodie stated that he first encountered Lawrence on the morning of his second day at Akaba (which must have been November 21). Anyone could be forgiven for inaccuracy after such an interval, and Brodie's statement in *Friends* cannot be treated as evidence unless it can be substantiated by contemporary sources.

At the head of the second page of the RFA diary, as is usual, Brodie repeated the latest date on the previous sheet: 21–11–17. Opposite this date there are eight lines of text describing not one, but a series of operations, as follows: 'Carried

411

out reconnaissance with Col P. Joyce and Col Lawrence, up Wadi Yetm. Carried out reconnaissance with Major Maynard in Wadi Araba towards Dead Sea. We reached a point five miles S.W. of Ain Gharandel and returned . . . Cars were used for transport of stores and personnel, including Sherif Fasil, to el Guierra, up Wadi Yetm and Maziaa . . . A working party was in Wadi Yetm making a road'. After this the *next* date given in the diary is a month later, '25–12–17 approx', when the RFA section left Akaba bound for Feisal's advance headquarters inland.

Even at first sight, Brodie's record of the first month at Akaba seems to be nothing more than a summary, and it is hard to see how anyone could take it to provide exact information about the dates of the unit's operations. However, the content of the page is, technically, ambiguous: it could mean that *all* the operations described in the first eight lines took place on a single day—November 21 —after which nothing happened for a month. This (physically impossible) claim is implicit in James's 'literal' interpretation.

A more reasonable view is that this retrospective section of the diary lists the operations that took place between the RFA unit's arrival at Akaba on November 21 (approx) and its departure on December 25 (approx). Military historians I have consulted all agree that after a sea voyage by freighter the unit would have needed several days to establish itself ashore before embarking on any kind of operation, and that it is virtually impossible that the unit began a reconnaissance up Wadi Itm on the day after SS *Ozarda* arrived at Akaba. There was, moreover, no urgency about this exploratory expedition.

The date of the Wadi Itm reconnaissance can be established with certainty by looking at other records that are truly contemporary with the events. Lawrence's pocket diary (now in the British Library) shows that he returned briefly to Akaba from his ill-fated northern expedition on November 26 (very briefly indeed, according to *Seven Pillars*). He left again the following day, spending subsequent nights in Wadi Itm and Wadi Hawara, and was back at Akaba on December 3. What had he been doing in the interval? He wrote to his family on December 14 that he had spent 'a few days motoring, prospecting the hills and valleys for a way Eastward for our cars'. This information tallies with the RFA war diary, except that instead of the single date '21–11–1917' the reconnaissance is shown to have begun on November 27 (by which time the unit would have had time to establish itself ashore) and ended a week later.

These dates for the reconnaissance do not rest on Lawrence's evidence alone: the seven-day absence from Akaba is borne out by the fact that Joyce, who accompanied him, dispatched no telegrams during that period. Indeed, the regular telegrams sent by Joyce to Cairo and Jidda provide absolute proof that Lawrence had not returned to Akaba by November 21. Lawrence's superiors in Cairo were extremely anxious for news of him, as his expedition northward behind enemy lines had been regarded as little short of suicidal. Clayton had written to Joyce on November 12: 'I am very anxious to get news of Lawrence to hear that he is safe'. If, as James argues, Lawrence had returned to Akaba by November 21, Joyce's daily messages on November 22 and 23 would certainly have mentioned the fact. However, they contain nothing more than a report from Arab sources that Lawrence and Ali ibn Hussein had attacked the railway somewhere between Deraa and Jerusalem. The first definite information Joyce could send was on November 24, after Lieutenant Wood, the Royal Navy officer who had taken part in the northern mission, had returned to Akaba, probably bringing Lawrence's detailed report to Clayton and other letters. Joyce's telegram read: 'L[awrence] left at Azrak. Found original objective impossible. On Nov 7 L[awrence] destroyed one train with two engines. Reported considerable casualties to Turks.' This message bears out Lawrence's diary dates and the chronology of his account in *Seven Pillars*. It can be found in file WO 158/634 at the Public Record Office—a file which James evidently consulted, since his references cite it as the source of several other documents.

Joyce was a highly responsible officer and, had he really spent November 21 with Lawrence, it is inconceivable that he would have failed to tell Clayton that Lawrence was safe. Had he done this, the information from Wood sent on November 24 would have been entirely superfluous, and the *Arab Bulletin* of December 5 would not have recorded in its 'Late News' section that 'Major Lawrence returned to Akaba at the beginning of December'. Therefore only one conclusion is possible: while the wording of Lt. Brodie's RFA diary, written up six months in arrears, is ambiguous, the interpretation James has put on it is shown to be incorrect by reliable documents that are truly contemporary with the events.

James's publishers make great play of his university training: according to the dust jacket of *The Golden Warrior* he was 'a founder member of York University, where he read History and English, and subsequently he undertook a research degree at Merton College, Oxford.' Likewise, Phillip Knightley wrote in the *Sunday Independent* on 19 August 1990: 'Lawrence James is an unlikely iconoclast. He is a historian, educated at York and Oxford, whose previous books have been meticulously researched histories of Imperial Britain'.

But how could any serious historian overlook such plain evidence while investigating the damning claim that his subject was a liar? The answer may be given in Phillip Knightley's article: 'James says he was always interested in Lawrence. "I was born in the West Country and over the years I came to know quite a lot of people who'd met him. I started to wonder where the truth lay, and, once I had read enough to realise that Lawrence was the only man this century to have made himself into a legend, I knew that one day I'd have to write a book about him." The key episode in Lawrence's life', Knightley continues, 'that struck James as false was the homosexual rape at Dera . . . "I felt that Lawrence's account did not ring true. But I saw no way of taking the argument any further." Then, ploughing through war diaries and intelligence reports for the period, James hit paydirt . . .' In other words, James was persuaded from the outset that Lawrence was a liar, and his mistaken interpretation of the 10th Motor Section RFA diary merely shows how easily a researcher can be blinded by preconceptions.

An enormous number of operational records from the First World War survive, and it is always rash to base startling conclusions on a single document. Correctly interpreted, the diary agrees with other surviving records. Far from proving that Lawrence gave a false account of his movements during November 1917, it adds detail to what is known from other sources. It also draws attention to something else, which James might have spotted if he had been less intent on proving Lawrence's dishonesty. Years later, Lawrence would write that it was in 1917 that he had decided, nebulously, to join the ranks, and that the 'friendly outings with the armoured car and air force fellows were what persuaded me that my best future, if I survived the war, was to enlist'. Might it not be significant that his first contact with British forces after the Deraa episode was a week-long expedition with the armoured car and RFA units from Akaba?

References and Notes

MANUSCRIPT MATERIALS: File and, in most cases, page number or document identification are given. In the case of the embargoed T. E. Lawrence papers at the Bodleian Library, file numbers are not listed as they will change when the papers become generally available.

In many instances originals or transcripts of documents are available in more than one location. The source listed here is the source I have used. For example, there are few references to the many original T. E. Lawrence letters held at the University of Texas because transcripts of these letters made for David Garnett's *Letters of T. E. Lawrence* (1938) were available to me among the T. E. Lawrence papers at the Bodleian Library.

Dates of letters and other documents are given in the standard British sequence: day-month-year, e.g. 9.11.1916 for 9 November 1916.

When quoting letters by T. E. Lawrence published in one of the standard collections, I have indicated this by using one of the abbreviations listed below.

Printed books: American as well as English editions are listed where the page references apply in both.

Abbreviations Used in the Notes

AB   *Arab Bulletin* (Cairo), secret Intelligence journal issued by the Arab Bureau, 1916–19. Facsimile reprint (Gerrards Cross, Archive Editions, 1984).

ADM   Archives of the British Admiralty in the Public Record Office, London.

AE   Archives of the French Foreign Office, Paris.

AFGG   [France] Ministère de la Guerre, Etat-Major de l'Armée—Service Historique: *Les Armées Françaises dans la Grande Guerre,* Tome IX—premiér volume, Volume d'Annexes (Paris, Imprimerie Nationale, 1935).

AIR — Archives of the Royal Flying Corps and Royal Air Force in the Public Record Office, London.

Arbur — Telegraphic address of the Arab Bureau, Cairo.

Ashmolean A — Ashmolean Museum Archives, Oxford.

B — Bodleian Library, Oxford

BL — British Library, London.

B:LH — *T. E. Lawrence to his Biographer Liddell Hart* (London, Faber & Faber, 1938; Garden City NY, Doubleday, Doran, 1939).

BM/A — Papers of F. G. Kenyon in the British Museum Archives relating to the excavations at Carchemish.

BM/WAA — Archaeological papers relating to the Carchemish excavations in the British Museum, Department of Western Asiatic Antiquities.

B(r) — Categories of embargoed material in the Bodleian Library, including the T. E. Lawrence papers embargoed until the year 2000.

B:RG — *T. E. Lawrence to his Biographer Robert Graves* (London, Faber & Faber, 1938; Garden City NY, Doubleday, Doran, 1939).

CAB — Archives of the British Cabinet in the Public Record Office, London.

CO — Archives of the British Colonial Office in the Public Record Office, London.

DBFP 1/4 — *Documents on British Foreign Policy 1919–1939*, First Series, Vol. IV, 1919, ed. E. L. Woodward and R. Butler (London, HMSO, 1952).

DG — D. Garnett (ed.), *Letters of T. E. Lawrence* (London, Jonathan Cape 1938; Garden City NY, Doubleday, Doran, 1939).

Dirmilint — Telegraphic address of the Director of Military Intelligence, War Office, London.

Durham — Durham University Library.

EoR — S. and R. Weintraub (eds.), *Evolution of a Revolt* [collected minor writings of T. E. Lawrence] (University Park and London, Pennsylvania State University Press, 1967).

ETEL — D. Garnett (ed). *The Essential T. E. Lawrence* (London, Jonathan Cape; New York, E. P. Dutton, 1951).

FO — Archives of the British Foreign Office in the Public Record Office, London.

Friends   A. W. Lawrence (ed.), *T. E. Lawrence by his Friends* (London, Jonathan Cape: Garden City NY, Doubleday, Doran, 1937).

Hedgehog   Telegraphic address of A. C. Dawnay's Arab Operations staff in Cairo. Some telegraph operators abbreviated this to 'Hedghog'.

HL   M. R. Lawrence (ed.), *The Home Letters of T. E. Lawrence and his Brothers* (Oxford, Blackwell; New York, Macmillan, 1954).

HGM   E. Brémond, *Le Hedjaz dans la Guerre Mondiale* (Paris, Payot, 1931).

Houghton   Houghton Library, Harvard University.

HRHRC   Harry Ransom Humanities Research Center, University of Texas, Austin.

Intrusive   Telegraphic address of the Military Intelligence Department, Cairo.

IWM   Imperial War Museum, London.

KCL   The Liddell Hart Centre for Military Archives, King's College, London.

LAA   K. Morsey, *T. E. Lawrence und der arabische Aufstand 1916–18* (Osnabrück, Biblio Verlag, 1976. A revised English edition is in preparation)

LH:*TEL*   B. H. Liddell Hart, *'T. E. Lawrence' in Arabia and After* (London, Jonathan Cape, 1934).

L-L   J. M. Wilson (ed.), *Letters from T. E. Lawrence to E. T. Leeds* (Andoversford, Whittington Press, 1988).

L/P&S   Political and secret papers of the British India Office in the India Office Library, London.

LTEL   A. W. Lawrence (ed.), *Letters to T. E. Lawrence* (London, Jonathan Cape, 1962).

MB   M. Brown (ed.) *Letters of T. E. Lawrence* (London, J. M. Dent, 1988).

The Mint   T. E. Lawrence, *The Mint* [revised unexpurgated text] (London, Jonathan Cape, 1973).

MOEP   *Military Operations in Egypt and Palestine* ('Official History of the Great War' series (Vol. I by Sir G. MacMunn and C. Falls; Vol. II (Parts I and 2) by C. Falls and A. F. Becke; with two cases of maps (London, HMSO, 1930–9).

OA			A. W. Lawrence (ed.), *Oriental Assembly* [collected minor writings of T. E. Lawrence] (London, Williams & Norgate, 1939; New York, E. P. Dutton, 1940).

PEF			Archives of the Palestine Exploration Fund, London.

PRO			Public Record Office, London. Also a file class at the PRO designating collections of private papers held there.

SIR			H. M. Hyde, *Solitary in the Ranks* (London, Constable, 1977; New York, Atheneum, 1978).

SP			T. E. Lawrence, *Seven Pillars of Wisdom* (London, Jonathan Cape; Garden City NY, Doubleday, Doran, 1935).

SP(O)		*Seven Pillars of Wisdom,* 1922 draft, known as the 'Oxford' text.

WO			Archives of the British War Office in the Public Record Office, London.

References for quotations are given in sequence for each page. Where a quotation runs across a page-break, the reference will be found under the page on which the quotation ends.

Prologue

p. xv The German work referred to is K. Morsey, *T. E. Lawrence und der arabische Aufstand 1916–18* (Osnabrück, Biblio Verlag, 1976). **p. xviii** TEL to V. W. Richards n.d. (1922), B(r) (transcript). W. S. Churchill, address given at the City of Oxford High School for Boys on the occasion of the unveiling of a memorial to T. E. Lawrence, 1936, *HL* p. xiii. **p. xix** TEL to R. R. Graves 28.6.1927 *B:RG* p. 58. **p. xxiii** P. Adam, *Les Echecs de T. E. Lawrence* (privately printed, *c.* 1962, p. 9) author's translation. **p. xxiv** TEL to C. F. Shaw 29.3.1927 BL Add. MS 45903. **p. xxv** W. S. Churchill, *Life of Lord Randolph Churchill* London, Macmillan, 1906, pp. x-xi.

Chapter 1. Childhood
December 1888–October 1907

p. 3 *Baedeker's Northern France* (London, 1894) **p. 21.** TEL to R. White 10.6.1931 *DG* p. 721. **p. 5** TEL, introduction to *Travels in Arabia Deserta* by C. M. Doughty (London, Jonathan Cape and the Medici Society, 1921) p. xxviii. *Ibid.* **p. 7** H. R. Hall, 'T. E. Lawrence' in *Oxford High School Magazine* (Oxford) 1935, pp.40–1. TEL to C. F. Shaw 24.8.1926, BL Add. MS 45903. TEL, amendments to the typescript of R. R. Graves, *Lawrence and the Arabs,* 1927, Houghton fMS Eng 1252 (367). E. F. Hall in *Friends* p. 46. A. W. Lawrence to J. E. Mack 1.11.1968, quoted in Mack's *A Prince of our Disorder* (Boston, Little, Brown, 1976) p. 474 n. 70. A. W. Lawrence to J. M. Wilson 12.5.1985. **p. 8** C. F. C. Beeson in *Friends* p. 52. **p. 9** T. W. Chaundy in *Friends* p. 41. C. F. C. Beeson in *Friends* p. 52. 'Report of the Keeper of the Ashmolean Museum to the Visitors', in *Oxford University Gazette* (Oxford) Vol. xxxvii, No. 1203, 30.4.1907, pp. 552–6. **p. 10** C. F. Bell, notes on LH:*TEL*, BL Add. MS 63549. **p. 11** A. W. Lawrence to J. M. Wilson 12.5.1985. TEL to his family 19.5.1911, B MS Res C13. **p. 12** TEL to C. F. Shaw 14.4.1927, BL Add. MS 45903. **p. 13** B. H. Liddell Hart's notes on a conversation with Lawrence, weekend of 12.5.1929, B(r) (transcript). TEL to D. Knowles 7.12.1927 *DG* p. 553. *The Mint*, Part 2, ch. 11, p. 132. TEL, written reply to B. H. Liddell Hart's 'Queries I' *B:LH* p. 51. TEL to C. F. Shaw 26.12.1925, BL Add. MS 45903. TEL, written reply to B. H. Liddell Hart's 'Queries I', B(r) (transcript). **p. 14** TEL to Mrs Rieder 8.3.1914, B(r) (transcript). **p. 15** TEL to his family 14.8.1906, B MS Res C13. TEL to his family 28.8.1906, B MS Res C13. TEL to his father 20.8.1906, B MS Res C13. TEL to his mother 24.8.1906, B MS Res C13. T. E. Lawrence to his father 20.8.1906, B MS Res C13. TEL to his mother 24.8.1906, B MS Res C13. TEL to his father 6.8.1906. B MS Res C13. TEL to his mother 26.8.1906, B MS Res C13. **p. 16** TEL to C. F. Shaw 10.7.1928, BL Add. MS 45904. TEL to his mother 14.8.1906, B MS Res C13. TEL to W. G. Lawrence 16.8.1906, B MS Res C13. TEL to his father 20.8.1906, B MS Res C13. TEL, 'Twenty-Seven Articles', *Arab Bulletin* (Cairo), 20.8.1917. **p. 17** TEL to his father 20.8.1906, B MS Res C13. T. E. Lawrence to his mother 24.8.1906, B MS Res C13. TEL to his mother 26.8.1906, B MS Res C13. TEL to his father 31.8.1906, B MS Res C13. TEL to his mother 28.8.1906, B MS Res C13. **p. 18** TEL to his mother 26.8.1906, B MS Res C13. C. F. C. Beeson in *Friends* p. 54. *Ibid.* TEL to his father 31.8.1906, B MS Res C13. **p. 19** TEL to his mother 24.8.1906, B MS Res C13. TEL to his mother 6.4.1907, B MS Res C13. TEL to D. G. Hogarth 14.1.1926 *DG* p. 491. TEL, written reply to B. H. Liddell Hart's 'Queries I' *B:LH* p. 51. **p. 20** TEL to D. Knowles 14.7.1927, B(r) (transcript).

Chapter 2. Oxford University
October 1907–December 1910

p. 22 A. T. P. Williams, 'Lawrence in Oxford' *The Oxford Magazine* (Oxford) Vol. 53, Feb.-June 1935, p. 696. A. G. Prys-Jones, 'Lawrence of Arabia: Some Personal Impressions' (typescript). Jesus College, Oxford. *The Mint*, Part 2, ch. 2, p. 109. **p. 23** *SP* ch. LXI p. 348. E. F. Hall in *Friends* pp. 46–7. TEL, written reply to B. H. Liddell Hart's 'Queries I' *B:LH* pp. 50–1. **p. 24** L. C. Jane to R. R. Graves 26.7.1927, B(r). *Oxford University Examination Statutes* 1908, p. 97. TEL to his mother 23.7.1908, B MS Res C13. TEL to his mother 2.8.1908, B MS Res C13. **p. 25** TEL to his mother 6.8.1908, B MS Res C13. **p. 26** TEL to his family 9.8.1908, B MS Res C13. TEL to his mother 28.8.1908, B MS Res C13. **p. 27** *Ibid.* C. F. Bell, notes on LH:*TEL*, BL Add. MS 63549. **p. 28** C. M. Doughty to T. E. Lawrence 3.2.1909 *LTEL* p. 37. TEL, written reply to B. H. Liddell Hart's 'Queries I' *B:LH* p. 52. **p. 29** W. Morris: *A Note by William Morris on his Aims in Founding the Kelmscott Press* . . . (London, Kelmscott Press, 1898) p. 1. L. H. Green in *Friends* p. 68. TEL to his mother 'about' 6.7.1909, B MS Res C13. T. E. Lawrence to his mother 2.8.1909, B MS Res C13. **p. 30** *Ibid. Ibid. Ibid.* **p. 31** TEL to his family 13.8.1909, B MS Res C13. TEL to his mother 29.8.1909, B MS Res C13. *Ibid.* TEL to his mother 7.9.1909, B MS Res C13. *Ibid.* TEL to his mother 29.8.1909, B MS Res C13. TEL to his mother 7.9.1909, B MS Res C13. **p. 32** TEL to E. T. Leeds 19.9.1909, Leeds papers. TEL to Sir John Rhys 24.9.1909 *DG* p. 81. TEL to his mother 9.10.1909, B MS Res C13. **p. 33** TEL to C. F. Shaw 12.5.1927, BL Add. MS 45903. TEL to his family 16.3.1916, B MS Res C13.

420 *References and Notes*

TEL to his mother late August 1910, B MS Res C13. **p. 34** TEL to V. W. Richards 10.12.1913 *DG* pp. 160–61. TEL to his family 24.1.1911, B MS Res C13. V. W. Richards, *Portrait of T. E. Lawrence* (London, Jonathan Cape, 1936) p. 20. **p. 35** Quoted in P. G. Knightley and C. Simpson, *The Secret Lives of Lawrence of Arabia* (London, Nelson, 1969) p. 29. V. W. Richards in *Friends* p. 383. TEL to his family 31.1.1911, B MS Res C13. **p. 36** Quoted in J. E. Mack, *A Prince of our Disorder* (Boston, Little, Brown, 1976) p. 65. TEL to W. G. Lawrence 11.5.1911, B MS Res C13. L. C. Jane to R. R. Graves 26.7.1927. B(r). **p. 37** C. T. Atkinson to the President of Magdalen College, Oxford 18.6.1935, Liddell Hart papers 9/13/33, KCL. W. H. Hutton to R. R. Graves 21.11.1927. B(r). E. Barker in *Friends* p. 62. TEL to E. T. Leeds 2.11.1910, Leeds papers. **p. 38** *Ibid.* D. G. Hogarth, 'The Excavations at Carchemish: First Report' in *The Times* (London) 1.7.1911, p. 5. D. G. Hogarth, *Carchemish* Vol. I (London, The British Museum, 1914), p. 12. **p. 39** D. G. Hogarth: 'The Excavations at Carchemish: First Report' in *The Times* (London) 1.7.1911, p. 5. E. T. Leeds, 'Recollections of T. E. Lawrence,' Leeds papers. **p. 40** D. G. Hogarth, *Accidents of an Antiquary's Life* (London, Macmillan, 1910) p. 1. C. F. Bell, notes on LH:*TEL*, BL Add. MS 63549. TEL to his family 24.1.1911, B MS Res C13. TEL to Herbert Baker 20.1.1928 *DG* p. 568. **p. 41** TEL to R. V. Buxton 22.9.1923, Jesus College, Oxford. TEL to his family 14.1.1911, B MS Res C13.

Chapter 3. Beginnings at Carchemish
December 1910–June 1912

p. 42 TEL to his family December 1910, B MS Res C13. **p. 43** F. G. Kenyon to the Lords Commissioners of the Treasury, late December 1910, BM/A. TEL to his family 26.2.1911, B MS Res C13. D. G. Hogarth, report to the British Museum 20.5.1911, pp. 3–4, BM/A. **p. 44** D. G. Hogarth to F. G. Kenyon 16.3.1911, BM/A. TEL to his family 1.3.1911, B MS Res C13. **p. 45** TEL to his family 20.3.1911, B MS Res C13. R. D. Barnett in *Carchemish* Vol. III (London, The British Museum, 1952) p. 258. **p. 46** TEL to E. T. Leeds 27.3.1911, Leeds papers. TEL to his family 31.3.1911, B MS Res C13. **p. 47** D. G. Hogarth to F. G. Kenyon 1.4.1911, BM/A. *Ibid.* TEL to his family 16.4.1911, B MS Res C13. **p. 48** TEL to his family 11.4.1911, B MS Res C13. D. G. Hogarth to W. M. F. Petrie 10.7.1911, Ashmolean A. **p. 49** TEL to his family 11.5.1911, B MS Res C13. D. G. Hogarth, *The Life of C. M. Doughty* (London, OUP, 1928) p. 176 n. 1. D. G. Hogarth, report to the British Museum 20.5.1911, pp. 39–40, BM/A. *Ibid.* p. 20. **p. 50** TEL to his family 23.5.1911, B MS Res C13. G. M. L. Bell to her family 18.5.1911 *The Letters of Gertrude Bell*, ed. Lady Bell (London, Ernest Benn, 1927) Vol. I, pp. 305–6. TEL to his family 24.6.1911, B MS Res C13. **p. 51** TEL, diary entry for 29.7.1911 *OA* p. 46. TEL, diary entry for 31.7.1911 *OA* p. 48. TEL to his family 24.6.1911, B MS Res C13. **p. 52** TEL to his family 6.1.1912, B MS Res C13. TEL to Mrs Rieder 4.7.1911 *DG* p. 115. 13. TEL to Mrs Rieder 11.8.1911 *DG* p. 119. TEL to D. G. Hogarth 24.6.1911 *DG* p. 114. **p. 53** TEL to N. Rieder postmarked 12.8.1911 *DG* p. 120. D. G. Hogarth to F. G. Kenyon 4.10.1911, BM/A. **p. 54** TEL to his family 11.1.1912, B MS Res C13. TEL to his family 18.1.1912, B MS Res C13. **p. 55** TEL to D. G. Hogarth 12.2.1912, B(r) (transcript). TEL to his family 18.1.1912, B MS Res C13. **p. 56** TEL to E. T. Leeds 18.3.1912, Leeds papers. D. G. Hogarth to F. G. Kenyon 10.5.1912, BM/A. D. G. Hogarth to F. G. Kenyon 19.5.1912, BM/A. **p. 57** TEL to Mrs Rieder 20.5.1912 *DG* p. 139. TEL to his family June 1912, B MS Res C13.

Chapter 4. Achievement at Carchemish
June 1912–August 1914

p. 58 TEL to his family 23.6.1912, B MS Res C13. TEL to his family 3.8.1912, B MS Res C13. H. Flecker (ed.), *Some Letters from Abroad of James Elroy Flecker* (London, William Heinemann, 1930) p. 59. **p. 59** TEL to his family 13.9.1912, B MS Res C13. TEL to M. R. Lawrence 12.9.1912, B MS Res C13. TEL to his family 18.9.1912, B MS Res C13. TEL to his family 22.2.1913, B MS Res C13. **p. 60** TEL to V. W. Richards 15.7.1918 *DG* p. 244. 'The Kaer of ibu Wardani,' by C. J. G. [pseud. of TEL] in *Jesus College Magazine* (Oxford) Vol. I, No. 2, January 1913, pp. 37–39. C. L. Woolley *Dead Towns and Living Men* (London, OUP, 1920) p. 188. TEL to Mrs Rieder 7.1.1913. B(r) (transcript). **p. 61** TEL, note for inclusion in Liddell Hart's biography, *B:LH* p. 87. TEL to his family 2.2.1913, B MS Res C13. TEL to D. G. Hogarth 2.2.1913, Leeds papers. TEL to his family 22.2.1913, B MS Res C13. **p. 62** TEL to E. T. Leeds 25.5.1913, Leeds papers. TEL to D. G. Hogarth end of February 1913, BM/A. TEL to his family 23.3.1913, B MS Res C13. **p. 63** TEL to his family 26.4.1913, B MS Res C13. C. L. Woolley in *Friends* p. 87. C. L. Woolley, report to the Trustees of the British Museum for April 1913, BM/A. **p. 64** TEL to E. T. Leeds 15.5.1913, Leeds papers. C. L. Woolley to D. G. Hogarth 6.6.1913, BM/WAA. TEL to his family 11.6.1913, B MS Res C13. TEL to his family 15.6.1913, B MS Res C13. TEL to his family 20.3.1911, B MS Res C13. TEL to his family 13.3.1913, B MS Res C13. TEL to his family 26.4.1913, B MS Res C13. **p. 65** TEL to his family 15.6.1913, B MS Res C13. W. G. Lawrence to a friend 14.10.1913 *DG* p. 158. W. G. Lawrence to his family 16.9.1913 *HL* p. 442. W. G. Lawrence to his family 27.9.1913 *HL* p. 447. **p. 66** TEL to C. F. Bell 1.10.1913, BL Add. MS 63550. TEL to W. G. Lawrence 21.10.1913, B MS Res C13. C. L. Woolley in *Friends* p. 89. **p. 67** *Ibid.* **p. 68** TEL to F. el Akle 3.1.1921, B(r) (photocopy). E. T. Leeds, 'Recollections of T. E. Lawrence', Leeds papers. TEL to R. R. Graves 28.6.1927, Houghton fMS Eng 1252 (347). **p. 69** TEL to his family 3.10.1913, B MS Res C13. C. L. Woolley to F. G. Kenyon 6.11.1913, BM/A. **p. 70** TEL to V. W. Richards 10.12.1913 *DG* pp. 160–61. TEL to R. V. Buxton 22.9.1923, Jesus College, Oxford. C. L. Woolley to F. G. Kenyon, telegram *c.* 10.12.1913, PEF. C. L. Woolley to F. G. Kenyon 17.12.1913, BM/A. **p. 71** TEL to F. Messham 20.12.1913 *DG* p. 162. TEL to his family 26.12.1913, B MS Res C13. TEL to C. F. Bell 26.12.1913, BL Add. MS 63550. **p. 72** Sir Charles Watson to C. L. Woolley 16.12.1913, PEF. S. F. Newcombe in *Friends* p. 105. TEL to his family 4.1.1914, B MS Res C13. TEL to E. T. Leeds 24.1.1914, Leeds papers. **p. 73** C. L. Woolley and TEL, *The Wilderness of Zin* (Palestine Exploration Fund *Annual* No. 3, 1914–1915, London, Palestine Exploration Fund, 1914) pp. xv-xvi. *Ibid.* pp. 11–12. **p. 74** TEL to E. T. Leeds 28.2.1914, Leeds papers. *Ibid.* D. G. Hogarth to F. G. Kenyon 8.2.1914, BM/A. **p. 75** TEL to his family 23.4.1914, B MS Res C13. TEL to his family 17.5.1914, B MS Res C13. **p. 76** C. L. Woolley to F. G. Kenyon 31.5.1914, BM/A. C. L. Woolley, preface to *Carchemish* Vol. III (London, British Museum, 1952) p.[5]. C. L. Woolley, *As I Seem to Remember* (London, Allen & Unwin, 1962) p. 93. TEL to D. Knowles 7.12.1927 *DG* p. 553.

Chapter 5. London and Cairo
August 1914–August 1915

p. 81 TEL to R. V. Buxton 22.9.1923, Jesus College, Oxford. **p. 82** TEL to F. G. Kenyon 2.11.1914, BM/A. TEL to E. T. Leeds 16.11.1914, Leeds papers. *Ibid.* **p. 86** Lord Kitchener to R. H. A. Storrs, for Sherif Abdullah, repeated in FO to M. Cheetham, telegram, 24.9.1914, FO 371/2768. **p. 87** TEL to D. G. Hogarth 20.12.1914 *DG* p. 190. Force in Egypt, GHQ General Staff, War Diary entry for 22.12.1914, WO 95/4360. TEL to W. G. Lawrence 21.1.1915, B MS Res C13. Diary entry by S. P. Cockerell, a close friend of Lloyd's, for 27.12.1914, Lloyd papers GLLD 9/1, Churchill College, Cambridge. **p. 88** *SP* ch. VI   p. 57. S. F. Newcombe, note, 1927 B(r). ('Lawrence' has been substituted where Newcombe wrote 'T. E.,' because Lawrence was neither referred to nor addressed in this way prior to 1923). **p. 89** Sir J. G. Maxwell to Lord Kitchener 4.12.1914 quoted in *MOEP*, Vol. I, p. 20 n. 2. Sir J. G. Maxwell to Lord Kitchener, telegram, 27.11.1914, FO 371/2139. Lord Kitchener to Sir J. G. Maxwell, 28.11.1914, FO 371/2139. **p. 90** Quoted in M. Fitzherbert, *The Man who was Greenmantle* (London, John Murray, 1983) p. 149. TEL to D. G. Hogarth 15.1.1915 *DG* p. 191. *SP* ch. CIII   p. 566. **p. 91** E. M. Dowson in *Friends*   p. 138. *Ibid.* p. 136. R. H. A. Storrs, *Orientations* (London, Ivor Nicholson & Watson, 1937) p. 229. S. F. Newcombe, note, 1927. B(r). **p. 93** TEL to D. G. Hogarth 18.3.1915 *DG* pp. 193–94. *Ibid. Ibid.* **p. 94** TEL to D. G. Hogarth 22.3.1915 *DG* pp. 195–96. TEL, 'Syria: the Raw Material . . . written early in 1915' *AB* , 12.3.1917, p. 110. *Ibid.* **p. 95** *Ibid.* pp. 110–12. *Ibid.* p. 112. **p. 96** *Ibid.* pp. 112–13. *Ibid.* p. 113. *Ibid. Ibid.* p. 114. *Ibid.* **p. 97** TEL to his family 4.6.1915, B MS Res C13. **p. 98** TEL to his mother, undated, B MS Res C13. TEL to his family 23.6.1916, B MS Res C13. **p. 99** TEL to his family 19.8.1915, B MS Res C13. TEL, note on the typescript of *Lawrence and the Arabs* by R. R. Graves, 1927, *B:RG* p. 82.

Chapter 6. The Arabs Revolt
September 1915–October 1916

p. 100 TEL to his family, 31.8.1915, B MS Res C13. **p. 101** D. G. Hogarth, 'Mecca's Revolt against the Turk' from *Century Magazine* (New York) Vol. 78, July 1920, p. 409. D. G. Hogarth, 'T. E. Lawrence,' in *Encyclopædia Britannica*, 13th ed., supplementary Vol. 2 (London and New York, 1922) p. 674. **p. 102** Sir A. H. McMahon to FO 26.10.1915, FO 371/2486. TEL to W. G. Lawrence 17.7.1915, B(r). TEL to E. T. Leeds 16.11.1915, Leeds papers. **p. 103** TEL to his family 24.1.1916, B MS Res C13. TEL, verbal statement noted by B. H. Liddell Hart *B:LH* pp. 61–62. **p. 104** B. H. Liddell Hart, notes made of a conversation with TEL, *B:LH* p. 141. TEL, 'The Politics of Mecca,' sent to the Cairo Residency on 1.2.1916. FO 141/461. **p. 107** Sir A. H. McMahon to Sir P. Z. Cox 20.3.1916, Houghton Library, bMS Eng 1252 (372). **p. 108** *SP* ch. VI p. 60. TEL, note on the typescript of B. H. Liddell Hart, '*T. E. Lawrence*' in *Arabia and After*, June 1933, *B:LH* p. 92. **p. 109** TEL, suppressed introductory chapter of *SP*, *OA* pp. 143–4. **p. 111** Minutes of a meeting of the Nicolson Committee, 21.1.1916, FO 371/2767. Draft of the Sykes-Picot terms enclosed with Sir A. Nicolson to Sir E. Grey 2.2.1916, FO 371/2767. Minute (headed 'Arab Question') of a meeting held on 4.2.1916, FO 371/2767. **p. 112** Intrusive Cairo to Dirmilint London, telegram, 3.5.1916, FO 882/2. **p. 113** TEL to his family 1.7.1916, B Ms Res C13. D. G. Hogarth, report, 10.6.1916, FO 882/4. Sir A. H. McMahon to Sherif Hussein 23.6.1916, draft letter to be telegraphed to Port Sudan for translation and transmission, FO 882/19. **p. 114** Sir A. J. Murray to Sir W. R. Robertson, telegram, 15.6.1916, WO 158/625. Sir W. R. Robertson to Sir A. J. Murray, telegram, 16.6.1916, WO 158/625. *SP*(O) ch. 22. *Ibid.* Sir A. J. Murray to Sir A. H. McMahon 19.6.1916, FO 141/738/3818. **p. 115** EEF Intelligence Diary 24.6.1916, WO 157/705. D. G. Hogarth, 'Arab Bureau report for June 1916,' 30.6.1916, p. 2, FO 141/738/3894. TEL to his family 1.7.1916, B Ms Res C13. **p. 116** War Office memorandum, 'The Sherif of Mecca and the Arab Movement,' 1.7.1916, FO 371/2773. Sir A. J. Murray to Sir W. R. Robertson 14.7.1916, CAB 44/15. **p. 117** *SP*(O) ch. 41. **p. 118** TEL to his family 22.7.1916, B MS Res C13. *Ibid.* **p. 119** *SP*(O) ch. 9. *Ibid.* G. F. Clayton to Sir F. R. Wingate 9.10.1916, Wingate papers W/141/3/35, Durham. *SP*(O) ch. 9.

Chapter 7. Intelligence Mission to the Hejaz
October–November 1916

p. 121 Arab Bureau, 'Summary of the Military Achievement of the Sherif of Mecca, June to October 1916', October 1916, FO 882/5 fos. 80–81. **p. 122** TEL, 'The Sherifs,' 27.10.1916, FO 882/5 fos. 40–41. **p. 123** TEL, memorandum 17.11.1916, Clayton papers 694/4/42–46 (misdated 18.11.1916), Durham. E. Brémond to A. Defrance 16.10.1916, quoted in M. J-M Larès: *T. E. Lawrence, La France et Les Français* (Paris, Imprimerie Nationale, 1980) p. 156 (author's translation). TEL, 'The Sherifs,' 27.10.1916, FO 882/5 fo. 40. **p. 124** TEL, report 29.10.1916, *AB* No. 31, 18.11.1916, p. 458. TEL, 'The Sherifs', 27.10.1916, FO 882/5 fo. 41. TEL, report 29.10.1916, FO 882/5 fo. 72. TEL to A. C. Parker 24.10.1916, Parker papers. **p. 125** TEL, 'Hejaz Administration,' 3.11.1916, FO 882/5 fo. 54. **p. 126** TEL, 'Military Notes,' 3.11.1916, FO 882/5 fos. 56–58 **p. 127** A. C. Parker, diary entry for 31.10.1916, Parker papers. TEL, suppressed introductory chapter of *Seven Pillars*, OA, pp. 139–46. **p. 128** Sir F. R. Wingate to Arbur, telegram 9, 7.11.1916, WO 158/603. Sir W. R. Robertson to Sir F. R. Wingate, telegram 24923, 11.11.1916, Wingate papers W/143/2/142–143, Durham. **p. 129** Arab Bureau Report 31.10.1916, FO 371/2781. Sir F. R. Wingate to G. F. Clayton, telegram 781, 12.11.1916, Wingate papers W/143/2/144, Durham. Sir F. R. Wingate to C. E. Wilson 12.11.1916, Wingate papers W/143/1, Durham. Arbur to Sir F. R. Wingate, telegram AB205, 13.11.1916, Wingate papers W/143/2/190–192, Durham. **p. 130** Sir F. R. Wingate to G. F. Clayton 14.11.1916, Wingate Papers W/143/2/193–4, Durham. TEL, note on the typescript of LH:*TEL*, June 1933, *B:LH* p. 93. **p. 131** TEL, memorandum, 17.11.1916, quoted from the text in Sir A. J. Murray (GOC-in-C Egypt) to DMI, telegram IA2629, 17.1.1916, WO 106/1511 fos. 34–35. *SP* ch. XVII p. 114. Sir F. R. Wingate to C. E. Wilson 23.11.1916, Wingate papers W/143/6/54–56, Durham. **p. 132** Earl of Cork and Orrery, *My Naval Life* (London, Hutchinson, 1942) p. 99. C. E. Wilson to G. F. Clayton 22.11.1916, Clayton papers 470/4, Durham.

Chapter 8. Temporary Posting with Feisal
December 1916–January 1917

p. 134 TEL, 'The Arab Advance on Wejh', *AB* No. 41, 6.2.1917, pp. 60–2. *SP* ch. XX p. 126. **p. 135** *SP* ch. XX p. 130. **p. 136** *SP* ch. XVII pp. 114–15. **p. 137** *SP*(O) ch. 24. TEL, 'The Arab advance on Wejh', *AB* No. 41, 6.2.1917, pp. 60–62. *SP*(O) ch. 23. *B:LH* p. 63. **p. 138** TEL, 'The advance on Wejh', *AB* No. 41, 6.2.1917, p. 62.

TEL to K. Cornwallis 27.12.1916, FO 882/6. TEL to R. Fitzmaurice 2.1.1917, Houghton fMS Eng 1252 (352).   **p. 139** TEL to C. E. Wilson, report, 8.1.1917, FO 882/6 fos. 127–28. C. E. Wilson to Arbur, telegram W126, 6.1.1917, WO 158/627.   **p. 140** TEL to his family 16.1.1917, B MS Res C13. TEL to S. F. Newcombe 17.1.1917, National Museum, Ankara. TEL, notebook entry dated 18.1.1917, BL Add. MS 45915 fo. 2.   **p. 149** Sir R. E. Wemyss to the Admiralty 30.1.1917, ADM 137/548 fos. 114–15. C. E. Vickery, 'Memorandum on the general situation in Arabia (Hedjaz) and the Policy and Organisation of the British Mission to Grand Sherif' 2.2.1917, FO 882/6 fo. 152.   **p. 142** *AB* No. 40, 29.1.1917, p. 41. Sir F. R. Wingate to Sir W. R. Robertson 21.2.1917, FO 882/6 fos. 189–90. C. V. Vickery *op. cit.* fos. 152–54.   **p. 143** *Ibid.* fo. 156. R. H. A. Storrs, *Orientations* (London, Ivor Nicholson & Watson, 1937) p. 221.   **p. 144** *SP* epilogue p. 661.   **p. 145** C. E. Wilson to Arbur, telegram W300, 25.1.1917, FO 141/736/2475.

Chapter 9. Looking Northwards
January–April 1917

p. 146 TEL to his family 31.1.1917 *HL* p. 334.   **p. 147** *SP* ch. XXVIII p. 168.   **p. 148** *SP* ch. XXXVI p. 214.   **p. 149** *SP*(O) ch. 115.   **p. 153** TEL, notebook entry dated 17.2.1917, FO 882/6 fo. 179. *SP*(O) ch. XXXII.   **p. 155** Note enclosed in a letter from G. F. Clayton to Sir F. R. Wingate of 7.9.1916, Durham 140/2/106. H. Garland, 'Report on the Raiding Party sent to the Hejaz Railway line under Bimbashi Garland, February 1917' 6.3.1917, FO 882/6 fo. 40. TEL, verbal reply to a question from B. H. Liddell Hart *B:LH* p. 63 (where the words 'not very good' are omitted).   **p. 156** C. E. Vickery, report, 1.3.1917, FO 886/6 fos. 47–48.   **p.157** B. H. Liddell Hart, notes on a conversation with TEL 31.10.1933 *B:LH* pp.188–89.   **p. 159** TEL to C. E. Wilson, undated, but 8.3.1917, Houghton bMS Eng 1252 (230). TEL, notebook entry dated 10.3.1917, BL Add. MS 45914.   **p. 160** *SP* ch. XXXI p. 181.   **p. 161** *SP* ch. XXXVIII p. 225. *Ibid.* ch. XXXIII p. 193.   **p. 162** TEL, notebook entry dated 22.3.1917, BL Add. MS 45914 fo. 34. B. H. Liddell Hart, notes after a conversation with TEL 31.10.1933 *B:LH* p. 188. J. C. Watson to GOC Middle East Brigade RFC 11.1.1917, WO 158/605. TEL, notebook entry dated 22.3.1917, BL Add. MS 45914 fo. 33.   **p. 163** TEL to C. E. Wilson 16.4.1917, FO 882/6.   **p. 164** TEL, report, April 1917, FO 882/6 fo. 340. TEL, 'Raids on the Railway,' *AB* No. 50, 13.5.1917, pp. 216–17. TEL to C. E. Wilson 16.4.1917, FO 882/6.   **p. 165** P. C. Joyce to C. E. Wilson 1.4.1917, FO 886/6. *Ibid.*   **p. 166** 'Note on Information received from Col. Newcombe dated 5th April', WO 158/606. *Ibid.*   **p. 167** G. F. Clayton, memorandum to the Arab Bureau 8.3.1917; copied to Sir F. R. Wingate, C. E. Wilson and TEL.

Chapter 10. 'A Useful Diversion'
April–July 1917

p. 168 *SP* ch. 38 p. 225.   **p. 169** TEL, 'The Howeitat and their Chiefs' *AB* No. 59, 24.7.1917, pp. 309–10. G. F. Clayton to Sir F. R. Wingate 29.5.1917, FO 882/6 fo. 388.   **p. 170** *SP* ch. XXXVII p. 226.   **p. 171** *SP* ch. XXXVIII p. 225–26.   **p. 172** Note by TEL on the typescript of LH:*TEL*, *B:LH* p. 97. C. E. Wilson, 'Note on the proposed military plan of operations of the Arab Armies' 1.5.1917, FO882/6 fo. 351.   **p. 173** Sir T. B. M. Sykes to Sir G. M. W. Macdonogh (DMI, War Office), telegram 18, 30.4.1917, FO 882/16.   **p. 174** *AB* No. 50, 13.5.1917 p. 207. Sir T. B. M. Sykes to Sir

F. R. Wingate 6.5.1917, FO 141/654 fo. 243. *Ibid.* **p. 175** C. E. Wilson to G. F. Clayton 21.3.1917, FO 882/12 fo. 198. Quoted in *HGM* p. 142. *Ibid.* 'Note by Lt. Col Newcombe D.S.O.' 20.5.1917, Wingate papers W145/7/66, Durham. **p. 176** TEL, pocket diary entry for 13.5.1917, BL Add. MS 45983. **p. 177** *SP* ch. XLII, pp. 246–47. **p. 178** *SP* ch. XLIV, p. 254. TEL, notebook entry, 2.6.1917, BL Add. MS 45915 fo. 56. *SP* introductory chapter, first published in *OA* p. 145. **p. 179** TEL, pocket diary entry, 5.6.1917, BL Add. MS 45983. TEL, notebook jotting, undated but *c.* 5.6.1917, BL Add. MS 45915 fo. 55v. TEL to V. W. Richards, undated but *c.* autumn 1922, B(r) (transcript). **p. 180** *SP*(O) ch. 51. *Ibid.* **p. 181** TEL to G. F. Clayton 10.7.1917 *DG* p. 225. Miscellaneous Military Report No. 148, 7.7.1917, L/P&S/11/24, file p. 2885. **p. 182** *SP* ch. XCIX p. 546. *SP* ch. XXX p. 174. *SP*(O) ch. 51. TEL, verbal answer to a question by B. H. Lidell Hart, 24.2.1933, B(r) (transcript). **p. 183** *SP* introductory chapter, first published in *OA* pp. 145–46. **p. 184** *SP*(O) ch. 57. G. F. Clayton to Sir G. M. W. Macdonogh 5.7.1917, FO. 882/7 fo. 2.

Chapter 11. The Consequences of Akaba
July–August 1917

p. 186 S. F. Newcombe, report, 4.5.1917, FO 686/6 Part 2 fos. 80–81. **p. 188** G. F. Clayton, memorandum, 15.7.1917, WO158/634. *Ibid.* Sir E. H. H. Allenby to Sir W. R. Robertson, telegram EA61, 16.7.1917, WO 158/634. *Ibid.* C. E. Wilson to G. F. Clayton 22.11.1916, Clayton papers 470/4, Durham. **p. 189** C. E. Wilson to Arbur for Sir F. R. Wingate, telegram W12.10, 13.7.1917, FO 882/7 fo. 28. Sir F. R. Wingate to Sir W. R. Robertson 11.7.1917, FO 882/7 fo. 21. Sir F. R. Wingate to TEL 14.7.1917, FO 882/7 fo. 29. Sir F. R. Wingate to Sir W. R. Robertson 14.7.1917, L/P&S/11/124, file P. 2884/1917. **p. 190** *SP*(O) ch. 65. **p. 191** Sir E. H. H. Allenby to Sir W. R. Robertson, telegram EA70, 19.7.1917, WO 158/634. C. E. Wilson to G. F. Clayton 29.7.1917, Wingate papers W146/2/26, Durham. **p. 192** G. F. Clayton to General Staff 'Operations' 9.8.1917, WO 158/629. C. E. Wilson to Sherif Hussein 22.7.1917, FO 686/35. Sherif Hussein to C. E. Wilson 28.7.1917, WO 158/629. **p. 193** G. F. Clayton (Brig. Gen., Cairo) to Sir G. M. W. Macdonogh (DMI) 28.7.1917, FO 882/7 fo. 44. **p. 194** TEL, 'Twenty-Seven Articles,' FO882/7. D. de St-Quentin to Guerre, report 70, Paris 20.8.1917, quoted in M. Larès, *T. E. Lawrence, la France et les Français*, Paris, Imprimerie Nationale, 1980, p. 158 (author's translation).

Chapter 12. The First Syrian Campaign
August–December 1917

p. 195 TEL to G. F. Clayton 27.8.1917, FO 882/7 fo. 89. **p. 197** TEL to G. F. Clayton 27.8.1917, FO 882/7 fo. 88. Sir T. B. M. Sykes to G. F. Clayton 22.7.1917, Sykes papers, St Antony's College, Oxford. *SP* ch. CI p. 556. Sir T. B. M. Sykes to G. F. Clayton 22.7.1917, Sykes papers, St Antony's College, Oxford. **p. 198** President W. Wilson, speech to the United States Senate 22.1.1917, published in J. B. Scott (ed.), *President Wilson's Foreign Policy: Messages, Addresses, Papers* (New York, OUP, 1918) p. 250. 'British reply to Russian Note regarding the Allied War-Aims,' undated, but responds to a Russian enquiry of 3.5.1917, FO 371/3062. **p. 199** TEL to G. F. Clayton 7.9.1917, Clayton papers 693/11, Durham (photocopy of original). **p. 200** TEL to Sir T. B. M. Sykes 9.9.1917, enclosed with the above, Clayton papers 693/11, Durham (photocopy of original). G. F. Clayton to TEL 20.9.1917, Clayton papers

693/11/9–12, Durham.   **p. 201** TEL to E. T. Leeds 24.9.1917, *L-L* p. 113.   **p. 202** D. G. Hogarth to W. G. A. Ormsby-Gore 26.10.1917, FO 371/3054 fo. 388. *SP* ch. LXIX   p. 385.   **p. 203** *Ibid. SP*(O) ch. 76. *Ibid.* D. G. Hogarth to W. G. A. Ormsby-Gore 26.10.1917, FO 371/3054 fo. 388.   **p. 204** G. F. Clayton to G. A. Lloyd 25.10.1917, Lloyd papers GLLD 9/10, Churchill College, Cambridge.   **p. 205** P. C. Joyce to G. F. Clayton 4.11.1917, FO 882/7 fo. 199.   **p. 206** D. G. Hogarth to his wife 11.11.1917, Hogarth papers, St Antony's College, Oxford.   **p. 207** *SP* ch. LXXVIII pp. 431–33.   **p. 208** *SP* ch. LXXIX   p. 435.   **p. 209** TEL to W. F. Stirling (DCPO) 28.6.1919 *MB* p. 166, B(r) (transcript). *SP*(O) ch. 87. *Ibid*, 'Him' has here been substituted for 'me' in Lawrence's text.   **p. 210** *Ibid.* TEL to W. F. Stirling 28.6.1918 *MB* p. 166, B(r) (transcript). *SP* ch. LXXX p. 447.   **p. 211** TEL to his family 14.12.1917, *HL* pp. 343–44. G. F. Clayton to War Office London 12.11.1917, WO 158/637. *SP*(O) ch. 87.   **p. 212** *SP*(O) ch. 88.

Chapter 13. The Dead Sea Campaign
December 1917–February 1918

p. 213 TEL to E. T. Leeds 15.12.1917, *L-L* p. 115–16.   **p. 215** Sir F. R. Wingate to Foreign Office London, telegram 1394, 24.12.1918, FO 371/3062, no. 243033. *SP*(O) ch. 115. *Ibid. AB*   **p. 216** TEL to G. F. Clayton 22.1.1918, WO 158/634.   **p. 217** *SP* chs. LXXXV-LXXXVI pp. 476 and 482.   **p. 218** *SP*(O) ch. 101.   **p. 219** A. G. C. Dawnay to Chief of the General Staff, General Headquarters EEF, 15.2.1918, WO 158/616. Comment by TEL on the typescript of *Lawrence and the Arabs* by R. R. Graves, 1927 *B:RG* p. 98. A. G. C. Dawnay to Chief of the General Staff, GHQ, EEF, 15.2.1918, FO 141/668/4322.   **p. 220** TEL to G. F. Clayton 12.2.1918, FO 882/7 fo. 267v.   **p. 222** *SP*(O) ch. 99. Note by TEL on the typescript of LH:*TEL*, 1933 *B:LH* p. 106.

Chapter 14. Dangerous Pause
February–June 1918

p. 224 G. G. Butler to Department of Information London, August 1917, quoted in a letter from an unidentified official at the Foreign Office to J. L. Fisher (War Office) 13.12.1917, FO 395/86. L. J. Thomas to J. Buchan, 10.12.1917, FO 395/86 no. 23678.   **p. 225** Sir T. B. M. Sykes to G. F. Clayton, telegram 32, 2.3.1918, FO 371/3383. TEL to his family 8.3.1918 *HL* p. 348.   **p. 226** H. W. Young, *The Independent Arab* (London, John Murray, 1933) p. 143. *SP* ch. XCII p. 508.   **p. 227** TEL to E. M. Forster 17.6.1925, King's College, Cambridge. War Diary, Hejaz Operations 30.3.1918, 'Summary of Arab Operations during March 1918,' WO 95/4415.   **p. 228** L. J. Thomas, *With Lawrence in Arabia* (London, Hutchinson, 1925) Foreword pp. vi-vii. TEL to E. M. Forster 17.6.1925, King's College, Cambridge.   **p. 229** *SP* ch. XCIII pp. 516–17.   **p. 230** TEL, comment on the typescript of *Lawrence and the Arabs* by R. R. Graves, 1927, *B:RG* p. 100. A. G. C. Dawnay to Chief of the General Staff, General Headquarters EEF, 1.5.1918, FO 882/7 fo. 283.   **p. 231** TEL, comment on the typescript of LH:*TEL*, 1933, *B:LH* p. 112.   **p. 232** *SP*(O) ch. 106.   **p. 233** *SP* ch. XCV   p.527.   **p. 234** *SP* ch. XCV p. 527. *SP*(O) ch. 110.   **p. 235** *SP*(O) ch. 106. TEL, 'Sidelights on the Arab War', unsigned article in *The Times* (London) 4.9.1919. B. H. Liddell Hart, notes on a conversation with Lawrence, 1.8.1933 *B:LH* p. 142. Foreign Office London to Sir F. R. Wingate, *c.* 9.1.1918, CAB 27/23.   **p. 236** G. F.

Clayton to Sir T. B. M. Sykes, 4.2.1918, FO 371/3398 fo. 620. TEL to G. F. Clayton, 12.2.1918. FO 882/7 fo. 268.

Chapter 15. Preparations
June–September 1918

p. 237 'Address presented by Seven Syrians to H.C. Cairo on the 7th May 1918,' FO371/3380. Foreign Office London to Sir F. R. Wingate, telegram 753, 11.6.1918, FO 371/3381 fo. 27. **p. 238** *Ibid*. Sir F. R. Wingate to Foreign Office, telegram 948, 16.6.1918, FO 371/3381 fos. 7–8. **p. 240** TEL to his family 24.9.1917, *HL* p. 341. **p. 241** TEL to V. W. Richards 15.7.1918 *DG* pp. 244–46. **p. 242** A. G. C. Dawnay to P. C. Joyce, 12.6.1918, Akaba Archive, Akaba/I M/26, KCL. **p. 243** *Ibid*. P. C. Joyce to A. G. C. Dawnay 20.6.1918, Akaba Archive, Akaba I H/82, KCL. A. G. C. Dawnay to P. C. Joyce 3.7.1918, Akaba Archive, Akaba I M/28, KCL. **p. 244** H. W. Young, *The Independent Arab* (London, John Murray, 1933). P. C. Joyce (Commandant Akaba) to A. G. C. Dawnay (Hedgehog Cairo), telegram 29301, 1.8.1918, Young papers 14, KCL. **p. 245** *SP* ch XCV p. 529. R. V. Buxton to an unidentified recipient, letter in the form of a diary, entry dated 4.8.1918, copy in author's possession. **p. 246** *SP(O)* ch. 113. TEL, comment on the typescript of *Lawrence and the Arabs* by R. R. Graves, 1927, *B:RG* .103. **p. 247** *SP* ch. XCIX p. 545. *Ibid*. p. 546. *Ibid*. ch. CI, p. 555. **p. 249** *SP*(O) ch 121. Message from TEL forwarded in Commandant Akaba to Hedgehog Cairo, telegram 518, 30.8.1918, FO 882/13 fo. 121. *SP*(O) ch. 121. *SP* ch. CVI p. 579. **p. 250** Message from P. C. Joyce forwarded in Commandant Akaba to Hedghog Cairo, 7.9.1918, WO 157/738.

Chapter 16. A Hollow Triumph
September 1918

p. 251 *SP*(O) ch. 122. *SP* ch. CVII, p. 586. **p. 252** *SP*, epilogue. *SP*, first stanza of the dedicatory poem. TEL to G. J. Kidston, undated but 1919, *MB* p. 169. *Ibid*. TEL, written answer to a question by B. H. Liddell Hart, 3.9.1933 *B:LH* p. 169. TEL to F. el Akle 3.1.1921, B(r) (photocopy of original). **p. 253** TEL, 'The Destruction of the 4th Army,' *AB* 22.10.1918. *SP* ch. CIX p. 593. **p. 254** TEL, 'The Destruction of the 4th Army' *AB* 22.10.1918. **p. 255** 'Message from General Allenby to Emir Feisal,' 20.9.1918, Young papers 19, KCL. A. G. C. Dawnay to P. C. Joyce, undated but 20.9.1918, Akaba Archive M11, KCL. *Ibid*. *Ibid*. **p. 256** *SP* ch. CXIII p. 615. **p. 257** Minutes of a meeting of the War Cabinet held on 20.9.1918, CAB 23/7 fo. 118. *Evening Standard*, London, 25.9.1918. A. J. Balfour to Lord Derby, telegram 805, 23.9.1918, FO 371/3383 fo. 482. **p. 258** A. J. Balfour, statement handed to P. Cambon on 23.9.1918, FO371/3383. Foreign Office London to Lord Derby, telegram 2015, 25.9.1918. FO 371/3383 fo. 489. **p. 259** TEL to A. G. C. Dawnay 25.9.1918, WO 157/738. Sir E. H. H. Allenby to Sherif Feisal, transmitted in L. J. Bols to TEL 25.9.1918, WO 157/738. **p. 260** Sir E. H. H. Allenby to Sir H. H. Wilson, telegram EA 1707, 30.9.1918, FO 371/3383 fo. 528. 'Special Instructions' issued by General Staff Australian Mounted Division, 29.9.1918, WO 95/4551. **p. 261** TEL, 'The Destruction of the 4th Army', *AB* 22.10.1918. *Ibid*. TEL, comment on the typescript of LH:*TEL*, 1933, *B:LH* p. 152. **p. 262** Sir G. de S. Barrow, *The Fire of Life* (London, Hutchinson, n.d.) p. 211. *SP*(O) ch. 135. TEL to W. F. Stirling 15.10.1924 *MB* p. 275. **p. 263** TEL, 'The Destruction of the 4th Army,' *ABD 22.10.1918*. *SP* ch. CXIX p. 643. W. F.

Stirling, *Safety Last* (London, Hollis & Carter, 1953)   p. 94.   **p. 264** TEL to General Staff, GHQ, 1.10.1918, WO 157/738.   **p. 265** 'Report by Lieutenant-General Sir H. G. Chauvel . . . on the Capture of Damascus, and the arrangements made for the Civil Administration thereof' 2.10.1918, WO 95/4371. TEL to General Staff, GHQ, 1.10.1918, WO 157/738.   **p. 266** TEL to General Staff, GHQ, 1.10.1918, WO 157/738. *SP* ch. CXX p. 651. War Office to General Headquarters, Egypt, telegram 67558, 1.10.1918, WO 37/960.   **p. 267** *Ibid. Ibid. SP* ch. CXXII p. 660.   **p. 268** Sir H. G. Chauvel, statement given to the Director of the Australian War Memorial, 1936.

Chapter 18. The Peace Conference
October 1918–September 1919

p. 270 TEL to W. Yale 22.10.1929 *DG* pp. 670–71.   **p. 271** Lord Winterton to Lord Robert Cecil 16.10.1918, Cecil papers, BL Add. MS 51094. Lord Robert Cecil, 'Memorandum,' 28.10.1918, FO 371/3384 fo. 424. Minutes of the 37th meeting of the Eastern Committee of the War Cabinet, 29.10.1918, CAB 27/24 fo. 150.   **p. 272** *Ibid.*   **p. 273** Sir A. J. Stamfordham to TEL 17.1.1928 *LTEL* p. 186. B. H. Liddell Hart, transcript of an interview with TEL, B(r) (transcript). *Ibid.*   **p. 274** TEL to F. R. Wingate for transmission to Sherif Hussein, telegram 1340, 8.11.1918, FO 371/3384 fo. 569. Anglo-French Declaration released on 9.11.1918, text in D. Hunter Miller, *My Diaries of the Conference of Paris* (New York, Appeal Printing, 1924) Vol. 15 pp. 507–8.   **p. 275** Note [to the Foreign Office] communicated by P. Cambon 18.11.1918, FO 371/3385 fo. 163. S. Roskill, *Hankey, Man of Secrets*, Vol. II (London, Collins, 1972), pp. 28–29.   **p. 277** Sir E. Crowe, minute, 5.12.1918, FO 371/3418 fos 406–7. Lord Hardinge, undated minute, FO 371/3418 fo. 407. TEL to G. Dawson 15.12.1918, B(r) (transcript).   **p. 278** 'Interview with Sherif Feisal' (minutes) 27.12.1918. FO 371/4162. TEL to C. F. Shaw 18.10.1927, BL Add. MS 45903.   **p. 280** J. T. Shottwell, *At the Paris Peace Conference* (New York, Macmillan, 1937)   p. 129. *Ibid.*   **p. 281** S. Bonsal, *Suitors and Suppliants, the Little Nations at Versailles* (New York, Prentice-Hall, 1946) p. 56.   **p. 282** From Feisal's diary, sold at Sothebys, London, on 28.3.1983. L. du P. Mallett, minute, late June 1919, FO 608/97 fo. 149. Sir R. Rodd to Foreign Office London, telegram 346, 18.5.1919, FO 371/3809. Sir R. Rodd to A. J. Balfour, telegram, 21.5.1919, FO 608/97 fo. 143.   **p. 283** Foreign Office London to High Commissioner Cairo, telegram 694 'personal,' 5.6.1919, FO 141/453/6347.   **p. 284** Quoted in F. W. Pember to TEL 18.6.1919, B(r) (transcript).   **p. 285** 'Aide-mémoire in regard to the Occupation of Syria, Palestine, and Mesopotamia pending the decision in regard to Mandates' 13.9.1919, FO 608/106.

Chapter 18. An Honourable Settlement
September 1919–August 1922

p. 286 D. Garnett, citing Lawrence's mother, *DG* p.294.   **p. 287** TEL to C. F. Shaw 14.4.27, BL Add. MS 45903. Quoted in J. E. Wrench, *Struggle 1914–1920* (London, Ivor Nicholson & Watson, 1935) pp. 363–4.   **p. 288** *Daily Telegraph*, London, 2.10.1919. TEL to E. M. Forster 17.6.1925, King's College, Cambridge.   **p. 289** *Strand Magazine* (London) Vol. LIX, January 1920. TEL to Sir A. J. Murray 10.1.20 Houghton bMS Eng 1252 (156).   **p. 290** 'Interview with Col. Lawrence: Sidelights on the Joys of Desert Warfare' in *The Globe* (London) 12.12.1918. TEL to P. Burton, quoted in Burton, *Adventures Among Immortals* (London, Hutchinson, n.d.)   p. 207.   **p. 291** R. R.

Graves in *B:RG* p. 10. **p. 292** TEL to F. Manning 15.5.30 *DG* p. 692. TEL to E. Garnett 26.8.22 *DG* p. 360. Comment on the draft of *Lawrence and the Arabs* by R. R. Graves, 1927, *BRG* p.117. **p. 294** TEL to W. Yale 22.10.1929 *DG* p. 671. TEL to C. B. Harmsworth *c*, 15.9.19, FO 371/4236. TEL to Lord Winterton 22.4.20 *DG* pp. 302–3. **p. 295** TEL to H. St.J. B. Philby 21.5.1920, Philby papers, St Antony's College, Oxford (photocopy of original). **p. 296** TEL to V. W. Richards, undated, but probably June or July 1920. B(r) (transcript). TEL to F. N. Doubleday 20.3.1920 *DG* pp. 300–01. **p. 298** TEL to F. N. Doubleday 29.3.1920 *MB* p. 176, B(r) (transcript). TEL to F. N. Doubleday 14.5.1920 *DG* p. 305. **p. 299** TEL to F. el Akle 3.1.1921, B(r) (photocopy of original). TEL, note on the typescript of *Lawrence and the Arabs* by Robert Graves, July 1927, *B:RG* p. 110. **p. 300** Note by B. H. Liddell Hart of a conversation with Lawrence 1.8.1933 *B:LH* p. 143. **p. 301** TEL to R. R. Graves, 1927 *B:RG* p. 114. TEL to R. R. Graves, 1927 *B:RG* p. 112. TEL to R. R. Graves, 1927, *B:RG* p. 80. **p. 302** Lord Curzon to TEL 7.7.1921, FO 406/47 p. 74. **p. 303** TEL to W. S. Churchill, telegram, 28.11.1921, FO 406/48 p. 160.

Chapter 19. The Decision
January–August 1922

p. 304 TEL to Sir H. M. Trenchard early January 1922 *MB* pp. 192–3. TEL to E. H. Kennington 16.2.1922, B(r) (transcript). **p. 305** TEL to R. R. Graves 12.11.1922 *DG* p. 379. TEL to V. W. Richards 15.7.1918 *DG* p. 244. TEL to D. G. Hogarth 13.6.1923 *DG* p. 424. **p. 306** TEL to H. G. Andrews *c*, 15.3.1934. B(r) (transcript). TEL, note on the typescript of *Lawrence and the Arabs* by R. R. Graves, July 1927 *B:RG* p. 91. TEL to Sir H. Baker 6.11.1928, B(r) transcript. **p. 307** *SP*(O) ch. 118. **p. 308** *SP*(O) ch. 87. *SP*(O) ch. 118. **p. 309** *Ibid. Ibid.* TEL to R. R. Graves 18.1.1923 *B:RG* p. 24. **p. 310** Sir H. M. Trenchard to TEL 11.1.1922, B(r) (transcript). Note by TEL on the flyleaf of his copy of *The Singing Caravan*, by R.Vansittart, B(r) (transcript). **p. 311** TEL to W. S. Blunt 23.7.1922, Fitzwilliam Museum, Cambridge. TEL to G. F. Clayton 15.8.1922, Clayton papers 693/11, Durham (photocopy of original). **p. 312** TEL to E. Garnett 26.8.1922 *DG* pp. 360–61. Sir O. Swann to TEL 16.8.1922 *LTEL* pp. 187–8. **p. 313** TEL to R. R. Graves 12.11.1922 *DG* p. 379.

Chapter 20. Aircraftman Ross
September 1922–January 1923

p. 317 *Daily Mail* (London) 4.9.1922. TEL, *The Mint*, Part 1 chapter 25 p. 90. **p. 318** TEL to S. C. Cockerell 15.10.1924, *DG* pp. 468–69. TEL to E. Garnett 7.9.1922, *DG* pp. 366–67. TEL to D. G. Hogarth 29.10.1922, *DG* p. 374. B(r) (transcript). TEL to E. Garnett 6.11.1922, *DG* p. 377. TEL to E. Garnett 12.11.1922, *DG* p. 380. **p. 319** *Ibid.* TEL to R. D. Blumenfeld 11.11.1922, *MB* pp. 211–12. **p. 320** TEL to W. Roberts 28.11.1922, B(r) (transcript). TEL to R. D. Blumenfeld 24.11.1922, B(r) (transcript). C. Findlay, 'The Amazing A.C.2.' in *The Listener* (London) Vol. LIX, No. 1523, 5.6.1958, pp. 937–38. TEL to E. Garnett [1.12.1922], *DG* p. 385. **p. 321** G. B. Shaw to TEL 1.12.1922, *LTEL* p. 161–62. TEL to R.V. Buxton 21.12.1922, *DG* pp. 388–89. TEL to H. Baker 25.12.1922, *DG* p. 389. *Daily Express* (London) 27.12.1922. **p. 322** R. D. Blumenfeld, *R.D.B's Procession* (London, Ivor Nicholson & Watson, 1935) p. 116. G. B. Shaw to TEL 28.12.1922, *LTEL* pp. 167–68. **p. 323** C. F. Shaw to TEL 31.12.1922, BL Add. MS 45903. G. B. Shaw to TEL 4.1.1923, *LTEL* pp. 168–70. **p.**

324 TEL to H. J. Cape 7.1.1923, *DG* p. 393. TEL to C. F. Shaw 8.1.1923, BL Add. MS 45903. TEL to E. H. Kennington 22.2.1923, B(r) (transcript). J. E. Mack, *A Prince of our Disorder* (Boston, Little, Brown, 1976) p. 323. **p. 325** Interview with A. E. Chambers 18.2.1968. D. Stewart, *T. E. Lawrence* (London, Hamish Hamilton, 1977) p. 276. TEL to R. A. M. Guy 25.12.1923, Houghton bMS Eng 1252 (233). **p. 326** TEL, *The Mint*, Part 2 ch. 2, pp. 109–10. TEL to E. H. Kennington 15.9.1927, B(r) (transcript). **p. 327** TEL to G. B. Shaw 30.1.1923, *DG* p. 397.

Chapter 21. Private Shaw, Publisher
January 1923–December 1924

p. 328 TEL to T. B. Marson, Trenchard's personal assistant, 28.1.1923, *DG* pp.394–95. TEL to E. Garnett 30.1.1923, *DG* p. 396. Sir P. W. Chetwode to TEL 17.2.1923, B(r). **p. 329** TEL to R. Isham 22.11.1927, *DG* p. 545. TEL to S. C. Cockerell 22.10.1923, *DG* pp. 437–38. TEL to L. G. Curtis 19.3.1923, *DG* pp. 410–11. *Ibid. DG* p. 412. **p. 330** TEL to L. G. Curtis 27.3.1923, *DG* pp. 412–14. TEL, *The Mint*, Part 2 ch. 18, p. 149. **p. 331** *SP* ch. CVII p. 586. A. Dixon, *Tinned Soldier* (London, Jonathan Cape, 1941) pp. 296–97. TEL to F. E. Hardy 25.3.1923, B(r) (transcript). **p. 332** TEL to E. Garnett 12.4.1923, *DG* p. 409. A. Dixon, *op. cit.* note 28 above, pp. 294–95. TEL to A. R. D. Fairburn 12.5.1923, Alexander Turnbull Library, Wellington, New Zealand. **p. 333** TEL to L. G. Curtis 14.5.1923, *DG* pp. 416–17. TEL to H. J. Cape 4.6.1923, B(r) (transcript). TEL to H. J. Cape 8.7.1923, B(r) (transcript). TEL to H. J. Cape 11.8.1923, B(r) (transcript). *Ibid.* **p. 334** TEL to F. E. Hardy 15.8.1923, *DG* p. 427. TEL to E. H. Kennington 15.8.1923, B(r) (transcript). TEL to G. L. Bell 18.8.1923, *DG* pp. 427–28. TEL to H. J. Cape 19.8.1923, B(r) (transcript). TEL to D. G. Hogarth 23.8.1923, *DG* pp. 428–29. TEL to H. J. Cape 13.9.1923, B(r) (transcript). **p. 335** TEL to R. V. Buxton 4.10.1923, *DG* pp. 434–35. TEL to L. G. Curtis 25.9.1923, All Souls College, Oxford. TEL to E. Garnett 4.10.1923, *DG* pp. 433–34. TEL to H. J. Cape 11.10.1923, B(r) (transcript). **p. 336** TEL to A. E. Chambers 5.11.1923, B. TEL to R. V. Buxton 5.11.1923, Jesus College, Oxford. **p. 337** TEL to R. V. Buxton 13.12.1923, *DG* pp. 442–43. **p. 338** TEL to R. V. Buxton 23.12.1923, Jesus College, Oxford. *Ibid.* TEL to D. G. Hogarth 21.1.1924, *DG* p. 451. TEL to A. P. Wavell 27.12.1923, *DG* p. 449. TEL to A. P. Wavell 23.1.1924, B(r) (transcript). **p. 339** E. M. Forster to TEL mid-February 1924, *LTEL* p. 60. TEL to G. W. M. Dunn 11.3.1931, *DG* pp. 715–16. **p. 340** TEL to C. F. Shaw 26.3.1924, BL Add. MS 45903. **p. 341** TEL to H. G. Granville-Barker 9.5.1924, Houghton bMS Eng 1020. TEL to A. E. Chambers 3.8.1924, B. TEL to E. Garnett [18.5.1924], B(r) (transcript). **p. 342** C. F. Shaw to TEL undated, but *c.* 6.10.1924, HRHRC Texas. G. B. Shaw to TEL 7.10.1924, *Collected Letters of Bernard Shaw* Vol.III, ed. D. H. Laurence (London, Max Reinhardt, 1985) pp. 884–86. TEL to C. F. Shaw 13.10.1924, BL Add. MS 45903. TEL to R. V. Buxton 25.11.1924, *DG* pp. 470–1. **p. 344** J. E. Mack, *A Prince of our Disorder* (Boston, Little, Brown, 1976) p. 446.

Chapter 22. Ambitions Fulfilled
January 1925–December 1926

p. 345 TEL to Sir Hugh Trenchard 6.2.1925, *SIR* pp. 105–6. TEL to R. V. Buxton 18.2.1925, Jesus College, Oxford. **p. 346** TEL to R. V. Buxton 26.3.1925 *DG* p. 472. *Ibid.* TEL to C. F. Shaw 26.3.1925, BL Add. MS 45903. TEL to R. V. Buxton

16.5.1925, Jesus College, Oxford. **p. 347** TEL to L. G. Curtis [May 1925], All Souls College, Oxford. TEL to J. Buchan 19.5.1925, *DG* pp. 475–6. **p. 348** TEL to E. Garnett 13.6.1925, *DG* pp. 476–77. TEL to E. M. Forster 17.6.1925, King's College, Cambridge. TEL to R. V. Buxton 20.6.1925, *DG* p. 478. TEL to C. F. Shaw 28.6.1925, BL Add. MS 45903. **p. 349** TEL to C. F. Shaw 4.7.1925, BL Add. MS 45903. TEL to C. F. Shaw 28.9.1925, BL Add. MS 45903. **p. 350** *Ibid.* TEL to E. Garnett 3.11.1925, B(r) (transcript). TEL to W. Roberts 10.12.1925, B(r) (transcript). **p. 351** TEL to H. J. Cape 25.5.1927, *DG* p. 518. **p. 352** TEL to M. Pike 18.10.1926, B(r) (transcript). Sir H. Trenchard to TEL 22.11.1926, *LTEL* p. 198. TEL to G. Brough 27.9.1926, *DG* p. 499. B(r) (transcript). TEL to D. G. Hogarth 19.5.1927, B(r) (transcript). **p. 353** E. Bishop, *The Debt we owe: the Royal Air Force Benevolent Fund 1919–1969* (London, Longmans, 1969) p. 121. TEL to D. G. Hogarth 1.6.1927, B(r) (transcript). TEL to his mother 1.12.1926, *HL* pp. 362–63.

Chapter 23. Voluntary Exile
January 1927–January 1929

p. 354 TEL to his mother 11.1.1927, *HL* p. 364. TEL to C. F. Shaw 28.1.1927, BL Add MS 45903. TEL to F. el Akle 28.1.1927, B(r) (photocopy). **p. 355** TEL to his mother 11.1.1927, B MS Res C13. Viscount Allenby to TEL 22.1.1927, B(r) (transcript). TEL to C. F. Shaw 4.3.1927, BL Add. MS 45903. TEL to C. F. Shaw 15.2.1927, BL Add. MS 45903. **p. 356** TEL to E. Garnett 1.8.1927, *DG* p. 533. TEL to R. V. Buxton (quoting Buxton) 4.3.1927, Jesus College, Oxford. *Ibid.* **p. 357** TEL to C. F. Shaw 7.4.1927, BL Add. MS 45903. W. L. S. Churchill to TEL 16.5.1927, *LTEL* p. 24. TEL to C. F. Shaw 4.3.1927, BL Add. MS 45903. **p. 358** TEL to E. M. Forster 27.4.1927, King's College, Cambridge. TEL to C. F. Shaw 24.11.1927, BL Add. MS 45903. **p. 359** TEL to E. Eliot 16.6.1927, *MB* pp. 333–4. TEL to C. F. Shaw 29.9.1927, BL Add. MS 45903. R. R. Graves to Tel 3.6.1927, B(r) (transcript). TEL to R. R. Graves 9.6.1927, *B:RG* p. 45. **p. 360** TEL to R. R. Graves 28.6.1927, Houghton fMS Eng. 1252 (347). TEL to L. G. Curtis 14.7.1927, All Souls College, Oxford. TEL to C. F. Shaw 29.9.1927, BL Add. MS 45903. TEL to F. N. Doubleday 16.6.1927, Princeton University Library. **p. 361** TEL to R. R. Graves 30.7.1927, *B:RG* p. 91. TEL to R. R. Graves 3.8.1927, *B:RG* p. 95. TEL to C. F. Shaw 4.8.1927, BL Add. MS 45903. TEL to R. R. Graves 17.8.1927, *B:RG* p 133. TEL to C. F. Shaw 18.8.1927, BL Add. MS 45903. **p. 362** TEL to C. F. Shaw 8.12.1927, BL Add. MS 45903. TEL to R. R. Graves 24.12.1927, *B:RG* pp. 141–2. W. M. M. Hurley (adjutant, RAF Karachi), *Friends* p. 401. TEL to C. F. Shaw 27.10.1927, BL Add. MS 45903. TEL to D. Knowles 30.12.1927, *DG* pp. 560–1. **p. 363** TEL to C. F. Shaw 8.12.1927, BL Add. MS 45903. TEL to C. F. Shaw 8.5.1928, BL Add. MS 45904. **p. 364** TEL to R. V. Buxton 10.6.1927, Jesus College, Oxford. TEL to C. F. Shaw 10.11.1927, BL Add. MS 45903. TEL to Sir H. M. Trenchard 17.3.1928, B(r) (transcript). **p. 365** B. Rogers to TEL 4.3.1928, B(r). R. Isham to TEL 6.12.1927, B(r) (transcript). TEL to R. Isham 2.1.1928, B(r) (transcript). **p. 366** *Ibid.* TEL to C. F. Shaw 2.2.1928, BL Add. MS 45903. TEL to C. F. Shaw 25.2.1928, BL Add. MS 45903. TEL to C. F. Shaw 16.3.1928, BL Add. MS 45903. *Ibid.* **p. 367** Sir H. M. Trenchard to TEL 10.4.1928, *LTEL* p. 200. TEL to E. Garnett 15.3.1928, *DG* pp. 579–80. G. B. Shaw to TEL 12.4.1928, *LTEL* pp. 175–76. **p. 368** E. Garnett to TEL 22.4.1928, *LTEL* pp. 96–78. TEL to Sir H. M. Trenchard 1.5.1928, B(r) (transcript). **p. 369** TEL to H. S. Ede 30.6.1928, *DG* pp. 614–5. **p. 370** TEL to R. Isham 30.6.1928, B(r) (transcript). R. Isham to TEL

11.8.1928, B(r) (transcript). *New York Sun*, late July 1928. **p. 371** *Evening News* (London) 26.9.1928. Letter from C. M. J. Barrington, an Army Reserve officer, to the editor of the *Sunday Express* (London) quoted in the issue of 30.9.1928. **p. 372** *Sunday Express* (London) 30.9.1928. Quoted in the *Sunday Times* (London) 9.12.1928. P. J. Patrick, minute, 12.12.1928, L/P&S/11/293/5310. **p. 373** *Empire News* (Manchester) 16.12.1928. *Free Press Mail Service* 27.12.1928, FO 371/13992. TEL to E. Walker 25.12.1928, Houghton bMS Eng 1252 (220). Sir F. H. Humphrys to Delhi and London, telegram, 3.1.1929, FO 371/13988.

Chapter 24. Plymouth
January 1929–February 1931

p. 375 TEL to his mother 19.3.1929, *HL* p. 376. TEL to H. S. Ede 20.3.1929, *DG* pp. 644–45. **p. 376** *John Bull* (London) 13.4.1929. TEL to H. A. Ford 18.4.1929, *DG* p. 650–51. **p. 377** TEL to B. Rogers 1.5.1929, Houghton bMS Eng 1252 (163). B. Rogers to TEL, undated retained copy or draft, Houghton bMS Eng 1252 (279). *Ibid*. TEL to B. Rogers 23.5.1929, Houghton bMS Eng 1252 (164). **p. 378** TEL to A. G. C. Dawnay 17.9.1929, B(r) (transcript). **p. 379** TEL to C. F. Shaw 19.11.1929, BL Add. MS 45904. **p. 380** TEL to C. F. Shaw 15.12.1929, BL Add. MS 45904. TEL to Sir H. M. Trenchard 18.12.1928, B(r) (transcript). TEL to D. Garnett 10.2.1930, B(r) (transcript). **p. 381** TEL to H. J. Cape 21.2.1930, B(r) (transcript). **p. 382** TEL to E. Thurtle 13.3.1930, *DG* p. 685. TEL to C. F. Shaw 27.3.1930, BL Add. MS 45904. TEL to C. F. Shaw 19.4.1930, BL Add. MS 45904. TEL to F. Manning 15.5.1930, *DG* p. 692. TEL to R. V. Buxton 10.9.1930, Jesus College, Oxford. **p. 383** TEL to C. F. Shaw 5.10.1930, BL Add. MS 45904. TEL to B. Rogers 1.11.1930, Houghton bMS Eng 1252 (184). **p. 384** From the manuscript notes known as 'Leaves in the Wind', B LAdd. MS 46355. TEL to C. F. Shaw 6.2.1931, BL Add. MS 45904. *Ibid*. Inquest of the Iris Flying Boat crash, 18.2.1931, Press cutting from an unidentified newspaper, 19.2.1931. TEL to B. Rogers 25.2.1931, Houghton bMS Eng 1252 (190).

Chapter 25. Last RAF Duties
February 1931–March 1935

p. 386 W. E. G. Beauforte-Greenwood to S. Smith 13.5.1931, published in *The Golden Reign* by C. S. Smith: (London, Cassell, 1940) pp. 144–45. TEL to C. F. Shaw 14.10.1931, BL Add. MS 45904. **p. 387** TEL to C. F. Shaw 28.11.1931, BL Add. MS 45904. TEL to W. E. G. Beauforte-Greenwood 20.1.1932, B(r) (transcript). TEL to G. Brough 5.3.1932, *DG* p. 739. TEL to C. S. Smith 6.3.1932, C. S. Smith, *The Golden Reign* by C. S. Smith (London, Cassell, 1940) pp. 182–3. TEL to C. F. Shaw 14.6.1932, BL Add. MS 45904. **p. 388** J. C. Walton to C. W. Orde 19.8.1932, FO 371/16188 fo. 89. *The Writers' and Artists' Year Book 1930* (London, A & C Black, 1930) p. 86. *Sunday Chronicle* (London) 28.8.1932. **p. 389** TEL to W. B. Yeats 12.10.1932, *DG* p. 744. TEL to R. A. M. Guy 18.10.1932, B(r) (transcript). **p. 390** TEL to B. Rogers 19.12.1932, Houghton bMS Eng 1252 (199). **p. 391** TEL to R. V. Buxton 16.2.1932, Jesus College, Oxford. TEL to G. W. M. Dunn 28.2.1933, B(r) (transcript). TEL: application for discharge from the RAF, *DG* pp. 762–3. TEL to C. F. Shaw 6.3.1933, BL Add. MS 45904. TEL to C. S. Smith 3.4.1933, quoted in C. S. Smith, *The Golden Reign* (London, Cassell, 1940) p.207. **p. 392** Extract from Lawrence's RAF personal file, B(r) (transcript). TEL to Viscountess Astor 1.6.1933, Reading University Library. **p.**

393 TEL to C. F. Shaw 23.8.1933, BL Add. MS 45904. TEL to David Garnett 3.11.1933, B(r) (transcript). TEL to C. F. Shaw 9.12.1933, BL Add. MS 45904. TEL to A. S. Frere-Reeves 25.9.1933, RAF Museum, Hendon. **p. 394** TEL to H. S. Ede 31.12.1933, B(r) (transcript). TEL to 'Captain L.-J.' 12.5.1934, photocopy in author's possession. **p. 395** TEL to 'Captain L.-J.' 17.5.1934, photocopy in author's possession. Sir O. E. Mosley, *My Life* (London, Nelson, 1968) p. 226. TEL to H. Williamson 20.12.1934, Exeter University Library. **p. 396** TEL to C. F. Shaw 31.12.1934, BL Add. MS 45904. TEL to B. H. Liddell Hart 12.9.1934, *B:LH* p. 225. TEL to H. J. Cape 6.8.1934, B(r) (transcript). TEL to H. J. Cape 3.5.1934, B(r) (transcript). TEL to C. F. Shaw 16.11.1934, BL Add. MS 45904. TEL to F. Manning 16.11.1934, B(r) (transcript). **p. 397** TEL to C. F. Shaw 26.1.1935, BL Add. MS 45904. **p. 398** TEL to R. R. Graves 4.2.1935, *DG* pp. 851–3. TEL to E. Garnett 23.12.1927, B(r) (transcript).

Chapter 26. Clouds Hill
April–May 1935

p. 400 TEL to T. W. Beaumont 25.2.1935, B(r) (transcript). **p. 401** TEL to T. B. Marson 6.3.1935, B(r) (transcript). TEL to Sir J. E. L. Wrench 1.4.1935, B(r) (transcript). TEL to E. Plamer 5.4.1935, B(r) (transcript). **p. 402** TEL to Bruce Rogers 6.5.1935, Houghton bMS Eng 1252 (210). Viscountess Astor to T. E. Lawrence 7.5.1935, B(r) (transcript, misdated 7.4.1934). TEL to Viscountess Astor 8.5.1935, *DG* p. 972. **p. 403** TEL to H. Williamson, telegram, 13.5.1935, *DG* p. 872.

Envoi

p. 405 Sir A. T. Wilson, *Thoughts and Talks, 1935–7* (London, Right Book Club, 1938) p.33. J. Buchan, *Memory Hold the Door* (London, Hodder & Stoughton, 1940) p. 229. C. F. Shaw, quoted in J. Dunbar, *Mrs G.B.S., A Biographical Portrait of Charlotte Shaw* (London, George G. Harrap, 1963) p. 300.

Appendix I

p. 407 In Latin, the Chapman family motto reads *'Crescit sub pondere virtus.'* **p. 410** T. R. Lawrence to TEL, draft, 8.3.1916, B(r) (transcript). 5. LH:*TEL* p. 14.

Appendix II

p. 412 Diary of the 10th Motor Section of the Royal Field Artillery, WO 95/4415. TEL to his family 14.12.1917, *HL* pp. 343–4. G. F. Clayton to P. Joyce 12.11.1917, FO 882/7, fo. 205. **p. 413** P. Joyce to Arbur, telegram 202, 24.11.1917 (received 25/11/ 1917) repeating message from Lieut. Wood, WO 158/634 fo. 168a. 'Late News', *AB* No. 72, 5.12.1917, p. 490. **p. 414** TEL, note on the typescript of *Lawrence and the Arabs* by R. R. Graves, *B:RG* p. 91.

Acknowledgements

I offer my heartfelt gratitude for the help I have received from many individuals and institutions, whose names are listed in the original edition of this book. I have valued not only their assistance, but also their courtesy and interest which were a constant source of encouragement.

For the use of copyright material and papers from particular collections I gratefully acknowledge the kind permission of the following: The Literary Executors of Lady Astor; Samuel French Ltd and the Literary Estate of J. M. Barrie (unpublished letter Copyright the Literary Estate of J. M. Barrie 1989); The Trustees of the British Museum (for material from the British Museum Archives and from the archives of the Department of Western Asiatic Antiquities, Copyright The British Museum 1989); Curtis Brown Ltd, London, and the Estate of Sir Winston Churchill (for the letter from Winston Churchill to T. E. Lawrence and the extract from Churchill's speech to the Oxford High School); Odhams Press Ltd and the Estate of Winston Churchill for the extract from Churchill's *Life of Lord Randolph Churchill*. The Controller of Her Majesty's Stationery Office (for Crown Copyright material in the Public Record Office and elsewhere); Lord Deedes (for W. H. Deedes); Gonville and Caius College, Cambridge (for C. M. Doughty); John Sherwood (for James Elroy Flecker); King's College, Cambridge, Executor of the E. M. Forster Estate (for E. M. Forster); The Literary Estate of Edward Garnett; A. P. Watt Limited for the Estate of Robert Graves; extracts from unpublished letters Copyright The Estate of Robert Graves 1989; Dr Caroline Barron (for D. G. Hogarth and L. V. Hogarth); The India Office Library and Records (for Crown Copyright papers in the India Office Library); The Fellows of Jesus College, Oxford (for material from the Jesus College Archives); Jonathan Cape Ltd and the *Seven Pillars of Wisdom* Trust (for passages from Lawrence's letters and the 1922 draft of *Seven Pillars of Wisdom* by T. E. Lawrence, unpublished text Copyright the *Seven Pillars of Wisdom* Trust 1989, and from *T. E. Lawrence by his Friends*); Professor A. W. Lawrence, Jonathan Cape Ltd., and the *Seven Pillars of Wisdom* Trust for passages from *The Mint*; The Bodleian Library, Oxford, and the Houghton Library, Harvard (for papers from their respective T. E. Lawrence collections); The Estate of E. T. Leeds (for material from the Leeds papers); The Trustees of the Liddell Hart Centre for Military Archives, King's College, London (for material from the Liddell Hart papers, the Akaba Archive, and the H. W. Young papers); Dr J. Charmley, the Estate of Lord Lloyd, and Churchill College, Cambridge (for material from the Lord Lloyd papers); The Palestine Exploration Fund (for material from their archives); The Estate of Bruce Rogers (for Bruce Rogers); The Trustees of the Will of Mrs Bernard Shaw (for Charlotte Shaw, unpublished text Copyright 1989.); The Society of Authors on behalf of the Bernard Shaw Estate (for Bernard Shaw); Durham University Library (for material from the Sudan Archive and from the Clayton Papers); The Royal Air Force Museum, Hendon (for the papers of Lord Trenchard), and the Estate of Lord Wester Wemyss and Churchill College, Cambridge (for material from the Wemyss papers). I apologise to any other copyright owner whom I have inadvertently overlooked. Brief quotations from published works are not listed separately above, and I gratefully acknowledge the owners of these copyrights. The source of material from all published works is stated in the references and has not been repeated here.

The illustrations have been reproduced by kind permission of the following: The Bodleian Library, Oxford (for photographs from the T. E. Lawrence papers); The Trustees of the British Museum (for photographs and drawings from Carchemish, and of Hypnos); Dr. Maurice Larès; The Trustees of the Liddell Hart Centre for Military Archives (for the photograph of Lawrence, Churchill, and Gertrude Bell at Cairo); The Hulton Picture Company (for the Cairo Conference group); Magdalen College, Oxford (for Lawrence's sketch for *Crusader Castles*); the family of Janet Laurie; Merton College, Oxford (for the OTC group); The Ashmolean Museum, Oxford (for Lawrence and Hogarth by A. John; Lawrence by W. Roberts); B. D. Thompson (for Dahoum by Dodd); The Imperial War Museum (for photographs from their T. E. Lawrence collection and the last radio message from Kut); The National Portrait Gallery (for Lawrence by A. John; Lawrence by H. Coster; Lord Allenby by E. Kennington; Lord Trenchard; Doughty by A. John); John Sims for the photograph of T. E. Lawrence by Wing Commander R. G. Sims; Rolls-Royce Motor Cars Ltd. (for Lawrence entering Damascus); Associated Press (for Mrs Shaw); The National Trust (for plans of Clouds Hill); a private collector for the head-and-shoulders sketch of Lawrence in uniform by A. John. The Fitzwilliam Museum Cambridge (for Thomas Hardy by A. John); other illustrations are from the author's collection.

Index

Abbreviations used in this index:

EEF   Egyptian Expeditionary Force
TEL   Thomas Edward Lawrence ('Lawrence of Arabia')
RD   *Revolt in the Desert* by T.E. Lawrence
7P   *Seven Pillars of Wisdom* by T.E. Lawrence
S–P   Sykes–Picot Agreement, *1916*
WWI   World War I, *1914–1918*

Dates of the lives of the main characters are given in parentheses following their names.